LA VILLETTE 1971–1995:
A HISTORY IN PROJECTS

LA VILLETTE 1971–1995: A HISTORY IN PROJECTS

Alain Orlandini

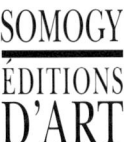

To Roger Taillibert, as a gesture of my friendship

This book is published with the support of:

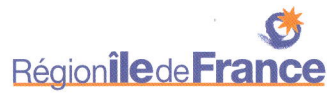

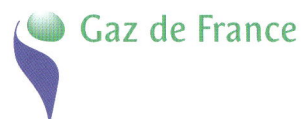

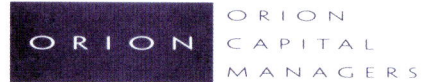

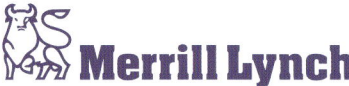

Book design
    Hugues Cornière, Graphic Garage

Revision and proofreading
    Cathy Lenihan

Translation
    Charles Penwarden
    John Tittensor

Managing editors
    Isabelle Dartois, Audrey Gregorczyk

Production
    François Combal

© Somogy éditions d'art, Paris, 2004

ISBN: 2-85056-680-2
Printed in Italy (European Union)
Copyright deposit: fourth quarter, 2004

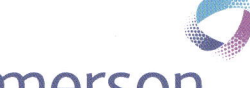

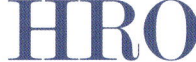

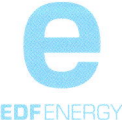

Acknowledgments

The author would like to extend his warmest thanks to the following people for their valued and prestigious support:
– **Mr. Jean-Paul Huchon**, president of the Île-de-France Regional Council.
– **Mr. Alain Van der Malière**, head of the Direction Régionale des Affaires Culturelles (French regional cultural authority) for Ile-de-France.

The author would also like to offer heartfelt thanks to the following public-sector sponsors, without whose financial support this book could not have existed:
– **Établissement Public du Parc et de la Grande Halle de La Villette,** and especially its chairman, Bernard Latarjet.
– **Établissement Public du Parc de La Villette,** and especially its chairman, Jean-Claude Moréno.
– **Établissement Public de la Cité des Sciences et de l'Industrie,** and especially its chairman, Jean-François Hebert.
– **Établissement Public de Maîtrise d'Ouvrage de Travaux Culturels,** and especially its chairman, Jean-Claude Dumont.

I am also grateful to the following private companies, whose generous contributions have helped make this publishing project a reality:
– **Accor** and its "Patronage, Sponsoring, and Public Relations" department director, Alain Caudrelier-Bénac.
– **Ægide** and its chairman and managing director, Jean-Marie Fournet.
– **Alcan Composites** and its sales manager, Christophe Pobles.
– **Alstom Entreprise Paris** and its chairman and managing director, Michel Cantet.
– **Altadis** and its co-chairman, Jean-Dominique Comolli.
– **AMO** and its chairman, Michel Macary.
– **Arcora** and its chairman, Dominique Queffélec.
– **Atis Real Auguste-Thouard** and its chairman and managing director, Alain Bechade.
– **Awon Group** and its chairman, Robert Waterland.
– **Axa Reim France** and its chairman and managing director, Pierre Vaquier.
– **Bateg** and its manager, Jean de Rodellec.
– **Baudin-Chateauneuf** and its chairman and managing director, Michel Colombot.
– **Bellechasse** and its chairman, Marc Pietri.
– **Bin** and its managing director, Michel Piovesan.
– **Bouygues Construction** and its chairman and managing director, Yves Gabriel.
– **Bouygues Immobilier** and its chairman and managing director, François Bertière.
– **Bredy SA** and its chairman of the board, Guillaume Bredy.
– **BTP Banque** and its chairman, François Desportes.
– **Café de la Musique** and its chairman and managing director, Alain Boudou.
– **Campenon Bernard Construction** and its chairman and managing director, Fernando Sistac.
– **Canauxrama Croisières** and its chairman and managing director, Michelle Colorado.
– **Capri Résidences** and its chairman and managing director, Alain Legrand.
– **Carré Noir** and its managing director, Pascal Beucler.
– **CDII Rey-Grange Concept** and its chairman and managing director, Dominique Rey-Grange.
– **Centre Immobilier Pastor** and its acting chairman, Michel Pastor.
– **Chambre Syndicale des Sociétés Anonymes de Crédit Immobilier** and its chairman, Claude Sadoun.
– **Ciments Calcia** and its chairman and managing director, Jean-Paul Méric.
– **Codepro** and its chairman and managing director, Yves Le Neveu.
– **Cogedim** and its chairman and managing director, Henri Caro.
– **Colas** and its chairman and managing director, Alain Dupont.
– **Colbert** and its chairman, Bruno Ledoux.
– **Compagnie EMGP** and its chairman and managing director, Jean-Paul Dumortier.
– **Compagnie Parisienne de Chauffage Urbain** and its chairman and managing director, François Dupoux.
– **Compagnie de Saint-Gobain** and its chairman and managing director, Jean-Louis Beffa.
– **Coprim SA** and its managing director, Christian Lefrançois.
– **DTZ Jean Thouard** and its chairman of the board, Philippe Leigniel.
– **Eiffage TP** and its managing director, Jean Guénard.
– **Eiffel** and its managing director, Jacques Huillard.
– **El.GCC** and its sales manager, Emmanuel Muguet.
– **Erdec** and its manager, Monsieur Jean-Claude Lacombe.

- **Eurogem SAS** and its chairman, Michel Platzer.
- **Euro RSCG Omnium** and its chairman and managing director, Stéphane Fouks.
- **Européquipements** and its chairman, Olivier Pelat.
- **Eurovia** and its chairman and managing director, Roger Martin.
- **Féau-Dauchez** and its chairman of the board, Paul-Louis Camizon.
- **Fédération Nationale des Travaux Publics** and its chairman, Daniel Tardy.
- **Financière Pinault** and its manager, François-Henri Pinault.
- **Financière Rive Gauche** and its chairman and managing director, Michel Bressot.
- **First Avenue** and its chairman and managing director, Jean-Louis Charbit.
- **Francelot** and its chairman and managing director, Michel Abelin.
- **France Quick SA** and its chairman and managing director, Alain Béral.
- **France-Sols** and its chairman and managing director, Marc Périn.
- **Franco-Suisse Bâtiment** and its chairman and managing director, Pascal Lorenzetti.
- **Freyssinet France** and its managing director, Bruno Dupety.
- **GA** and its managing director, Samir Rizk.
- **Gaz de France** and its chairman, Pierre Gadonneix.
- **La Générale de Promotion** and its managing director, Roger Berdah.
- **GET** and its chairman of the board, Pierre-Marie Faure.
- **Groupe Altarea** and its chairman and managing director, Alain Taravella.
- **Groupe Ancel** and its chairman and managing director, Patrick Sparfel.
- **Groupe Bureau Veritas** and its chairman of the board, Frank Piedelièvre.
- **Carlyle Group** and its managing director, Éric Sasson.
- **Groupe Crédit Coopératif** and its chairman, Jean-Claude Detilleux.
- **Groupe Fougerolle** and its chairman and managing director, Jean-Jacques Lefebvre.
- **Groupe Ginger** and its chairman and managing director, Jean-Luc Schnoebelen.
- **Groupe Hoche** and its manager, Richard Saint-Guilhem.
- **Groupe Meunier** and its chairman, Philippe Zivkovic.
- **Groupe Setec** and its chairman, Claude Néraud.
- **GTM Construction** and its chairman and managing director, Robert Hosselet.
- **G3A** and its manager, Jean-Pierre Matton.
- **L'Habitation Confortable** and its chairman, Jean-Yves Autexier.
- **Hammerson Europe** and its managing director, Gérard Devaux.
- **Horeto** and its managing director, Frédéric Boyer.
- **HRO France** and its international chairman, Howard Ronson.
- **Icade** and its chairman and managing director, Étienne Bertier.
- **IED** and its chairman and managing director, Christian Pellerin.
- **Immobanque** and its chairman and managing director, Luc Guinefort.
- **Inex BET** and its chairman, Miroslav Jorgacevic.
- **ING Real Estate Development France** and its country manager, Paul Koch.
- **Jean Lefèvre Ile-de-France** and its sales manager, Pierre Deniau.
- **Kaufman & Broad** and its chairman and managing director, Guy Nafilyan.
- **Lafarge** and its chairman and managing director, Bertrand Collomb.
- **Lazard Frères** and its executive vice-chairman-director, Georges Ralli.
- **Léon Grosse** and its chairman of the supervisory board, Léon Grosse.
- **Lucia** and its chairman and managing director, Sébastien Bazin.
- **SA d'HLM La Lutèce** and its chairman and managing director, Robert Domenget.
- **LVMH/Moët Hennessy – Louis Vuitton** and its chairman, Bernard Arnault.
- **LW Habitat** and its chairman and managing director, Stéphane Lacroix Wasover.
- **Merrill Lynch Invesment Managers** and its chairman of the board, Henri Vernhes.
- **Marignan Immobilier SAS** and its chairman and managing director, Hervé Manet.
- **MDB Promotion** and its executive vice president, Antoine Kieffer.
- **Nexity** and its chairman and managing director, Alain Dinin.
- **Les Nouveaux Constructeurs SA** and its chairman and managing director, Olivier Mitterrand.
- **Ocil** and its managing director, Robert Domenget.
- **Ogic** and its chairman and managing director, Jean Diaz

- **Orion Capital Managers (France SARL)** and its managing director, Aref Lahham.
- **Otis France** and its chairman and managing director, Bruno Grob.
- **Parquets Briatte** and its chairman and managing director, Gilles Briatte.
- **Philia** and its chairman, Gilles Lamarque.
- **Pierre Etoile** and its manager, Franck Delibéros.
- **Pierre et Vacances Promotion Immobilière** and its chairman and managing director, Gérard Brémont.
- **Pont Saint-Pierre Investissements** and its manager, Christian Garrel.
- **Profimob** and its chairman and managing director, Serge Kot.
- **Promaffine** and its chairman and managing director, Bernard Roth.
- **Promogim** and its chairman and managing director, Christian Rolloy.
- **Quinette Gallay** and its chairman and managing director, Gilles Ancelin.
- **Rabot Dutilleul** and its chairman and managing director, Jean-François Dutilleul.
- **Réalco** and its chairman and managing director, Paul Zasso.
- **Rem Finance** and its chairman and managing director, Ély Michel Ruimy.
- **Rothschild et Cie Banque** and its managing partner, Édouard de Rothschild.
- **Roxim Promotion SA** and its chairman and managing director, Marc Pigeon.
- **Sari** and its chairman and managing director, Daniel Valoatto
- **Satelec** and its chairman and managing director, Jean Magnaval.
- **SCIC SA** and its chairman and managing director, François Jouven.
- **Screg Ile-de-France Normandie** and its chairman and managing director, Bruno Chambon.
- **Sedaf Ile-de-France** and its chairman and managing director, Philippe Motte.
- **Sefri-Cime** and its chairman and managing director, Claude Cagol.
- **Ségécé** and its chairman and managing director, Éric Ranjard.
- **Semapa** and its managing director, Thérèse Cornil.
- **Sepimo** and its chairman and managing director, Alain Jesel.
- **SFL** and its chairman and managing director, Yves Mansion.
- **Sicra** and its chairman and managing director, Gilbert Legendre.
- **SMAC Acieroïd** and its chairman and managing director, Robert Lefevre.
- **Socfim** and its chairman of the board, Jacques Larretche.
- **Socotec** and its chairman and managing director, Yves Le Sellin.
- **Sogeprom** and its chairman, Jean Stern.
- **Sorif** and its chairman and managing director, Olivier de la Roussière.
- **Spie Batignolles** and its executive vice president, Maurice Guillou.
- **Spie Trindel** and its director of tertiary activity, Jean-Marie Camus.
- **Tertial** and its managing director, Inès Reinmann.
- **Thales Engineering & Consulting** and its "Building Engineering" department director, Maxime Mazloum.
- **Thyssen Ascenseurs** and its operations manager, Alain Béguin.
- **TWM France** and its chairman, Frédéric Haven.
- **Ugine & ALZ** and its chairman and managing director, Philippe Darmayan.
- **Unibail** and its chairman and managing director, Léon Bressler.
- **Unifica** and its director of development, Jean-Paul Antuori.
- **Urbaine de Travaux** and its chairman and managing director, Jean-Claude Lorang.
- **Vinci Park** and its regional manager, Paul Coiffard.
  Viry and its chairman and managing director, Bernard Viry.
- **Voyageurs du Monde** and its chairman and managing director, Jean-François Rial.
- **Le Zénith de Paris** and its managing director, Daniel Colling.

Finally, the author is beholden to the following individuals, who offered their amicable support for the publication of this book:

– **Agnès B.**, fashion designer.
– **Jacques Allemand**, former chairman and managing director of GTM Construction.
– **Henri de Castries**, chairman of the board of the Axa group.
– **Christian Chianalino**, former chairman and managing director of Constructa.
– **Jean-François Dubos**, general secretary of Vivendi Universal.
– **Paul Dubrule**, chairman and cofounder of Accor.
– **Christian Giacomotto**, chairman of the management committee of Gimar Finance et Cie.
– **François Grether**, town planner.
– **Henri Guitelmacher**, former chairman of the Fédération Nationale des Promoteurs-Constructeurs.
– **Daniel Kéravec**, vice-president of Zénith de Paris.
– **Nicolas Lefebvre**, managing director of SEMAEST.
– **Maurice Lévy**, chairman of the board of Publicis.
– **Daniel Marcovitch**, former deputy for the 19th arrondissement of Paris.
– **Philippe Meritte**, former general secretary of EPPV.
– **Pierre Milovanovitch**, managing director of Sagi.
– **Jean Nouvel**, architect.
– **Marc Pandraud**, chairman of Merrill Lynch France.
– **Jacques Pautigny**, former chairman of the Syndicat National des Aménageurs-Lotisseurs.
– **Christian Peene**, former chairman and managing director of Unimo.
– **Jean-Louis Richon**, former executive vice president of Coprim.
– **Jacques Séguéla**, vice chairman of Havas Advertising.
– **Jean-Louis Subileau**, developer-contractor.
– **Alain Treussard**, engineer (Socotec).
– **Jean-Baptiste Vaquin**, director of the Atelier Parisien d'Urbanisme.
– **Georges Vauzeilles**, acting director of the central commercial management of Bouygues Construction.
– **Bernard Weil**, developer-contractor.

The author would also like to warmly thank:
– **Jean Audouze**, former chairman of EPPGHV.
– **Patrick Broders**, director of communication for the Établissement Public de la Cité des Sciences et de l'Industrie.
– **Christian Brulé**, chairman of the Association de Prévention du site de La Villette.
– **Marie Chauvin**, MA student in urban geography at the Université de Paris-I, for her contribution to the interviews in chapter IV and to the text: *"Geographic Death": The Obsession with Geometry*.
– **Jean-Louis Cohen**, former director of the Institut Français d'Architecture.
– All the teachers at the **École d'Architecture de Paris-La Villette**, especially Jean-Louis Avril, Philippe Boudon, Georges Édery, Louis-Pierre Grosbois, Xavier Jaupitre, Jean-Pierre Le Dantec, Martin Van Treeck, Jean-Louis Véret and Inge-Lise Weeke.
– Everyone at the **EPPGHV**, and especially Vincent Poussou, director of communications, Marie-Vag Lugosi, head of the "Public Access" department, Pascal Denègre, head of technical documentation, and Michèle Zazzaron, head of the photo library.
– **Pierre Gaudin**, former director of the Maison de La Villette.
– **Frédérika Gérard**, former general manager of the Établissement Public de la Cité des Sciences et de l'Industrie.
– **Christian de Portzamparc**, chief architect of the Cité de la Musique; and the Atelier Christian de Portzamparc, especially François Barbereau, Bertrand Beau, Isabelle Nguyen and Étienne Pierres.
– All those who showed the way with their own committed studies, especially **Jean Sérignan** and **Roger Taillibert**.
– Everyone at **Somogy Éditions d'Art**, especially Nicolas Neumann and François Combal.
– **Jacques Terrière**, former head of the "Congresses and Commercial Events" department of the Établissement Public de la Cité des Sciences et de l'Industrie.
– **Bernard Tschumi**, chief architect of the Parc de La Villette.
– All the photographers whose work is used in this book.

Contents

Preface 11

Introduction 13

1. Chronology 16
From the Agony of the abattoir to the Inauguration of the Cité de la Musique
    Interview with Jean Sérignan 76
    Interview with François Grether 84
    Interview with Roger Taillibert 92

2. The Cité des Sciences et de l'Industrie 100
Adrien Fainsilber or the Ideal of Reason
    Interview with Adrien Fainsilber 110
    Interview with Jean Semichon 122

3. The Géode 128
Technical Prowess as Symbol
    Interview with Gérard Chamayou 134

4. The Parc de La Villette 136
"Geographic Death": The Obsession with Geometry
    Interview with François Barré 154
    Interview with Bernard Tschumi 160
    Interview with Rem Koolhaas 176
    Interview with Bernard Lassus 182
    Interview with Gilles Vexlard 190
    Interview with Alexandre Chemetoff 198
    Interview with Jacques Gourvénec 208

5. The Grande Halle de La Villette 214
Hymn to Versatility
    Interview with Bernard Reichen 222

6. The Zénith de Paris 230
A Venue for Rock
    Interview with Daniel Colling 236
    Interview with Philippe Chaix 242

7. The Maison de La Villette 244
A Place for Memory
    Interview with Pierre Du Besset 250

8. The Cité de la Musique 252
When Architecture Meets Desire
    The Conservatoire National Supérieur de Musique et de Danse . . 255
    The Pôle Public de Diffusion Musicale et Muséologique 275
    Interview with Pierre Boulez 286
    Interview with Christian de Portzamparc 290

Conclusion 313

Preface

The city is a theatre where society performs. It is therefore a mirror, a mirror held up to each one of us, and the reflection there is the image of our own lives. La Villette shows us that the symbols of consumerism are changing, and that daily anxiety over material survival can sometimes be replaced by an aspiration to culture and knowledge.

The history of La Villette, as described in painstaking detail by Alain Orlandini, teaches us how to read a particular moment in the architectural and urban history of Paris, a history in which the powers that be – political or otherwise – contradict each other, hesitate, then finally decide, thus reflecting a whole society, and a generation, whose certitudes have been shaken and that finds the future hard to foresee.

The remarkable architectural diversity of La Villette is now something of a graft that is brought to life by the alert steps of visitors from the urban region onto which the site is attached.

Perhaps one could argue that the suture should have been carried out with greater care, using finer materials?

Be that as it may, La Villette remains an example of what an urban space should be: the place where the city is reconstructed on the city, the miraculously fertile humus of a city that is forever being reborn.

It is vital that the city should once again become a place where the imagination can prosper. It must also be a space where rebellion and violence can be integrated.

And to be precise: to integrate means to accept, and even to desire a law common to all. It is also to identify with the urban forms that history is continually engendering.

Alain Orlandini's book shows us how the projects implemented on the site of La Villette have all responded, or tried to respond, to a fundamental set of issues. Fundamental, because historical and urban.

ANDRÉ ANTOLINI
Former chairman and managing
director of Immobilière Saint-Paul

Introduction

This book came out of a series of lectures commissioned from the author by the Établissement Public du Parc et de la Grande Halle de La Villette. The purpose of these lectures was to analyse the architectural projects built on the site of the old abattoir. Although numerous commentaries on these projects have been published by specialist journals, they have never been brought together in a single publication that would make it possible to compare the different pieces of architecture and the discourses surrounding them, or to follow the chronology of the building. The primary purpose of this book is thus to replace the usually fragmentary reading of these projects, with a historical account affording a view of the key dates in the rehabilitation of the Villette site, and shedding light on the diversity of the theoretical universes referred to by the architects and planners who worked on the site. In this eminently complex project, empiricism struggled with political rivalry, architectural diversity with the heterogeneity of the briefs. La Villette was in need of a book. Here it is.

The first forms of public appropriation of the abattoir as the starting point of this historical study – when "mere facts" give rise to history

The writing of this book implies another consideration: La Villette was not born with the competition to build the Parc de La Villette. And its eminently complex history cannot be reduced to a succession of dates linked to the organisation of prestigious architectural competitions. To understand La Villette, we need to go back into its history, the whole of its history; to the high-profile inaugurations, as well as to the "mere facts." And we must never forget what Cassirer taught us: the pertinence of historical research lies in the "devotion to the tiny detail." Take, for example, that strange period – that would have been all too easy to ignore, and yet turned out to be essential – when the inhabitants of Paris' 19th arrondissement took possession of the Villette site at a time when the modernisation of the abattoir meant reducing its scale of operations. It was, to be exact, in 1971 that the first forms of a cultural strategy aiming to back up the east Parisians' appropriation of the site began to appear. As we shall see, this process was closely linked to the typology of the terrain where it occurred. So 1971 was the date when the first programmatic experiments were sketched out for the site, under the aegis of Jean Sérignan, planning commissioner for the development of the Villette sector; while 1995 was the date when the inauguration of the Cité de la Musique by President François Mitterrand brought to a close an architectural and urbanistic adventure that had lasted nearly a quarter of a century. Hence the title of this book.

A necessarily exhaustive history

Understanding the history of a place means deciphering all the interpretations that have been made of it. It means reactivating an often sizeable production of forms and spaces that will never become reality and yet still constitute a body of knowledge that can help us understand its evolution. To examine it all, from the built projects to the ones history chose to ignore: this was the price to be paid in order to write the history of La Villette.

The usefulness of interviews

Finally, the idea behind this book is to let the architects have their say. There are too many of them who balk at publicly arguing the case for their projects. We went and talked with Adrien Fainsilber, Gérard Chamayou, Bernard Tschumi, Bernard Reichen, Philippe Chaix, Pierre Du Besset and Christian de Portzamparc. The long conversations we had with them are reproduced here in full. Readers with little taste for theory may prefer to start with them. The lively tone of all those we spoke to undoubtedly make it easier to understand their theoretical universe, even if the analytical and critical texts here are meant to be as didactic as possible. When the subject required it, we also spoke to people who, while not directly involved in the conception of the works built at La Villette are, by virtue of the functions they hold or have held, the best qualified to appreciate its developments. This is the case with Jean Sérignan, François Grether and Roger Taillibert, humble "pioneers" whose programmatic proposals showed great foresight. It applies as well to the main architect of the abattoir's meat market, Jean Semichon whom, logically, we asked for his opinion of the architectural qualities of the Cité des Sciences et de l'Industrie, since the rehabilitation of his work was the other architects' point of departure. Likewise, the director of the "Park Mission," François Barré, whom we asked to enlighten us about the philosophical postulates underlying the conception of the competition brief for the construction of the Parc de La Villette. As well as, finally, Daniel Colling, the true instigator of the Zénith project, who speaks with youthful passion of the combat for the "cause of rock"; and the director of the Ensemble InterContemporain, Pierre Boulez, the chief user of the concert hall at the Cité de la Musique, who agreed to go over the genesis of this project for the reader.

How the book is organised

The opening text, entitled "From the Agony of the Abattoir to the Inauguration of the Cité de la Musique," presents a rigorous chronology of the site's evolution. It pays particular attention to the competition briefs and the studies organised with a view to developing the site, as well as offering a comparative analysis of some of the projects submitted. It prepares readers for the analytical and critical texts in the following chapters. It contains three interviews, with Jean Sérignan, François Grether and Roger Taillibert. Jean Sérignan, who was made development commissioner for the Villette sector in 1973, evokes the first budding of a spontaneous cultural project, which found a space for itself in the disused land of a doomed industrial complex. François Grether, formerly an architect and planner at the Atelier Parisien d'Urbanisme – APUR (Paris Town Planning Office), goes over the vital role played by that office in the rehabilitation of the Villette site. Roger Taillibert, mandated in 1978 by President Valéry Giscard d'Estaing to study the conversion of the abattoir, proves a brilliant polemicist as he takes us through the eminently political and strategic dimension of an urban operation like the one at La Villette.

The chapters that follow consider, respectively, the Cité des Sciences et de l'Industrie, the Géode, the Parc de La Villette, the Grande Halle, the Zénith, the Maison de La Villette and the Cité de la Musique. Each of these chapters includes an interview with the main architect. In addition to a critical text on Bernard Tschumi's project, the chapter on the Parc de La Villette contains a series of interviews with some of those short-listed after the first round of the competition. For budgetary reasons, it was only possible to interview Bernard Tschumi, Rem Koolhaas, François Barré, Bernard Lassus, Gilles Vexlard, Alexandre Chemetoff and Jacques Gourvénec. The next reprinting of this book will, we hope, provide an opportunity to talk with Sven Ingvar Andersson, Andreu Arriola, Rich Bakker and Ank Bleeker, and to publish their comments. Readers will no doubt be surprised by the size of the chapter on the Cité de la Musique. They would, however, be quite mistaken to see this as sign of even the slightest favouritism. The extreme complexity of the competition brief and the great diversity of the Cité de la Musique's interior spaces naturally led us to carry out a highly detailed reading of Christian de Portzamparc's project.

Terminology

One final remark concerning the terminology used to describe Christian de Portzamparc's project. By "Cité de la Musique," I refer to all the buildings built on either side of Place de la Fontaine-aux-Lions. Rather than a legalistic reading of the project, which would distinguish the Paris Conservatoire National Supérieur de Musique et de Danse (National Conservatory of Music and Dance), to the west, from the Cité de la Musique, to the east, we prefer an "architectural" reading which embraces the entire complex built at the tip of the Villette site; in other words, the Conservatoire and what, because of the concert hall and the Instrument Museum that it houses, I have decided to call the Pôle Public de Diffusion Musicale et Muséologique (Public Music and Museum Complex).

CHRONOLOGY: FROM THE AGONY OF THE ABATTOIR TO THE INAUGURATION OF THE CITÉ DE LA MUSIQUE

Fifteenth of March 1974, and the last ox has just been slaughtered at La Villette. The wholesale butchers have left and the feverish activity of the scalding rooms has given way to the muffled creak of windswept metal. Is La Villette site – this "void with infinite potential,"[1] as Rem Koolhaas liked to say of it – destined to become the prey of property developers or, with architectural and urban thinking apparently bent on being defined exclusively in terms of opposition to the modernist discourse, the focal point of a fruitful ideological debate?

The public authorities had already asked Pierre-Yves Ligen and his Atelier Parisien d'Urbanisme – APUR (Paris Town Planning Office) to look into a partial conversion of the abattoir; in 1970, Prime Minister Jacques Chaban-Delmas had come down in favour of the continued use of the abattoir, though did not rule out a possible restoration of the unused facilities, and Jean Sérignan had subsequently been appointed "development commissioner for La Villette sector." Becoming managing director of the Société d'Économie Mixte de La Villette – SEMVI (La Villette Semi-Public Company) in 1971, Sérignan opted for an approach combining management of the abattoir and the drawing-up of a cultural programme. Since reorganisation of the abattoir was going to

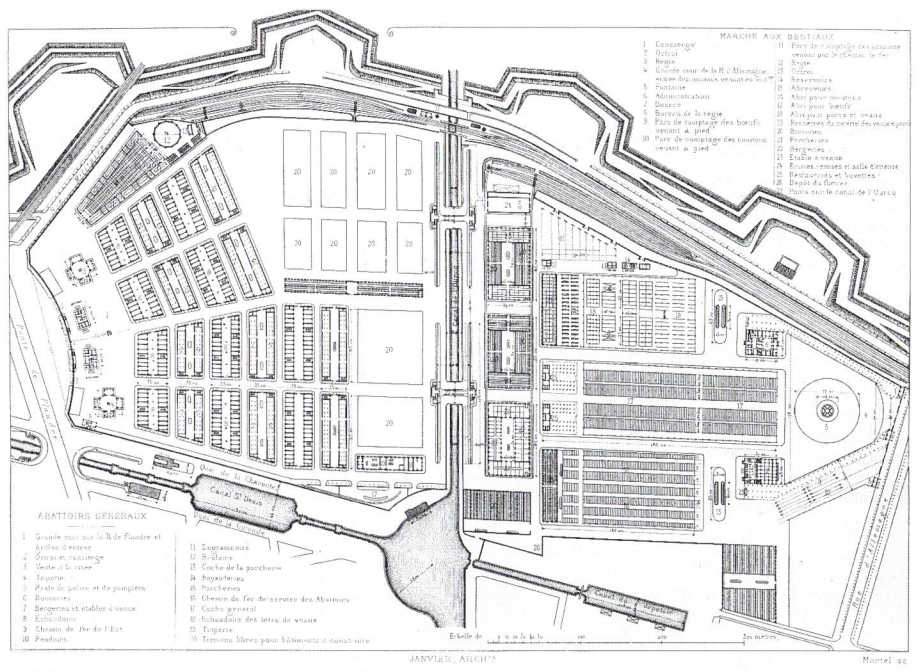

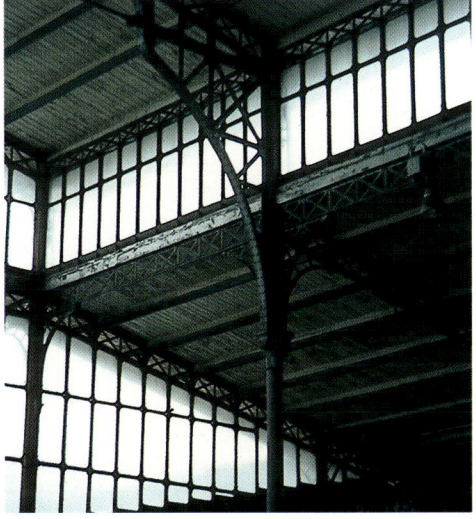

Above: Plan of the abattoir.
Left: The cattle shed.

CHRONOLOGY　17

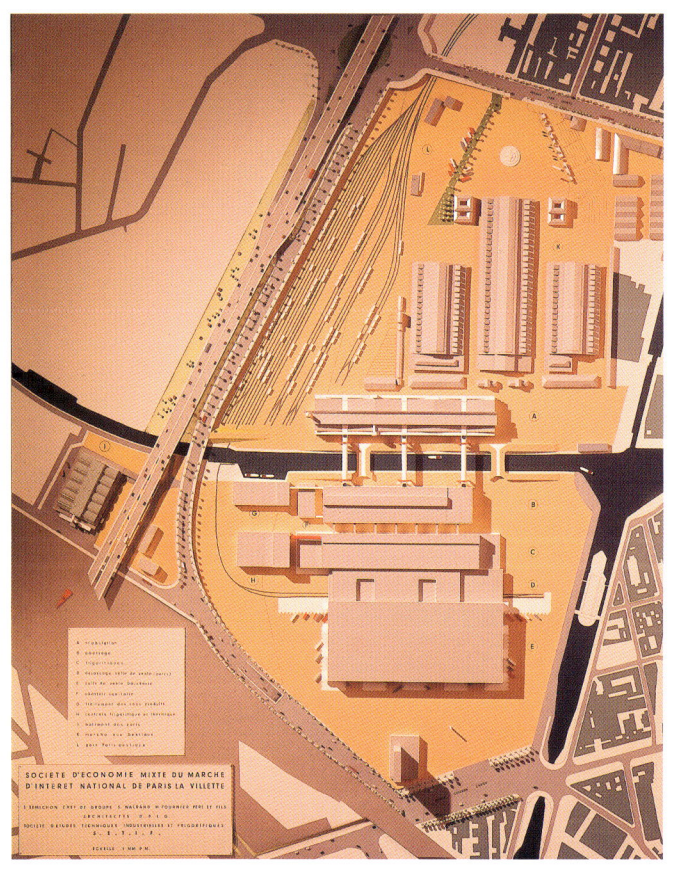
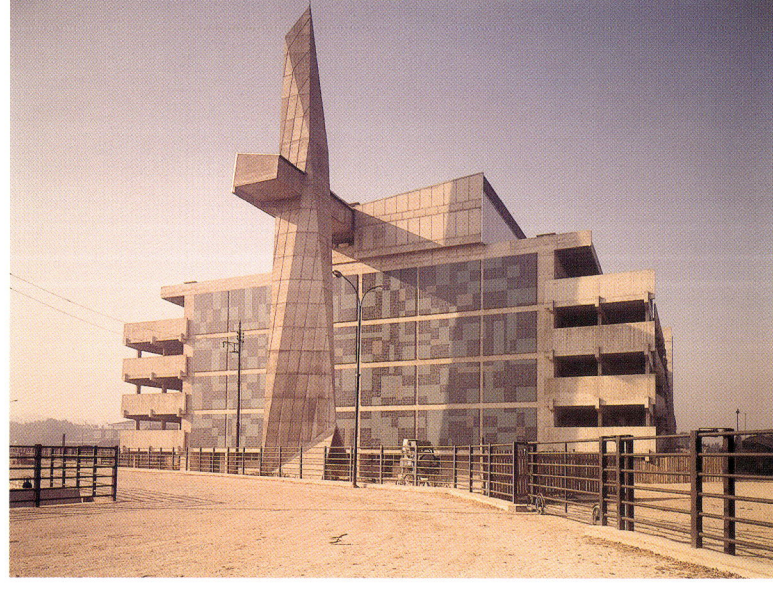

The industrial abattoir (architects: J. Semichon and S. Walrand).
Above left: Model.
Above right: The livestock stalls building or "hôtel à vaches" (foreground: The fodder lift).
Right: Model (foreground: The office tower and shopping centre, never built).
Below: The Villette site, early 1970s.

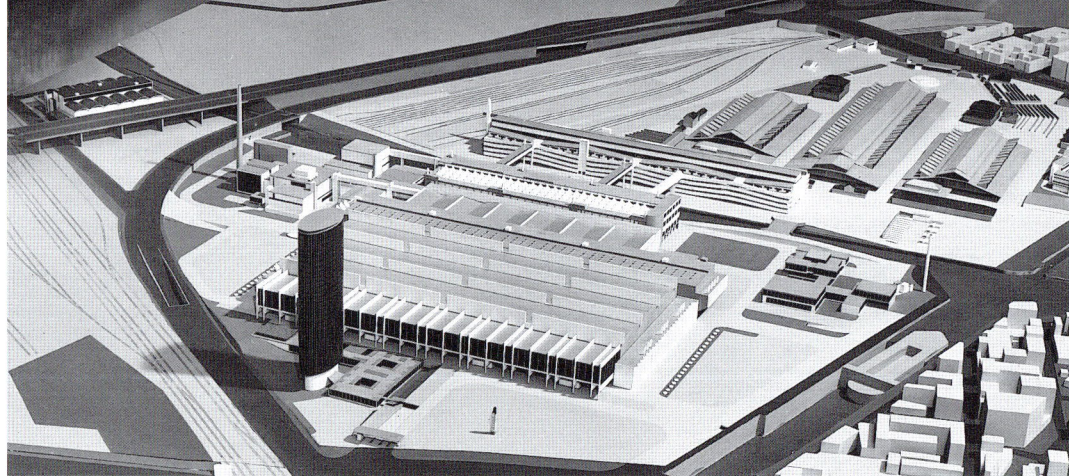
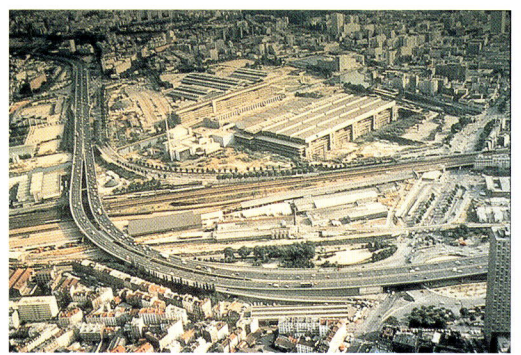

18   LA VILLETTE: 1971–1995

involve reducing its area – meat sales were to be partially transferred to Rungis – he undertook a detailed inventory of buildings with rehabilitation potential and encouraged the development of social-cultural projects for the site. These were to be aimed primarily at the residents of north-eastern Paris, where facilities of this kind did not exist.

Jean Sérignan's "development proposal for the Villette sector" (1975)

The development proposal for the Villette sector, submitted for approval to the Prefect of Paris in May 1975, focused on two core sites: the meat market, whose construction had never been completed, and a fifteen-hectare park. The meat market would house a technology training centre, a performance space and a sports facility – structurally it lent itself to this kind of diversity – and would counterbalance the presence of the cattle shed to the south. Sérignan saw this latter, a vestige of the old livestock market, as a venue for temporary exhibitions. To counteract the fragmentation of La Villette, cut in two by the Canal de l'Ourcq, the fifteen-hectare park would run north-south, its enormous area of greenery extending to the edge of Place de la Fontaine-aux-Lions flanked by apartment blocks, offices and shops. The park – "a major structural factor in the development, creating links between its different facilities and involving the organisational and the functional articulation of the brief's proposals for the area"[2] – would also include an enormous "resort complex" of skating rinks, boating areas and swimming pools. Serious consideration was given to the possibility of linking the park to suburban Paris by "extending it along the Canal de l'Ourcq to the sports complex on the other side of the Périphérique (outer ring road) and towards Pantin."[3]

In addition to achieving a balance between leisure areas and a new neighbourhood, and a brief offering an overall fit with city of Paris urban policy – lots of parkland, restrictions on the building of offices, and retention of non-polluting industries – the Sérignan proposal also included a particularly cogent finance plan based on the amortising of development spending, and clearing of the liabilities of the old meat market; on 1 January 1974, the latter totalled some 681.6 million francs (104 million euros). The project also had to have an appropriate legal status, and the Sérignan team opted for the Société d'Économie Mixte pour l'Aménagement du Secteur de La Villette – SEMAV (La Villette Semi-Public Development Company), to which was entrusted the development of the newly created ZAC (local government planning Project Zone).

The Atelier Parisien d'Urbanisme competition (1976)

The ideas competition launched by the APUR seemed to confirm Jean Sérignan's "development proposal for the Villette sec-

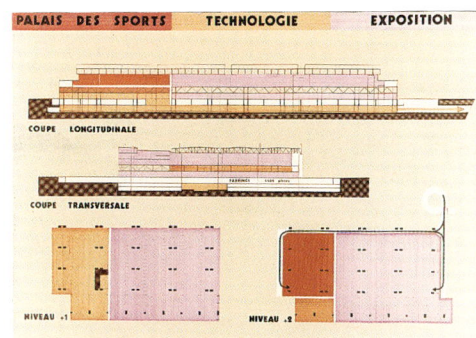

tor," despite the organisers' declared intention not to use the winning project or projects. The brief related to the rehabilitation of the meat market and the cattle shed in the context of a fifteen-hectare park, and an ensemble of residential and office accommodation. The choice of new func-

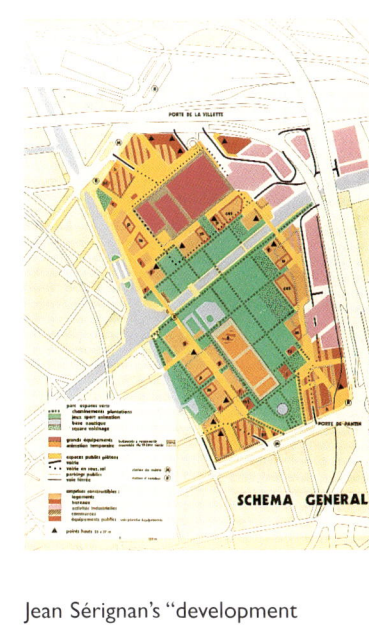

Jean Sérignan's "development proposal for the Villette sector" (1975).
Above: Site plan.
Below: Plans and sections of the meat market (also called the "grande salle"). Proposals for the brief.

Atelier Parisien d'Urbanisme – APUR (Paris Town Planning Office) competition (1976).
Above right: Project by L. Krier.
Below right: Project by D. Bigelman, B. Huet, B. Leroy, S. Santelli.
Below left: Project by the Groupe Arche (P. Dutard, D. Laroche, L. Leblanc, G. Loux, G. Maillochaud).

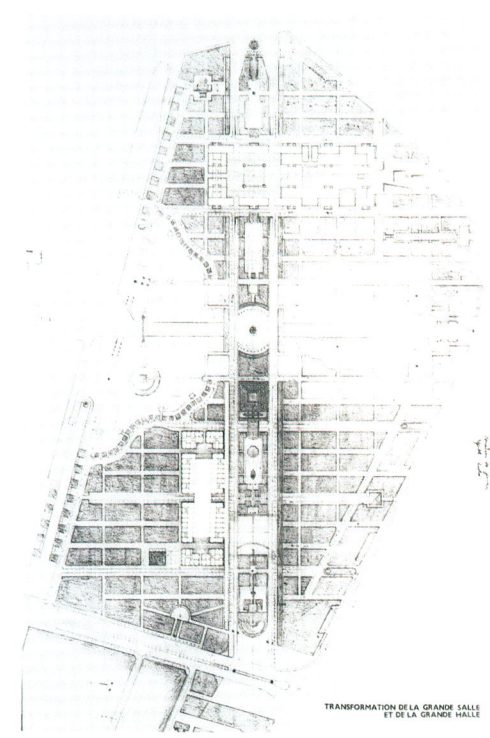

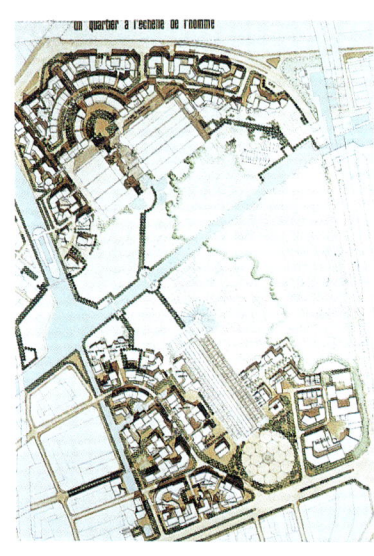

tions for the two buildings was left to the participants in the competition. The overall brief, then, closely matched Sérignan's except for the inclusion of a hospital complex that the minister of Health, Simone Veil, wanted on the old abattoir site.

One effect of the APUR competition was to highlight the sheer incapacity of postmodern urban thinking when forced to drink at the well of reactionary neoclassicism. Leon Krier went deliberately academic in opting for an approach that opposed the dominance of the axis to the most rigid of symmetries: the park ran along the banks of the Canal de l'Ourcq, at right angles to a "boulevard" cutting through the meat market. Succumbing to the "heritage preservation syndrome," Bernard Huet kept the three sections of the livestock market, which he fitted into a composition very much in line with traditional French taste. Denis Sloan proposed a monumental planted area perpendicular to the canal, while the Arche Group laid its buildings out mechanically along Avenue Corentin-Cariou and Avenue Jean-Jaurès, allotting the heart of the plot to a park redolent with failed baroque rhetoric.

More courageous projects countered the "axis cult" with something more appropriate to the context. The Atelier de Montrouge anchored its housing and office complex to the edges of Avenue Jean-Jaurès, cutting into it with "antennae" – landscaped sine curves extending out towards the adjacent neighbourhoods. To the east, two underpasses linked the park to the sports complex – renamed the "Sports Park" – in Pantin. This plea for a non-commercial planning approach was backed by the Riboulet-Thurnauer-Véret team's manifesto calling for "new relationships between space, nature and society." An immense grassed area, or "communal meadow" covered the eastern side of the site; the cattle shed was transformed into an open university focused on "revers-

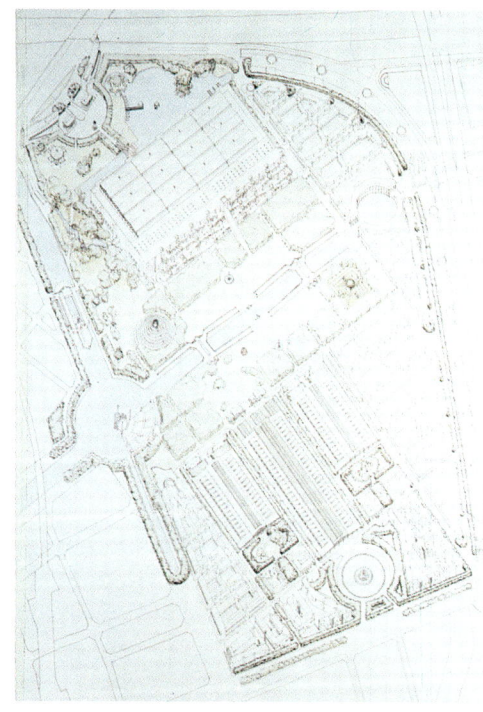

ing the power-knowledge relationship"; and the livestock stalls building became a "Community Association Centre" – a "ruin" dedicated to the celebration of "bureaucratic idiocy". Together they would add up to a public space "adaptable to the interests and needs of all." This uncom-

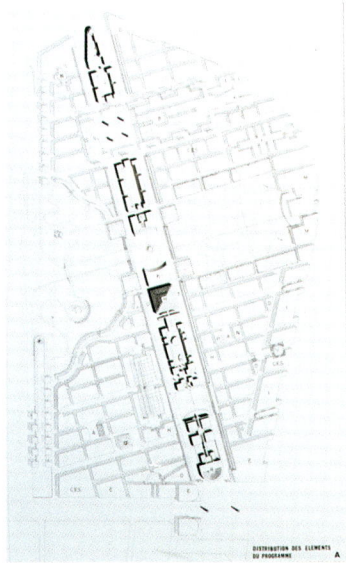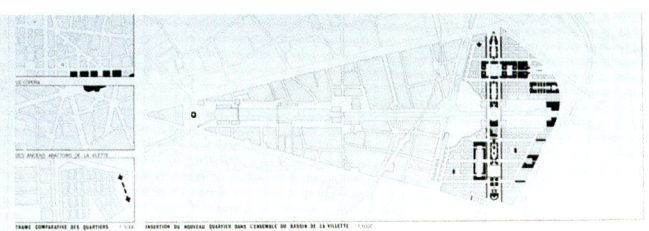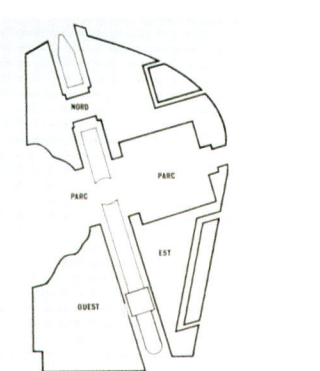

APUR competition (1976).
Left: Project by L. Krier.
Below left: Project by D. Sloan, A. Judet, J.-L. Mery.
Below right: Project by the Atelier de Montrouge (P. Riboulet, G. Thurnauer, J.-L Véret).

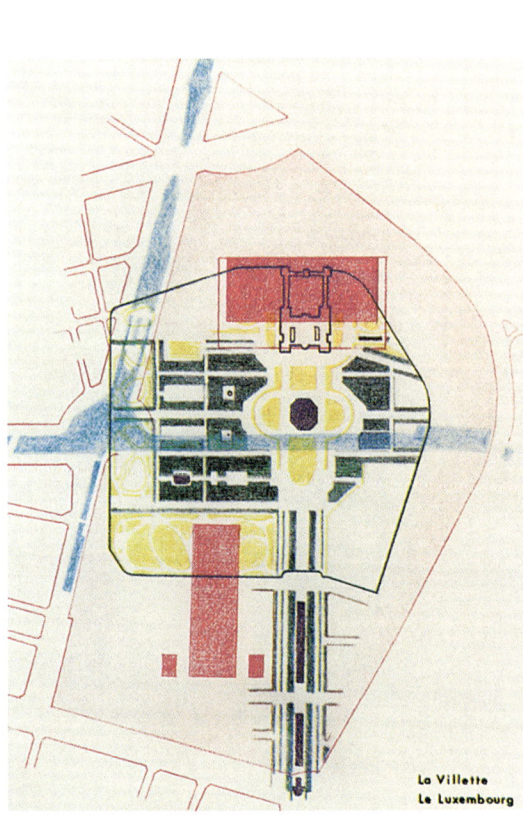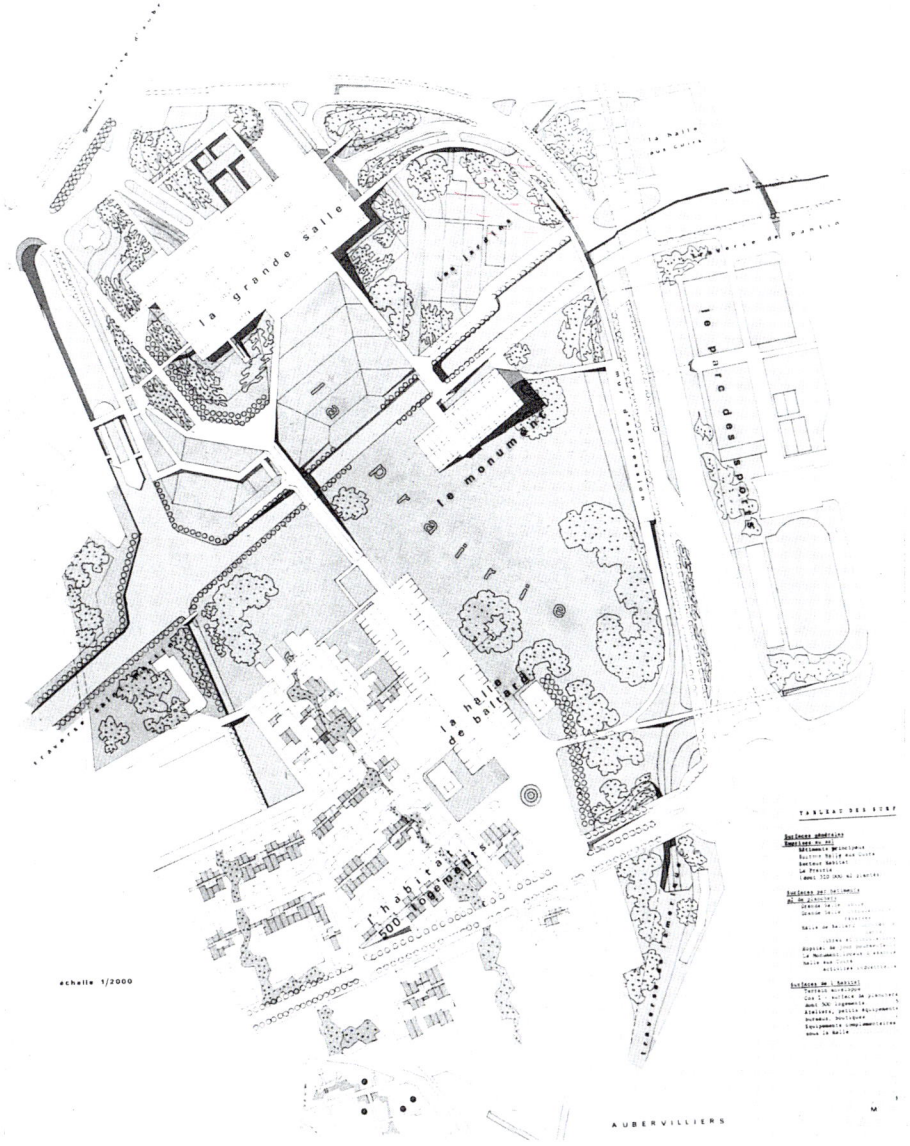

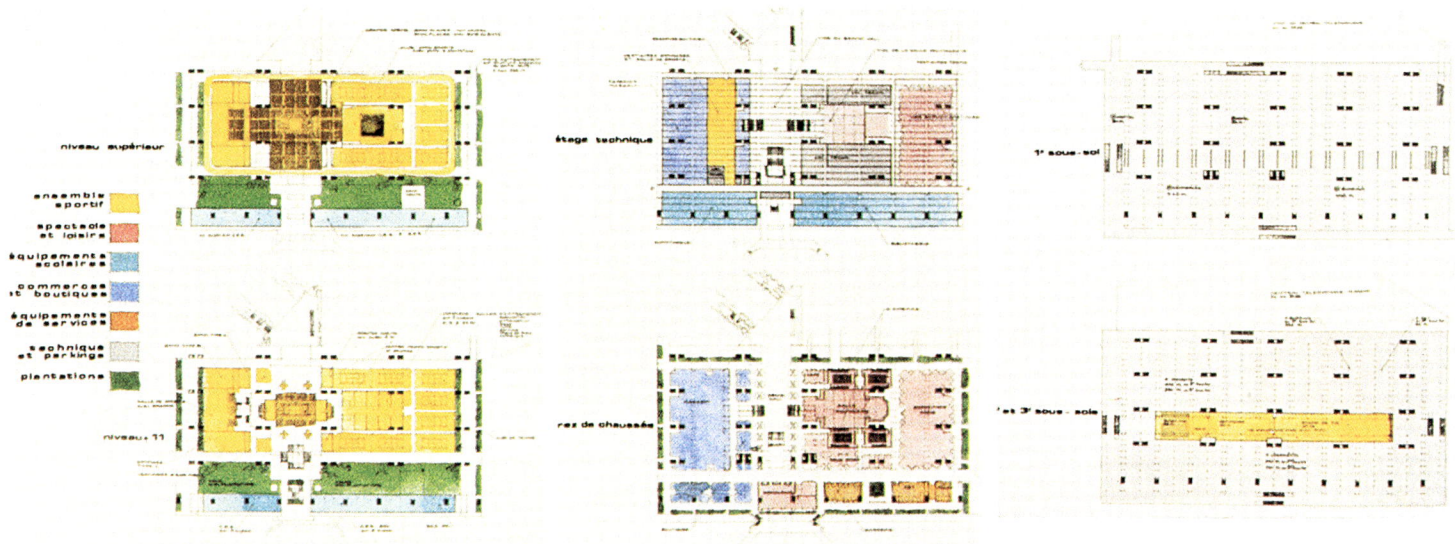

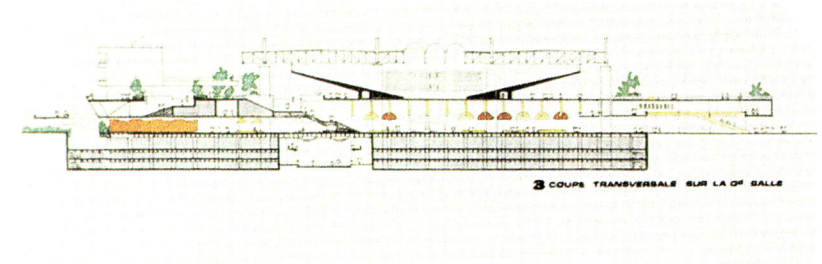

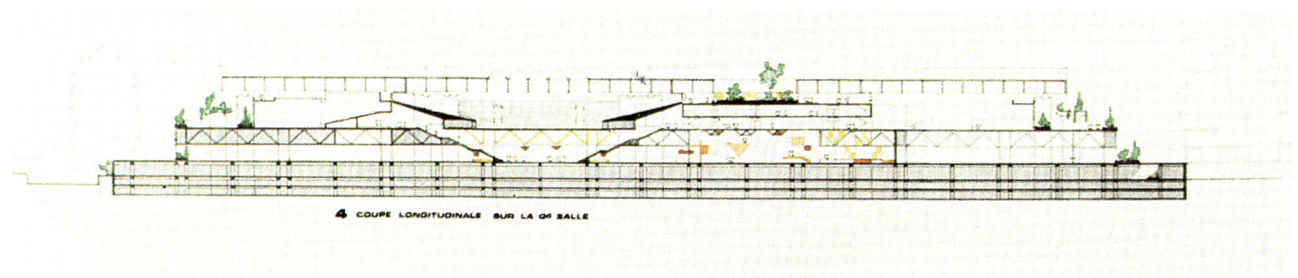

Above: APUR competition (1976).
Project by J. Haguenauer,
J. Chasseraud, B. Jacqueminet,
N. Franguiadakis, B. de Montety,
N. Yousri, Y. André.

promisingly ethical approach would be hallowed by the use of the retaining wall on Boulevard Serrurier as a "graffiti wall." Jacques Haguenauer concentrated his efforts on the meat market, mastering the colossal scale of its interior with crystal-clear planimetry. For their part, Joseph Belmont and Jean Prouvé heroically set out to domesticate the road running along the east of the site with a "housing screen" whose service areas were intended to neutralise traffic noise.

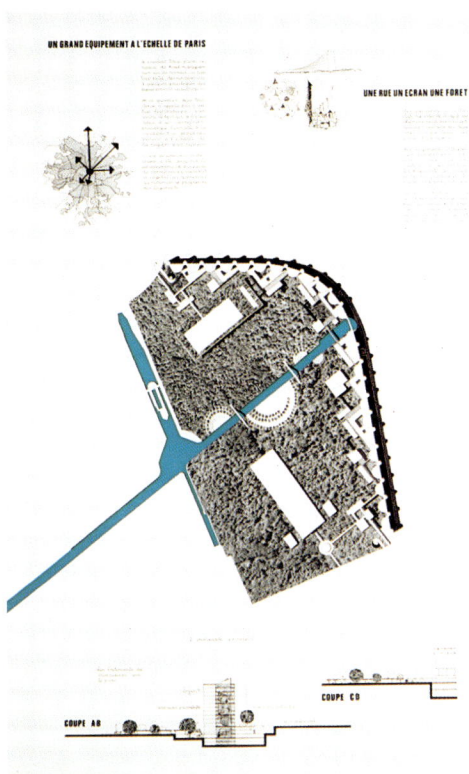

The APUR competition presented participants with three very tricky questions. The first had to do with the dimensions of the site. What kind of typology did such monumental scales call for? Some saw geometry as the answer, stressing access to the buildings via networks of thoroughfares. Others, doubtless unnerved by all the empty space, went for density, blitzing the site with architectonic confetti and producing lunar landscapes seemingly congealed by some post-nuclear deluge. This approach was in turn countered by projects that merged the buildings into enormous forests whose proliferation seemed beyond all control.

The second question had to do with the presence on the site of two extremely large structures: the meat market and the cattle shed. How was the brief to be applied to an area already over-provided with buildings? Some opted for swamping the meat market in a subtly chaotic mishmash of low-level volumes or encircling the cattle shed with stepped apartment blocks. Others, of a bolder cast of mind, spread the brief around in the form of minuscule architectural entities succeeding each other along strips that foreshadowed Bernard Tschumi's Folies (Follies) and Promenade Cinématique (Cinematic Itinerary) – when, that is, they did not simply disencumber the northern part by bulldozing the meat market.

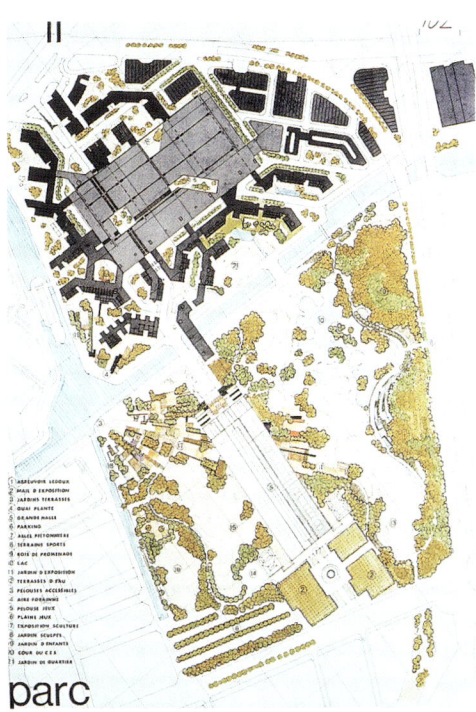

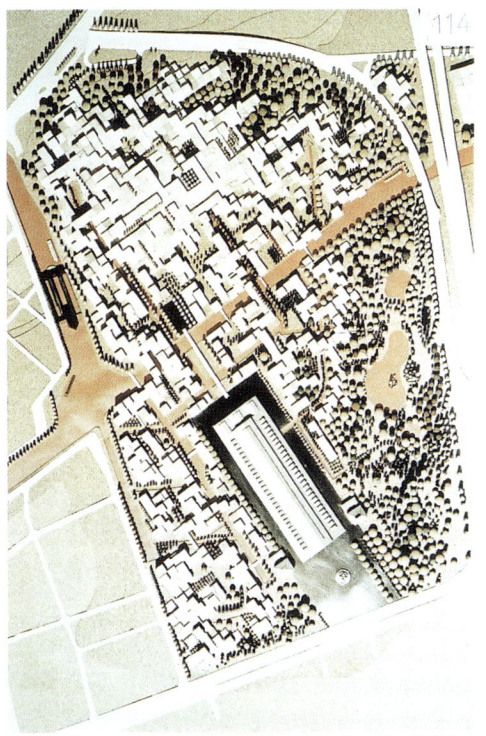

APUR competition (1976).
Left: Project by J. Belmont, J. Prouvé, M. Mercier.
Above right: Project by B. Néouze, Y. Clément, G. Duran, G. de La Personne.
Below right: Anonymous project.

CHRONOLOGY 23

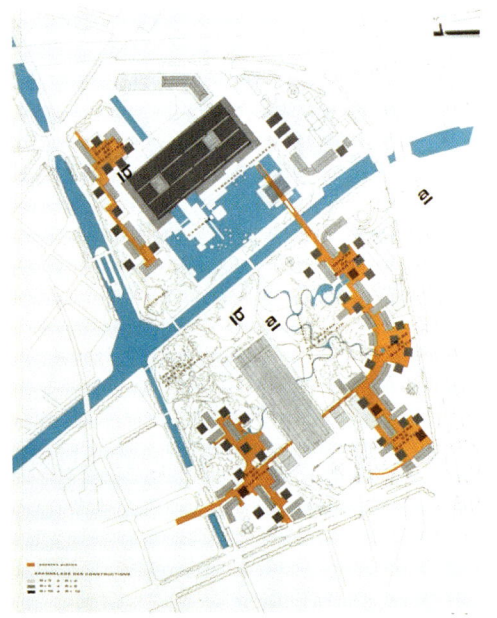
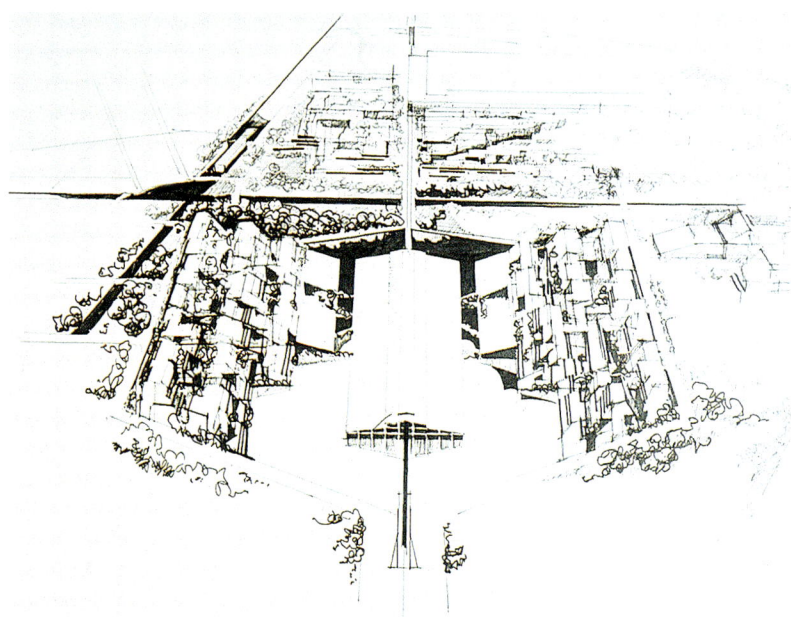

APUR competition (1976). Anonymous projects.

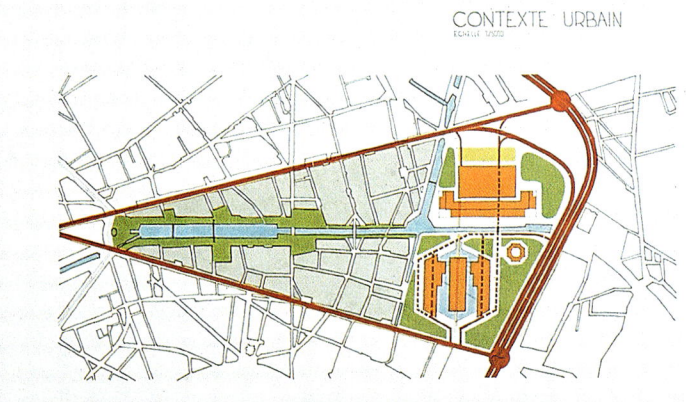

The Canal de l'Ourcq and the double roadway turned out to be reefs on which a good number of candidates foundered. Some mindlessly stuck the buildings along the banks of the canal, thereby exacerbating the scission of the site; others changed the canal's configuration, either to make their focus a hypothetical, out of scale "square lake," or to scarify the site with unravelling *canaletti* in an ultimate confusion of architecture with painting.

In addition to the fact that they irrevocably locked off the eastern extremity of the site and any possible link to the suburbs, the Boulevards des Maréchaux (inner ring road) and the Périphérique (outer ring road) were seen as sources of noise pollution. Some competitors responded with enormous buildings that either clung to the edge of the thoroughfares in question, or ran up to them at right angles. In some

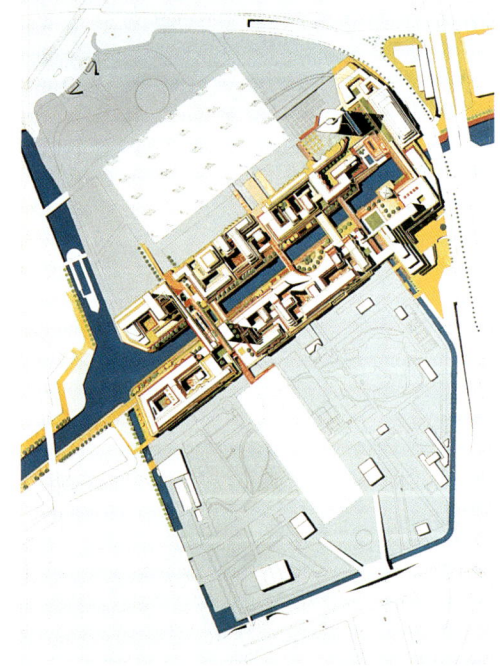

24 LA VILLETTE: 1971–1995

APUR competition (1976).
Above left: Project by D. Agrest,
M. Gandelsonas, J. Silvetti.
Below: Anonymous projects.

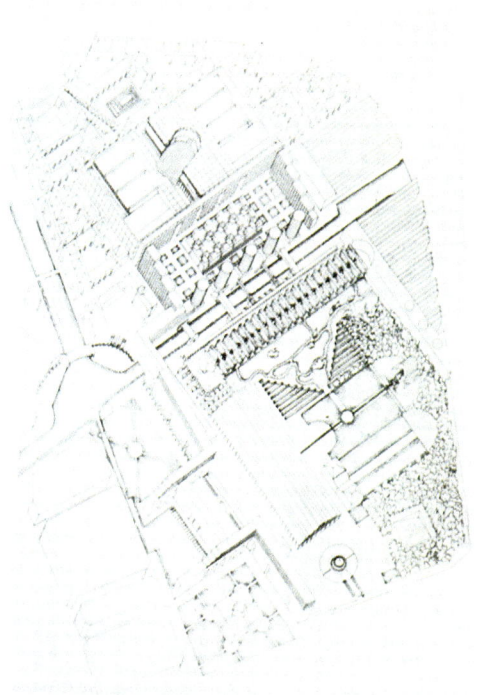

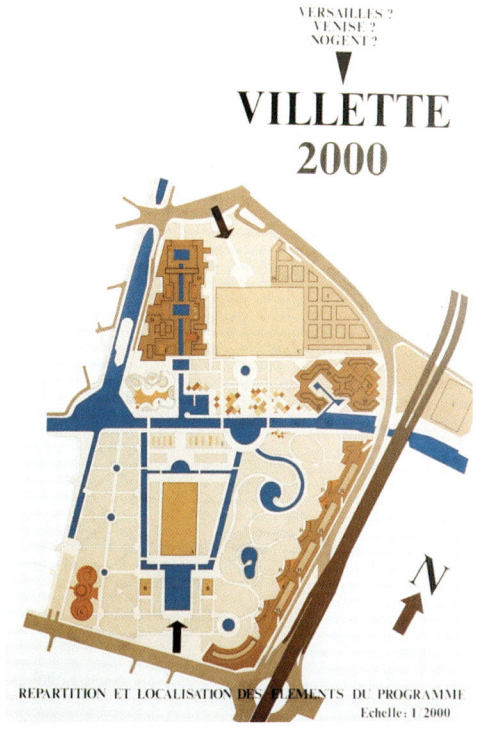

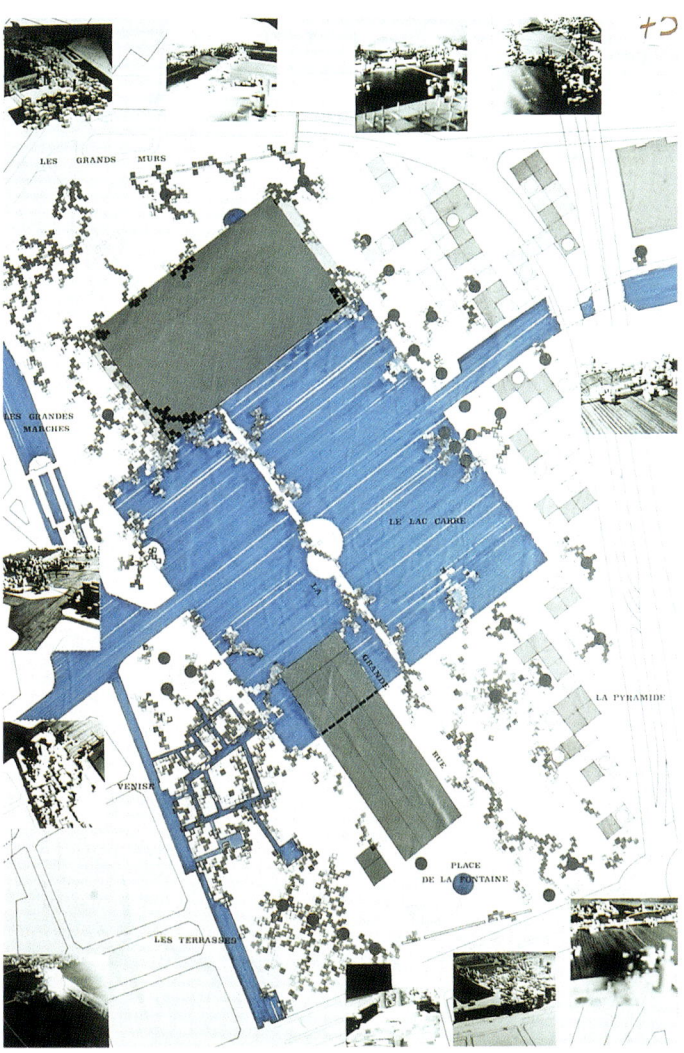

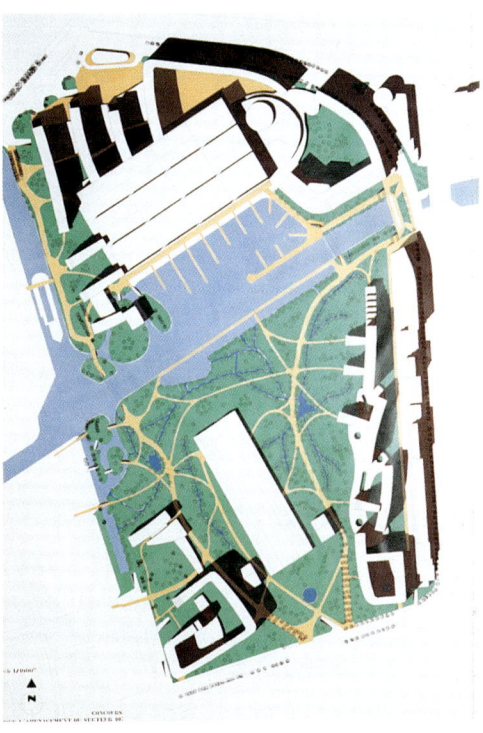

APUR competition (1976).
Above left: Project by B. Tschumi.
Above right and below: Anonymous projects.

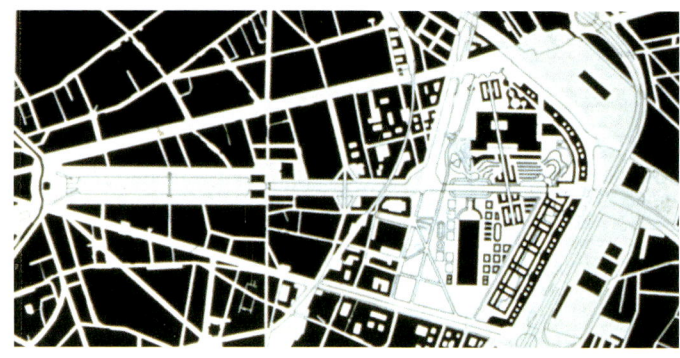

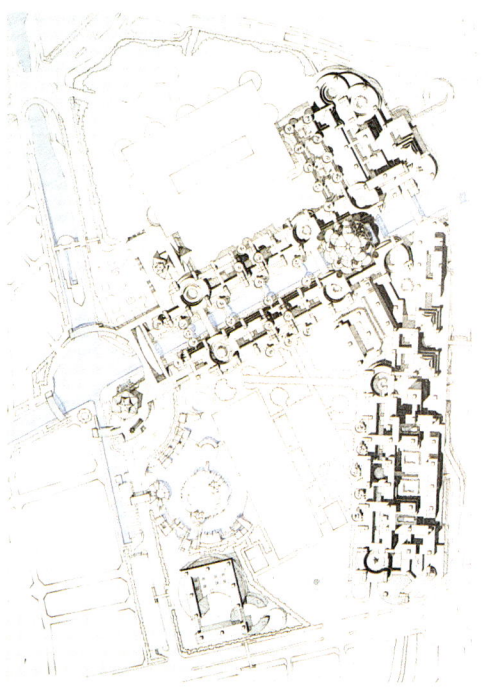

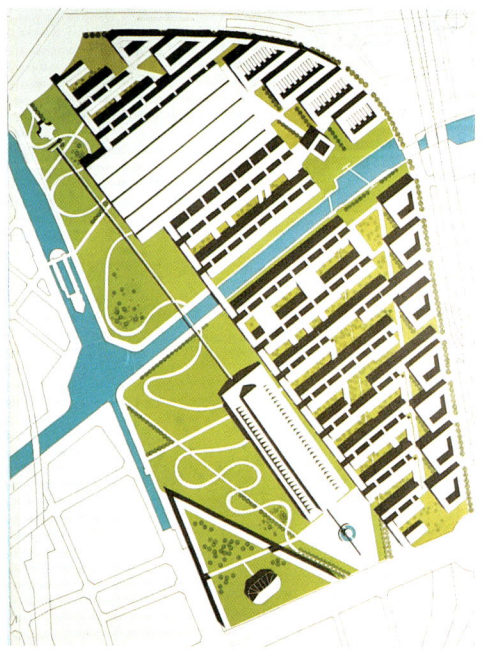

cases the task of damping down the traffic noise – more imaginary than real – was entrusted to luxuriant vegetation.

The Roger Taillibert study (1978)

Then, 1978 saw the arrival on the scene of Roger Taillibert, designer of the Parc des Princes sports stadium and architect-curator of the Grand Palais in Paris.

Appointed to oversee the "overall development co-ordination of the Villette sector as a whole," Taillibert was to become a militant advocate of the rehabilitation of the meat market into a science museum. He saw such a museum as providing an unparalleled opportunity to regroup – under one roof and one administrative body – the archives of the Académie des Sciences, the collections of the Palais de la Découverte, and the Musée des Techniques du Conservatoire National des Arts et Métiers. In addition, then, to a proposed reorganisation of the city's science-oriented museums, Taillibert came up with a unified site plan including an "observatory tower" topped with a panoramic restaurant. Like Jacques Haguenauer, Taillibert offered a rigorous layout for the interior of the meat market, with an endless run-through of the typological possibilities, and brought the same punctiliousness to his treatment of the exterior, volume, sketching out irresistible perspectives with a futurist touch. As it happened, a premonitory sphere crowned the south façade of the museum.

Paul Delouvrier steps in (1978)

If Jean Sérignan was unquestionably the man behind the decision to create a park on the abattoir site; and Roger Taillibert was the first to suggest a science museum to the authorities, and can also take the credit for convincing the French president

26 La Villette: 1971–1995

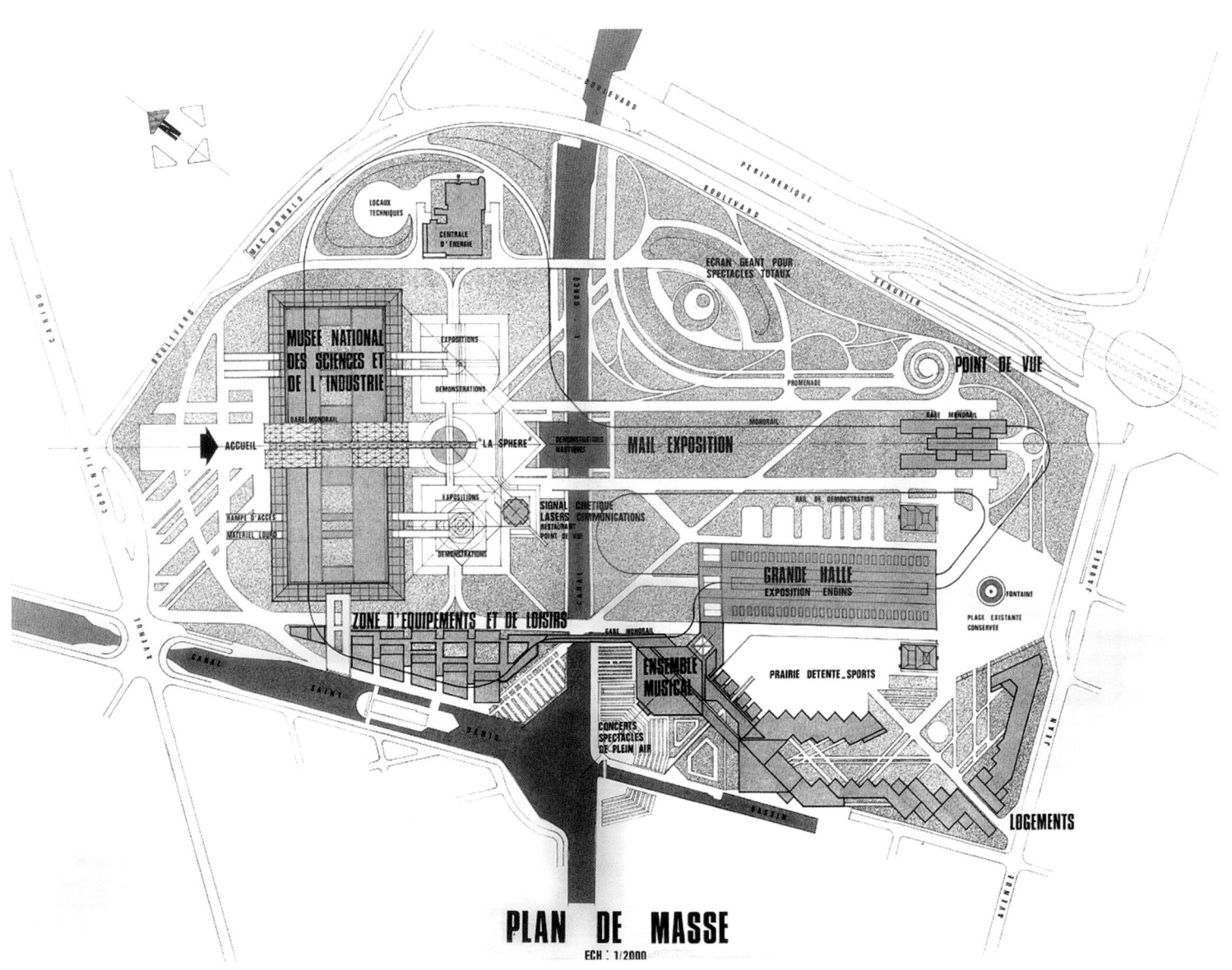

Development proposal of the Villette site (R. Taillibert, 1978).
Site plan.

CHRONOLOGY 27

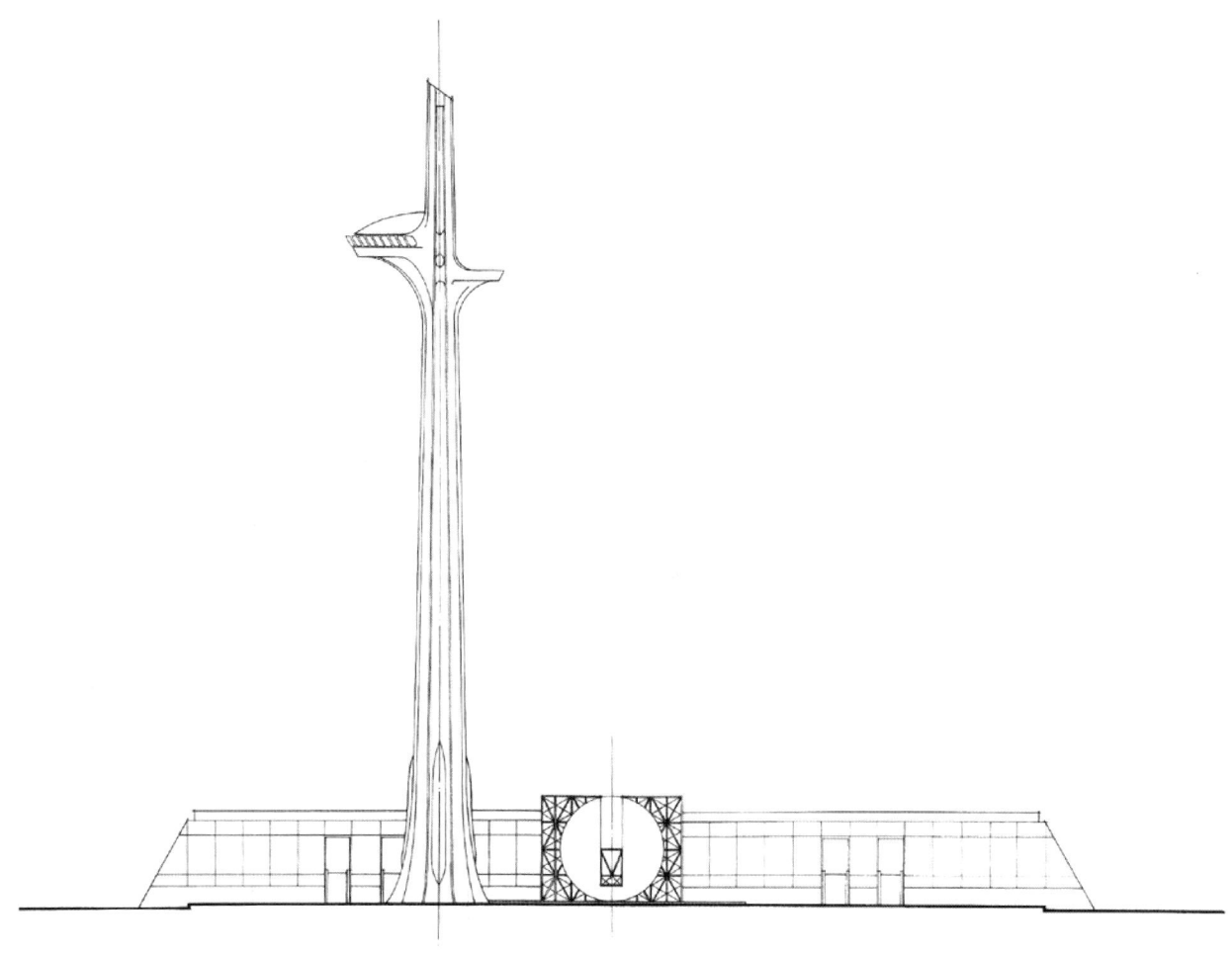

Development proposal of the Villette site (R. Taillibert, 1978).
Meat market (south façade).

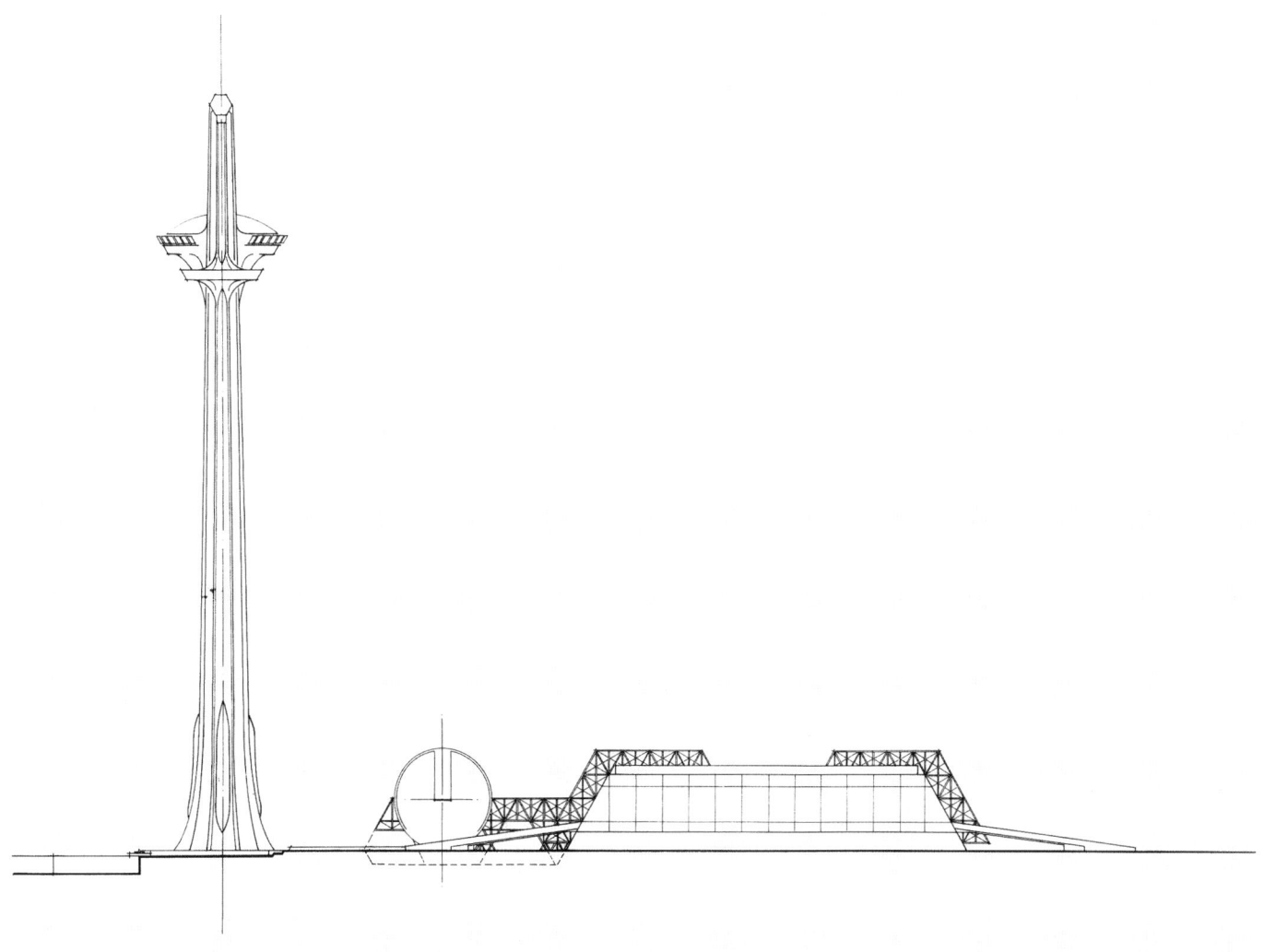

Development proposal of the Villette site (R. Taillibert, 1978).
Meat market (east façade).

CHRONOLOGY

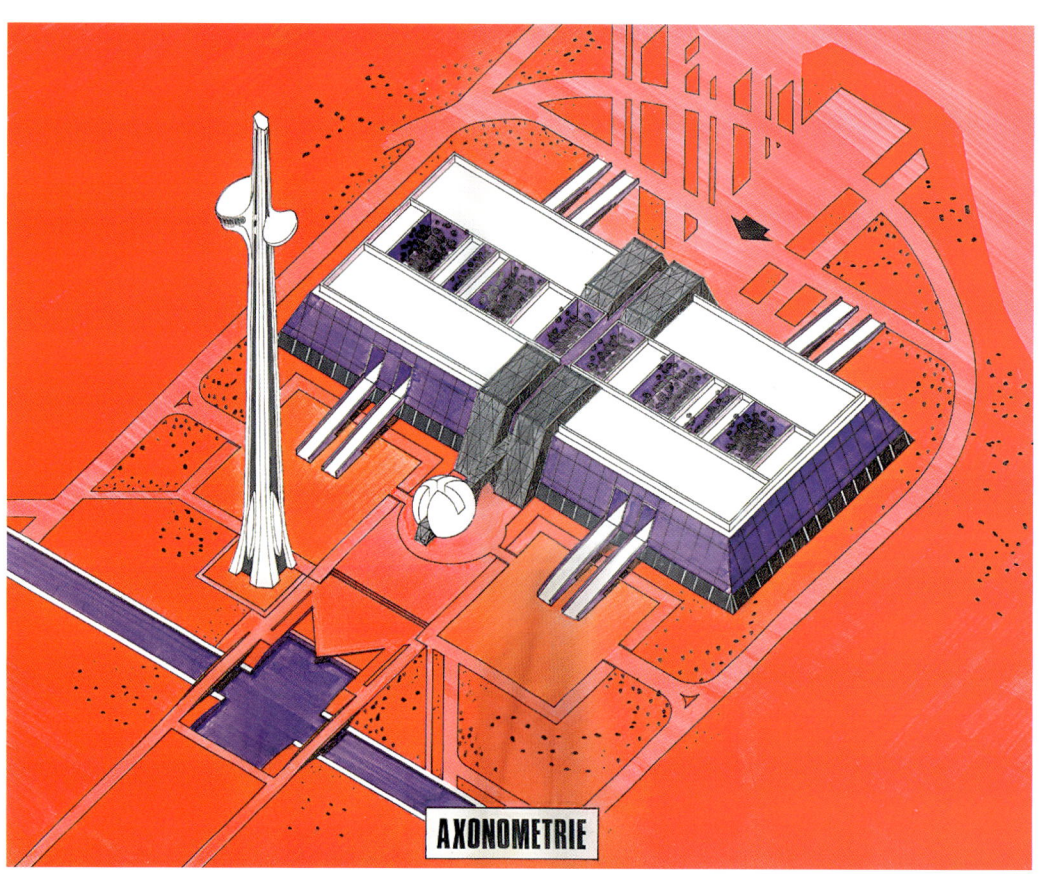

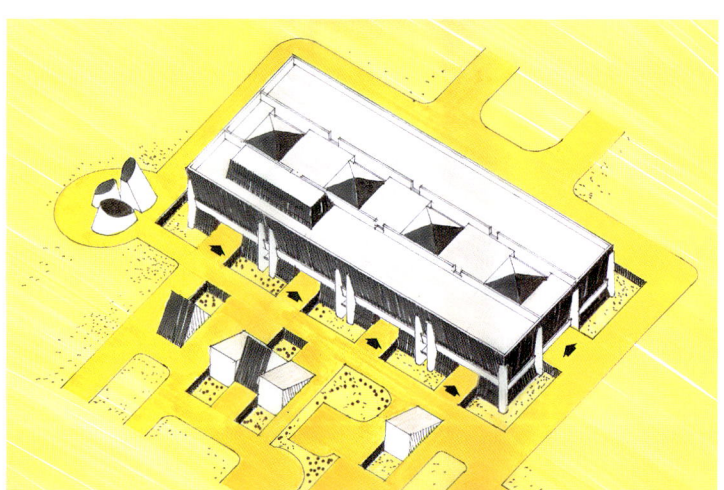

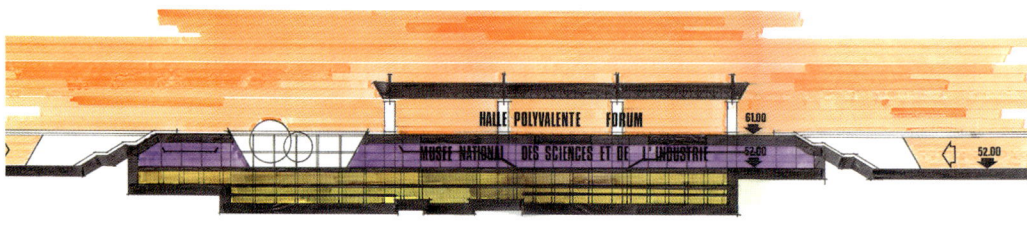

Development proposal of the Villette site (R. Taillibert, 1978).
From top to bottom:
Meat market (axonometric view);
Meat market (axonometric view);
Meat market (principle section).

30   La Villette: 1971–1995

to build at La Villette the major auditorium originally planned for Les Halles; then Paul Delouvrier's contribution was to set up and run the administrative body in charge of financing the cultural projects of La Villette.

But when leaving the president's office after having been appointed to "create La Villette" – Giscard d'Estaing's own words to him – in August 1978, was France's former national electricity CEO aware of the titanic nature of what he was taking on? True, a core cabinet meeting held at the presidential Élysée palace the following October, very quickly validated the plan for a "national museum of science and industry," a park and an auditorium on the abattoir site. And no less a figure than Maurice Lévy, professor of physics at the Université de Paris-VI, was chosen to define the goals of the museum. President Giscard d'Estaing was also the moving force behind France's "new towns," but it took all his political combativeness to have the Établissement Public du Parc de La Villette – EPPV (the public body in charge of the park), classified under national expenditure – a guarantee of funding by the Ministry of Finance – and thus overcome the last reservations of a political class that harboured doubts about the project's chances of success.

Paul Delouvrier, in charge of the EPPV from its foundation in July 1979 until 1984, also broadened its area of responsibility by resolving to include a dance school – a decision doubtless triggered by an impromptu visit to the site by a certain Isabelle de Lasteyrie Du Saillant.

When she remarked to Delouvrier that a complex devoted to music and dance could very well be part of La Villette, the French president's sister – who also happened to be a technical adviser to the minister of Culture and Communications, Jean-Philippe Lecat – was doubtless making known the minister's keenness to see the Rue de Madrid Conservatoire rebuilt on the abattoir site. Delouvrier checked out the idea with Sylviane Grange and Pierre Boulez, respectively, deputy director of music at the Ministry of Culture, and director of the Institut de Recherche et de Coodination Acoustique/Musique – IRCAM (Institute for Research and Coordination in Acoustics and Music). When both spoke up for reform of the Conservatoire curriculum and the building of new premises, Delouvrier drew up a competition brief for the creation of a "national museum of science and industry," adding a dance complex to the museum, park and auditorium projects.

This was a bold cultural venture: but with a determined and high-ranking civil servant overseeing the development body, La Villette could now get under way. There were stumbling blocks, however: Delouvrier was forbidden to entrust the design of the museum to Roger Taillibert – who nourished the hope of building it – after having been cited in connection with the Montreal Olympics finance scandal (he was later exonerated); and President Giscard d'Estaing refused to put Maurice Lévy in charge of the "Museum Mission" – there was disagreement over methods between Lévy, future CEO of the Cité des Sciences, and Alice Saunier-Séïté, Universities minister. Even so, the competition for the Musée National des Sciences et de l'Industrie opened in February 1980.

The competition for the "Musée National des Sciences et de l'Industrie" (1980)

The competition focused mainly on rehabilitation of the meat market. The gigantic metal structure would host 30,000 square metres of permanent exhibitions, a further 10,000 of temporary ones and a giant hemispheric screen. The museum would have to fit into an "overall devel-

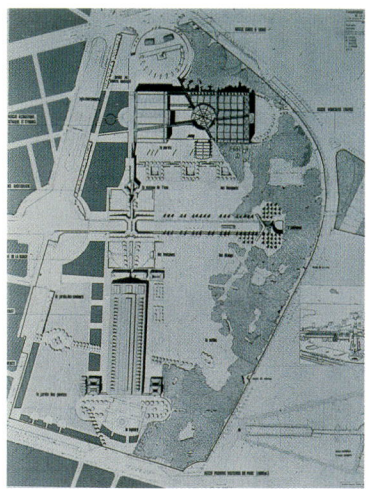

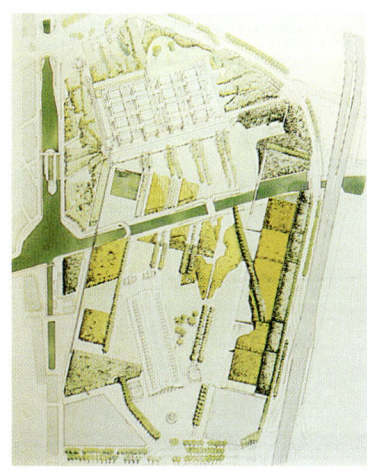

Musée National des Sciences et de l'Industrie competition (1980).
Above: Project by A. Zublena.
Below: Project by P. Chemetov.

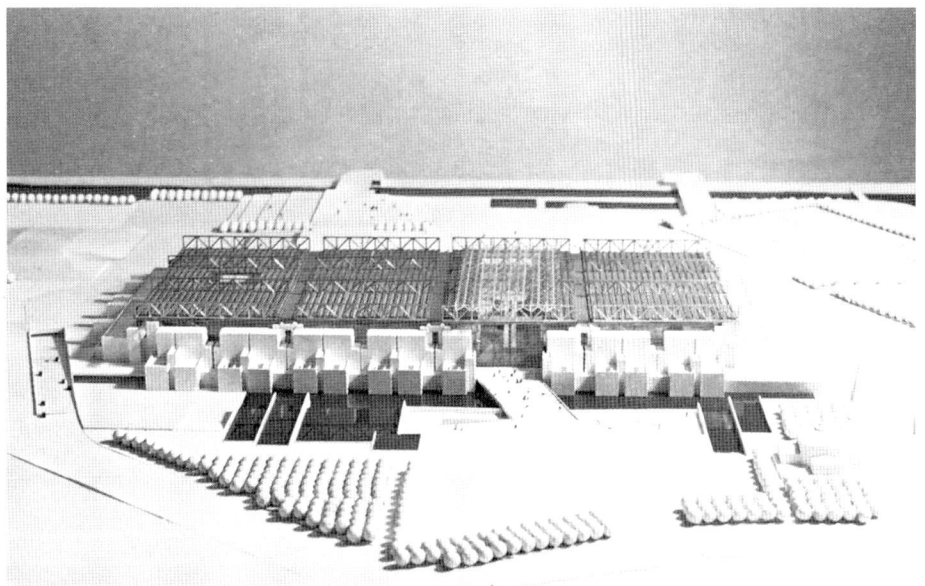

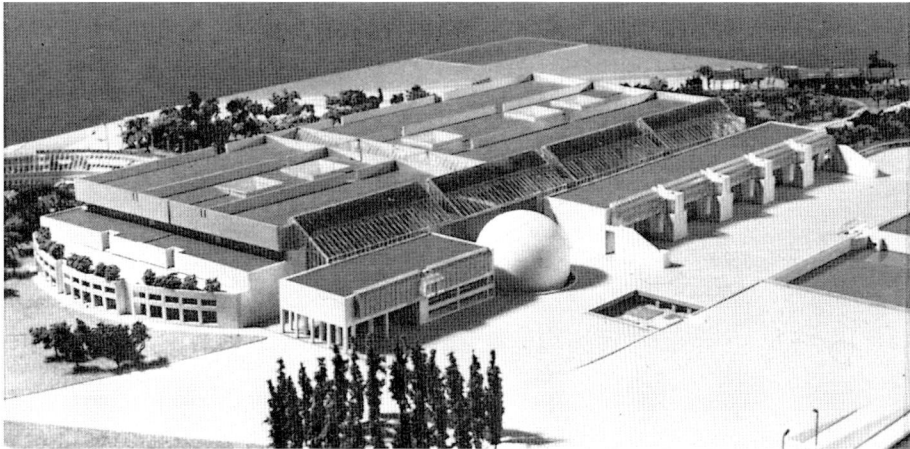

Musée National des Sciences et de l'Industrie competition (1980).
Above: Project by P. Lajus.
Below: Project by B. Bonnier.

Page right: Musée National des Sciences et de l'Industrie competition (1980).
Project by D. Badani.
Above left: Perspective view of the hall.
Above right: Site plan.
Middle right: Model.

opment layout" also including a park, an auditorium and a dance school. The brief stressed the importance of north-south passageways and welcomed suggestions regarding a use for the cattle shed, listed as an historical monument since 1979. The sadly dilapidated sheep and swine sheds were to be demolished.

Was the "swine area," a vast excrescence on the south façade of the meat market, to be restored? It was up to the competitors – all French, at the express wish of the president – to decide.

Would the winning architect get to create the park and the music and choregraphic complex? The answers to this question could not have been more evasive.

7 = 6 + 1

Ultimately the jury chose six projects.

Aymeric Zublena gutted the meat market, using enormous oblique lines converging on a circular entrance hall.

Paul Chemetov subdivided it into museum blocks accessible via a network of sky-lit passageways.

Bertrand Bonnier cut into the swine area to make way for his hemispheric space.

Pierre Lajus split the meat market in two, setting the thoroughfare for the exhibitions at the centre of the second bay.

Daniel Badani and the Reichen/Robert team both found a brilliant fit between architectural and urban scale. Badani, whose project was long a presidential favourite, offered access to the museum via a skilfully gradual ascent. Opposed to the swine area, which he saw as "bastardising" the south façade of the meat market, Badani proposed the demolition of its upper levels and the use of the remaining volume as terraces providing access to the museum. Visitors would then plunge into its very heart via monumental staircases in the second bay. Reichen and Robert used only the two central bays of the market, sending internal traffic lengthways along the façades. An "aqueduct avenue," also called "discovery avenue" was to be built with material from the demolished buildings and would link the museum to the park, the music complex and the very same cattle shed that Reichen and Robert would find themselves rehabilitating in 1983.

Among the unsuccessful projects was an odd proposal from Jean Balladur: suspended from the main beams of the megastructure, sails shaped like birds' wings plunged, as if liquefied, into large pools. Equally startling was Jean Willerval's proposal for what looked like an interstellar spacecraft ready for takeoff.

Members of Groupement d'Études Architecturales, for their part, shut the meat market away under an immense glass shell.

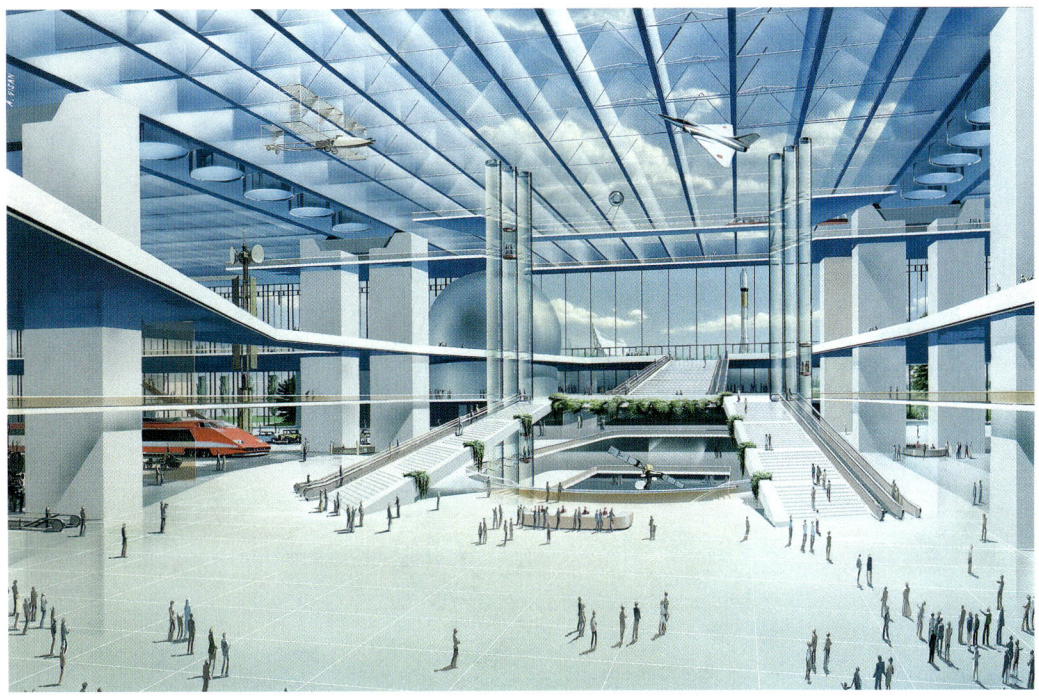
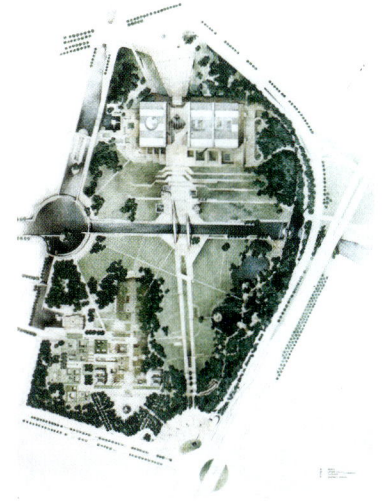
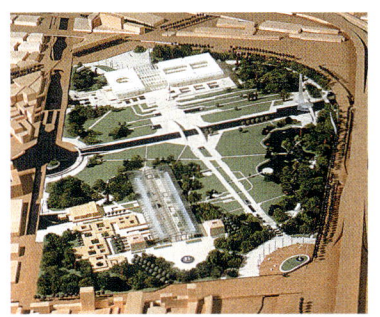

Still in the running, then, were Badani, Bonnier, Chemetov, Lajus, Reichen/Robert and Zublena: six projects for a museum. It was at this point that Paul Delouvrier proved a skilled strategist. By taking advantage of the fact that two members of the judging panel were absent: Bernard Rocher, deputy mayor of Paris in charge of Town Planning and Roger Taillibert – who had refused to take part in the competition – boycotted the voting sessions, finding the projects indefensible. With the backing of his director of Architecture, Joseph Belmont, a cleverly used figurehead, Delouvrier just managed to get the six projects through – and disregarding

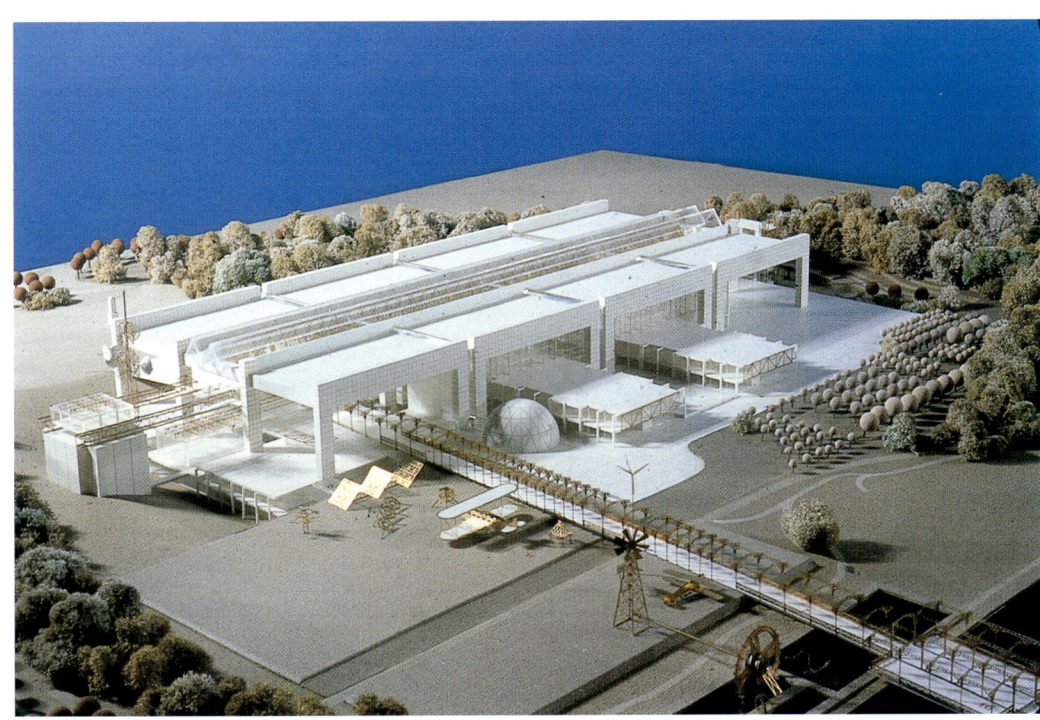
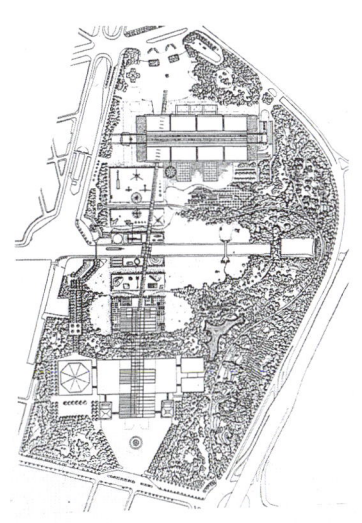

Musée National des Sciences et de l'Industrie competition (1980). Below left and right: Project by B. Reichen and P. Robert.

CHRONOLOGY 33

Musée National des Sciences
et de l'Industrie competition (1980).
Above right: Project by J. Balladur.

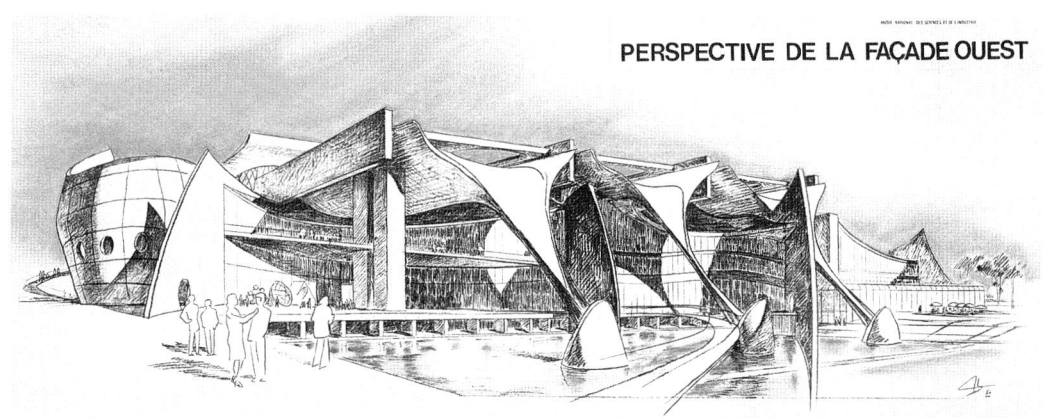

the panel's opinion, added that of Adrien Fainsilber. As for the second round – it never happened.

Delouvrier had made sure his case was legally watertight: the competition had been organised "under the responsibility of the EPPV president" which the judging panel, also presided over by Delouvrier, was to "assist in the choosing of the seven short-listed projects."

On 15 September 1980, Adrien Fainsilber was declared the winner.

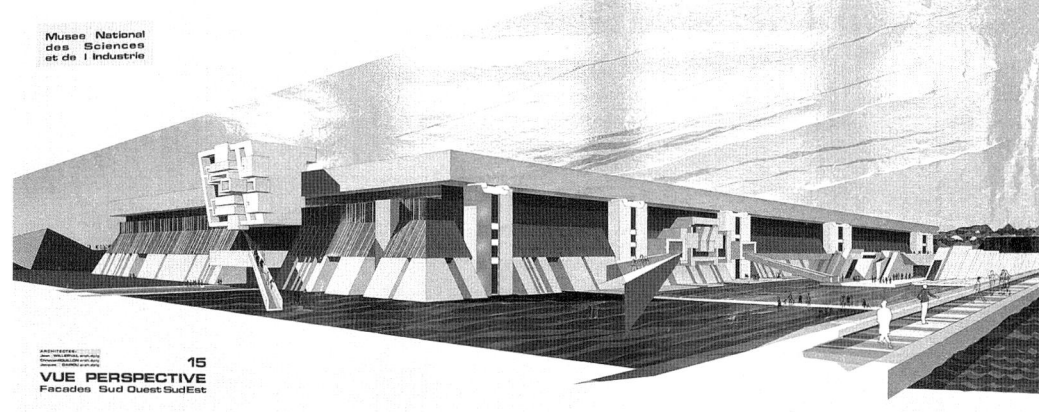

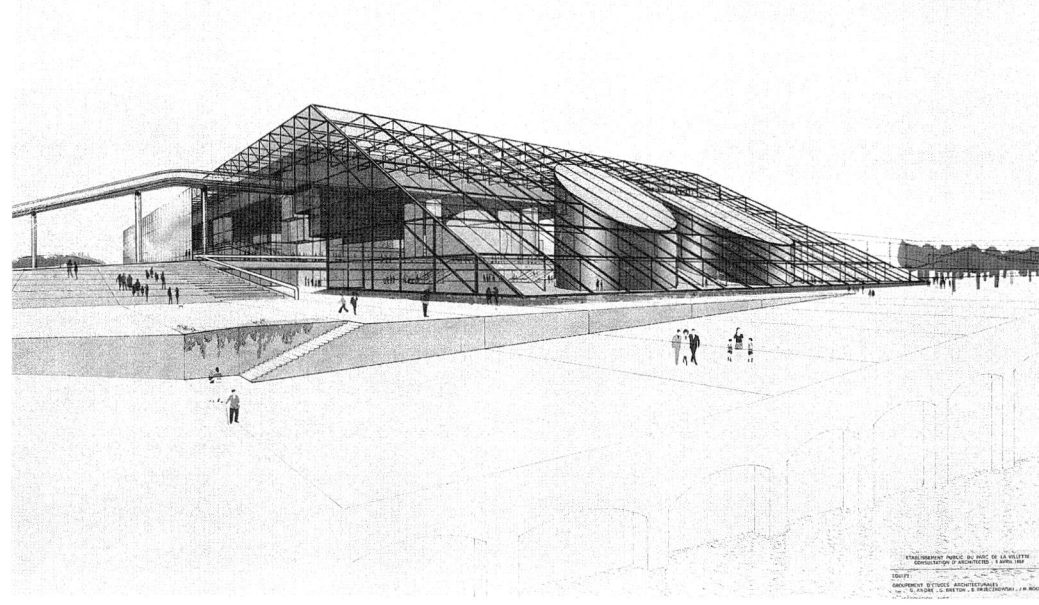

Musée National des Sciences
et de l'Industrie competition (1980).
Middle: Project by J. Willerval.
Below: Project by Groupement
d'Études Architecturales (G. André,
G. Preton, B. Bzgeczkowsky,
J.-R. Roques).

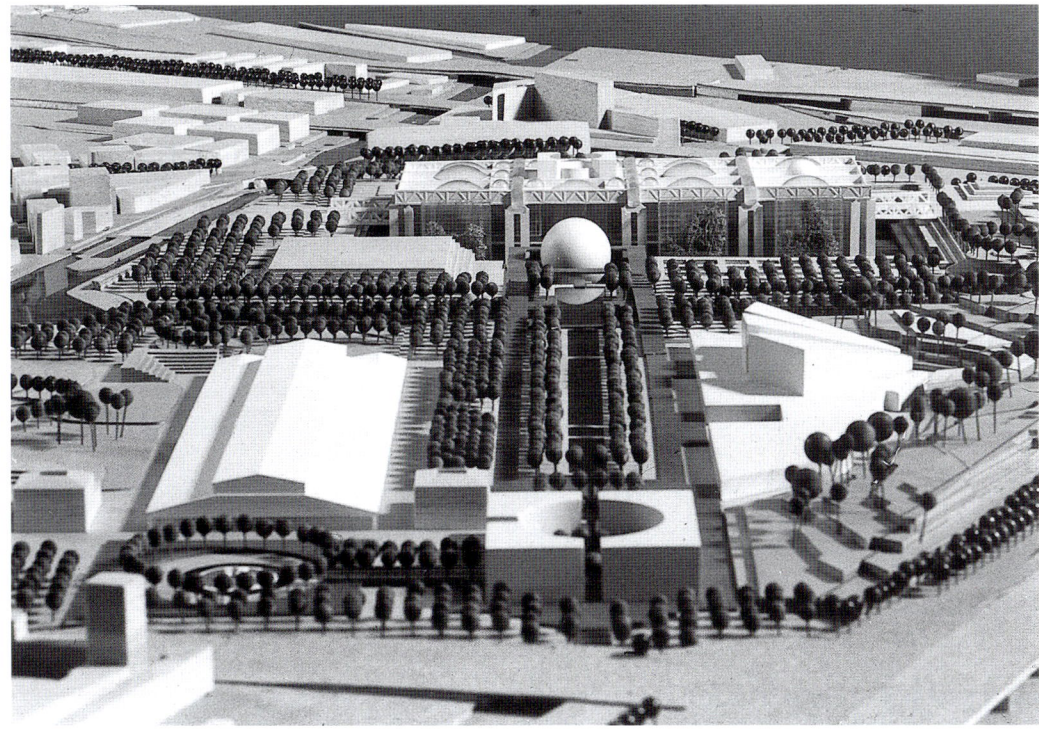
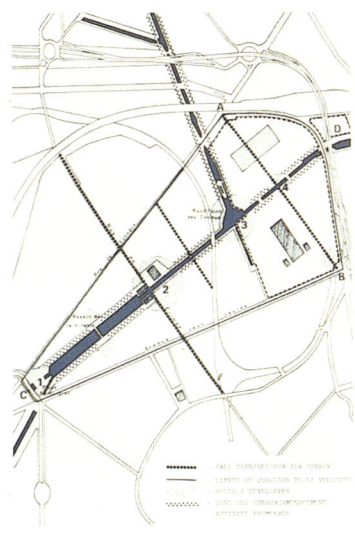

Musée National des Sciences et de l'Industrie competition (1980). Project by A. Fainsilber.
Right: The road network, 19th arrondissement, Paris.
Left: Model.

Adrien Fainsilber's project

Adrien Fainsilber's plan involved cutting into the heart of the meat market to make room for the entrance hall. Intersected by a pedestrian thoroughfare, the hall gave the impression of spreading towards the north and south forecourts. The Géode – the hemispheric cinema – was set against the south façade of the museum. At right angles to the Canal de l'Ourcq, a pool ran towards Place de la Fontaine-aux-Lions, ensuring visual and pedestrian continuity between the Porte de La Villette and the Porte de Pantin. Stripped of the clutter of the refrigeration rooms and swine area, the museum, now rendered more blatantly gigantic by the excavation of the adjacent land and its reflection in the surrounding moats, broodingly dominated the northern part of the site.

The combination of an overtly sober treatment of the building elements and a tendency to draw on the formal patterns of classicism made Fainsilber a worthy heir to Jean-Louis-Nicolas Durand. At the same time, he revealed an indisputably practical grasp of cutting-edge technology in the bioclimatic greenhouses designed in collaboration with Peter Rice; the use of the so-called "spider" technique for attaching the roof domes; the hollowing out of the load-bearing pillars to accommodate staircases conforming to construction standards; and the scraping-back of the porticoes leading to the interior, which allowed for exposure of the pillars to the north and subsequent visual compatibility between the two longitudinal façades. A kind of "high-tech Auguste Perret," Fainsilber had successfully untangled the maze of the meat market – he would later do the same in Clermont-Ferrand, transforming the old carcass of the Palais-Vieux into a resplendent museum – and would ultimately deliver a ready-to-go Cité des Sciences et de l'Industrie to Maurice Lévy, logically destined to become its director. Two feasibility studies – Janus I (1983) and Janus II (1985) – preceded the opening of the Cité in March 1986. Work had begun in early August 1982.

If the idea behind the Pompidou Centre was to plunge the visitor into the very heart of the process of cultural production,

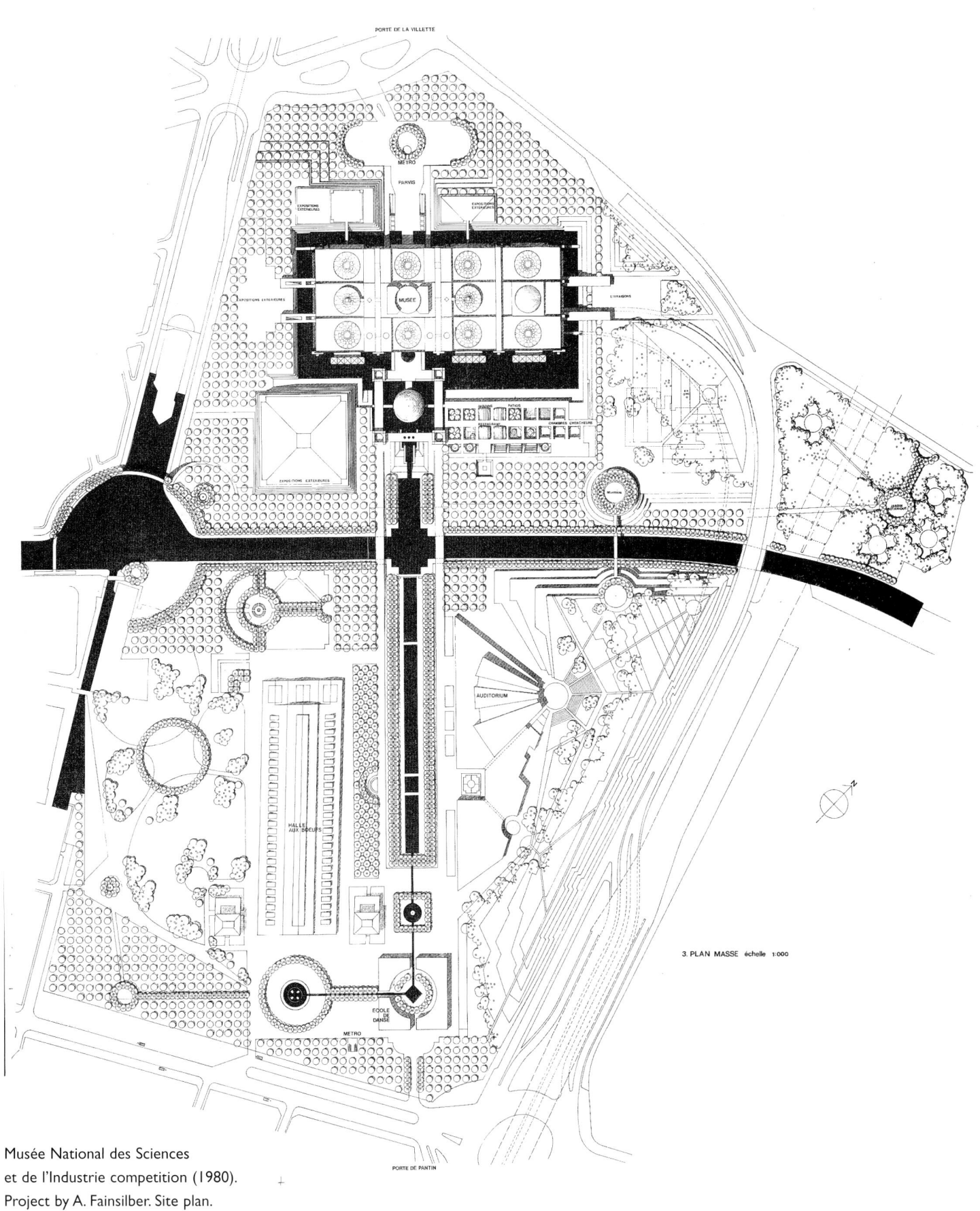

Musée National des Sciences et de l'Industrie competition (1980). Project by A. Fainsilber. Site plan.

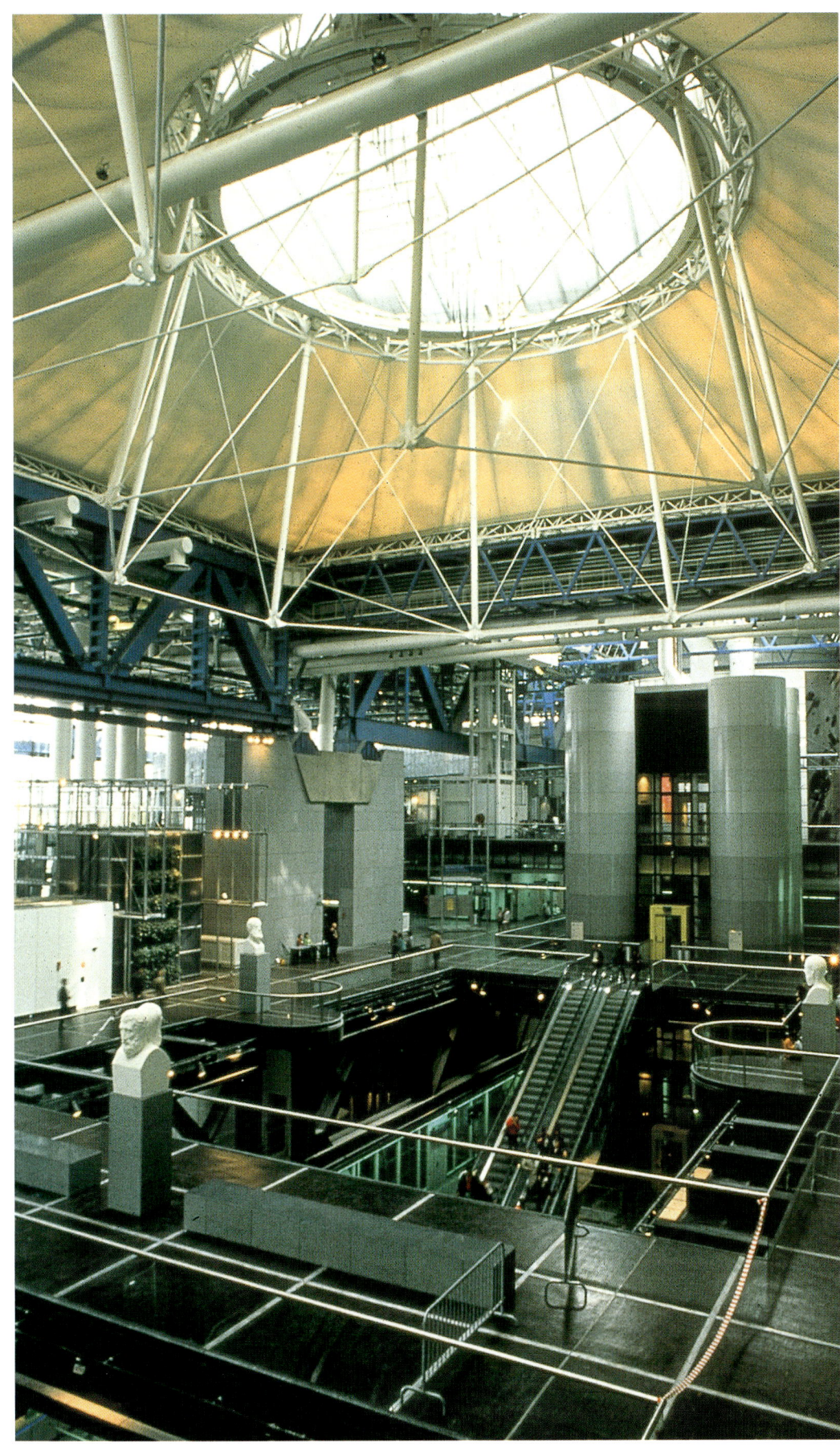

The Cité des Sciences
et de l'Industrie
(architect: A. Fainsilber).
View of the hall from the upper floor.

The Cité des Sciences
et de l'Industrie
(architect: A. Fainsilber).
Above: The north façade.
Middle: The columns of the façade.
Below: The north façade (final project).

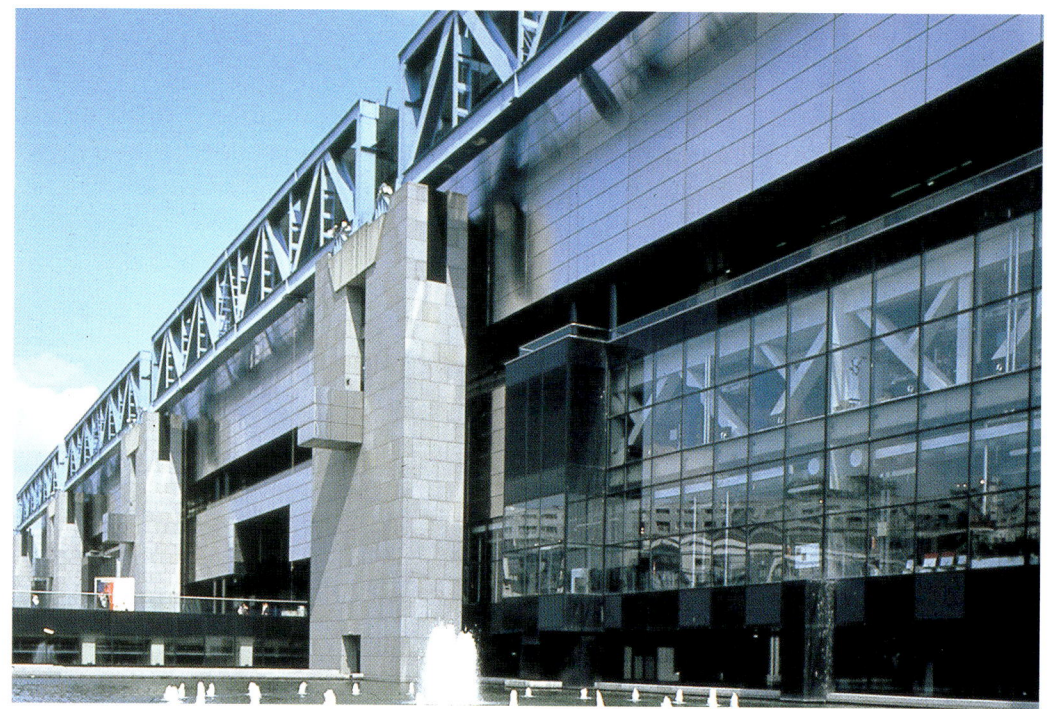

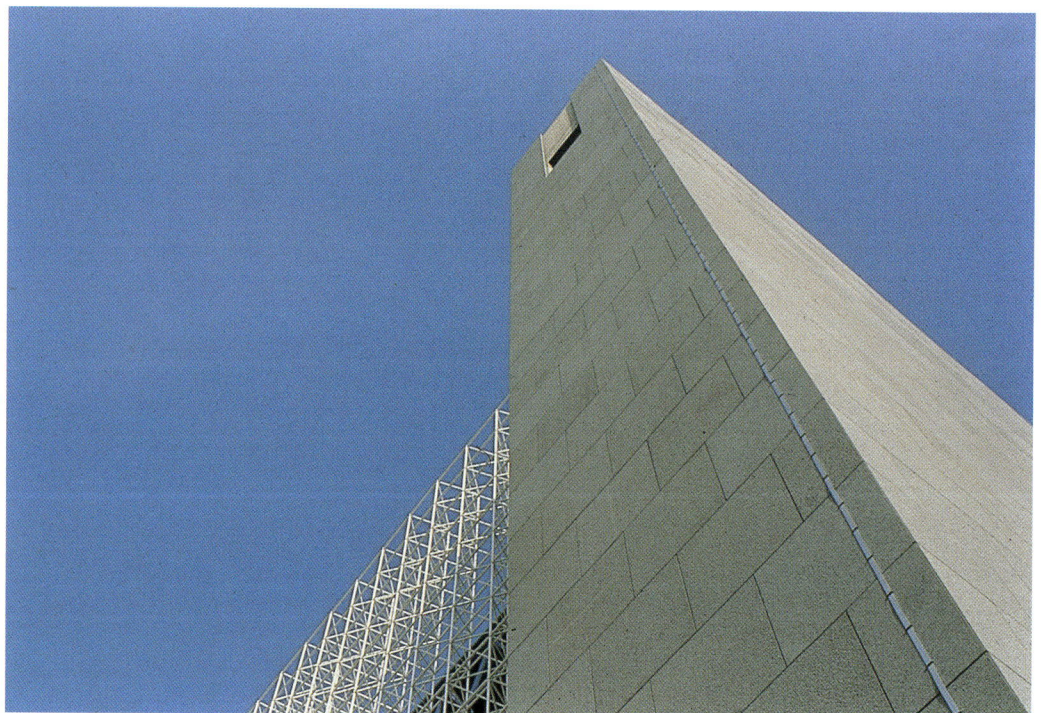

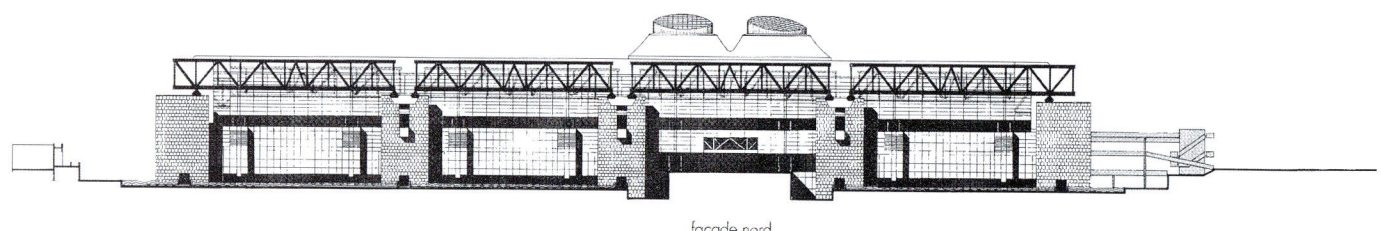

38   LA VILLETTE: 1971–1995

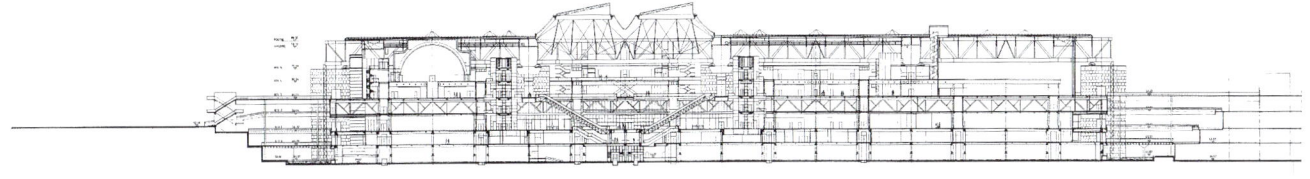

coupe longitudinale

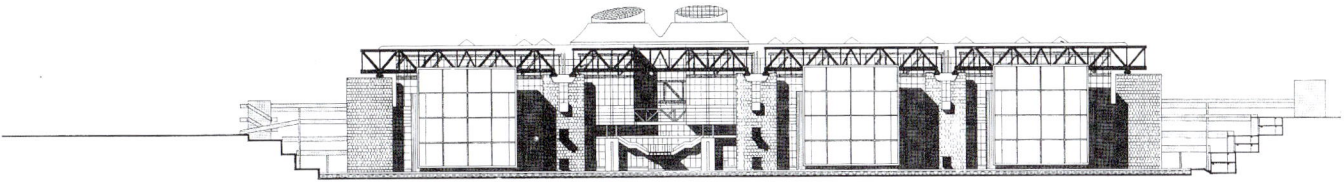

façade sud

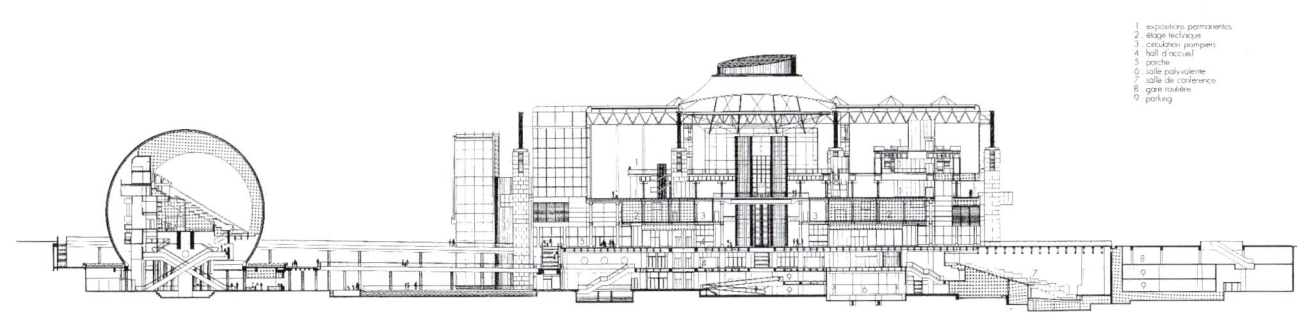

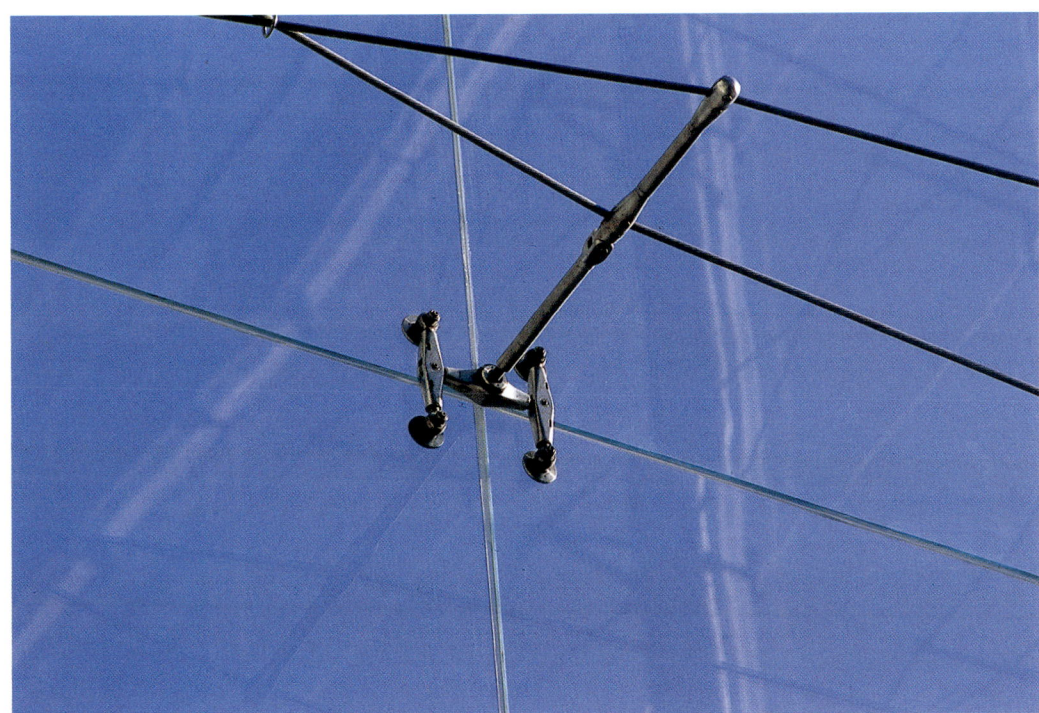

The Cité des Sciences
et de l'Industrie
(architect: A. Fainsilber).
Above: Longitudinal section, entrance hall; south façade; transverse section, entrance hall and Géode (final project).
Left: The bioclimatic greenhouses.

CHRONOLOGY 39

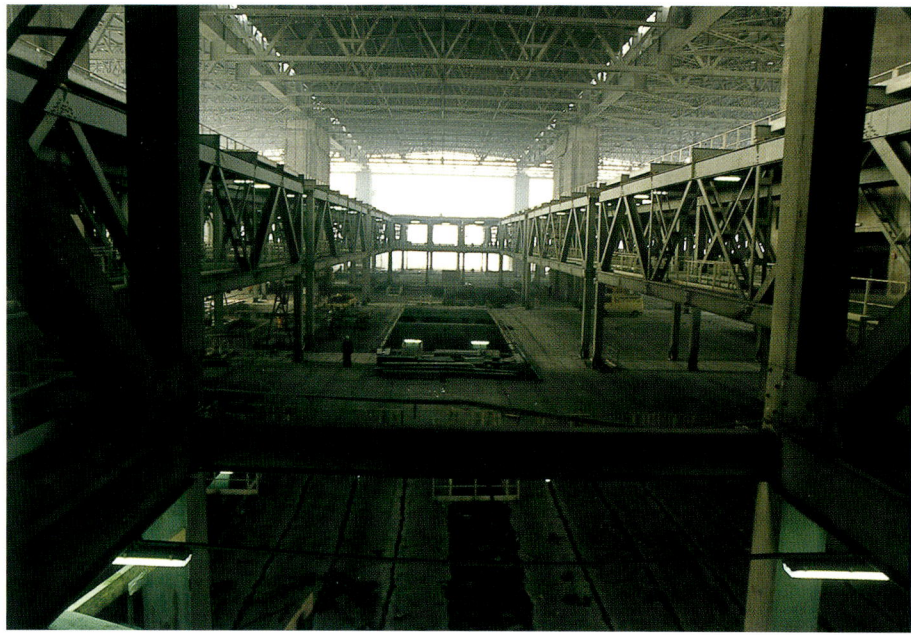

The Cité des Sciences et de l'Industrie (architect: A. Fainsilber). The entrance hall of the meat market during its construction.

then the Cité des Sciences et de l'Industrie was to be its scientific double. In allowing ordinary people to "see, touch and understand" – the three keywords of the Lévy Report – the Cité would work for a fresh perception of knowledge based on the sacrosanct concept of interactivity.

The Cité, then, had two main aims; the first of them philosophical: a simultaneous rethinking of the notions of truth and accuracy. The second was strategic: a reconsideration of the terms of the relationship between science and industry, with a view to dealing dispassionately with the competitive economic climate of the third millennium.

The Parc de La Villette competition (1982–1983)

While the terms of the 1980 competition clearly indicated the authorities' concern to articulate the Cité des Sciences and the Parc de La Villette, actually getting the latter under way remained very much a secondary matter. The park, it seemed, was reckoned a mere typological tool for reinforcing the presence of the museum to the north. Like Le Nôtre's gardens, it was intended solely as a foil for the architectural object.

The conclusions of the study the Centre Scientifique et Technique du Bâtiment – CSTB (Scientific and Technical Centre for Building) carried out for the EPPV were to confirm this neoclassical vision of the park. It would, they hoped, be a "vector for urban centrality," but competition participants were nonetheless encouraged to see it "in terms of the Versailles maze model."

The proposals of the working group chaired by Sylvie Barrau had very much the same tilt. While the park was not to be a mere "visual accompaniment to the museum," and had to be "attractive in its own right," it was also described as a "space for relaxation, play, encounters and celebrations."

The dominance of the baroque approach characterised most of the submissions, with participants gluing the park onto the museum as if it were a kind of lobby. After all, in his "explanatory note on the development agenda," Adrien Fainsilber had portrayed the park as "a natural extension of the museum"; while Daniel Badani had expressed the wish for a "monumental gate marking the park entrance."

The appointment of François Barré as head of the "Park Mission" in November 1981 coincided with the authorities' determination to reconsider the basic landscape approaches in light of the changed historico-philosophical scene of the late twentieth century. This shift was backed by newly-elected President François Mitterrand, who opted for an international competition for the park, leaving Fainsilber no real choice but to drop his overall development agenda and concentrate solely on the museum.

The inception report prepared by François Barré – nicknamed by Paul Delouvrier "the eye of the Élysée"– stressed the importance of a garden design redefining the age-old nature/culture link. Like the baroque park – "against nature" because geometrical – and its embodiment of Cartesian mind/matter dualism; like the Enlightenment park, in which nature seen as "pure proliferation" coexisted with an architecture-artefact, and its reminder of the self-containedness of nature and human understanding; like the Haussmannian park, that "therapeutic" Eden warding off the morbidity of the industrial city; and, like the *Ville Radieuse* with its isotropic landscape, the Parc de La Villette would stand as a social symbol, revealing – to quote François Barré – nature "modified" and "provided with a concept." The goal at La Villette was to resuscitate the nature/culture relationship that had once been central to the art of the garden.

Unity lost, uncertainty triumphant
But what kind of park would suit what some were calling postmodernity? What kind of symbolism would match what Isabelle Auricoste termed a "heady complexity"[4] which had "not yet produced the image of the world of tomorrow?"[5]

The belief no longer existed in "ordering the parts in terms of the One"[6] and the "cohesion of the All?" The Fainsilber site plan and its "passive" point of view were out of date. Acknowledging the dominant role of the Périphérique, Barré set out to "encourage dispersal,"[8] asserting that as a "form full of partial motifs, today's parks, like today's materials, are composite."[9]

With the loss of certain values leaving our age to endure the agonies of undecidability – Daniel Sibony's famous "contradictory statements" – what could be more natural than a park that had "the shifting character of a reflection"[10] and stood "at the crossroads of questions?"[11]

The competition brief
The wildly eclectic brief – La Villette as home to thermal baths, games areas and science discovery workshops – looked like the symbol of a postmodern social mix of hyperurbanisation, multiple affiliations and ideological abdication, with "particularist clamouring"[12] as the response to the hegemony of a "totally indifferent (non)culture."[13] The brief, designed by Barré to be open-ended and multifarious – "linked," he said, "to the rhythms and quests of urban life, and allowing for new kinds of activities, instead of a landscape in which grass and trees are sacred"[14] – also reflected the disappearance of the knowing/doing dichotomy and plumped for the underlying savvy of a new "culture of the everyday". For Jean Nouvel the brief set the seal on "a new poetics (born) of the necessary encounter between technology and nature: a poetics of reality."[15] For the flurry of architects drawn to the competition – four hundred and seventy-one submissions from some thirty-six countries – creation of the park had to be approached in the light of two main concepts: the "garden city" and the "garden in the city". This meant adopting a structural, morphological slant, while at the same time keeping the dream afloat via recourse to nature in a subtly domesticated form.

Participants also had to perpetuate the tradition of the urban composition in proposals fitting with the principles of historical layout. In its inception report the competition's technical commission was clear on this point: "The goal is a project significant not only in terms of use and the links established between the various activities, but by its form as such, independent of its use and the contingencies of its creation. This is what is meant by the term 'composition', with all its implications as to an urban landmark, a source of recognition and identity, a force capable of enduring beyond our epoch and taking its place in the genealogy of the great Parisian compositions."

Given that it extended to the northern and southern tips of the site – both waiting for

The Parc de La Villette competition (1982–1983).
Project by Latitude Nord (G. Vexlard, L. Vacherot).

their own briefs – and had to accommodate the cattle shed, the Pavillon Janvier, the Pavillon Bourse and the former Rotonde des Vétérinaires (Vets' Rotunda) – all of them listed as historical monuments – the park would also have to allow for a certain flexibility: the pool included in the Fainsilber site plan could be incorporated into proposals by other participants if they so desired.

The jury

The international jury, participants had to convince, was chaired by Brazilian landscape architect Roberto Burle Marx, and included architects Vittorio Gregotti and Renzo Piano, biologist Henri Laborit, musician Luigi Nono and urban sociologist Françoise Choay. It was assisted in its deliberations by a technical commission comprising nine "analysis units," each with two members and charged with analysing fifty projects. The units were overseen by transversal coordinators.

The rules did not allow the jury to choose an outright winner: twenty-four proposals were to be selected, with the architect in first place being put in overall charge of the site, and the details being entrusted to the twenty-three "second-place finishers." A shaky assemblage of incompatible sensibilities, the jury finally came up with a gutsy compromise: nine "winners" were told to rethink their proposals with a view to what promised to be a hard-fought second round. This decision reflected disagreement within the jury, but its significance was not fully appreciated by an uncomprehending French press.

Nine projects, three agendas

The nine winning projects embodied, in their own way, three quite distinct approaches: extreme densification of a site under the geometrical dictatorship of contradictory sets of regulations; concentration of the brief at a single point,

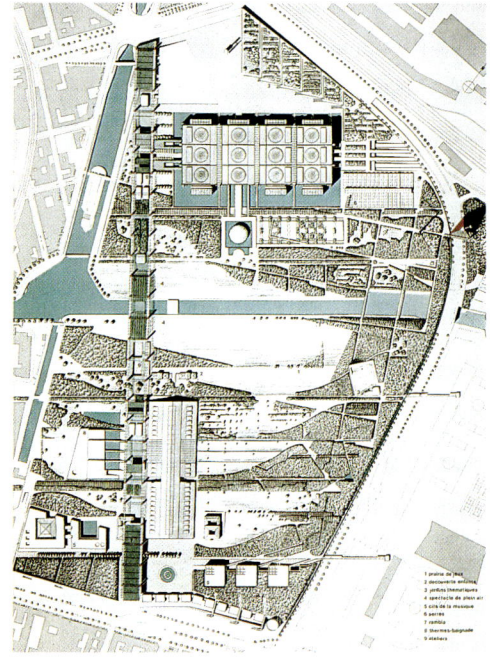

creating a third building to compete with the Cité des Sciences and the Grande Halle; and banishment of building in a tribute to emptiness.

The Latitude Nord project

With the assistance of architects Patrice Dutard and Jean-Paul Morel, landscapers Gilles Vexlard and Laurence Vacherot lauded the sheer extent of the site. A striated wooded slope led off towards the roads, with the metal-framed gallery or *rambla* organising the distribution of the brief along the north-south axis. Because it tended to merge the boundaries of the park with the horizon, this approach was described as "superlative" by its creators. With its promise of a "geographical" outpouring, this ode to emptiness long led the field, before finally coming in second: Renzo Piano saw in the *rambla* a pastiche of one of his own projects.

The OMA project

The genial mischief-maker Rem Koolhaas weighed in with a stunning project that was the front runner at the end of the first round. Considering that the density of the brief – while confirming the obsolescence of the classical, romantic and Haussmannian parks – set its seal on the arrival of an "era of excess," this architect from the Office for Metropolitan Architecture (OMA) set out to design the "supermodern" park, which – like the "monstrous ultra-city" dear to philosopher Jean-Luc Nancy – would be utterly dominated by the "oxymoronic" dynamics of congestion and dissemination. Strips of vegetation running east-west like a "horizontal skyscraper" gave the park a dimension at once abstract and kinetic, with the visitor's gaze drawn towards the periphery and meeting fragments of a brief distributed according to obscure mathematical laws. As if having fun at the expense of Fainsilber's classicism, the Géode – kidnapped by the Jardin Astronomique (Astronomical Garden) – was now decked out with a ring; the hide shed, squeezed between two roads, had a tea room up in its roof – the Dutch architect's way of symbolising a "generic city" swollen by totally unpredictable programmatic possibilities; and the enormous bridge linking the canal lock to the near suburbs seemed the ironic, disillusioned expression of a quest for unity incompatible with the hypercomplexity of the contemporary world. Amid post-glacial vapours rising out of Piranesi wells, the "fabricated nature" of the Forêt Circulaire (Circular Forest) plunged the visitor into an abyss of artifice, a mix of gadget utopia and gore-movie delirium pointing us to the new, networked global village. Junkspace was born – and "(would be) our tomb."[16]

The Bureau des Paysages project

Alexandre Chemetoff set out both to "reconcile the city with its territory" and to reveal a bounteous nature tamed by human genius.
Backing onto Boulevard Serrurier, the terraced theme gardens continued on to the "Plaine," a "bit of Ile-de-France country-

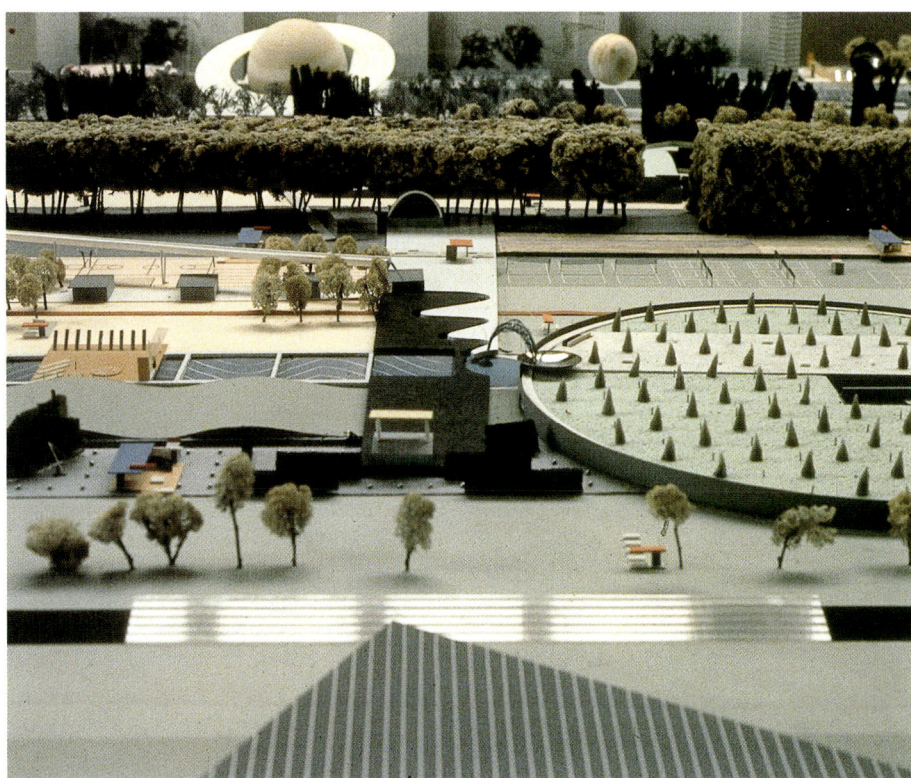

side" lorded over by various modern architecture manifestos. At once a "public collection of contemporary architecture" and a point of convergence for agricultural, building and technological inventions, Chemetoff's project heroically faced the site's metropolitan condition, challenging the role of utilities in the city by making

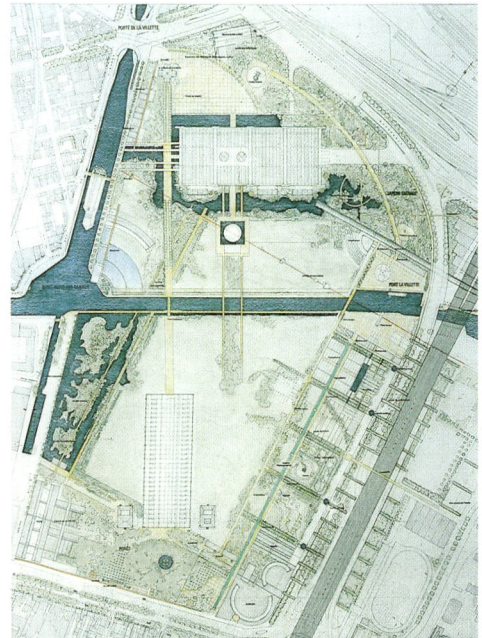

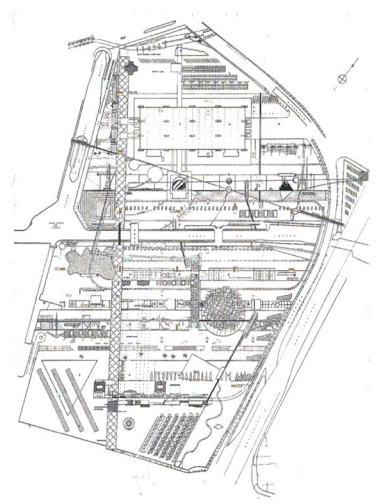

The Parc de La Villette competition (1982–1983).
Project by the Office for Metropolitan Architecture – OMA (R. Koolhaas, E. Zenghelis, S. de Martino, A. Wall, K. Christiaanse, R. Roords, R. Steiner, J. Voorberg).
Above right: Model.
Middle: Site plan.
Left: Project by Bureau des Paysages (A. Chemetoff, B. Althabegoïty, J.-L. Cohen, H. Bardsley, M. Massot).

them "part of the story." Because it "placed" the park in a stratified "urban geography" – its excavated edges gave Paris metro users a glimpse of the theme gardens; because it saw in the road infra-structure the "fundamental line of the project" – those same gardens, literally clinging to Boulevard Serrurier, ratified its utilitarian and aesthetic content; and because it reinforced the park's "limit" aspect by dotting its extremities with greenhouses and restaurants, Chemetoff's proposal was by far the most courageous of all those in the competition.

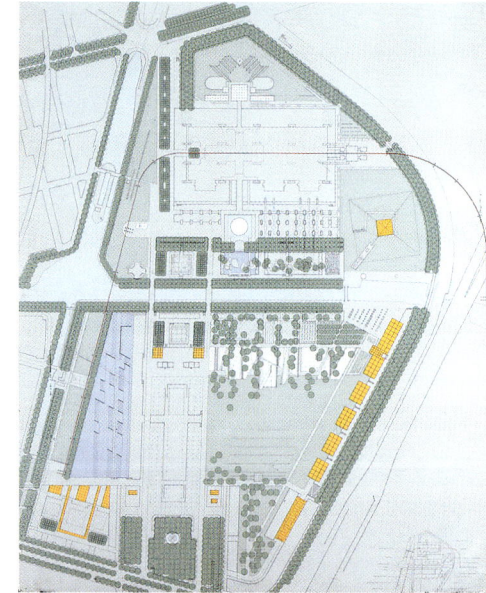

The Rich Bakker and Ank Bleeker project

Two more Dutchmen, Rich Bakker and Ank Bleeker, were about as hermetic as you could get, volunteering nebulous ramparts and the beginnings of a link between Porte de La Villette and Porte de Pantin.

The Andreu Arriola project

Andreu Arriola centred his composition on the Canal de l'Ourcq, striping the park

The Parc de La Villette competition (1982–1983).
Middle left: Project by S. I. Andersson.

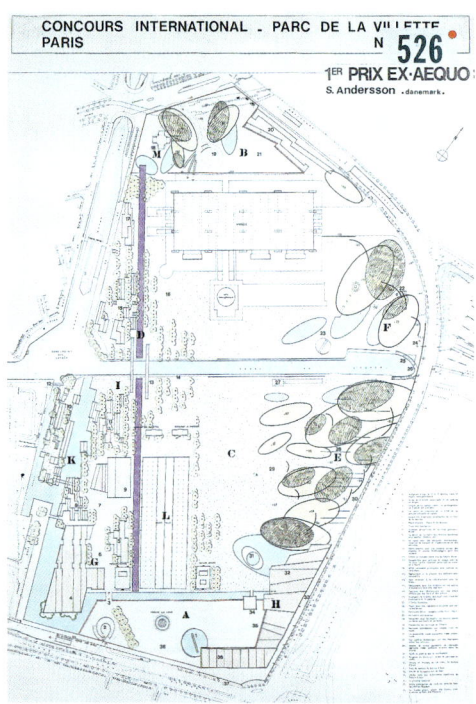

The Sven Ingvar Andersson project

The great ecologist Sven Ingvar Andersson offered a celebration of the encounter between man and nature. Peacocks and sheep were there in the heart of things, an artificial landscape of woods, ponds and "ellipsoidal hills" backed onto the roads and the park's "spinal column" – a rectilinear pedestrian thoroughfare known alternatively as the "Grande Chaussée" or the "Voie Lactée" (Milky Way) – tied its two extremities together.

The Parc de La Villette competition (1982–1983).
Above right: Project by R. Bakker and A. Bleeker.
Below right: Project by A. Arriola.

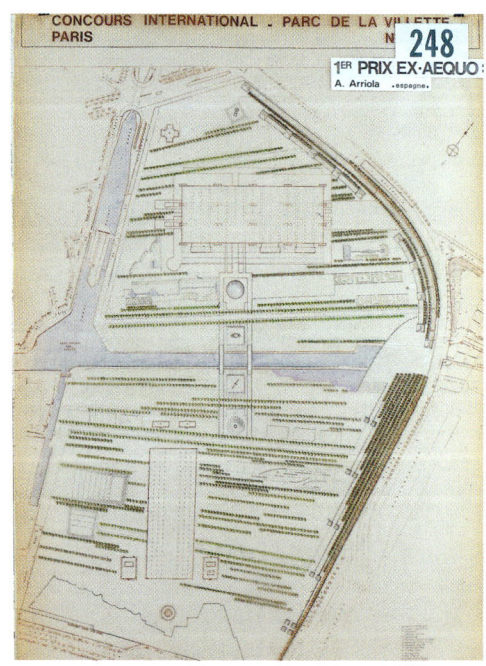

44   LA VILLETTE: 1971–1995

with rows of trees converging on Place Stalingrad. Its total lack of imagination drew the fury of the press when the results were announced.

The Bernard Tschumi project

For architect Bernard Tschumi the Parc de La Villette competition was the opportunity to call for the banishing of modernity and acknowledgement of a frankly incomplete postmodernity. Energetically drawing on Jacques Derrida, Gilles Deleuze and other kindred spirits, Tschumi submitted a project that, despite its quote-studded conceptualism, came with a deliciously refreshing aura of insurrection. He saw himself as

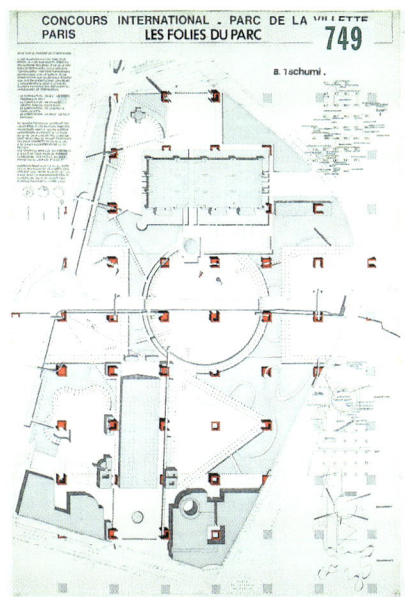

The Parc de La Villette competition (1982–1983).
Project by B. Tschumi.
Above and below right: Two of the plates presented in the competition.
Left: Site plan (final project).

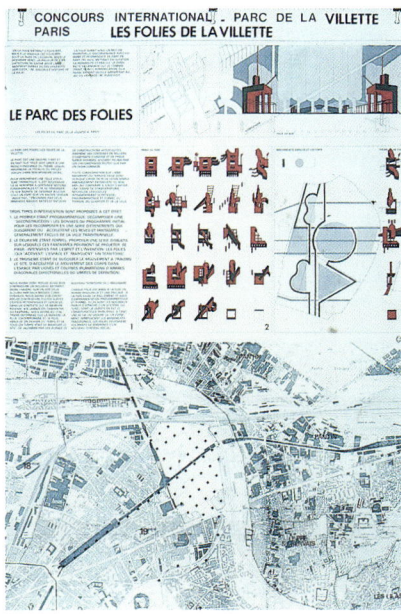

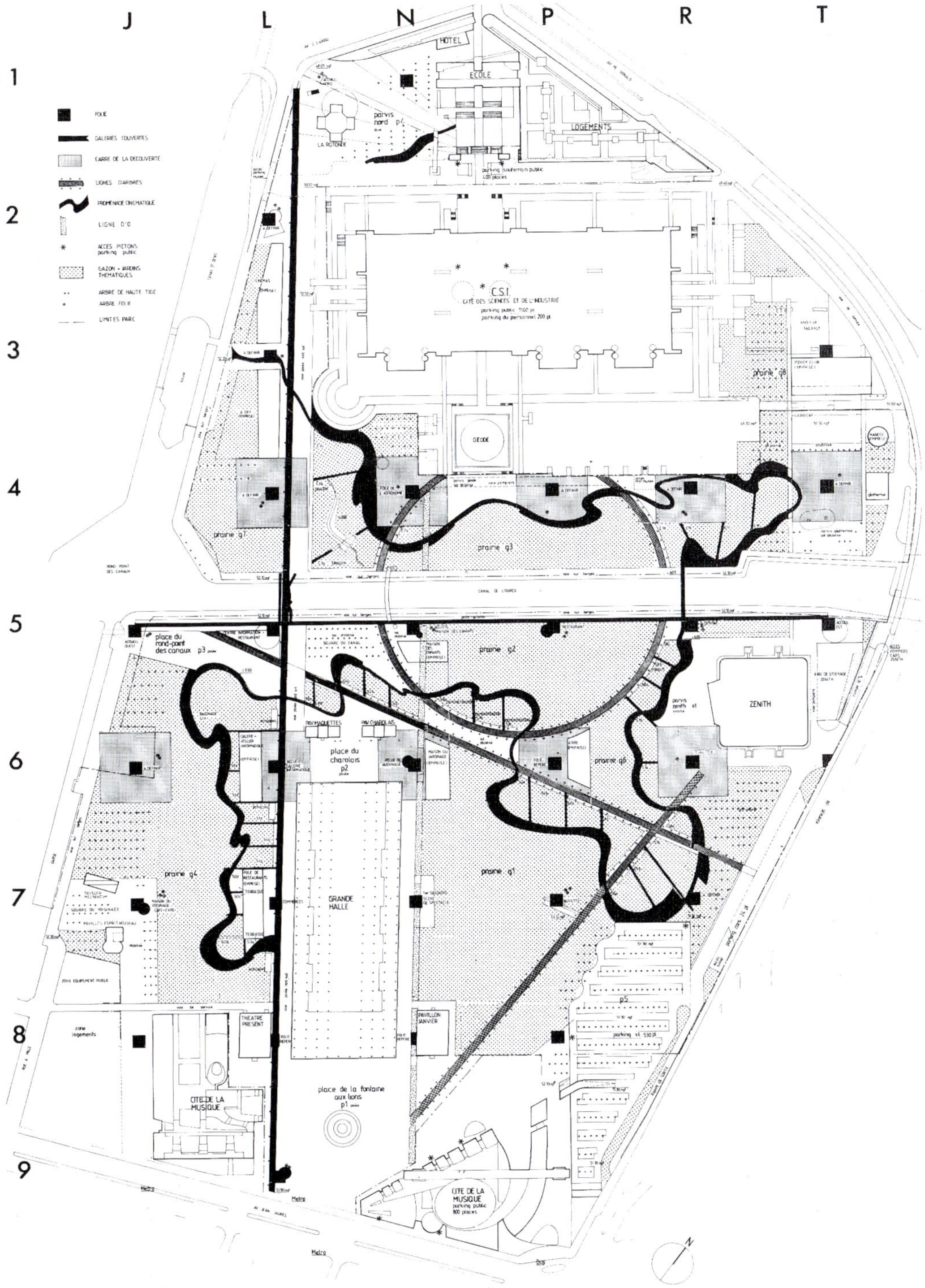

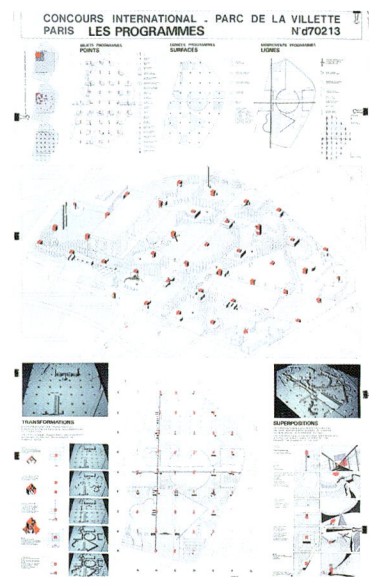

The Parc de La Villette competition (1982–1983).
Project by B. Tschumi.
Above: One of the competition plates.
Below: The Parc de La Villette (architect: B. Tschumi). Detail of a Folie.

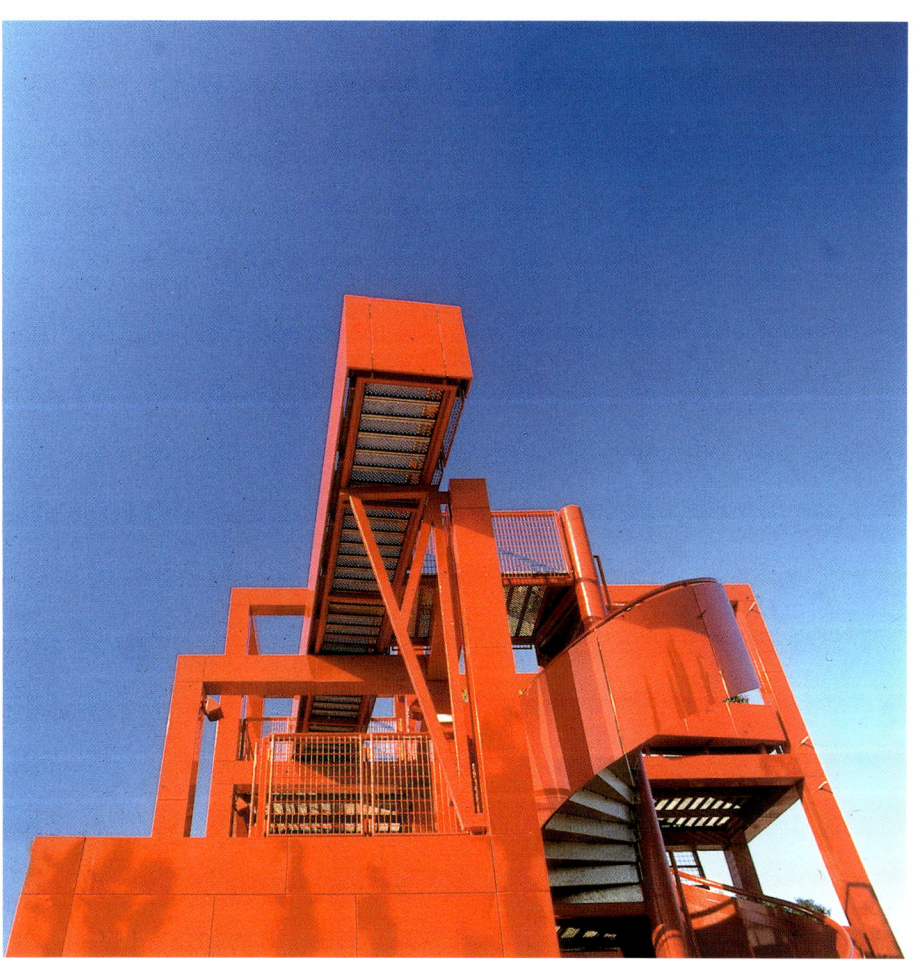

the destroyer of classical uptightness, and his theoretical *bricolage*, very much of its time, thoroughly vanquished a François Barré already swooning over the matchless eloquence of the chic playboy. Little matter that his architecture, awash with references, was in its own way symmetrical with the neomodernist excesses of a Ciriani (or the neoclassical equivalents of a Bofill); little matter the recriminations of those who, appealing to Michel Leiris, saw in this poet of the streets the architect of "Merdonité." Barré had found his man, and that man was Bernard Tschumi. But what exactly was this war of independence that was making Tschumi famous? What mould was this musketeer of the latest revolution looking to break?

Founded on the axioms that had been the starting point on the long road leading to the "simple facts," the seventeenth-century philosophical system had been replaced by the eighteenth century's Newtonian empiricism. The latter, busily deconstructing physical reality in line with the dual movement of analytical reduction and synthetic reconstruction, demonstrated the relationship between nature and reason. As an intellectual exercise, knowledge of nature led to a view of its subject as an intelligible, codifiable whole and to the discovery, behind the stunning diversity of its visible manifestations, of a founding principle, a single, universal law. Soundly structured by reason and borne along by the limitless flow of the vital process of the cosmos, the dynamics of knowing – the *libido sciendi* spoken of by Cassirer[17] – underscored an isomorphically inflected fit between nature and models rendered measurable by methodological convergence: a methodological convergence and measurability of models of which Newton's law of universal attraction seemed the unqualified emblem.

This failed to anticipate, however, the advent of a postmodernity running totally contrary to the dictates of reason. Perceived until then as an undivided whole, the world had split open – Nietzsche and Freud had had their say – and ultimately disintegrated into a juxtaposition of contextualities in which business and the market, the "new virtual nomads" touted by Jacques Attali, rubbed shoulders with the triumph of *dissensus*, political fickleness and definitive social instability. Total unpredictability in the rhythms appropriate to socio-economic change; narrative in its death throes; all received notions of progress shattered: the world had changed and Bernard Tschumi was there to spread the word.

His project, then, seemed torn between and straining against a host of divergent tensions.

An initial system of "dots" was mapped onto the entire site. The Folies (Follies), gleaming little cubes 10.8 metres on a side, set about the "deconstruction" of the brief into a series of "mooring points"[18] striving to establish a "territorial determination."[19] Gridded and undifferentiated, the Folies underpinned the "unity of the overall system"[20] – a unity some of them sabotaged. The "deviant" Folies departed from the stylistic neutrality proper to their status as manufactured objects, "contaminated" by a brief Tschumi manipulated like so many Surrealistic *cadavres exquis*.

A second system, of "lines" this time, gave the park direction using two dead-straight axes. Almost a kilometre long, the Galerie de La Villette walkway – a wild extravagance designed in collaboration with Irish engineer Peter Rice – lightheartedly spanned the Canal de l'Ourcq to connect Porte de La Villette and Porte de Pantin, while the raised Galerie de l'Ourcq walkway ran along the canal, slipping in between the Ledoux rotunda and the municipality of Pantin.

A third system – "surfaces" – was overlaid on the others in the form of two large grassed games areas, the Prairie du Cercle (Circle Meadow) and the Prairie du Triangle (Triangle Meadow).

Tschumi's overlaying of his Points, Lines and Surfaces systems, the circular layouts from Team Zoo, and the rectangular grid proposed by anti-establishment Roland Castro, reflected a tendency by competition participants to comprehend the size of the site in terms of geometrical syntax. To temper the excess of geometrical rhetoric, Tschumi's gardens were positioned according to the mysterious laws of the "frozen fortuitousness" of the Promenade Cinématique: the dreamlike atmospheres of the Jardin des Bambous, the Jardin des Brouillards and the Jardin des Frayeurs Enfantines (Bamboo Garden, Garden of Mists and Garden of Childhood Fears) yielded themselves up in the course of a stroll seemingly bereft of all logic. This was an evolving project for an evolving architecture – Derrida's "trans-architecture" – with the Folies, those "refuges for programmatic, formal experimentation," representing "architectural chromosomes"

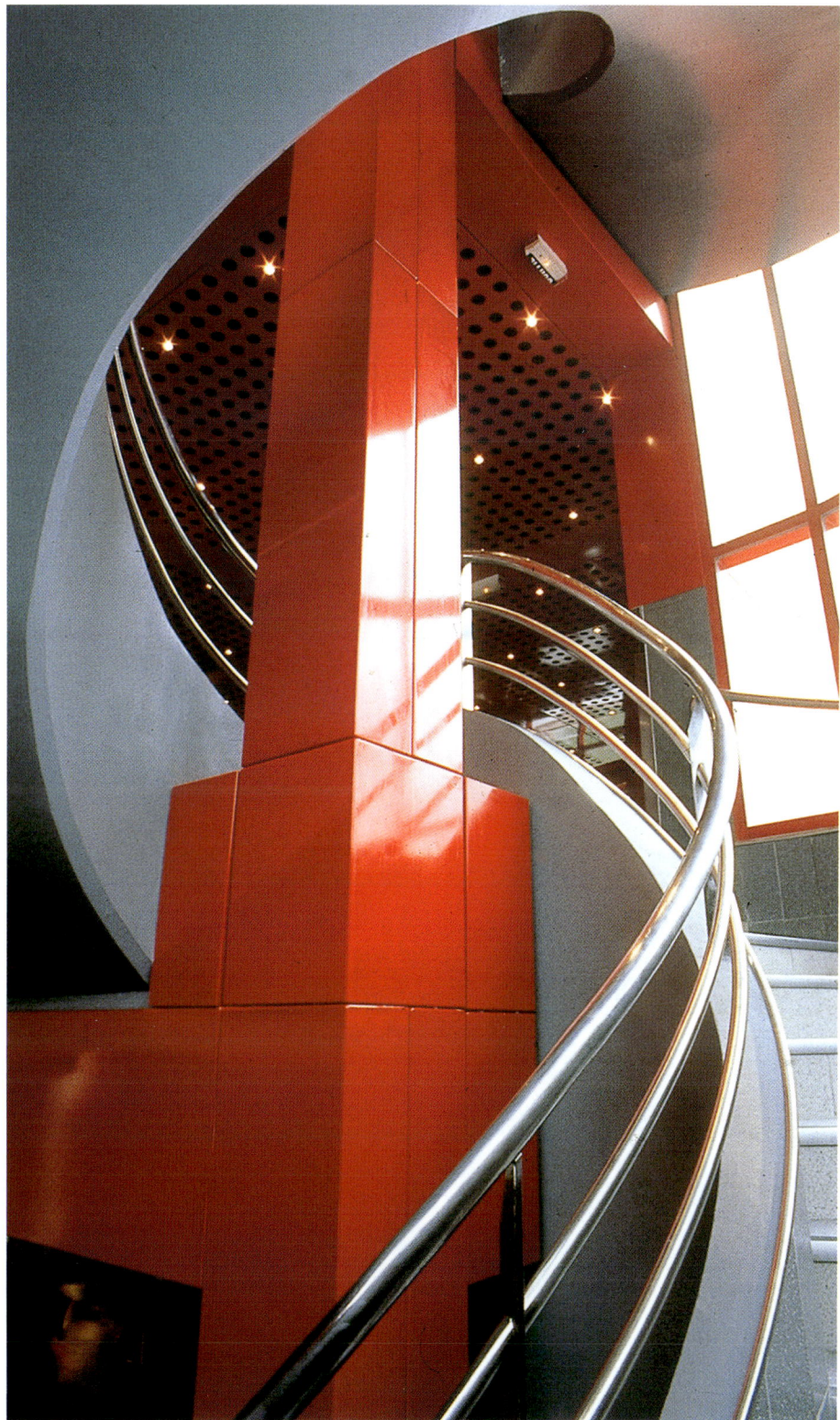

The Parc de La Villette (architect: B. Tschumi). Detail of a Folie.

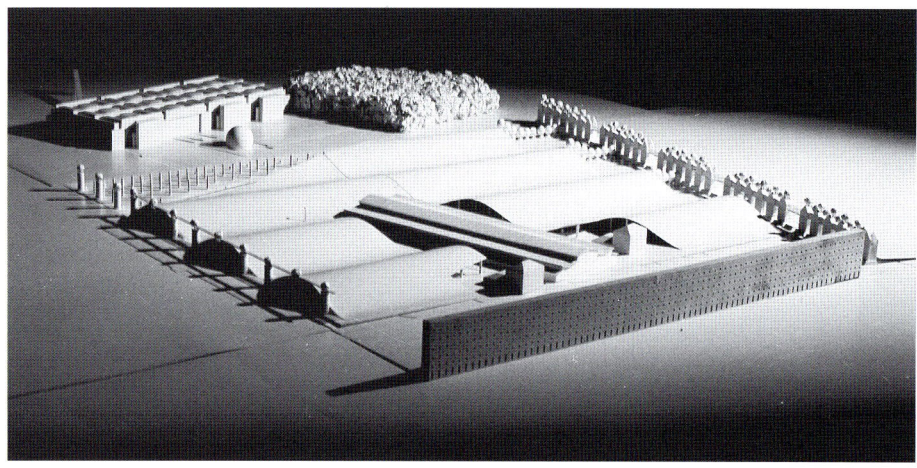

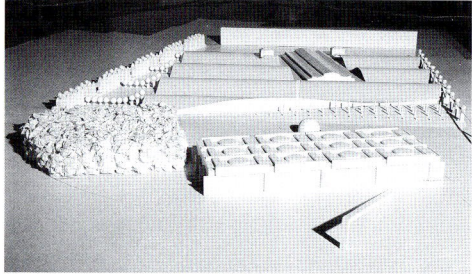

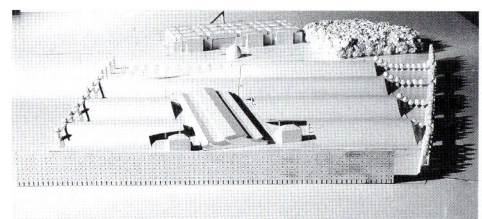

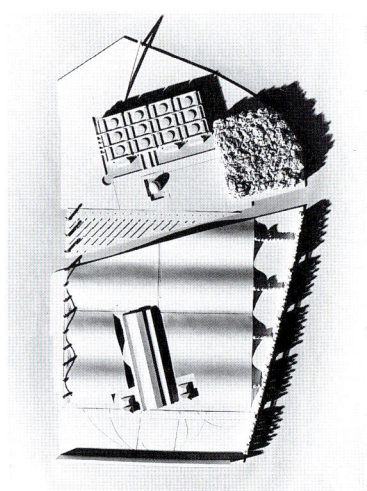

The Parc de La Villette competition (1982–1983).
Above: Models of the project by M. Lemarié and J.-P. Vallier.
Below left: Project by J. Gourvénec and J.-P. Raynaud.

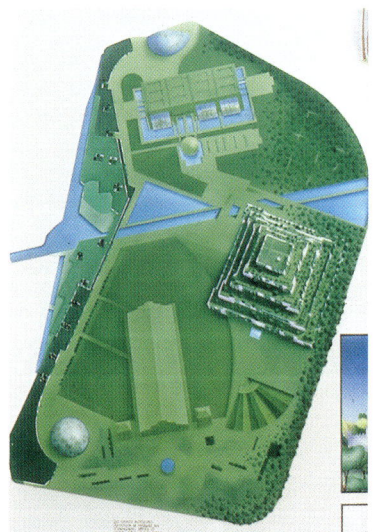

did raise certain questions: for instance, was a biologist, however gifted, qualified to assess the relevance of an architectural project? There was, too, the startling matter of jury president Roberto Burle Marx, verging on senility and prone to dozing off (!) during voting sessions; not to mention the internecine struggle between architects, landscapers and other "factions" that often resulted in nauseating settlings of old scores. Here, unquestionably, were legitimate grounds for controversy.

or "stem cells."

Tschumi's park finally turned out to be a deft compromise between the zanily conceptual Koolhaas project and the very "architectured" Vexlard proposition, of which it could be described as the fragmented double.

After a brilliant verbal presentation and a radical reworking of his first-round version, then, Bernard Tschumi came in first, ahead of Rem Koolhaas, whose new project disappointed the judges, with landscapers Bernard Lassus and Gilles Vexlard both coming third. The decision drew an angry reaction from Lassus, who saw himself as the victim of plotting by a jury with an exclusively pro-architect bias. And while these accusations had no basis in fact, the organisation of the competition and the overly eclectic character of the jury

The Bernard Lassus and Jacques Gourvénec projects

There can be no question that in taking an "anti-fragmentation" slant – the park as a miniature reproduction of the slope of the Seine Valley – Bernard Lassus was appealing too explicitly to a "naturalistic" vision: this could only mean a clash with a jury bent on hewing to the competition's ideological orientation in the inception report and its advocacy of an "urban" – that is to say "built" – approach (in reference to the "garden city" concept in the report).

For Lassus, the giant scale of the site led

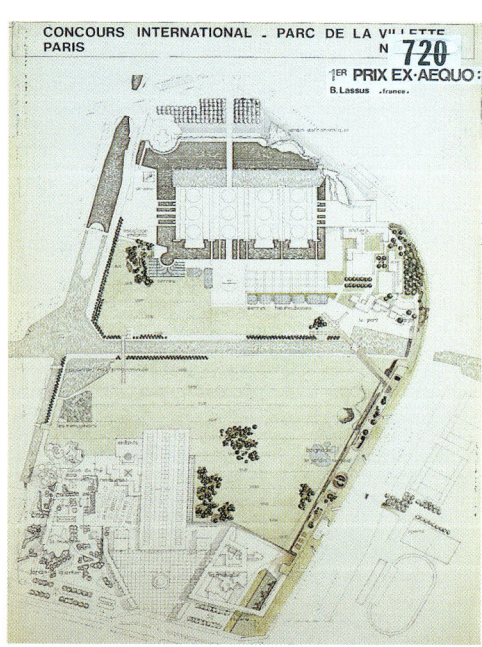

The Parc de La Villette competition (1982–1983). Project by B. Lassus.

48 LA VILLETTE: 1971–1995

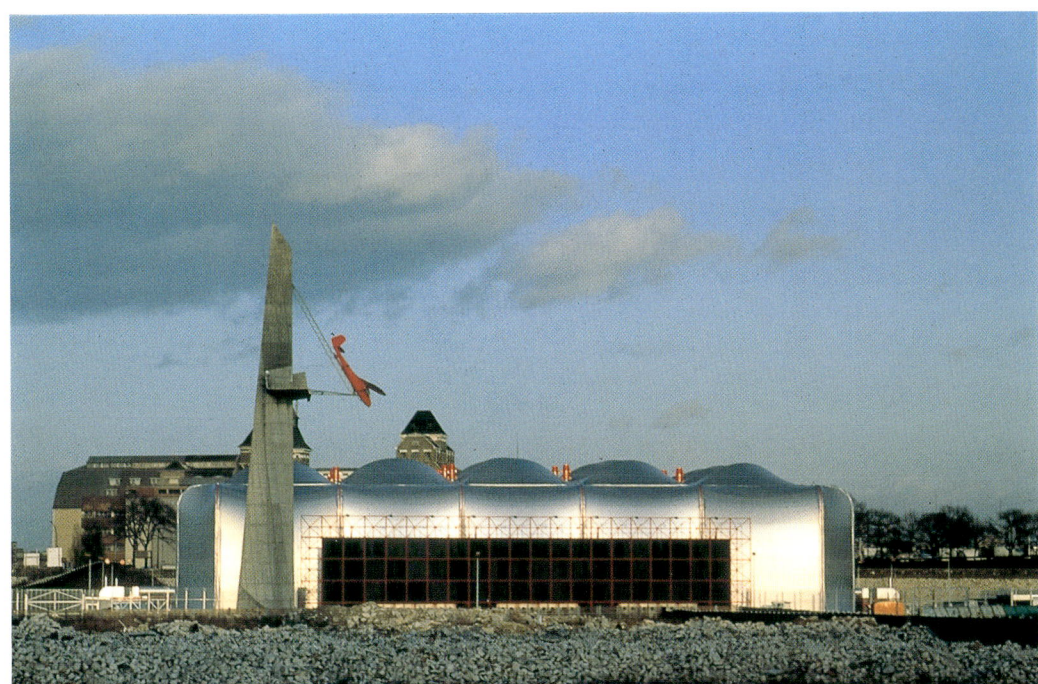

The Zénith (architects: P. Chaix and J.-P. Morel).

to a "geographic" perception which in turn saw the cattle shed, that metal monster hampering the gaze, vanishing as if by magic beneath a vast slope descending towards Place de la Fontaine-aux-Lions. This dizzyingly extensive park – the famous "living room of the poor" – could be taken as a flattened version of the Lemarié/Vallier proposal with its little valleys and dunes; unless, of course, it was the antithesis of the Jacques Gourvénec project which, at the risk of hypertrophy, included a monumental pyramid of greenery near the roadways.

The disconcerting opacity of the rendering, in marked contrast with Tschumi's sparkling sketches, ultimately led to the defeat of someone who had earlier drawn attention with a premonitory *arrangement of red dots*.

Bernard Tschumi: "modernist hanger-on"?

If the Galerie de La Villette walkway provided an imperturbable straight-line connection between Porte de La Villette and Porte de Pantin, merging with north-east Paris' road grid and inflicting on the west of the park the frenetic rhythm of the contemporary city, then the Promenade Cinématique countered this with an indisputably more shifting aesthetics of reptation. The grid of Folies, on the other hand, seemed stripped of any desire to "meet" the site, treating it with lofty disdain, as if to be preserved from any risk of contextual corruption. True, the Folies would slip astutely in among the enormous buildings – the Cité des Sciences, the Grande Halle and the

The Parc de La Villette (architect: B. Tschumi).
Plan of a Folie.

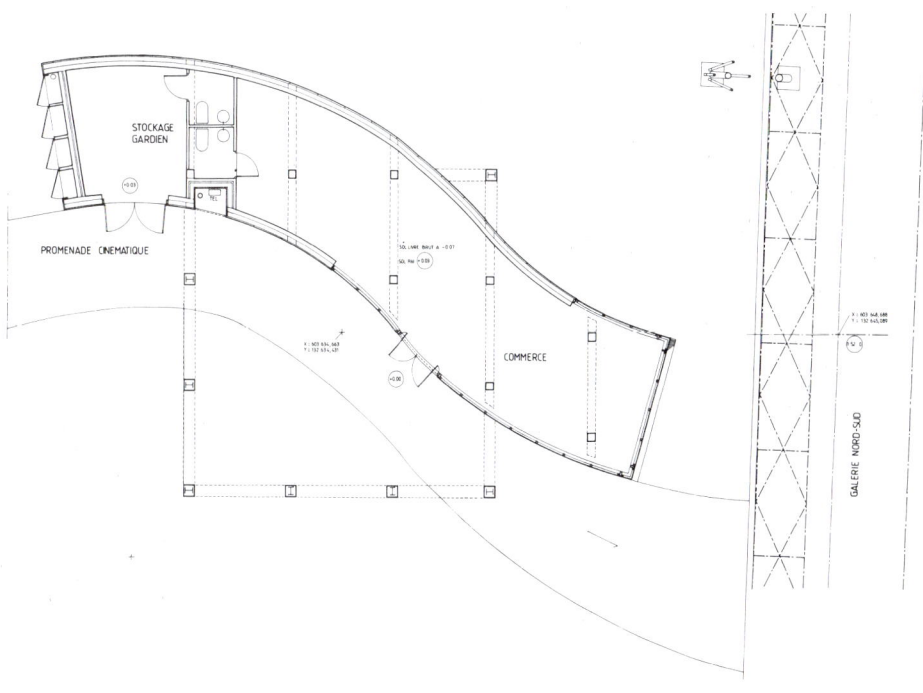

CHRONOLOGY 49

The Parc de La Villette (architect: B. Tschumi).
Right: The Jardin du Dragon (Dragon Garden).
Below: The Promenade Cinématique (Cinematic Itinerary).

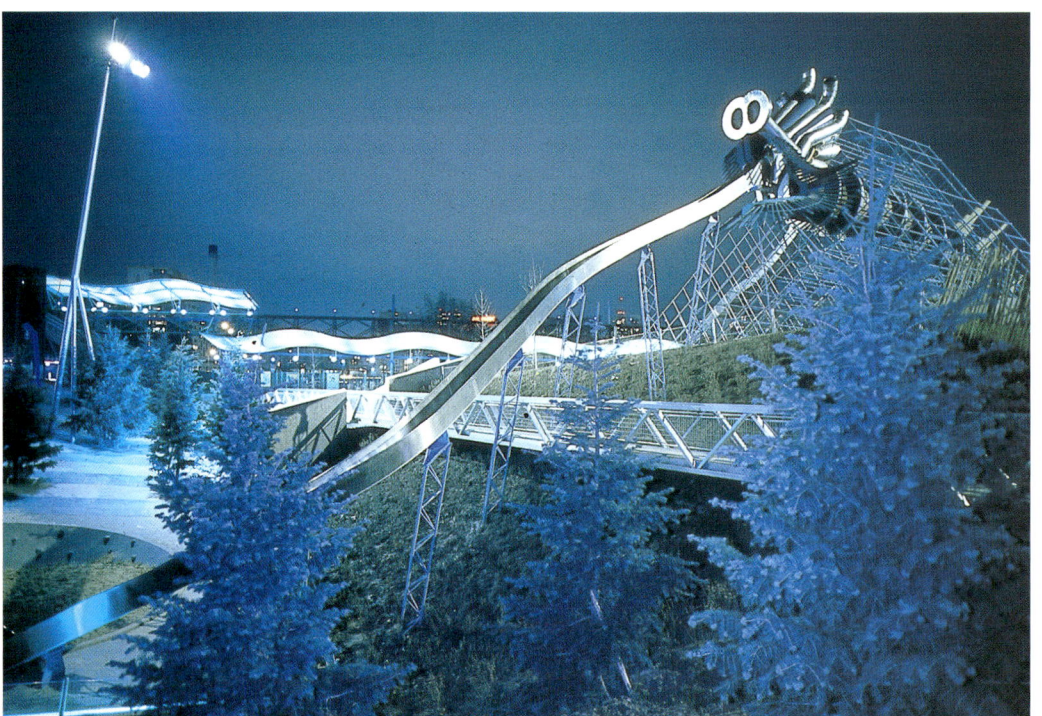

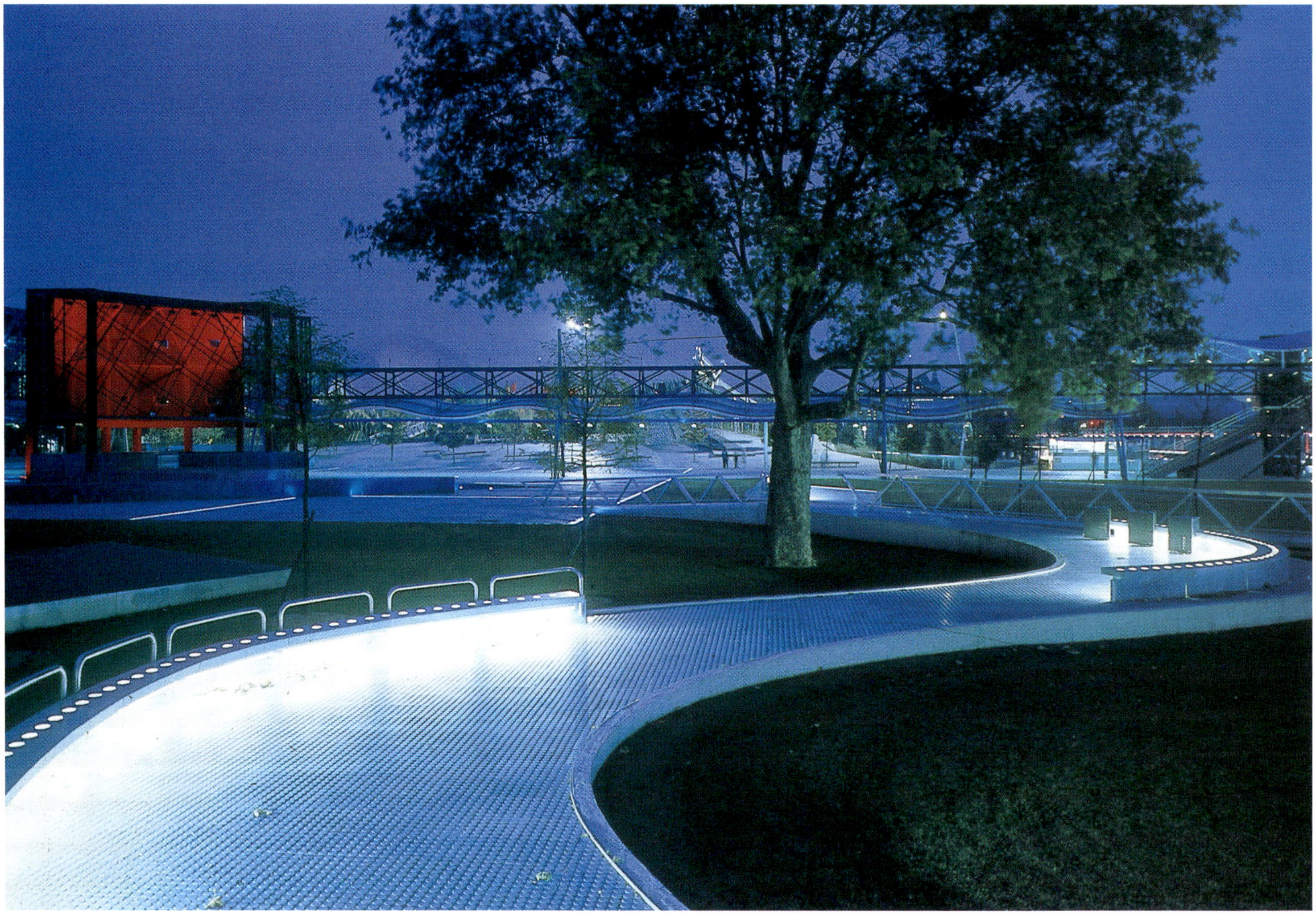

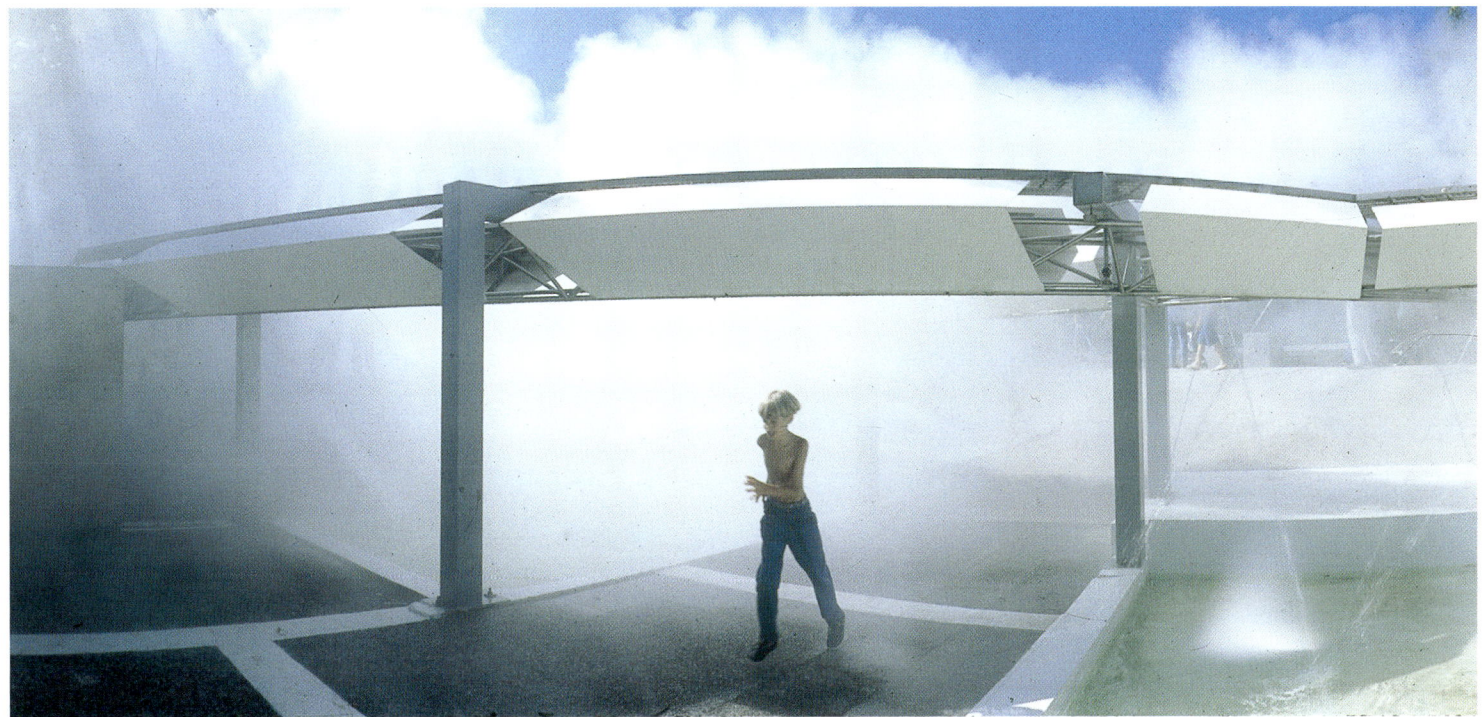

Zénith – but would fail to limit the "embarrassing emptiness"[21] of the site: the Folie de la Baguette et du Gros Rouge (French Bread and Cheap Red Wine Folly), the Folie Furieuse (Mad Folly) and the Folie du Chef de Gare (Station-Master Folly) cut through the park like blazing comets – but only on paper. In fact, wasn't the whole thing a reality-drained metaproject, in orbit above its site as it neutralised itself with its plethora of literary and philosophical references? When Alexandre Chemetoff called it a "superb carpet of green"[22] he did not forget to add that it was "devoid of interest."[23] The result, then: an abyss in which the severing of representation from realisation was symbolised by the Prairie du Cercle and the Prairie du Triangle – geometrical in name only, since their monumental proportions blocked any perceptual assessment; and a yawning gap between idea and execution that would lead Paul Scarcelli to qualify the Tschumi project as no more than a "cerebral neo-garden"[24] and others to see it as a failed three-dimensional transposition of Kandinsky (or maybe Mondrian?). Then again, perhaps the park's "nonexistence" had to do with Paul Virilio's "aesthetics of disappearance," its elusive contours highlighted by a sublimely nocturnal lighting, as if suspended in the "electronic void" of the "teletopic metacity."[25]

In addition to its "hyperrealisation," the Tschumi project also stood accused of keeping doubtful philosophical company. The methodical perfection of the grid of Folies made legitimate reference to "political over-regulation of society,"[26] biological over-regulation of the human body – with the "deviant" Folies symbolising "anomalous symptoms" – and the erosion of distinctiveness, now perverted as "the stubborn revolt of singularities."[27] The Galerie de La Villette and the Galerie de l'Ourcq, however – like the two Prairies – remained serious bones of contention.

In their hysterical acceleration of flow – an echo of ever-expanding mobility and information exchange – were the Galeries not dissolving memory in the "synchrony of all-place and all-time"[28] and thus nourishing an "avant-garde of oblivion?"[29] Were they not a call to some fearful "exit from history," like the shattered Folie-fragments at

The Parc de La Villette (architect: B. Tschumi).
The Jardin des Brouillards (Garden of Mists; architects: A. Pélissier and F. Nakaya).

The Parc de La Villette (architect: B. Tschumi).
Above and middle: The Galerie des Jeux Électroniques (Electronic Games Gallery; architect: J. Nouvel).
Below: The Maison du Jardinage (House of Gardening; architect: H. Gaudin).

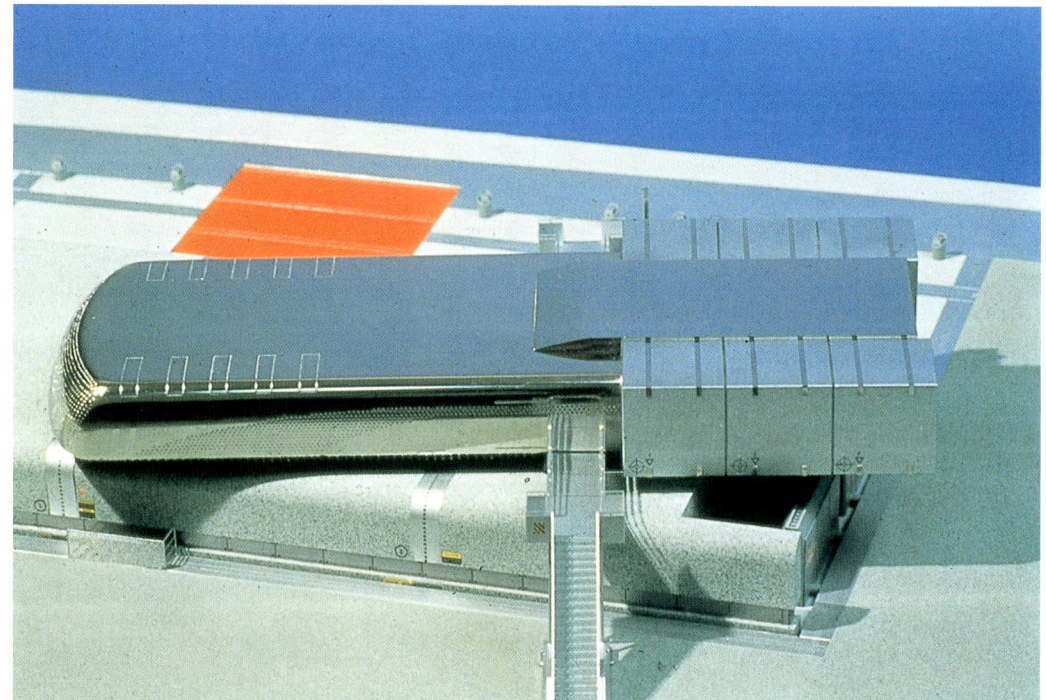

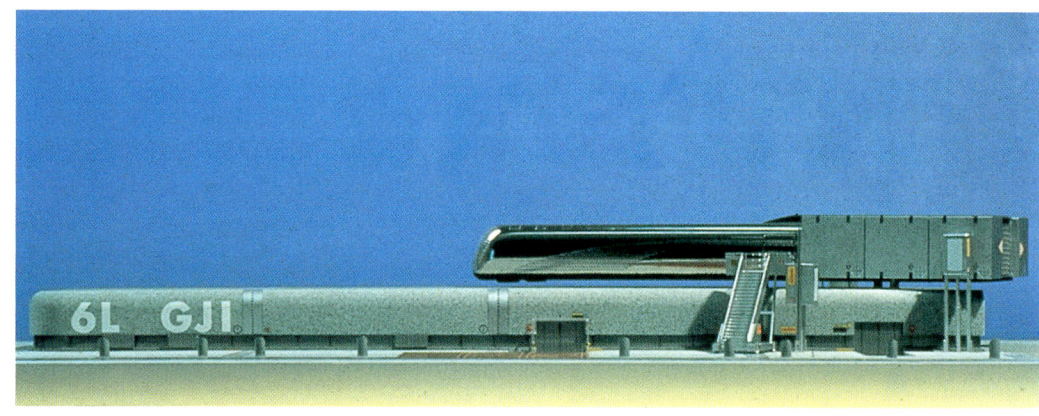

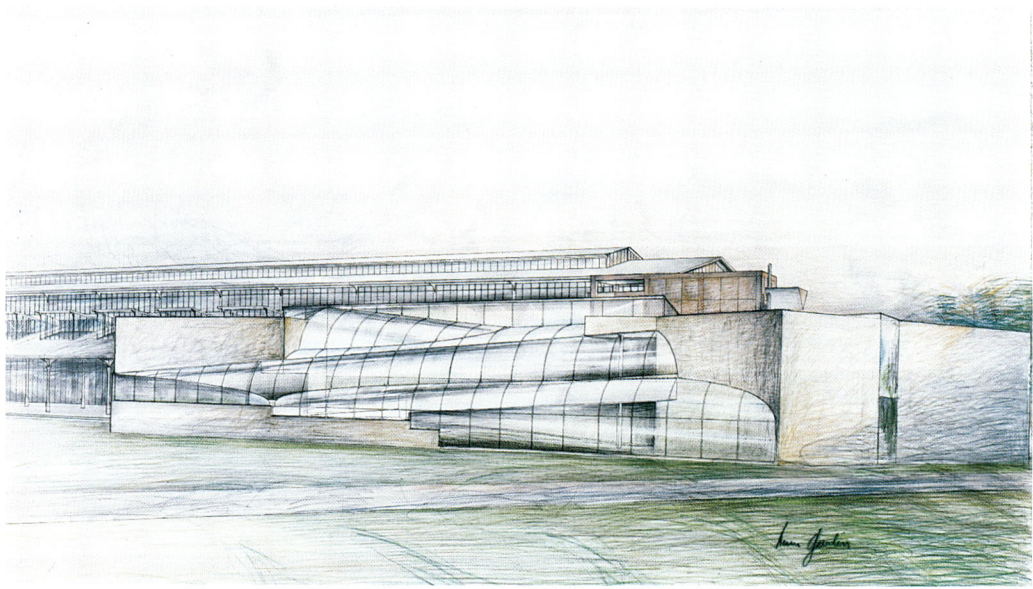

52   LA VILLETTE: 1971–1995

the Pavillon Bourse and the Pavillon Janvier? In their effecting of these collisions – as if signalling the advent of an "age of zapping" and the speeding-up of the process of social differentiation – were they not making the park a scene of probabilist disorder and a resonance chamber for social breakdown? And the Prairies – were they not the seal of approval for this breakdown, with their spatial neutrality a mirror of the uncertainty of the times, reflecting the "power of choice"[30] and the "lability of desire?"[31]

As a mindless transcription of reality, the Parc de La Villette would ultimately become a "kiddie-type zoo of everyday life"[32] and Bernard Tschumi a "modernist hanger-on."

The Cité de la Musique competition (1984)

The Cité de la Musique competition saw the laurels go to a young French architect called Christian de Portzamparc, who had already earned himself something of a reputation in 1975 with a bold reworking of the Haussmannian block in his Hautes Formes housing project in Paris. Combining Portzamparc's personal vision of the façade with the requirement of adjacency, the Hautes Formes seemed at the time tainted by the modern plan, transforming the "open block" into a hybrid typology. Unfairly beaten in the Opéra-Bastille competition, Portzamparc turned the École de Danse de l'Opéra de Paris into an exultant artistic triumph whose borrowings from Erich Mendelsohn and Le Corbusier did not exclude dips into Antiquity. The tousle-headed dream-worker that Roland Castro had dubbed "architecture's Rimbaud" – and whom some saw as pathologically eccentric – had succeeded in transcending the intemperate diversity of his references, in giving birth to an architecture of light/heavy contrasts in which Romantic fire went hand in hand with the tomblike hush of "inexpressible space." Stress on the fullness/emptiness antithesis, as in his famous "totem" and "clearing" concepts; celebration of an earth-rooted structure whose squat base was symmetrically counterbalanced by a splendid summit; and an immoderate passion for detail – these were among the predilections of someone who, early enamoured of painting and sculpture, had come to architecture by accident.

The competition provided Portzamparc with the chance to test his theories against the incredibly tough constraints of the space and the brief. The ugliness of the area allotted to the project – a few hectares on the very fringe of the city, split by a small square that could not be built on – was equalled only by the sheer hypertrophy of the massive programme.

The first phase of the competition was to cover the construction of the Conservatoire National Supérieur de Musique et de Danse at the south end of the site. Intended to match the changes taking place in the teaching of music and dance, this vast complex was to be complemented by a 1,200-seat concert hall, a main auditorium, a music education institute and a Galerie de l'Instrument (Instrument Gallery) that would house the collection of the Conservatoire de la Rue de Madrid in Paris. The second phase of construction would involve extensions to the concert hall and the Galerie de l'Instrument, for which, respectively, the auditorium and the musical instrument centre would represent significant continuations of the original brief. However, given the numerous budgetary uncertainties and the imminence of elections that boded ill for the Socialist Party, it quickly became clear that the large symphony hall, its two adjoining halls and the musical instrument centre were unlikely to go ahead. The authorities made a point of stressing to competition participants that there could be no guarantees as to the long-term development of the project, with Article V of the competition rules stating unambiguously: "The contracting authority makes no commitment concerning the later phases of the Cité de la Musique; this applies equally to the choice and engagement of the prime contractor and the dates of implementation of these works."

The logical outcome of the first round, then, was that competitors submitted a sketch for the Conservatoire, the concert hall and the Galerie de l'Instrument, but in the form of a site plan offering summary indications of the activities making up the second phase. Not only were the participants allowed very little time for project preparation – the brief was only made available in late January 1984 and proposals had to be in by 2 April of the same year – they also had to cope with a large number of constraints.

The two-phase approach to the Cité de la Musique meant that from the outset competitors had to think in terms of a project that could be extended without any disturbance to the functioning of the first-phase buildings.

A further complication was that the brief included areas for the public and others exclusively for students, which called for clear ranking of internal traffic zones. In town planning terms the main recommendation bore on achieving a fit with the layout of the park, ensuring views of the gardens, leaving Place de la Fontaine-aux-Lions strictly alone – the possibility of building on it was absolutely excluded – and sticking rigorously to alignment with Avenue Jean-Jaurès.

The Atelier de Portzamparc project

Confronted with all these traps, Portzamparc opted for an unexpected degree of limpidity. He situated the Conservatoire facilities to the west of Place de la Fontaine-aux-Lions and public areas to the east, where they would coexist with the elements planned for the second phase. This division was accentuated by an architectural treatment differentiating the two complexes. Blithely ignoring the alignment exigencies, Portzamparc sensibly grafted his project onto the layout of the park. Four solemn volumes topped with a monumental porch-roof – a motif he would return to for the law courts in Bordeaux – were set at regular intervals parallel to the Galerie de l'Ourcq. A forecourt discreetly slipped in between the Conservatoire and Avenue Jean-Jaurès revealed the southern tip of the Galerie de La Villette.

This seamless blending of the Conservatoire into the very heart of Tschumi's layout to the west was countered by upheavals to the east, where the public reception area showed the flaws in the

The Cité de la Musique competition (1984).
Project by Atelier de Portzamparc (C. de Portzamparc, F. Barberot, F. Borel, F. Chochon, F. Léonhardt, M.-E. Nicoleau, E. Pierres).
Initial proposal. Model.

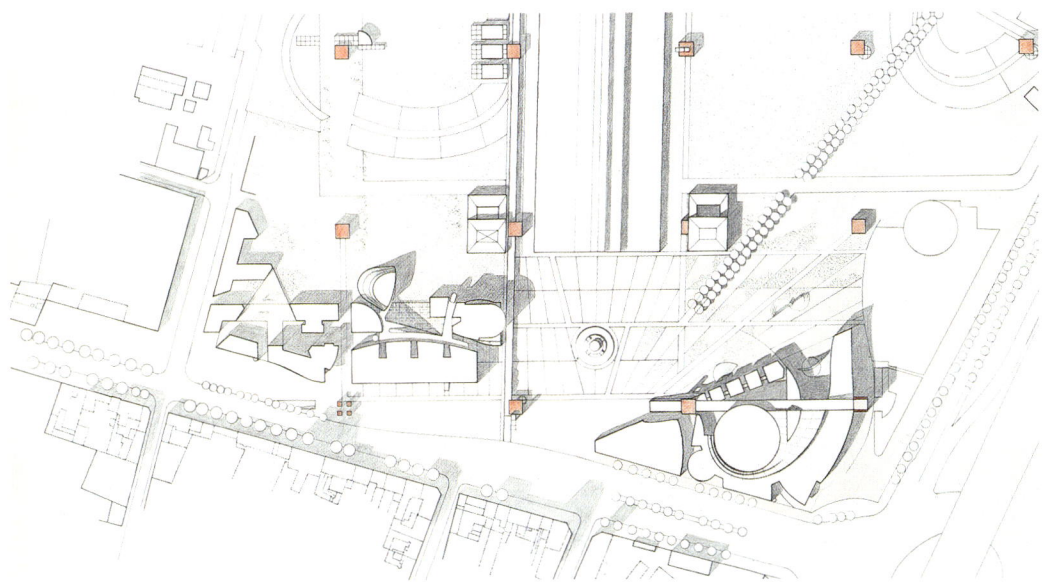

The Cité de la Musique competition (1984).
Project by Atelier de Portzamparc (C. de Portzamparc, F. Barberot, F. Borel, F. Chochon, F. Léonhardt, M.-E. Nicoleau, E. Pierres). Initial proposal. Site plan.
Below: Project by M. Ketoff and M. Petit. Initial proposal. Site plan.

park's framework; while a "hunting horn" passageway hotly embracing the concert hall pointed up the eloquence of the curve. The contagious fluidity of this kinetic, Mendelsohn-style architecture was, however, tempered by the straightness of the enormous open-work beam in the Galerie de l'Instrument overhanging the Rue Musicale. A gaping void – the "converse of fullness" as Portzamparc likes to call it – is set between the two segments of this asymmetrical project and, miraculously, succeeds in unifying them. Reverent towards Tschumi's project to the west, but cheekier to the east, Portzamparc won over the jury with his astute solution to the problem of the links with the Villette site: his arrangement deliciously chaffs the park's stiffness, while healthily taking the edge off that of the Grande Halle and splendidly opening up the site towards the soundless terrain of the periphery.

In addition to the project's capacity to structure, the jury was appreciative of its perspicacity in regard to the phasing problem. By grouping the first-phase elements around Place de la Fontaine-aux-Lions, Portzamparc ensured that the Place would rapidly take on its own architectural character; and by slipping the second-phase elements in along the Périphérique, he made extension of the project possible with no risk to the smooth running of the Pôle Public: the music performance and museum facilities. Lastly, the pertinence of a spatial organisation based on what Portzamparc terms "necessary dissociation" – the work is broken down into acoustically independent ensembles – demonstrated a quest for the primacy of architectural over materials-based acoustics; and this reinforced the convictions of a jury already mightily impressed by the project's sheer plasticity.

The Ketoff/Petit team's project

The Ketoff/Petit team tied its project symmetrically to the Grande Halle, at the risk

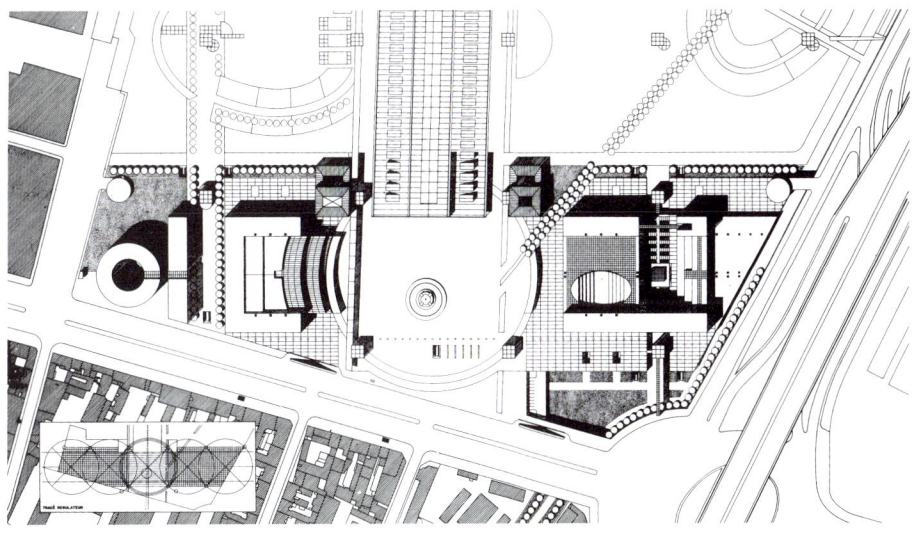

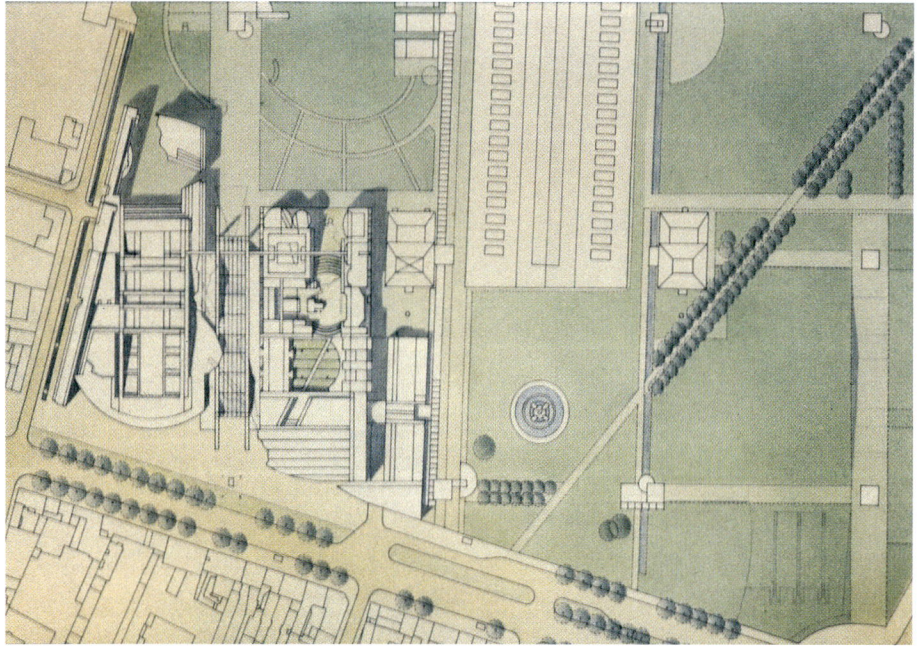

The Cité de la Musique competition (1984).
Above: Project by A. Sarfati. Initial proposal. Site plan.

The Alain Sarfati project

In this especially bold project, Alain Sarfati concentrated the entire brief to the west of Place de la Fontaine-aux-Lions, and thus succeeded in linking the south-east tip of the park – transformed into a venue for auditory experiment and discovery – to the neighbouring urban structure.

The Henri Gaudin project

Winner of the first round, Henri Gaudin encroached on Place de la Fontaine-aux-Lions, irregularly increasing the density of its surroundings. For reasons that remained obscure, the French president turned the project down flat, openly defying the jury's evaluation.

of seizing up the south end of a site for which the contracting authority wanted extreme flexibility. Despite its old-hat neo-classicism and the deadly opacity of its volumes, the project was much appreciated for its compositional rigour, actually winning over President Mitterrand, whose preference was for symmetry. The jury stressed the project's virtues when Commins-bbm, acoustics advisers to the technical commission, stated that the concert hall "offered extremely favourable conditions for the performance of classical music."

The Xenakis/Véret team's project

The Xenakis/Véret project was without doubt the most beautiful of all. On each side of Place de la Fontaine-aux-Lions the "birds" – replicas of the Pavillon Philips – topped the famous "potato-shaped" concert hall and the main auditorium. To the west a network of intersecting ramps connected the Conservatoire, the public music rooms and the museum buried crosswise under the Place. To the east, a craft village – a kind of miniaturised version of the Quartier de l'Europe, in Paris' 8th

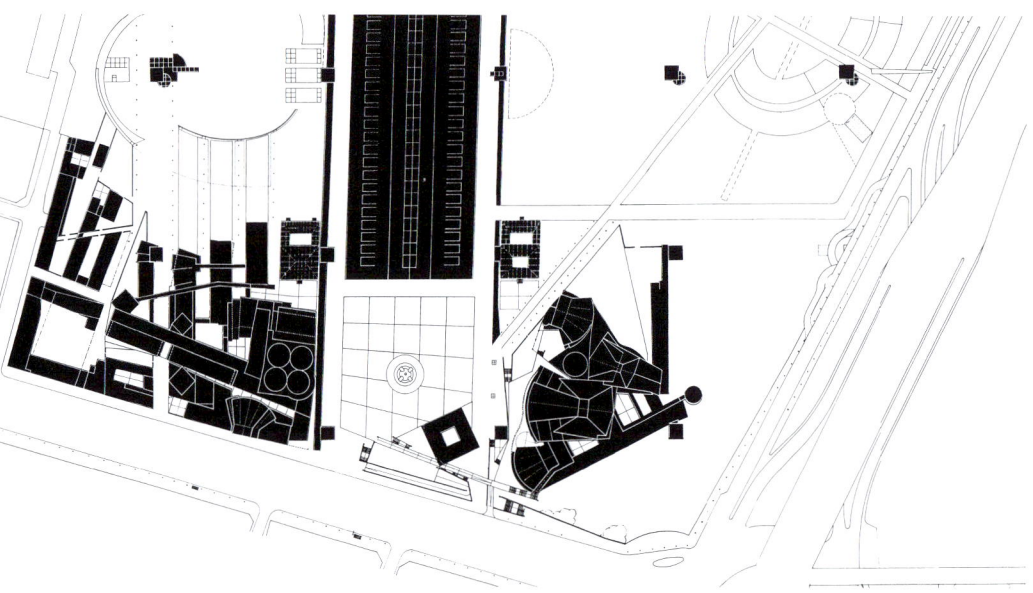

The Cité de la Musique competition (1984).
Project by H. Gaudin.
Initial proposal. Site plan.

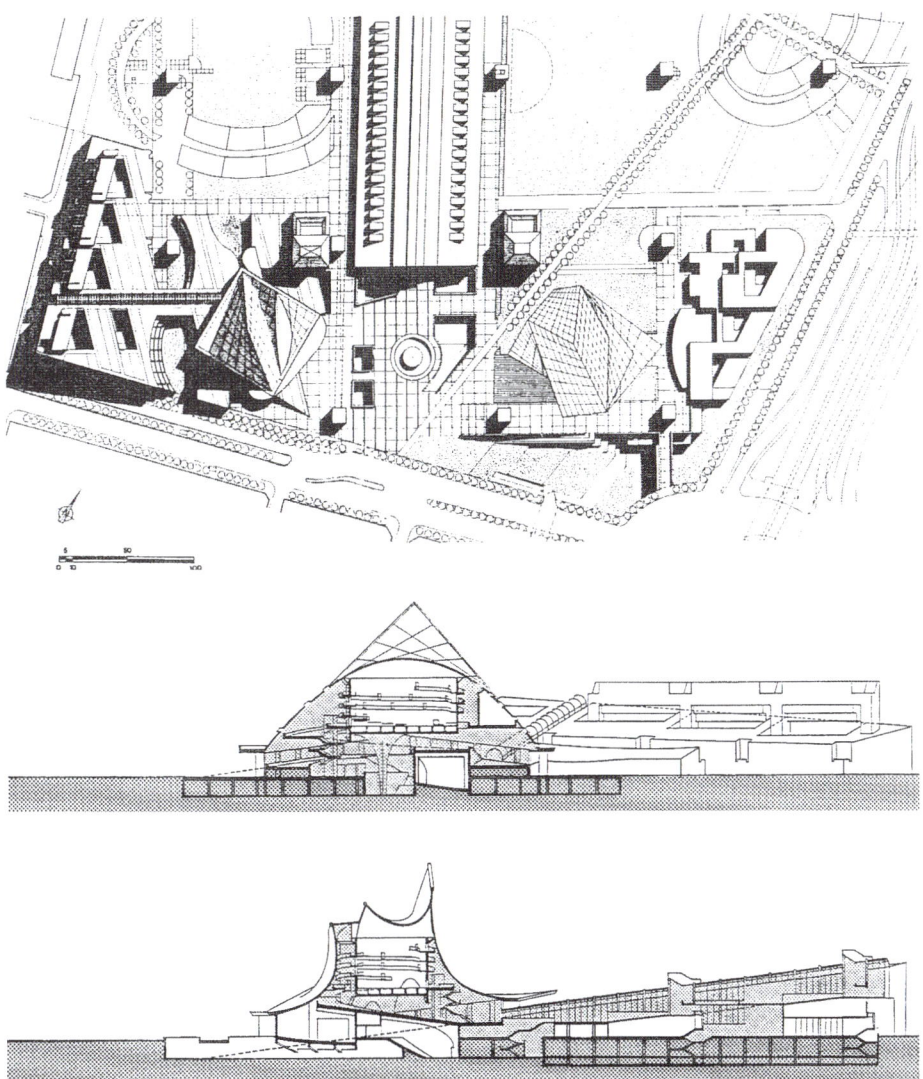

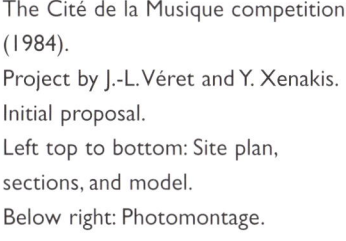

The Cité de la Musique competition (1984).
Project by J.-L. Véret and Y. Xenakis.
Initial proposal.
Left top to bottom: Site plan, sections, and model.
Below right: Photomontage.

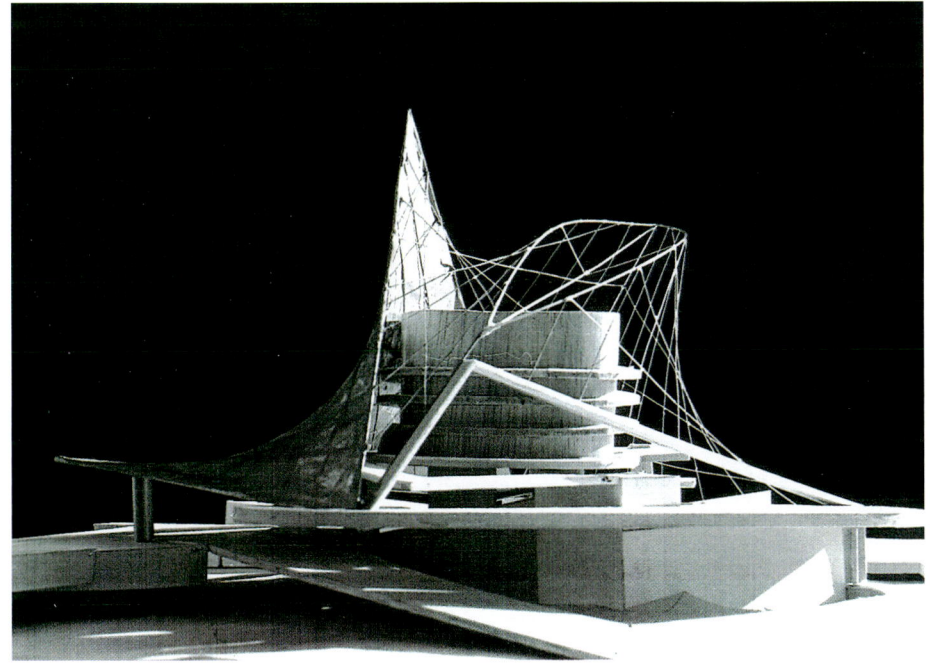

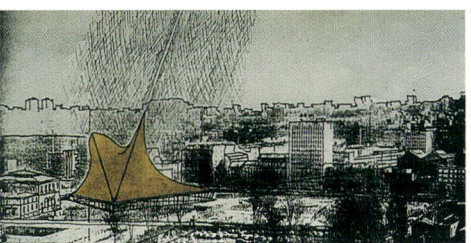

CHRONOLOGY 57

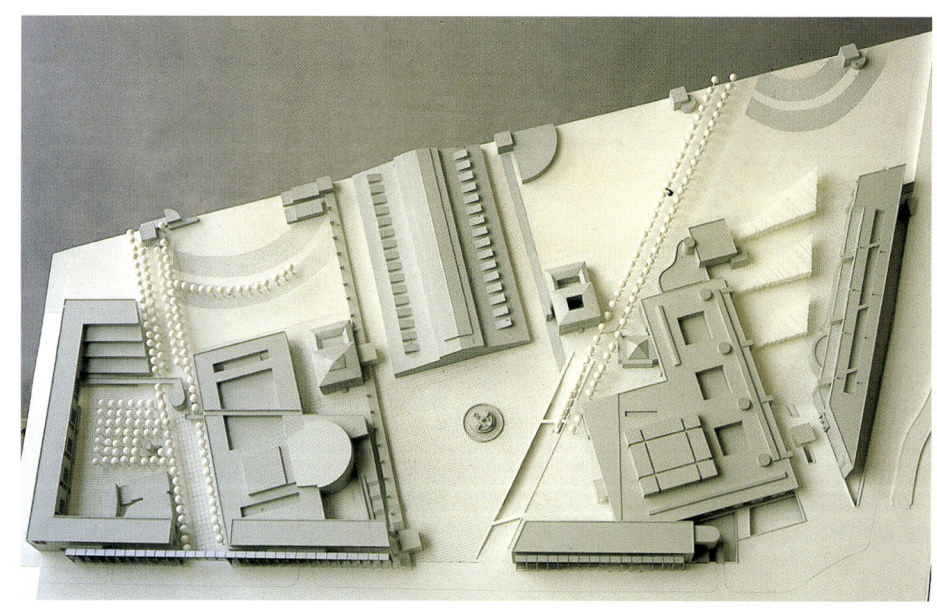
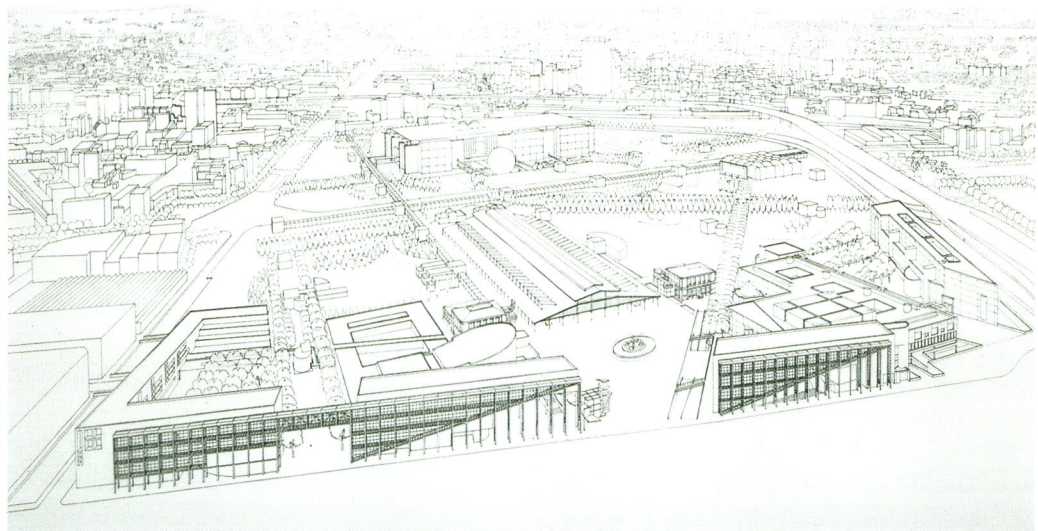
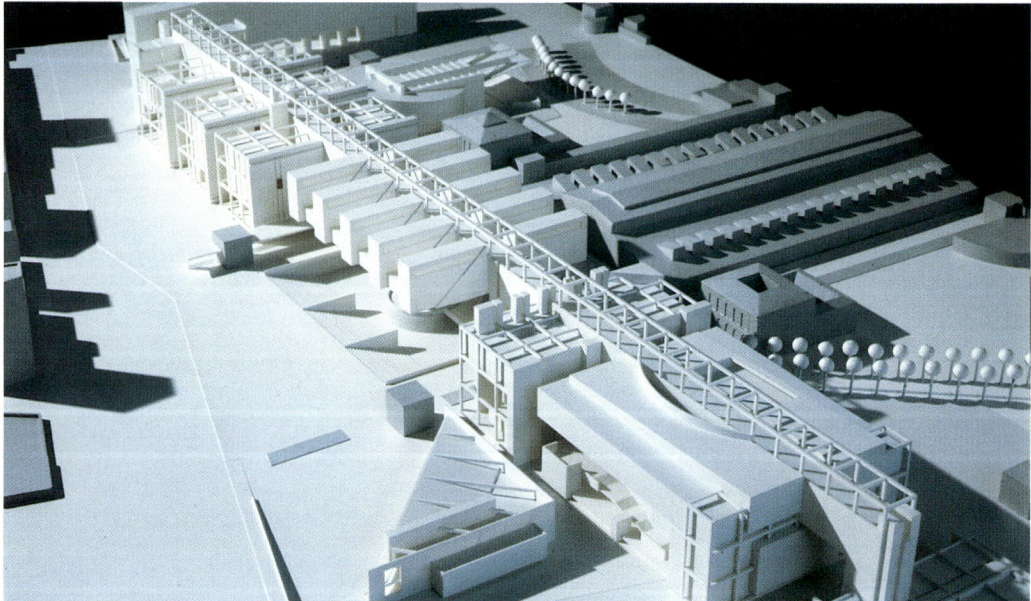

The Cité de la Musique competition (1984).
Above and middle: Project by G. Maurios. Initial proposal. Model and perspective view.
Below: Project by Archiplus (F. Soler, J. Bernard). Initial proposal. Model.

arrondissement – demonstrated an undeniable ability to transcend the constraints imposed by the brief. Acoustically interesting – the jury acknowledged "the originality and innovative character of the solutions for the spatial and acoustic organisation of the concert facilities" – the proposal made the "birds" two signals that fitted with the scale of the city and, while intensifying the symmetrical aspect, contained reminiscences of Martin Van Treeck's Orgues de Flandres project.

The Georges Maurios project
Determined to find a fit with the Haussmannian scale of the site, Georges Maurios positioned two large volumes on the edge of the avenue, setting back from it a surprisingly rigid architecture that embraced Place de la Fontaine-aux-Lions.

The Archiplus, Olivier Baudry and Michel Kagan projects
Notable among the rejects was a fantastic proposal from Archiplus. Levitating above Place de la Fontaine-aux-Lions and overhung by a belvedere-promenade linking the Conservatoire in the west to the main auditorium, in the east, the Galerie

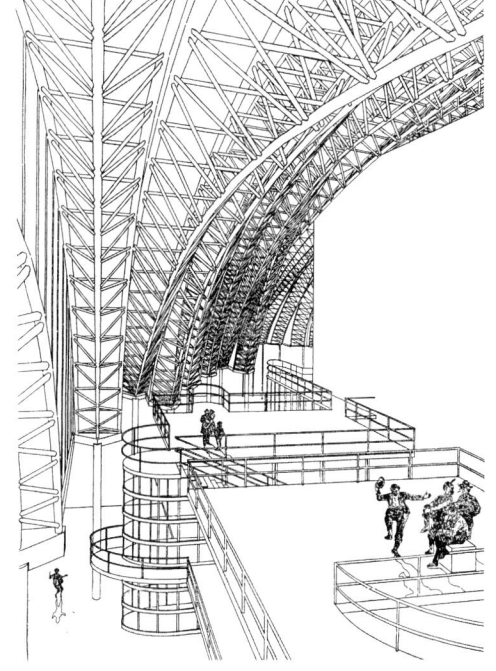

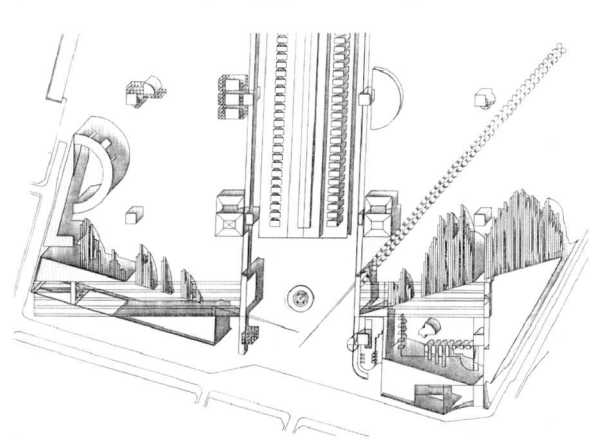

The Cité de la Musique competition (1984).
Project by O. Baudry. Initial proposal. Perspective views and site plan.

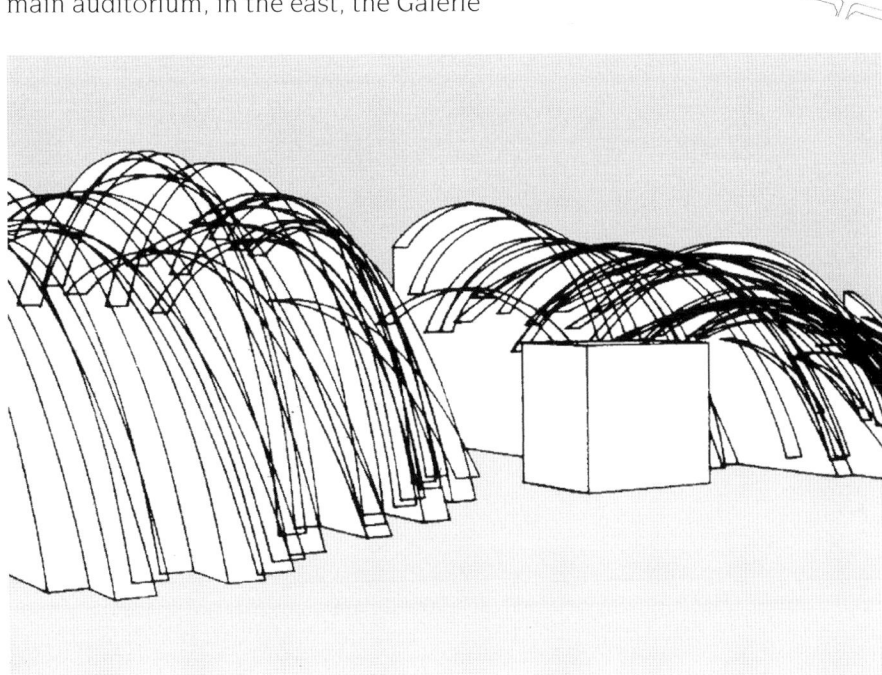

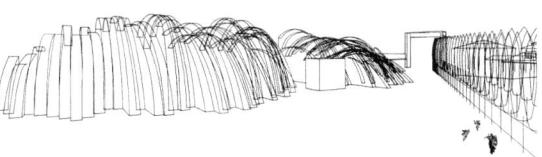

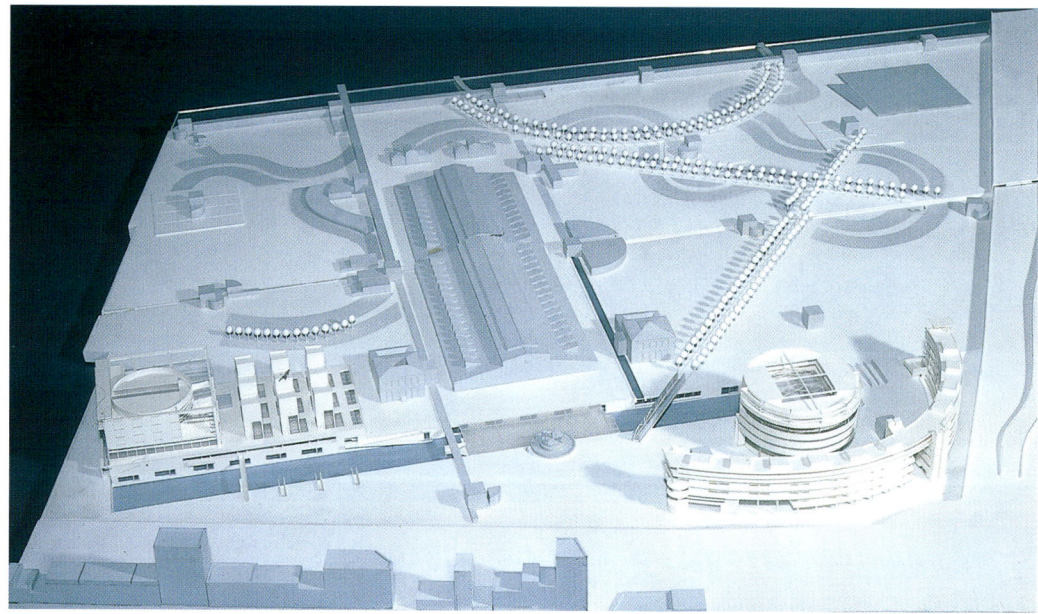

The Cité de la Musique competition (1984).
Project by M. Kagan. Initial proposal. Model.

de l'Instrument epically framed the south gable of the Grande Halle. With its flagrant inner tensions insolently pointing up the brief's contradictions – one demand was that candidates establish "a compositional correspondence between the two blocks," but without "seeking building continuity between east and west" – the project was turned down by a jury that focused unfairly on the dysfunctional placing of the annexes under the main auditorium. Olivier Baudry resuscitated Paul Scheerbart, sprinkling here and there what looked like fragments of Mies' glass skyscraper. This natural-morphic "Alpine Architektur" approach created a link between the park and the large geometrical volumes set along the avenue. Michel Kagan "protected" the main auditorium with a flagrantly Le Corbusier arc-shaped building. Lower down, a "sound and light canal" ran parallel to the south façade of the Grande Halle and hooked up the east and west blocks.

Modifications to the brief between the two rounds of the competition

From the outset it had been strongly suggested that student accommodation at the Conservatoire should be placed to the west of Place de la Fontaine-aux-Lions, doubtless because of the plans to include, on the same wing of the site, a social housing complex to be financed by the city of Paris. Between the two rounds of the competition, however it was decided to increase the amount of student accommodation; this led the contracting authority to opt for setting the Conservatoire to the west and the public facilities to the east – to the chagrin of Alain Sarfati, who had got through the first round and was now faced with a total revision of his project. The decision to separate the public facilities from the Conservatoire also worked against the Ketoff/Petit project – likewise short-listed – which put the Conservatoire and concert hall together on the east side. These unsettling changes to the brief forced François Trehen, of the technical commission, and Francis Le Doré, of the "interdepartmental unit for public sector building quality" to challenge the authorities: on what basis would the president of France judge the six projects – Gaudin, Ketoff/Petit, Maurios, Portzamparc, Sarfati, Xenakis/Véret – submitted for his approval? How could one avoid the suspicion that the three proposals singled out by the president for the second round would be chosen for their capacity to "cope with" the new changes – an unjust state of affairs in that the decision would thus be based on criteria unknown to first-round participants? Did not such modifications necessitate a fresh competition? These questions were made all the more embarrassing in that a further between-rounds resolution to add to the Conservatoire three teaching rooms open to the public – the interdisciplinary, organ and vocal arts rooms – only compounded the confusion. This was, however, a decision that allowed Christian de Portzamparc to hone his project considerably.

Atelier de Portzamparc, Alain Sarfati and Ketoff/Petit new projects

The three rooms Portzamparc had originally sited to the east were thus to be transferred to the west, and this enabled him to make something more concise out of a first-round Conservatoire plan that had seemed somewhat distended. The new arrangement was immediately notable for the strict organisation of its interior traffic areas. To the west, the public music rooms gave onto a patio surmounted by an oblong courtyard turned towards Place de la Fontaine-aux-Lions, while a large, sloping roof countered the project's horseshoe shape. To the east, the Pôle Public de Diffusion Musicale et Muséologique (Public Music and Museum Complex), as if totally indifferent to the

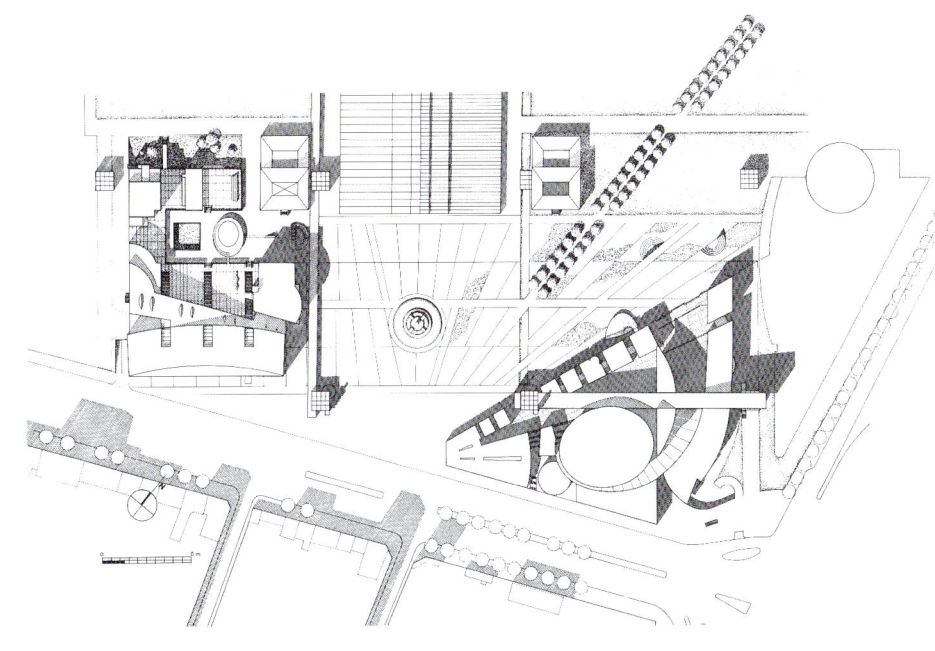

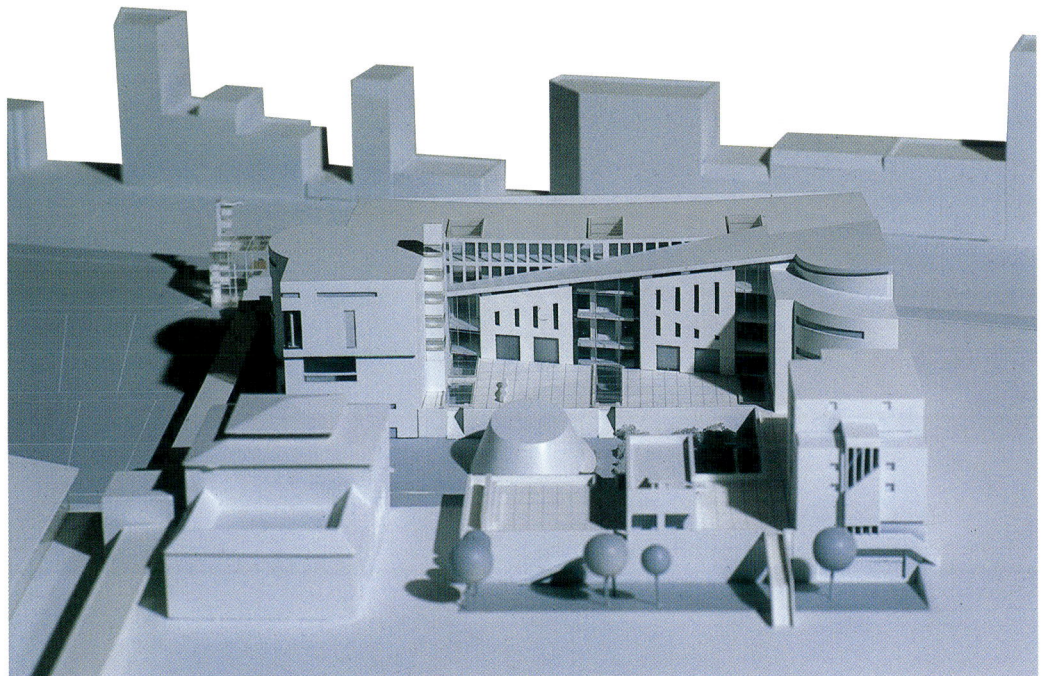

The Cité de la Musique competition (1984).
Project by Atelier de Portzamparc (C. de Portzamparc, F. Barberot, F. Borel, F. Chochon, F. Léonhardt, M.-E. Nicoleau, E. Pierres).
Second proposal.
Above: Site plan.
Below: Model.

The Cité de la Musique competition (1984).
Project by Atelier de Portzamparc (C. de Portzamparc, F. Barberot, F. Borel, F. Chochon, F. Léonhardt, M.-E. Nicoleau, E. Pierres). Above: Ground floor plan of the Conservatoire National Supérieur de Musique et de Danse de Paris – CNSMDP (National Conservatory of Music and Dance of Paris). Second proposal.
Below: First floor plan of the Conservatoire. Second proposal.

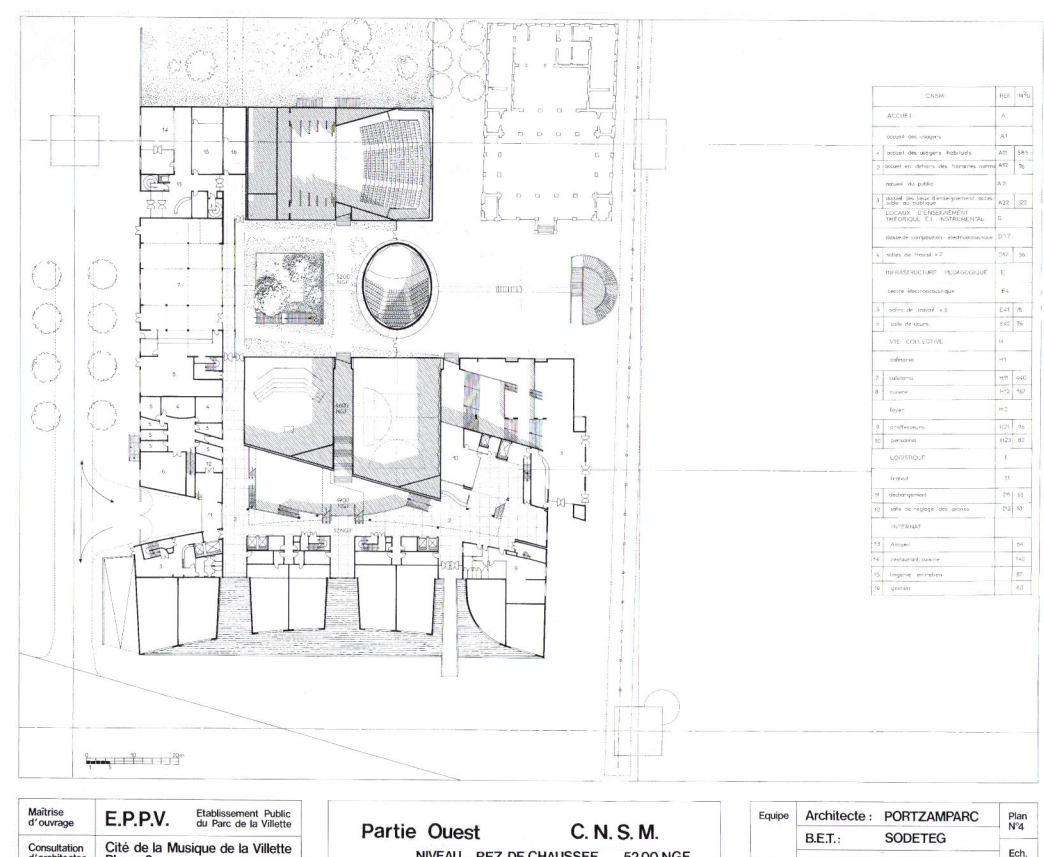

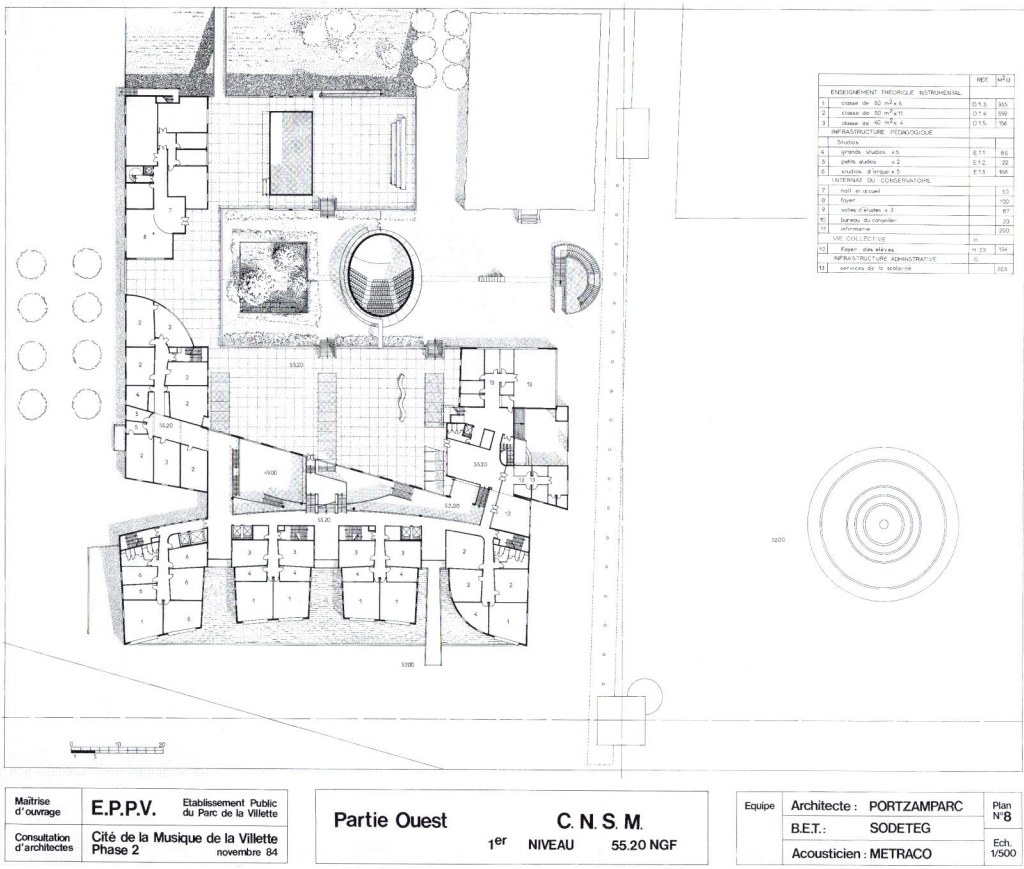

62 LA VILLETTE: 1971–1995

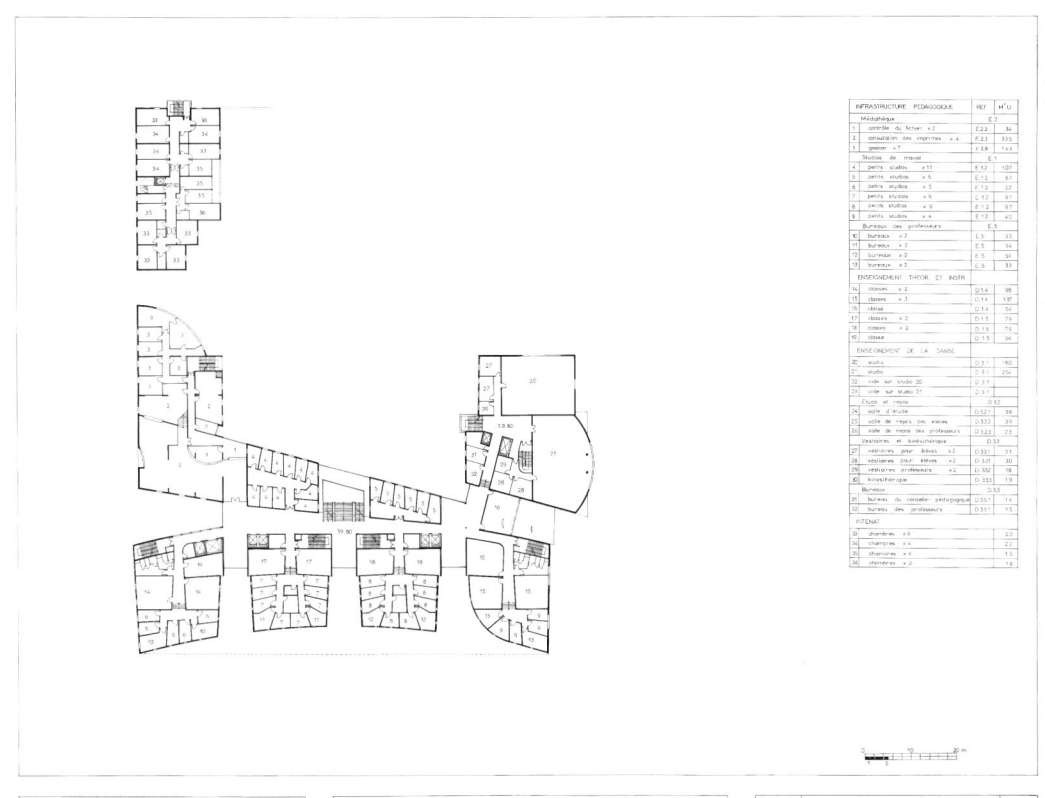

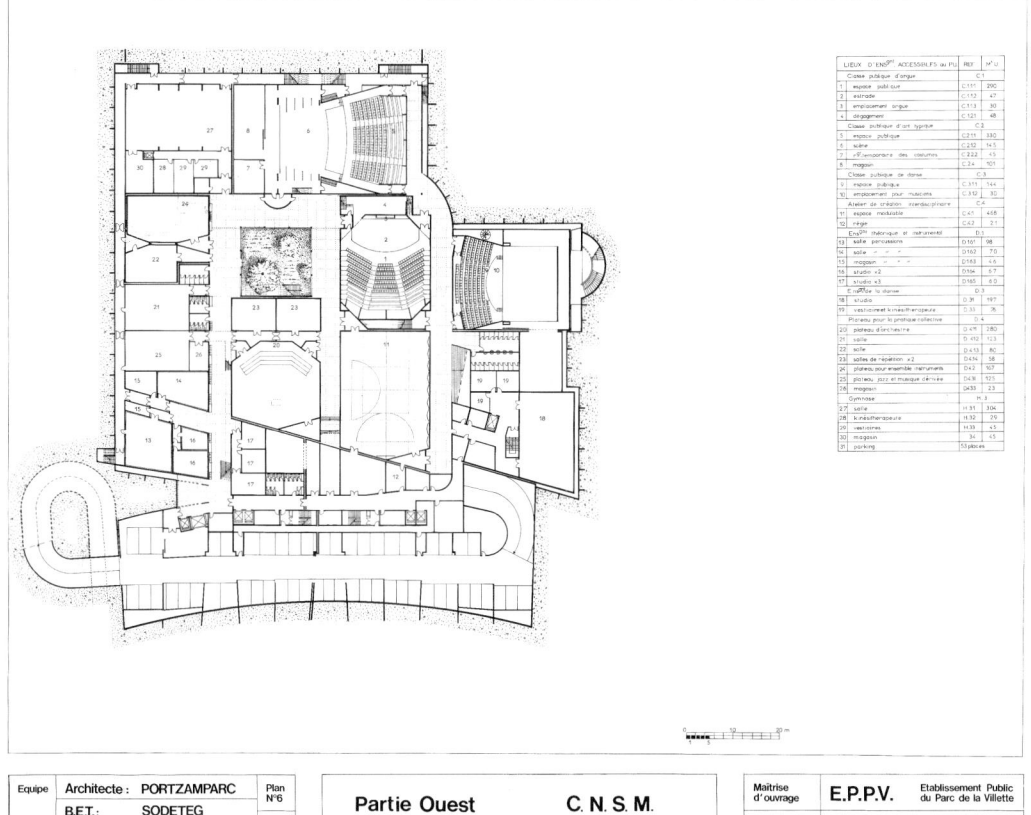

The Cité de la Musique competition (1984).
Project by Atelier de Portzamparc (C. de Portzamparc, F. Barberot, F. Borel, F. Chochon, F. Léonhardt, M.-E. Nicoleau, E. Pierres).
Above: Second floor plan of the Conservatoire. Second proposal.
Below: Second-level basement plan of the Conservatoire. Second proposal.

CHRONOLOGY 63

The Cité de la Musique competition (1984).
Above right and below: M. Ketoff and M. Petit project. Second proposal. Model and site plan.
Above left: Project by A. Sarfati. Second proposal. Model.

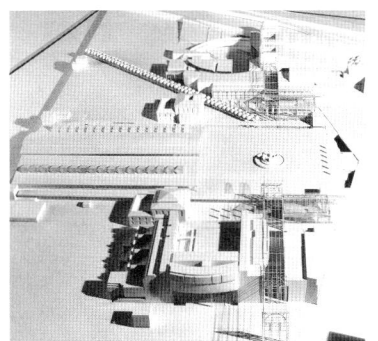

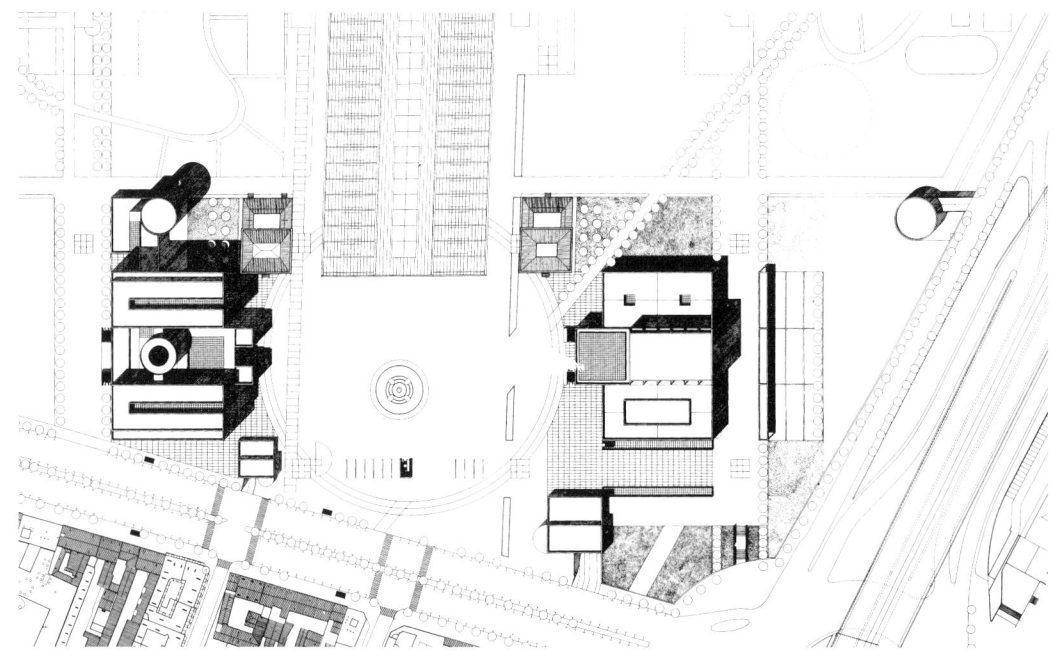

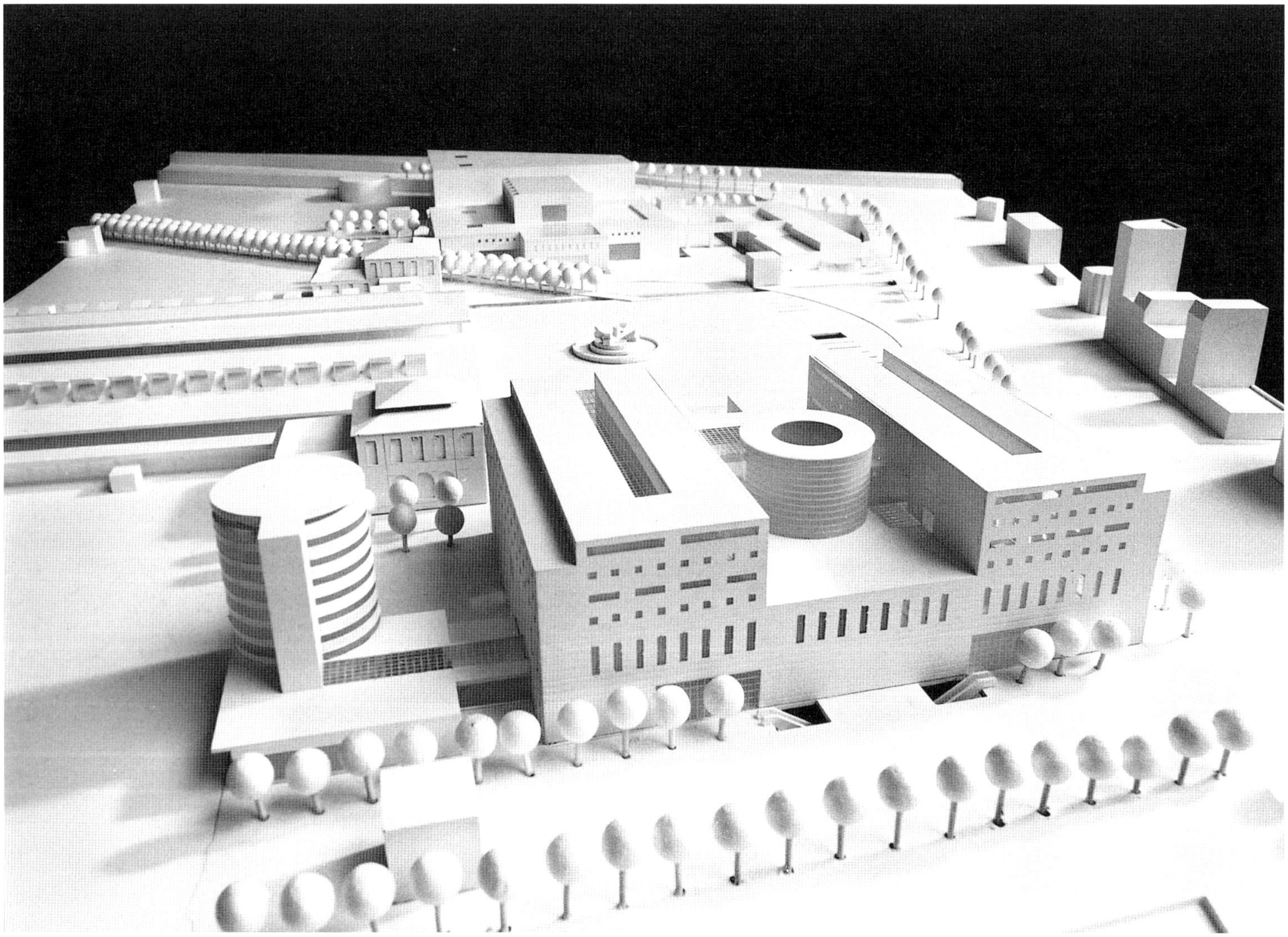

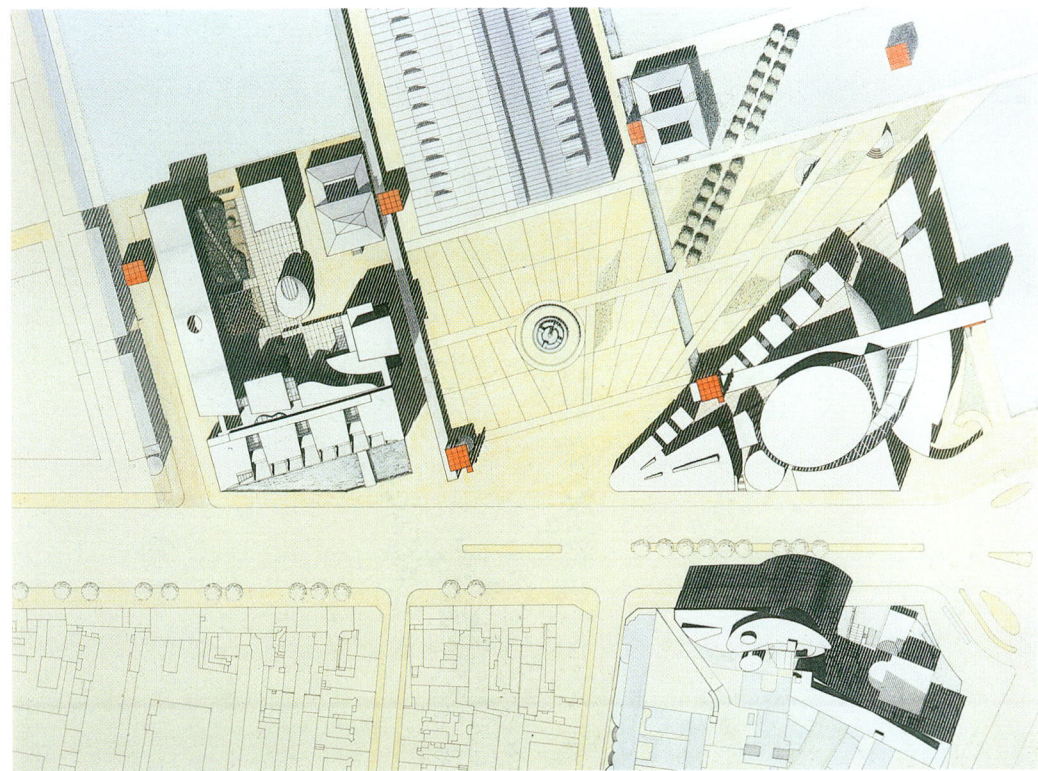

The Cité de la Musique (architect: C. de Portzamparc).
Left: Site plan. Final proposal.
Below: The Conservatoire. First-level basement plan. Final proposal.

tergiversations of the brief, proudly displayed its remarkable formal and organisational consistency. The technical commission's opposition to the siting of the Galerie de l'Instrument in an enormous, glassed-in metal structure would lead to the transfer of the museum spaces to small blocks set on the edge of the park – initially intended as public reception areas – without any consequences for the morphology of the project.

This was the proposal that earned Christian de Portzamparc first place in 1985, ahead of Alain Sarfati and Ketoff/Petit, whose new projects disappointed the jury: the Sarfati layout was seen as too symmetrical, while Ketoff/Petit had "rigidified their forms and thus isolated them from the city and the park."

Final modifications to the winning project

Christian de Portzamparc's project only achieved its full plastic and organisational

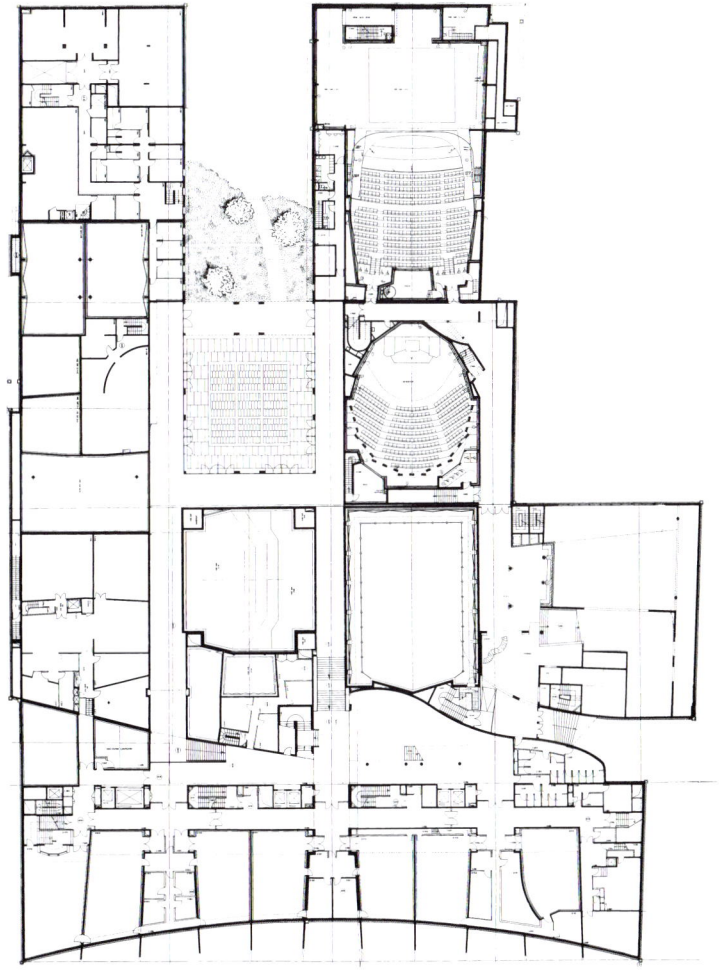

CHRONOLOGY 65

The Cité de la Musique (architect: C. de Portzamparc).
Above right: The Conservatoire. Sections of the two main staircases and the public music rooms. Final proposal.
In the middle: Model. Background: The symphony hall (not built).
Below: The Conservatoire. Axonometric view. Final proposal.

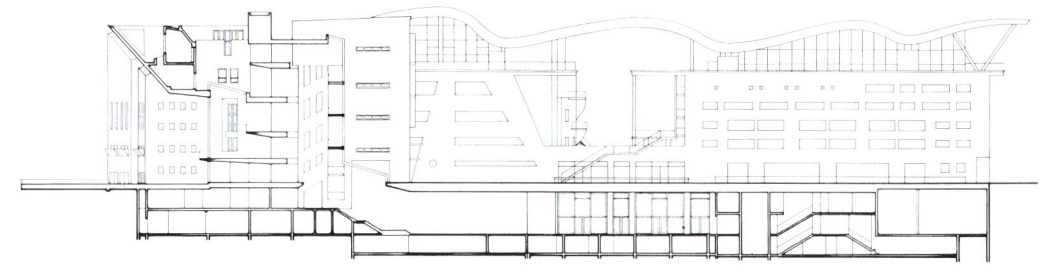

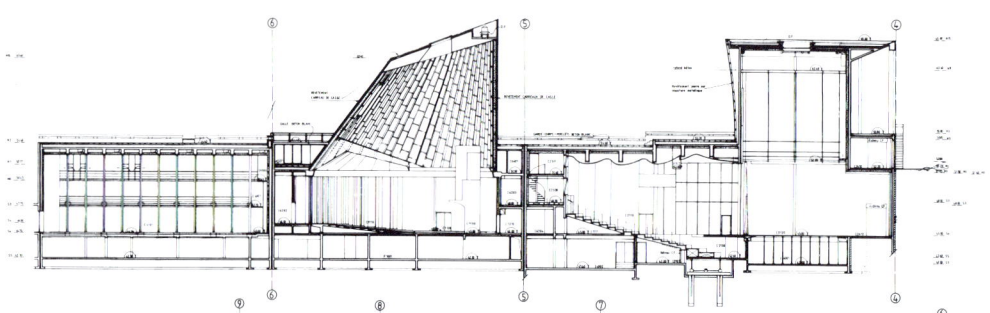

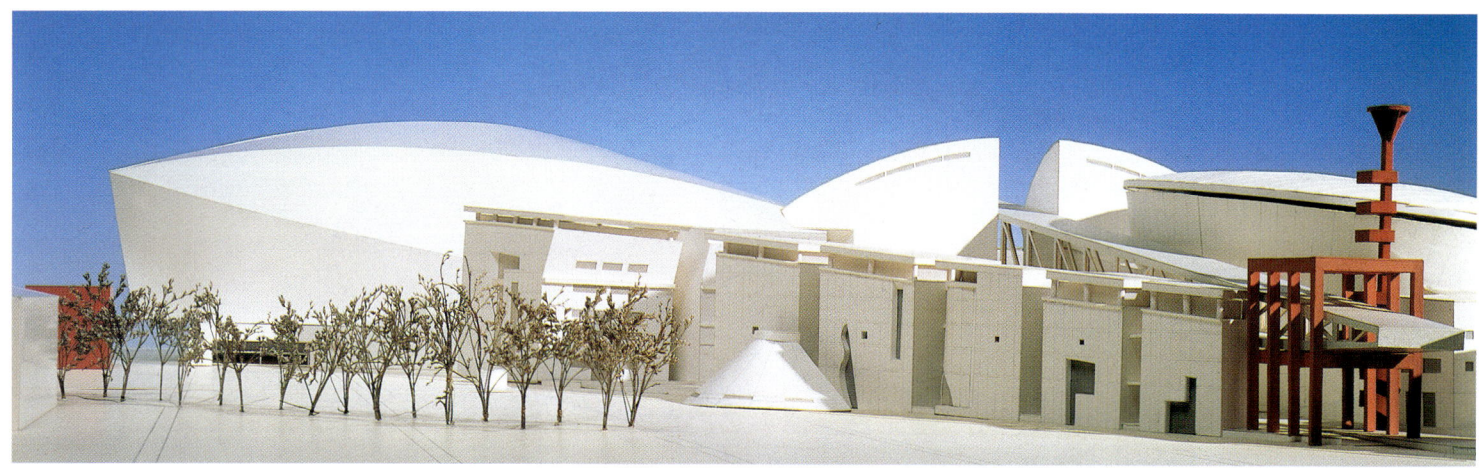

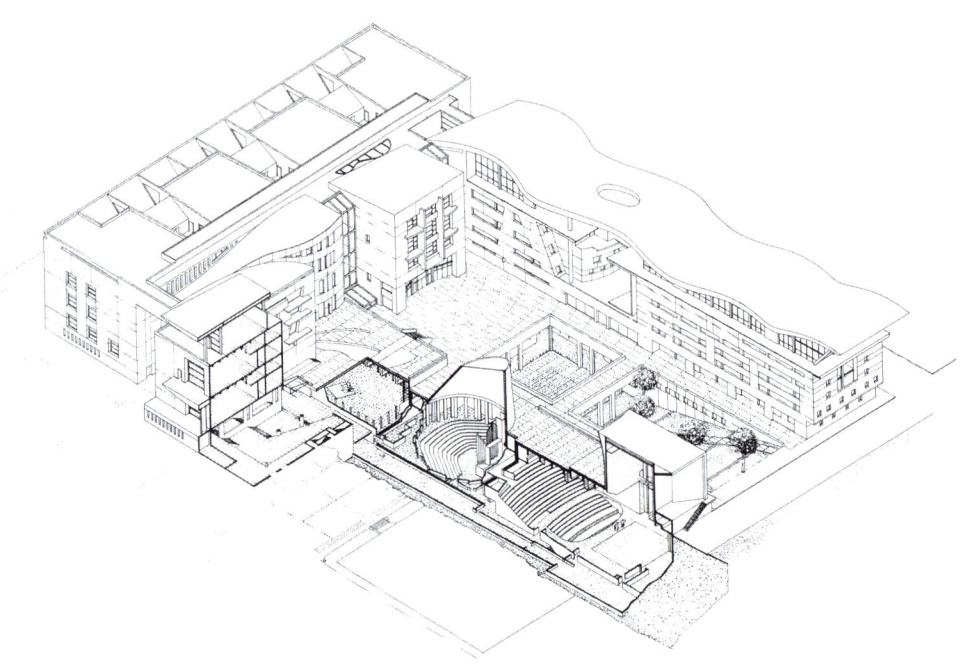

66   LA VILLETTE: 1971–1995

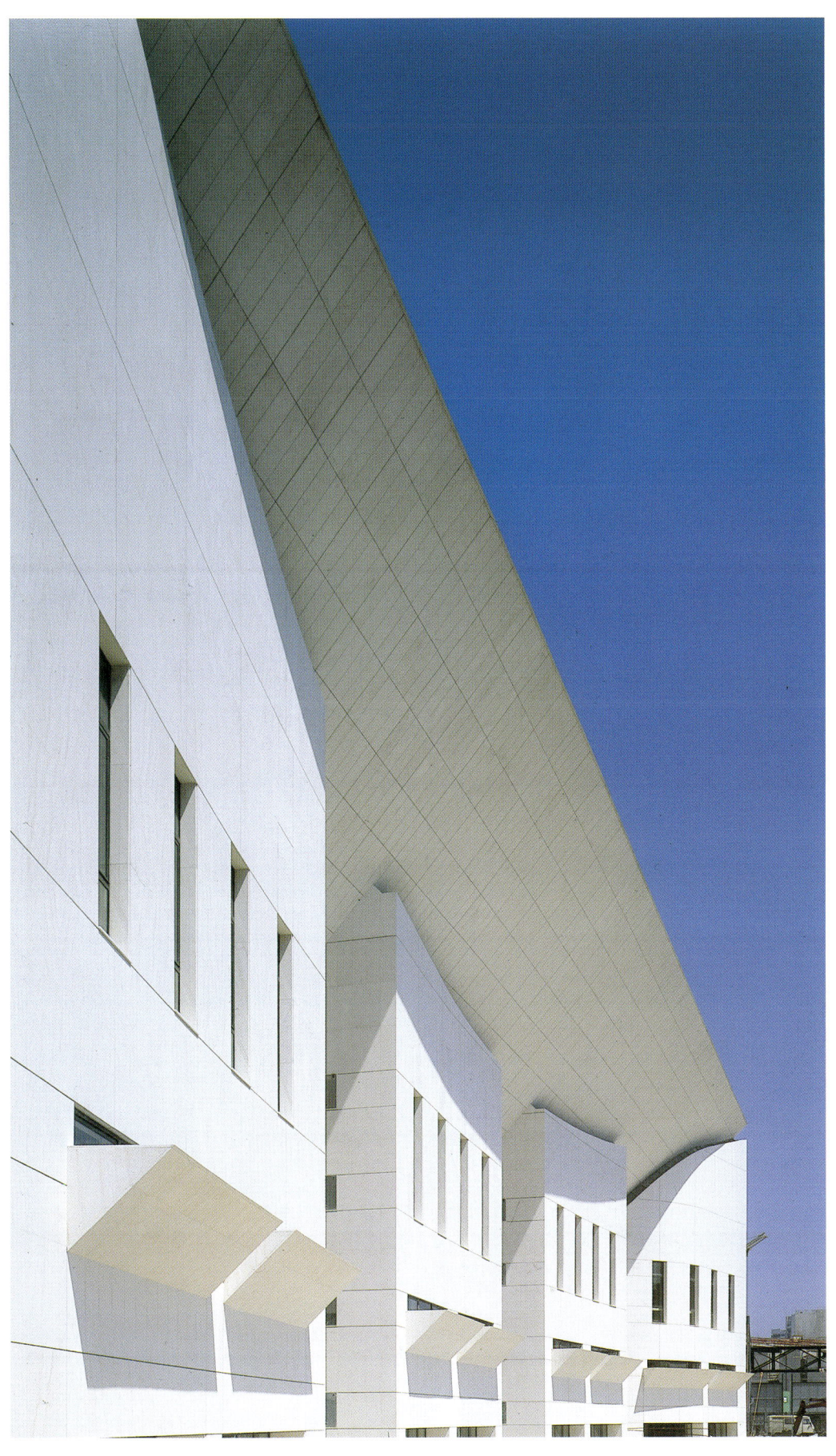

The Cité de la Musique (architect: C. de Portzamparc).
The Conservatoire's south façade.

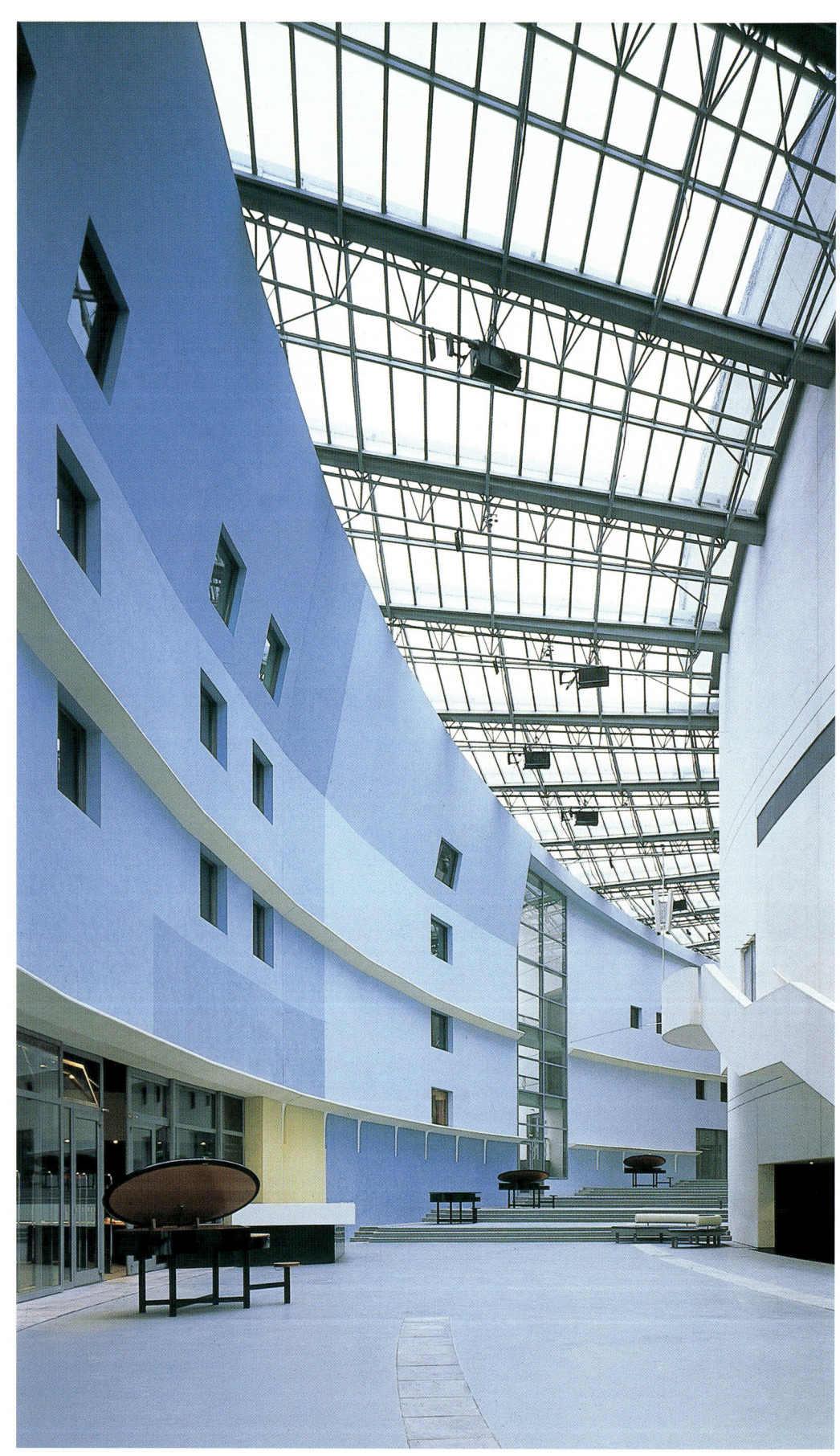

The Cité de la Musique (architect: C. de Portzamparc).
The Pôle Public de Diffusion Musicale et Muséologique (Public Music and Museum Complex): The "Conque" (Conch Shell).

proportions at the detailed design phase. Here the architect opted to open out the interior courtyard towards the park, whose north-south axis then energised the plan – especially at its lower levels, focused as they were on two majestically hypnotic interior streets. Meanwhile the Pôle Public de Diffusion Musicale et Muséologique brought a timely note of brightness to a Villette site suffocating under the weight of all its standardised spaces.

Disconcerting it may be, but the Cité de la Musique's internal dichotomy remains a core contribution to rigorous urban composition. Unquestionably a new territory has been created at La Villette. Mingling the static and the dynamic, the stolid and the lyrical, the site is demarcated and subjugated by the irresistible power of a geometry which, nonetheless, never succeeds in rendering it sterile. Does not the flagrant jumble to the east reveal a peaceful alliance of shapes curled up inside a basic geometrical figure – the triangle? And conversely, is not the highly geometrical character of the Conservatoire to the west sublimated by the multiple shifts of level and the endless variety of the materials? Playing on the dual register of "geometrical translation of architectural problems"[33] and "architectural semanticisation of geometrical operations,"[34] Christian de Portzamparc adroitly mastered the conjunction of architectural and urban scale, and in doing so achieved a formal coherence that no amount of political unpredictability or mind-boggling changes to the brief ever succeeded in undermining. Effortlessly ductile and thoroughly organic, this project subtly highlighted the inherent violence of the development of La Villette-North sector, where two colossal buildings by Gérard Thurnauer throw up an opaque barrier between the Cité des Sciences and its urban setting.

The official opening of the Cité de la Musique

The official opening of the Pôle Public on 12 January 1995, set the seal on a sovereign generation of architects with its own freely-established set of doctrines, and on the transmutation of La Villette – once a "city of blood" – into a new

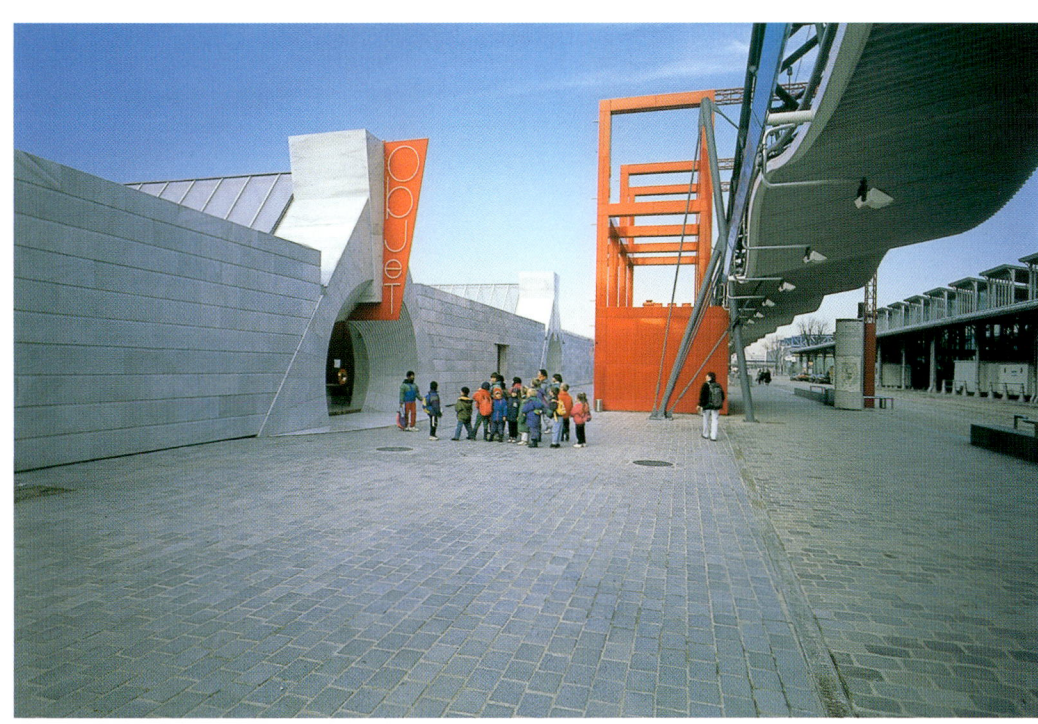

The Pavillon Paul-Delouvrier (architect: O. Tusquets).

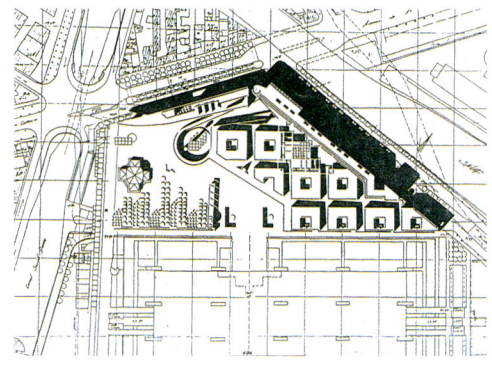
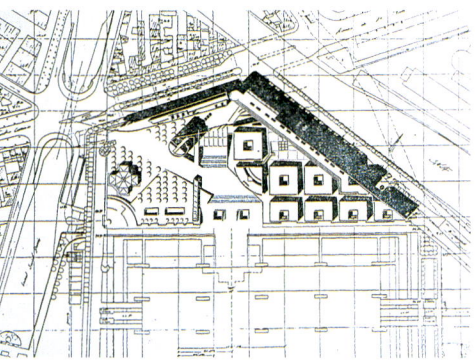
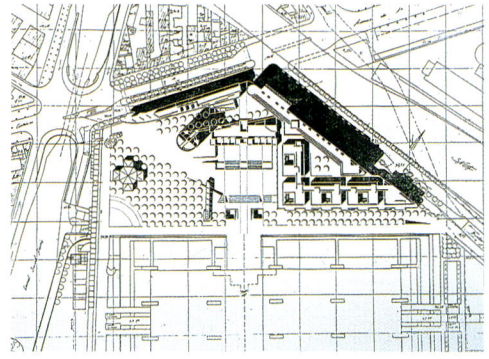
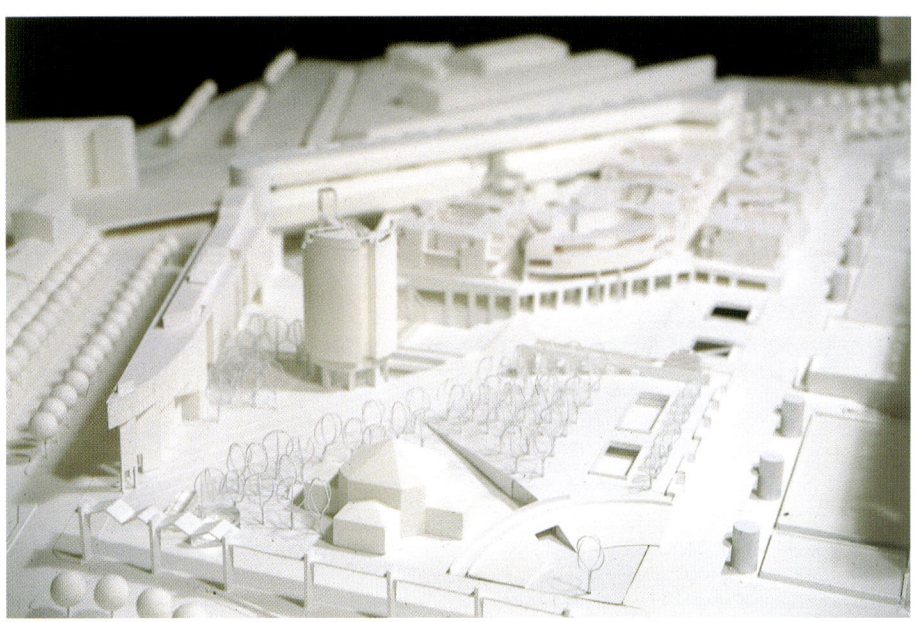
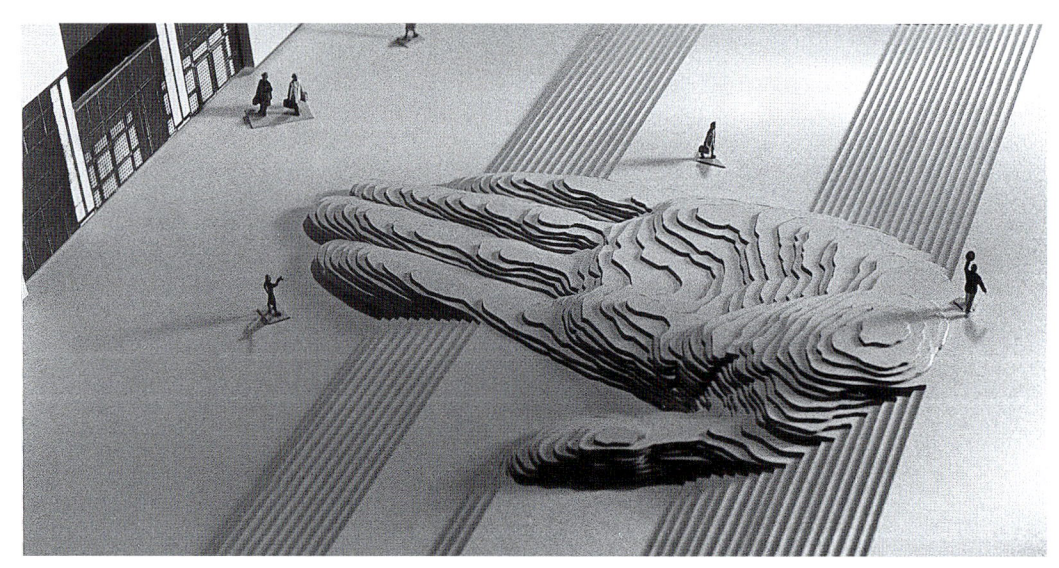

Competition for the development of La Villette-North sector (1985).
Above left: Project by G. Thurnauer. Model.
Above right: Project by G. Thurnauer. Site plans:
Phase 1 (top);
Phase 2 (middle);
Final proposal (bottom).
Below right: Project by G. Thurnauer. The "Main Géante" (Giant Hand); (in collaboration with J. de Gaspary).

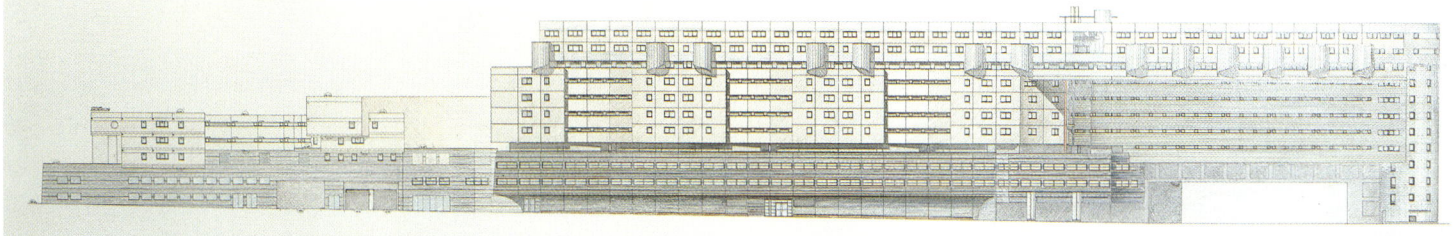

Competition for the development of La Villette-North sector (1985). Above: Project by G. Thurnauer. The Boulevard Macdonald façade.

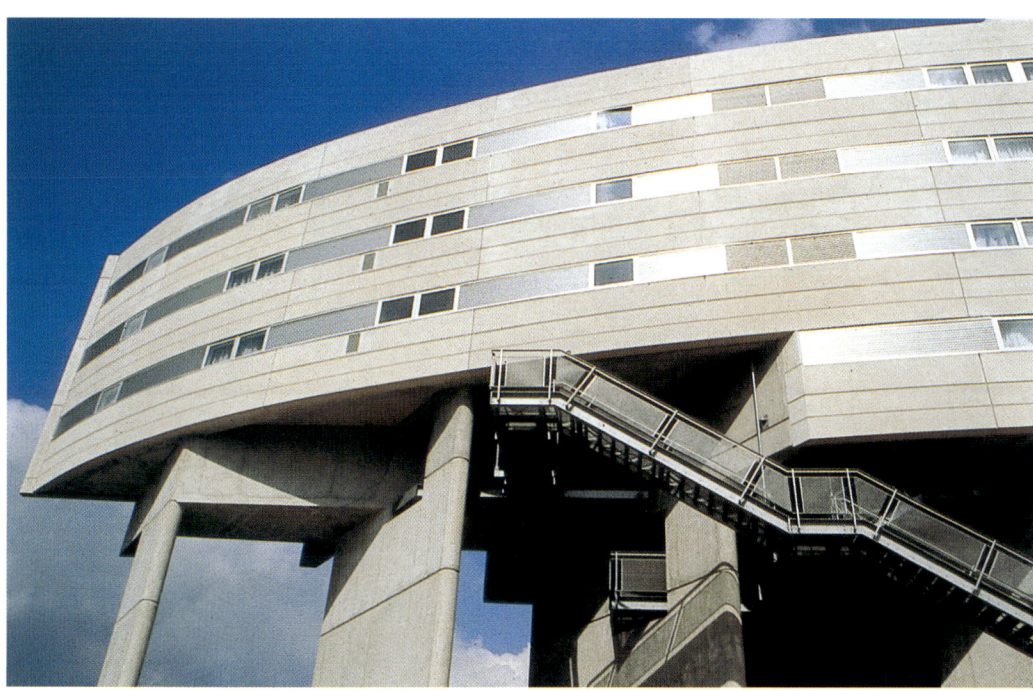

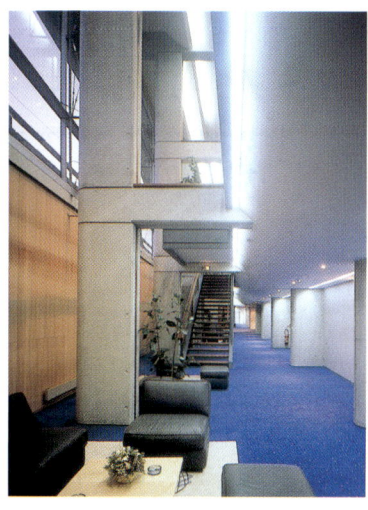

Künstlerkolonie. A Künstlerkolonie (Artists' Colony) whose protagonists would no longer be called Peter Behrens, Joseph Hoffmann or Joseph Maria Olbrich, but rather Adrien Fainsilber, Bernard Tschumi and Christian de Portzamparc.

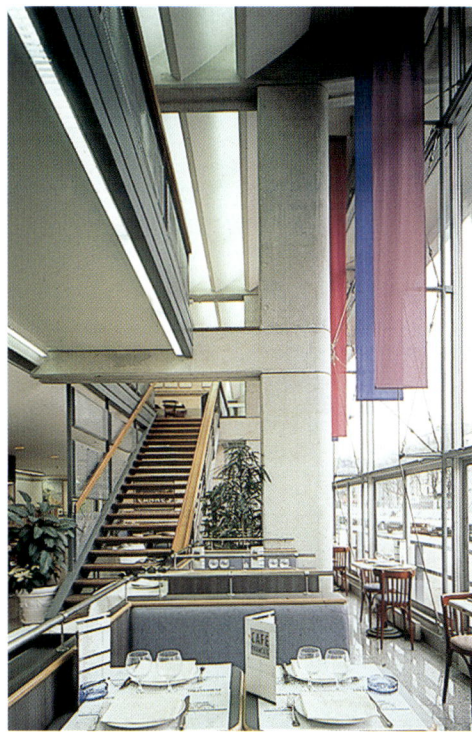

The Hôtel Maeva (architect: G. Thurnauer).
Forecourt façade and interior views.

CHRONOLOGY 71

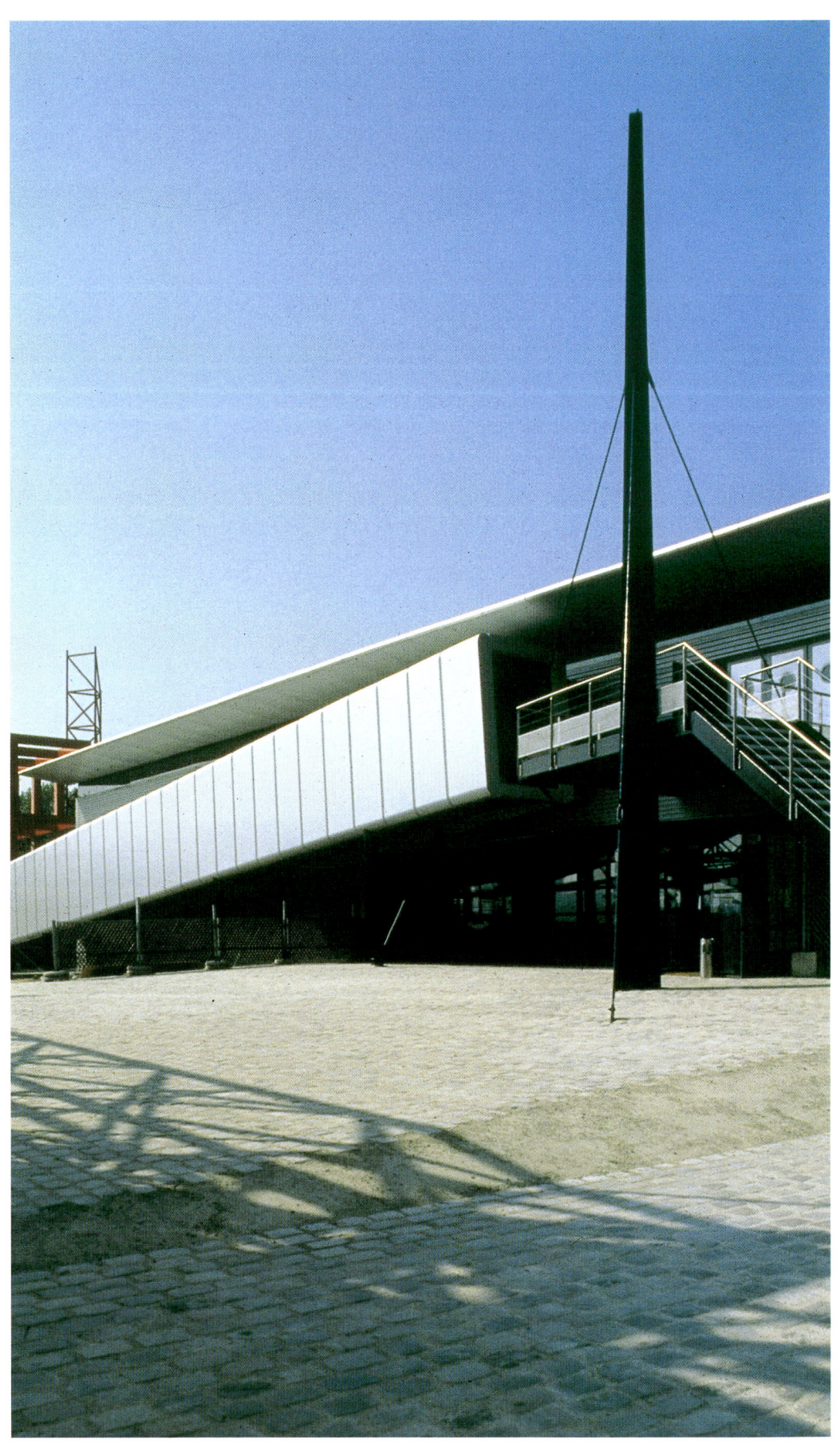

The Cinaxe (architect: B. Tschumi).

Notes

1. Rem Koolhaas, "New York/La Villette", in Jacques Lucan, OMA – *Rem Koolhaas* (Paris/Milan: Electa France, 1990), p. 67. (English translation: Jacques Lucan, OMA – *Rem Koolhaas*, Birkhauser, USA, 1999).
2. See note 2 ("Le Parc") in the presentation of the *Proposition pour l'aménagement du secteur de La Villette*.
3. Ibid.
4. Isabelle Auricoste, "De l'espace urbain", in Isabelle Auricoste, Hubert Tonka, *Vaisseau de pierre/Architectures : Parc-Ville Villette*, (Seyssel: Champ Vallon, 1987), p. 116.
5. Ibid., p. 116.
6. Ernst Cassirer, *La Philosophie des Lumières* (Paris: Fayard, 1966), p. 73. (English translation: Ernst Cassirer, *The Philosophy of the Enlightenment*, Princeton University Press, 1968).
7. Ibid., p. 108.
8. François Barré, "Aux portes du parc", in *L'Invention du parc*, (Paris: Graphite/Établissement Public du Parc de La Villette, 1984), p. 15.
9. Ibid., p. 16.
10. Barré, "Des préliminaires théoriques à la conception du programme et à la réalisation du parc de La Villette", in Isabelle Auricoste, Hubert Tonka, op. cit., note 4, p. 106.
11. Ibid., p. 107.
12. Marc Augé, *Non-Lieux*, (Paris: Seuil, 1992), p. 48. (English translation: *Non-Places: Introduction to an Anthropology of Supermodernity*, Verso, 1995).
13. Jean Baudrillard, "Le mondial et l'universel", in Jean Baudrillard, *Écran total* (Paris: Galilée, 1997), p. 178. (English translation: Jean Baudrillard, *Screened Out*, Verso, 2002).
14. See the report on the objectives for the competition to build the Parc de La Villette.
15. Jean Nouvel, in *L'Invention du parc*, op. cit., note 8, p. 81.
16. Rem Koolhaas, "Junkspace", in Rem Koolhaas, Stefano Boeri, Sanford Kwinter, Nadia Tazi, Hans Ulrich Obrist, *Mutations*, (Barcelona – Bordeaux: Actar/arc en rêve centre d'architecture, 2000), p. 747. (English translation: Rem Koolhaas et al., *Mutations*, Actar Editorial, 2001).
17. Ernst Cassirer, op. cit., note 6, p. 49.
18. Bernard Tschumi, *Le Parc de La Villette : cinégramme folie*, (Seyssel: Champ Vallon, 1987), p. 5. (English translation: Bernard Tschumi, *Cinegram Folie: Le Parc de La Villette* [New Designs], Princeton Architectural Press, 1988).
19. Ibid., p. 8.
20. Ibid., p. 5.
21. François Barré, op. cit., note 10, p. 107.
22. Alexandre Chemetoff, "Paris, le vendredi 30 janvier 1987", in Isabelle Auricoste, Hubert Tonka, op. cit. note 4, p. 110. (The French expression, "tapis vert", is the term for the green baize used for gambling.– *Trans*.)
23. Ibid., p. 110.
24. Paul Scarcelli, "Le 'Bois Sacré' de Tolbiac", *Libération*, Paris, 17 January 1996.
25. Paul Virilio, *La Vitesse de libération*, (Paris: Galilée, 1995), p. 40.
26. Jean Baudrillard, "Le Sida : virulence ou prophylaxie?", in Jean Baudrillard, op. cit., note 13, p. 14.
27. Baudrillard, "Le mondial et l'universel", in Jean Baudrillard, op. cit., note 13, p. 179.
28. Baudrillard, "Disneyworld Company", in Jean Baudrillard, op. cit., note 13, p. 173.
29. Paul Virilio, "L'avant-garde de l'oubli", in Paul Virilio, *Un paysage d'événements* (Paris: Galilée, 1996), p. 39. (English translation: Paul Virilio, *A Landscape of Events* (Writing Architecture), MIT Press, 2000).
30. Pierre-Henry Jeudy, "Miroirs d'un enclos sans clôture", in Isabelle Auricoste, Hubert Tonka, op. cit., note 4, p. 109.
31. Ibid., p. 109.
32. Jean Baudrillard, "Préface", in Isabelle Auricoste, Hubert Tonka, op. cit. note 4, p. 5.
33. Philippe Deshayes, "L'embrayage comme correspondance à l'espace", in Philippe Boudon, *De l'architecture à l'épistémologie. La question de l'échelle* (Paris: PUF, 1991), p. 210.
34. Ibid., p. 210.

INTERVIEWS

Jean Sérignan

François Grether

Roger Taillibert

Interview with Jean Sérignan

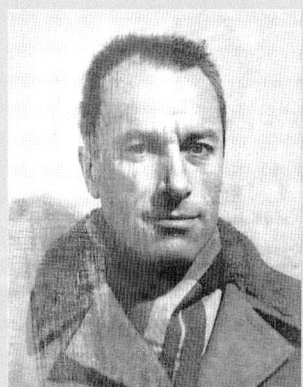

Jean Sérignan came to La Villette in early 1971 with a twofold mission. First, as director of the SEMVI (La Villette Semi-Public Company), he was involved in running and rationalising the workings of the abattoir. Second, arising directly from the first task was the rationalisation of the abattoir complex leading to a redefinition of its spatial organisation. Because this process meant reducing the area in use, it was possible for local inhabitants to appropriate the spaces that were freed up, and consequently the strategy of architectural development could be based directly on an analysis of the way these spaces were used. It is this strategy, which was both flexible and directive, that the commissioner for the development of the Villette sector describes below.

When did you come to La Villette?

I came to La Villette at the end of 1970. And I arrived on the site of the abattoir as the representative of the Ministry of Finance. My mission was to develop ideas for the site's fifty-five hectares. At the same time, I was at the head of the SEMVI, which was in charge of managing the abattoir – this was still functioning at the time. I formed a team with several architects, a few technicians and an engineer from the Ponts et Chaussées. This was the team that conceived ideas for the development of the site. But before I say any more, I would like to tell you something: contrary to what some say, the history of La Villette did not begin in 1970, nor even in 1980. The truth is that it began a hundred years earlier, when Napoleon III decided to build a big abattoir on the edge of Paris, along with a livestock market. It is important to understand that the whole history of the site can be explained by this beginning. For it was during this period that the territory became shaped by a series of lines of force and points that are still in evidence today. To understand the site of La Villette, one needs to evoke its history. And this is intimately linked to the construction of the Canal de l'Ourcq under Napoleon Bonaparte. The aim of that, as you know, was to ensure the capital's water supply. Originally – and this was its main objective – the canal was there to provide Paris with drinking water. And if it turned out to be navigable, this was simply a consequence – welcome but not premeditated – of the water supply project. This project was paralleled by two major historical events: in 1860, the assimilation by Paris of a number of outlying towns – La Villette, Vaugirard, Passy and Grenelle – which of course increased the area of the capital; and the construction, just before the war of 1870, of an abattoir complex and, with it, an enormous livestock market. That's not what we're here to talk about, but I did want to point out that the plans of the abattoir and livestock market complex were very intelligently worked out. Alleys of trees led from each of the Portes towards the different poles of activity. The complexes were extremely hierarchised – urbanistically, that is. So we can see that La Villette very quickly became an enormous space filled with various installations laid out on each side of the Canal de l'Ourcq, which, it should be made clear, was seen as an obstacle to the smooth working of the installations. Then came the great project to modernise the abattoir, starting in 1960. This project grew out of an economic strategy that proved to be totally incompatible with

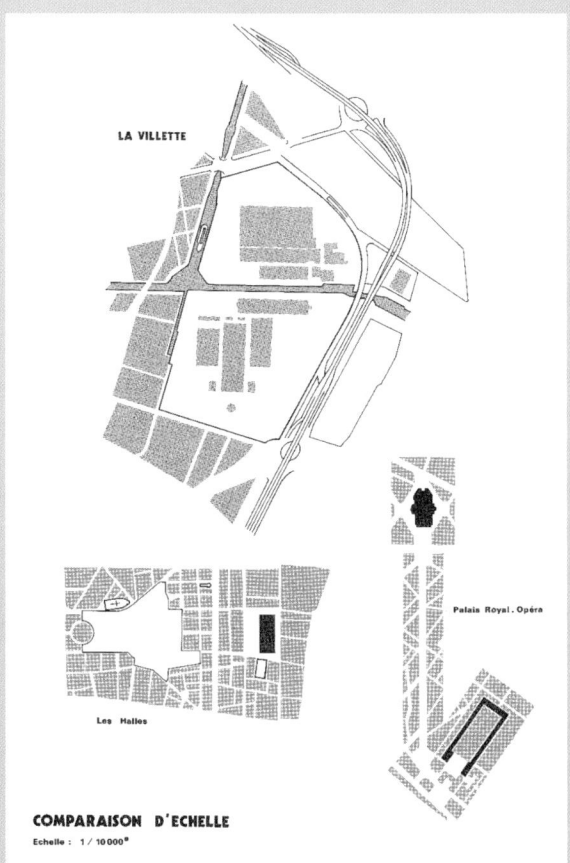

Development proposal for La Villette (J. Sérignan, 1975). Studies.

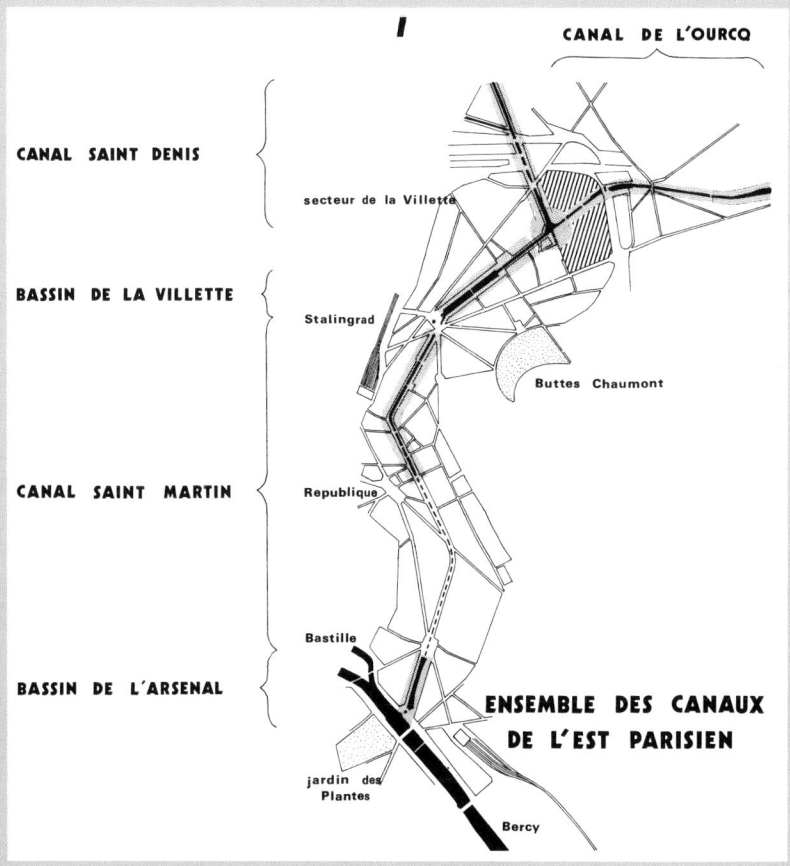

the new refrigeration techniques – hence the scandal of the abattoir. However, I should add that when the modernisation of the slaughterhouse complex was undertaken, the refrigeration industry was in its infancy and it wasn't yet possible to transport carcasses in refrigerated wagons. In those days, then, an industrial project like the one at La Villette was totally justified, but the developments in transport technology made that kind of monolithic concentration obsolete because it was now possible to slaughter animals where they were reared and to transport the carcasses directly to the place of sale in refrigerated trucks. So what could be done? At first they decided to leave the livestock market, which was still functioning, and to reorganise the abattoir complex while planning for a market that would absorb the one in the central sheds. A huge station was also built with more than fifteen railway lines going all the way up north, passing under the Canal de l'Ourcq, and arriving in the lower levels of the meat market that had just been built parallel to Avenue Corentin-Cariou.

Yes, the famous meat market, which was left unfinished and never really got working.

Exactly. To build the meat market they had to destroy all the old cattle stalls that were initially located to the north. In addition to the big hall – which later became the Cité des Sciences et de l'Industrie – they added new slaughterhouses, refrigerated chambers and a series of metal footbridges over the Canal de l'Ourcq, linking the abattoir to the cattle stalls built along the southern bank of the canal. Logically enough, the slaughterhouses were the first part to be completed – they had to go on slaughtering animals – while the meat market was still unfinished when the new abattoir was opened in 1969. This meant that they had to create a temporary meat market. To do this they chose to use a small building near the cattle shed as a stopgap. As a result, all the site's activity, which historically was located on both sides of the canal, was now grouped together on the southern part of the site. This was when questions began to be asked about the final cost of the whole operation. Especially since, in the meantime, the state had made a bid to buy the whole site. The scandal of La Villette, I would like to say, has nothing to do with any kind of corruption. Nobody got rich at La Villette. The story of La Villette is simply one of a huge economic mistake.

Was the closure of the abattoir implicit in the state's purchase of La Villette?

I think I can say that it was. But the dimensions of the site should be considered: the distance from Porte de La Villette to Porte de Pantin is more than a kilometre. The length of the Canal de l'Ourcq – the part flowing through the site – is about five hundred metres. And the area of the site is close to fifty-five hectares. That's a lot. As for Place de la Fontaine-aux-Lions, its area is identical to that of Place des Vosges. It would be amusing to continue this little game of comparisons. The thousand metres separating Porte de La Villette from Porte de Pantin are the length of Avenue de l'Opéra. And the area of the cattle shed is comparable to that of the garden at Palais-Royal. So, given these huge dimensions, what did the managing organisation decide to do? It very naturally decided to rationalise the space. Rationalising the space means getting rid of installations that are useless or in the way. As of 1971, therefore, I decided to destroy a certain number of buildings. At the time, a letter from Prime Minister Jacques Chaban-Delmas gave me full freedom to act. Given the very financial nature of the operation, which implied extremely rigorous management, I was, as a senior civil servant at the Ministry of Finance, put in charge of the SEMVI – whose role it was to manage and build the abattoir and the market at La Villette. But my mission went beyond the activities of the SEMVI. At the time I was asked to consider ways of developing La Villette, which could mean many different things. Later on, the appointment of a commissioner for development confirmed what was stated in that first mission letter – in other words, proposing development solutions. In fact, this turned out to be a happy coincidence because I had also served at the Ministry of Infrastructure and had been vice-president of the commission of the Sixth Plan for cultural affairs, both nationally and in the Paris region. So, acting on these mandates I had been given, I started opening up the site. But, not in any old fashion. You have to respect the nature of the site on which you are acting. The plan to get rid of certain buildings has to be accompanied by a consideration of the way in which the vacant spaces thus created will be used. Therefore, destroying buildings at La Villette quickly came to mean progressively opening up the site to the local inhabitants, while thinking about the functions to be performed by the new places under consideration. I should mention as well that in those days nobody had access to the abattoir site. The whole fifty-five hectares were surrounded by huge metal railings. It was therefore physically impossible to get onto the site. People suddenly realised that in the north of Paris there was a reserve of property that could play the role of what I would be inclined to define as an air pocket. Once the railings along the periphery had been opened up, Place de la Fontaine-aux-Lions quickly became a place of social interaction.

Is that when the idea of the park emerged?

Yes. Especially since the closure of Les Halles had just shown very clearly that old industrial land could be spontaneously transformed into an extraordinarily lively spot. Also, there was a fashionable idea at the time – I am thinking in particular of the Sixth Plan – that there was a need for breathing spaces, to create parks and gardens. There were a lot of trees at La Villette, even when the abattoir was in use. We were certainly reluctant to fell them. Then the Historical Monuments department weighed in, listing the cattle shed and the two pavilions flanking it as heritage sites. One of them, which was unused at the time, was given a new lease on life by a theatre troupe. The Théâtre Présent was inaugurated on 31 December 1972. The first play performed there was called *La Chevauchée burlesque des Saigneurs de La Villette* (The Burlesque Odyssey of the Pig-Stickers at La Villette). The inauguration of the theatre ushered in an extraordinary period that saw the cohabitation of different activities – theatre, abattoir and political rallies. The quarter now became a place of assembly and encounter for inhabitants of the 19th arrondissement. But I must be honest and say that the cultural dimension of the site was never planned in advance. It simply emerged from a very favourable combination of circumstances, and particularly from the will to explore the potential of the site at La Villette in an honest way without making further investments.

But did you know when you arrived that the abattoir was going to close?

I knew that they needed to reduced activity. Take the meat market, for example. I knew that it cost too much to build. But I couldn't rule out its being converted and serving other purposes. Indeed, the final decision to close the abattoir was only made in March 1974. When I started out on the site, I knew that the complex was running at a loss and that I would have to reduce its activity. And so that the site wouldn't simply die, I planned to transform its components as and when they were closed down. But the final closure in 1974, showed that the end of the livestock market, abattoir and meat trade there was irrevocable. Nevertheless, some of the activities did continue, for example the leather warehouses and the refrigerated containers, thanks to which the SEMVI went on making money. But the fundamental consequence of the official closure was the presence of these three big and now empty halls. That was when we decided to organise the Foire à la Ferraille et à la Brocante (Scrap and Bric-a-Brac Fair) that was held in the cattle shed in May 1974. We were trying to show that the livestock market could be remodelled.

One of the sheds even housed a concert by the Rolling Stones.

The concerts were held in the sheep shed. The Rolling Stones weren't the only group to perform there. Others also came and played. La Villette had over a million visitors a year during this interim period. And the great victory here was that the thinking about the site was carried out in parallel with practical experiments. The sense of the way a space works when it comes from lived experience of the site is very different from a mental projection based on plans.

What was the main thrust of the development project submitted to the authorities in May 1975?

The project followed the appointment of a development commissioner for the Villette sector in 1973. The text instating the commissioner vested considerable powers in him. He could, for example, act by delegation for government ministers. But before developing that point, let me go back to the period prior to the 1975 project. So, we had to go on then analysing the possibilities of the site. We had to make it clear that we were thinking seriously about the kinds of activities that the site was capable of handling.

It was important to proceed carefully. At the time, the property developers were really "drooling." Some of them had a burning desire to build at La Villette. The first decision we took was therefore to not sell the land of the old abattoir complex. It was imperative that it remain in the hands of the public authorities. There would be no fire sale at La Villette. We went on clearing the site by demolishing the installations we judged useless. For example, we took down the metal footbridges over the Canal de l'Ourcq. The site was suddenly cleared to the north. We were then able to join the two banks of the canal by means of a big pedestrian bridge. In fact, it cost virtually nothing because we reused the old functional footbridge of the by-products building. But the consequence of all this was that we suddenly became aware of the importance of the water. The canal was no longer an obstacle between the two parts of the site but an urban feature worthy of interest in its own right. Then an important event occurred: Valéry Giscard d'Estaing came to power. This was important because the new president's ideas on urban development were very different from those of his predecessors. Valéry Giscard d'Estaing wholly rejected the tower model of urbanism practised under General de Gaulle and Georges Pompidou. La Villette thus quickly became a part of the president's special prerogatives. Decisions were now taken according to a very particular process in which the French president regularly called upon his civil servants to imagine together how the site should evolve. That was how the decision was taken to lay out a four-hectare garden at the roundabout by the canals. But I should tell you about the Jardin du Dragon (Dragon Garden). That was quite a business. It was the park's main attraction. To make it they used cable reels that the children there were used to playing on. I must say that what François Ghys did there was remarkable. Just think, the dragon's tongue was made with sheets of steel left lying around in the abattoir. The dragon cost less than seventy-seven thousand euros.

And it so impressed Bernard Tschumi that he wanted to keep it.

Absolutely. And it is a great success.

So, in fact, you can claim to be the father of the Parc de La Villette.

You could put it like that. The idea for the park came from the first development team. And it came out of the realisation that a reduction in the area of land used by the abattoir complex was accompanied by an appropriation of the space as a public area. It was, I must admit, a rather empirical approach. Jean Richard, whose circus was set up on the land now occupied by Conservatoire, turned up one day with the dung from his horses and we decided to use it as fertiliser. Then, the following day this little old-age pensioner from the area came along wanting to plant a few rosebushes there. Old building site huts were even used as photography galleries! It was vital to prove that the site really could attract people. Near the meat market we created a skateboard park. An industrialist was experimenting with a technology for making light-weight concrete walls, so we gave him a free hand. That's how the skateboarding track came into existence. All these activities were carried out without the need to lease out the land in any way. It was imperative that we steer clear of any rigid engagements with concession stands. They would have been the surest way to compromise the site's future.

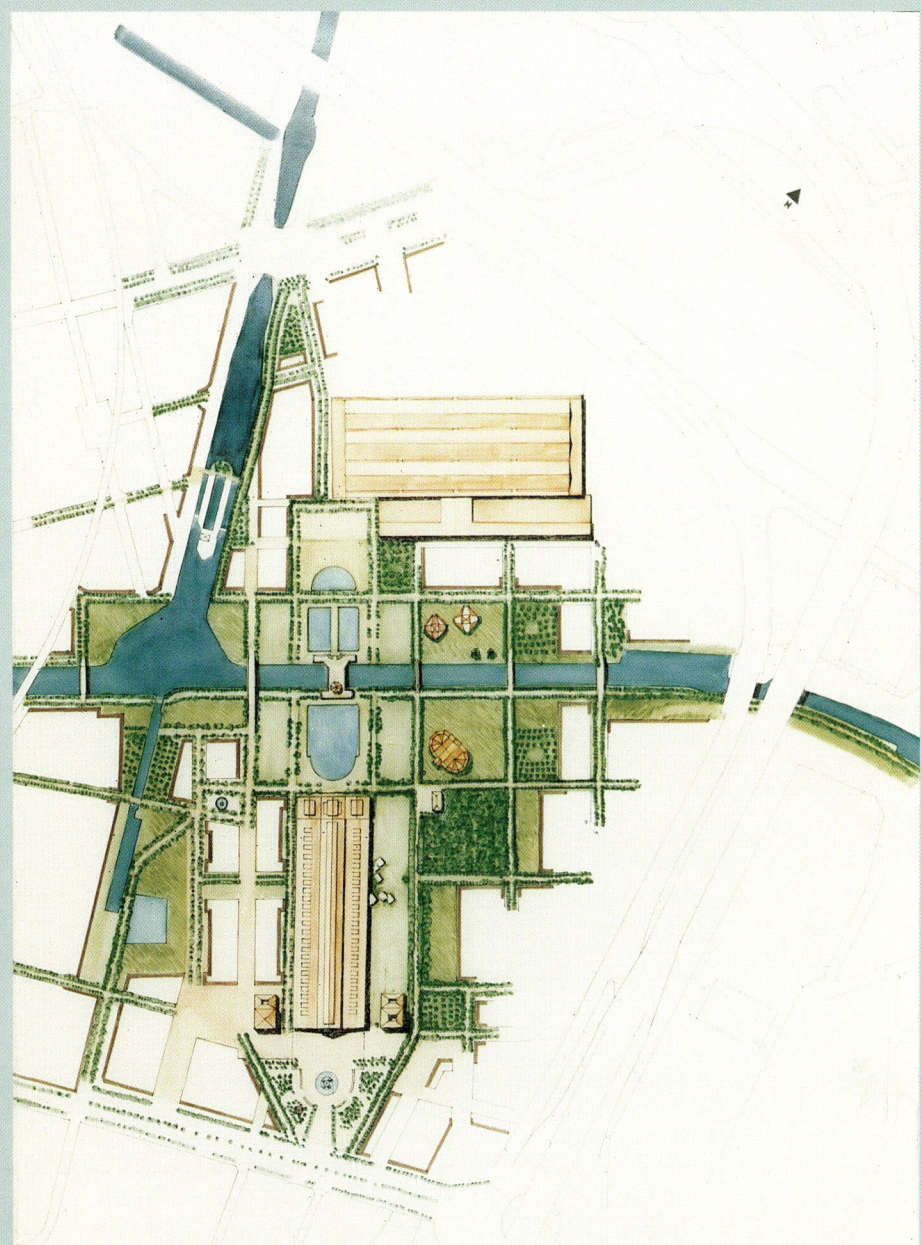

Development proposal for La Villette (J. Sérignan, 1975). The Parc.

INTERVIEW WITH JEAN SÉRIGNAN   81

The skateboarding track you mention represents the first cultural activity organised in the northern part of the site.

Yes. In the north there was the meat market, which was still being built. So there was not much we could do. It was huge. An enormous mammoth over two hundred and fifty metres long. But, in the end – and this was what made our approach such a success – we managed to create a park at a cost of about four and a half euros per square metre! At La Villette we were "anti-unused space." We could have closed off the site or prohibited access pending the decision taken by the authorities. On the contrary, we chose to open the spaces that had been freed up, and to define their new function on the basis of an analysis of the way the spaces were used.

Let's talk about the meat market. Your development plan suggested rehabilitating it as a multi-cultural centre housing a sports facility, a technology training centre and exhibition spaces. How did you conceive of the programming?

Unlike the proposals for the park, which led to its actual construction, the proposals for the transformation of the meat market were purely hypothetical because we didn't have the budget to carry out the rehabilitation work. Our development proposals were theoretical – and not experimental – in the sense that we knew no decisions could be taken without a more comprehensive process of analysis. We hadn't reached that stage yet. The meat market was a modern ruin, and nothing more. Also, it should be emphasised that the massive dimensions of this market ruled out any thought of experimentation. But there were a series of studies that touched on the market's structure and the dimensions and the possible cost of its rehabilitation. Nothing was put forward without prior study of the points that I have just mentioned. We also studied the cattle stalls building. We very soon concluded it was unusable. Whereas the Rotonde des Vétérinaires (Vets' Rotunda) could be fixed up.

Your development project also made provisions for housing around the site.

Yes, and I regret that now. I remember that at the time we wanted to go along with the fashion of the day. We envisaged building a new quarter. It was utterly unrealistic. On the contrary, what we should have done was guarantee the creation of a landscaped ensemble. So let's forget that point. The other idea was to create a link between the park created at La Villette and the Buttes-Chaumont park. To this end we suggested converting the old railways between the inner ring road and the abattoir complex. This was when the "coulée verte" (green belt) idea came up. We had to generate all kinds of solutions in order to win over the public authorities. The fact of listing certain buildings as historical monuments meant that we could impose a series of rights of way, thus giving rise to the hope that future programmatic choices would take a direction that today is commonly described as cultural. And of course there was the other function that we wanted to see the site perform, that of the landscaped area. Again, I want to emphasise the fact that experiment was the key factor in our thoughts about La Villette. We did a lot of thinking throughout Giscard d'Estaing's presidency. At the end, though, I must admit that no clear-cut decision was really taken. The definitive programme was only established at a later stage.

The EPPV (the public body in charge of La Villette) did however come into existence during Giscard d'Estaing's mandate. As for the decree setting it up, it clearly defined the activities that the site would soon be supporting.

You're right. But the text in the decree is still pretty general. The developments came later.

Did you join the new EPPV team?

No, because that was a different mission. Legally, my mission as development commissioner ended with the creation of the EPPV, whose function, remember, was to carry through the programme laid down in the decree of 1979. My mission was by its very nature temporary. There could be no question of my influencing the choices made by the developing authority. But I did go on directing the SEMVI until it was wound down, in 1980. Which means that there was a short period during which I sometimes had occasion to work with Paul Delouvrier, the president of the EPPV. I set two conditions for me to come to La Villette: the first was financial independence. I didn't want to be paid for the task I was about to take on because I was still working for the Ministry of Finance. Not being paid for this type of mission is, as I see it, essential if one is to see it through properly. Knowing that one day you are going to relinquish the mission that has been vested in you puts paid to any careerist fantasies. The second condition was that I be granted adequate powers. For I had to be free to act. And from that point of view, I think that I can say that it was possible to carry out my mission in a satisfying way. The conditions that I set for my coming were totally accepted.

Interview by Alain Orlandini.

Interview with François Grether

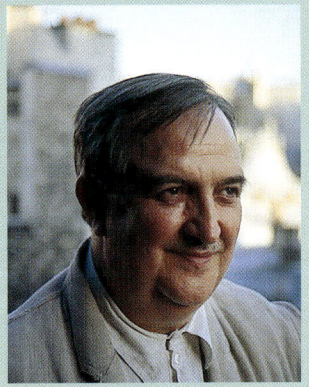

The architect and urbanist, François Grether, joined the Atelier Parisien d'Urbanisme – APUR (Paris Town Planning Office) in 1970. There he was put in charge of studies for La Villette and north-eastern Paris. Two years later, he joined Jean Sérignan, with whom he worked on preparing a first development project. In 1978, Grether returned to the APUR, where, up to 1991, he led numerous projects in eastern Paris. Today, François Grether divides his time between teaching at the École Spéciale d'Architecture, the EPF in Lausanne and the École d'Architecture in Nancy, and working on major urban projects (Boulogne-Renault, Plaine Saint-Denis, Brest harbour, among others).

When did you come to La Villette?

I joined the APUR in 1970. La Villette was my first planning project, just when the abattoir scandal was breaking out. I was soon being asked to put a general framework in place for the project. This required a fair degree of prudence because at the time we didn't know if the abattoir complex was going to close or not. We therefore came up with a number of scenarios: the abattoir limited to the centre of the site, with urban spaces laid out around the edges; the abattoir complex occupying the entire plot; La Villette totally "freed" of the abattoir complex and housing different kinds of activities, and so on. After the state had bought up the land – originally, it belonged to the municipality – the Ministry of Finance exerted its authority over the whole abattoir operation, including the abattoir project then under way, the debt (over one hundred and fifty million euros), and the management of the SEMVI. The first studies were carried out in 1970. Jean Sérignan arrived at the end of the year and contacted the Atelier Parisien d'Urbanisme, which was preparing the master plan for the development of Paris. In 1971, I made a partial switch from the APUR to work with Jean Sérignan. He already had two advisers with him. One was the financial manager of the Centre National d'Études Spatiales, the other was from the Ministry of Culture. I set up a little team responsible for planning the development of the old abattoir site.

What was your function when you got involved with the abattoir complex?

I was in charge of the Development Planning unit for La Villette under Jean Sérignan.

Were you still attached to the APUR?

Yes, the rest of my working time. This meant I was dealing with two very distinct scales: that of the abattoir complex, and the larger one being that of the city of Paris. In 1978, the president of France decided that La Villette would be managed by the state alone, while Les Halles was to be within the purview of the municipality. After that, relations between Paris and La Villette became rather prickly.

Did you take part in the organisation of the ideas competition organised by the APUR in 1976?

Yes, but I should add that the competition was preceded by the elaboration of a

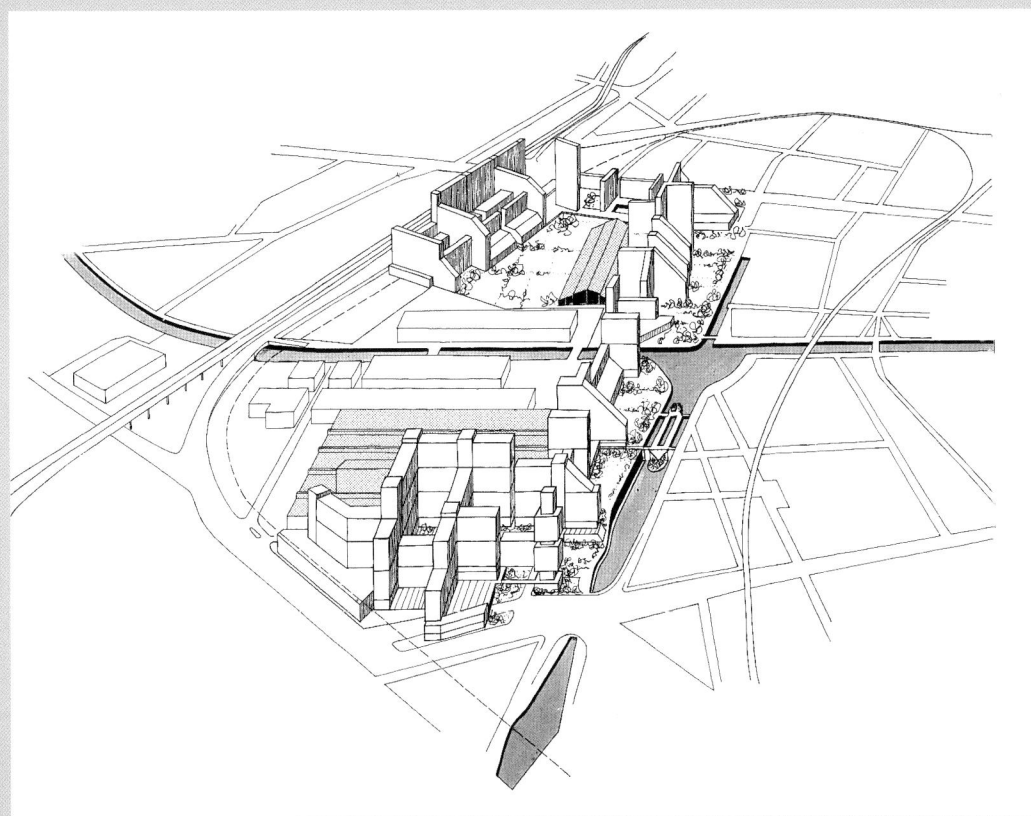

Development proposal for La Villette (F. Grether, 1970). Study.

development plan under the authority of Jean Sérignan. At the time, there was a lot of pressure from the Ministry of Finance because the development plan was to generate property revenues on a scale with the old debt. There was even a financial study team working on the site for a while. It came to some astonishing conclusions: by playing on the discount and bid rates, the state would have broken even – a century after completion of the site development! But, in 1974, the former Finance minister became president and the financial conditions surrounding the project were suddenly lifted. The priority now was to create a park, and a budget of over seven hundred and fifty thousand euros was made available to that end. Since 1970, we had been suggesting that the cattle shed and the two pavilions flanking it should be kept, and that the structure and volume of the unfinished meat market should be converted into a museum of science and technology. So, we now started thinking about the nature and role of the Cité des Sciences et de l'Industrie, which at the time we called the Musée des Sciences et des Techniques (Science and Technology Museum); and which was to be created by transferring the Conservatoire des Arts et Métiers to La Villette. We also decided to create a fifteen-hectare park. From very early on, we argued for an idea of the site that involved making the most of the canals and developing ways of linking the park, the neighbouring districts and the boroughs of Aubervilliers and Pantin. The creation of the park would be compensation for the closure of the abattoir complex, just as the creation of the Buttes-Chaumont park had compensated for the creation of an abattoir complex in Paris' 19th arrondissement. There were some at La Villette who wanted to urbanise and build a new La Défense. For us, that was an absurdity because the transport was inadequate. A big space like La Villette needed to include a park. When Roger Taillibert came on the scene in 1977,

INTERVIEW WITH FRANÇOIS GRETHER

the idea of building a big auditorium was put forward because the Salle Pleyel concert hall was no longer adequate. Roger Taillibert took up our idea of creating a park, and of converting the cattle shed, but he wanted to simplify our approach by cutting out the housing and office projects. It was of course thanks to Taillibert's intervention that what would later become the Cité de la Musique took a decisive step forward. Then Paul Delouvrier came along and initiated the competition for the Cité des Sciences.

Before setting up the competition for the construction of the "Musée National des Sciences et de l'Industrie," there was, in 1976, that famous ideas competition organised by the APUR. I'd like now to talk about the brief for that competition and the projects that were presented. To begin with the brief: why did it put such an emphasis on housing?

Jean Sérignan was not a builder, so his reservations about the contents of the development project are understandable. But housing was the main concern of the Paris City Council. You have to imagine the situation back then: the population of Paris was falling sharply and there was an urgent need to initiate a pro-active housing policy. The big empty sites – land belonging to the SNCF and RATP rail and municipal transport groups – were the most obvious places to build housing, because the older operations to renovate insalubrious buildings were dragging on inconclusively, and were often bogged down in endless legal wrangling. The brief for the competition organised by the APUR, in close collaboration with Jean Sérignan, was a compromise, with the park and major structures on one side and housing and activities on the other. This competition enjoyed a certain degree of success because among the designers present in 1976, there were some figures who would later become famous.

Who are you thinking of here?

I am thinking of Bernard Tschumi; Christian de Portzamparc as well. This competition attracted architects from different generations, both veterans and greenhorns, and the result was a debate that illustrated the new ideas emerging at the time.

What about the quality of the proposals?

The 1976 competition revealed the change in thinking about urban planning that was manifest at the time. Since 1968, the "blank slate" approach to renovation had been challenged and criticism of the effects of modernism had become almost ubiquitous. Some had reverted to neoclassicism. In those days, the propositions being made by Bernard Huet and Leon Krier seemed innovative, even though today they seem historicist. In contrast, others continued to borrow from the modernist lexicon. Joseph Belmont, for example. So, the 1976 competition told us a lot about the new tendencies emerging in France.

Did any proposals make a particularly strong impression on you?

I remember being surprised by Antoine Grumbach's proposal, which cobbled together a recreation of the Parc Monceau. Leon Krier's ultra-classicism also surprised me. But it was a big competition, and the propositions were very diverse. Indeed, that's why three types of prizes were awarded: one for the composition of the ensemble, one for the park and one for the built elements. Urban development projects are very difficult to organise. Few competitions of this kind had in fact been organised before La Villette. The only one I can remember before La Villette was the one for La Roquette. It was the first competition to really make a link between architectural and urban problems. Urban issues and architectural form were very closely associated in that competition. Before then, there were two opposing logics: urban planning and architectural projects. The competition for La Villette was organised with the same vision as the earlier one for La Roquette. It too sought to make a link between architecture and urban thinking. I remember that, to help the jury deliberate serenely, we set up an apparatus making it possible to examine every proposal. The projects were all displayed on panels inside the sheep shed and slid along a rail. We were assisted by a company that specialised in exhibition displays. Taking a rational approach, the jury defined a typology of projects, and each proposition was classified in accordance with it.

Who were the jury members?

Among the jury were James Stirling, who was particularly influential, and the painter Pierre Soulages, who was constantly referring to the rules and regulations. The jury was chaired by the prefect, Jean Taulelle.

Did you think of implementing the competition brief?

No. Some of the prize-winning architects hoped they would be able to carry out their projects, but they were disappointed. Although it was never officially admitted, the ideas competition did not go any further. Or rather, not in any direct sense, because it no doubt influenced the competitions that were organised afterwards. The period that followed the competition was a period of disenchantment.

Jean Sérignan took a very restrictive approach, concentrating only on the cultural activities that could occupy the site. He thought that the site had to be "brought alive" – which was my view, too – and decided to organise various events in the cattle shed, notably the Foire à la Brocante et au Jambon (Bric-a-Brac and Country Produce Fair). He was also a big skateboard fan and organised competitions. Jean Sérignan should definitely take the credit for the idea of bringing cultural activities to La Villette.
But the defining of development projects only really began with the organisation of the competition for the construction of the Cité des Sciences et de l'Industrie. Paul Delouvrier and Michel d'Ornano, then minister of the Environment, held a press conference to announce the launch. At the end of the competition, they posed

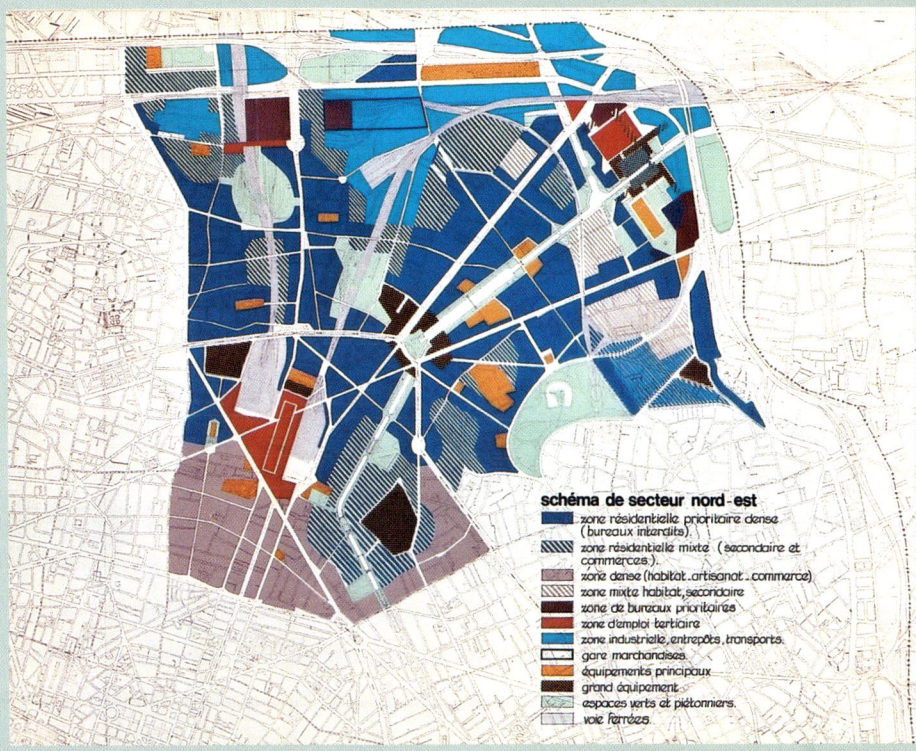

Master plan for North-East sector (architects: B. Antonini, F. Grether, D. Touche). Date unknown.

Guideline studies for the APUR competition (1976).

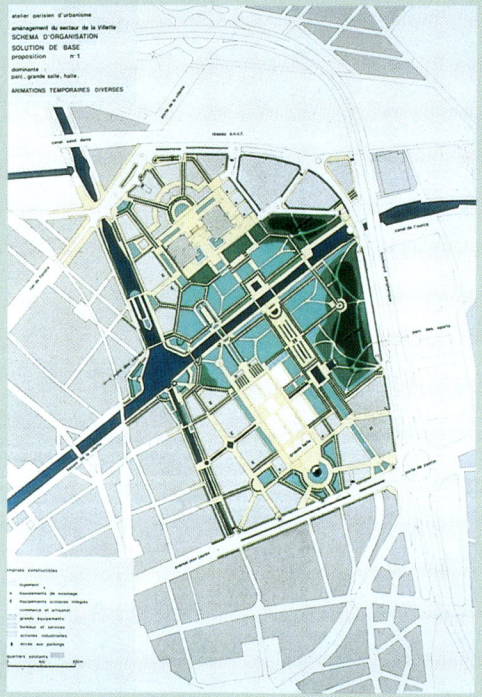
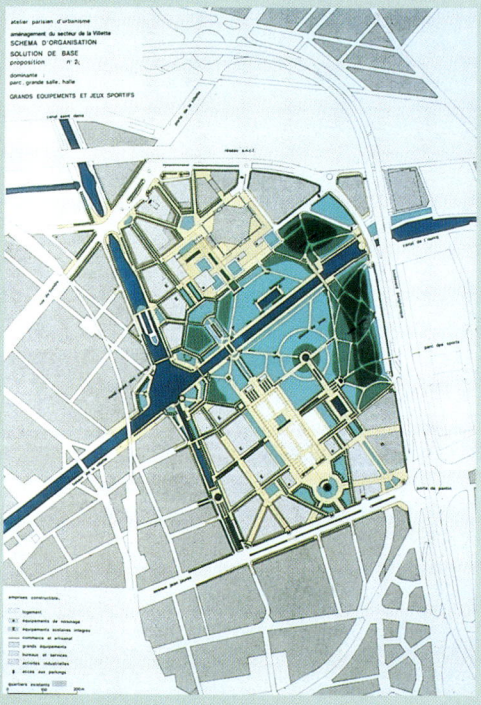

for photographers in front of the livestock stalls building, which they were in the process of demolishing. Just as the photo was being taken, they were engulfed by a cloud of dust. Michel d'Ornano was livid.

Let's talk now about the competition for the Parc de La Villette. How did that proceed?

It was a difficult competition because there was a large number of propositions. Also, the jury was very eclectic, and some of the renderings were very hard to read. In the end they managed to come up with nine projects. I can remember that Bernard Tschumi's project was very hard to understand on a first reading. I was only able to appreciate it later. Between the two rounds, François Barré was in favour of the propositions by Rem Koolhaas and Bernard Tschumi. Rem Koolhaas' project was quite provocative. The positioning of the volumes was calculated by means of rather complex mathematical operations. As for myself, I preferred the project by Bernard Tschumi.

It was more accessible than the one by Rem Koolhaas.

You were on the jury for the Cité de la Musique competition. Which projects did you argue for?

I only voted in the second round, when I replaced Alain Grellety-Bosviel, who was ill. And I argued on behalf of Alain Sarfati's project.

Although the project he presented for the second round was less apposite than the one in the first round.

That's true. But I didn't find the Ketoff/Petit project very convincing. The proposal they made in the competition for the Parc de La Villette in 1982 was much better. As for Christian de Portzamparc's project, it was finely conceived. But, for me, Alain Sarfati's project offered a more fitting response to the issues raised by the brief. But maybe my vision of things was mistaken. I have to admit that Christian de Portzamparc's project did turn out to be particularly interesting. Its qualities became manifest during the process of building it.

Some people complained that Christian de Portzamparc was given an unfair advantage in the competition.

The project Portzamparc submitted for the Opéra-Bastille was rejected, even though it was very good. The competition for the Cité de la Musique might consequently have been seen as a sequel to that earlier competition, as an opportunity to compensate Christian de Portzamparc for that injustice.

Were you at any point pressured to choose one project rather than another?

No. But I wasn't at the dinner given by Paul Delouvrier for the jury members before the afternoon vote. The jury was chaired by Maurice Fleuret who, I think, supported Alain Sarfati's proposition. Whatever happened there, I don't imagine there was any need to put pressure on the jury because, as I said, Christian de Portzamparc's project was a very good one. However, the jury presentations during the competition for the Cité des Sciences was more turbulent. I remember that the projects were presented in the salons at the Gare d'Orsay. Paul Delouvrier took me by the arm and said, "There aren't any interesting projects." I replied, "Monsieur le Président, one must take the time to look." To which Delouvrier responded: "No. These projects are bad. We must therefore choose a man. And that man is Adrien Fainsilber." After that there was the problem posed by the Géode. Giscard d'Estaing literally tore it out of the model because, he said, it wasn't on the right scale. And there was that famous debate about the beams, which François Mitterrand wanted to be blue.

Let's talk about the projects as they stand today. How do you judge the Parc de La Villette?

Today, with the passage of time, the judgement one would make is different from the way one would have seen things at the time. Because of the presence of the abattoir, there was a very large territory – Paul Delouvrier often said that the site at La Villette was as big as the Vatican's. As a place, therefore, La Villette was out of the ordinary and the element most capable of playing a linking role was undoubtedly the park, which was therefore central. Today the park interests me mainly for the way it is used. Its conception is uninteresting, hard to interpret and sometimes provokes some pretty heated discussions, but what is really fascinating is that the practices that developed there eventually pushed the theoretical discourse into the background and managed to subvert the expected uses, thus changing the value of some of the spaces. The Parc de La Villette is symptomatic of a certain ideological ambition and a certain kind of appropriation. The Parc de La Villette – and this is a fundamental point – is different from other parks and, in that sense, we can say that François Barré's gamble came off. It is not so much Bernard Tschumi's theoretical discourse as the appropriation of the park by the public that is interesting. The problem with the Folies is different. If the Folies didn't exist, there would definitely be something missing. But in their actual form they pose the problem of the way the space is structured. They seem too artificial. This is no doubt because the secondary Folies, which were supposed to stand near the main ones, were never built. I am thinking in particular of the projects by Henri Gaudin and Jean Nouvel, for which no funding was forthcoming.

It's not so much the Folies as the rather awkward way the park connects with the surrounding urban fabric that is problematic. I am thinking, for example, of the western part of the park, which is awkwardly articulated with the local neighbourhood. This is typified by the Folie that is located at the intersection of the two canals and blocks any perspective view of the roundabout.

> The canals never interested Bernard Tschumi, and they don't really seem to interest the municipality either. It is obvious that the relation to the canals is one of the weak points of Bernard Tschumi's project.

The criticism I am tempted to make of the Parc de La Villette is that its shape is not a very good expression of the modern world. If postmodernity is made up of ruptures and dissociations, the park fails to appear as a symbol of that, even if the images chosen to represent it suggest that it is. The park's postmodern dimension is more in evidence in the way it is used. Here we can see the emergence of unprecedented individual singularities, miniaturised and hyperspecialised localisations of interests. The Parc de La Villette is indeed the site of a new dissemination of social activities.

> But you shouldn't forget the thematic gardens. They introduced another scale into the park. And this play of scales is something that is very positive.

Isn't the best image of the Parc de La Villette the one we get at night, when the lighting delicately underscores the contrast between the linearity of the arcades and the massive forms of the Folies, contributing to the emergence of a reality that really does seem to back up these notions of dissociation and rupture that I mentioned earlier?

> Perhaps.

What do you think of the Cité des Sciences et de l'Industrie?

> It's a project that I appreciate. I like the way Adrien Fainsilber made use of the structure's big spans, and the way the Géode announces the park. However, I do have a few reservations about the internal itinerary. You go in and you see everything at once. The architectural promenade is a bit short. At the time, I argued strongly for the ancillary programmes that were supposed to make the transition with respect to the neighbourhood. In this regard, I think what Gérard Thurnauer did to the north is rather violent. As for the south, Aldo Rossi's housing, for which part of the brief was cancelled, doesn't completely meet the desired objectives.

What is your opinion of the Cité de la Musique?

> The Cité de la Musique is a very fine architectural ensemble, well used and an undeniable public success.

And the Grande Halle?

> For me, Bernard Reichen and Philippe Robert were a bit heavy-handed. The Grande Halle has become opaque.

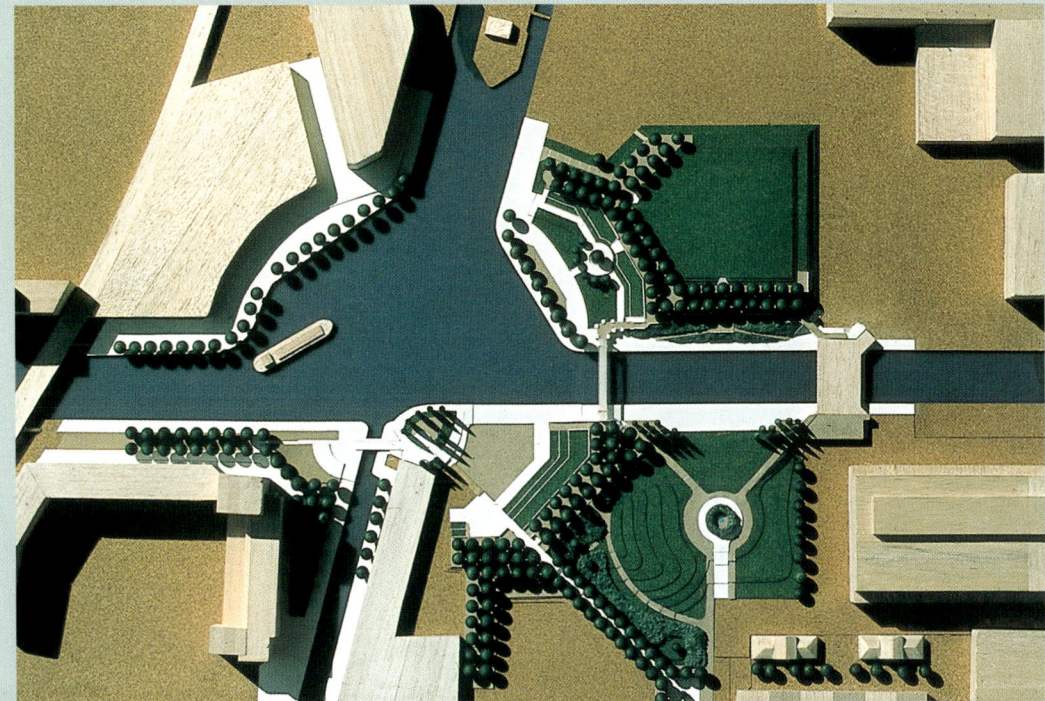

The Jardin du Rond-Point (Roundabout Garden; architects: G. Charlet, F. Ghys, F. Grether, 1978).

Originally, the spirit of the Grande Halle was that of an umbrella, transparent and very fluid below.

Isn't the site at La Villette too broken up?

Overall, there remains the power of the big, public infrastructure projects. La Villette is a centre of architectural projects that continues to play an emblematic role. It's true, there have been a number of peripheral additions, but that doesn't detract from the power of the ensemble. However, there's still a lot to be done, notably around the park and along the canals.

Is La Villette a success?

In the main, yes. The great success of the thing is the general conception of the park with its new practices and cultural openness. And that is something for which François Barré must take much of the credit. There are certainly failures here and there, but the power emanating from these major undertakings, supported throughout by the state, is important for this area of Paris and will, in the future, represent a major chapter in the history of contemporary urban transformations.

Interview by Alain Orlandini.

Interview with Roger Taillibert

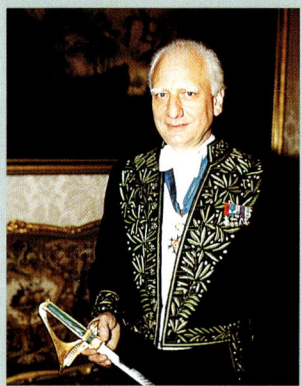

Roger Taillibert designed the Parc des Princes soccer stadium in Paris and the Olympic Village in Montreal. In 1977, he was asked by President Valéry Giscard d'Estaing to carry out a study of the site at La Villette. Here he goes through the main aspects of the work.

When did you come to La Villette?

I came to the site a little while after the ideas competition organised by the Atelier Parisien d'Urbanisme. An absurd competition because the brief envisaged a lot of housing construction. So, as soon as I arrived, in early 1977, I rejected the idea of the housing and said that La Villette should be made into a place for the propagation of knowledge. I remember writing an article about this in *Le Monde* at the time. Some people wanted to build housing, others to construct a hospital. Today's Hôpital Debré, located at Porte des Lilas, was originally supposed to be built where the Conservatoire National Supérieur de Musique et de Danse de Paris – CNSMDP (National Conservatory of Music and Dance) now stands.

Why would they want to build a hospital at La Villette?

Simone Veil, the minister of Health at the time, was looking for land. That is why she wanted to build on the site of the old abattoir. I argued the case for a cultural facility at ministerial meetings. These were also attended by the prefect for the Ile-de-France region, who supported me; by Alain Lamassoure, who was later a member of Alain Juppé's government; and, of course, by Simone Veil. And it was this refusal to build the hospital at La Villette that gave rise to the idea of setting up the Conservatoire on the abattoir site. We knew at the time that the Conservatoire couldn't stay in Rue de Rome; the building was too run down and the students were cramped. As for the hospital, the prefect suggested that it be built where it indeed now stands, near the Porte de Lilas, where land was available.

La Villette must have looked pretty surreal in 1977.

I can remember this rather mad scene, with President Giscard d'Estaing arriving on the site in a helicopter, and all his staff with him. Before the president came, I had made a series of studies which pointed to the need to raze the livestock stalls building and to keep only the meat market. The president was doubtful, "Do you think we can keep that?" he asked me. I answered, "Yes, it will be a nod to history." Then I hastened to add, "There are posts all over the place, but it can be rehabilitated." The least one can say is that he had his reservations. Today, seeing how the park works, I think we should have destroyed the cattle shed because it blocks the view southwards. Or perhaps it should have been moved towards the east?
The fact is, anyway, that its present position is a problem.

And the two sheds flanking the cattle shed?

I told the president that they had to be demolished. They were in a terrible state.

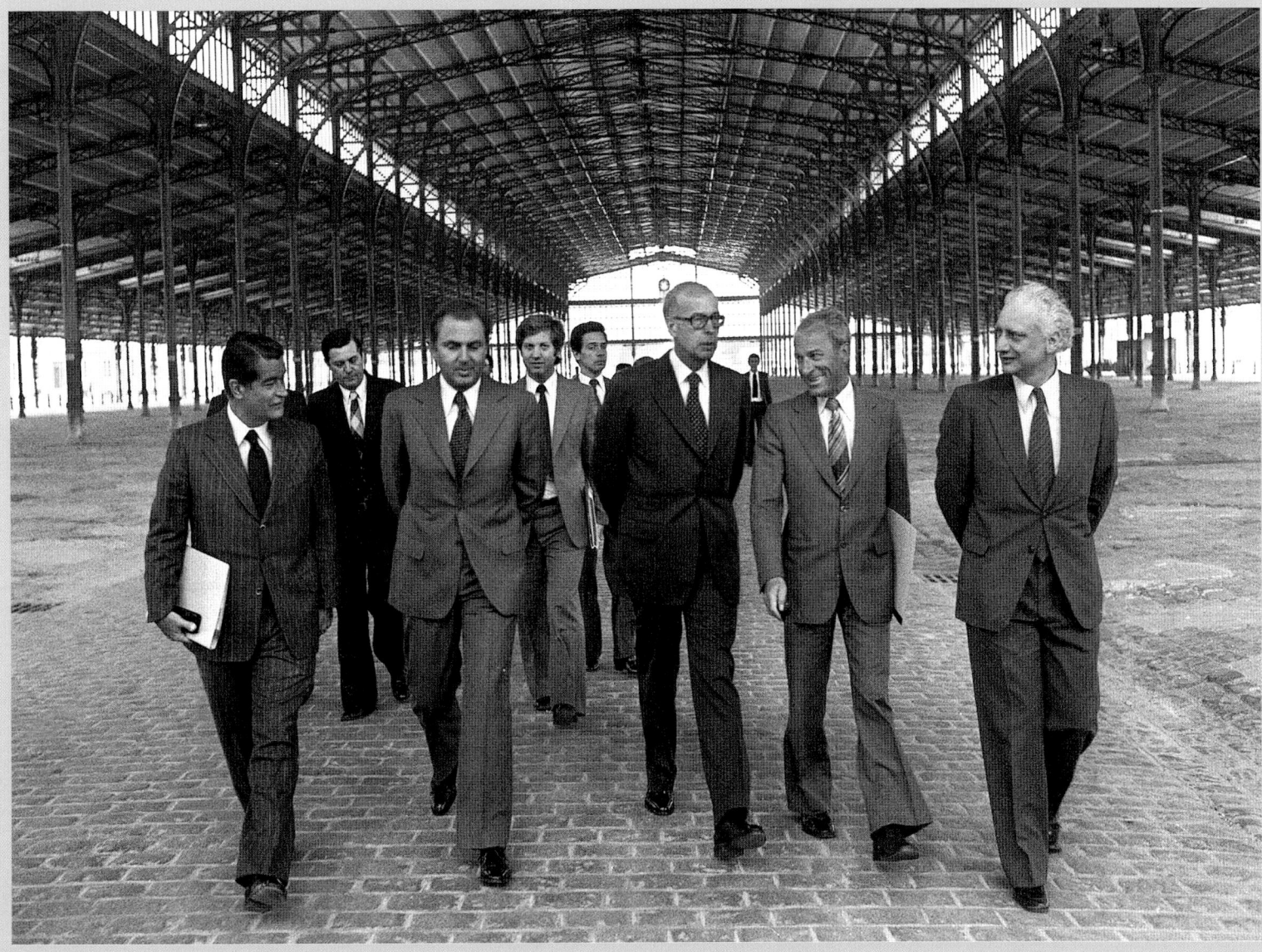

Your study centred on the meat market building.

Yes, it's a huge hall. One could have envisaged all kinds of uses for it. Also, I often wondered why Adrien Fainsilber positioned the Géode outside the meat market. As far as I am concerned, I would have built it inside. The market was big enough to house it.

Positioned outside the Cité des Sciences, the Géode breaks up the linearity of the south façade, which is almost three hundred metres long. It also opens up toward the park.

Indeed. But the play of scale you mention could have been established in another way, notably by a suitably laid out ensemble of fountains and gardens. I should remind you that the market hall has an area of one hundred thousand square metres. Everything could have fitted inside. The science museum in London is only forty-two thousand square metres, the museum in Munich is thirty-eight thousand square metres, and the one in Toronto is thirty-five thousand square metres. I have been to all these museums.

French president Valéry Giscard d'Estaing visiting La Villette accompanied by, from left to right: Lucien Lanier, prefect of Ile-de-France; Jean-Philippe Lecat, minister of Culture and Communication; Michel d'Ornano, minister of the Environment; Gilles Ménage, prefect chief of staff; unknown; President Valéry Giscard d'Estaing; Jean Sérignan, development commissioner of the Villette sector; Roger Taillibert, architect.

INTERVIEW WITH ROGER TAILLIBERT

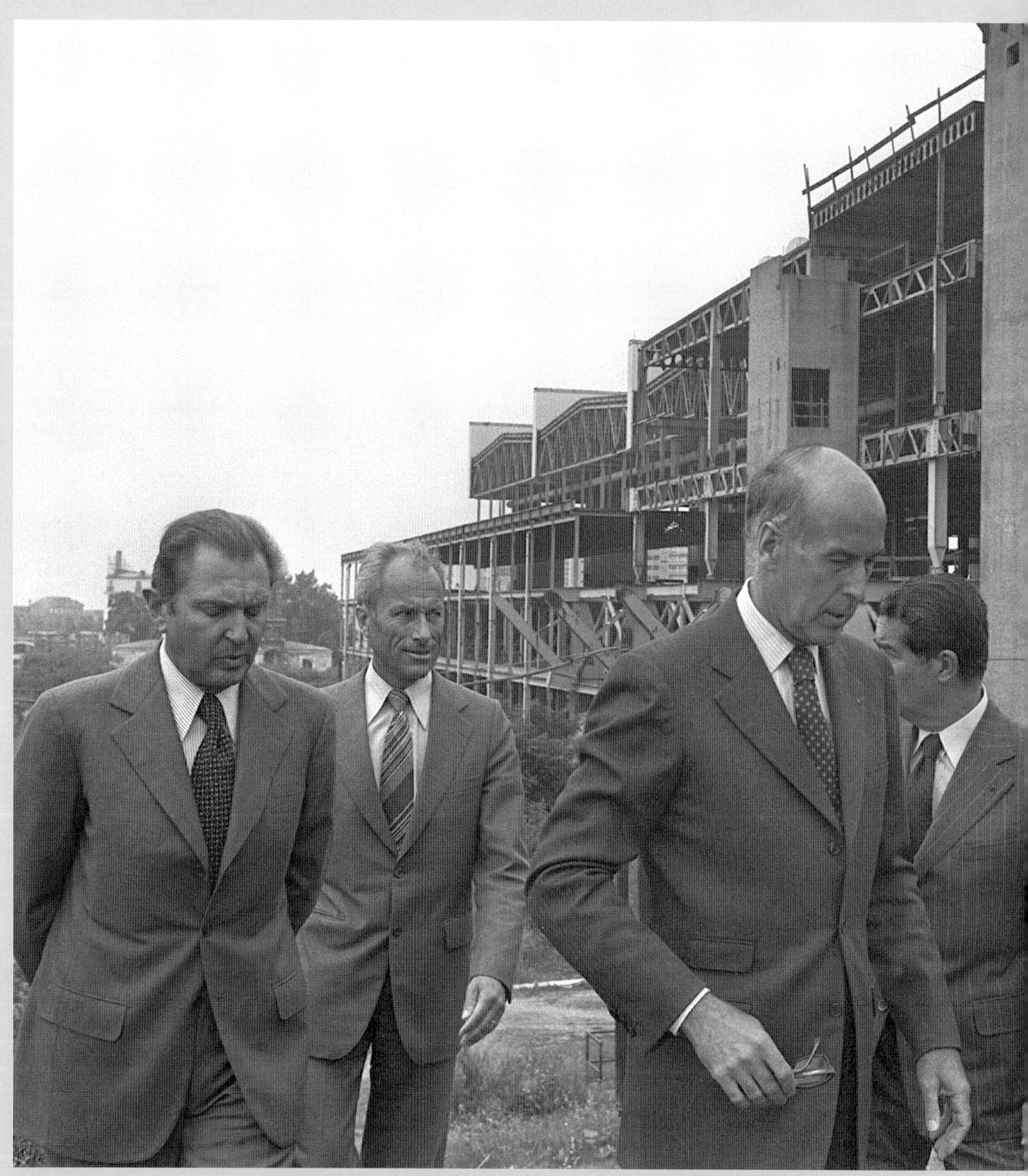

94   LA VILLETTE: 1971–1995

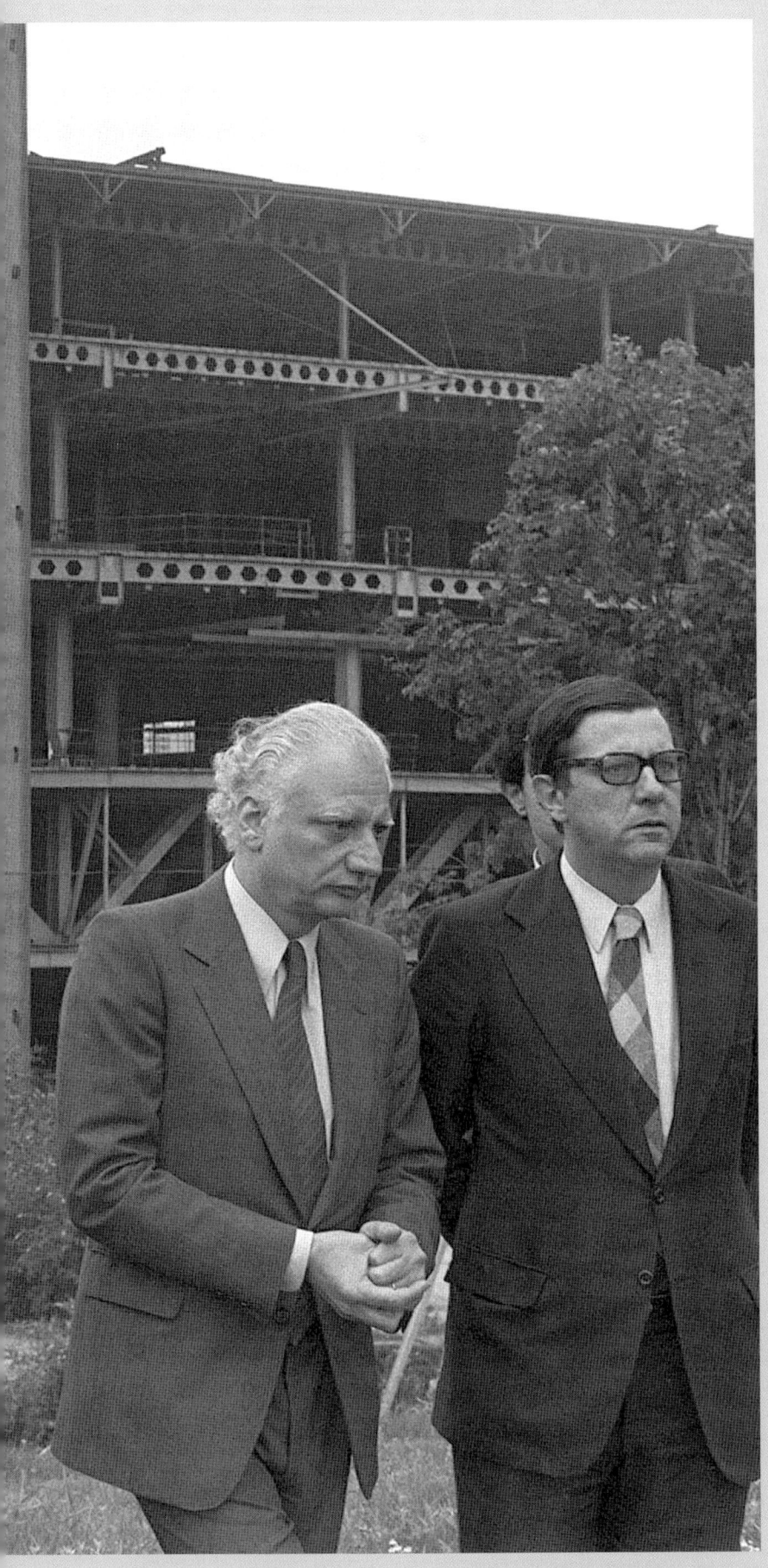

President Valéry Giscard d'Estaing visiting La Villette with his staff, from left to right: Michel d'Ornano, Jean Sérignan, President Valéry Giscard d'Estaing, Lucien Lanier, Roger Taillibert and Jean-Philippe Lecat.

The figures I am giving you are not invented. The Géode could therefore have fitted inside the meat market.

What was your function when you came to the site of the abattoir complex?

The president asked me to continue with the operation begun at La Villette. That meant making an inventory of the buildings on the site, and drawing up a programme of activities in accordance with the ones that could be rehabilitated. My idea was to transfer the Palais de la Découverte to the meat market. There is no good reason for having the Palais de la Découverte in the Grand Palais, whose vocation is essentially artistic. The meat market became a kind of huge technology centre. The Conservatoire des Arts et Métiers could also have been housed there. At the time, I told the president that we must forget the idea of the centre being state-run. "You can't mean that!" he replied. I stuck to my point, telling him that it was up to the big French companies to run this kind of complex. There needed to be a board of directors comprising heads of French companies in the technological and industrial sectors permanently present on the site to manage and decide programming for the complex. Its organisation needed to be entrusted to the SNCF (railways), EDF (electricity), Dassault (aviation, military) and Aérospatiale. For too long now, France has been a country of literary types. French youth must get into the sciences. The countries that are forging ahead in today's world are the ones that have succeed in training technicians.

Your approach was in total contrast to that of the Atelier Parisien d'Urbanisme.

The APUR programme was, as I have said, absurd. You don't build ten thousand housing units on land that belongs to the state. Especially since the Villette site is very interesting from an urbanistic point of view. And don't forget that in 1977, the Pompidou Centre had only just been built. As soon as he had decided to go ahead with La Villette, President Giscard d'Estaing mandated me to present the development project I had drawn up to the mayor of Paris. He wasn't very pleased. I said, "Let La Villette go forward and buy up the land around it. That will extend the effect." And I added, "If you build ten thousand housing units at La Villette, that will mean twenty thousand votes against you."

When was the decision taken to convert the abattoir into a science complex?

The decree instating the creation of the Établissement Public du Parc de La Villette (the public body in charge of the park) dates from 1979. But the decision was taken in 1977. A budget was even ratified that same year. At the cabinet meeting I proposed a budget of almost two hundred million euros. The president set the budget at one hundred and thirty million. I recommended that he choose Paul Delouvrier to direct the new development organisation. I had three names suggested to me. Paul Delouvrier struck me as the best qualified to make a success of La Villette. When I met him, he told me that the president was thinking of setting up an administrative public establishment to see through the operation. I told him this was a mistake. To make a go of La Villette we needed a commercial structure. This was the only kind of structure that could get Peugeot, Renault on board, along with the aeroplane and arms merchants – in other words, all our industry. Free admission to the centre with card-access activities at each stand – to be paid for, of course. That was the ideal modus operandi.

ASSEMBLÉE NATIONALE

GILBERT GANTIER
DÉPUTÉ DU XVIᵉ ARRONDISSEMENT
CONSEILLER DE PARIS
ADJOINT AU MAIRE DE PARIS

RÉPUBLIQUE FRANÇAISE
LIBERTÉ - ÉGALITÉ - FRATERNITÉ

PARIS, le 30 Avril 1980

Monsieur le Secrétaire Général,

    L'Etablissement public du Parc de La Villette présente dans l'ancienne salle à manger de l'Hôtel d'Orsay, la vingtaine d'esquisses réalisées par les architectes qui ont été consultés sur l'aménagement du futur Musée des Sciences et de l'Industrie.

    Cette présentation est, dans son ensemble, catastrophique. Elle ne saurait, me semble-t-il, servir de point de départ aux recherches plus poussées prévues pour les idées jugées "les meilleures".

    Je regrette donc, pour ma part, que les intéressantes propositions d'aménagement faites antérieurement par M. Roger TAILLIBERT n'aient pas été retenues au nombre des projets soumis à l'examen des membres du Conseil d'administration de l'Etablissement public.

    Je souhaiterais, dans ces circonstances, que vous puissiez prendre personnellement connaissance des esquisses présentées au Palais d'Orsay, ainsi que de la maquette de M. Roger TAILLIBERT que j'avais vue, voici de nombreux mois, au Grand Palais.

    Votre point de vue, si vous vouliez bien me le faire connaître, me serait précieux pour préciser la nature du concours qu'il me paraîtra possible d'apporter à la mise en oeuvre d'une idée qui me semblait appeler des réalisations rapides et relativement simples.

Je vous prie d'agréer, Monsieur le Secrétaire Général, l'expression de mes sentiments très fidèles et cordiaux —

Gilbert GANTIER

Monsieur François POLGE DE COMBRET
Secrétaire Général Adjoint
Présidence de la République
Palais de l'Elysée
75008 PARIS

Letter from the deputy mayor of Paris, G. Gantier, to the assistant secretary general to the President's Office, F. Polge de Combret about the "catastrophic" presentation of ideas for the competition for the Musée National des Sciences et de l'Industrie.

INTERVIEW WITH ROGER TAILLIBERT

Development proposal for La Villette (R. Taillibert, 1978). Perspective views of the meat market.

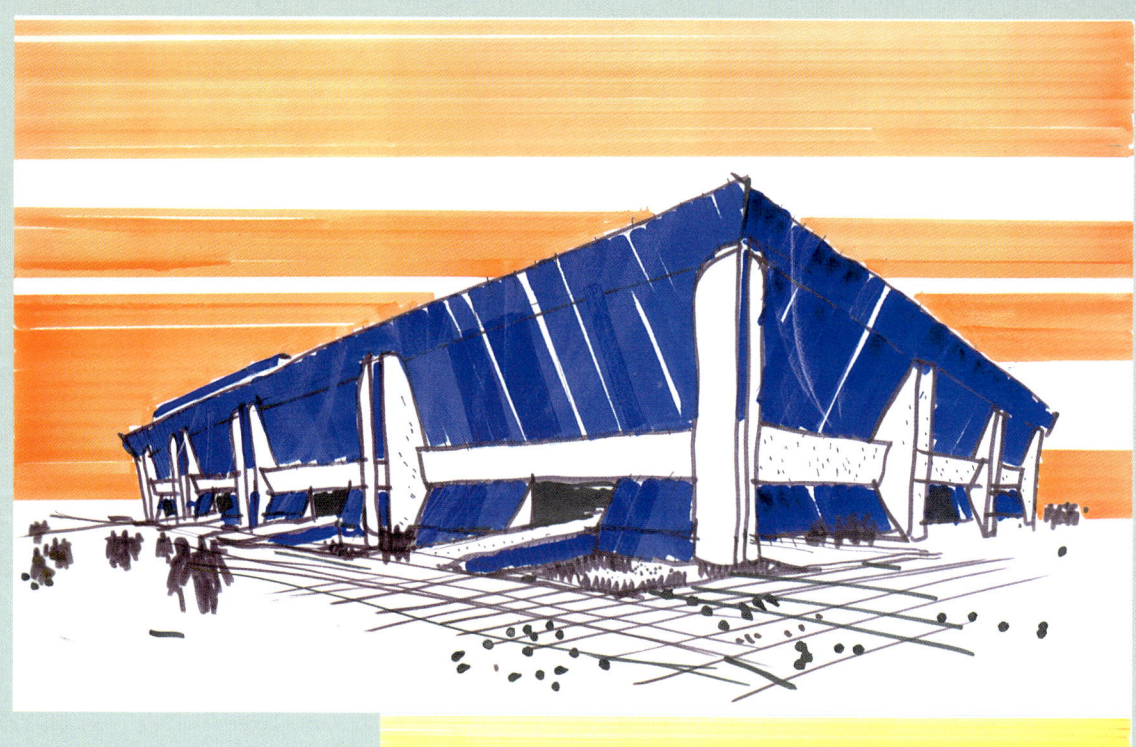

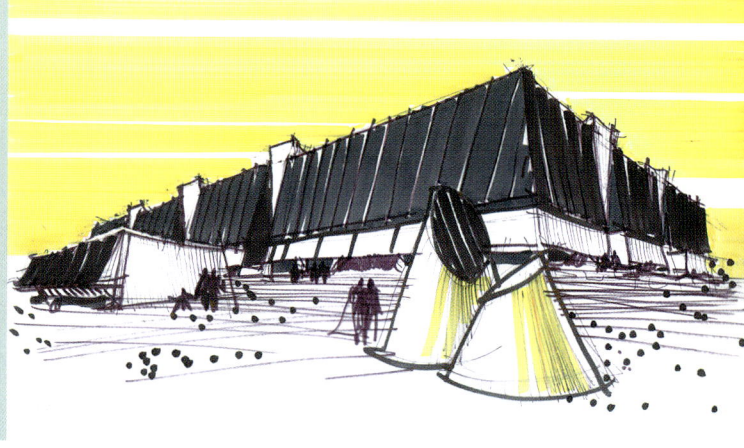

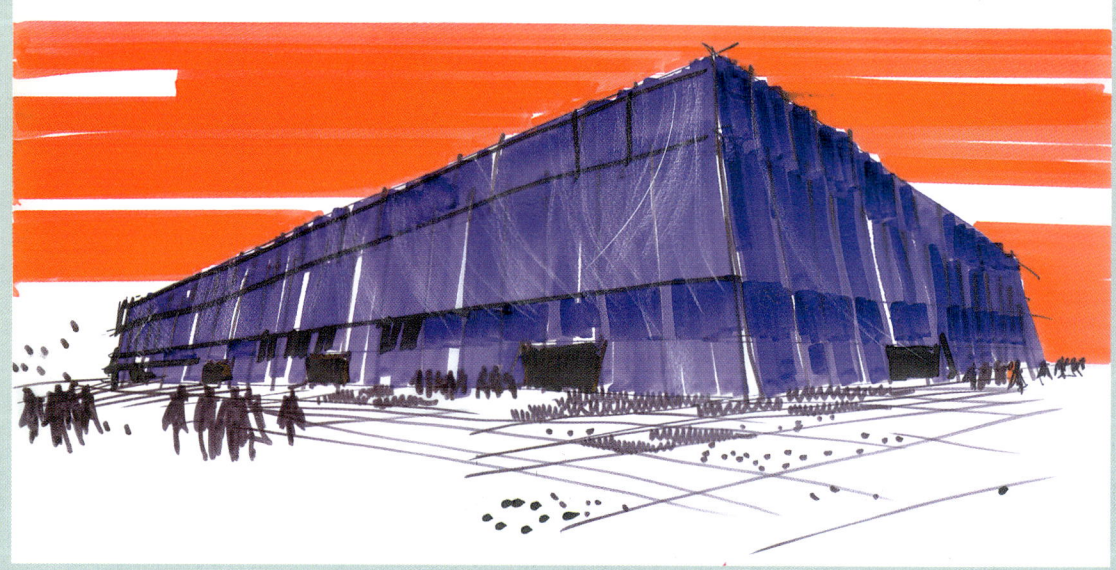

When you met Paul Delouvrier, you were getting ready to build the Cité des Sciences et de l'Industrie. What happened next?

Paul Delouvrier told me one day that the president wanted to organise a competition to build the museum and the park. He also told me that he was very keen for me take part in the competition. I refused, categorically. Then he insisted that I sit on the jury. Eventually I agreed. At the end of the session, the jury – which included the directors of some big international museums – refused to name a winner. That was when Paul Delouvrier managed to get the president to accept the project that he thought most appropriate – that is to say, Adrien Fainsilber's project. Bernard Rocher, who was also on the jury, came to see me at the end of the session, and said he didn't understand why I hadn't been chosen to manage the operation because I had been very closely involved in the preparatory studies. The only memory I have of the presentations to the jury is that the projects were rather weak. The great majority of architects proved incapable of using the structure of the old meat market. And yet the key point of the project was to make the most of it. A piece of architecture is above all a structural system. If you have a structure, you have architecture. What is a cathedral? It's a simple stone structure. The big architectural monuments are essentially the expression of valid structural systems. Architecture is not just theatre sets.

Let's imagine that you had been given responsibility for the construction of the Cité des Sciences. How would you have gone about things?

First of all, I would have handled the façades of the building in such a way that they

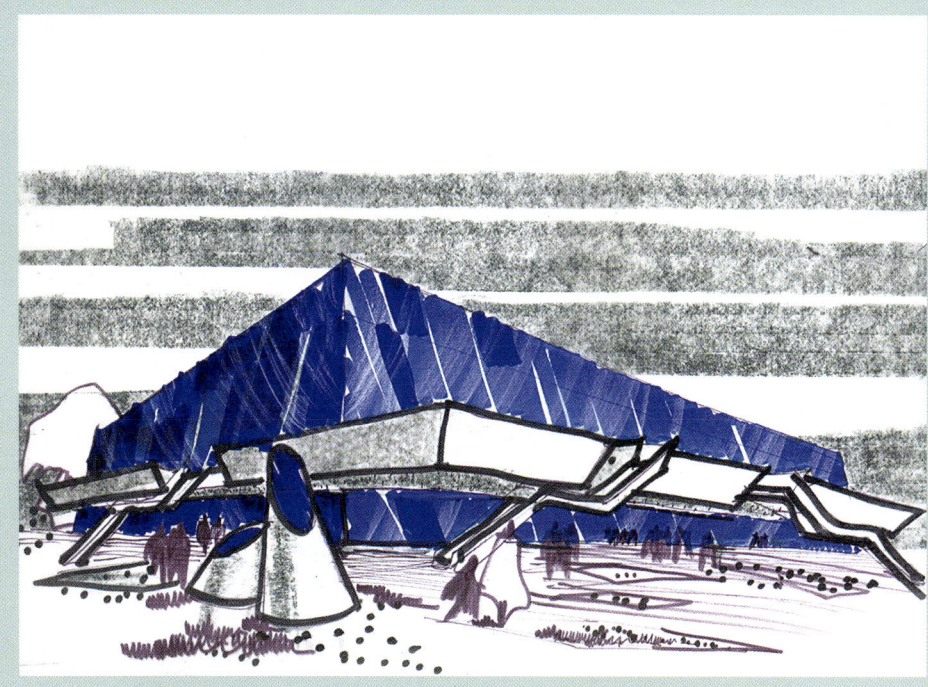

Development proposal for La Villette (R. Taillibert, 1978). Perspective view of the meat market.

showed the parallelepipedal form of the original structure. Second, I would have linked the building to the Canal de l'Ourcq through a whole series of fountains. Third, I would have conceived each level as a big, empty floor that could be extended by an outdoor exhibition platform. And finally, I would have devised the plan in such a way as to make very evident the existence of a big interior street serving all the different activities.

And the park?

On this subject I would like to read an extract from a report I submitted to the president: "The park should not be a historical pastiche of the different styles of gardens, but, on the contrary, a resolutely modern composition in which the synthesis of the mineral, the vegetal and the built will accompany that of the arts and technology, of science and fine crafts."
By virtue of its internal dynamic, its significance in the city and in Europe, it will provide a powerful stimulus for the revitalisation of north-eastern Paris."

Any regrets?

None.

Interview by Alain Orlandini.

THE CITÉ DES SCIENCES ET DE L'INDUSTRIE: ADRIEN FAINSILBER OR THE IDEAL OF REASON

> "Who possesses the real birthright, if not reason?"
> Ernst Cassirer

In 1978, the government decided to rehabilitate the immense steel ogre formed by the meat market of the industrial slaughterhouse. This decision marked the conception of what, over the years, has become one of France's main centres for the popularisation of science: the Cité des Sciences et de l'Industrie.

In 1979, the Établissement Public du Parc de La Villette – EPPV (the public body in charge of the park) was set up and tasked by decree with the organisation of an architectural competition. A shortlist of twenty-seven French architects was drawn up on the strength of the submissions. Adrien Fainsilber was the eventual winner.

A combination of scales

Initially chosen to rehabilitate the meat market and to integrate it into an ensemble comprising a park, an auditorium and a dance school, Adrien Fainsilber took special care to offset the inevitable dispersion of what was a disparate architectural programme laid out over a huge terrain (fifty-five hectares), and to draw

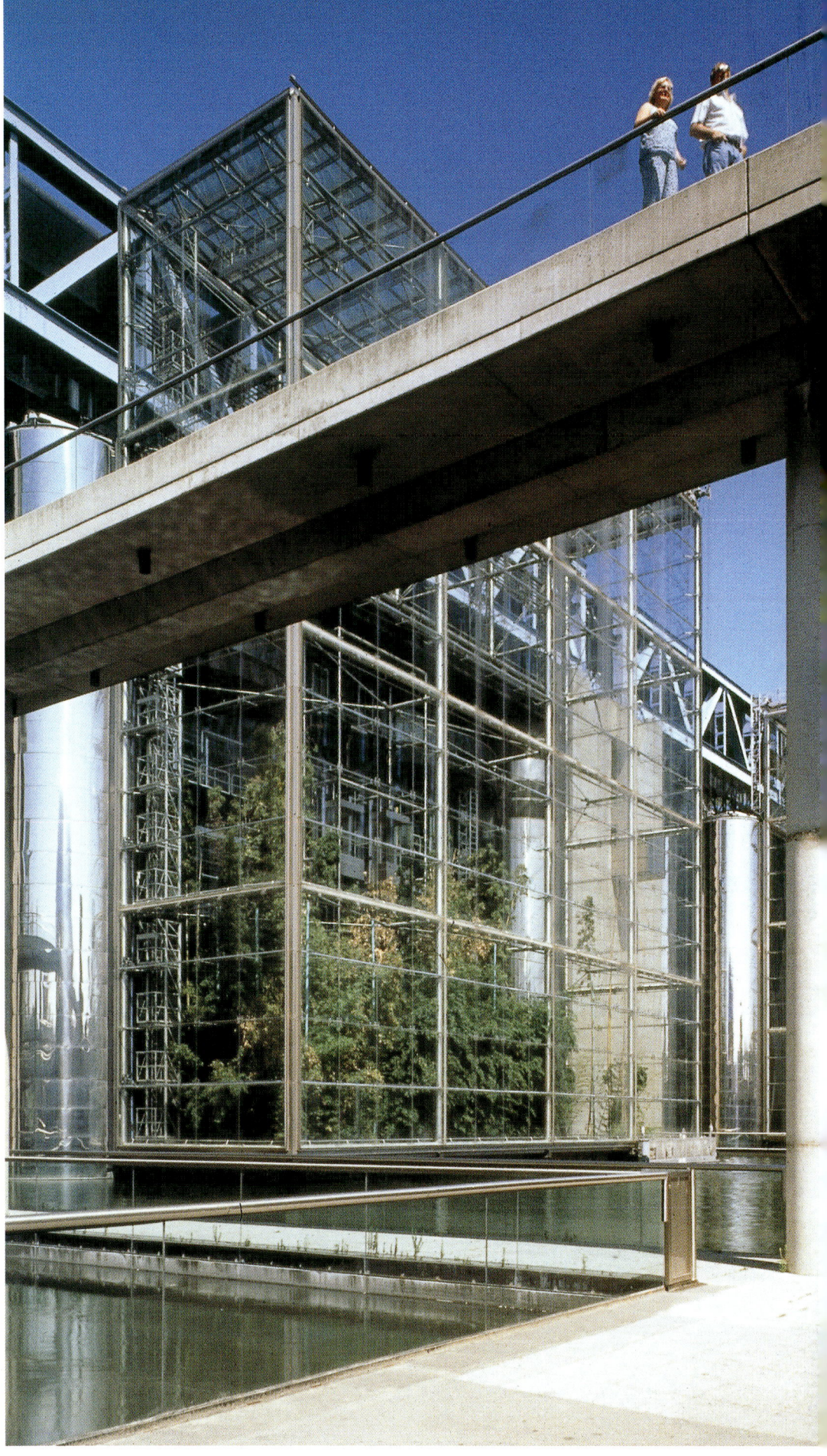

The Cité des Sciences et de l'Industrie (architect: A. Fainsilber).
One of the bioclimatic greenhouses of the south façade.

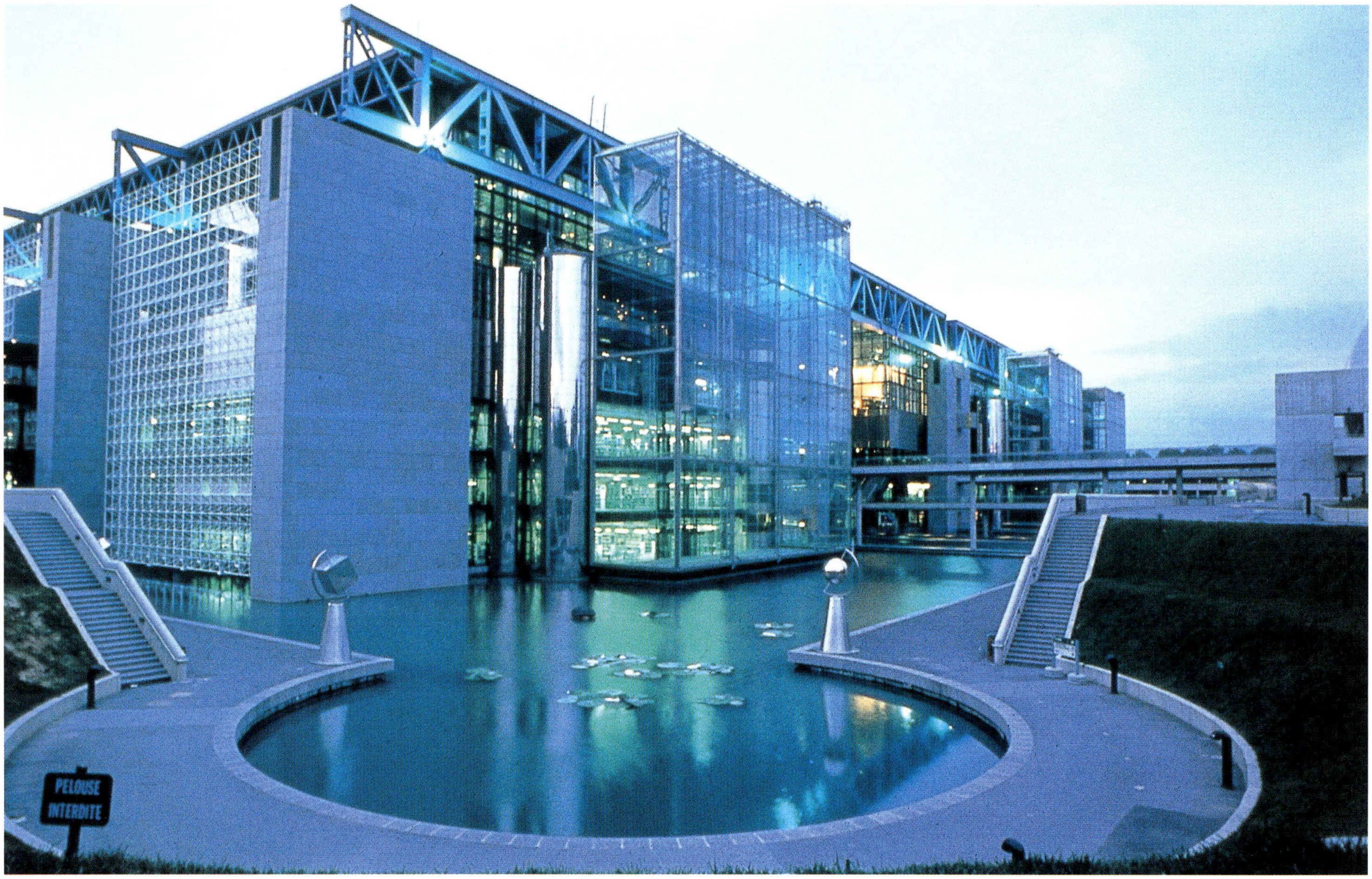

The Cité des Sciences
et de l'Industrie (architect:
A. Fainsilber).
Above: The south façade.
Below: Plan of the ground floor.

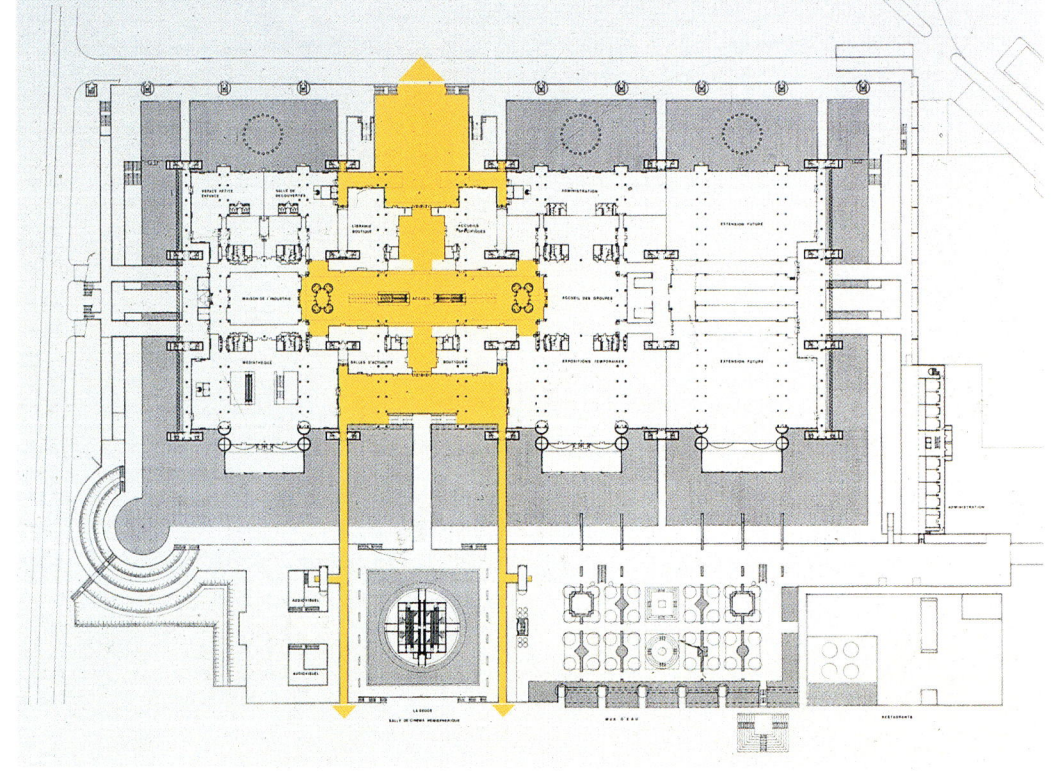

102   LA VILLETTE: 1971–1995

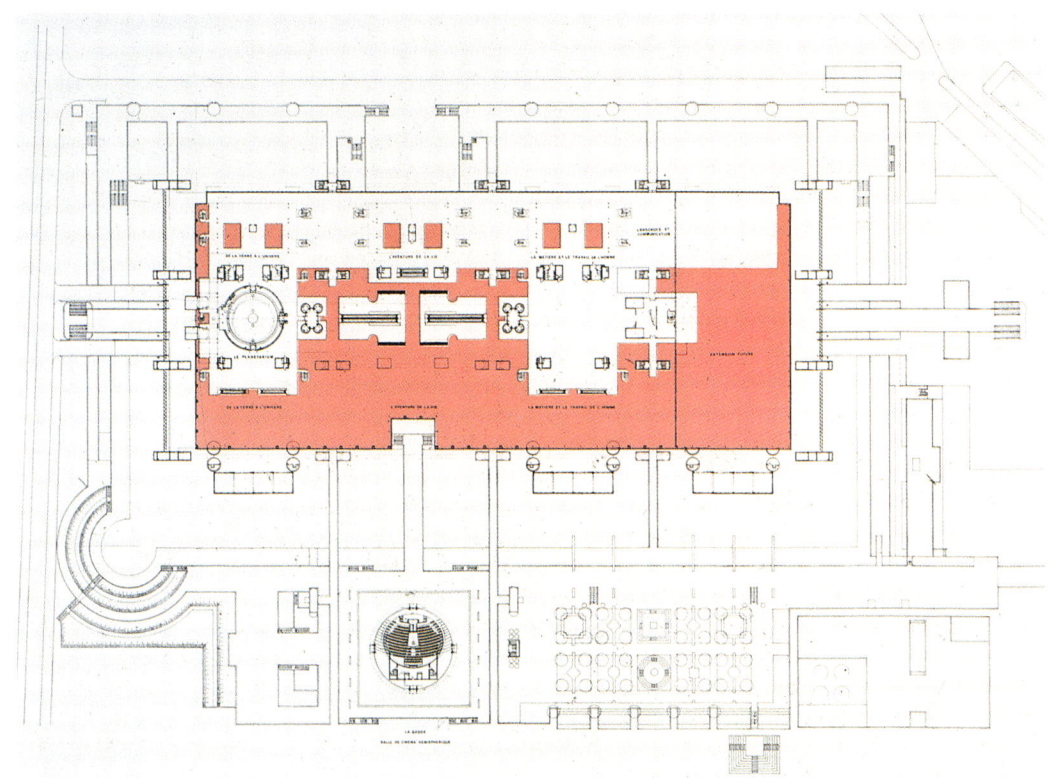

The Cité des Sciences et de l'Industrie (architect: A. Fainsilber).
Left: Plan of the first floor.
Below: Cross section of the entrance hall.

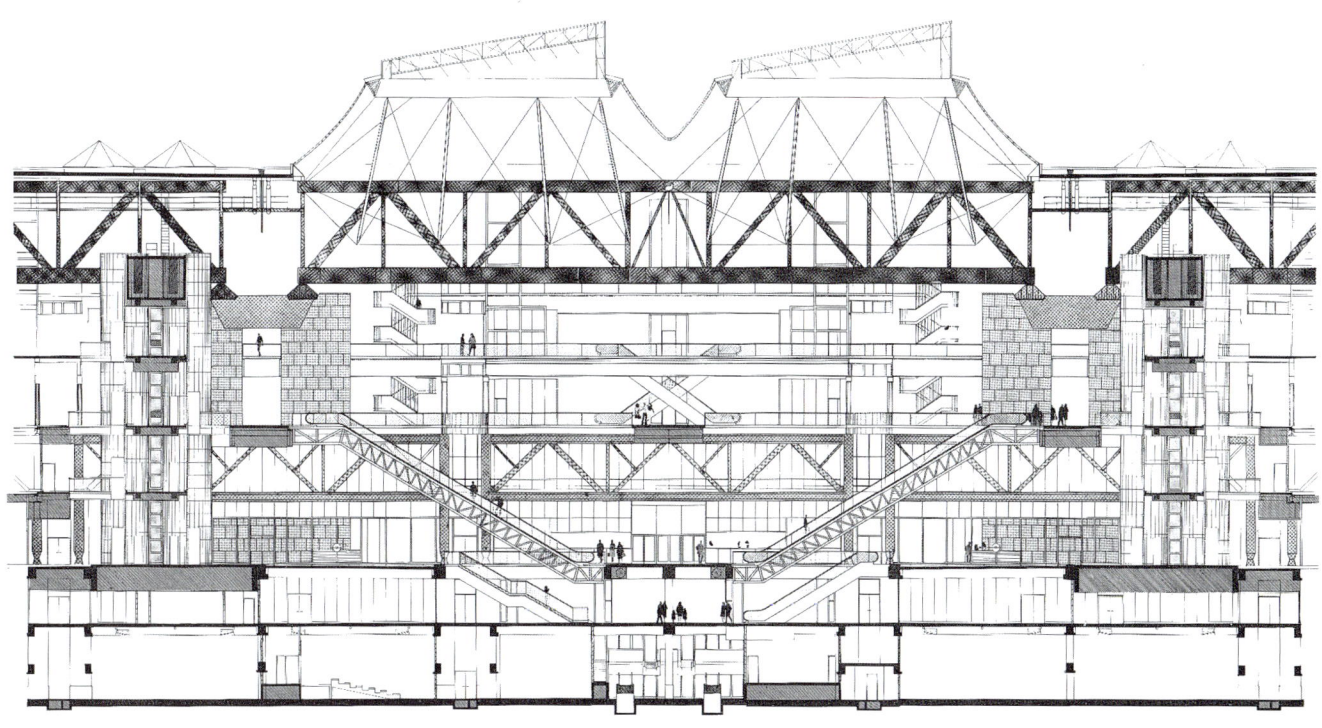

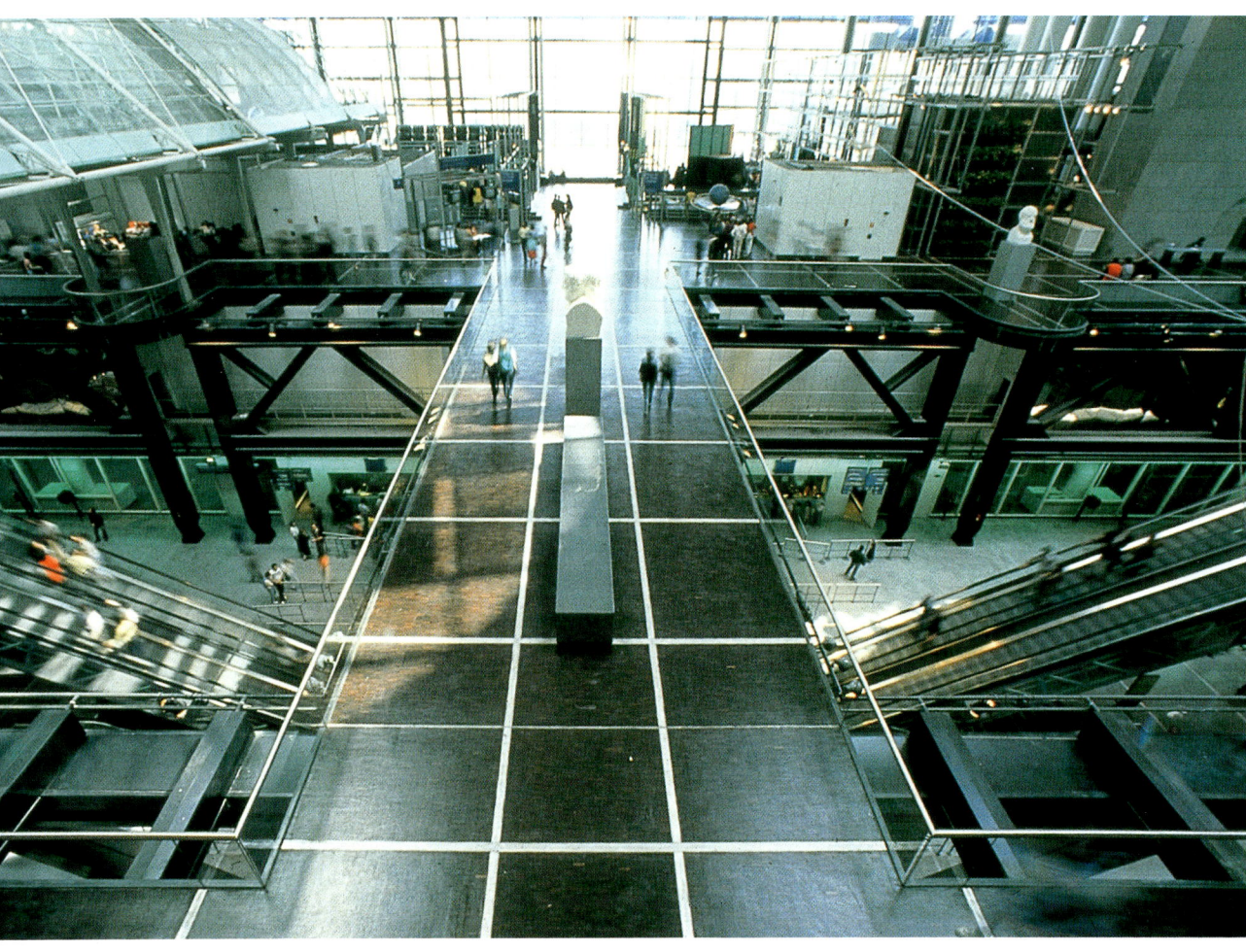

The Cité des Sciences et de l'Industrie (architect: A. Fainsilber).
Left: The first floor walkway.
Below left: One of the escalators in the entrance hall.
Below right: Plan of the entresol.

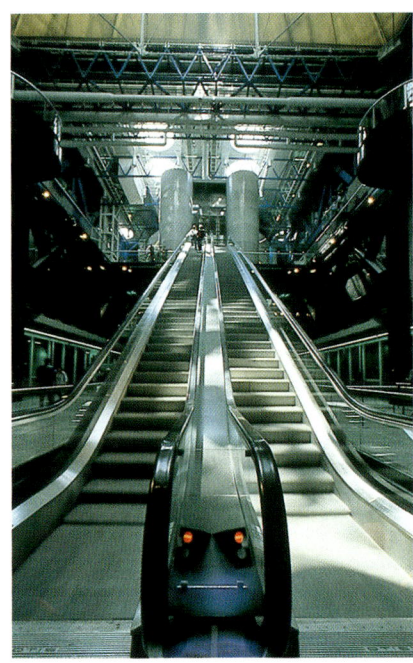

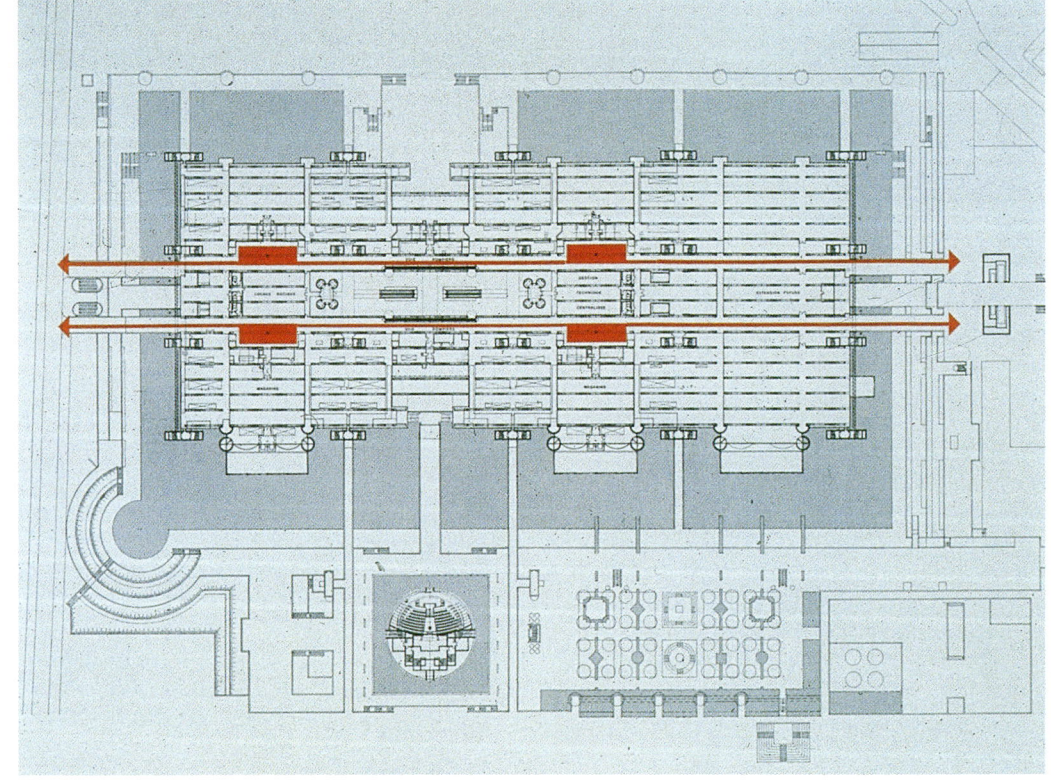

104   LA VILLETTE: 1971–1995

a site plan that opened up a plurality of perceptual scales.

By boldly placing the hemispheric auditorium outside the Cité des Sciences, Fainsilber began by breaking up the latter's monstrous size, and allowing the former to serve as a courteous invitation to venture into the park. Multiple footbridges over the "moat" reinforced the dialogue set up between the two buildings, while an indoor street continued the axis established by the pool reaching towards Place de la Fontaine-aux-Lions, on either side of which stood the auditorium and the dance school.

An austere plan, a building with integrity

This judicious cohabitation of scales seemed inseparable from a highly rigorous conception of the plan, one that made it possible both to understand the spatial organisation of the Cité and to exhibit its constructional system.

Above the entrance hall, lit by vast rotating cupolas, two indoor streets serve the exhibition areas laid out around the sides of the façades, leaving an impressive empty space at the heart of the Cité that has great structuring power. The right angle is' master here; the mezzanines of the upper levels fan out in tiers, perpendicular to the perspective lines of the passageways, and the lift shafts echo the verticality of the main pillars.

This very open plan, due in fact to a subtle interpretation of fire safety regulations – two firemen's passages, fitted between the ground floor and first level, ensure access to every nook and cranny of the Cité, thus removing the need to divide up the spaces with fire partitions – cohabits with a rationalist approach to the building constraints which prompted the architect to reveal the armature of the meat market hall, this being preserved almost in its original state (only the secondary trusses of the metal framework were replaced with lattice girders which, fixed to the upper part of the main beam, made

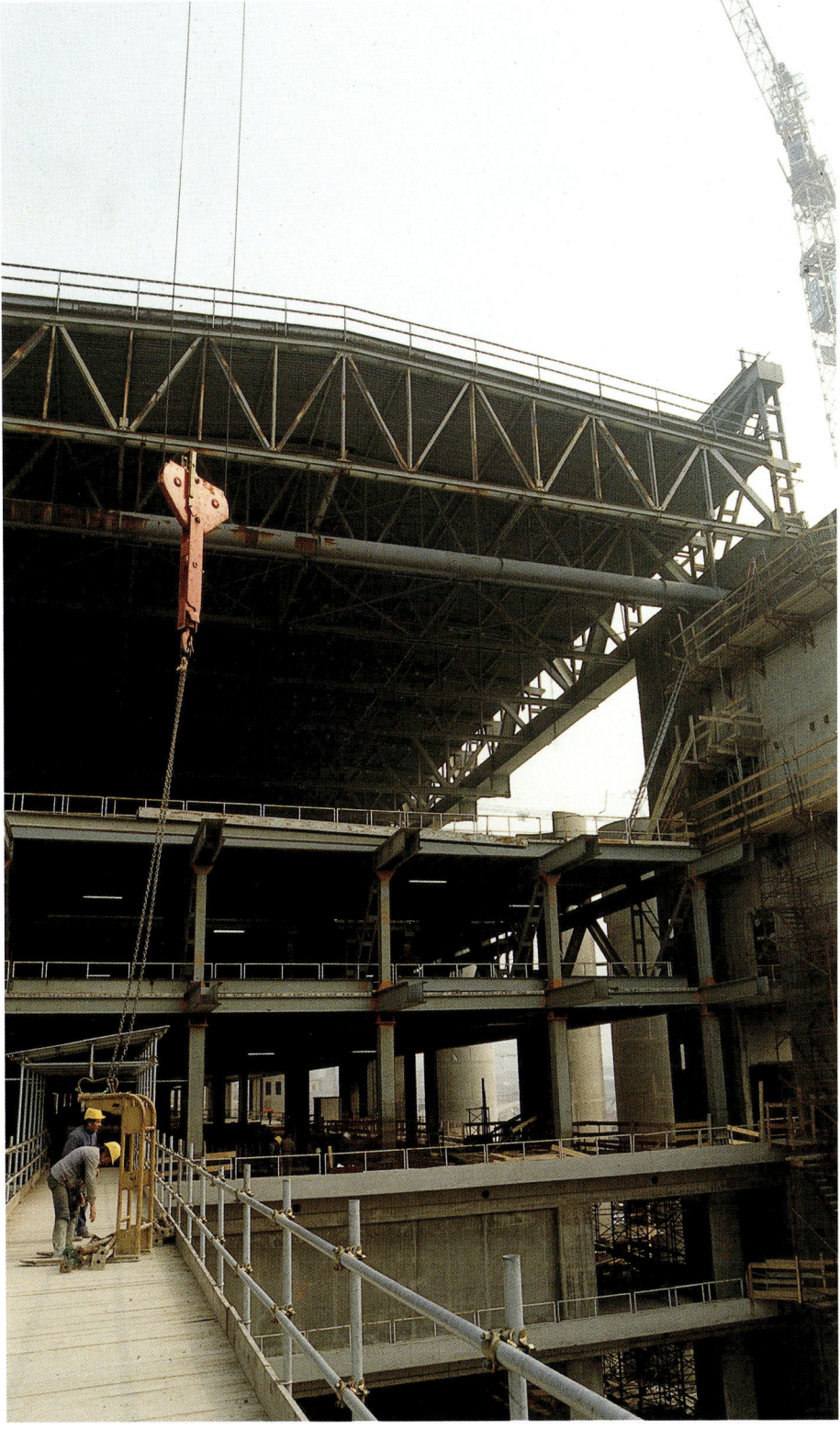

The Cité des Sciences et de l'Industrie (architect: A. Fainsilber). The construction site.

THE CITÉ DES SCIENCES ET DE L'INDUSTRIE 105

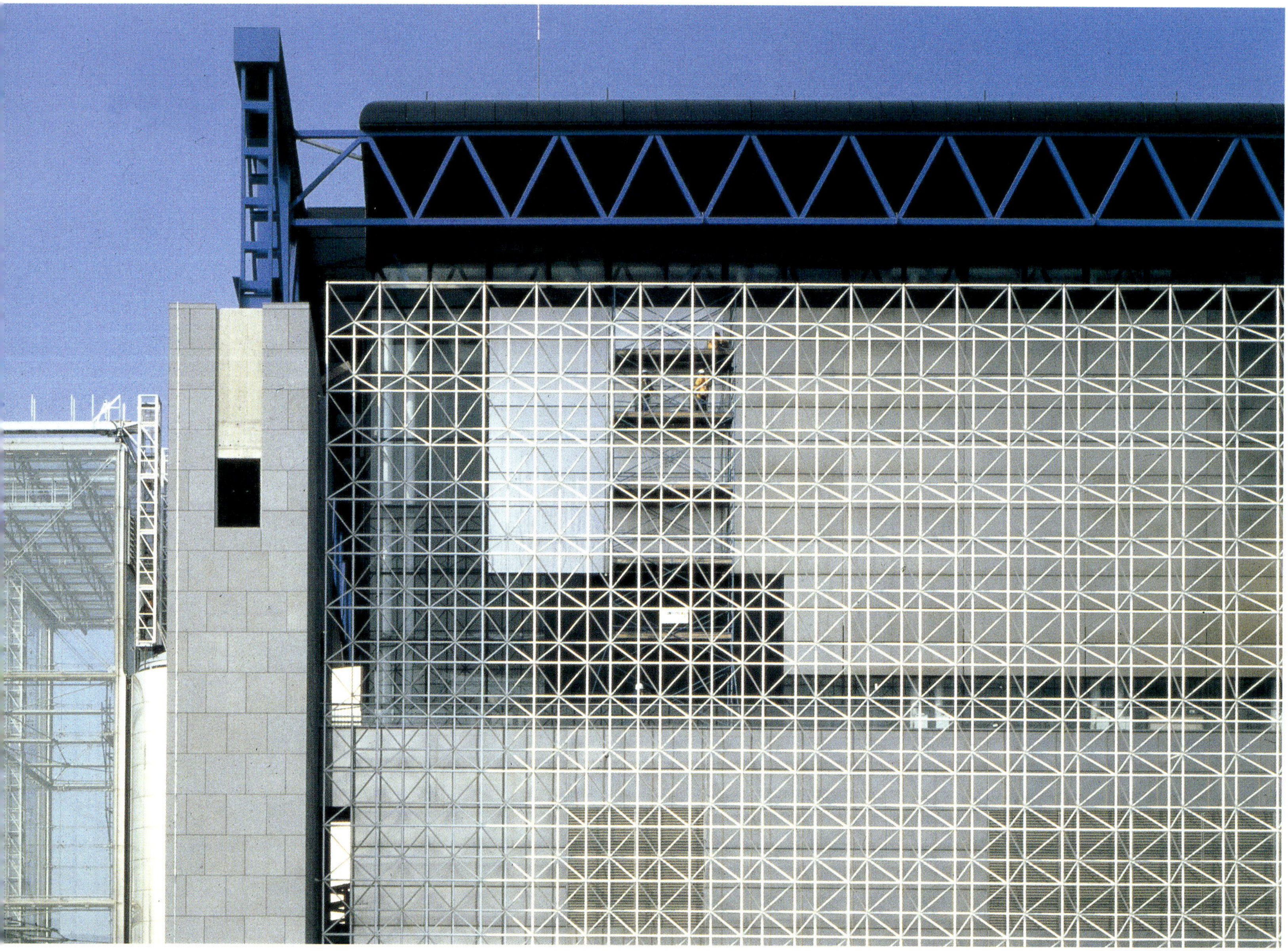

The Cité des Sciences et de l'Industrie (architect: A. Fainsilber).
Above: The east façade.
Below: Detail of the south façade.

it possible to add the two exhibition mezzanines).

By freeing the main pillars (these proudly proclaim their heroic straightness, evoking an idea of architecture as construction), and using load-bearing systems to regulate the spaces (the ground floor porticoes carefully delimit the area of the entrance hall), Fainsilber was perpetuating the constructional integrity of the moderns, adding to one of the most glorious pages in the history of architecture.

The façade as emanation of the plan

However, Fainsilber's allegiance to modernity is at its most manifest in the design of the north and south façades.

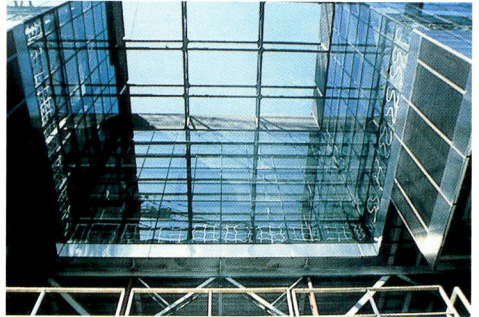

Whereas the south façade is entirely glazed, allowing the daylight to reach the emblematic features of *Explora*, the permanent exhibition; the north façade is clad in stainless steel, behind which there is a peaceful atmosphere appropriate to an interactive museum and the intense, hands-on activity that this inevitably generates.

The contrast between the façades, dictated by the brief, is tempered however by the similarity of the main entrances, those gaping holes that reveal the sparkling minerality of the Cité – the "great gem."

By judiciously setting the façades back from the main pillars, Fainsilber gives us an idea of the depth of the structure, in keeping with the eminently pedagogical approach of his practice.

Classical rationalism

While Fainsilber's architecture drinks at the well of a classicism that some may deem superannuated, and while it asserts the pre-eminence of proportion as if echoing the geometrical order of the universe, it is impressively radical in formal terms since it is founded on the geometry of pure solids, "in which proportion adheres completely to form."[1] Basing himself on mathematics and perspective – the science of representing space – Fainsilber tends towards a normative aesthetic form in which simplicity becomes an ideal and is linked to a conception of architecture as an aesthetics of rules, all of which protects his work against subjectivist indulgence.

Crushing in its authority but marvellous in its balance, Fainsilber's architecture shines with the sun of reason. We can forgive the formalism that presided over the conception of the east and west façades. Indeed, when draping these in an immense metal lattice, this "maniac of exact relations"[2] that is Adrien Fainsilber, was no doubt trying to cope with the heterogeneity of the construction of the meat market. Architecture, after all, should first and foremost be a pleasure for the eye.

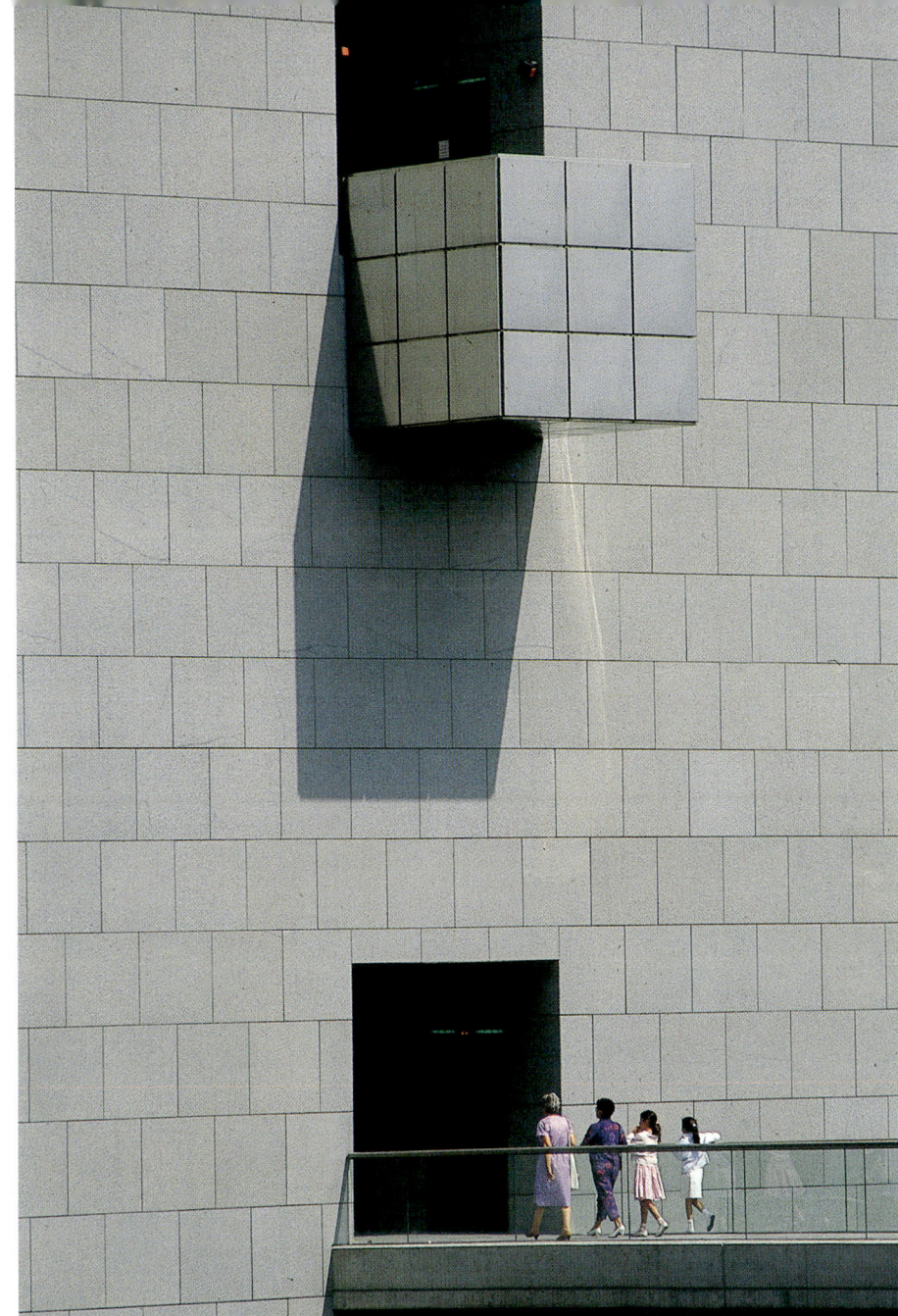

The Cité des Sciences et de l'Industrie (architect: A. Fainsilber). Detail of the south façade.

Notes
1. Françoise Fichet, *La Théorie architecturale à l'âge classique* (Brussels: Mardaga, 1979), p. 16.
2. Frédéric Edelmann, "Le grand prix d'architecture à Adrien Fainsilber", *Le Monde*, 4 March 1987.

INTERVIEWS

Adrien Fainsilber

Jean Semichon

Interview with Adrien Fainsilber

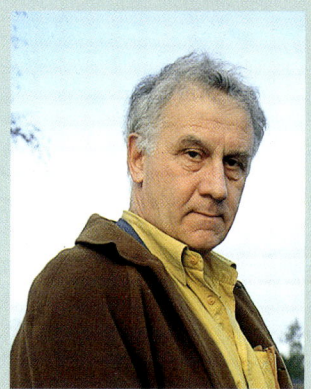

Adrien Fainsilber studied architecture at the École Nationale Supérieure des Beaux-Arts in Paris and, after graduating, began his career as a *chargé d'études* at the Paris Region Development and Planning Office. While working as a consulting architect for the Ministry of Infrastructure and Housing and the Architecture and Town Planning department, he designed a large number of buildings, including the Université de Technologie at Compiègne, the molecular interaction and high pressure laboratory at Villetaneuse, and the hospital complex in Évry. In 1980, Fainsilber won the competition to build the Cité des Sciences et de l'Industrie. In 1986, the year of its inauguration, he was awarded the French Grand Prix for Architecture. In recent years, Fainsilber has conceived and built an impressive number of projects, including the wastewater treatment plant at Valenton, the Musée des Beaux-Arts in Clermont-Ferrand, and the Musée d'Art Moderne et Contemporain in Strasbourg.

What impression did you have when you went and saw the meat market of the abattoir? Did the solutions for remodelling it come to you quickly?

The first surprise was the building's monumental scale; a monumentality that is in fact less visible from outside – because the meat market was partly obscured by a number of low buildings – than from the inside, where you could see the giant main pillars and the great spans of the metal structure. So, I was impressed, but also frightened. A few days later, I went back to the site and I realised that the perimeter walls of the lower level areas were not load-bearing. That meant we were able to dig all around the building and open up the lower levels to the daylight. In doing this, we also gave the building monumental proportions that it didn't originally have.

The relation between the structure and its urban context seems to be really fundamental for you. How does the Cité des Sciences fit into the city?

I didn't want the museum to be an obstacle to pedestrian movement between Porte de La Villette and Porte de Pantin. Hence the presence of this axis that you emphasised. An axis that runs parallel to the whole network of paths running alongside the Canal de l'Ourcq. The two main goals driving my approach to La Villette were to make the Cité des Sciences open to its neighbourhood, and to integrate the fifty-five hectares of the site into the surrounding fabric. If you look carefully, you will see that the museum entrance hall is a real public square.

Is the Géode, which you placed outside the museum, part of this approach?

It was necessary to use the Géode to create a powerfully symbolic sign, and shatter the linearity of the museum façade. But basically, as you know, the Géode was there to close off the vista from the Porte de Pantin. My initial project did indeed plan to place a waterway across the site, linking the Géode to the southern extremities. The Géode thus constituted the culminating point of an itinerary linking Place de la Fontaine-aux-

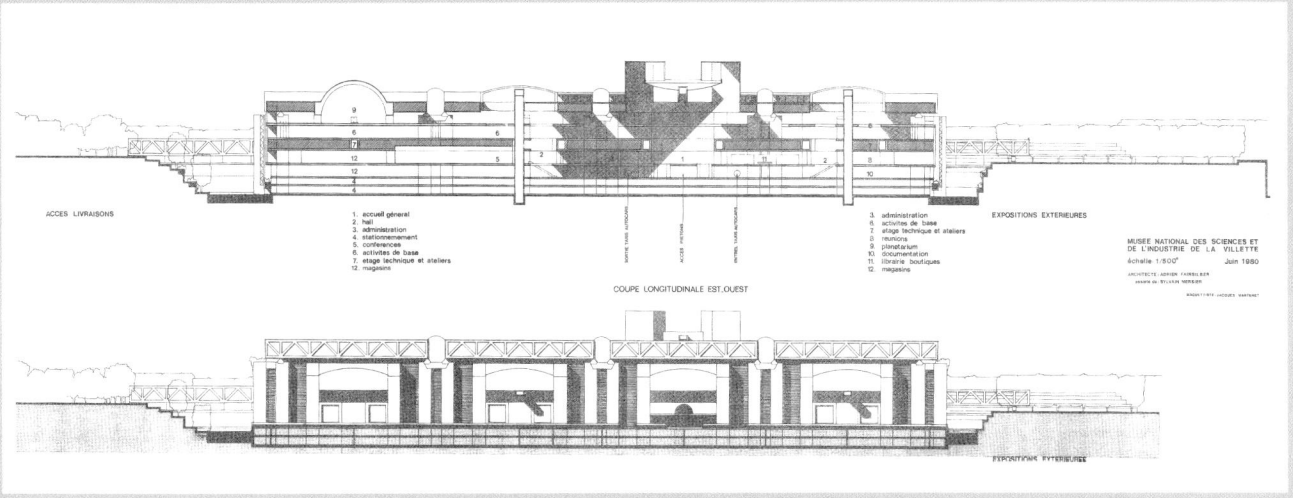

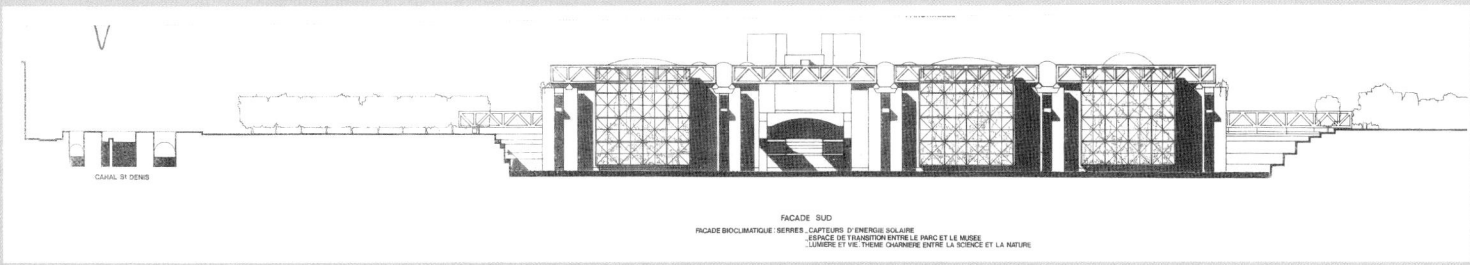

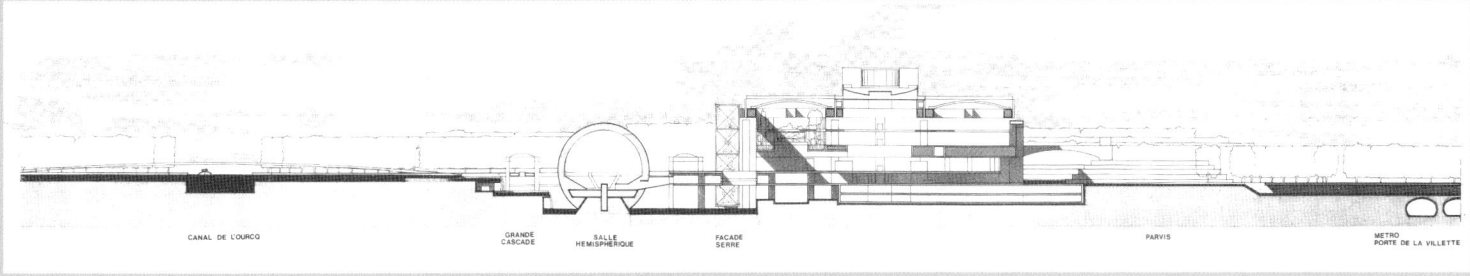

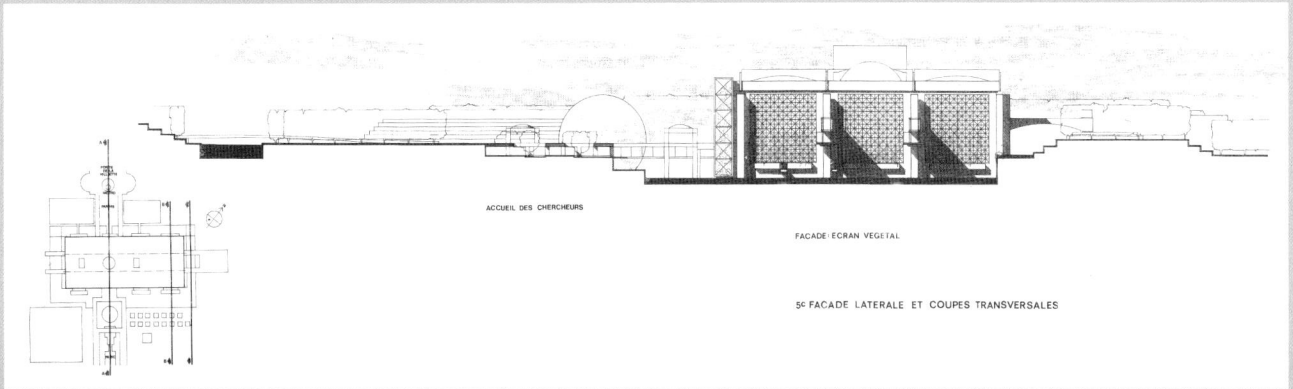

Lions to the area round the museum. It should be clear that when the competition to rehabilitate the meat market was opened in 1980, the architects were expected to accompany their proposals with a general plan featuring a park, an auditorium and a dance school.

The option that was subsequently chosen, with a main contractor for each project and no overall manager, unfortunately prevented a

The Musée National des Sciences et de l'Industrie competition (1980). Project by A. Fainsilber.

INTERVIEW WITH ADRIEN FAINSILBER

Letter from Alain Lamassoure, technical advisor to the secretary general to the President's Office, addressed to Paul Delouvrier, chairman of EPPV.

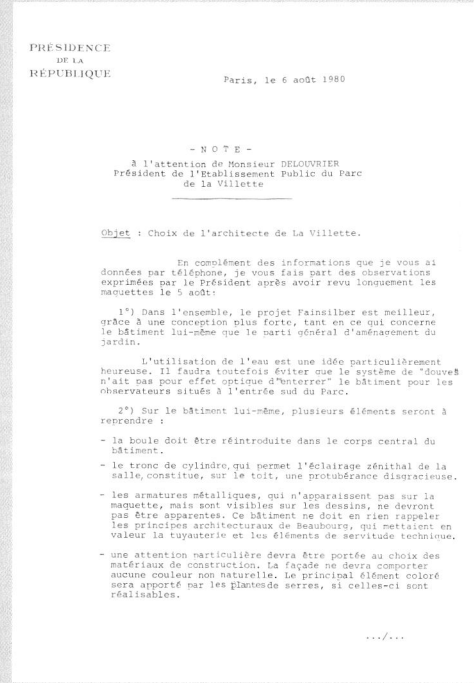

coherent ensemble from emerging, even if the Parc de La Villette and the Cité de la Musique are projects of real quality. The city is not about fragmentation. It is primarily a thing of continuity and composition. That's something people often tended to forget at La Villette, all the more so now with all the building happening along Porte de La Villette and Porte de Pantin, with the end result being a total fragmentation of the site – in other words, a kind of anti-town. Facing the museum, for example, there should be a totally bare forecourt on a scale matching that of the Cité des Sciences. There are now two big buildings along Avenue Corentin-Cariou which totally mask the museum's north façade. Let me make a confession: when the competition was opened I dreamed of doing the park. Control of the overall composition, that's what interested me most.

Did the fact that the cattle shed was to remain on the site bother you?

Not in the least. In fact, my development project made the future Grande Halle an essential element of the overall composition. Be that as it may, though, the cattle shed was there, on the site, and it was going to stay there. The authorities had made their decision.

Tell us about your way of always revealing and even celebrating the structure. There seems to be a kind of wish to make the work comprehensible.

At La Villette it would have been absurd to mask the constructional elements. On the contrary, they needed to be revealed. In fact, there are people who believe that I myself built the huge load-bearing pillars and metal beams that can be seen on the façade. If La Villette is a success, that is precisely because we always kept to the discipline imposed by the structure. In the competition, lots of architects wanted to camouflage the load-bearing elements. As I see it, this was a mistake. As far as I am concerned, I preferred to follow the constraints imposed by the existing structure. If I hadn't done that, the museum would have been virtually unfeasible.

This effort to celebrate the structure seems to be tied to a quest for bareness. Your style is very pared-down.

I don't like ostentatious architectural gestures. If you look attentively at the façades of the Cité des Sciences, you will realise that the existing structure never enters into conflict with the new elements. And that too is a way of attaining spareness.

How did you approach the problem of interior traffic?

In a museum, I think, it is vital that there should be a "major" space that ties together the vertical and horizontal pasageways, so that visitors know where they are and can find their way around. That is essential. The building was very big and in the end the role of the entrance hall was to make the scale accessible.

A word about the façades, and particularly the east and west façades, which are clad with a metal lattice.

The east and west façades of the meat market were like a vertical section of the building, revealing the concrete structure of the lower levels and the metal structure of the upper levels. The lattice you mention

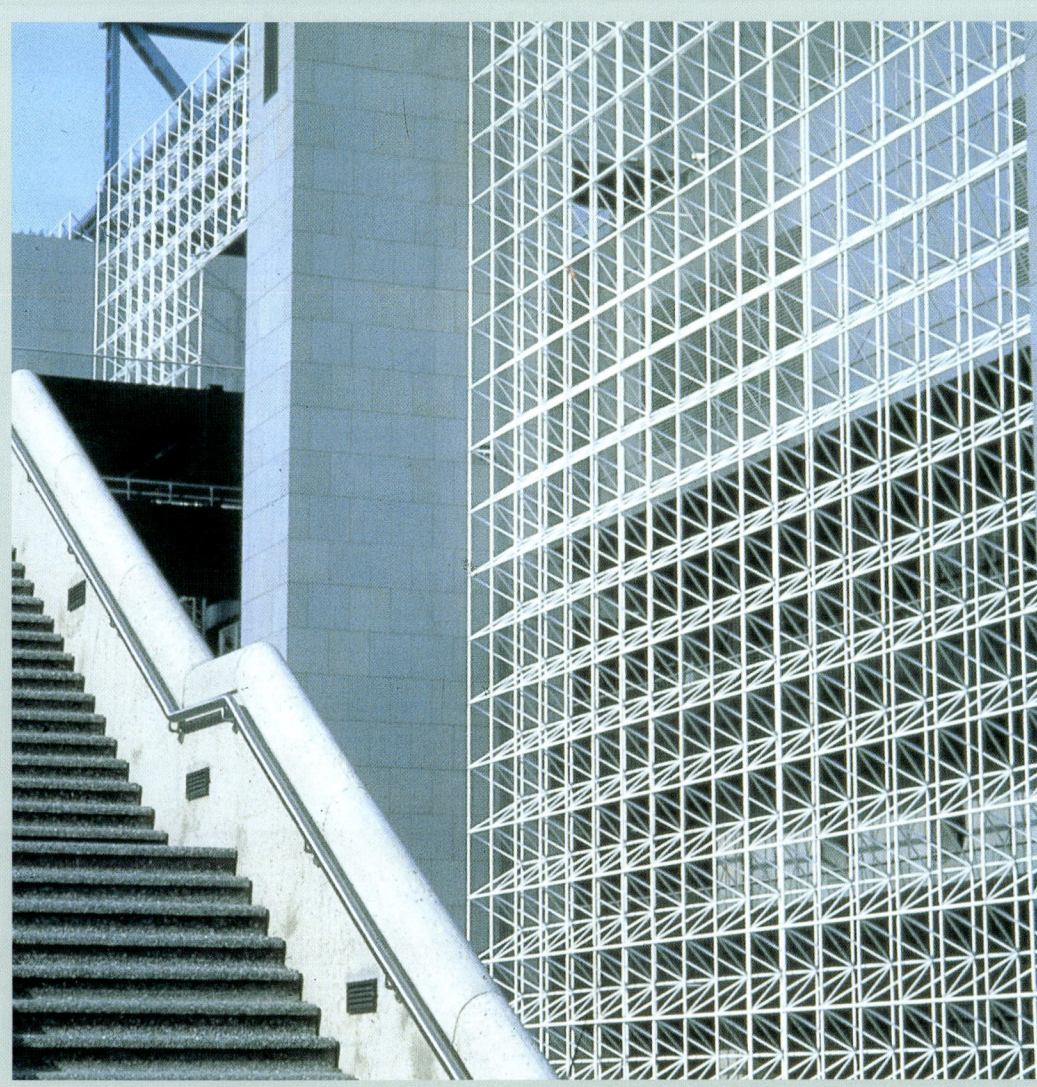

The Cité des Sciences et de l'Industrie (architect: A. Fainsilber). The west façade.

thus has a very precise function. It masks the heterogeneity of the meat market's structural system. It is there, in a sense, to unify the façades.

The Cité des Sciences is governed by the right angle. It would seem that there is not much room for curves in your architecture.

And the Géode?

It's outside the building.

And the columns containing the lifts? At La Villette, I think, this potency of the right angle that you refer to came from the structure itself. But it is true that I use the curve rather sparingly. I must admit that it doesn't often feature in my main choices when it comes to formal composition. There are a few exceptions, though, notably the town hall at La Flèche, whose form follows the curve of the island on which it was built.

Your architecture borrows constantly from classicism. What is your relation to the architecture of antiquity and the Renaissance and baroque periods?

I do undeniably have a real admiration for classical architecture.
But I am not sure that the references you mention are always conscious in my work. I believe that the unconscious reveals itself much more in such matters than we think. In architecture you never invent, you articulate; because you are always steeped in a given culture. Classical culture certainly had a big influence on my work, there's no denying it, but that doesn't necessarily mean I want to mechanically reproduce its architectural patterns.

Today, though, when walking around at La Villette, there is a huge stylistic difference between your architecture and that of Bernard Tschumi or Christian de Portzamparc. There is no reference to classicism in the work of your two colleagues – not, at least, in Bernard Tschumi's – whereas your architecture goes about sacralising the concept of proportion.

Yes, I have always been in awe of the big classical compositions, but my approach remains primarily an urban one. What interests me is the relation to the immediate urban environment, the relation to the city. After that comes volumetry, the relation to space, the way one catches the light. And this is where references to classicism may sometimes come in.

Is not your allegiance to the baroque mode of composition – that constant concern you have to integrate the buildings by means of a spatial staging celebrating the architectural itinerary and the architectural object – another way of referring to classical language? One gets the impression that there are two Adrien Fainsilbers: on one side, the architect, deeply attached to rationalism, and on the other, the landscape designer or the planner, who borrows copiously from classicism.

There is a misunderstanding. I see inside and outside as part of the same whole. The proposition for the park that I entered for the 1980 competition was quite simply the result of an urban problematic: the idea was to create a development project that could organise a site of fifty-five hectares and conceive the museum in relation with the park, and vice versa.

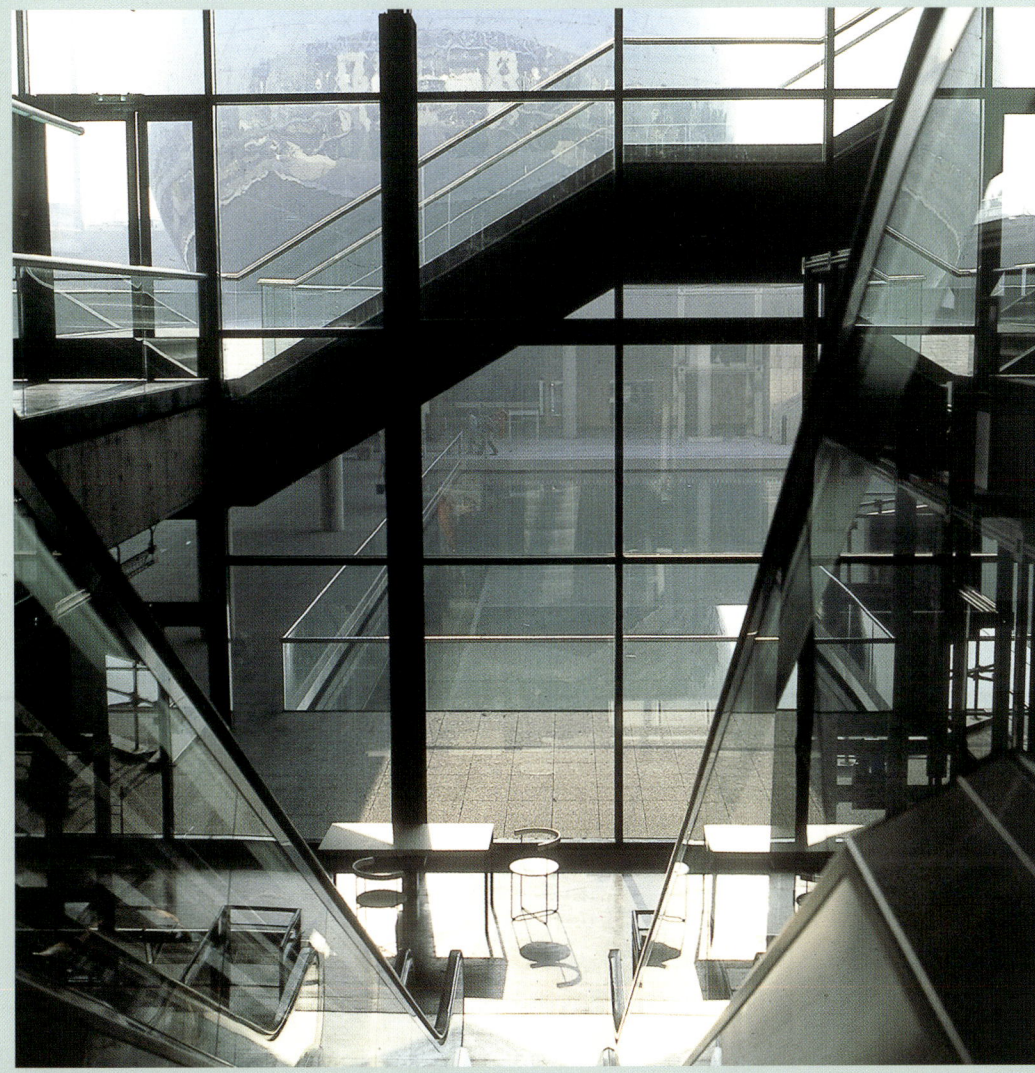

The Cité des Sciences et de l'Industrie (architect: A. Fainsilber). The surrounding areas of the Géode as seen from the first-level basement.

Even so, you could have chosen a fragmented approach, like Bernard Tschumi. But no, your proposition was very hierarchised, with a major axis running from north to south, linking the Cité des Sciences to Porte de Pantin. The logic here is one of order. For Bernard Tschumi, the architect of the Parc de la Villette, the complexity of the contemporary world makes such big structural schemes obsolete.

I don't share this theory of fragmentation. I would even be inclined to say that it is the complexity of today's world that makes such hierarchised urban patterns necessary. At La Villette there was no ignoring the structure of the site. The conception of a building and of an urban layout stem from the environment. Often, you have to make the most of what already exists.

But do you acknowledge the cult of axiality, of the theatricalisation of buildings by means of urban procedures playing on the effects of perspective?

Yes, of course. But we must avoid confusing the classical spirit with academicism. Sasaki, who worked with Saarinen on some very contemporary projects, was also steeped in that great French tradition. To be able to see a building that is several kilometres from

INTERVIEW WITH ADRIEN FAINSILBER

where you stand, to observe the relation between the construction, the water and the forest all around, as at Chantilly, is one conception of town planning. Town planning is not just "sticking" a pre-established solution on a site and ignoring its specificities.

Could you cite three buildings that marked you as a student?

The first building that comes to mind is Le Corbusier's Swiss pavilion, built at the Cité Universitaire. A very moving building that I discovered before I became a student. At the time, although totally incompetent in matters architectural, I was struck by the beauty of the proportions. And it was after that discovery that I started reading the complete works of Le Corbusier. The second building, I would say, could be by Alvar Aalto.

The Villa Mairea?

The Villa Mairea. Or the town hall in Säynätsalo, a brick building articulated round a patio. And then, let's say, the Kimbell Art Museum of Kahn.

Alvar Aalto is something of a model for you.

Aalto works with the grand material called light. You should go and look at his projects in Finland. They're extraordinary. You should know that the documents at an architects disposal don't always allow you to show the way the light enters the building. And this is even more true in the case of Aalto. He taught me more than Le Corbusier. When I went to visit him in Finland, I saw the plans for the Square House that he was preparing to build near Paris. I found the plans interesting but it was only after I'd visited the site that I understood the project. When I was there I realised that the large roof served to frame a landscape that was more than three kilometres away from the house and that the big copper gutter cleverly lifted up the ridge on the horizon. The theatrical inclination is really under control here. From the edge of the plot the house is hardly visible. Then you move round it, through a grove of trees, and it's only when you're inside that you get the view of the landscape.

And Mies van der Rohe?

Mies was a big influence when I was a student. I particularly appreciated the refinement of the technological solutions in his architecture. I visited practically all the buildings he made in Chicago. And then the pavilion in Barcelona, and the Nationalgalerie in Berlin.

One senses that you feel less admiration for Mies van der Rohe than you do for Alvar Aalto.

The problem with the Nationalgalerie is that you have to go to the lower level to find spaces suited to exhibitions.

At the risk of making Jean-Louis Cohen mad, one has to admit that Mies is very much a formalist.

Yes. And ultimately, his architecture is haunted by the Greek temple.

Let's talk now about Le Corbusier. Christian de Portzamparc and Bernard

Tschumi are ambivalent about the creator of the Ville Radieuse. On the one hand they acclaim his genius for form, on the other they condemn the theoretician, deeming him sometimes dictatorial. What is your take on Le Corbusier?

I am rarely critical about Corbu. Indeed, the dogmatism of certain projects is there only to underscore the manifesto aspect of his propositions. And don't forget that Corbu never built his most controversial projects. Believe it or not, I've read all his books. They are really quite impressive. I have also visited a good number of his buildings. I was at Harvard when the Carpenter Center was being built. It's a building with a ramp running through it that makes it possible to connect several blocks on the campus. I like this idea of an architectural promenade. When I was a student, Le Corbusier really was the master of a whole generation. All the more so since one could sense he was very isolated in France.

And the radical dimension of his projects never bothered you?

It was difficult to be critical in those days. Only later were we able to judge the misinterpretations of his doctrine. But look at Venice: when he planned the hospital there, Corbu respected the site. He cast aside all his urban theory. The structure, a very low fabric, fits perfectly into the surrounding urban fabric. And that is what is great about Le Corbusier: on the one hand, he lays out the theory of the right angle, and on the other he builds Ronchamp.

In your work one finds the fascination that Corbu had with service elements – ramps, staircases, lifts, and so on.

Of course. The ramp is a dynamic element. At Clermont-Ferrand, as at La Villette, or at Strasbourg for the Musée d'Art Moderne et Contemporain, it was necessary to facilitate visitors' movement and help them get their bearings in space. The ramp is a prominent element, which facilitates orientation. At Strasbourg there is no ramp, but there is a big escalator which ensures a certain fluidity of movement. This is particularly important because it is a public building.

Not long ago, when visiting the Conseil Économique et Social, I got a sense that there were several points that your work shares with that of its architect, Auguste Perret. What do you think of that?

I don't think so. Auguste Perret is neoclassical. I don't see myself as neoclassical. In fact, I don't like his architecture that much. But I do recognise that he is a great architect.

So you are more Corbu than Perret?

Without a doubt.

I believe you studied in Boston. Now, the Cité des Sciences looks to me to have been greatly inspired by the Boston City Hall, built by Kallmann, McKinnel and Knowles. What lessons did you learn from your stay in the United States?

When I was working in Boston, the city hall hadn't been built yet. But what you say is amusing because at the time I was working in an agency that was entering the competition to build it. The agency in question belonged to two neoclassical architects, Shepley and Bulfinch, who went on to build the Capitol in

INTERVIEW WITH ADRIEN FAINSILBER

The Cité des Sciences et de l'Industrie (architect: A. Fainsilber). One of the escalators in the entrance hall.

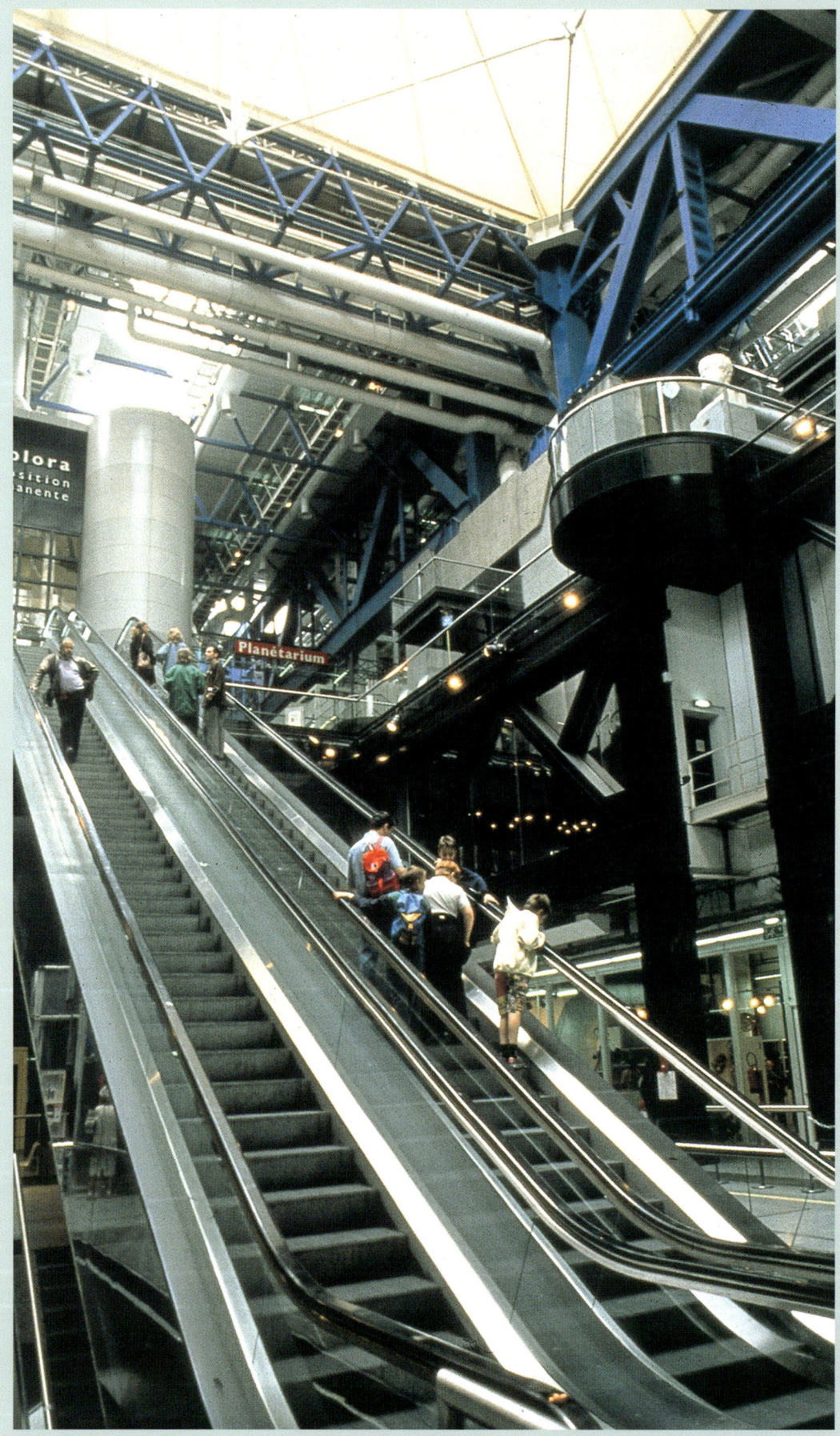

Washington. I didn't stay in their agency long, in fact. I worked mostly at Sasaki and Walker – they were the two landscape architects who were my real influences.

I mentioned the Boston City Hall, but I could also have mentioned the engineering building by Stirling and Gowan at Leicester University.

It's a magnificent building. I would even say that it is James Stirling's finest building. After that he moved towards postmodernism.

Have you ever thought of settling in the United States?

I thought about it for a short while. I was offered a job with José Luis Sert, who designed the Fundació Joan Miró in Barcelona. José Luis Sert worked a lot with Corbu. He was also the executive architect on the Carpenter Center. He designed a number of buildings around Boston. He's a very interesting architect. But the main thing I brought back from my stay in the United States is the idea that it can sometimes be important to learn far from home. Having to deal with other approaches can often help you to question yourself. The way architecture is taught and practised is very different abroad. Getting away from the French context can be very salutary.

What do you think of contemporary French architecture? Flipping through the specialist magazines, one gets the impression that the level is in fact pretty high. Indeed, it's a paradoxical situation: on one side, the lecture rooms, often abandoned by the students; on the other, production that seems to be getting better by the day.

That's true. In the 1960s, things were different. French architecture was no good. In fact, I was in the United States when I got wind of the Maine-Montparnasse project. In the States, they found it hard to imagine such a project being built. Today, the trends have been reversed and American architects are now coming to France in search of modernity.

How do you explain the renaissance of French architecture since the early 1980s? One gets the impression that the numerous competitions organised during François Mitterrand's two seven-year mandates did something to raise the level of architectural production.

The negative aspects notwithstanding, the competitions did undeniably contribute to the development of architecture in France. And then there were the *grands projets* (major building projects). In the 1960s you would go to the United States and the Scandinavian countries because that's where modernity was. In France, at the time, the institute still had a monopoly on commissions. Winners of the Grand Prix de Rome automatically became the architects of civil and state buildings. In the 1960s, I would never have been able to build a hospital or university because public commissions went automatically to the Grand Prix winners who, let it be noted, had no knowledge of building techniques. It was May '68 that did the most for the development of architecture in France, notably by ending the caste of mandarins. For the *grands projets*, it must be said, the authorities really were determined to give us the resources we needed to succeed. That was very important. The *grands projets* contributed meaningfully to the progress of architecture and construction techniques. Real progress was also made in matters of landscaping. Nowadays, people are even showcasing buildings at night. It was Sasaki who initiated me to landscaping. It was in the United States that I discovered the big compositions *à la française*. In France there was – and still is – a kind of allergy to this *grande composition* spirit. And yet Paris is Paris only because it is articulated around major vistas, major axes opening a passage towards the Seine. In the town planning of the seventeenth and eighteenth centuries there was a taste for theatre which, to my mind, will always be relevant. Town planning is also about articulating non-constructed spaces, articulating hollow and empty spaces.

How do you go about choosing your competitions? Why did you take part in the one for the Cité des Sciences et de l'Industrie and ignore the competition for the Opéra-Bastille and La Défense?

La Villette preceded the competitions for La Défense and La Bastille. But anyway, they would never have given two *grands projets* to the same architect. The only exception is Paul Chemetov who after he had put up the Ministry of Finance building, rehabilitated the Grande Galerie at the Musée d'Histoire Naturelle. Materially, it is very difficult to work on several major projects at the same time. When I did La Villette, my agency was wholly dedicated to building the Cité des Sciences. Winning a major project doesn't always bring you good luck. After La Villette, I had a real barren patch.

Is there any piece of architecture built as one of the grands travaux that has particularly impressed you?

I would be inclined to cite the Grande Arche at La Défense. Johan Otto von Spreckelsen's arch gave credibility not only to La Défense, but also to the possible westwards extension of the historical axis, in which few people had taken an interest. Without that arch, La Défense is nothing. I like the shape of the building, and I also like the way it fits into the site. But yours is a trick question. An impressive number of extraordinary buildings went up from the 1930s to the 1960s. Today there are a lot of great buildings, but there is no more great architecture.

Does the Cité des Sciences et de l'Industrie still stand as your best project?

Without a doubt, the Cité des Sciences is still my finest project. It is the expression of my conception of architecture: quality of interior space, maximum light and the assimilation of new building technologies.

A word about the Parc de la Villette: Bernard Tschumi, who designed it, argues that because of the increasing complexity of the contemporary world we need to give up on "totalising architecture." For Tschumi, the idea of architecture that needs to prevail is more modest, less triumphalist. This is ultimately a way of calling on us to abandon those big orderly schemes that were the reference for so long, and that you yourself often invoke.

Bernard Tschumi's project is too conceptual. There are never any clear-cut revolutions in architecture. There are rules, which some deem backward-looking, but which you cannot transgress. True architecture is the kind that can move us while taking into account a given urban environment. The Parc de la Villette is certainly an interesting project, as its success attests to, but it cannot be denied that Bernard Tschumi failed to take into account those major features of the site that are the canals, the Cité des Sciences, the Géode and the Grande Halle. One gets the impression that Tschumi's project could just as well have been built anywhere else. It is important to insist that the natural environment will always exist and that it will never be possible to erase it, not even with concepts.

A word about the competition to build the Cité de la Musique. Suppose you had been obliged to enter, what approach would you have taken? Would you have opted for a project positioned symmetrically in relation to the Grande Halle, or an asymmetrical one, like Christian de Portzamparc?

It's hard to answer. You can't enter a competition with a priori ideas, otherwise you're heading straight for disaster. You need to assimilate the brief, and you also need to assimilate the constraints of the site. Above all, you need a fairly long lead-time so you can do some thinking. Only after this period of maturation does the idea eventually emerge. But, I am sure that if I had taken part in the competition I would have found Bernard Tschumi's grid very restrictive.

As it happens, Christian de Portzamparc comes out of it pretty well.

He has come out of it well. I would simply say that from Avenue Jean-Jaurès the frontage of the buildings makes it hard to see the park behind. I personally would have "opened" the project to the park a bit more.

Did you know that Alain Sarfati, who entered the competition, had the – in my opinion – very clever idea of concentrating the entire programmatic content to the west of Place de la Fontaine-aux-Lions so as to leave the eastern part of the site completely bare. The park could thus extend all the way to the edge of Avenue Jean-Jaurès.

That's a very intelligent proposal. In my 1980 project, I situated the music complex opposite the Grande Halle. The park could thus stretch all the way to Avenue Jean-Jaurès and, in a sense, run alongside it. Today the park is no longer visible from the major thoroughfares that are Avenue Jean-Jaurès and Rue de Flandre.

No interviews, even fewer writings: why this extreme discretion?

I don't like to talk about my work. True work goes beyond commentary.

Interview by Alain Orlandini.

Interview with Jean Semichon

Jean Semichon is the architect who built the abattoir at La Villette. This complex, designed to replace the old abattoir built in the Second Empire, was acclaimed by the specialist press as one of the most efficient ever built. In this interview we go back over its conception, and especially that of the meat market building rehabilitated by Adrien Fainsilber.

In what circumstances were you commissioned to build the new abattoir and meat market complex at La Villette?

During one of my stays in Abidjan, when I was working on the design of the Abidjan and Bouaké abattoirs with the help of an industrial company, this company, SETIF, suggested that I join them to form a group to enter the competition for the modernisation of the abattoir at La Villette. Although I was a nobody at the time, my proposal was chosen.

The structural system of the meat market sports some pretty impressive dimensions – the main beams have a span of nearly sixty-six metres, and their height is nearly nine. Why such colossal dimensions?

The meat market had to provide the butchers with a whole series of large spaces. It needed to take the form of huge bays, each of which could be divided up into a multitude of sub-spaces. Hence these beams that can cover wide spans and that inevitably limit the number of supports. From this system of beams were hung the offices plus a system of rails along which the carcasses could be moved from one point in the building to another. From east to west, the meat market divided up into four halls, each one sixty-six metres long. From north to south, there was a succession of three spans each thirty-three metres deep.
The levels located below the meat market were used for conveying the meat, from the stands where it had been bought in the market, to the parking areas. At the lowest level were the loading platforms, the car parks and a railway. It was thanks to the presence of engineers paid by my agency that we were able to make this building. I should add that, because the floor was very bad, it

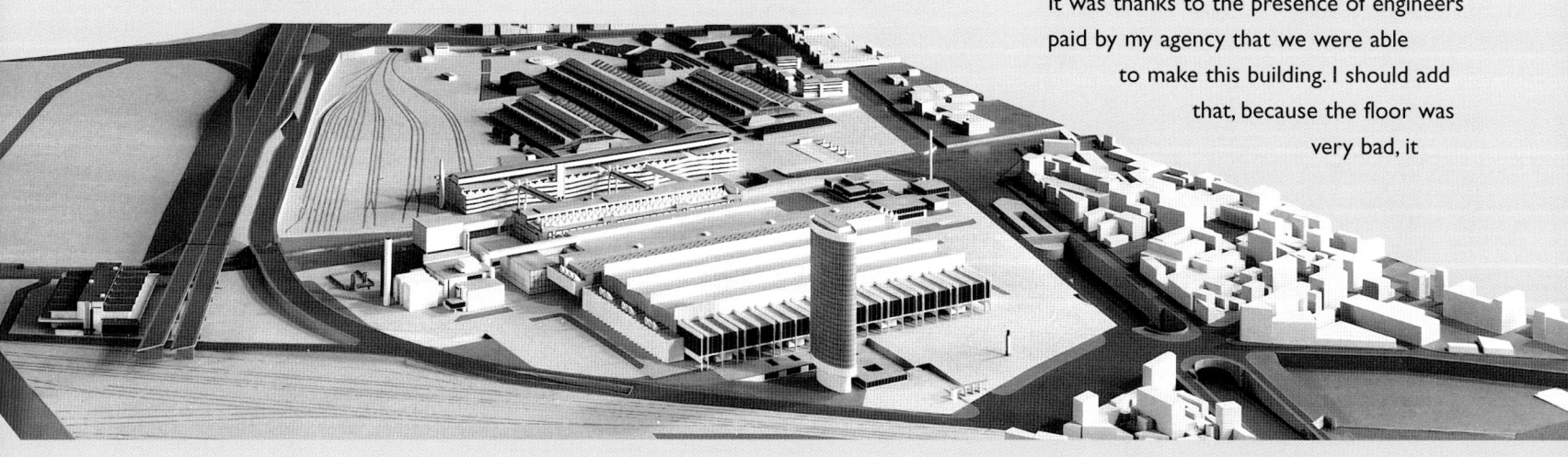

The industrial abattoir (architects: J. Semichon and S. Walrand). Model.

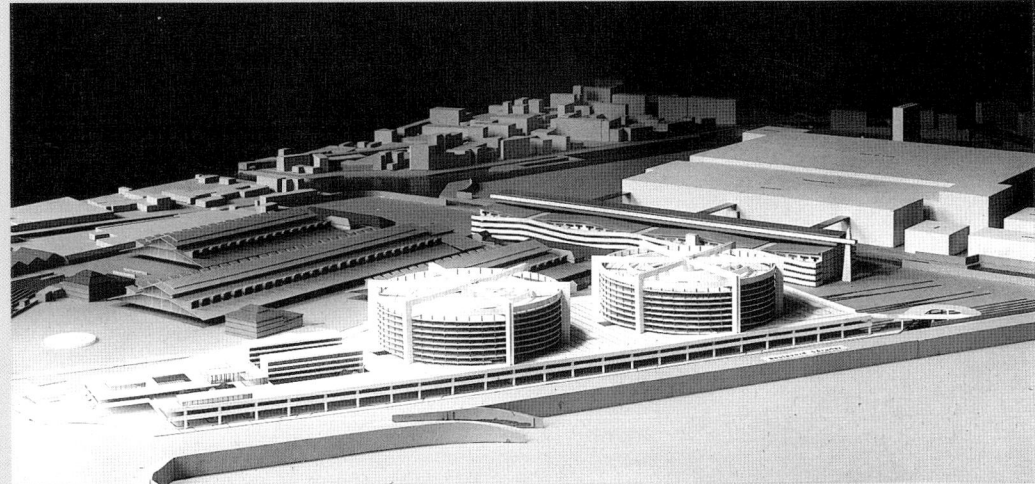

The industrial abattoir (architects: J. Semichon and S. Walrand). The car parks.

immediately meant that we had to find a solution that would use a very limited number of load-bearing elements.

What were the other elements constituting this new complex?

The new complex comprised the cattle stalls building, the cold storage chambers plus an administration tower and a heating station. Given the immensity of the site, we made the proposal to include car parks and commercial premises. These car parks, which constituted a kind of "centre of dissuasion" so that the trucks didn't venture off into Paris, and which we planned to locate in the south-eastern part of the site, were not directly linked to the site's activities. This complex, and indeed the shopping mall that we planned to add on to the north façade of the meat market, were in fact never built. As regards the livestock stalls building, we proceeded as follows: on the site of the old abattoir, we had noted the presence of six percent gradient ramps laid out on either side of the Canal de l'Ourcq so that the animals could be taken across to the scalding chambers located to the north, where they were slaughtered. The livestock stalls building therefore reproduced this ramp system, but this time over four levels. Now, I would like to make two points here. The first concerns the work on the new complex. This had to be staggered since the old abattoir at La Villette needed to remain in operation, both for the sale of the animals in the livestock market and for the slaughter of the animals in the scalding chambers – and to do so until the new complex was finished. That, as you can imagine, was not easy. Especially since the wholesale butchers put pressure on us so that the quantities exported could rise from one hundred and ten thousand to six hundred thousand tonnes per year, this due to the creation of a Marché d'Intérêt National – MIN (Market of National Interest) for exports. Because of that I had to suggest a new schematic design. The second point concerns the nature of the contract that was signed between the project owner and the main contractor for the construction of the new abattoir. This was the first contract signed in France after the decision to raise fees for art specialists working in the public sector, in whatever discipline, from four to six percent. But when I signed this clause I didn't realise that they had omitted to include a clause on damages, which turned out to be mighty unfortunate because the project was terminated and two hundred and eighty thousand square metres of new flooring were destroyed.

Above and below: The industrial abattoir (architects: J. Semichon and S. Walrand). The office tower: Perspective view and plan.

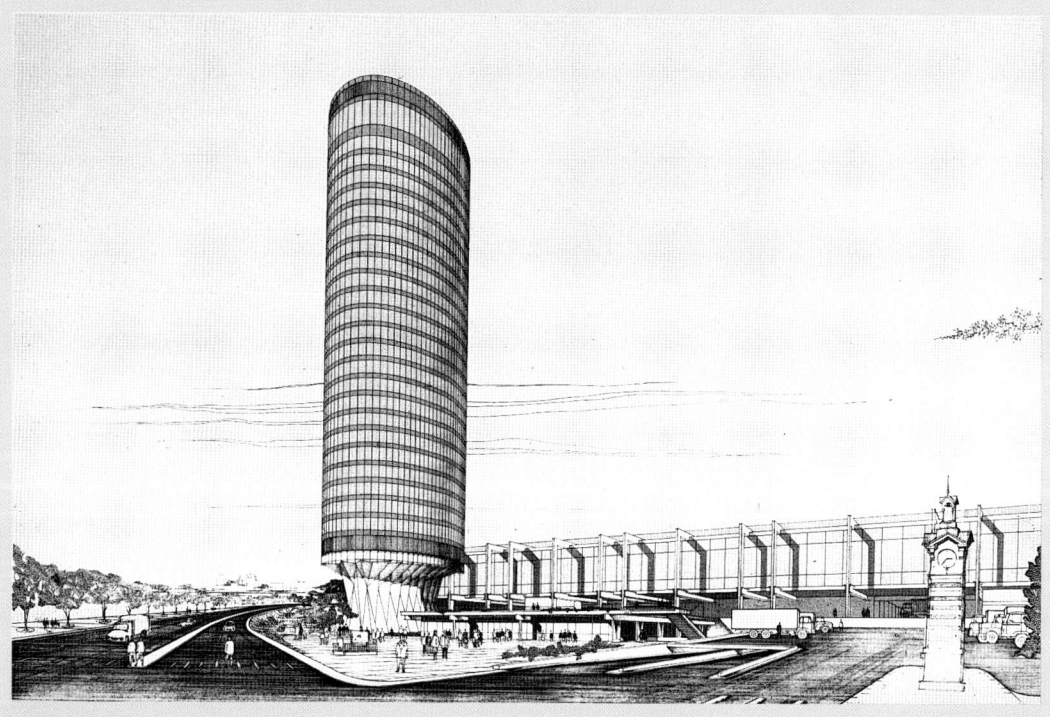

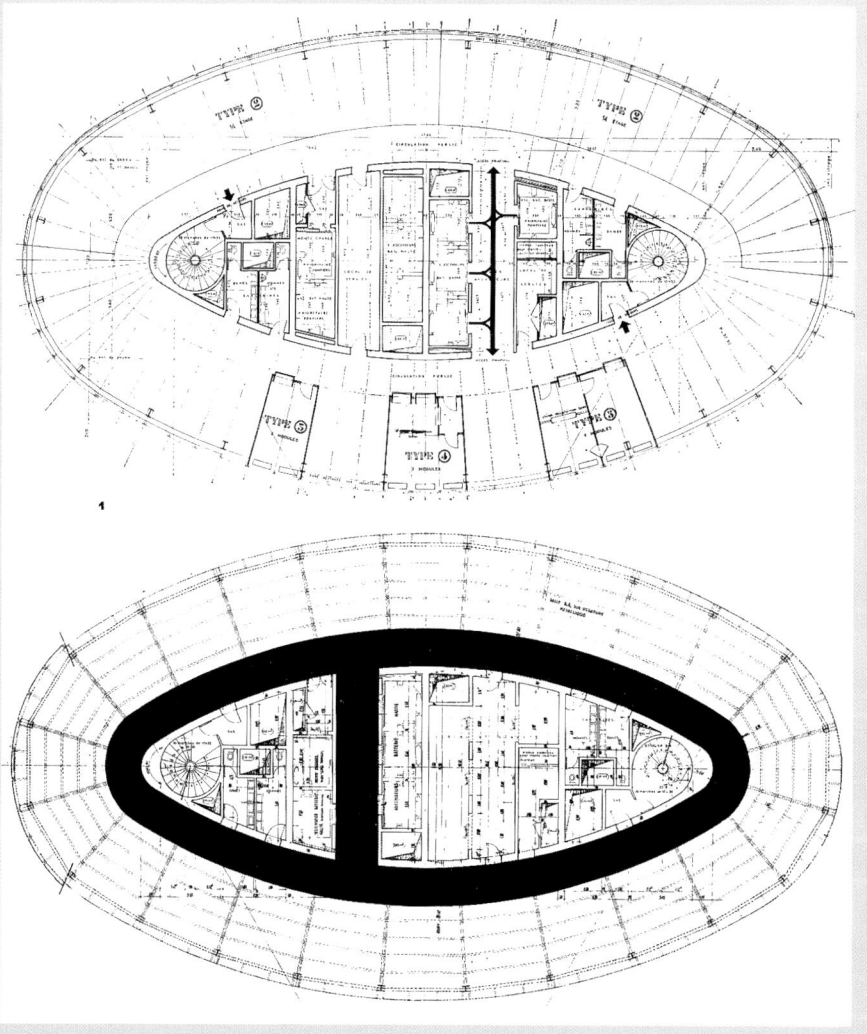

124   LA VILLETTE: 1971–1995

The plan of the meat market was made up of two distinct volumes. The first was constituted by a rectangle with three bays, the second took the form of another, longer rectangle, whose structural system was laid out at a right angle to that of the first rectangle. Why was that?

The buildings positioned against the big rectangle, which were smaller, included cold storage chambers, the processing centre for the "fifth quarter" (offal) and a meat market for swine. They required a lower ceiling than the hall which sold sides of meat.

Let's talk now about the competition for the Cité des Sciences et de l'Industrie. Why didn't you enter?

Paul Delouvrier was totally opposed to it.

Why?

At the time, the construction of the abattoir at La Villette was seen as a big economic failure. No doubt it was to erase this poor image that Paul Delouvrier did not want the rehabilitation of the meat market to be given to the architect who had designed it in the first place. Indeed, when I asked him to explain why he prohibited me from taking part in the competition, he replied that I had failed and that it was inconceivable that I should continue to do anything at all at La Villette.

Paul Delouvrier's argument is strange because the closure of the abattoir had nothing to do with a design flaw.

Like you, I still don't understand.

Would you have agreed to enter the competition if you had been allowed?

Of course. Especially since I had written to the French president to offer to rehabilitate the meat market. I never got an answer.

When did you write to the president?

In August 1978.

Between 1974, when the decision was taken to close the abattoir, and 1978, when it was decided to rehabilitate the meat market hall, several development studies were made. Jean Sérignan's study was submitted to the prefect of Paris in May 1975. The Atelier Parisien d'Urbanisme organised an ideas competition in 1976, and Roger Taillibert sent his proposals to Valéry Giscard d'Estaing in 1978. All these studies envisaged the rehabilitation of the meat market. Did you try to contact the people who developed these proposals?

No. I didn't think there was any point. However, I certainly do reproach all those people for not having seen a need to contact me. They must have forgotten that the law on artistic property states that the person who conceived a work must be consulted if his creation is modified or demolished, and this over a period of fifty years. The heirs, too, are affected.
I have already pointed out that the penalties faced under this law are not sufficiently dissuasive and that it was absolutely necessary to make provisions for penal action.

I would like to talk about the Cité des Sciences which, as you know, resulted from the decision to rehabilitate the abattoir meat market. What do you think of Adrien Fainsilber's project?

Before discussing that point, I would, if you don't mind, like to go back for a moment to the abattoir at La Villette, to give you the exact reason why that decision was taken. It's important to know that Rungis enjoyed the status of a protected market, so that authorised agents are obliged to use it. La Villette did not have this privilege. It was the minister of Agriculture, Edgar Pisani, who wanted things that way. He also decided to attribute funds to abattoirs outside the city. Also, because the MIN at La Villette had set up a system of taxes that were higher than those for the abattoirs outside the city, justified by the necessity of more complex sanitary control and a colossal export programme, it was logical that the butchers should stop using the abattoir facilities at La Villette. And so more and more of them moved out to the suburban abattoirs until, having dipped below fifty thousand tonnes a year, the slaughterhouse at La Villette was considered financially unviable. The closure of the slaughterhouse at La Villette was thus the result of a political decision and not an economic mistake. Having made these points, I can now answer your question. But before telling you what I think about Adrien Fainsilber's project, I would like to say that if I had been in his place I would probably have thanked the architect of the meat market for having given me such a limpid structural system. I think that the conversion was greatly facilitated by the clarity of the load-bearing system. Adrien Fainsilber did in fact tell me that the structural system of the meat market was admirable. The floors, made from moveable prefabricated elements, gave great freedom to play on volumes. Industrial architecture can sometimes allow for surprising aesthetic results, which is part of its particular appeal.

The constructive system of the meat market was particularly well showcased by Adrien Fainsilber. One of the great achievements of his project was to magnify the old structure, yet without producing an overly imposing building.

Yes. I think the decision to leave a whole row of beams visible outside the building was visually very clever, even if I wonder how these react to the cold. The other interesting point is the moats laid out round the museum. The building seems more distinct now. But of course it would have been absurd to adopt that approach for the meat market because the lower levels didn't need to be lit.

The celebration of the constructive system also happens inside the building. All around the entrance hall, there are these big porticoes that facilitate a longitudinal reading of the museum.

The volume of the meat market has been put to very good use, there's no doubt about that.

Suppose you had to take part in the competition to build the Cité des Sciences et de l'Industrie. How would you have gone about it?

As in the approach chosen by Adrien Fainsilber, I would have opted for an interior

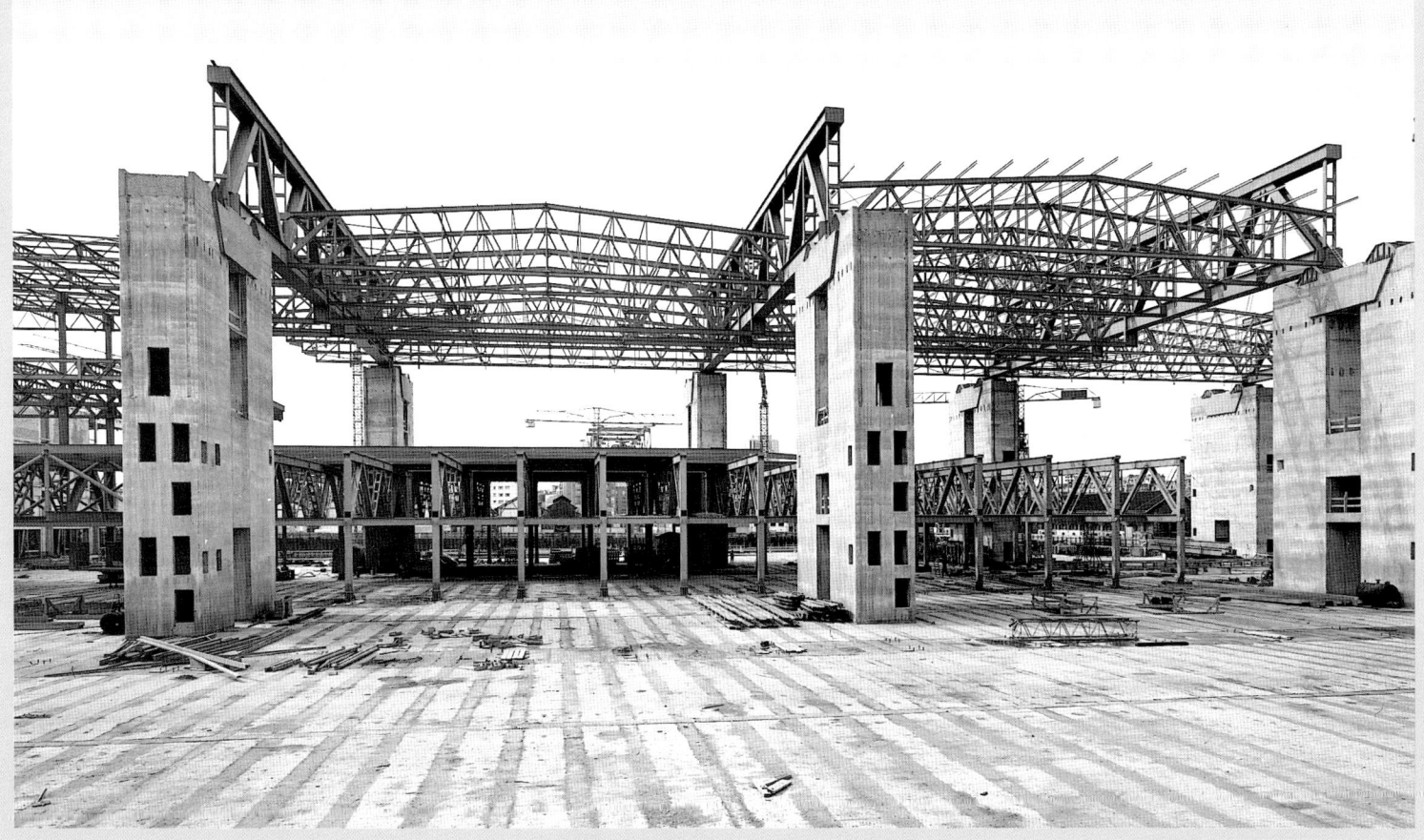

distribution emphasising the east-west axis, and for paths through it going from north to south. And I would of course have put the Géode outside the museum. In architecture, it is important to know how to be frank.

Interview by Alain Orlandini.

The industrial abattoir (architects: J. Semichon and S. Walrand). The meat market.

THE GÉODE: TECHNICAL PROWESS AS SYMBOL

The Géode comprises two distinct structural systems. The first consists of an immense pillar in reinforced concrete, from which, like branches on a tree, beams fan out to support the tiers. The second is in metal and uses a geodesic structure of steel tubing held together by rings, onto which a superstructure of stainless steel, curving triangles has been laid, thus forming the sphere's reflective skin.

Impressions of scale

With its diameter of thirty-six and a half metres, the Géode affords a serene vision of the gigantic Cité des Sciences. Like fingers on the same hand, small and large cohabit here without clashing. Although, when looking from the park, it seems to abut the south façade of the Cité des Sciences, the Géode superbly ignores its surroundings, abstracting itself from any geographic contingency to silently revel in its geometric perfection. The Géode's location outside the Cité also serves to draw the gaze southwards, towards the park, and helps map out an architectural itinerary linking the site's extremities.

Symbolic architecture

We know that in all ages thinkers have been fascinated by the sphere; because of its perfect regularity, it was long seen as a symbol of a world believed to be structured according to number and measure. Confronted with this temple of scientific knowledge that is the Cité des Sciences et de l'Industrie, Adrien Fainsilber wished to celebrate the permanence of nature's laws, in which he intensely believes. Thus the Géode refers at once to antiquity and the Enlightenment, the Platonic universe of the *Timaeus*, as well as Boullée's cenotaph to the memory of Newton.

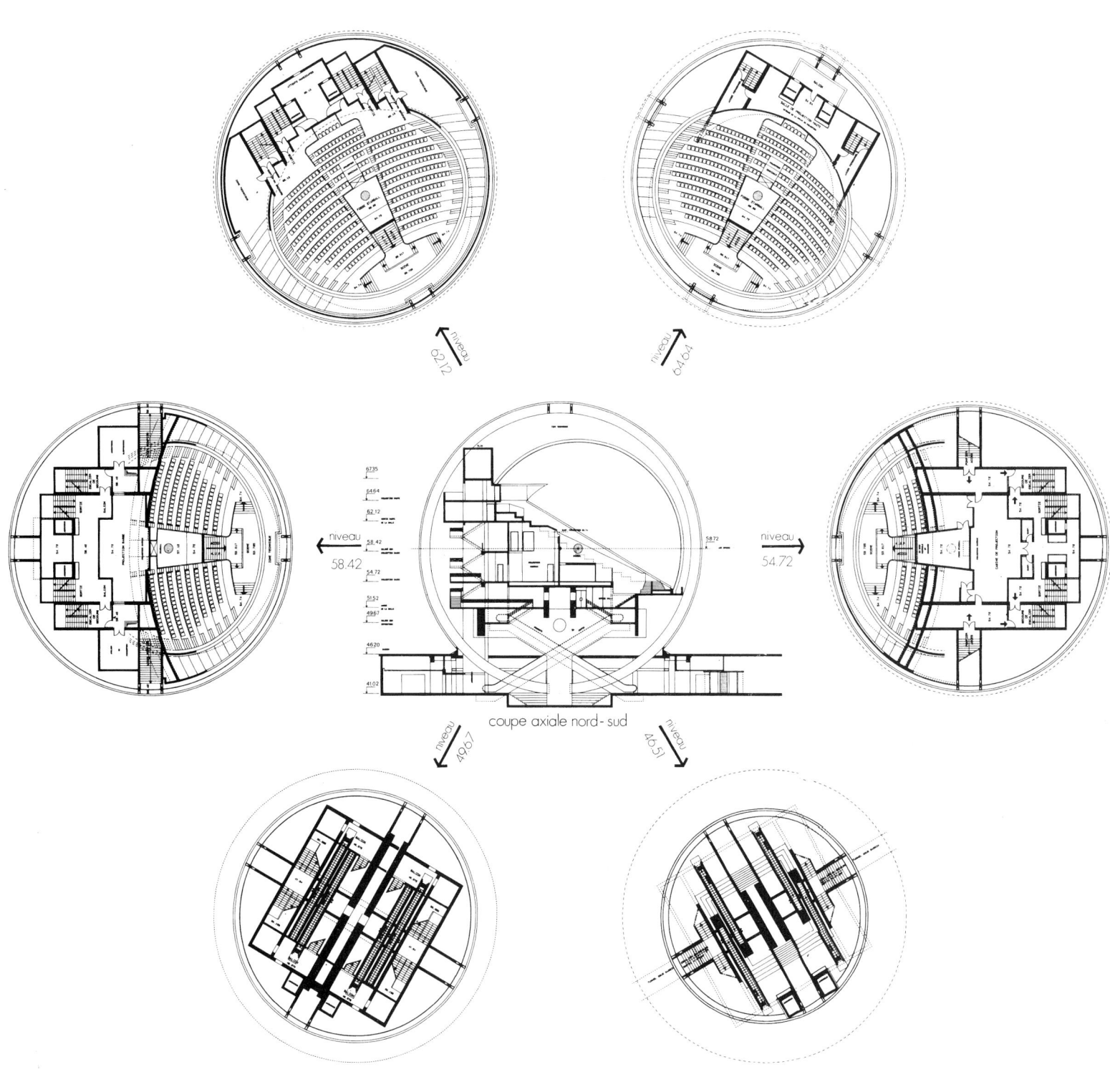

130   La Villette: 1971–1995

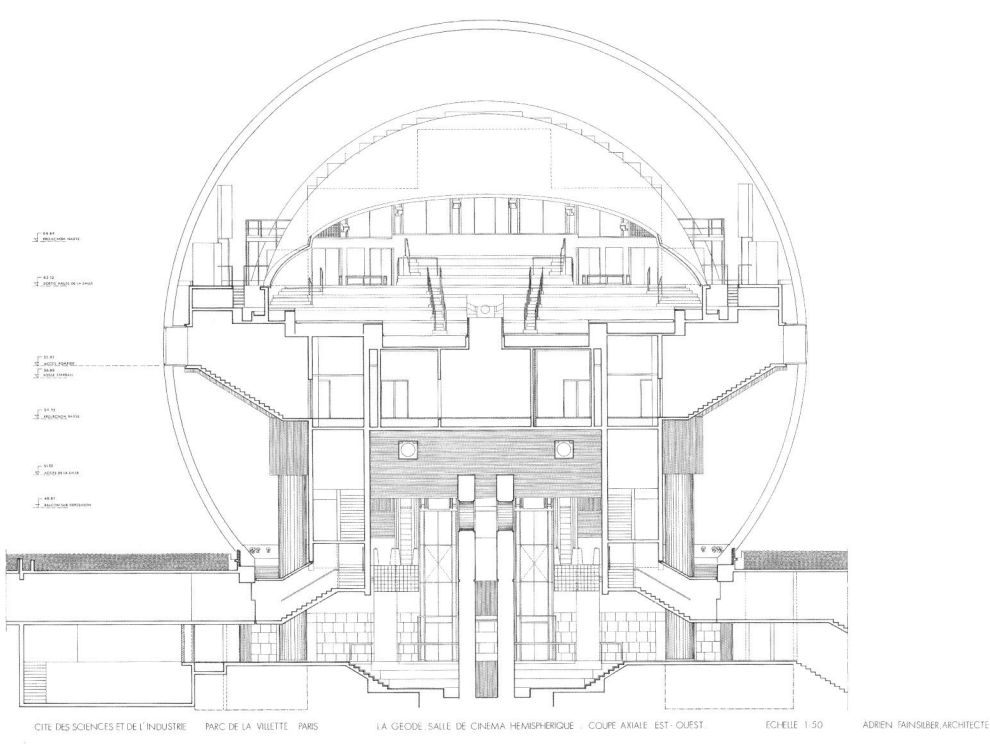

The Géode (architect: A. Fainsilber).
Page left: Plans of levels and section of the auditorium.
This page: Sections of the auditorium.

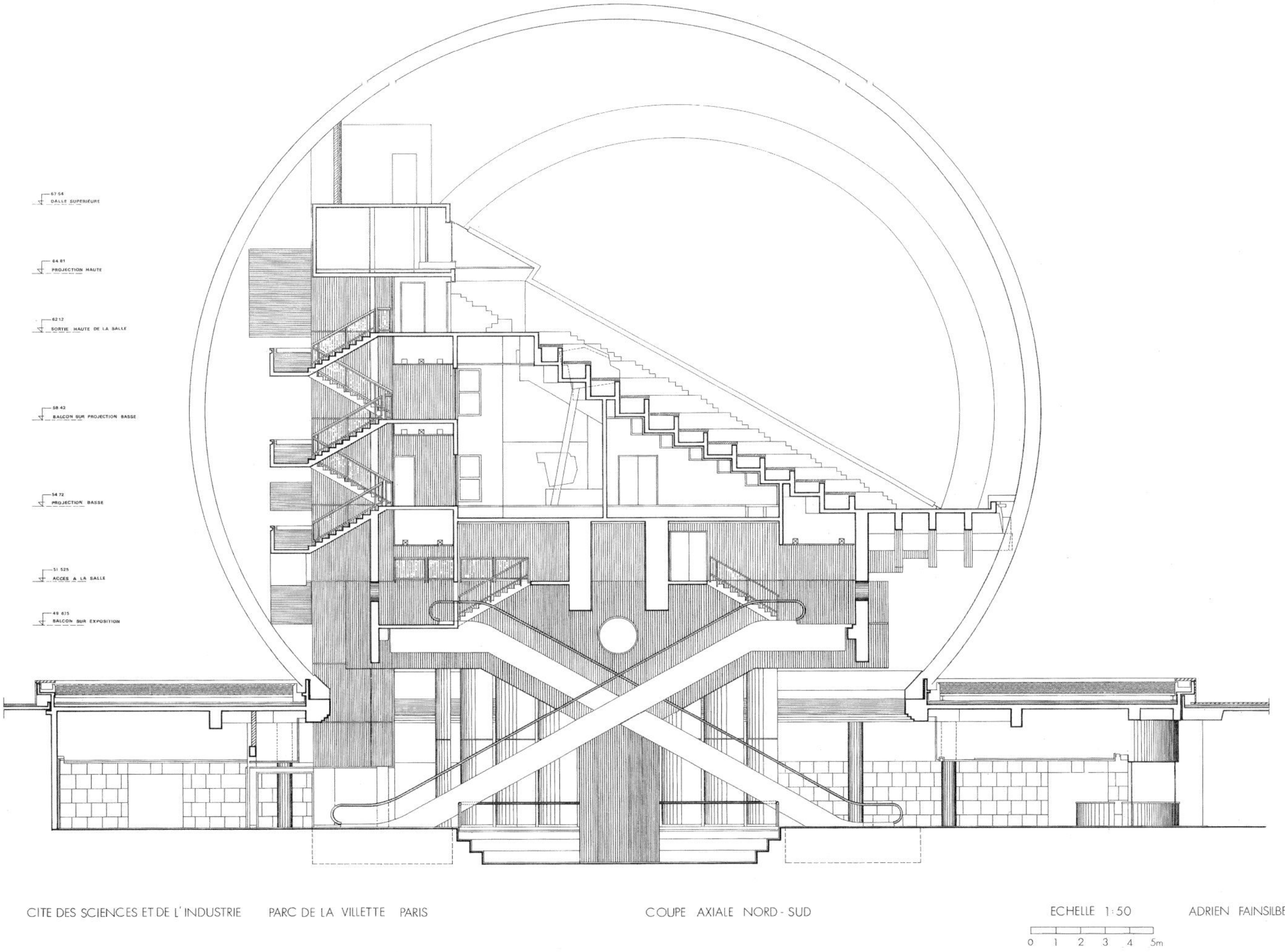

THE GÉODE 131

INTERVIEW

Gérard Chamayou

Interview with Gérard Chamayou

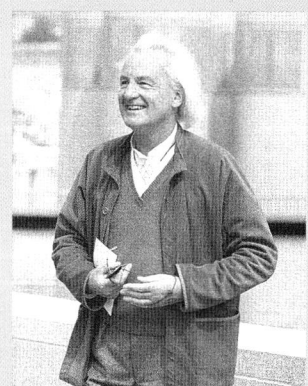

Artist and engineer, man of arts and sciences, Gérard Chamayou, known as "Felix", is the author of an eclectic body of work, to say the least. From construction to jewellery, and ballet and theatre sets to sculpture, the whole spectrum of human activity is covered with frenetic enthusiasm by this iconoclastic graduate of the École Centrale des Arts et Manufactures.
The interview below is an opportunity to go back over the conception of the Géode's reflective sphere, for which Chamayou received the *Brevet d'or*.

How was the Géode's mirror-sphere designed?

If you ask an organ to perform too many functions, it will inevitably resist. The same applies to physics. With the Géode's mirror-sphere, we needed to imagine a system combining several sub-systems, each capable of solving specific problems such as impermeability or static. The mirror-sphere is thus conceived like an onion, with its different layers of skin. The initial structure consists of a triangular geodesic mesh in steel tubing held together by what we call Saturn rings. This structure, whose only function is to take weight, is dressed with rock wool, ensuring thermal and phonic insulation. On top of this is fixed a secondary, aluminium frame, which carries the plates making up the mirror-skin's outer face. The joints make sure that any strain due to dilatation is never passed on to the carrying structure. That is one of the Géode's greatest successes, along with, of course, the resolution of complex problems such as the stamping and polishing of the reflective plates. You should bear in mind that there is a whole set of details that seem unimportant at first, but which make spherical construction impossible if you ignore them. I'm thinking in particular of the assembly stage of a geodesic structure, when a single misplaced metallic bar would make closing the sphere impossible. Around twenty years ago in Montpellier, I ran up against that problem. We were unable to finish a sphere I had designed. We had to completely take it apart and assemble it all over again. Those incidents were quite useful to me afterwards, particular at La Villette. I knew that for the Géode's mirror-sphere construction, there was no room for error, since the required precision was measured in tenths of millimetres. The level of precision was so high for the simple reason that we were about to lay polished stainless-steel mirrors on the structure that would inevitably and disproportionately magnify any errors. Some people said that I would never be able to close the Géode.
I answered that I could close it without any problem, if only they would let me work in peace.

The Géode is made up of two independent structural systems. The first one, in concrete, supports the tiers, and the second, in metal, carries the spherical envelope. What do you think of the structural scheme adopted by Adrien Fainsilber?

If it had been up to me, I would probably have opted for a different structural scheme. Building an *opercule*, that is to say placing an inclined circle inside the sphere, would have been another and, I think, cheaper way of supporting the tiers. The sphere reacts incredibly well to compression. The mirror-sphere weighs nearly seventy tonnes, and its structure was calculated to support a total load of around four hundred and fifty tonnes. When it is supporting these kinds of loads, the Géode only sways one centimetre at its summit.

You seem surprised by the structural scheme adopted by Adrien Fainsilber. But considered on its own, doesn't it refer back to the diversity of materials used, that is, of concrete and metal?

You are quite right to see things that way.

Perceiving the Géode is a real aesthetic experience, to such an extent that one sometimes forgets the technical mastery that has gone into the design.

It's true that this sphere has an absolutely magical side to it which makes any questions about its structural system seem ridiculous. What's more, it presents certain characteristics that the Institut Supérieur d'Optique is even today unable to explain. They realised for example that the Géode concentrated ultraviolet rays. As for the images it reflects, they are quite literally sublime. From afar, these images are hyper-realistic. From mid-distance, they are impressive. And from close up, they are definitely abstract.

Interview by Alain Orlandini.

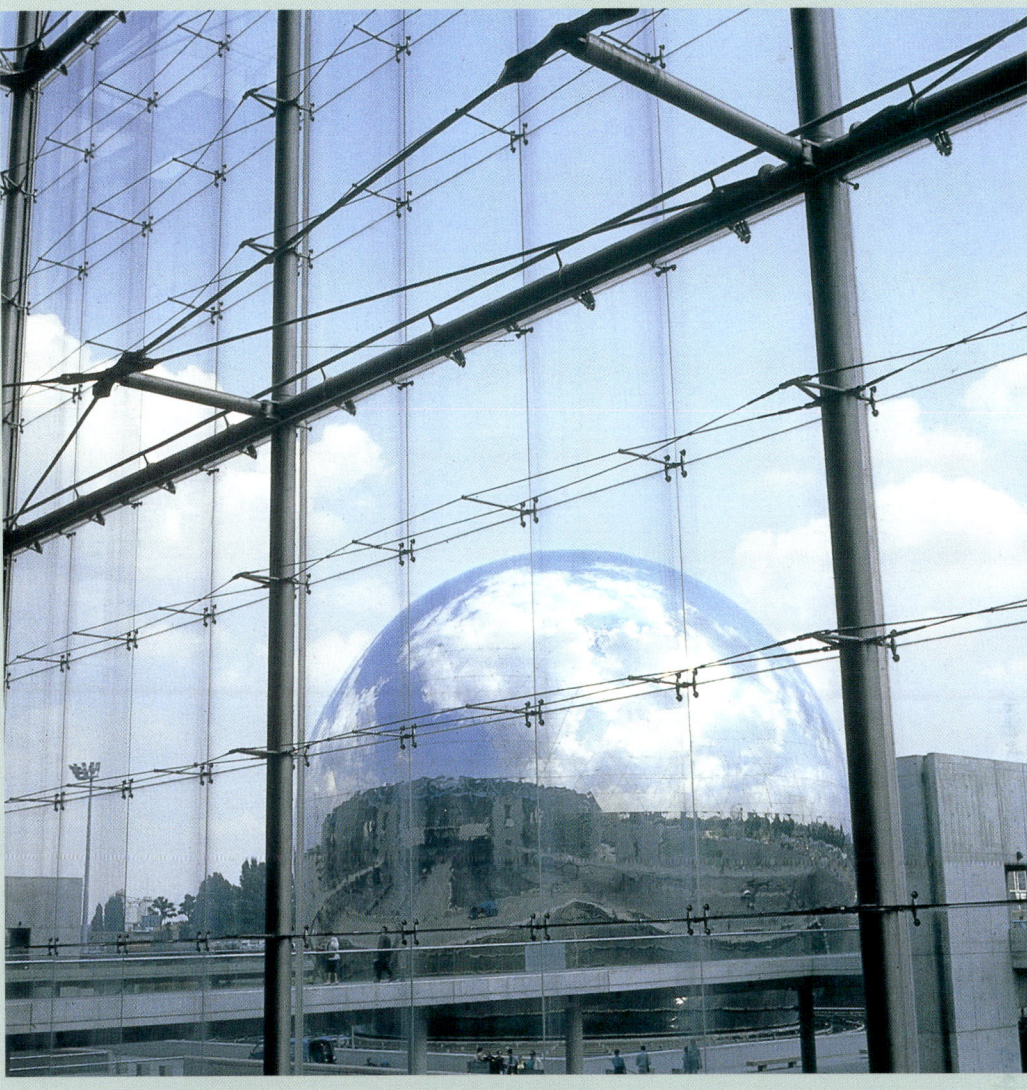

The Géode (architect: A. Fainsilber). View from the bioclimatic greenhouses of the Cité des Sciences et de l'Industrie.

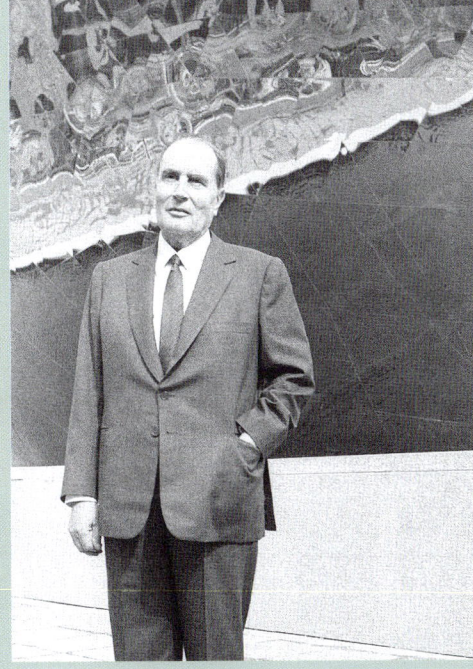

President François Mitterrand in front of the Géode during its inauguration.

THE PARC DE LA VILLETTE "GEOGRAPHIC DEATH": THE OBSESSION WITH GEOMETRY

Anyone who takes a close look at Bernard Tschumi's project will observe that there is a huge gulf between its representation and its actualisation. On one side, the images of the Parc de La Villette, on which the fragmentation into three autonomous systems (Points, Lines, Surfaces) can be seen; on the other, its "reality," its transcription into constructed form, in which it is hard to make out the separation of its three functors. What becomes of this once the huge expanses of the park have been occupied? What becomes of the play of tensions between the orthogonal structuring of the Villette site by the Folies (Follies) and the undulating layout of the Promenade Cinématique (Cinematic Itinerary)?

Virtual symbolisation

But why begin by insisting on the discrepancies between the images of the park and its built reality? Because Bernard Tschumi's entire project was based around the idea of "dislocating" his project, of subjecting the whole enterprise to a dynamics of fragmentation, and thus of confronting us with the advent of a post-modernity that is itself dislocated.

Thus it seems that the idea of nature as an intelligible totality governed by a found-

"Don't forget that when you mark out a plan it is the human eye that registers the effects."
Le Corbusier

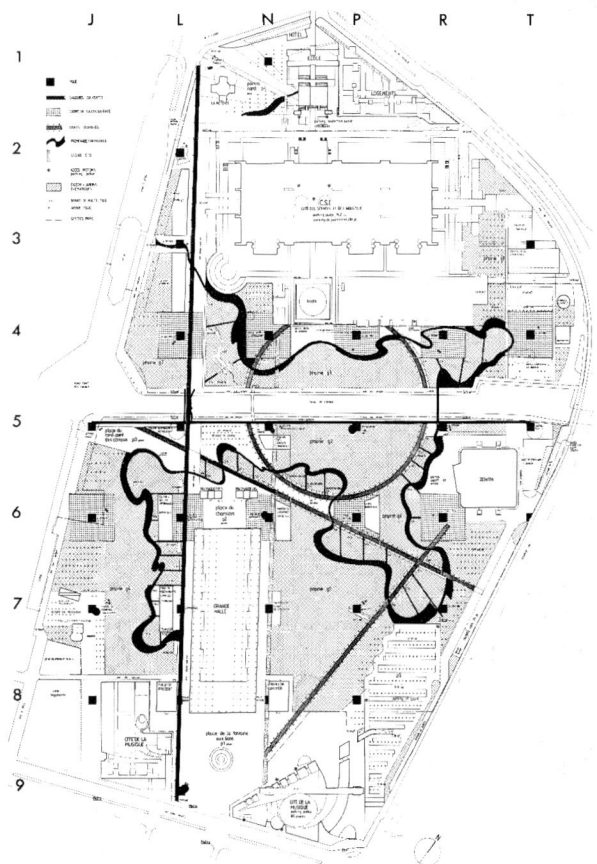

The Parc de La Villette (architect: B. Tschumi). Site plan (final project).

THE PARC DE LA VILLETTE   137

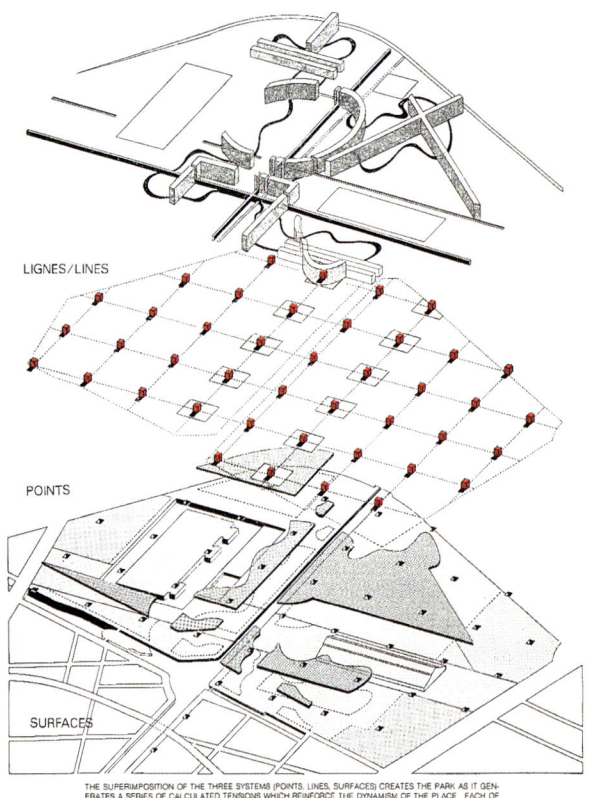

ing principle has been replaced by a world made up of constellations and contextualities, in which the *dissensus* has triumphed over reason. That the "supreme power of man"[1] has been substituted by a human psyche torn between the three Freudian categories of the id, the ego and the superego, and that Rousseau's utopia of the *Social Contract* has been wrecked by the Nietzschean superman. The Parc de La Villette is intended as an allegory of this new reality. Disjunction, dissociation, fragmentation: these are the concepts that inform its splintered aesthetic, seen as confirming the disappearance of the "one world and oneness of being."[2]

Now, as has been stressed above, this tensing of the park's functors exists only as an image, a design. And given that, by virtue of its gigantic scale, the Parc de

The Parc de La Villette (architect: B. Tschumi).
Above: Plan of general composition.
Right: Visualisation of the disjunction concept functioning in the organisation of the park.

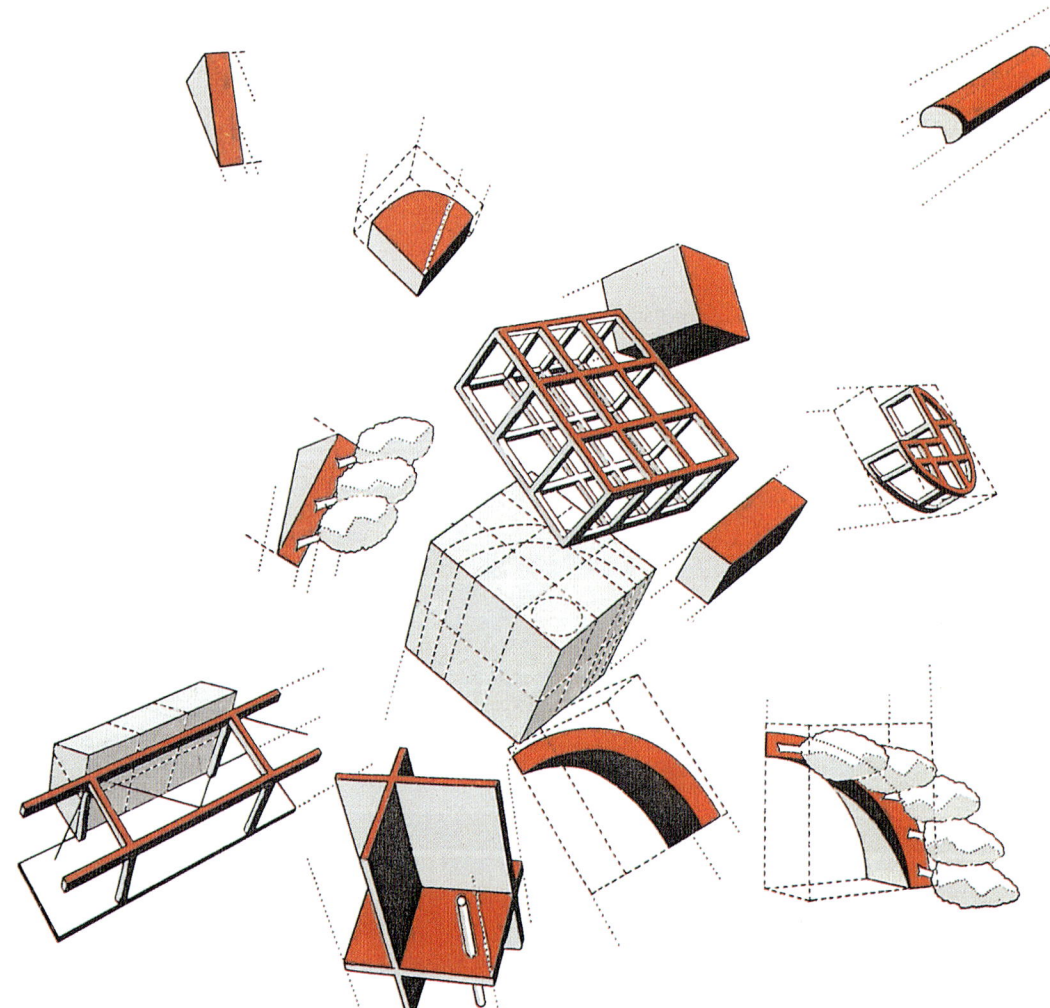

138   LA VILLETTE: 1971–1995

La Villette eludes any kind of globalising perception, who indeed would venture to claim they could grasp its materialisation on-site?

Urban formalism

In seeking to explain the primacy of the image of the park over its reality, we must begin with the surprisingly constant concern with "composition" that, from the Renaissance to the modern era, has led many designers to confuse architectural with urban scale, succumbing to the illusion that they could circumscribe the space of the *Großstadt* by means of plans that appeared to provide a structure. Thus, while an architect is able to refer his designs to forms of knowledge other than purely "formal" ones, the urban planner seems doomed to have to ward off the fear of the void and of large dimensions by devising geometrical plans, in the mistaken belief that these will guarantee spatial continuity. But then Bernard Tschumi's project has less to do with baroque rhetoric than it does with the functionalist urbanism of the early twentieth century, insofar as it places abstract motifs and other geometrical figures over something that cannot take the place of tangible reality: the blank space of the drawing sheet. Such a project is incredibly de-realising, in that it consists in rifling the pockets of a modernism once rashly besotted with abstract painting, only to come up with an interpretation that is even more formalist (!). Indeed, this was noted by the competition's technical committee, which in its analytical report emphasised the striking number of projects that "had the character of drawn figures rather than a reality capable of ordering the site of La Villette and making it come alive." It is hard not to detect here the same kind of reproach that Corbu once levelled at the upholders

> "No more time-lags, no more relief, volume is no longer the reality of things: this is now concealed by the flatness of figures. From now on, life-size is no longer the yardstick of the real, which is hidden in the reduction of the images on the screen."
>
> Paul Virilio

of Beaux-Arts academicism: "They have not thought in space, but they have made stars on paper, and drawn axes forming a star. They worked with intentions that do not belong to the language of architecture. They transgressed the rules of the plan by an error of conception or an inclination towards vanities."[3]

Scale is not proportion

The most telling example of this hyper-geometricisation of the Parc de La Villette is provided by the grid of Folies. This grid, which offers a fiction of unification – it appears to be there to delimit a site whose contours are hazy, but in the end fixes only its image – turns out to be the result of dilating the concept of the *free plan* theorised by Le Corbusier to fit the scale of a site of fifty-five hectares.

It is clear, then, that the confusion of image with reality mentioned above is compounded by a confusion between the concepts of scale and proportion. Surely, to take a scheme suited to architectural design and, having scaled it up propor-

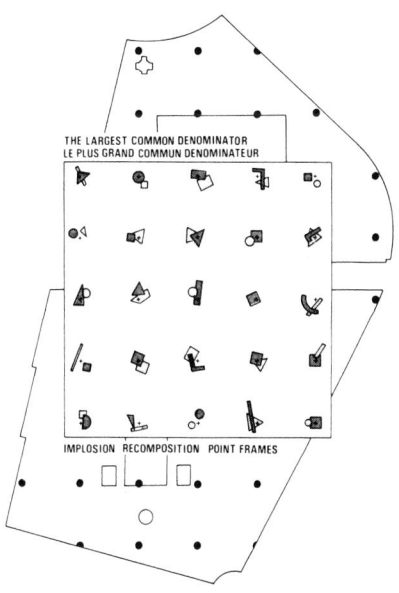

The Parc de La Villette (architect: B. Tschumi).
Study for the distribution of the brief.

THE PARC DE LA VILLETTE

tionally, apply it to the layout of a site whose dimensions are more those of a neighbourhood than of buildings – in other words, to implement only the proportional version of the concept of scale – is to ignore the very nature of architectural conception; that is to say, the fact of entering into a plurality of "levels of conception," for each of which there are corresponding measures and modes of representation. To suppose that one can think about the city the same way as one does about a building, to believe that what is valid for *a* is necessarily so for $n \times a$ – in a word, to imagine that "big" may be no more than "a little bigged-up" and to forget that "geometrical conceptualisation is, by its very principle, free of all quantitative considerations,"[4] means that you are bound to fail to make the "leap in scale" that was so necessary at La Villette. For Philippe Boudon, this confusion between scale and proportion is due to the fact that, as most commonly used, scale "is linked to the proportions that it accompanies: for the cartographer, 2 is to 4 on the map just as 200 is to 400 on the territory, once it is established that the map is at 1:100."[5] Because it focuses solely on the arithmetical relation linking the concept of the *free plan* to its translation onto the scale of the Villette site, and because it consequently fails to consider the body as the central actor of the perceptual phenomenon, the grid of Folies is above all the fruit of a search for proportional equivalence.

Tschumi has something of the attitude of the Chicago School architects who, by means of what Claude Massu calls a "dilation of European orders,"[6] sought to apply the tripartite division of the Renaissance palazzo to the design of late nineteenth-century skyscrapers. Except that for La Villette the reference used was Sullivan, Root and Company – that is to say the Palazzo Strozzi – that has been replaced by the aforementioned concept of the *free plan*. The grid of Folies was, without a doubt, conceived primarily as a tool for apprehending the dimensions of the Cité des Sciences and the Grande Halle, but in the end it was used on a very different scale, that of the entire site of La Villette. It suggests, therefore, that measurements specific to one level of conception – in this case, having to do with the apprehension of the dimensions of the Cité des Sciences and the Grande Halle – can "connect" with another level of conception, the one linked to the apprehension of the dimensions of the Villette site, without this "transfer" bringing about any changes in those same measurements. Now, the complexity of the act of conception – which lies in the necessary and difficult articulation of the measurements particular to

The Parc de La Villette (architect: B. Tschumi).
Studies for the distribution of the brief.

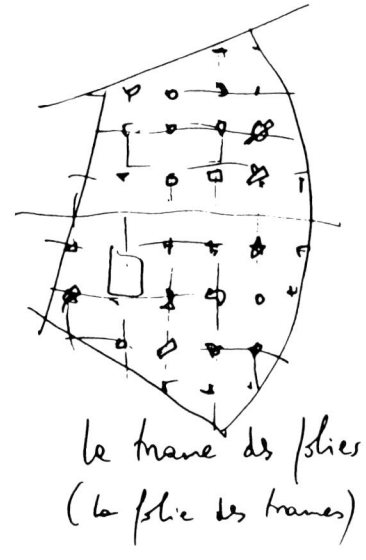

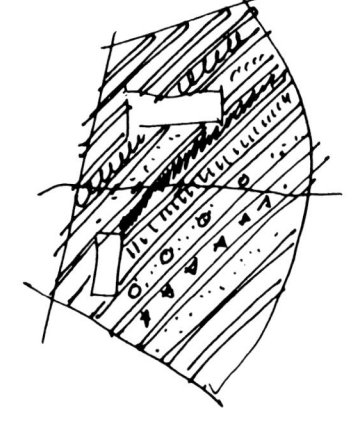

the different architectural scales that he has to deal with – oblige the architect to produce a plurality of images, each one relating to a particular level of conception, with its own appropriate type of measurement, and therefore to reject the simplified geometrical schemas that – this being the price of architecture's high media profile – the architect has got into the habit of submitting to competition juries. To conclude this paragraph, we could note that if geometry does appear in this way when an architect thinks in terms of large-scale dimensions, then this is no doubt because of the considerable indeterminacy with which these are perceived. Extensive space is seen as that "negative" space mentioned by Jean Cousin, an *elsewhere* space with vague and uncertain limits, and therefore conducive to regulatory systems with pronounced geometrical contents that are essentially reassuring (even though they may give the misleading impression that what is presented is what will be perceived on-site); whereas a small space is seen as "positive" in that it is akin to protective space, to the cave, and allows the identification and matching of representation with perception.

Architecture = the articulation of conceived space with "real" space

However, it would be wrong to attribute the cadaverous stiffness of the park at La Villette to the use of theoretical models. After all, many architects make frequent and perfectly creditable use of such models. Regarding which, note that the concept of the Folie was first exhibited at Documenta in Kassel, a long time before the competition was held for the park at La Villette. No, what is upsetting here is the lack of relation between the model that is invoked – the *free plan* – and the site of La Villette. Whereas with the architect Stanislas Fiszer, for example, the model and plot of land are subtly articulated, the scheme serving as the unit of measure for the plot and the plot engendering deformations in the scheme, at La Villette the grid of Folies is only rarely inflected. It floats weightlessly over a site that it snubs quite outrageously. From the Canal de l'Ourcq to the Périphérique (outer ring road), from the Bassin de La Villette to Place de la Fontaine-aux-Lions, there are many strategic points (in the sense that

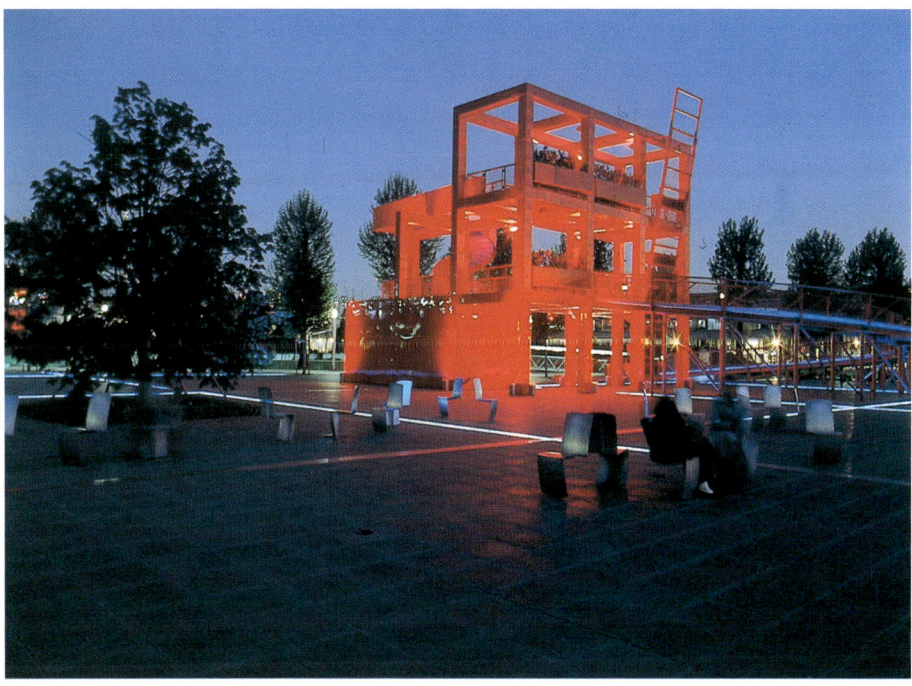

they constitute key strata of the site's memory) that deserved a more appropriate treatment. As Philippe Boudon appositely reminds us, "To articulate conceptional space onto real space is an indispensable function of the architect's work."[7]

The Parc de La Villette (architect: B. Tschumi).
The Folie Belvédère.

Seditious nature

The grid of Folies is indeed a troubling one. Although it does have some positive sides – spread over the whole site of La Villette,

The Parc de La Villette (architect: B. Tschumi).
The Théâtre Paris-Villette (formerly the Pavillon de la Bourse), and a Folie (or what remains of it).

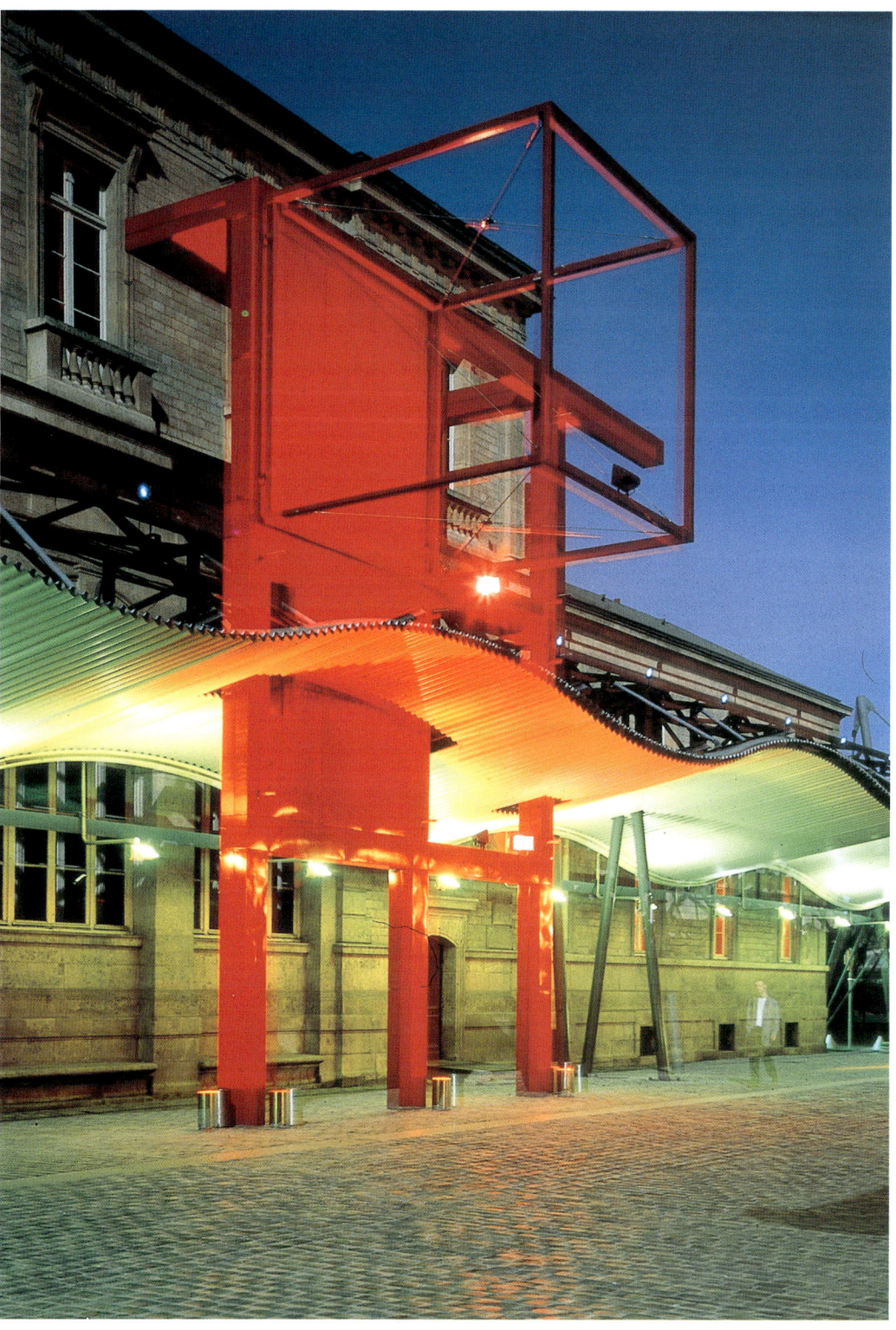

it encourages visitors to explore all fifty-five hectares, while guaranteeing a spatially equitable distribution of the programme, and with its kaleidoscopic combination of architectural styles it expresses the loss of the sense of historical continuity that is characteristic of postmodernity – it nevertheless claims, falsely, to structure the park (the "garden-city" mentioned in the inception report), a role that, strange as it may seem, is actually played by the Prairie du Cercle and Prairie du Triangle (the Circle and Triangle "meadows"): two vast expanses that are conducive to our burgeoning awareness of immensity and that, by flowing into the interstices of the grid of Folies, triumphantly draw out its legislative sap. Too bad! A hymn to abstraction, the park seemed to want to proclaim a final divorce from the elements, to doom us to a "geographic" death, and now, like the return of the repressed, here is seditious nature, refusing to bow down to the virtual and reaching out a friendly hand! Consequently, Tschumi's statements about the so-called exhaustion of the concept of nature will be read as simple suppositions of questionable validity. "The inadequacy of the civilisation versus nature polarity under modern city conditions," he wrote in Le Parc de La Villette : cinégramme folie, "has invalidated the time-honoured prototype of the park as an image of nature."[8] That history can be read as the story of nature being supplanted by culture, and that the concept of the "urban park" will arise as a response to this situation, is a reality that it would be absurd to ignore. But can we therefore conclude that the garden, understood simply as the place where the vegetal has primacy over any kind of constructed form, is obsolete? It is a moot point.

Thematic gardens versus Folies

Without a doubt, the thematic gardens constitute the other big success in Tschumi's project. The success is visual but above all functional, in that they – or at least some of them – really do come across as the spatial markers of the park. In contrast, the grid of Folies fails to delimit the park's emptiness. The multiplication of selves in the Jardin des Miroirs (Mirror Garden) is a sublime moment; sublime as the Jardin des Bambous (Bamboo Garden), where the verticality of the trees resonates with the horizontality of the footbridges perilously thrown out across the void. But in proceeding by juxtaposition, when it would have been better to use disarticulation – in other words, to try to link the gardens, if only imperceptibly, by means of recurring narrative fragments – does not the Promenade Cinématique (Cinematic Itinerary) fail to symbolise the fragmentation of the modern

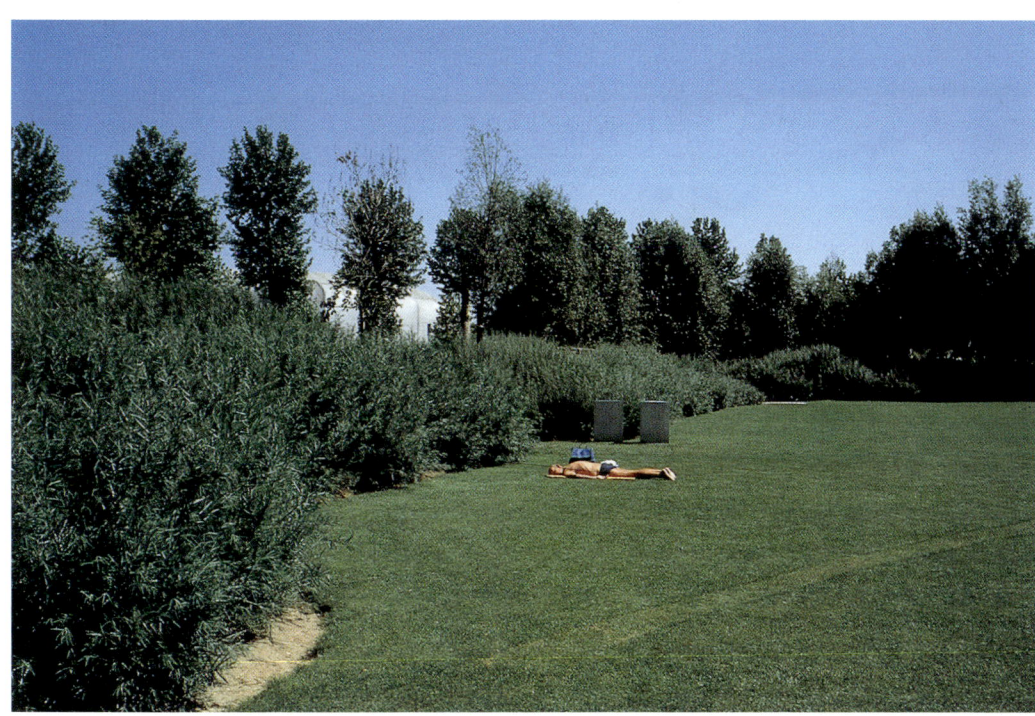

The Parc de La Villette (architect: B. Tschumi).
The Prairie du Triangle (Triangle Meadow).

world? And if À *bout de souffle* (*Breathless*) is the obvious cinematic reference here, this is clearly because the Promenade Cinématique is, as its name suggests, an attempted transcription of filmic language into landscape. But, above all, it is the reference because of the aesthetic of fragmentation that informs the entire filmic substance of Godard's masterpiece À *bout de souffle* and that immortal dialogue between Jean Seberg and Jean-Pierre Melville that Godard films in a succession of angle/ reverse-angle shots, which is such a rough ride that the soundtrack struggles hopelessly to match the image-track (or maybe vice versa). This thoroughly distorted sequence is itself only the expression "on a smaller scale" of the screenplay, which is itself prone to fragmentation. Godard seems to be grieving for a certain kind of cinema just as, today, Rem Koolhaas is mourning a certain idea of architecture.

To the Promenade Cinématique, which is itself virtual, might we not then prefer the Galerie de La Villette walkway, the most important of the park's vital organs, whose urban character is intensified by the hypnotic repetition of its constructional elements?

Surrealism to the rescue of architecture?

Finally, we need to consider the central idea in Tschumi's doctrine, the concept of programmatic contamination, for this very much conditioned the conception of the Parc de La Villette and, beyond that, is found throughout Tschumi's work.

If there is one idea that can be said to have really guided the planning of the park, it concerns the architect's power to morph into a "producer" of programmes by the simple act of juxtaposing distinct programmatic activities. It is an idea to which Tschumi very much subscribes in putting forward what he calls his "combinatory"

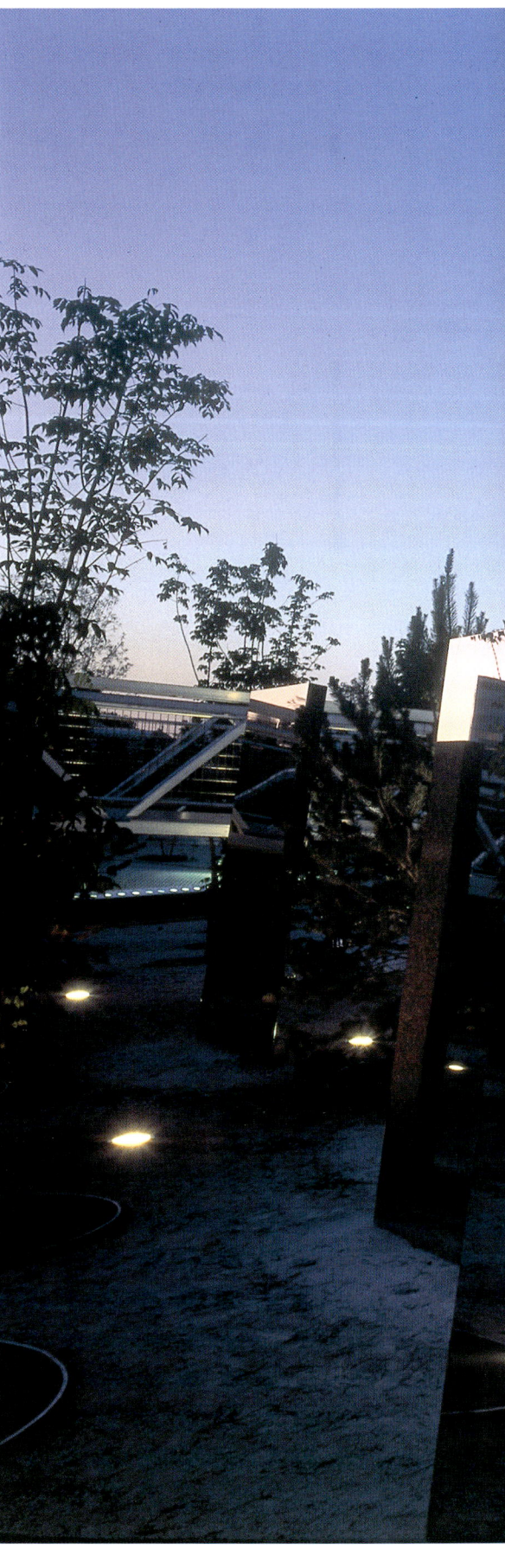

The Parc de La Villette (architect: B. Tschumi).
The Jardin des Miroirs (Mirror Garden).

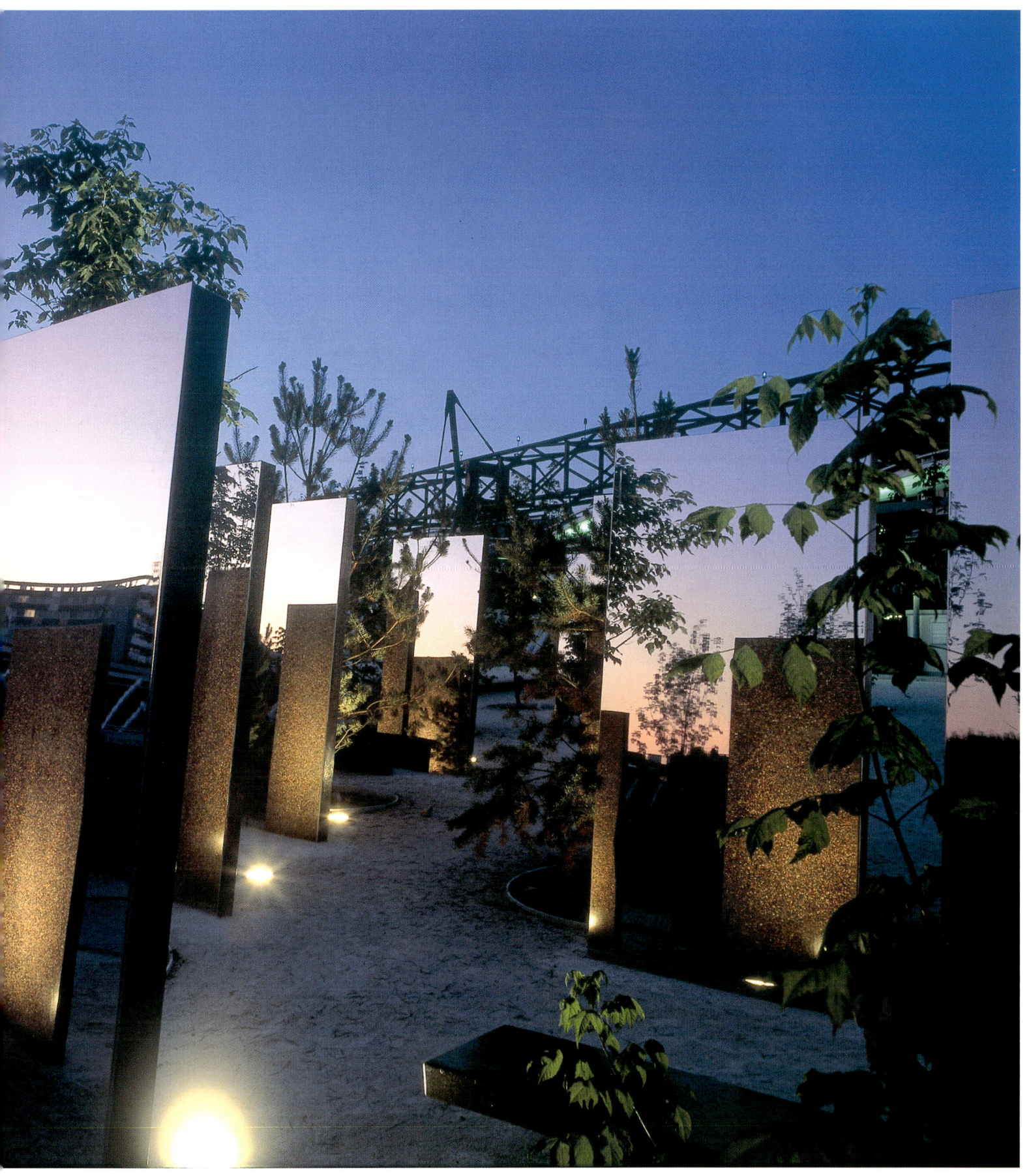

The Parc de La Villette (architect: B. Tschumi).
Above right: The Jardin du Dragon (Dragon Garden).
Below: The Jardin des Brouillards (Garden of Mists; architects: A. Pélissier and F. Nakaya).

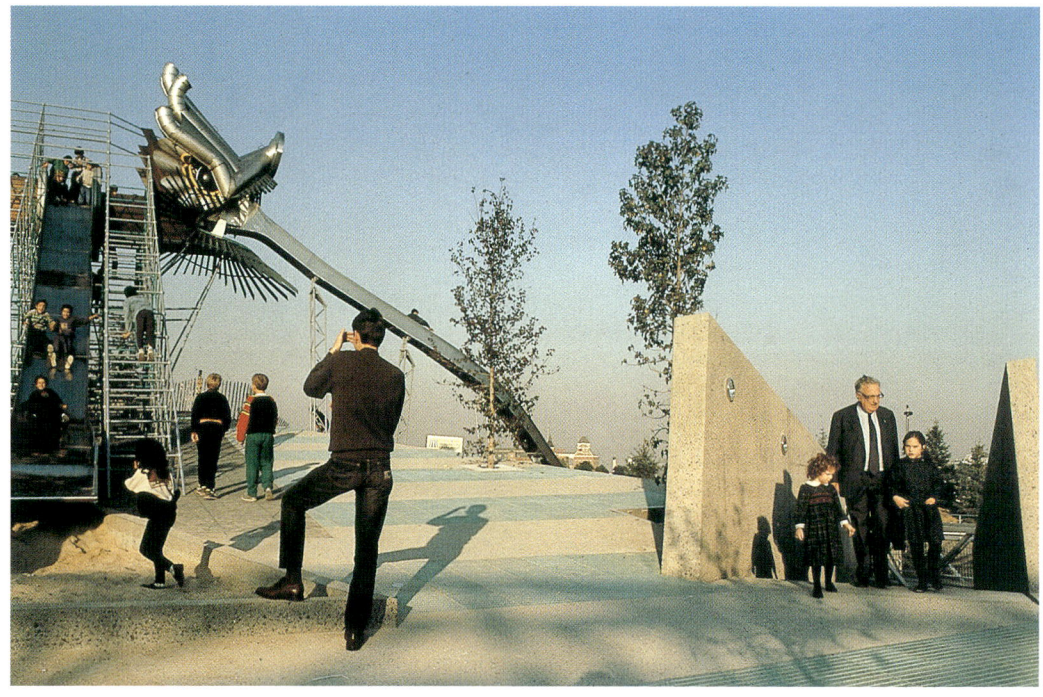

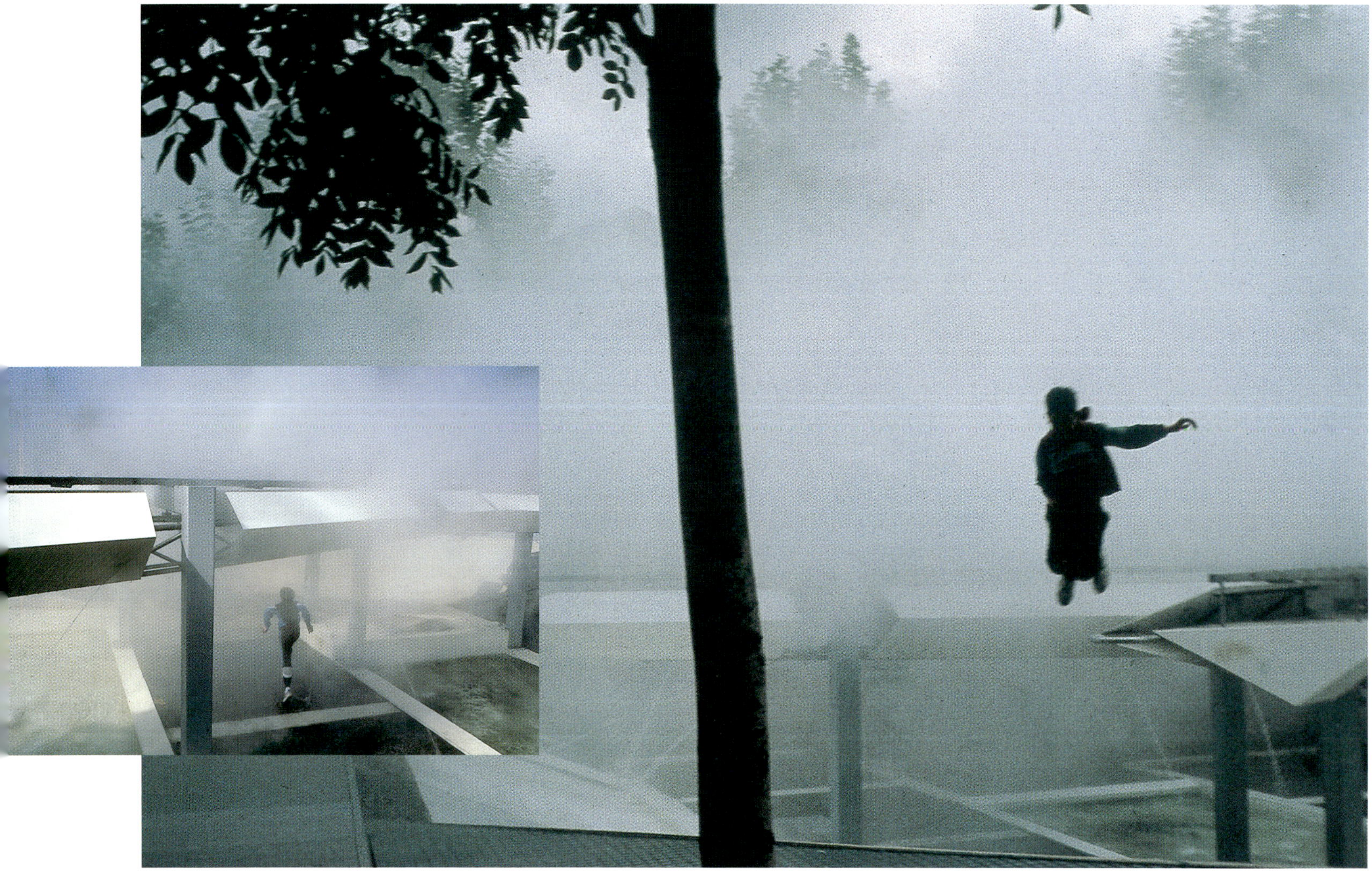

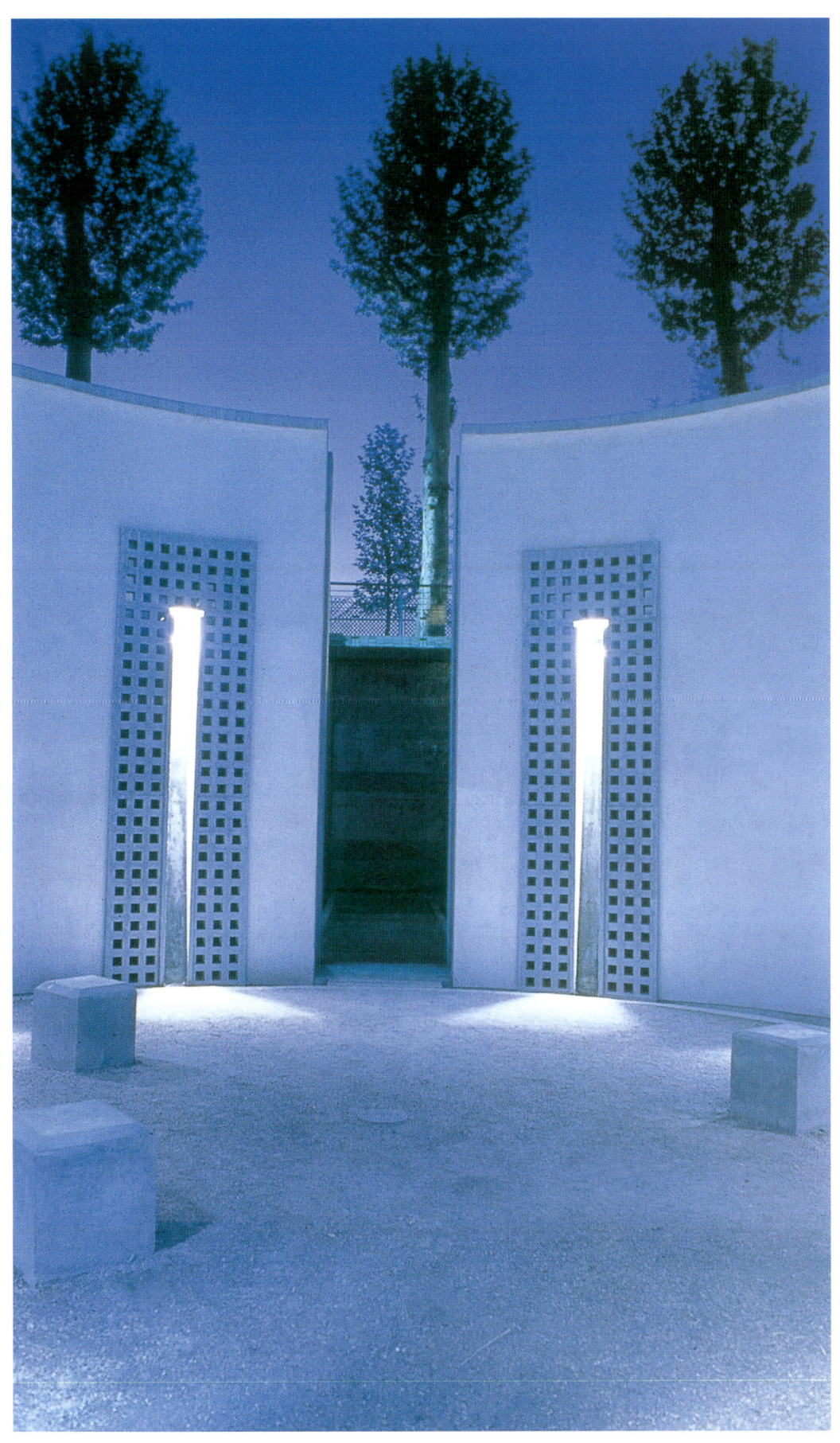

The Parc de La Villette (architect: B. Tschumi).
The Jardin des Bambous (Bamboo Garden; conception: Bureau des Paysages).
The Cylindre Sonore (Sound Cylinder; B. Leitner).

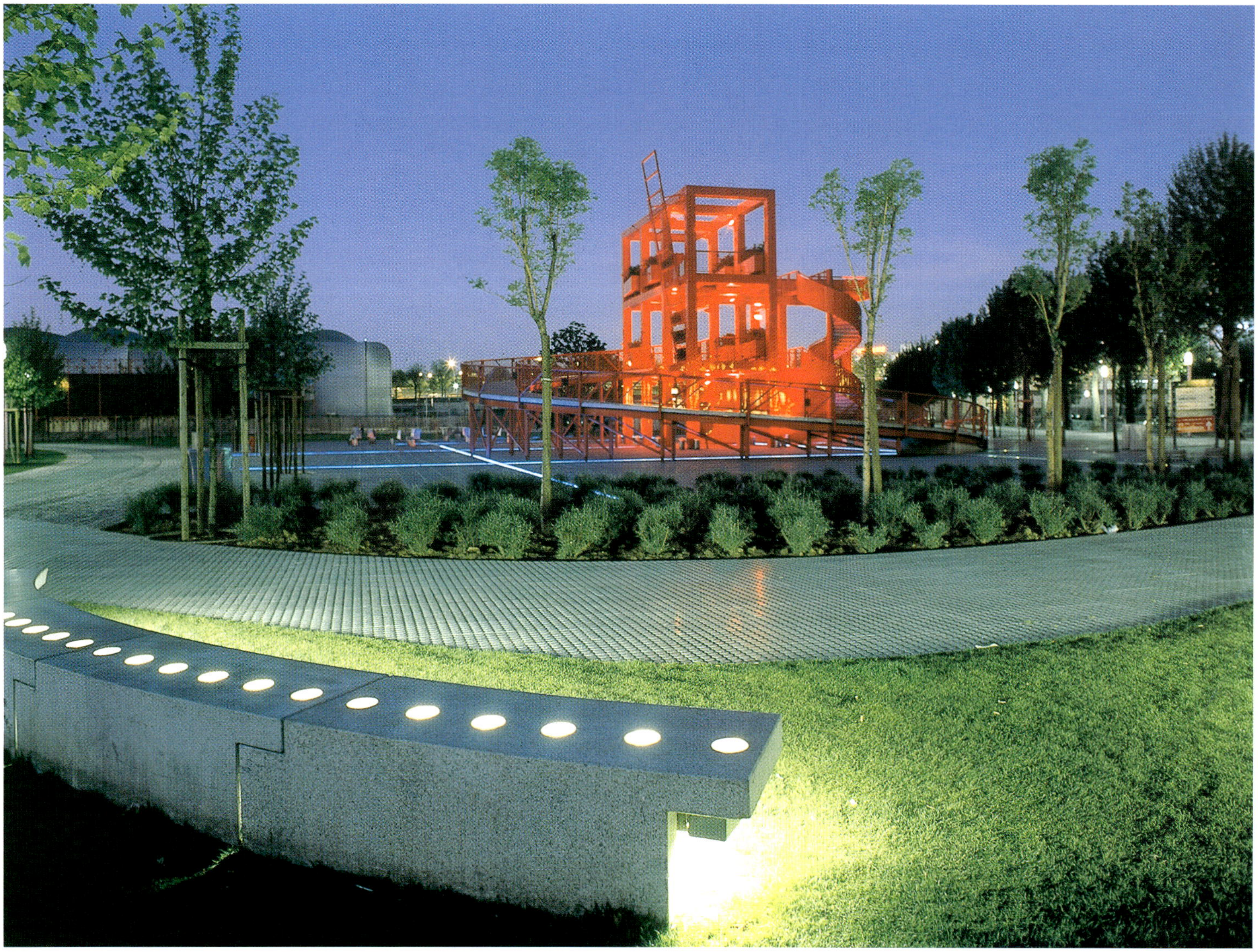

The Parc de La Villette (architect: B. Tschumi).
Above: The Promenade Cinématique (Cinematic Itinerary) and the surroundings of the Folie Belvédère.
Right: The Galerie de La Villette walkway.

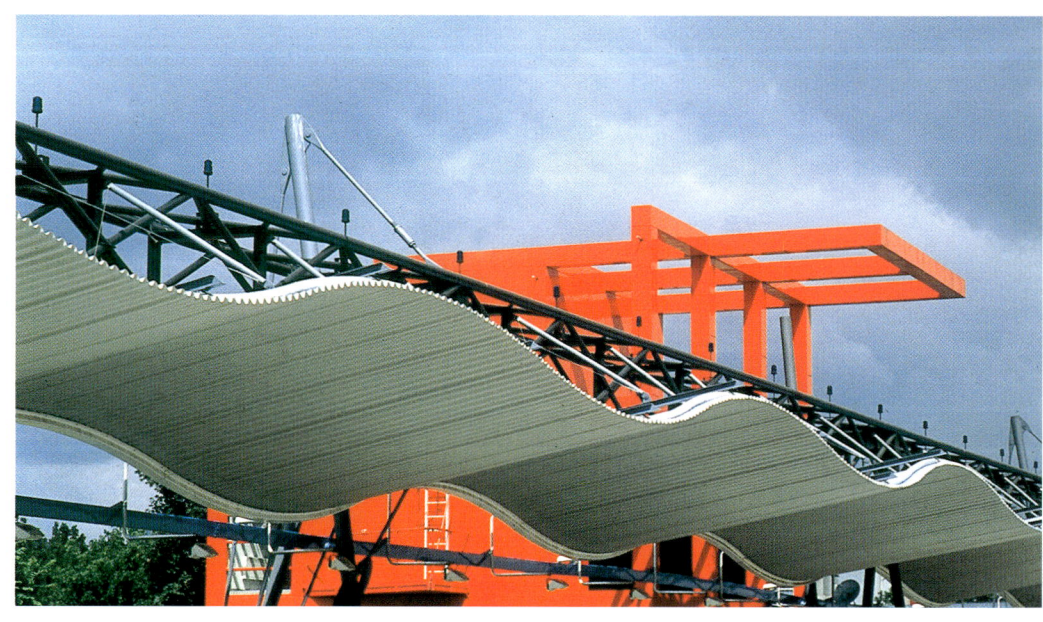

architectural concept. Tschumi's discourse thus leads us to suppose that the architect can and even must be, if only indirectly, the agent of that contamination.

Now, does not even the most elementary observation of the ways in which spaces are appropriated show that "acted space is not conceptualised space,"[9] and that these ways are often responses to logic that even architects would find it hard to explain. The most telling example of this illusory "spatial prefiguration of actions" – and the words chosen here are justified, for, whatever he may think, the programmatic alchemy attempted by Tschumi shows a desire to control the events liable to occupy the architectural space – is, I would suggest, the quickly-abandoned project for a Folie with a cycle track running through it. To this "prospective" approach that is high on Surrealism ("The pony-club skating on the Géode,"[10] clearly harking back to the Surrealist *cadavres exquis*), an approach which has on occasions interacted successfully with the field of architectural design (see the bold project that Tschumi entered for the Très Grande Bibliothèque competition), one might prefer that of Rem Koolhaas, based as it is on what the architect and director of the Office for Metropolitan Architecture – OMA, calls "relative neutrality."[11] This should be understood as a "decontextualisation" of paradigmatic architectural schemes that, when surgically grafted onto a site whose potentialities have been milked dry – what Koolhaas defines as an "automatic sublimation of the existent"[12] – can constitute a framework that is conducive to the emergence of new and unpredictable programmatic combinations. One need only remember Koolhaas' strange response to the competition brief for the park at La Villette: he "cut up" the land into strips of vegetation whose porous, "open" sides would no doubt have authorised all kinds of programmatic clashes.

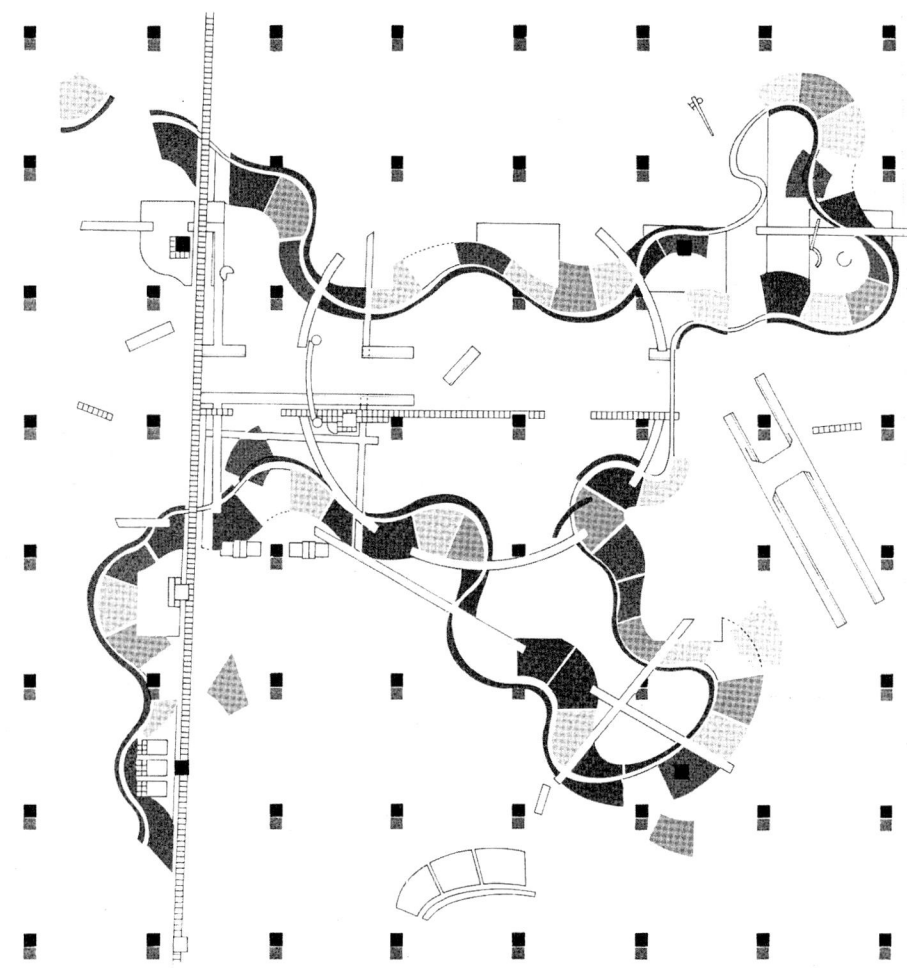

The Parc de La Villette (architect: B. Tschumi).
Plan of the Promenade Cinématique.

Utopia and spatial normalisation

To explain the stiffness of the Parc de La Villette, we must ultimately look to the powerfully utopian dimension of the competition brief itself. For as we know, utopia is a great source of geometrical plans, and systematically (and paradoxically) neutralises the subversive character of its ideas by its repeated invocation of the normative.

Rem Koolhaas: architect of postmodernity

In fact, it is Rem Koolhaas who has produced the true architectural manifesto of postmodernity. At the Kunsthal in Rotterdam, he has laid down what seems

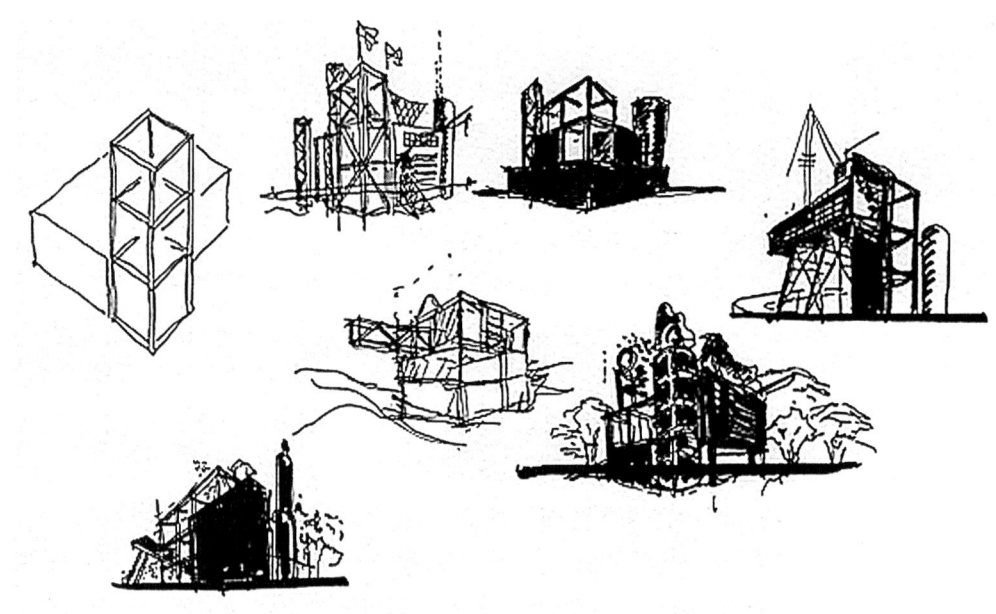

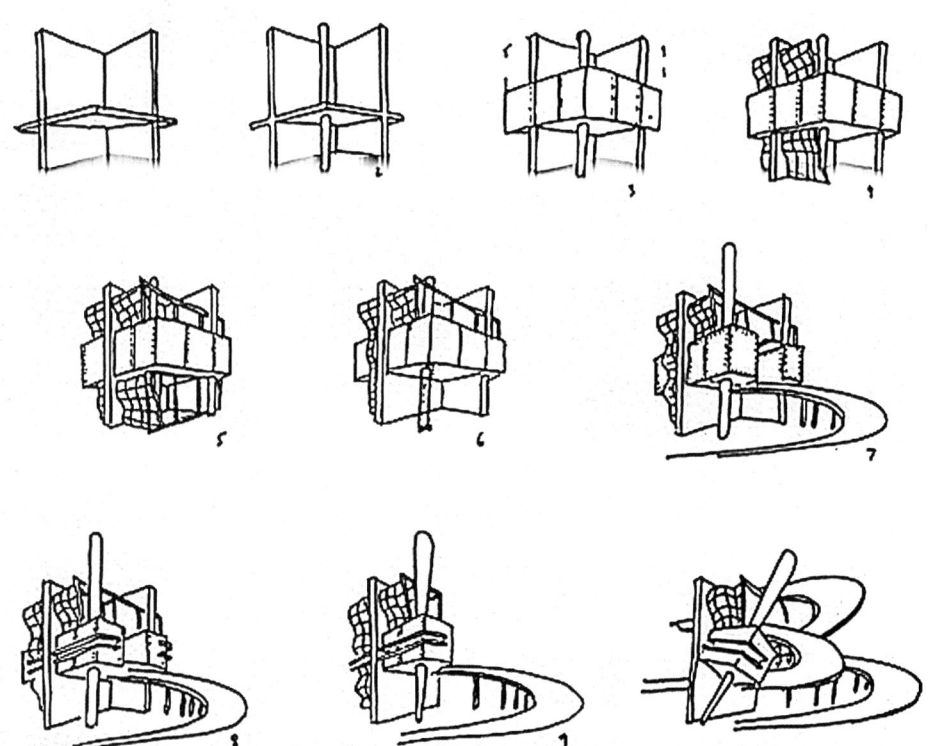

The Parc de La Villette (architect: B. Tschumi).
Proposed typologies for Folies.

like a model of non-architecture: a completely transparent and porous work pierced at its centre by a wide pedestrian street around which it desperately tries to articulate itself. This work of suture, this falsely reparative graft onto a heterogeneous urban fabric, is surely the kind of thing to be aimed at by contemporary architects, who will henceforth conceive of their work as a hymn to absence, to the self-effacing. This self-effacing quality is brilliantly repeated with the Grand Palais in Lille, a metal monster on a Cyclopean scale placed arbitrarily amidst the undifferentiated space of the generic city, leaving others to control its dizzying complexity ("We know nothing of vast multiplicity. We cannot come to grips with it – not as architects, planners, or anybody else,"[13] warned Aldo Van Eyck in 1966). The "discontinuous edifice that yet possesses a single structure"[14] is to be found here in Lille. In Lille, once again, where Le Fresnoy, a ramshackle tangle of wandering roofs, exhibits a lethal ballet of footbridges fleeing hysterically into nothingness, as if in response to a world heading for ruin.

(Text written in collaboration with Marie Chauvin).

Notes
1. Ernst Cassirer, *The Philosophy of the Enlightenment*, Princeton, 1968.
2. Ibid.
3. Le Corbusier, *Vers une architecture* (Paris: Flammarion, 1995), p. 157.
4. Gilles Gaston Granger, *Pour la connaissance philosophique*, in Philippe Deshayes, "L'embrayage comme correspondance à l'espace", in Philippe Boudon, *De l'architecture à l'épistémologie. La question de l'échelle* (Paris: PUF, 1991), p. 219.
5. Philippe Boudon, "Avant-propos. Pourquoi l'échelle?" in Philippe Boudon, op. cit., note 4, p. 5.
6. Claude Massu, "Changements d'échelle à Chicago", in Philippe Boudon, op. cit., note 4, p. 35.
7. Philippe Boudon, op. cit., note 5, p. 7.
8. Bernard Tschumi, *Le Parc de La Villette : cinégramme folie* (Seyssel: Champ Vallon, 1987), p. 4.
9. Philippe Boudon, Philippe Deshayes, Frédéric Pousin, Françoise Schatz, *Enseigner la conception architecturale* (Paris: Éditions de La Villette, 1994), p. 22.
10. Bernard Tschumi, op. cit., note 8, p. 26.
11. Jacques Lucan, "L'architecte de la vie moderne", in Jacques Lucan, *OMA–Rem Koolhaas* (Milan/Paris: Electa Moniteur, 1990), p. 38.
12. Rem Koolhaas, "La terrifiante beauté du XXe siècle", in Jacques Lucan, op. cit., note 11, p. 159.
13. Aldo Van Eyck, in Kenneth Frampton, *Modern Architecture: A Critical History* (London: Thames and Hudson, 1985), p. 276.
14. Bernard Tschumi, op. cit., note 8, p. 4.

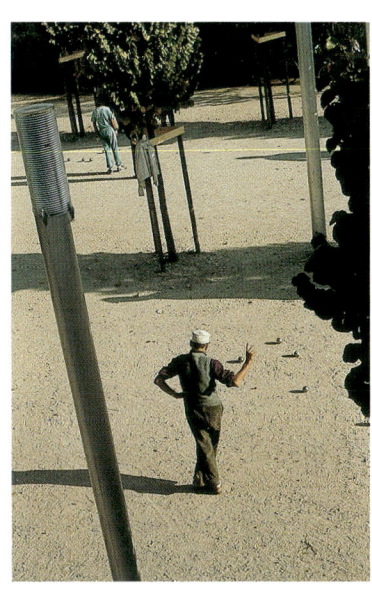

The Parc de La Villette (architect: B. Tschumi).
A "between" space.

INTERVIEWS

François Barré

Bernard Tschumi

Rem Koolhaas

Bernard Lassus

Gilles Vexlard

Alexandre Chemetoff

Jacques Gourvénec

Interview with François Barré

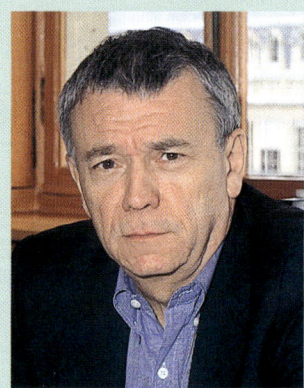

François Barré studied at the École Nationale d'Administration and the Institut d'Études Politiques in Paris. In 1967, he joined the staff of Jacques Chaban-Delmas in Bordeaux. A year later, he and François Mathey founded the now famous Centre de Création Industrielle. Editor-in-chief of the journal *Architecture d'aujourd'hui* in 1977, adviser on architectural policy to the chairman of Renault from 1977 to 1981, François Barré joined La Villette organisation in November 1981 as director of the Park Mission. In this capacity, he drew up the brief for the competition to build the park at La Villette and also organised the competition. François Barré was president of the Pompidou Centre from 1993 to March 1996, when he became director for Architecture and Heritage at the Ministry of Culture. Here he recalls the organisation of the competition for the Parc de La Villette and evokes some of the projects that were submitted.

What were the underlying philosophical assumptions of the brief for the construction of the park at La Villette?

The contents of the brief were induced by a series of premises that were made clear in the inception report. The first of these premises was conceptual. It reflected the desire to create a park that could be seen as a place capable of housing both scientific and artistic activities. Our country suffers from an excessively rigid division between scientific culture and the world of art. This dichotomy is the cause of, on the one hand, a magnification of what one might call the humanities – artistic creation, the literary world and fiction, and, on the other, a depreciation of so-called "technological" culture. We forget all too often that the Renaissance worked hard for the advent of what at the time was called the *total work*, a kind of hybrid element born of both the world of technology and the world of art. The first idea that we tried to articulate in the competition brief was to say that there could be a new alliance between these two spheres of activity, art and science, that are currently separated. The work being done by Pierre Boulez at IRCAM, to take an example from the world of music, offers convincing proof that this is feasible. At La Villette – one could put it like this – the aim was to create a huge *Gesamtkunstwerk*. The second idea put forward in the programme was the creation of a genuine urban space. By urban space, I mean a space at the confluence of square, street and public garden, in other words, a space inhabited by multiple dynamics linked to the presence of diverse activities. At the time, we considered it necessary to break with this notion of the park as a natural paradise. Indeed, after studying various gardens developed in Paris and abroad, we were convinced that the functions they performed were obsolete. Public gardens function only incompletely. They are open by day but never accessible at night. And that, as I see it, is highly regrettable because one of the interesting things about the public garden is precisely the fact that, when night falls, a good number of its daytime activities are perverted by various uses in phase with the fantasies and fears of the day. If urban life is fascinating, it is precisely because it is the theatre of a sudden switch in everyday behaviour, which, come evening, gives way to something more deviant.

Still, the rules and regulations of the Parc de la Villette stipulate that it is closed between one and six in the morning. That might be thought absurd, given that there is no "physical" barrier separating it from the adjacent urban fabric.

That's true. I must admit that I didn't know about that rule. But however that may be, we all know that rules are made to be broken. Still, I should tell you that when we drew up the brief in question, the plan was to have the park open day and night.

In addition to this first uncertainty about when the park can be used there is a second, spatial one. Near Place de la Fontaine-aux-Lions a low wall has been built with the words Parc de la Villette on it. We found that amusing. It's like an attempt to delimit a space that is by nature labile. The characteristic of urban space – and, as we have seen, the Parc de La Villette is meant to be an urban space – is to be perpetually evolving, and therefore indeterminate.

You have a point. I too have noticed that little wall near Place de la Fontaine-aux-Lions. Its shape, I believe, is that of an arc. But let's get back to the public garden. We had observed that the squares and gardens in Paris were used mainly by children and elderly people. Teenagers generally ignored them. Also, on too many occasions there was a break between the summer and winter periods. Because the activities available in Parisian parks were mainly open-air, they were abandoned during the cold months. This dichotomy of periods of use had to be broken. On the basis of these observations, we decided to create a park that would meet four objectives. First objective: to make a park that would unite scientific and artistic cultures. Second objective: to design a space that would come across as an urban space, in the sense that I defined above. Third objective: to figure out a place that would be seen as active – that is to say, designed for adults as well as for children, that would be open day and night, and, fourth, whose functions could be permanent. Regarding the last objective, this concerned the pedestrian links between north and south. The abattoir had destroyed any kind of link between the extremities of the site. Rue de Crimée was the only link between Avenue Jean-Jaurès and Rue de Flandre. It was imperative that the propositions submitted to us should recreate a link between the two ends of the site.

This was proposed quite explicitly in Adrien Fainsilber's project. I am thinking of that waterway running perpendicular to the Canal de l'Ourcq, linking the Géode area to Place de la Fontaine-aux-Lions.

Yes, but we deliberately ignored the projects presented during the competition for the Cité des Sciences. On the contrary, we considered it necessary to organise a new competition for the park, with the architectural propositions being judged in relation to the orientations in the new brief. The 1982 competition was intended to create a new generative logic that would make it possible to reintegrate some of the elements to the north – I am thinking, notably, of the Cité des Sciences et de l'Industrie. What seems clear now is that it would have been more judicious to begin by organising the competition for the park, and then to take proposals for the Cité des Sciences and the Cité de la Musique. But unfortunately history decided otherwise. Now I would like to deal with another issue, different from the ones I have just discussed. This issue is the site's geographical location. La Villette is first and foremost a place that is out of the centre. And that's what interested me when I came here. I could have decided to manage the competition for the Opéra-Bastille. Jack Lang invited me to choose from among the projects that constituted what, in those days, were called the *grands travaux* (major building projects). If I chose to come to La Villette, it is because of this "limit" aspect to the site, which I found fascinating. In the statement of objectives for the competition, we therefore stated explicitly that the candidates should give careful thought to the relation with the periphery, and particularly to the roadways – by roadways I mean the Périphérique and Boulevard Macdonald. Here, I have to admit that the responses failed to meet our expectations. But, as the organisers of the competition, we share some of the responsibility. We should have gone into that point at greater depth, either with financial studies that would have enabled us to cost the different solutions for treating these arteries, or by having a real policy of discussion and co-operation with the mayors of the neighbouring municipalities. There, I must admit, we were guilty of a lack of daring.

The lack of daring on the part of the organisers was matched by the timidity of the architectural proposals. Very few of them attempted to solve the problem posed by the presence of the periphery and roadways.

There was no lack of daring in the projects by Bernard Tschumi, Rem Koolhaas and Bernard Lassus. The urban grid proposed by Tschumi was perfectly in keeping with the ideas of rationality and irrationality put forward in the inception report. Koolhaas' project also covered the main points of the brief. As for Lassus' project, its ideas were articulated around large-scale landscape and relief. I think that these were three very fine projects.

By lack of daring, we mean the absence of relevant propositions for the treatment of the roadways. One gets the impression that the candidates were frightened of them. In fact, this is a point we raised with Bernard Tschumi. We pointed out to him that he called one of the gardens to the east of the site the Jardin des Frayeurs Enfantines (Garden of Childhood Fears). He smiled.

You're right, in a way. But look at the Prairie du Triangle (Triangle Meadow); it gets a great deal of use.

The Prairie du Triangle is still a long way from the Périphérique…

That's true. I must admit that the proposals that tried to confront the problem posed by the presence of the Périphérique head-on weren't always feasible. I am thinking here of Michel Corajoud, who wanted to put "workers' gardens" on the edge of it. His project was too explicit in its references to images of popular leisure. Some of the candidates suggested some very fanciful ways of spanning the roads. But let me tell you sincerely what I think: the strength of Bernard Tschumi's project lies in its capacity to propose multiple temporalities of use. The Promenade Cinématique is a very subtle echo of the Galerie de La Villette walkway. There are several ways of appropriating the park in Tschumi's project. This multiplicity of times for use must also be accompanied by a multiplicity of uses. The park must be able to offer a great choice of activities. That's fundamental. I've just got back from Tokyo. It's a city in which an incredible number of activities are concentrated. It's a polycentric city.

Yes, let's take this concept of polycentricity a little further. Do you think that modern society has reconciled itself to the end of the traditional European city? Do the new generations perceive the city as a polycentric space?

My opinion on this point has changed a bit since the competition. Towns in Europe are characterised by great historical density, so historic centres continue to be perceived as highly attractive places. In fact, I am inclined to think that they will remain essential reference points for the citizens of the big metropolises for many years to come. But that doesn't prevent us from hoping that our big cities will produce polycentricity one day. Like Roland Castro, I would have liked the Très Grande Bibliothèque to have been built in Saint-Denis. We have to get used to the idea of having major cultural facilities out in the suburbs. Don't forget that the area occupied by Paris is negligible compared to that of the Paris region. But neither should we kid ourselves. The new centralities that we create will never have the same historical dimension as the old centres. The presence of infrastructure may redress the balance in certain ways, but they can't cancel history. I am sure that centrality will continue to be an important symbolic referent. Look at Rome. It's a city that has developed tremendously over the last ten years, but it's centre remains very attractive.

One somehow gets the impression that candidates felt as if pivoting the park's dynamic eastwards would have been tantamount to "killing" the city, robbing it of the century-old prestige that it derives from its concentric configuration. Not many candidates dared to "open" their project eastwards.

Well, there was Rem Koolhaas, who proposed to use the roof of the leather hall as a restaurant. In fact, between the two rounds I was sure that Koolhaas was going to win. But it so happens that Tschumi's and Koolhaas' projects evolved in very different ways during the two months that preceded the second round of the competition. Koolhaas in a way "domesticated" the manifesto dimension of his project. The presentation of his project during the second-round oral was not very good. Whereas Tschumi's proposal gained in concision.

Wasn't it the grid of Folies that swung it for Tschumi? On paper at least, it does seem to give the site a certain spatial coherence. There's something reassuring about it.

Tschumi's project, no doubt because of its configuration with the superimposed grids, struck us as being immediately operational. From that point of view, you are quite right. Also, Tschumi's project embraced a whole series of notions – contamination, indeterminacy, chance – that Koolhaas' project had pushed into the background by the time of its second presentation. But, as you can imagine, the debates were very lively. I can remember that the musician Luigi Nono even walked out on the discussion. I can't really remember why, in fact. It was impossible to get him to return. He had gone back to Venice! I called him several times, but there was nothing we could do.

INTERVIEW WITH FRANÇOIS BARRÉ

Let's come back to Bernard Tschumi's project, and in particular to that grid of Folies. For us, it's the source of a paradox. On the one hand, it takes possession of the site in a way that is almost dictatorial. You could even say that it carries a set of imaginary associations related to conquest. On the other, it is intended to be the main tool of an intellectual dynamic that sees the Parc de La Villette as an architectural transcription of postmodernity, which, as we know, is essentially a matter of uncertainty, of randomness. Isn't that paradoxical?

> There's nothing paradoxical in that. What is supposed to express the feeling of uncertainty that you mention is the superimposition of the three grids. It is the tension between the three systems – Points, Lines and Surfaces – that is meant to translate this feeling of uncertainty characteristic of the age.

On several occasions we found ourselves thinking that what elicited the grid of Folies was the fact that the cattle shed had been kept on the site of La Villette. What do you think?

> In a way, one can in effect say that the park is "deduced" from the large structures present on the site. But then in that case you could also say that the big slope proposed by Bernard Lassus was induced by the local relief. What comes from the site? What comes from the architectural project? Those questions are hard to answer.

If there had been a way of deploying the grid of Folies beyond the limits of the Parc de La Villette, in other words, towards the towns of Aubervilliers and Pantin on one side, and to Ledoux's rotunda on the other, then no doubt a project of great ideological power would have been possible. Are you sure you did all you could to ensure that Bernard Tschumi's project developed in that way?

> If you are trying to tell me that we weren't brave enough, my immediate answer is that you are quite right. But you also have to imagine the atmosphere at the time. Not many people were interested in a competition to build the Parc de La Villette. Everyone was talking about the Grande Arche and the Opéra-Bastille. The Parc de La Villette was a project for the suburbanites. Also the Paris municipal council was putting the pressure on because they wanted to build housing on the south-western extremity of the site.

That's another paradox. The intellectual convictions of the competition organisers were very close to those of the people then in power, so one could logically suppose that the Parc de La Villette project would be resolutely defended.

> You could see it that way.

Let's talk about the competition brief. The inception report insisted on the two notions of the garden-city and the garden in the city. The idea was to call for the creation of a park articulated around both landscaped and built elements. Didn't most of the candidates miss this point?

Absolutely. And I must say, too, that it was the landscape architects who were found most wanting here. Most of them were incapable of taking on board the point you mention. And that, ultimately, is where everything was decided. Because the grid of Folies constitutes an architectural response to the concept of the garden-city laid out in the programme. In fact, the vast majority of jury members – and, given their very diverse backgrounds, the jury could hardly be suspected of partiality – were struck by the weakness of the proposals put forward by the landscape architects. Also, during the voting sessions, we realised that the renderings of the landscape architects' projects were very poor. The drawings were very hard to read. During this competition there was, undeniably, a real problem with the landscape renderings.

The one by Bernard Lassus was extremely abstruse.

Yes, but I must say that nearly all the renderings submitted by the landscape architects were unconvincing.

To conclude, let's come back to the position taken by Bernard Lassus. His line of argument wasn't as "anti-urban" as one might think. He explained to us that the big empty space that he wanted to deploy on the site needed to be read on the scale of the city itself. If we allow that the spatial referent is not the site of La Villette but Paris, then the big void in question is totally justified in that it constitutes a fully-fledged urban element, like a block of towers or a set of housing blocks. Ultimately, it all depends on the scale on which you read it.

The point of view put forward by Bernard Lassus was very interesting. And perfectly arguable. Indeed, his oral presentation during the second round was extremely impressive.

Interview by Alain Orlandini
(with the participation of Marie Chauvin).

Interview with Bernard Tschumi

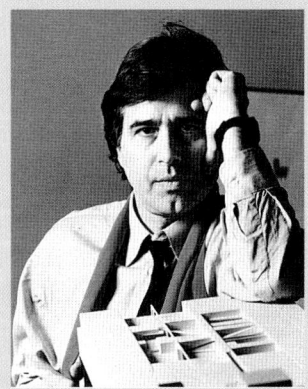

Bernard Tschumi was born in Lausanne in 1944. After graduating from the École Polytechnique Fédérale in Lausanne in 1969, he taught at the Architectural Association in London from 1970 to 1980, then at Princeton University between 1980 and 1981. Published in 1981, his key theoretical essay, *The Manhattan Transcripts: Theoretical Projects*, reflected his longstanding interest in the relations between architecture, philosophy and cinema. Bernard Tschumi won the competition to design the park at La Villette in 1983. Now Dean at the Graduate School of Planning and Preservation at Columbia University, New York, he recently built the Studio National des Art Contemporains at Le Fresnoy (Tourcoing/Lille), the architecture school at Marne-la-Vallée, and the Zénith in Rouen.

Your attachment to a conception of architecture as essentially representation is well known. For you, it is essential to link architectural thought to contemporaneous philosophical thought. In light of which, the question that we must ask is this: does the morphology of the Parc de La Villette – a morphology that is fragmented, dissociated – mean that the world we live in is no longer the mathematically ordered world that the Greeks and moderns believed in, but a world ruled by numerous, complex dynamics that cannot be reduced to any unitary representation? Is the world of Bernard Tschumi one where the fading of the myth of modernity – characterised by the claim to unity, universality and totality – has opened onto a new, irrevocably disarticulated reality, onto what Baudrillard likes to call the passage of social collectivities into the state of a mass comprised of individual atoms engaged in an absurd Brownian motion?

There are two types of architecture. On the one hand, architecture as form, and on the other architecture as event. On the one hand, architecture as object, an architecture in which the visual aspect is paramount – an architecture that strives for the handsome, static object; on the other, an architecture conceived as essentially dynamic, as the movement of bodies in space, as programme and activities, in which the reading of the work is articulated around those two complementary notions that are use and space (that is to say, ultimately, the opposite of static architecture, of an architecture of façades, and therefore of a frozen architecture). Today, there is an ongoing – and in fact highly polemical – debate opposing not only two generations of architects, but also differing sensibilities within the same generation of architects. At La Villette we tried to lay out a certain number of circumstances, either architectural or programmatic, in order to create an architecture that is liable to become event. The approach is organised mainly around the search for trajectories and vectors of movements, on inciting multiple programmatic choices that can lead to the perception of an intense programmatic density.

Like that curious project proposed for the Très Grande Bibliothèque – TGB (Grand Library project), which showed a running-track winding round the reading rooms.

Exactly. In fact, the members of the jury came to see me after their deliberations. They thought I was being provocative. But for us there was nothing provocative about it at all. The idea was simply to set up a contamination between programmatic activities that had very little in common with each other, as a way of stating that functions are never categorical but always in motion, always on the point of being modified by the close and unexpected presence of other functions. This logic, which was taken to extremes for the TGB project, was already present at La Villette. Concerning the Folie standing at the confluence of the two canals, the original plan was to make it into a piano bar-cum-greenhouse crossed by a running track. Of course, this kind of approach isn't always compatible with the user's requirements, but it's a way of thinking, a philosophy that needs to be constantly updated and reformulated as and when new programmatic opportunities arise.
A colleague once said that the Prairies in the park were "flat and devoid of imagination." No, they are deliberately bare in response to the density of the Promenade Cinématique, thus allowing a "free" appropriation of their surfaces. A free appropriation, that is to say, an appropriation by certain kinds of activities that it was impossible for us to imagine a priori. One must provide conditions for use, not *condition* use.

Avoid what the philosopher Pierre Ansay calls a "spatial prefiguration of acting."

It's an interesting formula.

This notion of the programme constitutes one of the main points of your doctrine. But you mention it as if it were contemporaneous with us. But already, years ago, when Bruno Zevi defined modern architecture, he mentioned the notion of the "inventory." For Zevi, it is a defining trait of modernism to see the programme as the necessary preliminary to all architectural thought. It is the programme that must induce the form and the form that, as prior given, bends the programme to its laws.

The notion of the programme really begins to emerge in the seventeenth century. Architecture then was conceived as a sum of functional elements that had to be linked (in passing, I'd like to insist that the importance suddenly acquired by the programme engendered an awareness of the powers devolved on the architect since, by giving his personal interpretation of a given "programme," he makes his own modifications to reality). Indeed, there is a twofold definition of the term "programme." One can speak of a programme as a "series of habits" repeating themselves over time (here there is repetition in use), and one can also speak of the programme as an "event," that is to say, as a moment when various activities collide in such a way that new activities appear as a result. Playing football near a Folie where musicians are performing is already a new way of perceiving everyday life.

Let's talk about the competition brief. This placed particular emphasis on the notion of the garden-city, on the idea that the park should above all be "built." Not many candidates seemed to have understood this. Is your layout grid a response to this concept of the garden-city?

INTERVIEW WITH BERNARD TSCHUMI   161

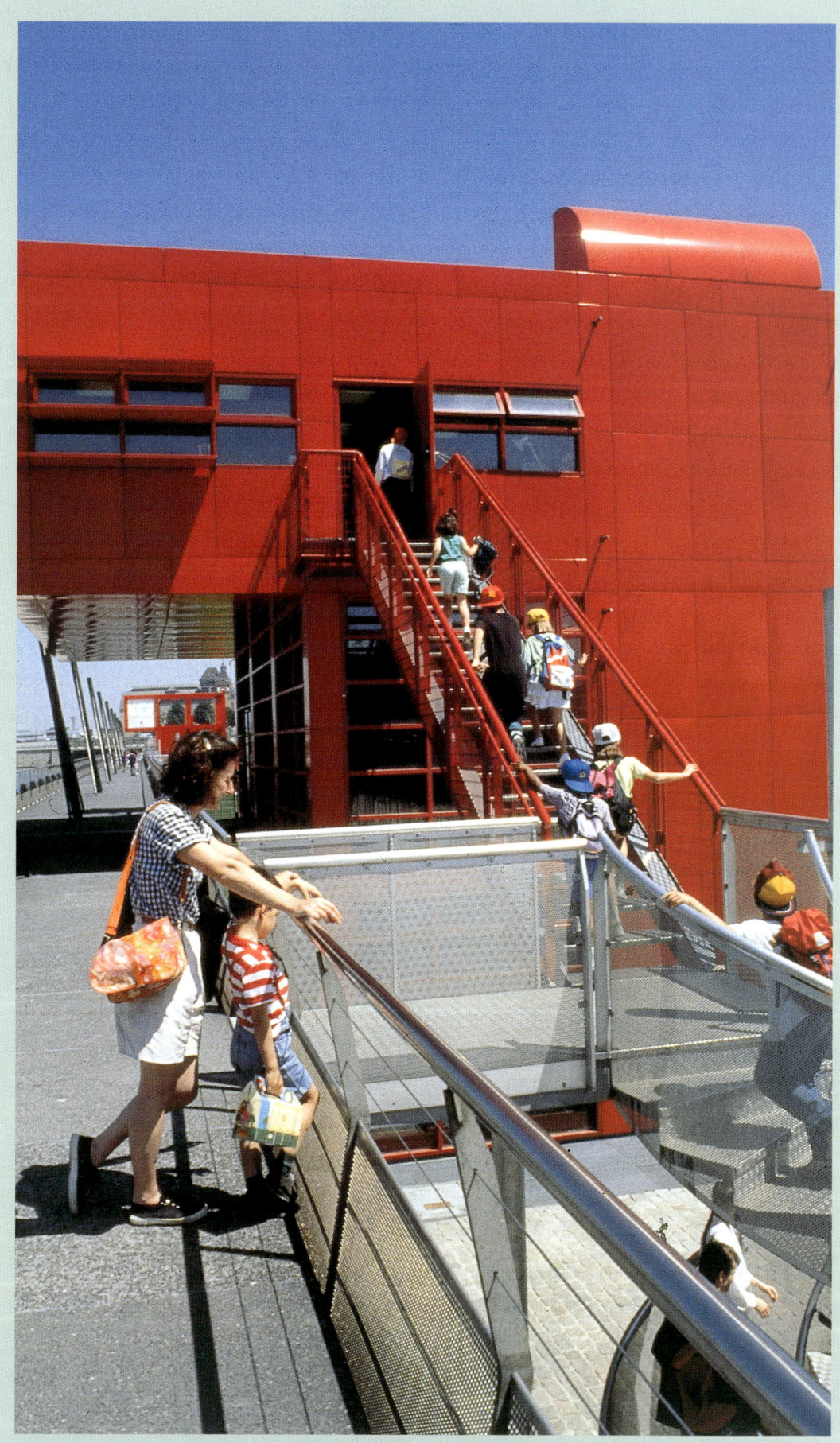

The Parc de La Villette (architect: B. Tschumi).
The Galerie de l'Ourcq walkway.

The grid is the expression of a certain architectural neutrality which, little by little gives way to a form that expresses the programme. But the grid is also the expression of an urban strategy. La Villette is a piece of city, which is why it needed to have something of the density of the built. This density is expressed by the grid. A grid that, in fact, could very well have been random. The choice of regularity here was a purely strategic one. To make the grid regular was to ensure that all the Folies would be built. And in the end this choice turned out to be the right one. But the fundamental point is the scale of the various buildings on the site. Absolutely incredible scales – almost three hundred metres for the Cité des Sciences, about two hundred and fifty metres for the Grande Halle. To these, outside elements must be added: the Périphérique, the Canal de l'Ourcq and Boulevard Macdonald. The presence of these elements annulled any eventual composition. To compose using these elements would have meant generating an academic, pompous space that would have uselessly celebrated them. So, on the contrary, we opted for a more conceptual approach. For a common denominator that made it possible to apprehend the different scales of the site and, mapping out the fifty-five hectares of the park seemed to us the most coherent approach. But to this reality – the presence of the grid – we need to add another one which has its own logic and which I call the Promenade Cinématique. This is a carefully orchestrated succession of atmospheric landscapes laid out along a winding circuit. A multiplicity of sensations: that is what we were trying for at La Villette. Right from the start there was this desire to avoid creating an overly homogenous space. It is characteristic of formalism to seek homogeneity.

Looking at the huge masses constituted by the Cité des Sciences and the Grande Halle, one wonders if their presence didn't lead naturally to the search for an architectural module of limited size, to enable their assimilation. Would the grid of Folies have existed without those big forms?

That's a good question. What are the models of urban development that we know? Should we have continued the grid of the streets, laid out a new grid for the site or, on the contrary, tried for a free layout of the site? Something tells me that without the presence of these great masses we would probably have used these concepts of fragmentation and discontinuity, but that the greater freedom we would have had in that case would have been somehow prejudicial to us. In the end the obstacles present on the site were conducive to success. I'll take an example. If you look attentively at the park plan, you realise that the grid is lined up parallel and perpendicular to the Canal de l'Ourcq. As for the Galerie de La Villette walkway, it runs parallel to the Grande Halle which itself stands at an angle to the canal. Which means that the Galerie shatters the grid. At the southern end, there aren't any Folies to the west of the Galerie, and at the end of the itinerary, near the northern square, some of the Folies have ended up round to the west of this. Between the two ends, there was quite a lot of damage. So one can see quite clearly that it was the restrictions of the site itself that enriched the chosen architectural language.

The grid of the Parc de La Villette reproduces Le Corbusier's free plan which, as everyone knows, is a theoretical tool suited to architectural conception – by architectural conception, we mean the reflection prior

to the realisation of buildings whose size is relatively limited. Now, the site at La Villette presents a pretty sizeable scale – a bit more than fifty-five hectares. Do you think that a conceptual tool appropriate to a given scale can, by simple proportionality, remain operational on a bigger scale, in this case, the scale of the city? Somewhere one gets the impression that you proceeded in the manner of the Chicago School architects, who used the tripartite division system of the Renaissance palazzo in designing their skyscrapers. Isn't there something here like a confusion of scale, or rather, a confusion between, on the one hand, the notion of scale – which brings in what Philippe Boudon calls "the impression of grandeur," that is to say, the almost affective, sensorial way in which we perceive architecture – and, on the other, the notion of proportion which subtends an idea of ratio, of number?

I don't agree. In fact, on several occasions Le Corbusier uses the concept of the *free plan* for urban developments. Think of the *plan voisin* of 1922 and its huge cruciform skyscrapers laid out in a rectangular grid. I also like very much that idea of architectural elements placed on virgin ground. But at La Villette – and this is a fundamental point – a whole series of conflicts come in between the grid of Folies and the other elements that constitute the park. The contemporary town is above all the place of the irreconcilable. And that is what the three superimposed grids in the park are meant to express. On this point, don't forget that, to a very considerable extent, the *plan voisin* passed over a whole dimension of complexity that is specific to the modern town. The *plan voisin* was a utopia in the sense that it denied the interweaving of the historical strata that constitute the city.

Still, there is something rather troubling about this grid. It takes over the site in an almost dictatorial way, but, curiously enough, it is the gardens of the Promenade Cinématique that ultimately seem to emerge as winners of this duel between the three systems: Points, Lines and Surfaces.

I don't know if you have noticed this, but our perception of the grid changes with the seasons. At certain times of the year, the grid disappears almost completely behind the vegetation. Whereas at other times, notably in winter, it is present with all the force of the self-evident.

Even so, it is the Prairie du Cercle and the Prairie du Triangle (Circle and Triangle Meadows) that visitors tend to go to.

You have no idea how much those Prairies were criticised. At the time people were constantly telling me that they were too flat. And I tirelessly repeated that they were designed, precisely, to be flat, in order to allow for all kinds of uses.

In the book on the Parc de La Villette that you published at Éditions Champ Vallon there is this rather surprising sentence: "The inadequacy of the civilisation versus nature polarity under modern city conditions has invalidated the time-honoured prototype of the park as an image of nature." Do you think that society today has really said its goodbyes to the idea of the park as a place of nature? When one sees how visitors flood into the park's gardens, it is difficult to share your point of view.

That there are still traces of nostalgia for the park as it was conceived by town planners in the nineteenth century doesn't bother me at all. But to want to patch together a recreation of the Buttes-Chaumont park strikes me as totally senseless. At Bercy, to take a recent example, they should have tried to make more of the proximity of the expressway. It's a shame. At La Villette, in contrast, the gardens were conceived as bits of city. But bits of city whose elements are not asphalt, street furniture or pedestrian crossings but a whole series of events involving water, plants and noise. I would like to say that what is fascinating about designing a park is that one day or another the natural elements will prevail over all the things you planned for during the conception phase. Speaking of which, I'll never forget the shock I felt when the first birds arrived on the site. It really made a big impression.

At the risk of seeming insistent, we must repeat that it's the Prairie du Triangle that serves as a landmark for the public. Which somehow contradicts this idea of a negation of the park as place of nature.

Yours is not the only possible reading here. The Prairie du Triangle owes its success to its strategic position on the site. And its strength lies in the fact that it opens the park to the periphery. Just as the eastern wing of the Cité de la Musique does, in fact. The great strength of Christian de Portzamparc's project is that he understood the need to establish an eastward dynamic. Place de la Fontaine-aux-Lions stretches the space towards the extremities of the site — which is very good.

There you have touched on a key point that we need to take further. François Barré once observed that there was something utopian in trying to recreate an urban space like a public square. As he saw it, in fact, we need to learn to renounce a whole set of places that we mistakenly continue to believe can be conceived as spaces of encounter and exchange. That is also what we were saying to Christian de Portzamparc a little while ago. Place de la Fontaine-aux-Lions may represent an intelligent "opening" towards the east, but it also fails to come across as a place that forges citizenship. People don't hang around the square very much.

Place de la Fontaine-aux-Lions is the place of the interstice. It acts as a magnet on various urban elements. It is the opposite of a space as forum. Interstitial places are very important. The landing on a staircase or the turn in a corridor are spaces that can become places of exchange when people take them over. Their strength is due to the fact that the functions they perform have not been institutionalised.

Looking at the site plan, you tell yourself that if the client had been a bit more daring and allowed you to extend the expanse of the Folies towards Ledoux's rotunda and the cities of Aubervilliers and Pantin, your project would probably have become an ideological manifesto of great significance. What's your view on this?

Yes, of course. However, here the word is not client, but the powers-that-be. You have to realise that at the time the different authorities weren't talking to each other. The park is the state. And the part that extends from the meeting of the canals to Ledoux's rotunda is the Paris town hall. In the climate of the day there was no way one could envisage any kind of agreement. Agreement could only be reached where it was indispensable. I'll give you an example. If the Galerie de La Villette walkway is not covered along the Canal de l'Ourcq, that's quite simply because the regulations concerning the canals of Paris prohibit this. There is no architectural intention at work there.

Yes, but even so, let's imagine that the Folies were deployed all the way to Ledoux's rotunda. That would have been quite impressive: on one side, the approach of the famous Enlightenment architect and his combinations centring on the syntactical elements of classicism, and on the other your Folies, invoking the International Style and Constructivism.

Say that to Bernard Huet. He'll strangle you.

Horizontal windows, pillars, the free plan – the Folies in the Parc de La Villette evoke the International Style, and more specifically Le Corbusier. What is the relation of your architecture to the creator of the Ville Radieuse?

The Folies at La Villette are the result of a game. A combinatory game, as it happens. Combinatory, because it draws on different languages and periods so that, precisely, the object avoids the apparent link to a given moment of architectural history. The basis was a work on the dynamic elements – lifts, staircases, ramps – to which was added a meditation on the structure of the cube and, of course, a reflection on the envelope of the cube in question. The link with the modern movement exists on the level of a certain fascination with all the elements allowing passage, and notably the ramp, which is an ubiquitous feature in Le Corbusier. But, more specifically, what was interesting here was the deconstruction of the elements. The term "deconstruction" should be understood here in the literal sense of dissociation, of taking apart, following which the elements were reorganised into a multiplicity of different spatial configurations. It was the dissecting that interested me, not any hypothetical synthesis. La Villette is all about fragmentation, rupture and dissociation. But to come back to Le Corbusier, it has to be admitted that some of his choices remain truly fascinating. What is less so is this approach that consists in trying to systematically codify everything, this propensity to rigidify the approach to the project. One should not seek to reduce the range of possibilities. There is something akin to a formal doctrine in Le Corbusier. And formal doctrines are dangerous.

Let's talk about the way your project relates to the extremities of the site, and more precisely the eastern and western extremities. A good many of the projects presented in the competition seemed to give priority to the western part of the site over the eastern part, so much so that it seems legitimate to ask if this wasn't the expression of an almost unconscious fear of the "nethertown" on the other side of the Périphérique. Doesn't the fact that one of your gardens, located to the east, was called the "Garden of Childhood Fears" express this anguish that the proximity of a chaotic urban fabric is liable to generate – in this case, the fabric of the bordering towns of Pantin and Aubervilliers?

You have touched on a very sensitive point. And I am inclined to answer that it is up to the Zénith to play the role of reorienting the park's critical mass towards the east. But

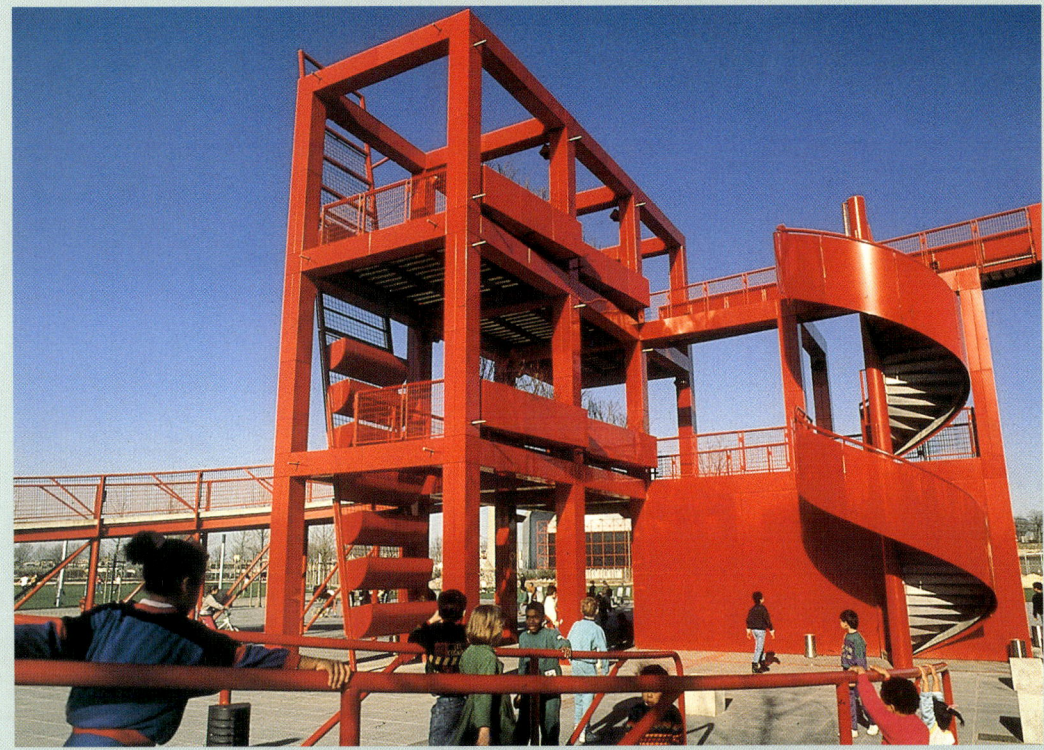

The Parc de La Villette (architect: B. Tschumi).
The Folie Belvédère.

that's not enough. However, there is, near the pony-club, between the Boulevard Macdonald and the Périphérique to be precise, a "pending" zone, which, once occupied by a programme, will become a "magnetic pole." Also, the fact that the construction huts were for many years located to the west, which made it possible to institute an eastwards dynamic. Remember that the Trabendo is also located to the east and that it too is part of this re-centring. But there is one fundamental thing that I have observed: to the east, contrary to what one might expect, the Périphérique is a real factor for silence. The park is silent on the eastern side. And I like that fact. I like that idea of a change of atmosphere. It's great to have a space that is unsettling. And, whatever else one might think about it, the Périphérique is a fully-fledged urban element.

Do you mean that you could live at the top of a tower-block between two motorway slip roads?

Yes. I'd rather like that.

Your proposition for the ideas competition organised by the Atelier Parisien d'Urbanisme in 1976, involved a high-density constructed front facing the Périphérique. Rather like Adrien Fainsilber who, in the proposal he made in 1980, also tried to mask its presence by using large terraces. Whereas today the park never tries to hide the presence of the Périphérique. How do you explain the fact that there can be such a fundamental difference of approach between two projects conceived less than six years apart?

The 1976 project should be put in brackets. It's a glitch. A useful glitch, certainly, but a glitch nevertheless. At the time, I don't think I had the theoretical tools to cope with a programme as complex as that of the APUR. But that was when I became aware of the weakness of the compositional approach. Strategically, methodologically and formally, I really didn't like the project presented in the 1976 competition at all. You could say that it was a student piece.

INTERVIEW WITH BERNARD TSCHUMI

But after that I did a lot of work, mainly at a theoretical level, which was a wise course to take because I won the 1982 competition.

Your 1976 project wasn't that backward-looking. One axis hit the meat market at an angle, as if calling for the abandonment of classical syntax.

Yes. But in those days if you said that you were breaking with a certain mode of thought it meant you had to take a position in relation to those modes and, so, in a way, to go on taking them into consideration. The 1976 project marks the end of my student career. A bit late, too.

The striking thing in your 1976 project is the poor quality of the rendering. When you compare the drawings of that project to the ones presented in the 1982 competition, the difference is bewildering.

The 1982 project is already a different world. Between the two projects, there was clearly a generational leap. Take the Leon Krier project, for example. It was a very good project. A bit historicist, it's true, but very rationalist. This was the kind of proposal that would be seriously running out of steam six years later. A new generation was emerging. In fact, it's no coincidence if, at the time, two competitions were won by a new theoretical tendency: the Park competition and the Peak competition, won by Zaha Hadid.

I would like to talk about Michel Foucault who, as you know, gave a great deal of thought to the notion of madness ["folie" in French – Trans.].

For Foucault, madness is linked to what he defines as an "excess of meaning," which, he argues, is at the origin of the new obsolescence of images. The image is above all the place of a balance between knowledge and figuration, between information and arrangement. In the modern period, things in the world are inter-linked by a whole series of extremely complex relations that attest to the advent of a multiple, plural meaning. And it is this multiple meaning that is, he says, smothered by the reductive limits of the image. With modernity, he argues, a void has been ineluctably hollowed out between signifier and signified. The power of the image ceases here to be an instructive power but becomes a power to fascinate that can lead to madness. The plan of the park and the considerable condensation of information that it plots out – a condensation expressed by the superimposition of the three grids – illustrates Foucault's argument. The park can be read as the intertwining of multiple information that escapes every form of interpretation, like a chaos of signs conducive to madness.

What are the implications of making architecture today? In answer to this question it needs to be said that the quantity of rules and restrictions facing an architect nowadays is absolutely staggering. In fact, there's no way you could cite all these rules. It is now impossible to reduce this ensemble of constraints to a marvellous common denominator that would be called architecture. On the contrary, you have to work with the complexity of systems that are very often contradictory. Architecture nowadays consists in working with dissociation. And it is this new reality that is expressed by the de-structured plans of the Folies.

In Discipline and Punish, Foucault gives an interesting definition of the notion of progress. This, he says, must be understood as the expression of the growing complexity of the production process. This dynamic of progress, because it induces an individualising breakdown of the workforce, is accompanied by the distribution of bodies in a space that, in order to meet the new demand for rationality, inevitably becomes disciplinary. Progress could thus be seen as the advent of the age of restrictive objectification and of the universality of the normative. The park, and the interlacing of grids that it displays, is very much in the image of this new hyper-specialisation of space. It is tempting to define your project as an aggregate of ordered multiplicities, like an analytic swarming of normative systems. And in the end that is what Jacques Derrida is saying when he defines the park as an "over-sedimented textuality."

Yes. And I would add that one always ends up being confronted with normative systems of order. The fundamental thing, though, is that the superposition of two normative systems does not necessarily lead to the birth of a super-norm. You can have fun playing one norm off against another so as to observe the different possible reactions. That is what the overlaying of the park's three grids is meant to do. But I would like to come back to the notion of the Folie. I can tell you a very funny story about that. After announcing the results to the press and the candidates, Paul Delouvrier took me aside and said, "Monsieur Tschumi, we are about to start out on a long period working together. So why don't we get going right away and replace the term 'Folie' by that of 'fabrique'?" I was surprised, to say the least. I told him that I found that course of action a little bit risky because everybody already knew about the terminology used in my project. "Don't worry," he said, and he started sticking little labels on the drawings of the presentation with the word "fabrique" (factory) on them. After that, the members of the client organisation started discussing what kind of terminology they should use. Anyway, in the end the various kinds of documents that were going around – photos, sketches, collages – simultaneously showed the words "folie" and "fabrique"! And to think that all this was due to Paul Delouvrier's worries that *Le Canard enchaîné* [a satirical and investigative newspaper—*Trans.*] might come up with the headline, "Mitterrand's Folly"! Which of course they did.

We are quite sure that Paul Delouvier failed to grasp the meaning of your project. He was from a different generation.

Yes, but like all self-respecting technocrats, Paul Delouvrier had a great deal of respect for new building techniques.

The two things aren't mutually exclusive. Neoclassicism and an avant-gardist approach to building have often gone hand in hand.

Absolutely. But the successive project owners at La Villette strongly encouraged innovative building. Serge Goldberg, an engineer from Polytechnique and the Ponts et Chaussées, was very understanding when we were trying out various construction systems with Peter Rice.

We should talk about the Galerie de La Villette. Its morphology is strangely

INTERVIEW WITH BERNARD TSCHUMI

The Parc de La Villette (architect: B. Tschumi).
Detail of a Folie.

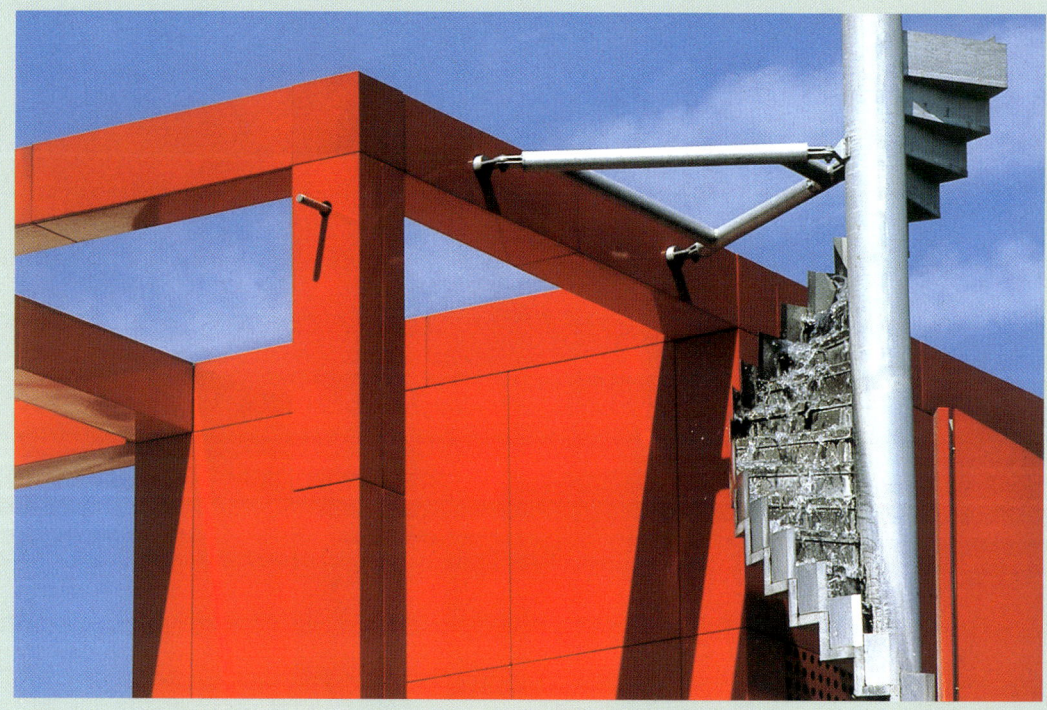

redolent of the "bar tower" project conceived some years ago by Mart Stam. Is it a nod to history?

No. The design of the Galerie de La Villette reflects our determination to shatter the sacred value of certain formal canons. The structure of the Galerie is an illustration of what physicians call an unstable equilibrium.

You say that its highly disarticulated constructive system symbolises today's world, where any attempt to achieve synthesis is doomed to fail. How do you reconcile the effort to achieve architecture that can be understood by its users with the need for this same architecture to be seen as an expression of the period in which it is created?

There are always different levels of interpretation for a given work. In no circumstances can one understand all the information that it evokes. Architecture is like a film, there is always something obscure, but this doesn't make it impossible to read, to decipher. However, what you do need to avoid is a wrong interpretation. You must avoid "projecting" an interpretative grid that has very little to do with the work under study. Architecture journals have this unfortunate tendency to impose a certain kind of reading. And that, I think, is very dangerous.

Let's talk about the rendering of your project. Undeniably, as early as 1982 you were clearly determined to affirm your project by means of meticulously produced images. At the time of the competition, did you sense that the 1980s and 1990s were going to be a time when communication was emphatically visual?

The rendering was obsessed with the idea of making obvious the concept of the Folie. Of course, a rendering can't say everything. You have to select a few ideas and try to represent them perfectly. Otherwise you lose the competition.

There's a story going round that when President François Mitterrand, was at the Élysée looking at the drawings for your project, he pointed at one of your sketches of a park in the classical period and said, "It wasn't bad in those days, either." What exactly happened? Were people in high places really in favour of a redefinition of the park concept, a redefinition advocated by the then director of the Park Mission, François Barré?

On the big sheet in the rendering presented to the president – it was over three metres long – there were four drawings, each representing a park from a particular period: the seventeenth century (Versailles), the nineteenth century (the Buttes-Chaumont), the twentieth century (Brasilia) and then the twenty-first century, which was of course La Villette. When I presented the project to the president, he did indeed come up to me, and pointing to the sketches of the seventeenth-century park and the Buttes-Chaumont say, in an aside, "They weren't bad either, were they." But after that I must acknowledge that the president was unfailingly supportive of the project. "Time must be given time," he used to say. Don't forget that six different governments came and went while the park was being built.

Wasn't choosing your project the bravest decision taken by the public authorities during the Mitterrand decade? For the Grande Arche they opted for a very neoclassical proposition, by Johan Otto von Spreckelsen; and in the competition for the Opéra-Bastille it was Carlos Ott who won. Christian de Portzamparc's proposal was judged too bold and rejected.

The park at La Villette was, with the Cité des Sciences et de l'Industrie, the first major project carried out by the new government. And the team at La Villette – I am thinking of François Barré in particular – was very young and very ambitious.
If we analyse the competition brief attentively now, we will find a multitude of contradictions, all of which reflect the intensity of the theoretical debate at the time. At La Villette – and this is a key point – the dynamic is specific to the brief, whereas for other competitions the dynamic was more political in nature. If you add to that the permanent worry that the government would drop the park project, then you know the reasons why the project was, to put it mildly, a tense one, and therefore very much alive! I would add, in conclusion, that the competition brief was very open, very indecisive, a bit like the geographical limits of the site itself, which were also very blurred.

Why didn't the competition to build La Villette give rise to the kind of architectural debate one could legitimately have expected? We put this question to François Barré recently and he admitted that, yes, unfortunately, the differences in the competitors' theoretical standpoints did not lead to a debate.

During the 1980s, architectural debate was focused on the choice between hi-tech architecture and classicism. And the real issue, as I'm sure you realise, lay elsewhere. It's a great pity.

You were a member of the jury judging submissions for the Cité de la Musique. Which project did you support?

In the first and, indeed, second rounds, I fought to get the Cité de la Musique project attributed to Christian de Portzamparc. He had far and away the best project.

Still, the park was more effectively set off by Alain Sarfati's project, which left the plot of land to the east of Place de la Fontaine-aux-Lions completely empty.

In opening up towards the park by means of geometries that were never brutal, and by resisting the temptation of symmetry, Portzamparc's project celebrated the park in its own way, too. Also, the architecture of the Cité de la Musique was so different from ours that it was possible to establish a non-conflictual dialogue between these two forms of expression.

Rem Koolhaas said that Portzamparc's project still owes something to classicism in the sense that it aims for a balance between the fullness constituted by the buildings of the Cité de la Musique and the emptiness of Place de la Fontaine-aux-Lions. What do you think?

I'm sure that Christian de Portzamparc wouldn't rebut a word of what Rem Koolhaas said.

Were there other projects that caught your interest?

The project proposed by Iannis Xenakis. I remember his famous "potatoid" very well. I would love to invite Iannis Xenakis to Columbia University. More and more, the students there are fascinated by the geometry of formlessness.

There is a point we would like to discuss with you: the way architects conceive of the idea of beauty. Your conception of beauty strikes us as fairly close to the Surrealist one, in that it rejects the notions of the canon and of order, in favour of the concepts of clashes and plurality. You regularly quote Lautréamont's marvellous definition of beauty: "as beautiful as the chance encounter between an umbrella and a sewing machine on a dissection table." Is this Surrealist conception of beauty a way of saying that the idea of beauty, as the ancients conceived of it, is somehow hopelessly stale?

An architectural operation is nothing other than a montage. Architecture is nothing other than an aggregate of combinations. And no aesthetic value concerning these transformative operations carried out by architecture can be established in advance. I often say that one should never photograph the Folies independently of their environment, even if this may sometimes be no more than a simple van beside them. Beauty is a matter of dynamism and not stasis.

When someone asked him what should be done with the Panthéon, Tristan Tzara replied that it should be sliced in two vertically and the two halves set fifty centimetres apart. Would you go as far as André Breton and ask that you be driven to the cemetery in a removal van?

Yes. And I would also say that those words should be written over the door of architect's offices everywhere.

In addition to being a practising architect, you teach architecture at

***Columbia University in New York.
I believe that you direct a seminar there
on the relation between literature and
architecture. How do you approach this
subject with your students?***

The idea is to bring two disciplines into relation with each other in order to set up the play of correspondences. I might for example give architecture students a theoretical text on biochemistry and ask them to elaborate architectural concepts that could function by means of mechanisms comparable to the ones observed in that field.

***One of your favourite novelists is Franz
Kafka. Is that because of the almost
obsessive way he traps his heroes in
stifling spaces?***

Absolutely, yes. We tend to think of space too much in terms of positivity. Architects are always talking about handsome spaces. But an endless corridor is also an architectural space. When Jean-Luc Godard does a long travelling shot down a corridor in *Alphaville*, he is showing new architectural spaces.

***Let's try to define the new architecture.
One gets the impression that, discreetly,
day by day, new forms of language are
falling into place or, more precisely, new
ways of representing reality telling us
that a new era is born, that one world
has displaced another, ushering in a
reality that is now elusive, ungraspable.
In fact, isn't the world slipping away
from us? Is architecture, whose primary
function is to transcribe the social
reality of the day in spatial terms, still
capable of representing a world that
now seems irreducible to any form of
representation?***

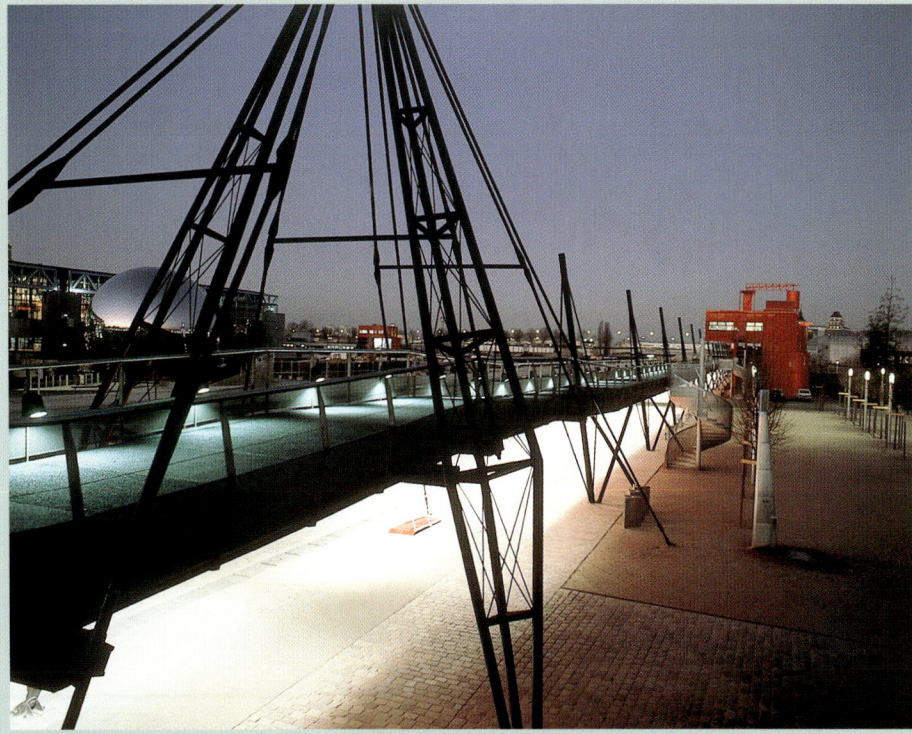

The Parc de La Villette (architect: B. Tschumi).
Night view of the Galerie de l'Ourcq walkway.

Architecture can — at its own particular level, of course — hold back the social evolution of a given period. The conception of a plan, for example, can accompany or counter certain evolutionary tendencies. But architecture can also accelerate social evolution. As far as I personally am concerned, I have always thought the best way of influencing a politico-social dynamic is to precede it, to anticipate it and then try to control it. The world can't escape us if we run faster than it does and if we then try to inflect its evolutionary dynamic. But it's true that in architecture, and indeed in other disciplines too, we are now sailing very close to the wind.

No more five-year plans.

No more five-year plans.

***Are there any architects in France
whose theoretical approach is close to
the one you yourself champion?***

INTERVIEW WITH BERNARD TSCHUMI

A lot of important things have happened in the last fifteen years. And most of them, in fact, because of the works of architecture that have been built. France is a country with a great intellectual tradition but, paradoxically, the way it has managed to improve its architecture – and substantially so – has been almost totally empirical. And so there are, here and there, fragments of thought – I am thinking notably of Jean Nouvel and others – that are of great interest for our architecture. But there is no role model. In fact, I don't set much store by this notion of the *maître à penser*. If there are to be role models, I prefer to look for them in other disciplines, such as cinema or painting. I should also emphasise the coming of a new generation of project owners who are ready to take risks. That's a very good thing. If there is a term one could use, I suppose it would be the term "climate." In France we have an aggregate of wills that are divergent but intense.

The city is at the centre of contemporary debate. How would you define the city of the twenty-first century? Is its evolution as chaotic as some maintain?

Rather than the notion of chaos, I prefer the notions of complexity and quantity. In today's world every activity has become complex, in the sense that we are seeing a phenomenal multiplication of the regulations designed to control procedure. The sum of constraints that an architect has to deal with nowadays is ten, twenty or even thirty times greater than what it was in the past. For many years architectural and urban theory aimed for harmony, for synthesis. The purpose was always to achieve a global image. Today, this kind of approach is no longer envisageable. We have entered the era of the confrontation of multiple logics.

Architecture today is made up of tensions. The public that walks along the Promenade Cinématique is not the same as the one that crosses the park via the Grande Galerie laid out from north to south. One must look for conflicts. Adrien Fainsilber said one day that the park was an organised chaos and that, in this sense, it was quite the opposite of traditional French architecture. Well, believe it or not, I took that as a compliment! For that is exactly what we have here: an organised chaos. But you need to create the right conditions so that this chaos will not be useless.

Adrien Fainsilber is a classicist, and at the same time a rationalist. He probably finds it hard to accept that today's world has less and less time for the old ideologies. But that's the way it is. This epoch is riding roughshod over the ground of the old quarrels.

I myself think that those old quarrels still have a lot of life in them.

So the future is bright for Ricardo Bofill's friezes?

For Ricardo Bofill's friezes and for the whole formal language used by the Ricardo Bofills of the early twentieth century, too.

Are you thinking of Henri Ciriani?

Who knows? In France, Le Corbusier still dominates architectural thinking. This continues to hamper thought, hemming it in with a few dusty dogmas. People who talk about *pensée unique* (one-track thought) have got a point. But let's get back to the park project. My approach is different to that of Adrien Fainsilber, for example. His park was the Versailles of the museum. But a different approach was needed. It was necessary to avoid hierarchy. My position was to shatter forms of authority.

What would be the proper definition of architecture?

Architecture is both space and the event that occurs there. Architecture equals space plus the movement of bodies. Architecture is a dynamic thing.

Can architecture today be optimistic?

In the United States, the big industrial groups are increasingly imposing their way of looking at things on architects. There is a very solid entente between the political world and the industrial world, which regularly results in a series of political decisions that are whittling away the architect's power a little bit more each day. A number of building processes have been codified by laws and regulations in order to protect various corporations in the world of construction. Now, we cannot allow an industrial standard established by a corporation to become the tool without which you cannot put up a building. For the construction of the cultural centre at Columbia University, the most inventive part of the project was given to a French company. We refused to work with the Americans.

Interview by Alain Orlandini
(with the participation of Marie Chauvin).

Interview with Rem Koolhaas

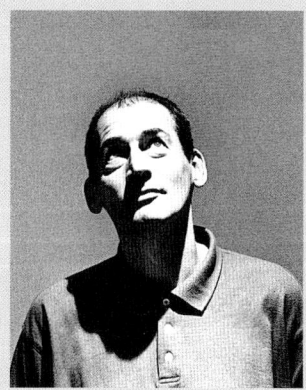

As we remember, in *Delirious New York*, the "retrospective manifesto" published by Rem Koolhaas in 1978, the Big Apple is presented as the laboratory of a "culture of congestion." Today, Koolhaas and his three colleagues at the Office for Metropolitan Architecture – Elia and Zoe Zenghelis and Madelon Vriesendorp – enjoy a world-wide reputation and their constructions include the Netherlands Dance Theatre in The Hague, the Kunsthal in Rotterdam and the Lille-Grand Palais, conceived as part of the Euralille operation on which Koolhaas was chief architect. In the interview published below he goes back over OMA's participation in the competition for the park at La Villette and considers the role of the architect in contemporary society.

The development that you proposed effected a horizontal stratification of the Villette site. The park was legible in the form of a juxtaposition of strips of vegetation laid out at right angles to the Périphérique. Was this a way of establishing a link to the suburbs?

If you look attentively at the layout of Paris, you will see that the fifty-five hectares of La Villette do not so much constitute the extremity of Paris as a chunk of urban fabric transpierced by a motorway ramp. So we must stop seeing the site of La Villette as a peri-urban one, especially since the terminology itself is dangerous in that it nearly always implies a reference to a centre, thus invalidating any attempt to put in place a true urban strategy. Only by forgetting the notions of centre and hierarchy can you hope to generate urban life. Our 1982 project called for a relativisation of the notion of centrality, notably by proposing to position the buildings of the future Cité de la Musique to the west of the Grande Halle and not on either side of its southern gable, which is what the competition asked us to do in 1984. By proceeding in this way, we avoided instituting a built/non-built opposition around the square, like the kind prized by the classics. Despite the subtly asymmetrical volumes elaborated by Christian de Portzamparc, the project for the Cité de la Musique that we have today is still somehow indebted to classicism. To let the park develop all the way to the south-eastern edges of the site, as we proposed, was a way of declaring that the non-built constitutes the urban in the same way as the built does.

One might find it tempting to read the strips as horizontal and also urban versions of the ramp. The comparison may sound rather bold, but one has to admit that the ramp does constitute a recurrent theme in your architecture.

I am fascinated by ramps because they allow for continuity. Going from one floor to another is very banal and with the ramp you can create spatial conditions that are less clear-cut. To get back to the strips, I would add that their orientation along the east-west axis made it possible to heighten the presence of the Périphérique, which can be likened to a natural element. Like nature, it too has its seasons. The high variability of traffic flow generates very different effects. Conversely, one could say that the presence of the strips impacted the way the park was seen from the roads. What most interested

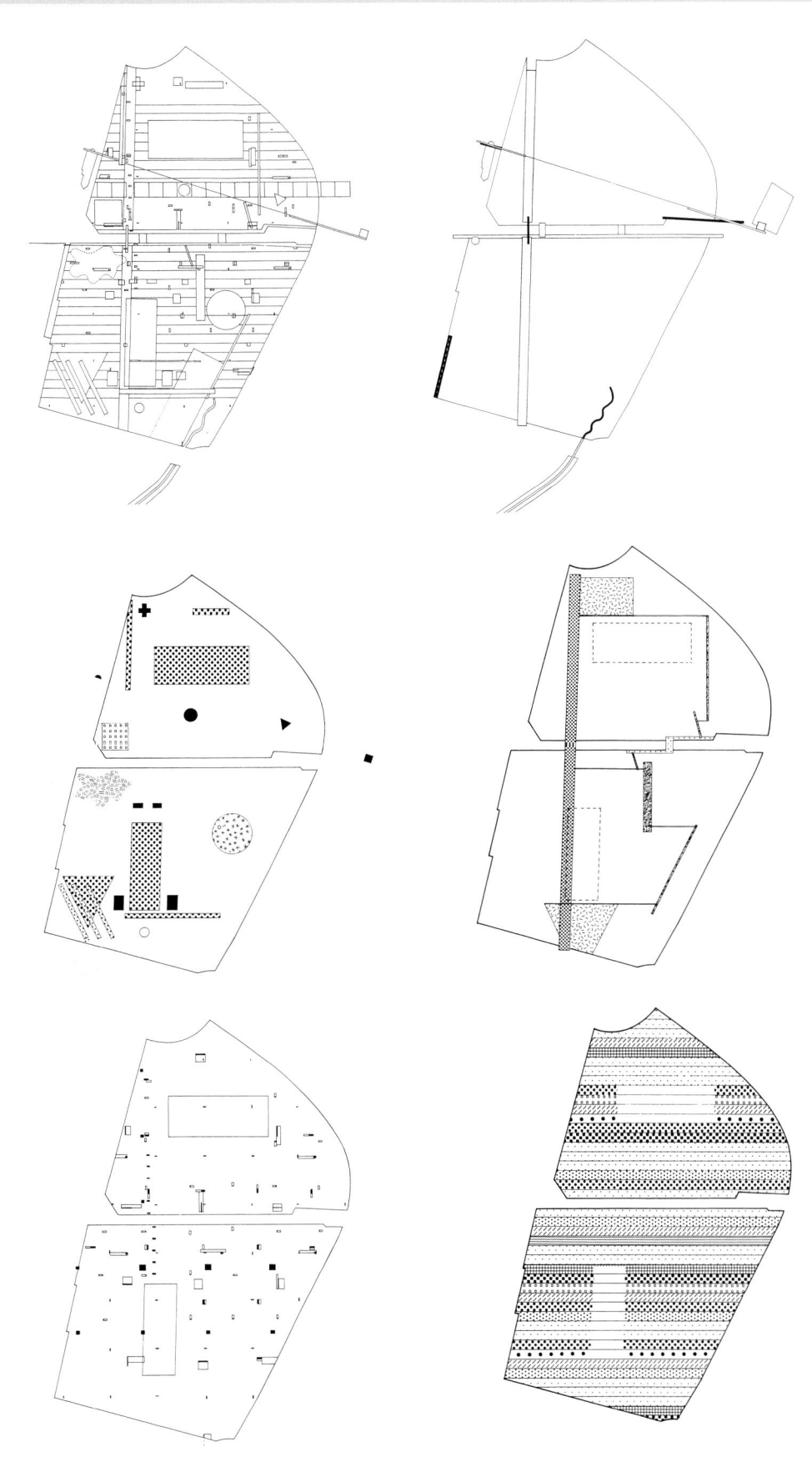

Competition for the construction of the Parc de La Villette (1982–1983).
Project by the Office for Metropolitan Architecture – OMA (R. Koolhaas, E. Zenghelis, S. de Martino, A. Wall, K. Christiaanse, R. Roords, R. Steiner, J. Voorberg).

Competition for the construction of the Parc de La Villette (1982–1983). Project by the Office for Metropolitan Architecture – OMA (R. Koolhaas, E. Zenghelis, S. de Martino, A. Wall, K. Christiaanse, R. Roords, R. Steiner, J. Voorberg). Model.

me was the handling of the park's impact on the Périphérique. From a car, the succession of strips is conducive to a perception in which the transformations in the park take on their full importance. The direction of the strips was determined by that of the Canal de l'Ourcq. This canal is a strip in itself. The logic of the strips concept makes it possible to integrate the canal into the project. We also considered a random deployment of light sources, which would have made the perception of the park from the Périphérique even more attractive.

The problem with the strips is that they almost never bring in any architectural elements. One has a feeling of being surrounded by abstractions.

It's true that I am often criticised for not deploying form. In fact, the criticism has some foundation. What I do think, though, is that the question of form should be posed last of all. At La Villette, the strips allowed us to question the way it was possible to define the city, without bringing in fully constructed elements. The density of the modern world is not necessarily the result

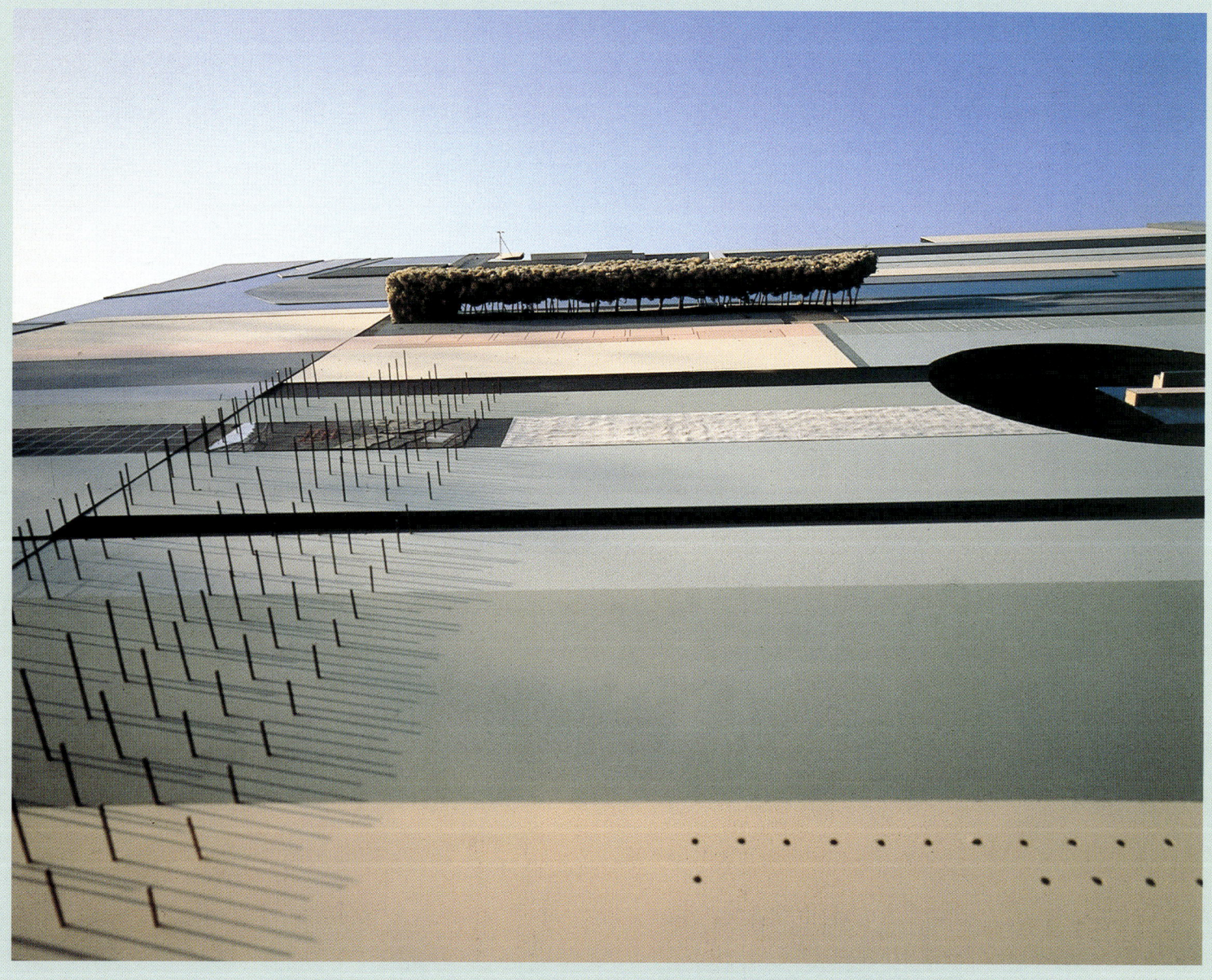

178   LA VILLETTE: 1971–1995

of built elements. Today's town can be understood as the place of a dispersion of programmatic elements. And when you say programmatic elements, that doesn't necessarily mean architecture.

Let's talk about the relation that your proposal tried to establish between the park, the Cité des Sciences and the Géode. Why did you plan to wrap a Saturn's ring around the Géode? Was there an intention to show that the neobaroque schemas favoured by Adrien Fainsilber are definitely a thing of the past?

The competition brief made provision for a Jardin Astronomique (Astronomical Garden). We chose to deploy this opposite the Cité des Sciences, parallel to the east-west axis. But, it so happened that the position of the Géode in this garden turned out to correspond to Saturn's. More metaphorically, I would say that this ring is a little bit an image of our relation to France, a relation that combines fascination and reprobation. Fascination, because our architectural imagination borrows copiously from French culture, but also reprobation because there is a whole set of specifically French tics, like the insistence on axiality, that are still invariably invoked. The ring you mentioned allowed us to recontextualise the Géode element so that it didn't look too solitary, as it does in the configuration proposed by Adrien Fainsilber. I could add that if history can be conceived as a set of temporal strata, then our idea of wrapping a Saturn's ring around the Géode was an architectural act being superimposed over Adrien Fainsilber's. Linkage with the elements on the site was also ensured by the strips we were talking about, and by the Forêt Circulaire and Forêt Linéaire (Circular and Linear Forests). Their vegetal aspect made it possible to reduce the impact of the two huge masses that are the Cité des Sciences and the Grande Halle. In fact, we also planned to reduce the latter to a simple roof, which would have facilitated deployment of the strips.

This idea of "capturing" part of the Périphérique by laying out a garden on either side of its lanes was a bit macabre, don't you think?

We had to show that the Boulevard Périphérique belongs to the park. The Périphérique is a really fascinating urban element. It's true that the spectacle it offers is quite radical, but I don't think that there is any antinomy between it and the site that precedes it. In my opinion, they are even complementary.

In your work there is a fascination with the chaotic dimension of the city. You seem to appreciate ruptures of scale, tangled networks, precarious spaces. Your rendering was itself like this metropolitan condition: dense, overcharged, ignoring all formal considerations.

Yes. You could say that I have kissed beauty, as formulated by the ancients, goodbye. During the 1970s there was an attempt to deny the conception of the metropolis as a source of signs and place of programmatic density and to get back to a more classical conception. Whereas we think that congestion is the sine qua non for the existence of a town. Congestion is the fundamental condition of modern culture.

What did you think of the competition brief? A lot of people said that it was exemplary.

There was something socially avant-garde about the competition brief. It called for the construction of what I would be tempted to define as a theme park with a strong social theme. It aimed to encourage the concentration of the different social actors on the same site. This programme was like anti-Disney. Paradoxically, it was proposed to us at a time when collective values were beginning to fade, to the advantage of a purely liberal conception of the modern world.

placed on a fabric governed by the laws of chance. But to get back to Bernard Tschumi's project, it has to be said that this was an experimental project, and that in this respect it is a success, because in 1982 people only built hi-tech or neoclassical. But if the grid of Folies bothers you, that may be because of the overly limited scale of the Folies, which makes it difficult to establish a dialectical relation between the rigour of the built elements and the freedom of the vegetation.

What do you think of Bernard Tschumi's project?

I think it's a very elegant project, although some of the theoretical aspects, like the grid for example, struggle to exist spatially. The problem, I think, had to do mainly with the difficulty of defining programmatic "charges" that would make it possible to intensify the appropriation of the space by the Folies. But I must admit that we all face this kind of difficulty in making theory and practice match up.

Recently we pointed out to Bernard Tschumi that the grid of Folies can be read as an urban declension of the free plan. We told him about the danger of thinking that a spatial scheme conceived for a certain kind of scale can be dilated or reduced in accordance with the dimensions that the architect has to deal with. What do you think about this?

The idea of using the *free plan* on an urban scale is not beyond the realm of possibility. For example, I could cite Singapore, which in a way functions on the model of the *plan voisin*. That town is composed of very tall buildings and extremely rigorous plans

Do you mean to say that if you had taken an identical approach to Tschumi's you would have tried to build more?

The first thing we realised during the competition is that the built is the minority. There is a lot more empty space than full at La Villette. That's what made me think that Tschumi's project might have gained from accentuating the volume of built elements. A built/non-built ratio of around 50:50 would surely have produced something even more fascinating. Or at least that's one possible reading. To simplify, one could say that the relation between a building and its surroundings can take on two very different forms. The first sees the work as a simple product of its surrounding reality. The struggle between the building and the site then tends to favour the latter. But sometimes too the work dominates its context, and even ends up absorbing it. In that situation, it is the building that triumphs in the confrontation with the site. That is what the term *bigness* is meant to express.

In which case Kunsthal would embody the first of these situations, and Lille-Grand Palais the second.

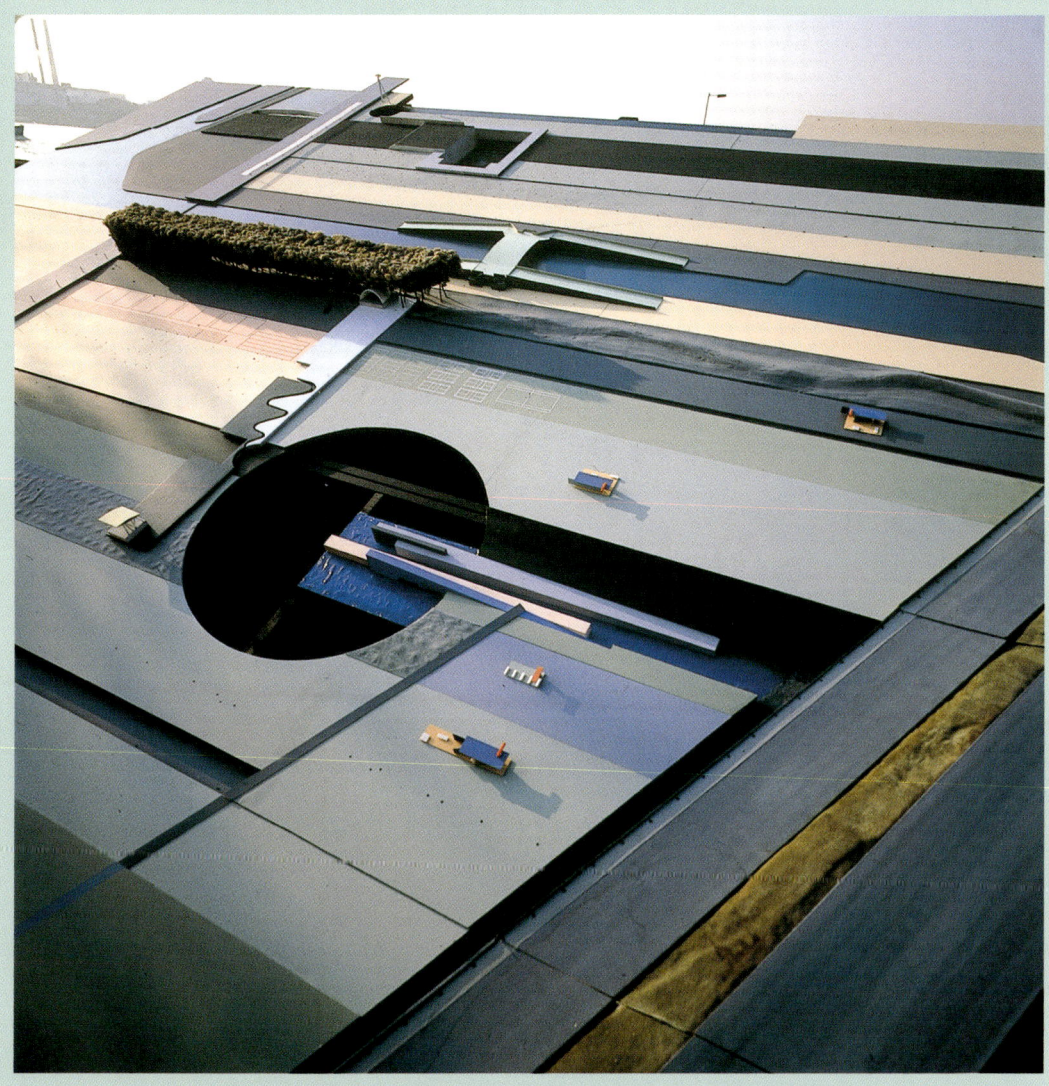

Competition for the construction of the Parc de La Villette (1983–1983). Project by the Office for Metropolitan Architecture – OMA (R. Koolhaas, E. Zenghelis, S. de Martino, A. Wall, K. Christiaanse, R. Roords, R. Steiner, J. Voorberg). Model.

Yes, and in the second scenario the architectural object is a kind of urban site in its own right. Its plan becomes a kind of mini-town.

Interview by Alain Orlandini (with the participation of Marie Chauvin).

Interview with Bernard Lassus

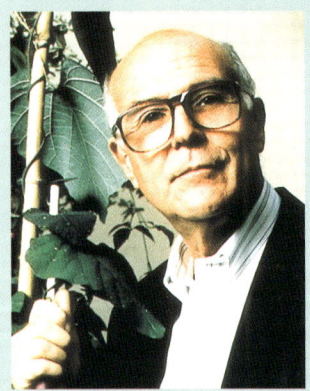

A former student of the École Nationale des Beaux-arts in Paris, Bernard Lassus combines his career as a landscape architect with teaching activities. He is director of the postgraduate course in "Gardens, Landscapes, Territories" at the Paris-La Villette architecture school and of the Charles-Rivière-Dufresny workshop at the École Nationale Supérieure du Paysage in Versailles. He also teaches at the University of Pennsylvania. Bernard Lassus won the competitions for the Corderie Royale park at Rochefort-sur-Mer and for the construction of the memorial centre at Oradour-sur-Glane. In 1983, he came equal third in the competition for the park at La Villette, along with Gilles Vexlard. Here he talks about that competition and the winning project by architect Bernard Tschumi.

What ideas was your plan for the layout meant to promote?

I would like to start by making the following remark: contrary to what was stated in the programme, the terrain at La Villette has never been flat. When the competition was organised, we discovered that the slope of the land occupied by the abattoir was originally that of the Boulevards des Maréchaux (inner ring roads). If the lie of the land was modified – the modifications took place when the abattoir was built – this was done simply to ensure that the cattle arriving on the site didn't break their legs when they came out of the wagons! That is the main reason for the alteration of the terrain. Originally, this followed the slope of the Seine Valley. Since the project had to be integrated into the urban fabric – that was one of the points laid out in the brief – we thought it was relevant to reproduce the site's original declivity with a big sloping area.

What visual artifices did you use to make this considerable difference in level between the highest point and Avenue Jean-Jaurès visually and functionally accessible?

The slope you are referring to was a slab. Below there was an incredible number of local premises. From Place de la Fontaine-aux-Lions you could get to some of the spaces located below. There was, therefore, no wall facing the avenue. Elsewhere, an alley ran alongside the east façade of the Grande Halle, linking Place de la Fontaine-aux-Lions to the area round the Canal de l'Ourcq. Its function was to provide the link between the centre of the plot and the surrounding fabric.

Was your rendering sufficiently explicit?

We gave a lot of thought to the notion of the ground, and no doubt this was to the detriment of the rendering. Our representation was literal and not sufficiently imagistic. That was the great weakness of our project, I must admit. We also spent a lot of time on noise-related problems. The two main ideas were, on the one hand, to aim for a geographical perception of the site and, on the other, to get rid of the noise pollution from the Périphérique. This latter problem was solved by having a vertical garden positioned on the edge of the traffic lanes. If you analyse the nine projects selected for the second round of the competition, none of them treated the problem of noise pollution as we did.

Gilles Vexlard's project proposed the construction of a sloping plane going down towards the Périphérique. This was in many ways almost identical to your idea, except that it chose a different direction for the axis of the slope.

That's true. But there was something paradoxical about that project: on the one hand, it appealed to a geographical perception of the site by highlighting its dimensions through the use of this slope you mention, and on the other it authorised the "seizure" of the space via a raised gallery walkway. The gallery is an architectural concept, not a landscape one.

I only recently became aware of the similarity between your two projects. That gives an idea of the time you need to assimilate the information contained in a layout plan.

You do need a lot of time. And the competitions happen too quickly.

Let's get back to your proposal, and particularly this notion of geographical scale.

The great strength of this site was its sheer extent. Paris had no other site with the dimensions of La Villette. The value of this place was above all the immense expanse of its surface, and for us it was logical to keep that. But in those days, the notion of emptiness wasn't as fashionable as it is today. Proof of that was provided by the jury, who chose Bernard Tschumi's project, a project that, articulated as it was around the criss-crossing of the site by a series of built elements, explicitly rejected the primacy of the void that we were calling for. Our option was a great emptiness. An emptiness whose limits were infinite because the crest line of the slope merged with the sky. To work within the original slope and extend the surface of the terrain – that's the idea we wanted to promote. The other point was the handling of noise. I have the impression that the perception we have of the Prairie du Triangle is denatured by noise. The noise pollution from the Boulevard Périphérique and the Boulevards des Maréchaux come together too violently there. Let me give you an example. I am currently finishing a small square in the 11th arrondissement of Paris. This square, which gives on to Rue de Charonne, was designed to include an anti-noise embankment three metres high. Quite simply, A place only means something if it gets you away from the noise. If there is noise, your space no longer exists.

Wasn't the idea of making the Grande Halle disappear beneath a slab a bit provocative?

Absolutely not. And even today I am sure that the idea would have allowed for some astonishing visual perceptions. On one side, to the south, the Grande Halle completely disappearing; on the other, to the north, the Halle rising up silently above the slab. But that frightened people, I know.

Quite a few candidates were troubled by the presence of the cattle shed. Bernard Tschumi told me that he worked out the grid of Folies as a way of grasping its monstrous dimensions.

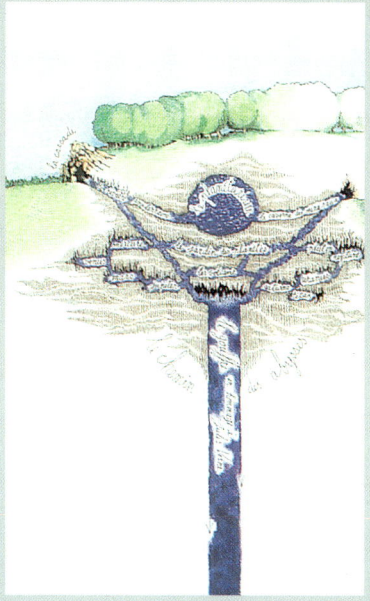

Competition for the construction of the Parc de La Villette (1982–1983). Project by B. Lassus. The Jardin Vertical (Vertical Garden).

INTERVIEW WITH BERNARD LASSUS

Competition for the construction of the Parc de La Villette (1982–1983). Project by B. Lassus. The Jardin Vertical (Vertical Garden).

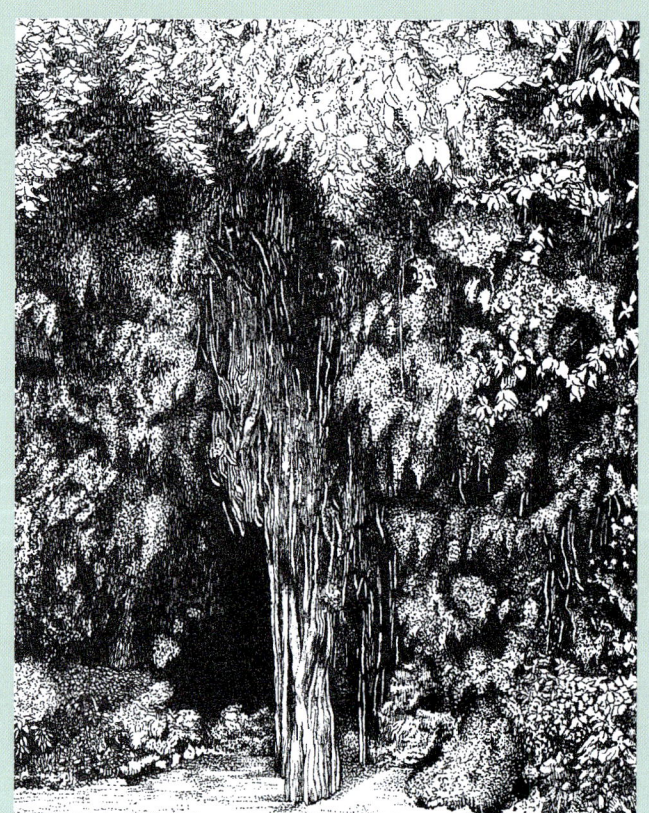

Which suggests that in a way it disturbed him too.

For me, Bernard Tschumi's project doesn't take into account the problem of the ground. And that's why I can say that the concept of landscape has too often been approached via the notion of the vegetal. La Villette was essentially about relief. I'd like to use an image here. In architecture, there is the carcassing on one side and the light work on the other. When it comes to landscaping, you could say that the relief is the carcassing, and the vegetation the light work. And I set great store by the relief. In the end, the jury failed to pick up on the metaphorical dimension of the slope. If the Grande Halle was swallowed up under the slab, the idea was precisely to insist on the importance of the relief.

Even so, burying the cattle shed beneath a slab did mean that you wanted to *privilege a geographical perception of the site to the detriment of its built elements.*

The project had to allow the place to exist. And that meant – a fundamental point, this – restoring the credibility of the canal. What is a canal if not a gauge of the slope? By creating a slope, I was giving meaning to the presence of the canal. It became a canal again. More than that, in fact: even though it was metaphorical, the slope restored meaning to the canal and lock. One must understand that La Villette was an artificial place. Artificial in that its morphology was codified by a canal and a lock. The presence of these two elements inevitably signified the site's immersion in the world of artificiality. Once meaning was restored to the canal and lock, the site became associated with the notion of urban mastery. The slope that we wanted to make was originally meant to restore the artificiality of the site by redefining the specific space constituted by the canal and the lock.

The competition brief insisted heavily on the notion of the urban park. The idea, it seems, was to call for the construction of a park, the perception of which would be closely linked to the idea of activities. Now, you seem to have adopted a "naturalist" intellectual logic that consecrated the primacy of the reality of nature over that of culture.

Can a town exist without empty spaces? I would say not. And I don't see how the fact of infusing empty spaces with tension need inevitably be antithetical to the notion of urban space. Look at London. Or take the example of Central Park in New York. There cannot be an opposition between these two notions that are emptiness and urban space. But, don't forget, our project integrated a whole series of activities. Local activities – which we located on the site of today's Cité de la Musique – and more general activities, which were positioned inside the Jardin Vertical (Vertical Garden). My proposition thus took on board the two notions of landscape and activity. But in my opinion, people have always found the idea of emptiness a bit frightening. It is certain that nowadays they would think long and hard before putting an empty space of over fifteen hectares in front of Invalides. In 1982, we weren't very much at home with all these ideas of before and beyond, of self-contained spaces, of interior or exterior spaces. Things have changed a lot since then.

The problematic that you raise there is the one that Christian de Portzamparc argues for. For him, there is fullness on one side – the totem – and emptiness – the clearing – on the other. And between the two, is architecture, whose role it is to provide the link. But let's get back to your project. Wasn't the positioning of the Jardin Vertical on the edge of the Périphérique a way of denying the reality of the urban world, which is also made up of motorway ramps? Isn't living in a city also about recognising what Jean Nouvel calls "the poetics of reality"?

I am not denying the reality of the Périphérique, I am denying the noise. That's not at all the same thing. At La Villette the noise had to be got rid of. Indeed, this problem is very topical because the recent law on noise pollution now allows us to build the necessary structures around roads that are considered noisy. As for our concept of the Jardin Vertical, it offered a highly relevant solution because it took into consideration both the deep- and high-pitched noises coming out of the different sources on the site. In fact, eminent scientists backed us up on this point when we were designing it. We had dreamed up a system that could transform the noise of the Périphérique into the croaking of frogs. But I'd like to come back to this idea of the twenty-first-century park. In the classical era, there was an opposition between the architect's building, which was perceived as the sanctuary of finitude, and the landscaped garden, seen as a space to be conquered. Remember Cook's famous words: over the horizon. In the classical era, the perception of horizontality was thus intimately linked to the notion of infinity. But today we are in a system that is entirely measurable – horizontally, I mean. Whereas what is incommensurate is depth, verticality. That's why I thought it was fundamental to substitute the concept of the classical garden, which was defined as the place of opposition between the measurability of the château and the measurelessness of the forest, with the concept of the "vertical" garden, in other words, a garden no longer understood as a "garden to be conquered" – that is, horizontally measurable – but more as a garden that has effected the transformation of its horizon into a vertical horizon. The Jardin Vertical was a kind of theoretical manifesto whose purpose was to illustrate the new period that we have now entered.

Your project has an underlying logic of order. It aims to articulate a series of locations within a unifying plan. Don't you think that a proposal of this kind

tends to give a misleading image of the postmodern world, which is made up essentially of ruptures, of disjunctions? As Jean-François Lyotard would say, we have to learn to say goodbye to our meta-narratives.

But, the notion of heterogeneity that is often associated with the concept of post-modernity was a constitutive point in my proposal. By answering the big slope running from north to south, the vertical garden gives rise to multiple perceptions. It all depends on the scale on which you are reading it. I'd like to come back to Bernard Tschumi's project for a moment, then you'll understand better what I mean. This project proves one thing. It proves that the urban has been able to conquer the site of La Villette. The notion of fragmentation has managed to take over the fifty-five hectares of the site. Fine. As for me, I am saying something else. I say that space – space as an expanse of emptiness – is perfectly capable of finding its place in the urban system. And this in no way invalidates the idea of a fragmented urban reality. When you undertake a reading of Tschumi's project, you understand that the idea was to show that urban space is to be seen as a dissociated space articulated around fragments of architecture arbitrarily scattered around the territory-world. But look at New York. I don't see what there is to stop me from saying that Central Park is a big void on the scale of the city. Does saying that mean that I refuse to recognise the fragmentary nature of today's city? Not in the least. It is important to understand that everything is related to the notion of scale. Like Tschumi, I too work in terms of empty and full forms. But I personally reasoned as follows: since La Villette was surrounded by fullness, it was fitting to put a big emptiness there.

This notion of scale proved very complicated for the candidates.

I would like to quote you a little aphorism from an old treatise on Chinese painting: to balance a house in a landscape, there must be six times its volume in trees. This idea is still relevant today. The vegetal and the built must answer each other as a feather answers lead, bearing in mind that the latter, for the same weight, fills six times less space than the former. Once you have understood that, the fifty-five hectares of the site at La Villette become insignificant. So insignificant that there was no reason to fragment them. I repeat: La Villette has been conquered by the urban system. But there's no way the Parc de La Villette can lay claim to the status of element of urban space.

A confusion of scale.

In a way.

In fact, to be precise, we ought to speak of artificial scale.

That's right. The urban has artificially taken over the fifty-five hectares of the site. But I wouldn't want there to be a misunderstanding. I am not saying that I banish the notion of heterogeneity. I am in favour of a certain acceptance of the heterogeneous. My project, all emptiness, sought to provide a counterweight to the over-fullness of the neighbouring urban fabric. As for Bernard Tschumi's project, it is none other than an image of the way in which the town conquers rural spaces. That is exactly how it must be read. As the image of the urbanisation of a territory. But still, one must be prudent. We forget all too often that only seven percent of the French national territory is urbanised. The importance

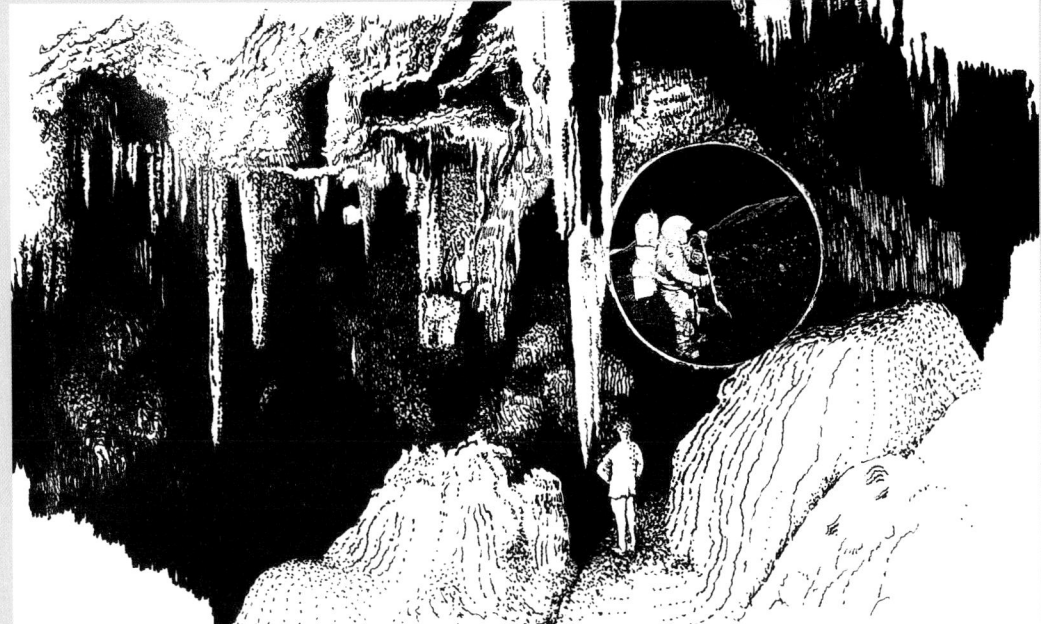

Competition for the construction of the Parc de La Villette (1982–1983). Project by B. Lassus. The Jardin Vertical (Vertical Garden).

of urbanisation should not be exaggerated. As for myself, I sincerely believe that the presence of a big empty space in a working-class quarter is something of fundamental importance for sensorial experience.

The phenomenal success of the park's Prairies could be taken to prove your point. The Prairie du Cercle and Prairie du Triangle seem to be the most popular with the public.

Absolutely.

Does the idea put forward by Bernard Tschumi, according to whom, "the disappearance of "the civilisation versus nature polarity under modern city conditions has invalidated the time-honoured prototype of the park as an image of nature," seem arguable to you?

You can't "weigh" the built as you "weigh" planted areas. That's what I want to say. Going from there, it's all a matter of discourse. I often say that when you have botched a landscape you build a staircase. It's a way of saying that it's all in the slope. The slope must come all the way to the threshold of the house. For it is an element of the sensible. I once wrote a text entitled *L'Eloge de la Pente* (In Praise of the Slope). The slope is fundamental because it summons up two notions: the visual and the tactile. And in fact I would tend to think that the notion of tactility is the more important of the two. We are heading towards an age when perception will tend to become multi-sensorial. The phenomenon of ambience is going to become very important.

What you are saying there is interesting. Just think, today we are seeing the resurgence of a musical genre once known as "Kosmic Music" and now known as "Ambiant." This movement intensively explores aural matter and is thus conducive to that tactile sensibility you mention.

INTERVIEW WITH BERNARD LASSUS 187

The tactile will increasingly be grafted onto the visual.

At a time when the technological tools for visualisation seem to be proliferating ad infinitum.

Exactly.

To conclude, we would like to go back to what happened during the competition to build the Parc de La Villette. Was the oral presentation to the jury as agitated as the press made out at the time?

The day after the competition, Roberto Burle Marx phoned me to arrange a meeting. What he told me was in substance this, "I am responsible for your defeat, and I am going to tell you why." He then went through a number of points that I would like to go over with you. After defending my project to the jury during the second round – I think this was sometime in March [March 1983—*Editor's note.*] – Vittorio Gregotti joined me as I was leaving the room where the jury sat, and told me that he was going to support my project "fifty percent." I found the words rather ambiguous. And I must confess to you that I didn't really understand what he meant by this. It was only later that I understood what he meant. I must remind you that at the beginning, the presentation to the jury in the second round – that's to say, in March 1983, once the nine candidates had been selected – was supposed to be in two phases. The candidates had to present their project to the jury – we had only a few minutes, which was very little – then the jury was to meet the following morning to choose the winning project with, I repeat, voting done in two phases. That was when, because of the absence of Burle Marx – his plane had been delayed – the jury decided that the voting would be done in only one round. And, in fact, the jury had every right to take this decision because it was authorised by the competition rules. This decision, which made the chairman, Burle Marx, furious – and while I'm on this let me add that, contrary to what some people let on, he was far from senile – quite simply caused me to lose the competition. I'll explain why. The group around Gregotti and Renzo Piano didn't like Bernard Tschumi's project. They preferred the project by the Dutch architect Rem Koolhaas. But – and this is when I understood the meaning of Gregotti's words – although this group didn't plan to vote for me in the first round (they were going to choose Rem Koolhaas), they would opt for my project, and not Bernard Tschumi's, in the second round. With a procedure involving only one vote, I was bound to lose. But with a procedure involving two rounds things would no doubt have been different because the people who had voted for Rem Koolhaas in the first round would have voted for me in the second. Gregotti actually published my project in the Italian journal *Casabella* a few months after the competition. It was, you will agree, a very unambiguous way of saying that he appreciated my project. Indeed, everything I have just told you was in a sense confirmed to me by Roberto Burle Marx. I remember very well that he told me he had clearly understood that only an architect could win the competition for the Parc de La Villette.

Can we say that the competition jury wanted to see an architect win rather than a landscape architect?

For an architect not to be chosen as winner of the competition was in some sense tantamount to saying that the layout of outdoor spaces in an urban context was beyond the range of architects. In fact, Lucius Burckhardt told me this quite openly once Bernard Tschumi had been announced the winner. Not, let me be clear, that this takes anything away from the quality of the competition. The work done by François Barré and his team was really impressive. The inception report is a real museum piece. With the competition for the Parc de La Villette, the notion of the programme became fully meaningful for the first time. The competition brief, as conceived in 1982, prompted the competitors to choose a schematic design. That is fundamental. Today, most programmes impose a design, even before reflection about the programme starts. That's totally absurd. It is the interpretation of the brief that leads to the choice of design. That should never be forgotten.

*Interview by Alain Orlandini
(with the participation of Marie Chauvin).*

Interview with Gilles Vexlard

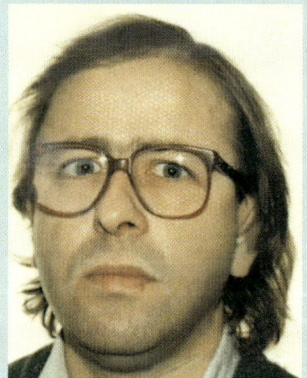

Gilles Vexlard trained as a landscape architect. In the numerous development missions he has been entrusted with, his approach to the project has invariably been based on the formulation of an appropriate conceptual vocabulary that enables him to assimilate the variety of scales encountered. Vexlard's most important projects include the layout of Place Charles-de-Gaulle in Vichy and Place de la Comédie in Montpellier, the Grande-Ile quarter in Guyancourt and the landscaped park at Riem, near Munich. State adviser on landscape to the department of Infrastructure in France's North region and professor at the École Nationale Supérieure du Paysage, Vexlard, assisted by Laurence Vacherot, was short-listed in the competition for the park at La Villette in 1983. In the final vote he came equal third with the landscape architect Bernard Lassus. Here, Gilles Vexlard, designer of the Jardin de la Treille (also known as the Garden of Gardening) talks to us about the competition brief for the Parc de La Villette and about the various propositions presented on that occasion.

What was your opinion of the competition brief? What, in your view, were its underlying ethical and philosophical assumptions?

The competition for the Parc de La Villette was a catalyst, a watershed that saw the transition from certain kinds of project practice to others. As for the programme, I was amazed when I read it. There was a kind of over-programming, like a dumping of ideas, words and surfaces. Everything intersected, linked up and formed layers – organisation charts were very fashionable in those days – and in the end all that constituted something very positive because we had to make choices and think about the final destiny of the terrain while at the same time, of course, distinguishing between what was fundamental and what was not. For my part, I was soon arguing that the project wasn't feasible. For there were two things in the brief: there was the inception report, that is to say, a series of philosophical and social intentions; and then the reality of the site, cut up and then assembled like something from the caterer, and never likely to provide the empty space needed for a proper grasp of the place. This is something I could understand from my experience of laying out big spaces. This experience made me aware that you need to be able to "hit hard" in order to engage with the terrain, while being capable of doing sufficiently little for things to happen, eventually, of their own accord. A real balancing act, in fact. The brief was a hyper-dense assemblage of contradictions and impracticalities linked to the nature of the terrain.

There were people who got carried away with the content and laid out all kinds of incredible things – furniture, games, lamps, chandeliers, galleries, and bandstands. Everything was in the same vein, whether it was something to do with potentiality, with becoming, or whether it was a matter of the purest materiality. The park was in fact turning into a giant mishmash. The situation for which this brief was paving the way was quite simply indescribable. The architects we were working with, who were used to dealing with programming problems, decoded the competition problem and eventually realised that the terrain was jam-packed. There was no room left for the imagination. Most of all, something fundamental had been lost, that is, the idea that the size of a place is what inspires the project. It is not a matter of occupying space, of positioning things next to each other or doing design. The real question that needs to be asked is whether the terrain – a very specific terrain, located here and not elsewhere – contains a situation that can be transcended, that can be exploited so that this place becomes unique. Unique not because you have built one, twenty, thirty or a thousand bandstands there, but unique because that territory there, will, as an integral whole, be able to express a body, a body that is its main quality.

You mean that it is the spatial conditions of the place that must dictate the reflection behind the project, and not the brief?

Yes, of course. In Versailles, where I teach, I run a workshop. The theme of this workshop is: "without a brief." The question we ask is: how do you make a project without a programme? At La Villette, I soon realised that the terrain was evacuated by the brief, as was the very idea of landscape. The work of the landscape architect consists in taking up a series of ideas concerning a very specific terrain and the place where that terrain is located. A terrain is unique because it stands in a precise spot. If the site of La Villette was in Vladivostok, it wouldn't even exist. In the middle of the Urals, the fifty-five hectares of the Parc de La Villette would be nothing. Nowadays, the area of a medium-sized cereal farm is two hundred hectares. So you have to relativise things. You have to be able to "weigh up" the situation you are in.

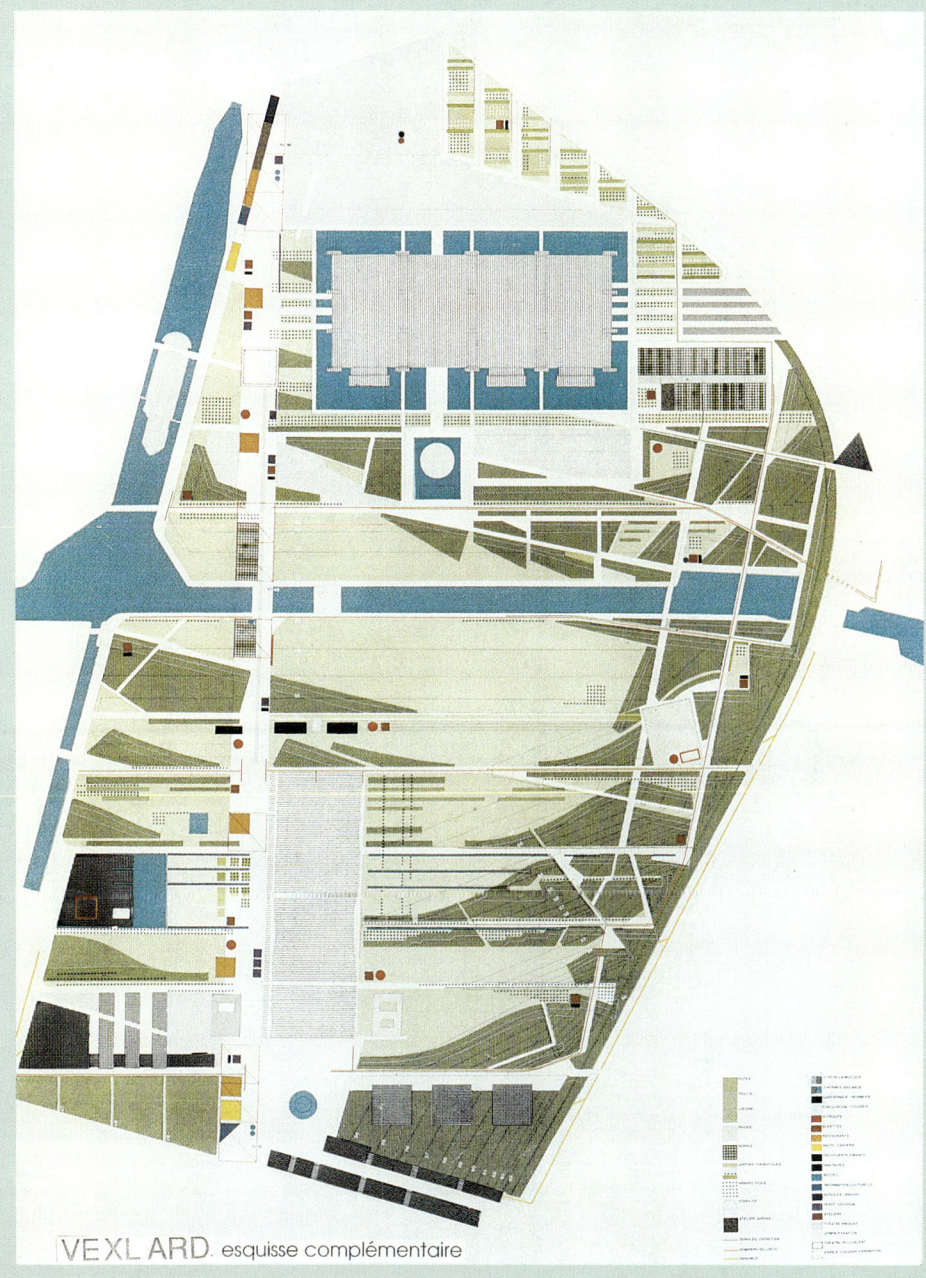

If I understand you correctly, it is not only the nature of the site that generates the project, but also its scale.

Of course. If the scale is not taken into consideration, there can be no project. The project is something that is engendered by the terrain that grafts itself onto the terrain. The identity of the place isn't just plucked out of a magician's hat. It comes from a capacity for keeping intact a series of potentialities that a place, and no other,

Competition for the construction of the Parc de La Villette (1982–1983). Project by Latitude Nord (G. Vexlard, L. Vacherot). Site plan.

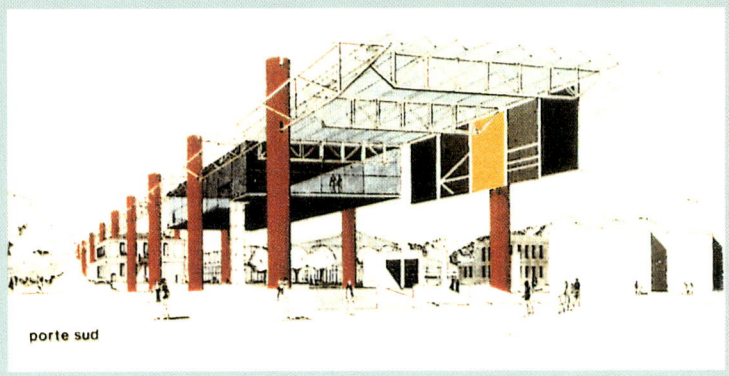

Competition for the construction of the Parc de La Villette (1982–1983). project by Latitude Nord (G. Vexlard, L. Vacherot). The Rambla (the "events" space).

possesses at its very foundation. To come back to the competition brief, we soon decided to get rid of it. If we hadn't abandoned the programme, we would have ended up doing composition. Or what I call "assemblage." Which, in fact, is what a lot of people end up doing. Taking the brief into consideration made it impossible to plot out places that would unify the terrain. La Villette's capital is its extent. It is also the Périphérique and the canal. Linkage to the suburbs is possible mainly because of the canal. Not "stuff" crossing the Périphérique. We should also remember that the competition to build the park at La Villette was a professional competition. The proposals had to be feasible. In this sense, it was an illusion to put roofs over the Périphérique with three or four hundred metres of underpinning. None of these peremptory – and simple – solutions are suitable for urban contexts like that of La Villette. When we got the brief we were aware of its unfeasibility and we rejected it, observing that this park project had other responsibilities. The first of these was to establish a link between the Porte de La Villette and the Porte de Pantin. The Parc de La Villette will not be urban because it has bandstands and chip stands dotted around it, but because it is laid out in the city, with a responsibility for linking those two points of ingress/egress to and from Paris. Hence the walkway running from north to south. The canal also plays this role, as it divides – or unites – the place. As for the problem posed by the presence of the suburbs, we can answer that they are there, beyond, on the other side. You have to try to set up a relation of the "here" to the "elsewhere." It is not simply a matter saying that you can get over the roads by making footbridges. We know very well that a footbridge does only one thing: show you that you can't cross it. We also know very well that all these things made to link no longer do link. They are merely urban prostheses that don't work. The point is that people exist on both sides of the roads – that they exist beyond. How is a landscape architect going to translate that, if not by raising the earth to indicate that there is an "elsewhere"? As with any pass: you go back down into the valley, over on the other side. Hence this need for a slope.

So it's not the structure that makes the link, but simply the fact of announcing, by means of an appropriate architectural or landscaping procedure, the existence of something beyond the limits of the terrain under consideration.

Yes. What makes the link is the fact of knowing that there is something equivalent beyond. And this relation of equivalence is instituted by the very fact of changing the horizon. Some horizons serve to say that there is an "elsewhere." And the elsewhere is always interesting, always imaginatively evocative. The elsewhere is something that asks questions. Our project aimed to install the site of La Villette geographically. Speaking of which, about the Canal de l'Ourcq, I must point out that it is devoid of meaning. Or rather, it has no a priori meaning since its role is simply to link the catchment areas. The canal blithely ignores the little detours that it happens to frequent. The canal must exist as a body of water that needs to be able to have a direction. It is our duty to direct the canal. Otherwise it no longer means anything and becomes mute. It says nothing beyond the fact of containing water. With its system of strips, our project was about weaving together the terrain's directions, destinations. The work on length is almost atavistic. It is consubstantial with notions of the vernacular, of territory. My references are not supermarket references, they are more like a farmer's references. What counts is the work on the terrain, maximising its receptiveness. It's like for an architect, for whom what counts is the carcass of the building, that is to say, that which enables the volumetry to exist, through which the volumes can enter into a dialogue. We therefore worked in strips in order to orient the terrain, and thus make available a principle that goes beyond the simple play of perpendiculars set up between the two buildings placed on the site, the Cité des Sciences and the Grande Halle. If we didn't set up an autonomous system capable of entering into a correlation with the major components of the site, like the canal and its east-west orientation, it was clear that the park would no longer be able to assert its status as park. Our system of strips was an agricultural system. It is the lengthways direction of a terrain that matters. The other advantage of this system of strips was that it saved us from having to confront the volumes present on the site. On the contrary, it allowed us to set them up, to cohabit with them, through the friction between parallels. We preferred that to a full-on clash. The relation between man and the terrain emerges from closeness alongside rather than through a gaze cast from a fixed point. Working on being alongside, on the friction between a building and a terrain, implies establishing the means. This system of strips united what could be united, that is to say, the distribution of the terrain and the optimisation of the surface. For we should not forget the notion of yield. What is yield? It is the number of furrows needed to optimise production. If you do not have this concern with the terrain's yield, then you cannot know that piece of land. You can't talk about it. Because the point, ultimately, is to ensure that the land attains a certain plenitude in terms of its use. The aim for us was to set out a demonstration of the place's consistency, and to do so by working on levelling. The reconstituted slope offered surfaces that were brought into the light and an expansion both of its occupancy and of the uses that we considered fundamental. Once this work had been done, once we had said that there was a beyond, an "elsewhere," it was clear that the movement through this instated territory would be something interesting, capable of generating a programme. To sum up, the project panned out as follows: in the first place, we established the programme. Next, we installed the terrain. And, third, we enabled frequentation, movement. Once this line of traversal existed, it was logical that it should be near the Grande Halle and the Cité des Sciences. Its role was to be alongside. Today, we don't know how the Grande Halle "rubs up against" the park. We don't know where it stands, how it positions itself. But our mistake at the time was to want to give form to something that was still in the realm of becoming, that was still to be invented and about whose nature and *facture* we knew absolutely nothing. We knew what this axis could not be, but we still didn't know what this thing might look like. I personally represented this crossways axis as a simple line of posts. The architects in our team gave the problem a formal translation, which underplayed the qualities that this transversal axis could have brought to the site. This axis would have made crossing the site into something contemporary. Indeed, instead of making things visible in keeping with a recognised order, it would have been about making the pedestrian the true actor.

In your critical text on the Parc de La Villette, you mention the Nouvelle Vague. In terms of landscape, the Nouvelle Vague means having your camera over your shoulder so that you're really there in the landscape.

The slope that you wanted to lay out on the site from east to west was a way of ensuring that the limits of the site fuse with those of the horizon. But didn't this effort to annul the spatial limits of the park contradict the definition of the garden, which emphasises the finished aspect of its constitutive lines. It was Marc Le Bot who said that a garden is a closed space, that it draws back into itself to complete itself and revel in its sufficiency.

For me, the garden is a personal stylistic exercise. It is a surrounded, closed space with precise limits, one that is not accountable to what happens around it. The garden implies no responsibility other than that of its maker and the person who goes there. To simplify, that's just about it. But I am not a gardener, I am a landscape architect, which is to say that I install relations on a terrain. The garden is something intimate, very egocentric. Most beautiful gardens, in fact, are inaccessible to the vast majority of people. What interests me is the social space of landscape. Landscape is a project in which everyone plays a part. But it should be made clear even so that, whatever the terrain you work on, you have to lay out, construct, impart meaning.

Wasn't this way of brushing aside the existence of the brief, the better to assert the landscape approach, in conflict with one of the objectives of the competition, that is to say, this idea that the park should be a constructed park above all.

What you are saying is partly true. But I would like to say that there are different levels of construction. Henri Gaudin says that construction begins with the furrow. I often quote Roupnel, too. He talks about "this ditch that unites and separates." The furrow constitutes an act of construction of the territory, one that is key, hugely important. What remains of old cities today? The sanitation networks and all the traces of installation and distribution of the territory. They withstand much better than all the superstructures. Construction is not only building, it is not simply bringing forth, raising or showing, it is also that which installs, furrows, that which lays down deep foundations in the terrain. I believe more in the grading, that is to say, the mass of earth on which things rest, than in the things themselves resting on a flat terrain.

Listening to you, one could easily come to the conclusion that you opted for an approach that was the opposite of Bernard Tschumi's, which consisted in placing a series of constructed objects that, in a sense, show little consideration for the place that they are occupying.

Yes. I am even at the antipodes of that approach. No doubt a landscape artist is frightened of the built, but it must also be admitted that the architect is frightened of the void. I have the feeling that this culture of empty space was annihilated by today's culture, which is an essentially urban culture. And the corrections that agricultural society could make no longer exist. Up until 1945, France was an agriculturally-based country. In those days there was still a culture of roots that countervailed the culture of construction. This culture had a sense of the land, of space, of distance.

Your arguments are very close to those of Bernard Lassus. Like him, you evince a great respect for emptiness, for immensity. Do you agree with him when he says that the grid of Folies broke up the space?

The grid of Folies is the expression of the loss of the knowledge linked to the notion of emptiness. Think of those people who went to Holland or Moscow on foot, and whose unit of measure was the league and not the metre. Those people had a territorial awareness that was very different from ours today. The Folies are in some sense an admission of impotence when it comes to mastering the void.

And mastering large-scale space, as well.

Yes. There is the feeling that you are going to possess the terrain because you've fixed on it. Why mark out the site of La Villette with Folies? As far as I am concerned, the surveyor's markings would have done. A point with a nail suits me fine. We are increasingly dispossessed of space, whereas people from the countryside know it better. To want to possess space by means of systematic marking shows that one has ceased to possess it.

When Bernard Tschumi asserts that cultural reality has won out over natural reality; when he says that – I am quoting him – "the inadequacy of the civilisation versus nature polarity under modern city conditions has invalidated the time-honoured prototype of the park as an image of nature," how do you answer?

I don't think he's right. The competition brief linked the idea of nature to a reactionary, backward-looking idea. The people who conceived the brief thought that by abandoning the principles of the traditional park they would inevitably come upon the principles of a new way of acting in space. And we can say that they were mistaken. They were mistaken for the very good and very simple reason that they were inexperienced, because we hadn't produced a park for nearly a century, except for complacent, unthinking parks. The reason why we try to establish a relation with plant life, with nature, is that it asks questions about life, that is to say, about a part of ourselves. The city, which has been unable to recover the pleasure of space, needs to ask questions about these radical solutions predicated on the belief that if you pile up objects on a site something is bound to happen there. Today there is something lacking in man and in life. And yet human beings are beautiful in space. Grids and the deployment of a strip are things that have

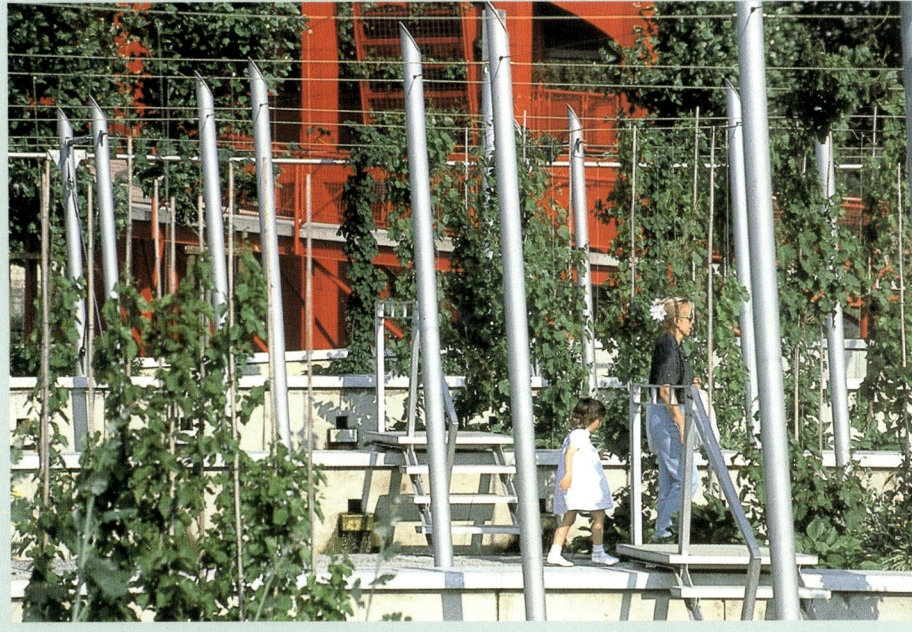

The Parc de La Villette (architect: B. Tschumi). The Jardin de la Treille (Garden of Gardening); conception: Latitude Nord (G. Vexlard, L. Vacherot).

INTERVIEW WITH GILLES VEXLARD   195

nothing to do with the site of La Villette. Points, Lines, Surfaces – it's true that they reassure all the devotees of reason, of forms.

Of abstract painting.

Of abstract painting. And also all those who hanker after the period from 1910 to 1920. Ultimately, Bernard Tschumi's project consists of a spatial representation of things that have remained in the domains of painting, abstraction and poetry. But they are a thing of the past. They're fifty, sixty, seventy years old. There is nothing modern about them.

To conclude, we would like to come back to this notion of the slope. Bernard Lassus wanted to have a slope running from north to south across the site, in order to reintegrate the park into slope of the Seine Valley. Whereas you proposed one running from east to west. Which slope was to be emphasised, the one following the north-south axis, or the one going from east to west?

My university training is as a geographer. I came to landscape because there were no projects in history/geography. So I have a fairly natural feeling for notions like relief, or slopes. The landscape architect's job is to put in order, on a given site, a certain number of things, so that this place can meet precise objectives. When you look at the site of La Villette, it is clear that it is the canal that initiated the landscape.

Your discourse is identical to that of Rem Koolhaas. Rem said that it was the east-west orientation of the canal that should guide the perception and organisation of the site.

When I saw Rem Koolhaas' project, I said that this was the project I would probably have made if I had been an architect. And I was very disappointed to have eliminated him. Because we were the ones who eliminated Rem Koolhaas, and not Bernard Tschumi. We eliminated Rem Koolhaas because we had a position that was the antithesis of his, even if some of the questions we asked were very similar. Like him, we treated the Grande Halle as a simple umbrella. In fact, it would be amusing to place one project over the other. Rem Koolhaas moved the site towards an absolute programmatic dynamic.

The other thing your propositions have in common is the quest for emptiness. Rem Koolhaas often says that he never envisages his projects in terms of volume, but always in terms of the programme.

Yes, but at the time Rem Koolhaas had a big advantage over us because he had an army of formidable draughtsmen who did some fantastic things. His rendering was stunning. The judging of the projects in the second round gave rise to a debate that focused on him and us. The debate was all punch and counter-punch. A punch-up between architects and landscape architects, between poets and programmers. In a debate there are always losers. But this time we both lost. In the end this opposition between our two proposals killed off the debate. But to get back to this notion of the slope, which you mentioned a while ago, I don't think that the slope of the Seine Valley went all the way to the canal. I think it stopped before that. It was therefore pointless to reposition it onto the site. However, to fold the terrain in order to make the canal meaningful, and to make the space slope, struck me as rather attractive. The vocabulary that interested me was a varied vocabulary that took advantage of the spatial situations created by the terrain and the vegetation. Thinking on landscape at the beginning of the 1980s was pretty impoverished. The references were always to the past. Today, when I hear talk about the Prairie du Triangle, as a landscape artist I find it pretty frightening because a triangle is by nature something that has no spatial rendering. Angular configurations always tend to reduce the field of spatial perception. In fact, it would be interesting to talk about optics, in the sense of optimising what is there to be seen. Optics is not just taking photos.

You mean that what we see in the image of the park in fact has very little in common with the park as it exists in situ?

In architecture, there are spaces that are impossible to develop, spaces without qualities. Le Corbusier's *free plan* was about this idea of the optimal use of space. As we saw it, it was necessary to restore the terrain's depth and length, and that's why we worked in the east-west direction. The strips played this role of optimising the constructed spaces, unlike Bernard Tschumi's Prairie du Triangle, which ends up losing its vanishing points and becoming totally flat. The Parc de La Villette is a kind of *tabula rasa*, like a kind of destruction of the terrain's vitality, authorising the positioning of various objects. The idea of the slope, in contrast, is the idea of a landscape architect. The idea of the slope is a landscape architect's idea. The idea of the slope comes from the landscape. Beneath the sky, one is always on a slope. Flatness is an obligatory architectural principle. Whereas the slope constitutes the beginning of the landscape. The Paris Basin is not the Seine. The Paris Basin is the earth allowing the Seine to exist.

So the notion of horizontality is a kind of fiction specific to architectural language.

Yes. When I say horizontality, I mean something that is going to show the slope. The slope is beneficial in many ways. It drains the water, it corrects distances, it exacerbates dimensions. The sine curve of the Promenade Cinématique isn't going to compensate for these ideas of thickness and dimensionality.

Interview by Alain Orlandini
(with the participation of Marie Chauvin).

Interview with Alexandre Chemetoff

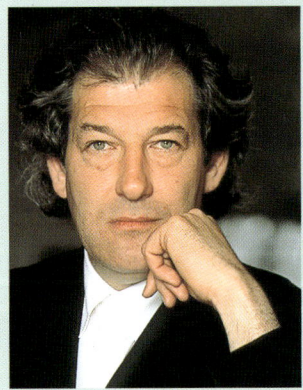

Born in 1950, Alexandre Chemetoff studied at the École Nationale Supérieure d'Horticulture in Versailles from 1970 to 1973 and became a DPLG landscape architect four years later. In 1983, he created the Bureau des Paysages, with which he conceived a number of projects. He intervenes in both urban and rural contexts and his varied portfolio of creations includes a number of gardens: the French Embassy garden in New Delhi, the famous Jardin des Bambous (Bamboo Garden) at La Villette, the water garden at Nancy; and various urban zones: the Hautes-Bruyères and Murigny-Sud development areas in Villejuif and Reims, the spaces around the Ministry of the Economy, the Budget and Finances at Paris-Bercy; and the conception of outdoor areas and gardens for the renovated Montrouge site of Schlumberger. Visiting professor at the Institute of Architecture at Geneva University, Alexandre Chemetoff is regularly invited to sit on competition juries. Here he comments on his own proposition for La Villette and discusses the brief.

What did you make of the competition brief?

The programme was extremely rich in terms of ideas. There was that phrase, "an idea behind each blade of grass." It was an exact reflection of what the competition organisers wanted, in other words, a programme full of contradictions, but generous.

What do you mean by a programme full of contradictions?

The programme wanted the cake *and* to eat it, too. It forced candidates to think differently about the very idea of the park. That was the quality I saw in it, anyway. Its major failing, however, was that it totally disregarded the terrain. The brief never came close to the site. And you can say the same thing about Bernard Tschumi's project and the Cité des Sciences as well as the various housing developments on the site. All that finally led to the choice of a project, a project that tended to disregard the site and was at the same time fairly generous. What lives on at La Villette, independently of the flaws and qualities of Tschumi's project, is this generosity in the programme.

What do you mean?

There is a wager this park manages to pull off, which is its attempt to open up to the city, to life. The Parc de La Villette is not like other parks – that is to say, in the etymological sense of the term, a closed place – but, on the contrary, a place that is open to the city. From that point of view, the park is a success.

What you are saying there is surprising. We tend to think that the links between the Parc de La Villette and the adjoining quarters are not sufficiently emphatic.

When I talk about the link with the city, I am talking about use. And that's where the contradiction lies. For the park is totally closed in on itself. If, in contrast, our

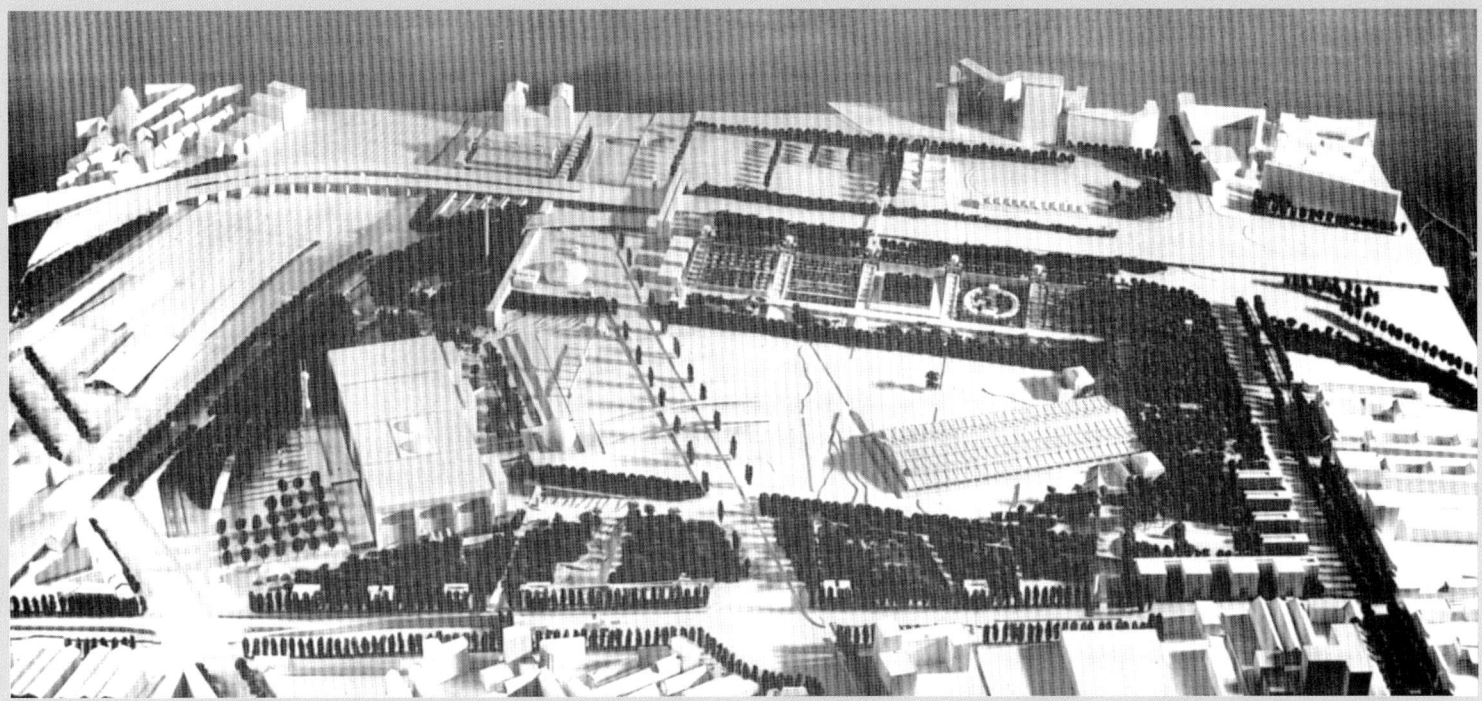

Competition for the construction of the Parc de La Villette (1982–1983). Project by Bureau des Paysages (A. Chemetoff, B. Althabegoïty, J.-L. Cohen, H. Bardsley, M. Massot). Model.

proposal oriented thoughts about the park towards the question of the Périphérique, it did so precisely so that the site would become a dimension of the park.

Was the brief really the cause of this plurality of uses you mention? Isn't the explanation to be found in the urban situation of the park, the multi-ethnic character of the people who go there?

The Parc de La Villette is an active park, a lively park. When walking around in it you can sense that there are lots of people who are responsible for the site, and these people are not only guardians. The energy deployed by the Établissement Public (public body in charge of the park) is perceptible.

Most of the Folies are empty, though.

Even so, something of the programme is still there behind it all. As far as I am concerned, I find the park a rather likeable place. But it's true that that's not enough. For, once again, the project never comes together with the site. Not even programmatically. The linkage with the major infrastructure, like the Périphérique, doesn't work, nor does the linkage with the Avenues Corentin-Cariou and Jean-Jaurès. You can establish a parallel between the programme and the organisation of the Établissement Public, which is like a kind of phalanstery. The park is a built utopia. And behind the notion of utopia, there is that idea that we are outside the site, that we are removed from the place.

It seems that whenever a utopian programme is formulated you inevitably get a markedly geometric architectural project. Wasn't it the utopian dimension of the brief that lay behind the geometrical feel of Bernard Tschumi's project?

Utopian means outside context, abstracted from the *topos*. Whereas place is all about contingency. Utopia engenders the use of self-sufficient geometry that composes its

The Parc de La Villette (architect: B. Tschumi). The Jardin des Bambous (Bamboo Garden; conception: Bureau des Paysages; A. Chemetoff, B. Althabegoïty, J.-L. Cohen, H. Bardsley, M. Massot).

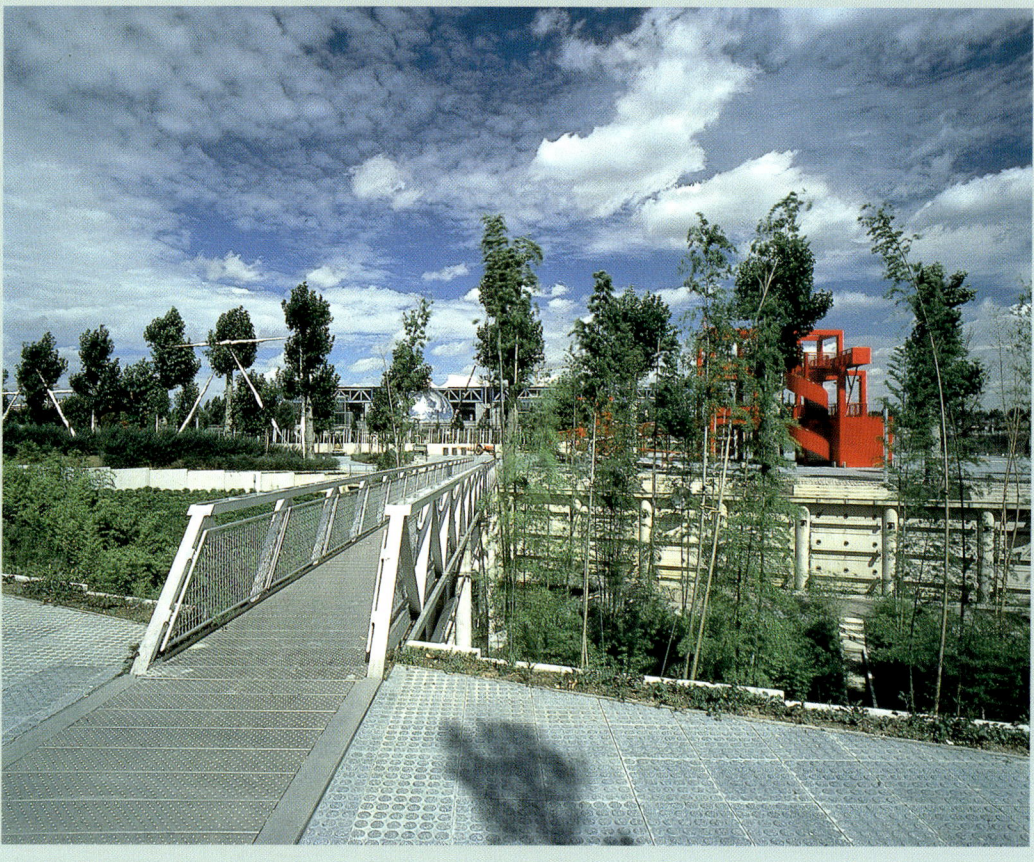

own narrative. Bernard Tschumi responded to the programme with a system of interlocking geometrical elements, of superimposed and non-superimposed figures that constituted the narrative of his project. The Folies and the literary, philosophical and cinematographic references propose an autonomous story line. So one can hardly be surprised if the park fails to bond with its site.
That's what Bernard Tschumi's project was always going to do. Retrospectively, one can understand why it was chosen. For in a way, it is the one that best illustrated the spirit of the programme.

When you say that Bernard Tschumi's project doesn't bond with the site, are you formulating a critique?

It is a critique. I personally tried to respond in a different way, almost in total contrast to that kind of approach, by showing that the elements of a narrative existed on the site.

What were the main points of the proposal?

There was a very simple idea in our project, which was to consider that this apparently flat terrain had its own relief, that of the networks constituted by the Boulevard Périphérique, the Boulevards des Maréchaux, the canal and the Métro (Underground). When you measure the magnitude of that relief, that is to say, measuring it from the depths of the Métro to the high point of the Périphérique, you get more than thirty metres. At La Villette, therefore, you have this relief which is not the relief of the natural topography, but that of the city floor. One way of inserting the park into its site was to insert it into the stratification of the city. By acting in this way, we were installing the park in a geography, which was that of the city's networks, and bringing to light this stratification. In fact, that's what we did on a natural scale with the Jardin des Bambous. It is a manifesto garden in the sense that it constitutes a way of showing what we wanted to do with the proposal we presented at the 1982–1983 competition, in other words, to reveal the networks running through the garden, and install a programme that had depth, and rather than being merely flat. We wanted to hook into an aspect of the history of gardens, that of productive gardens, and at the same time we wanted to take a position in relation to the city's networks. From that point of view, the proposition that we made found a different way of solving the question of modernity and locality. This was a way of saying that there could be a narrative rooted in the site. That there could be a project based on the site, and that bringing out the relief of the site is a way of composing a park. The idea was to say that on this section, or rather, on this vertical section, we could install the elements in the brief, and that we could devote the layout of the ground to plants and meadows.

How was this work on depth done?

We dug down at the site of Place de la Fontaine-aux-Lions to reach the floor of the Porte de Pantin Métro station, and we also dug on the Porte de La Villette Métro side. One could thus see the park when using the two Métro lines.

Do you think that the RATP (Paris transports body) would have accepted such a proposal?

Yes.

Knowing how difficult Bernard Tschumi is now finding it to get the Paris municipal authorities to give public access to the little canal lock to the west of the site, we find it rather hard to believe you.

Who knows? But let's go on. To the east, we rose up in tiers to the level of the Périphérique, which made it possible to enter into a relationship with the sporting grounds over on the other side, in Pantin. At the top of these terraces, we placed a car silo that made it possible to park along the Boulevards des Maréchaux. Also to the east, there was this big building that made it easier to cross the roads. Many of the elements in the brief were located on the edge of the park, and even on the other side of the Périphérique, so that there would be elements on either side of the roadways. Basically, the plan for our park consisted in freeing up a central space and having all the thematic gardens on the periphery, thus acknowledging the axis of the Périphérique as the founding line of the project. Thus, the Périphérique was like the site's biggest building. And our park was moored to it.

In the end, your and Rem Koolhaas' proposals were the only ones to seriously consider the question of how to handle the presence of the Périphérique. By attaching a system of gardens and tiers to its western flank, by laying out pedestrian walkways perpendicular to it, by replicating the same system of passageways on its eastern flank, and by delving into the depths of the gardens, starting from the Boulevards des Maréchaux, you were literally taking the Périphérique over.

The Parc de La Villette (architect: B. Tschumi). The Jardin des Bambous (Bamboo Garden); conception: Bureau des Paysages (A. Chemetoff, B. Althabegoïty, J.-L. Cohen, H. Bardsley, M. Massot)

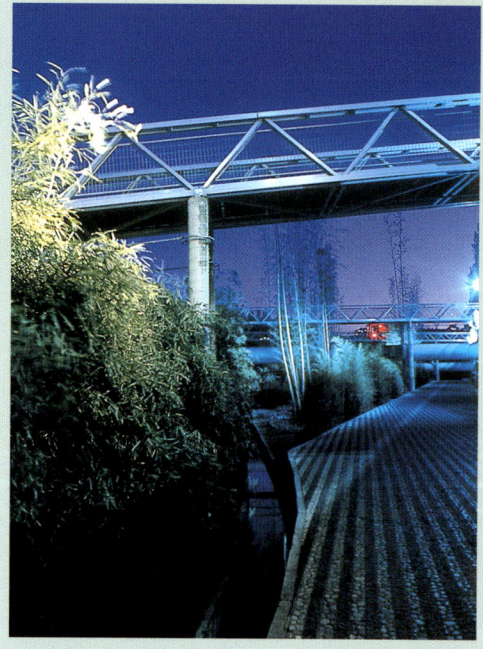

You don't seem very convinced of the soundness of his proposal. We ourselves found his system of strips very convincing. In any case, more convincing than Gilles Vexlard's slope.

The central element of Gilles Vexlard's project is the gallery walkway running from north to south. And in fact it was built.

Bernard Tschumi pinched the idea from him between the two rounds of the competition.

Bernard Tschumi's system allowed for all kinds of borrowings. But, to come back to our proposal, I should also point out that the fact of excavating the terrain to the south led us to locate the future Cité de la Musique between street level and the hollow constituted by the access to the Métro.

Yes. That was the strong point of our proposition. To recognise the existing site, however difficult it might be, is a fairly optimistic way of working. That, today, is the condition for being able to produce projects. It is a way of going beyond modernity because it asserts an aesthetic position. An aesthetic position that dares to confront a reality that is multiple. Nowadays we are plunged into towns that are constituted by a process of collage, assemblage and juxtaposition, and we can't just present projects that simply mimic this situation. On the contrary, we need to see the situation as containing something other than this fascination that motorway landscapes sometimes held for us in the 1980s – I am thinking particularly of the cinema of the late 1970s which, in films like *Kings of the Road* and *Alice in the Cities*, showed us characters wandering Europe's major infrastructures. But as far as Rem Koolhaas is concerned, what he wanted to do was to interiorise in the site some of the landscape elements formed by the networks and infrastructures.

Yes. In fact, we realised that there was a certain correspondence between your proposition and the one by landscape architect Bernard Lassus. But whereas he tried to fit his project into a natural relief, that of the Seine Valley, you were setting your proposal in a relief that was artificial. And both your propositions came up against the same difficulty, that of the relation to the land on which the Cité de la Musique was going to be built. Lassus envisaged a considerable difference in level between the high point of his slope and the level of Avenue Jean-Jaurès, whereas your proposal condemned the Cité de la Musique to be situated far short of the road level. Were your and Lassus' proposals feasible? Wouldn't they have confronted the architects

who were preparing to enter the Cité de la Musique competition with overwhelming functional constraints?

But the Cité de la Musique could have benefited by this difference in levels. Part of the Conservatoire programme is totally underground, which is what makes it possible to give the volumes a certain elegance. The approach chosen by Christian de Portzamparc is exactly the same as our own. As in our proposal, Portzamparc's project has a level corresponding to the water line of the city, with part of the project happening below it and another part above. Our difference in level would have multiplied the views and let in more light.

No doubt, but what I am trying to explain is that your approach introduced a further constraint for the future participants in the competition to build the Cité de la Musique. That is to say, they would have had to take into account a major difference of level between the low point of the space, which you had dug out, and the level of the roadway.

Another restriction in the site, who would have complained?

While we are on the question of networks, I cannot help mentioning Pierre Riboulet, the author of a highly detailed study of the relation between the park and its border zones, notably the Périphérique. This study very rightly points out that the problems posed by the development of peri-urban spaces have shown the incapacity of classical and Haussmannian languages when it comes to working on the scale of networks. According to Riboulet, we need to define new rules of volumetric organisation that will allow the emergence of what he calls a "modern monumentality," that is to say, a very discreet monumentality that confirms the existence of a city in which "the emblematic and the functional are reconciled," in which networks become monuments seeking "not to separate, but to gather." How did you approach the presence of those major infrastructural elements that are the Boulevards des Maréchaux and the Périphérique? And, more generally, do you have a doctrine that enables you to grasp the very anxiety-inducing presence of these elements?

There is nothing to say that these major networks have to be monofunctional. I don't think there is some fatal law dictating that the Périphérique be only a thoroughfare. The Périphérique should be able to serve simultaneously as a road system, an embankment and a system of service roads. It should be possible to appreciate the

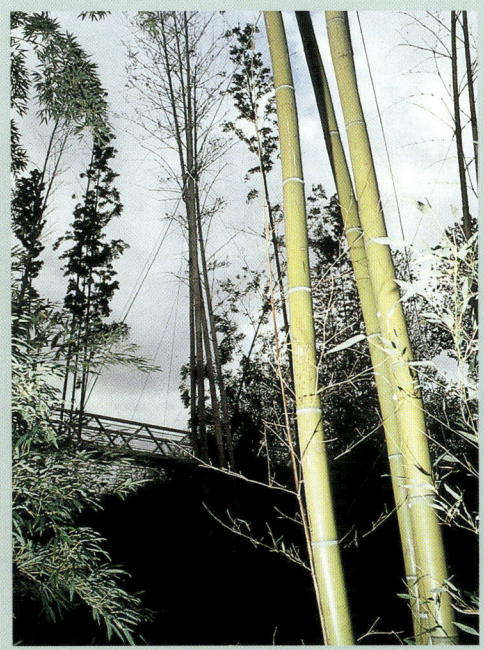

The Parc de La Villette (architect: B. Tschumi). The Jardin des Bambous (Bamboo Garden); conception: Bureau des Paysages (A. Chemetoff, B. Althabegoïty, J.-L. Cohen, H. Bardsley, M. Massot).

INTERVIEW WITH ALEXANDRE CHEMETOFF

motorway ramps for their capacity to generate urban space. There is, then, a double movement that needs to be set up. The first movement would be to ask how to design infrastructures in such a way that they can guarantee contact with the different parts of the urban fabric. I think indeed that there is no specific architecture that should be set up alongside the motorways. On the contrary, the motorways must teach us to make do with what already exists. In fact, there are plenty of examples to prove that we know how to do this. I am thinking of the very first sections of the Périphérique in particular, at the Porte d'Orléans, or on the first westwards motorway, which crosses the western suburbs of Paris around the Parc de Saint-Cloud and the Forêt de Marly. These examples show how major infrastructures manage to generate a landscape system that is, in a way, a system for linking up with what exists. As for the second movement to be instated, it is one that seeks to analyse constructions accurately, with a view to generating situations that are less one-dimensional than those arising from the encounter between Haussmannian fabric and the periphery, for example. Now, do I possess a doctrine that enables me to deal with these elements? Yes, in the sense that I think a good road infrastructure cannot be just monofunctional. It must develop "shouldering" systems, systems that ensure it is "feasibly" in the town. I would also like to point out, while we're on the subject, that in most cases it is not the infrastructure itself that is problematic but more the linkage systems, the interchanges and loops. What one therefore needs to learn to do is domesticate these infrastructures. The proposal we made in the competition, which consisted in treating the Périphérique as part of the park's reality, answered this question of what to do so that the Périphérique was no longer an alien or hostile presence for the park but a part of it.

We would like to talk about that big space situated at the centre of your proposition, entitled the "Plaine." What was its function?

We thought there was a possible relation between the theme of the museum and the theme of the park. There is one thing that I find extremely interesting about the future of parks: the theme of controlling the climate – the acoustic climate, the hydrometric climate – I thought we could present this mastery in the park itself. This took us away from horticultural, floral or landscaping references and into a kind of *mise-en-scène* of agricultural themes. The aim was to present scientific progress in matters of cultivation.

Was this huge plain meant as a celebration of the site's vast dimensions?

The point of this plain was to free up a large space in the centre of the site. We were making the link between the Grande Halle and the Cité des Sciences very clear. These seemed somehow to be resting on a large flat plain, all the more so because the other buildings in the programme were to be positioned on the various changes of level that we laid out. Ultimately, our project was centred around three elements: the Cité des Sciences, the Grande Halle and the Périphérique.

In your proposal you had the idea of presenting on the site a number of important buildings from the history of modern architecture. Why was that?

There was the idea that, as part of the park structure, we could build a number of buildings that were important to the history of Paris. The idea was to get back to the tradition of parks being often places for experimenting with new technologies. The first metal building in Paris, Verniquet's rotunda, is located at the top of the maze in the Jardin des Plantes. Our park would have been a place where we could have talked about new technologies. What bothered me about the Folies in the Parc de La Villette is that they really are not proper constructions. They are concrete buildings clad in sheet metal. The pavilions we wanted to exhibit would have demonstrated the connection between construction technology and architecture. Renzo Piano's IBM pavilion would have been perfectly at home in our park.

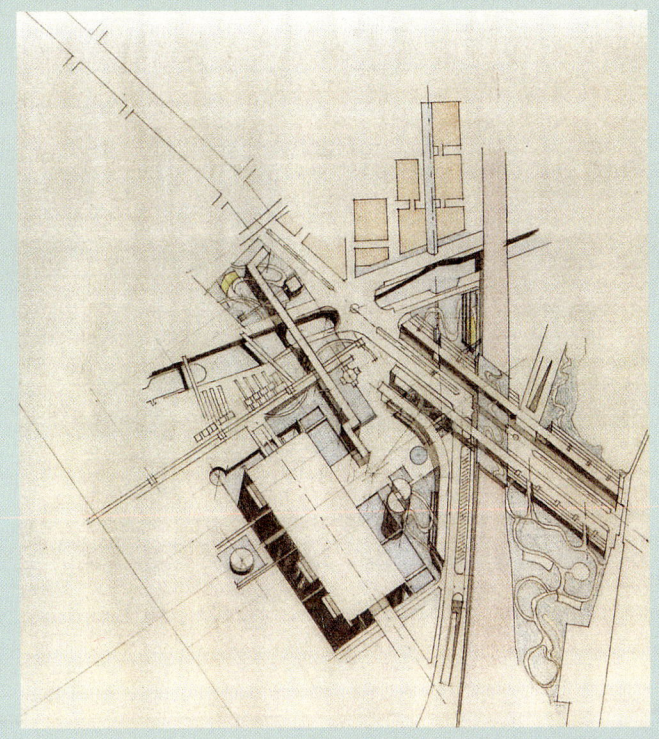

The programme called for the construction of a new kind of park, one free from the usual neoclassical, neo-Romantic or neo-Haussmannian references. Weren't you worried that an approach founded partly on a reference to history would be accused of historicism or even postmodernism.

The reference to Melnikov's pavilion is not what one could call a postmodern reference.

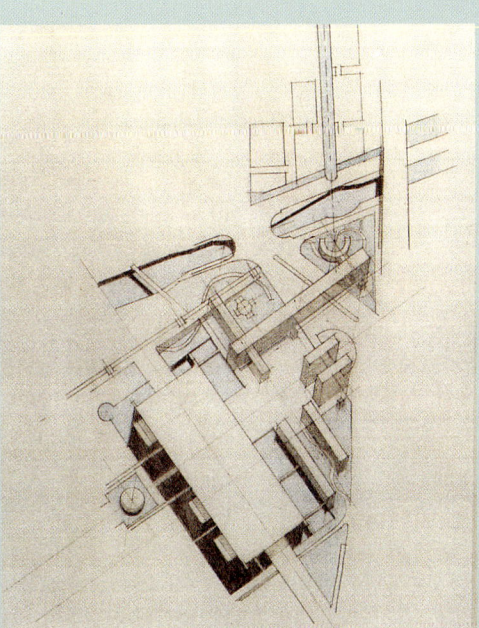

Development proposals for the northern and southern extremities of the Villette site. Studies (architect: P. Riboulet).

By postmodern we mean an approach playing on the invocation and juxtaposition of a variety of historical languages.

Like an idea of collage?

Yes. Postmodernity as a loss of the sense of historical continuity.

I don't know, but in the end I tell myself that our project was difficult to explain because it tried to reconcile the city with its territory. And that is something that still hasn't been achieved today. These days we are seeing the emergence of an urban geography that still has to be explored. When you look at the Périphérique in Paris, or the motorways,

INTERVIEW WITH ALEXANDRE CHEMETOFF

Development proposals for the northern and southern extremities of the Villette site (architect: P. Riboulet).

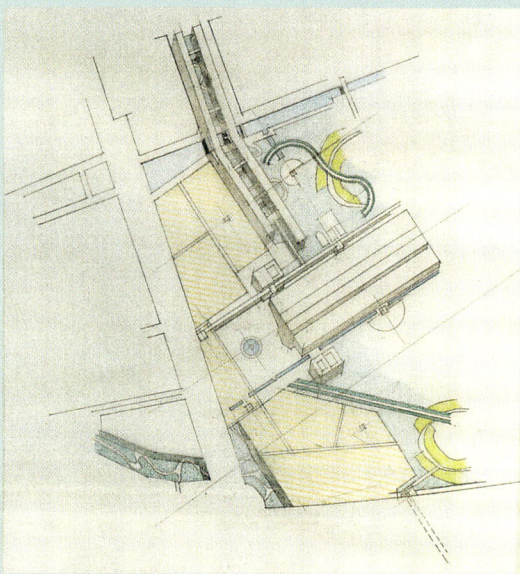 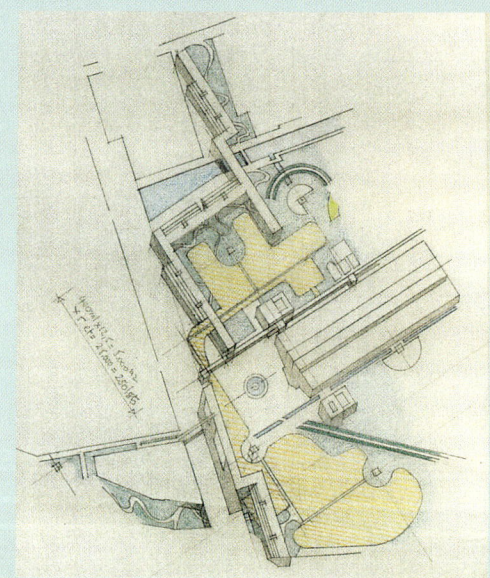

you realise that we still haven't solved the problem of the way major infrastructure relates to the territory. The competition for the construction of the Parc de La Villette should have raised the question of how to transform Paris around the Périphérique, how to transform a given of the site into a project.

Most of the proposals submitted by landscape architects asserted the superiority of the vegetal over the constructed, thus going against the brief, which, through the concept of the garden-city, called for the creation of a park that was constructed. Now, your proposition, which is also that of a landscape architect, managed to grasp the urban dimension of the programme in a very contemporary – and therefore very convincing – way. Did your approach, which was both landscaped and urban, constitute a way of calling for the coming-together of all the various architectural professions whose hyper-specialisation is such a bane nowadays for project developers?

Yes. If you think about it, you realise that we have nearly always made gardens against towns. And that is precisely why Bernard Tschumi's project is interesting: it shows another way of thinking about the city. Here, the park becomes one of the places for thinking about the city, or rather, the place where the rules of the future quarter are marked out. The garden here is no longer the antithesis of the city but a prefiguration of it. That, today, is where the meaning of the work done by the landscape architect is to be found, in this effort to find a kind of foundation, an extensive viability that makes it possible to ask questions about how to prepare a site that will house a city, be transformed into a city. How, by first taking into consideration the topographic elements and existing infrastructures, can we help the work on urban form? How, by taking them into consideration, can we ask questions about the way we conceive buildings, for example? Why indeed not think of substituting a systematic and regulatory approach with a situation-based approach that allows a different way of conceiving the project? The work of the landscape architect is of interest only to that extent, in that it becomes a way of going beyond the differences between the various disciplines and, to a certain extent, positing the very conditions of construction in a new way. The point is to argue for what I call a situational logic.

Interview by Alain Orlandini (with the participation of Marie Chauvin).

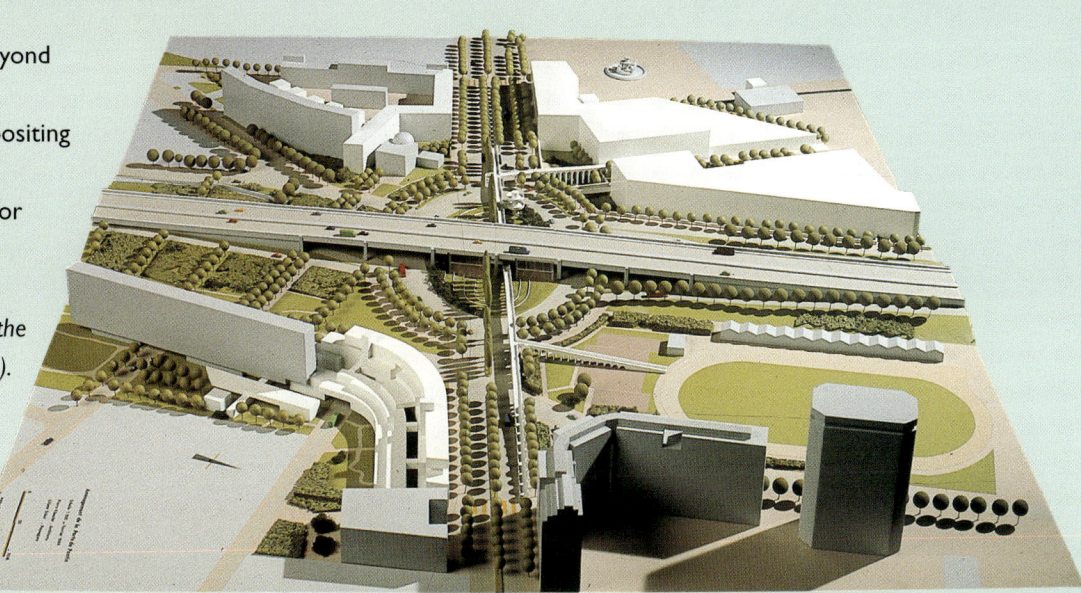

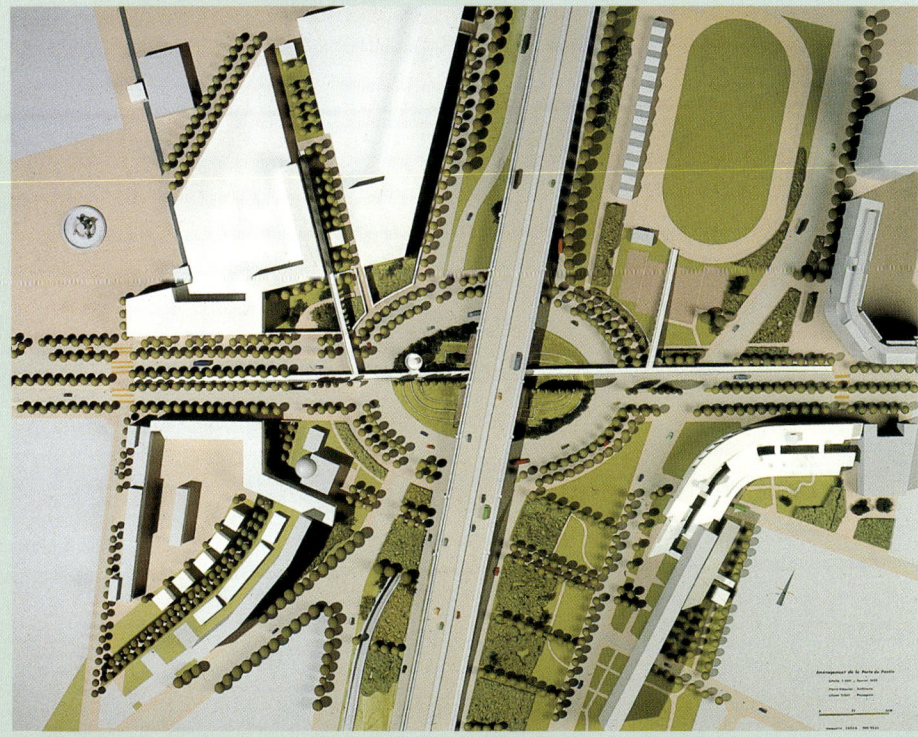

Development proposals for the northern and southern extremities of the Villette site (architect: P. Riboulet).

Interview with Jacques Gourvénec

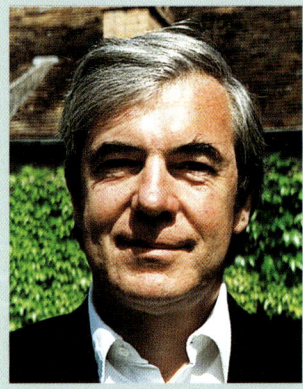

Jacques Gourvénec received his degree in 1974 and opened his agency four years later after a stint working in Brazil with the architect Oscar Niemeyer. In France, he has designed the Musée Cointreau in Angers, the archaeological museum in Tende and the Vigée-Lebrun school in Paris. Jacques Gourvénec is consulting architect for the Haute-Marne region and also a designer with the "Inclassables" furniture collection. Here he looks back on the brief and his proposal for the Parc de La Villette competition, which he won in 1983 in association with the artist Jean-Pierre Raynaud.

What was your view of the competition programme?

The contents of the brief were very precise. And, in the end, it didn't leave us much freedom. The conception of the park expressed in the brief was not romantic but, on the contrary, very rational, very scientific. To my taste, the programme lacked poetic ambition and generosity.

Strangely enough, your point of view goes against the one formulated by most of the participants, who praised the "open" quality of the programme.

When I say that the programme didn't leave much liberty, I mean in relation to its objective. The objective of the brief was very precisely defined. And Bernard Tschumi's, and Rem Koolhaas' propositions were, it turned out, the ones that made the best political reading of it. As far as we were concerned, we preferred to subvert the programme – like Bernard Lassus. But I must admit that the jury had the sense not to insist that the candidates offer a faithful transcription of the brief. Here I would like to recall the intelligence of Pierre Riboulet, a member of the technical commission, in the way he clarified the debate. His thematic analysis of the projects was remarkable.

The most relevant proposals were the ones that didn't offer a direct response to the brief. Gilles Vexlard was telling me that he simply disregarded it.

Yes. But our proposition disregarded the intention behind the brief. As for its contents, they were fully a part of our proposition. We were careful to answer all the points in the brief, because we didn't want to be eliminated.

Listening to you, we can understand why Bernard Tschumi won. With the grid of Folies, he endowed his project with a quasi-scientific dimension. While with the Promenade Cinématique he was acting as a dreamer, an artist.

Absolutely.

What applies to Bernard Tschumi also applies to Rem Koolhaas. Rem acted as a technician when he laid out his strips, and mutated into a poet when he made the Forêt Circulaire (Circular Forest).

Yes, but the strength and the weakness of these two projects is that when you see

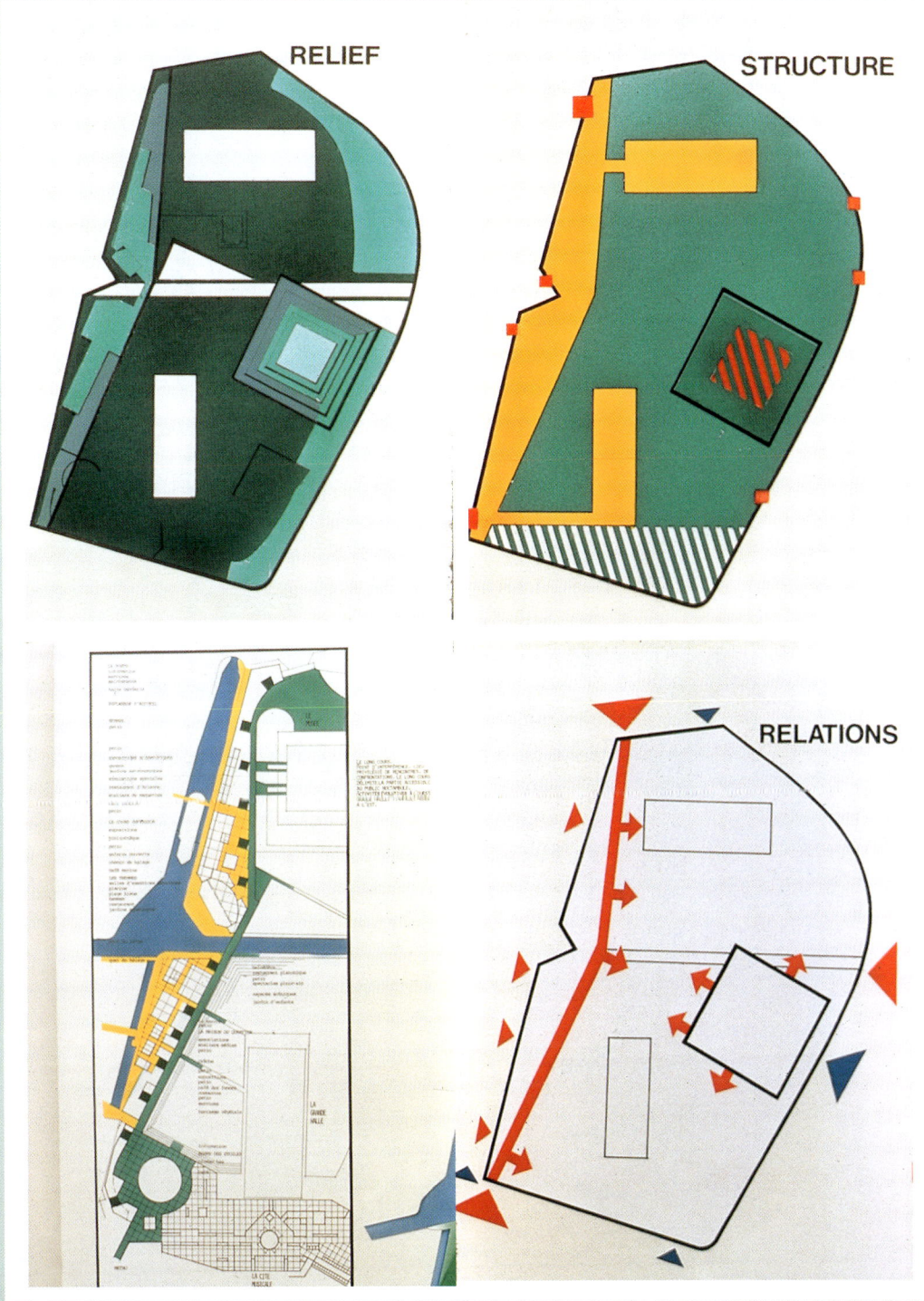

Competition for the construction of the Parc de La Villette (1982–1983). Project by J. Gourvénec and J.-P. Raynaud. Relief, structure, relations and passageways.

them, you very quickly feel you know what their purpose is.

There are two ways of reading the programme. The first is to recognise its avant-gardist dimension, since it boldly broke with neoclassical, neo-Romantic and neo-Haussmannian conceptions that were still in vogue at the time. But there is another reading which must lead us to recognise that perhaps the competitors weren't given all the resources they needed to meet some of the brief's objectives. We are thinking in particular of the handling of the

INTERVIEW WITH JACQUES GOURVÉNEC

relationship with bordering municipalities, which was impossible through lack of any understanding between the client organisation and the local authorities affected by the construction of the park.

One must admit that the competition programme had no nostalgia for the neo-classical or neo-Romantic conceptions of the garden. The brief was intended to break with the past. That is obvious. But I would make two criticisms. The first is that the vegetal element didn't get much attention.

It was in fact an "architectural" programme.

Yes. It was an architect's programme; or an urbanist's. The other criticism is its overly directive aspect. In fact, I would like to point out that it is the unmanaged spaces in the park that are the most alive. It turns out that the happening bits of the park are the ones where the brief had nothing planned.

A lot of people have said that the programme was bound to lead to a fragmentation of the space, which could only occur by undermining the immensity of the site – an immensity which they saw as one of its key qualities. For some, notably the landscape architect Bernard Lassus, building meant that one was "chipping off" the space.

Bernard Lassus is right. There were, on the site of La Villette, some very strong elements: the Grande Halle, the Cité des Sciences, and then a third element that we all too often forget, which is the Périphérique. Bernard Tschumi responded to this reality with a very subtle punctuation system, but one that is not to scale. One could indeed go on densifying the park without it changing anything. The Jardin des Roseaux, the Jardin des Nuages (Reed and Cloud Gardens) – it's all rather tiring. The power of an urban park lies in the creation of emptiness, in its creation of a space for dreaming. You have to have the courage to demand a big space. The gaze needs to be able to appropriate the space. The other problem with the park is that it has no effect on the extended periphery, because it doesn't extend beyond the limits of the motorway. The Parc de La Villette remains a neighbourhood park. The brief didn't put sufficient emphasis on this problem. And that's a real shame.

Do you think it is really necessary for the park to extend beyond the Périphérique? To establish a link with the suburbs, Gilles Vexlard thinks that it is enough to "raise up the earth." Then the gaze finds itself being drawn towards the Périphérique and the virtual link that is established with the periphery makes you want to go and see what's happening on the other side.

Yes. Our proposal planned for a big vegetal pyramid over fifty metres high. This pyramid was a signal. A signal stronger than the Périphérique. It made it possible to visually appropriate the site.

Let's move on to your project, and particularly this famous pyramid. What was its function?

Our project was a kind of invitation to dream. It also expressed our faith in the individual. We reject answers that use architectural gadgets and we opted for a big void, in counterpoint to which there was this pyramid of plants that I just mentioned.

A very big pyramid that balanced the site. This pyramid, which included gardens, offered an initiatory movement around the park.

We asked Bernard Tschumi if the grid of Folies would have existed without the presence of these great built masses that are the Cité des Sciences and the Grande Halle. So, allow us to ask the same question: would that pyramid have existed if they had gone ahead and demolished the meat market and the cattle shed?

Never. For it was because of the cacophony of the place that one had to be assertive — to redress the site's balance. One had to be present. This pyramid was a balancing factor. And its scale was urban, unlike that of the Parc André-Citroën. The Citroën park is not big enough. It is too small, too mannered. A park is not a garden with a few wild flowers and a few groves. A park is more than a "green breathing space."

How did you view the presence of the Canal de l'Ourcq?

Water is a fundamental element in itself, but at La Villette it existed only through the presence of the canal, which ultimately constituted only one of the signs of the place. In fact, our pyramid passed over the canal to the east. For me, the canal wasn't really very important.

In contrast, Rem Koolhaas saw the Canal de l'Ourcq as one of the site's key elements.

In my opinion, the canal has no weight compared to the Périphérique. In terms of the issues on the site, the water is minor.

How did you handle the Périphérique?

There is no way of preventing noise from getting into the park. But there are ways of ensuring that the noise of cars is digested. If one builds fountains, it is so that they will mask the noise of the cars. Even if that causes confusion. One is more receptive to the first noise one hears, the noise in the foreground.

Bernard Tschumi once told us that the Périphérique was a factor for silence. And walking around near it, we understood he was right.

That may be so. But the presence of the Périphérique wasn't taken into account by the brief at all. And just think that, although the inception report did see the park as being there for people from the outer suburbs, the programme didn't make provisions for a single parking space. That really astonished me. As I see it, acting like that meant that they were cut off from reality.

On this question of car parks, we would recommend that you look at the project by Jean-Pierre Vallier. He proposed to build a linear building near Place de la Fontaine-aux-Lions. This building was meant exclusively for parking cars. It was designed in such a way that the car headlights would light up the park at night.

That's very funny.

Let's now consider the theme of movement around the park. Many of the propositions included straight lines following the north-south axis.

INTERVIEW WITH JACQUES GOURVÉNEC

Your proposal distinguished itself by its adoption of angled lines. Why was that?

Our approach was emphatic, but no less respectful of the site for all that. When you are confronted with a building like the Cité des Sciences, it's ridiculous to stick pathways up around it. You need to be able to stand back and see it in half-profile. Not all the elements that structure the park are equal. When it came to the Cité, we preferred to stand back.

Most of the propositions made abundant use of geometry. What do you think was the reason for this?

Fear of the void. And yet the void is what is interesting. The problem raised by the use of geometry is that of a lack of thought. When you stop thinking, you pick up your pen. But a project is something you construct in your head.

It was Rem Koolhaas who said that he never thinks in terms of constructed volumes, because he wants to privilege analysis of the brief.

What he has done at Lille is very intelligent. Three things in one, and everyone in Lille can identify with his building. It doesn't much matter if the concrete wasn't properly vibrated or the sheet metal doesn't hold up. None of that has any importance in absolute terms. At Lille, you can sense that Rem Koolhaas has done some thinking. And that's what's most important. But Koolhaas eliminated himself between the two rounds of the 1982 competition. He was eliminated by his own lack of *gravitas*.

He no doubt made a strategic mistake by joining up for the second round with Michel Corajoud, whose proposal wasn't selected. François Barré can't have been very happy.

Maybe. But all considerations on matters of architectural design always remind me of what some architect said about the Pompidou Centre: "I would no doubt have produced a finer project than Renzo Piano, a better integrated one, but in my project there would have been one thousand two hundred people a day, whereas there, there were ten times more." Which means that it's all a matter of how you analyse the brief.

François Grether told us once about a very surprising scene he witnessed when Christian de Portzamparc came to see the people at Renault to talk to them about his project for redeveloping the Ile Seguin. They were a bit worried because he hadn't drawn anything and the management had been waiting for his proposal for several weeks. A few days later, Portzamparc went back to show them his project, drawn this time, and it was in total conformity with what he had said earlier.

Of course. That's how one should proceed. So I say that the drawing should only come afterwards, once everything has been made clear. Once all the dominant themes have been listed and you have thoroughly analysed all the consequences.
An architectural project is conceptualised without a pencil. You may sometimes make a mistake. But generally you don't need much more. Geometry, too, is sometimes the servant of a desire to control space. Take the architecture of the château of Versailles, everything is organised so that the king can control everybody, wherever he is. Geometry is made for domination.

Geometry also accompanies utopian discourse. As soon as you have a political utopia, there is a geometric city plan, whose rigidity paradoxically undermines the utopia it was supposed to serve.

Yes. That's always what happens. Because there eventually comes a point when you have to sit down and finalise things – to terminate the dream, in a way. That is where another dream begins. You were saying a moment ago that our proposition was geometrical. Perhaps. But our geometry is a geometry of necessity. Not a geometry of survival.

Ultimately, then, geometry should only be brought in as a last resort?

That's right. As a last resort. In fact, everyone finds geometry reassuring. It reassures the person who made it and the person who buys it.

Your proposal, which is above all landscape, wasn't selected. In the end, they chose Bernard Tschumi's – a proposition with high-density construction. Do you think that this choice indicates a change in perceptions of the concept of nature which, according to Tschumi, has been supplanted for good by that of culture?

Is that where we're headed? I see no proof. The concept of nature can't be swept aside just like that. I certainly don't think it is a normal or natural aspiration. That kind of thinking is more a mental game. But maybe it suits a lot of people to think that way. As far as I am concerned, I believe our aspirations are also directed towards nature.

Interview by Alain Orlandini
(with the participation of Marie Chauvin).

THE GRANDE HALLE DE LA VILLETTE: HYMN TO VERSATILITY

The abattoir is gone. But just as the meat market has been transformed into a dazzling tribute to scientific knowledge, so the cattle shed has survived to become a vast multidisciplinary venue.

A "gift of space" – despite the built-in obstacles

At two hundred and forty-one metres long and close to eighty-six metres wide – not all that much smaller than the meat market – the cattle shed is a kind of enormous metal umbrella resting on a host of cast iron colonnettes. Formerly open to the elements and thronging, every Monday and Thursday, with cattle under sentence of death, this was the perfect embodiment of the spidery, crystalline grace of the nineteenth century's triumphs in ironwork.

It was precisely this "spatial plenitude," so characteristic of industrial architecture, that Bernard Reichen and Philippe Robert set out to preserve at La Villette, in spite of the countless technical procedures rehabilitation of this metal cathedral would call for. How were they to provide the building with an internal circulatory network that would not disfigure its virginally benevolent emptiness? How were they to reconcile their determination to make a "gift of space" with the necessity for a fully equipped, multidisciplinary venue? So superbly did they meet these challenges that Reichen and Robert have since been the recognised, across the board champions in the rehabilitation field.

Burying the technical facilities

To keep the nave of some six thousand two hundred square metres unencumbered, Reichen and Robert decided to concentrate equipment space in the basement, leaving the ground floor available for a reception area, cafeteria, boutiques, shops and so on. Worth noting here is the planimetric similarity between the Cité des Sciences and the Grande Halle, each of which consigns its technical infrastructure to a single level completely cut off from the public.
The basement also houses the Salle Boris-Vian, a conference, discussion and screening venue. Access is via the interior or exterior of the building and there is direct contact with the entrance hall and the restaurants.

Offsetting the off-square

The cattle shed having been built off-square, it made sense to bring a relatively free approach to the new plan. Thus the six studios spread along the façade on each

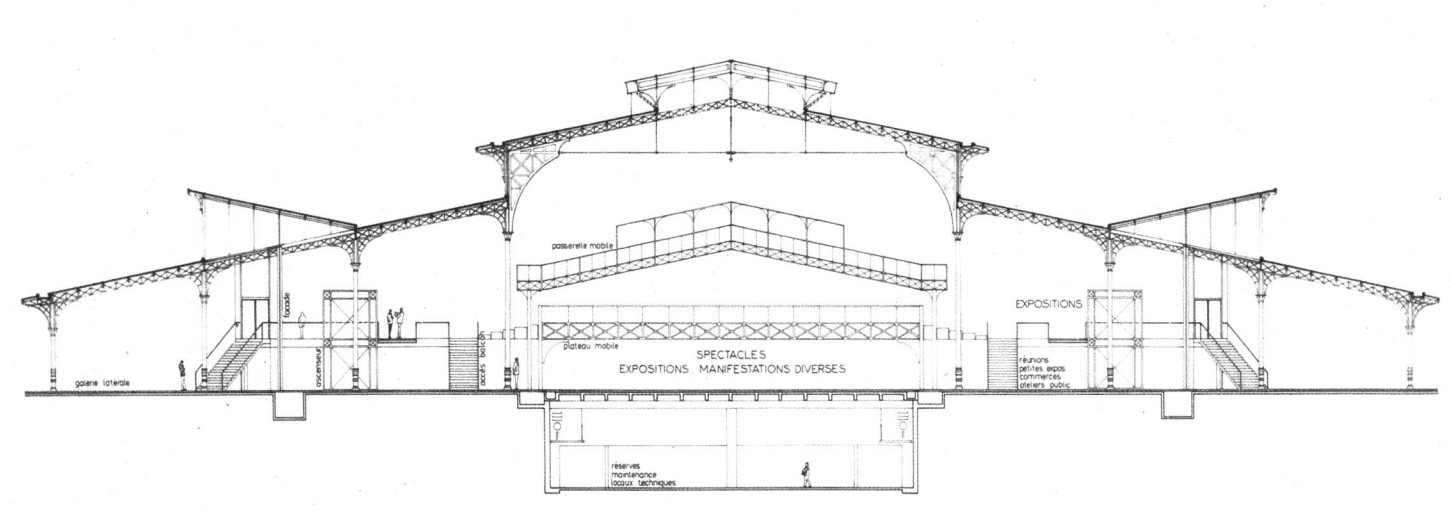

The Grande Halle (architects: B. Reichen and P. Robert).
Above: Cross section.
Below: The Galerie Mérindol.

side of the nave and linked by a system of walkways meticulously framing the central area, create no conflict whatsoever with the original structure. Served by lifts and staircases both inside and outside the building, the studios run parallel to the Galerie de La Villette, generating a full/empty spatial interplay with brief openings onto the park. For certain events walkways and mobile platforms – the latter attached to travelling cranes and allowing for suspension of sound and lighting equipment – can be used to connect the studios transversally. When necessary, an electrically operated tympanum rising out of the basement can divide the central area into two independent sub-spaces, cutting off the nave from the four thousand four hundred square metres of the Espace Charlie-Parker.

A plan reflecting the scale of the city

Facing Place de la Fontaine-aux-Lions and frequently used for exhibitions requiring outdoor space, the large peristyle extends the nave out into the city. It is matched by two covered walkways – the Galerie Janvier and the Galerie Mérindol, each two hundred and forty metres long – running parallel to the Galerie de La Villette.

When rehabilitation equals pure creation

Success all round: integration of the Grande Halle into its site, with the peristyle seeming to take the nave out towards Place de la Fontaine-aux-Lions, while the Galerie Janvier and Galerie Mérindol harmoniously reinforce the north-south character of the park; a rigorous plan, whose internal organisation in no way suffers from the off-square alignment of the original building; and attention to detail – for

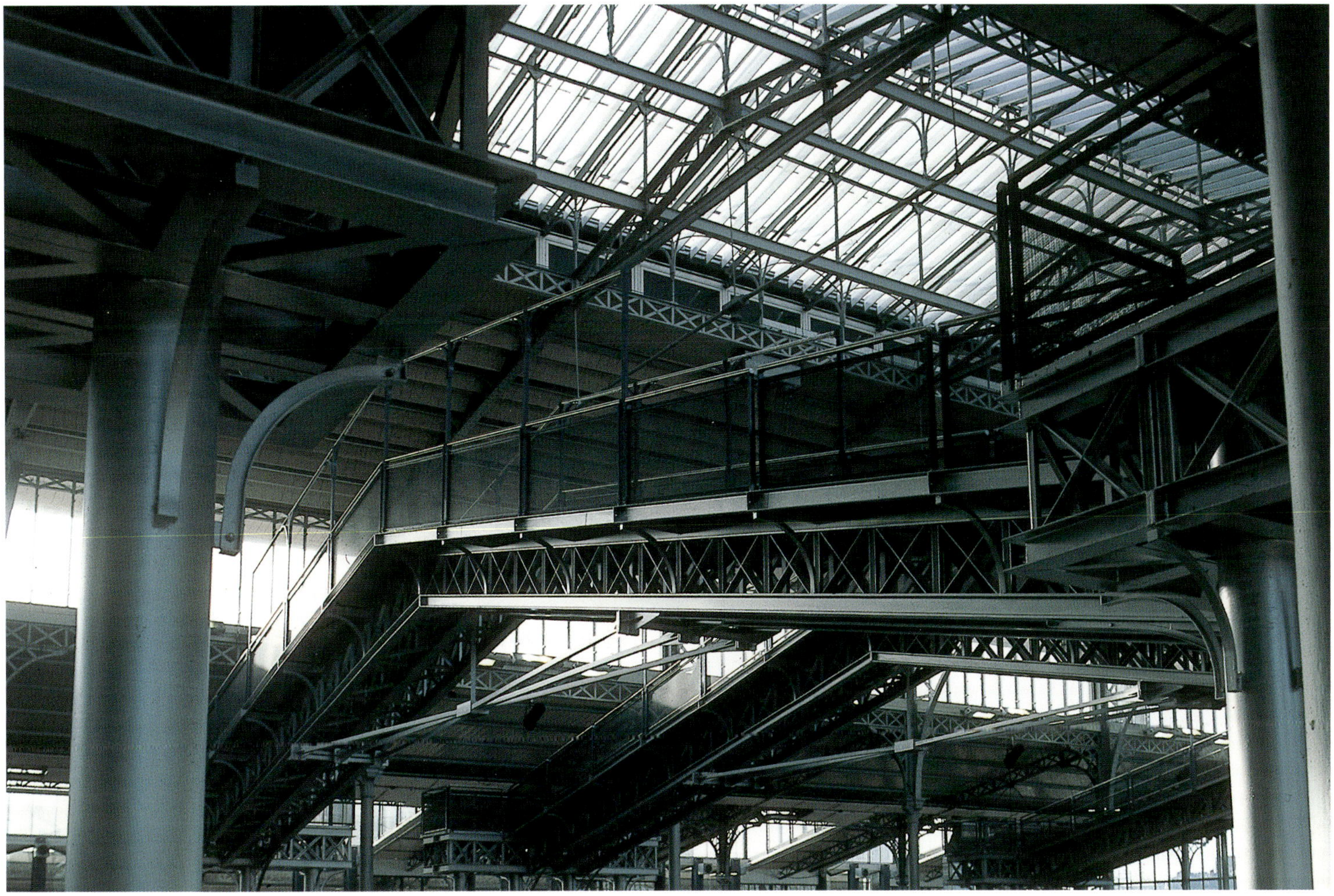

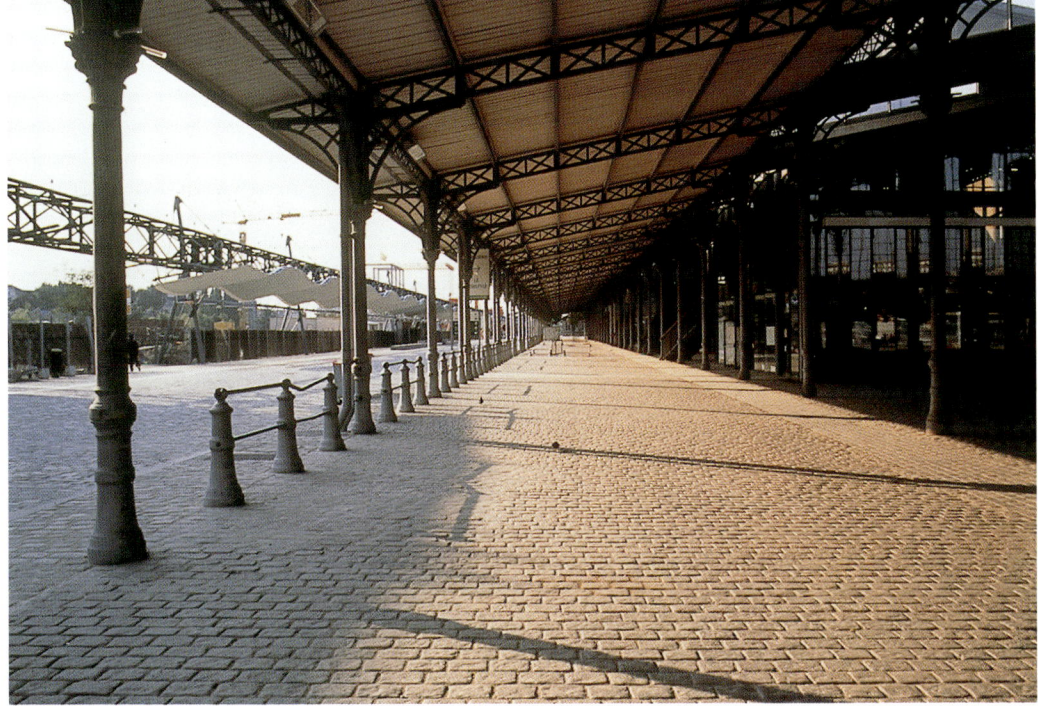

The Grande Halle (architects:
B. Reichen and P. Robert).
Above: The nave and one of the
travelling cranes.
Left: The Galerie Mérindol walkway.

THE GRANDE HALLE DE LA VILLETTE   217

The Grande Halle (architects: B. Reichen and P. Robert). Lighting on the columns.

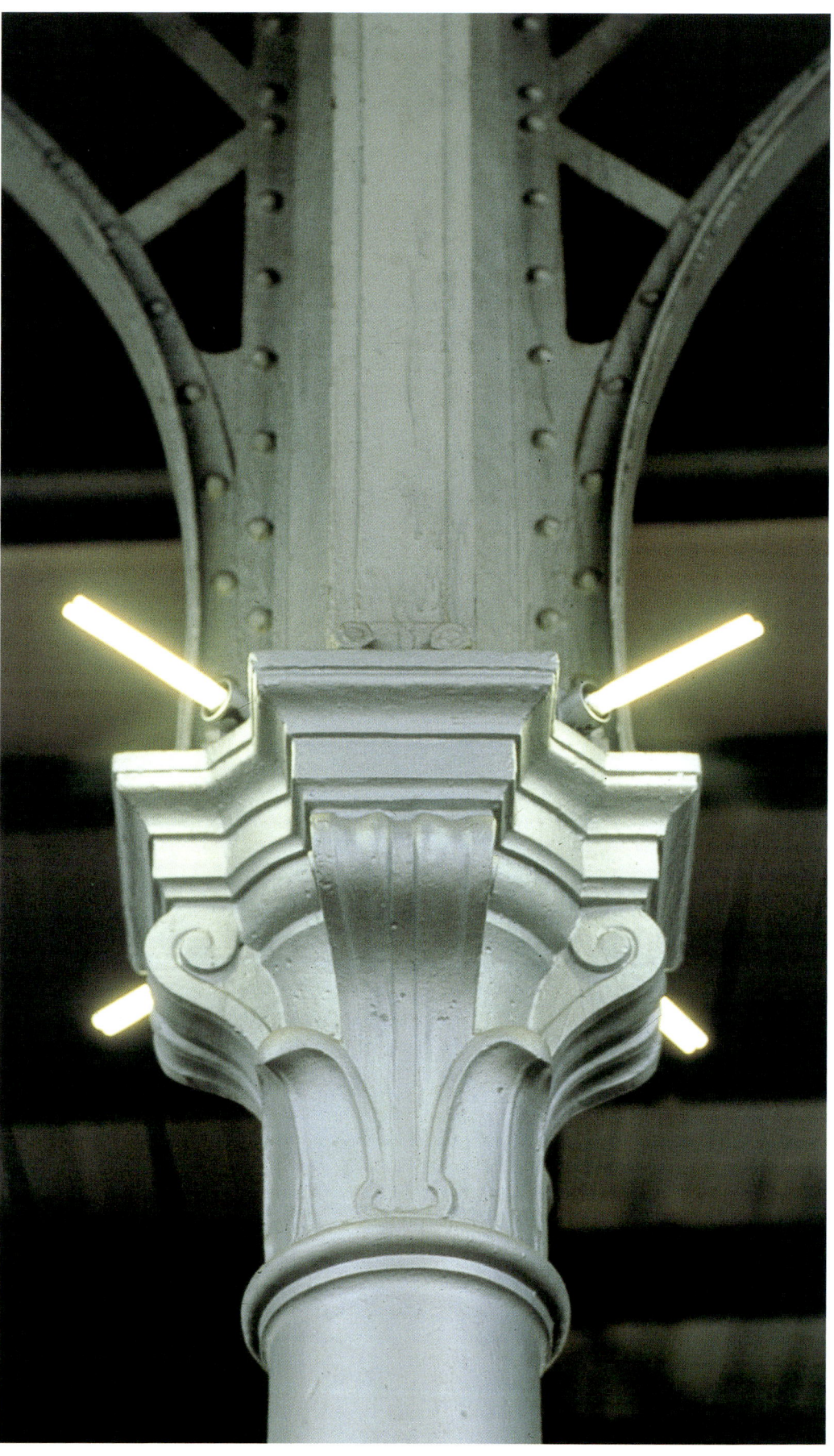

218 LA VILLETTE: 1971–1995

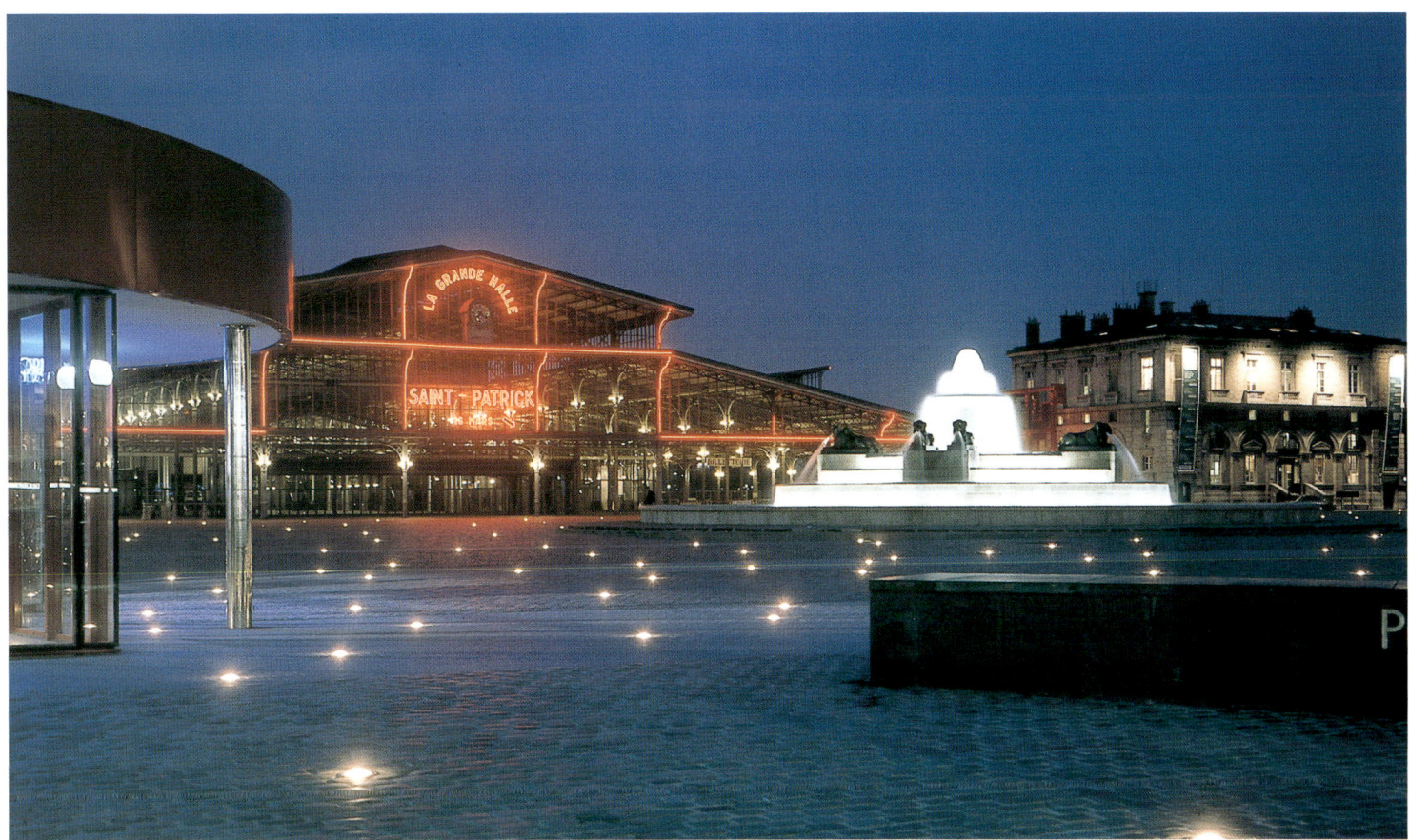

example, the slenderness of the columns highlighted at night by the opalescent tubes mounted on the capitals. Here Bernard Reichen and Philippe Robert demonstrate how well design and rehabilitation can go together, and that to consider the latter as no more than architecture's poor relation would be illogical.

The Grande Halle (architects: B. Reichen and P. Robert). South façade. Night view of Place de la Fontaine-aux-Lions.

INTERVIEW

Bernard Reichen

Interview with Bernard Reichen

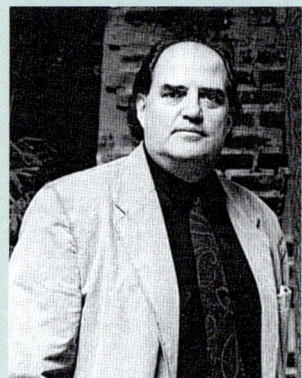

Both graduates of the École Spéciale d'Architecture, Bernard Reichen and Philippe Robert founded their Reichen & Robert agency in 1973. Their first project was the transformation of the former Leblan spinning mill into a multifunctional ensemble containing housing, offices and community facilities. This was followed by numerous rehabilitation projects, the Reichen & Robert team now being acknowledged specialists in conversion operations. Beyond their indeniable talent for transforming buildings, they are still "real" builders – witness the American Museum at Giverny, the French Embassy in Doha, Qatar and the Ruhr Environmental Technology Centre at Oberhausen. The following interview looks back to their conversion of the cattle shed of the abattoir at La Villette and their proposal for the Musée National des Sciences et de l'Industrie competition.

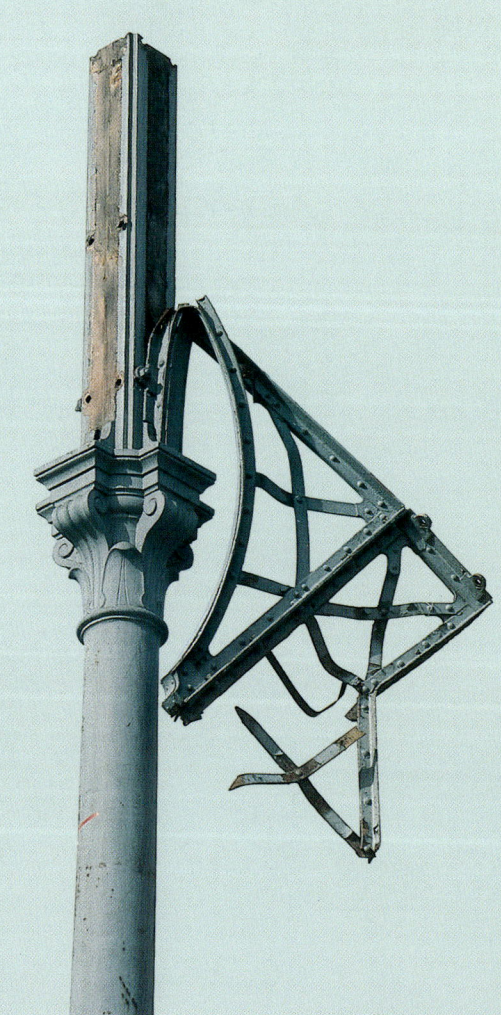

Before moving on to the Grande Halle at La Villette, I'd like to briefly consider your project for the Musée National des Sciences et de l'Industrie competition. Could you give me a general outline of the proposal?

We opted for a layout very different from those of the other participants. The brief comprised two phases, the first covering some eighty thousand square metres and the second a further forty thousand. We based our proposal on our belief that the second phase would never happen, which made a finished project of eighty thousand square metres preferable to a phased one of one hundred and twenty thousand. The outcome was that we completely emptied the first bay and turned it into a kind of information centre. This bay was also to be the end-point of a large arcade created by dismantling the swine shed, which itself linked the old meat market to the cattle shed. In addition, we emptied the bay at the opposite end. Between the two bays we put the museum, traversed by a longitudinal interior street. Our approach was intended to dissociate the project from the space we had to work with. Any conversion job involves taking two factors into account, the first being that space and function are not the same thing: the architecture remains, outliving the function it was originally created for. When you're dealing with the large covered markets of the nineteenth century, you have to take care not to petrify the interior. These kinds of buildings must lend themselves to appropriation and a covered market is first and foremost a public place with a roof on it. The second point is to beware of the euphoria that always comes with large, virgin spaces. The euphoria is due to the fact that they provide enormous, readily perceptible perspectives – but when you set out to appropriate them, you realise that you've really got your work cut out for you in terms of scale. Problems of scale are always very hard to solve.

Your project was the only one to suggest the system of an interior street running parallel to the site's east-west axis.

The aim was a sequence whose perspective would be entirely legible without being entirely filled up. This street ran the whole length of the old meat market, but took up only a part of it. The work we'd already done

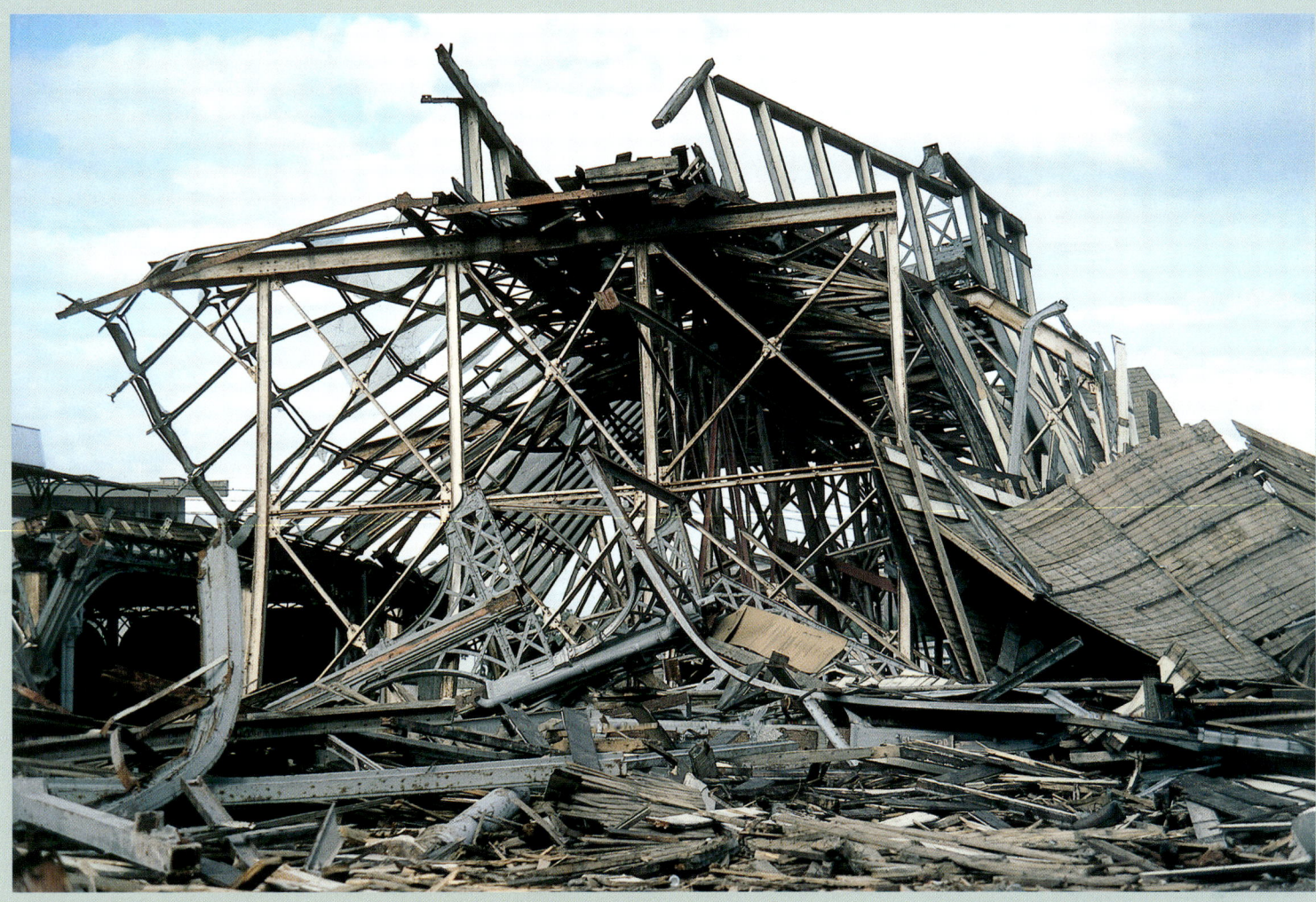

Above and page left: Demolition of the sheep shed, and the swine and calf shed.

on rehabilitation of nineteenth-century covered markets had given us an instinct for repetition. The rhythms of nineteenth-century architecture are the rhythms of metal, and these involve a whole lot of sub-scales whose mode of development is always repetitive. Even when we're designing new buildings we make considerable use of this street rationale and repetitive sequences.

What do you think of Adrien Fainsilber's project?

Very fine. But it seems to me that the treatment of the interior spaces tends to block your perception of the sheer immensity of the building. The longitudinal perspectives in the Cité des Sciences are quite weak. Philippe Robert and I like to stress the longitudinal perspectives, so we prefer the principle of the street to that of the focal point. The scale provided by the Cité des Sciences is as much that of the city as of the architecture, and the street concept seemed to us better suited to this kind of situation. But talking about the Cité more precisely would mean doing a space-by-space analysis.
Each time I go into a space I ask myself if it's smaller or bigger than I thought at first.

What's your opinion of Bernard Tschumi's Parc de La Villette?

The approach is very interesting. It seems to me that the mix of scales resulting from

INTERVIEW WITH BERNARD REICHEN

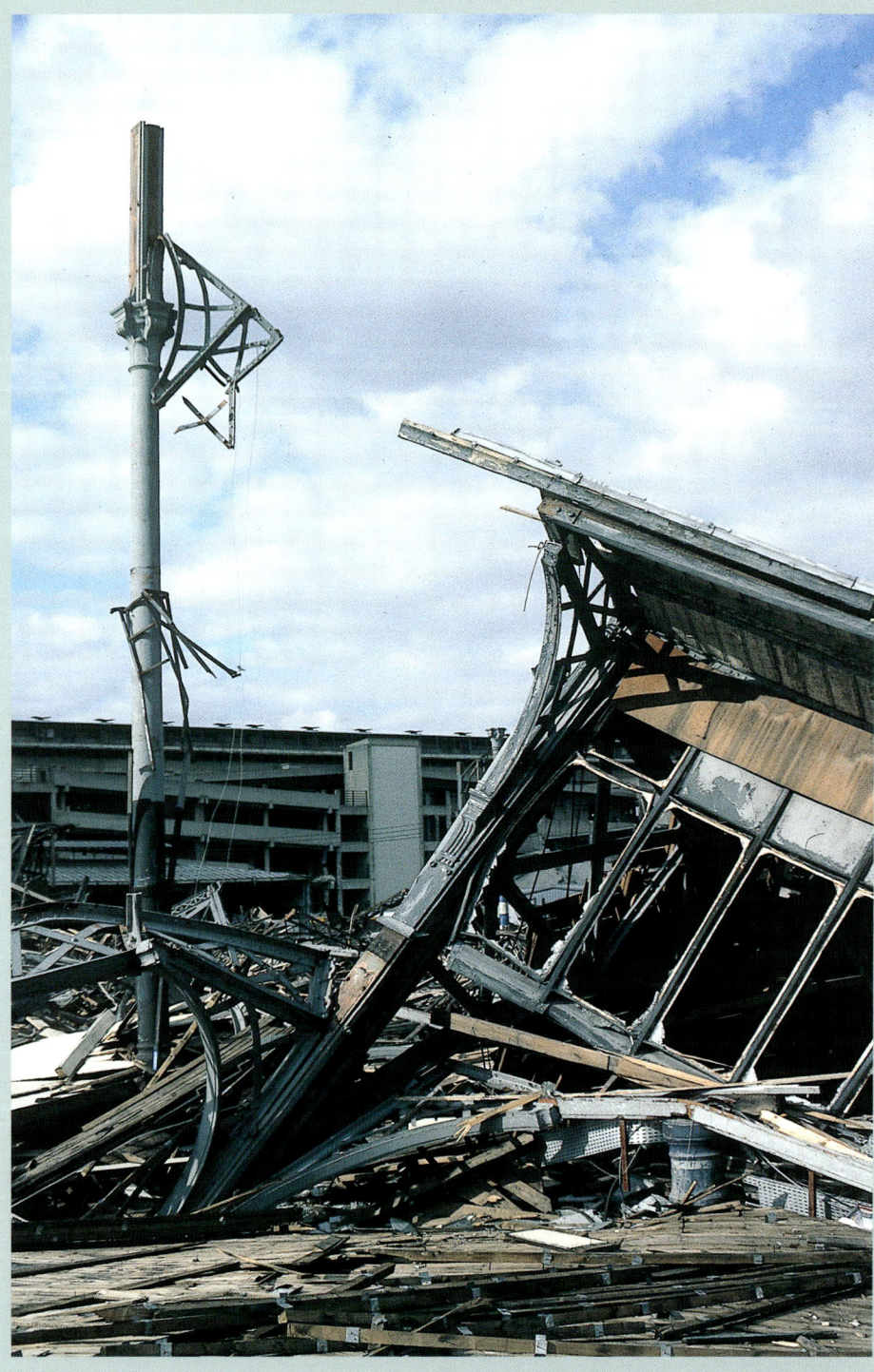

Demolition of the sheep shed, and the swine and calf shed.

the juxtaposition of the large "Prairies," the theme gardens and the Folies gives rise to a very convincing town planning system. I think that the project chosen was the best one. I often compare the Parc de La Villette and the Parc Citroën. The Parc Citroën is solemn, while the Parc de La Villette brings together large-scale facilities and areas of vegetation with micro-facilities and micro-areas of vegetation. Vegetation and stone are handled according to scales that never mix with each other. What you've got is a system of overlaid grids which functions very well. One scale for built objects, another for the false clearings and yet another for the theme gardens: the Parc de La Villette is a collage

— and a very astute one, given the enormousness of the buildings on the site. But Tschumi's project has another virtue, which is its project as process side. The Parc de La Villette is an "evolving" project; a project in movement, in the sense that it has to adapt to spatial appropriations not initially planned for. Now that these appropriations have emerged, I say, let's privatise the Folies; let's create a little building plot around each one and really break up La Villette. The basic problem is that the park was laid out over a site that had no prior, built-in use. There's an investigative method you can use for this kind of site, which consists of letting the reigning disorder organise itself. You open up the site and watch it turn into the kind of urban squat you find all over the place these days. The space ends up being shaped by a series of chance factors, and eventually finds the right clientele. So producing a space is one thing, and appropriating it is another. At La Villette the state put a lot of money into building major facilities, but life ultimately appears in the interstices — in the form of new uses for which, paradoxically, appropriate spaces are lacking. This is the role I'm saying the Folies could play. Instead of becoming sententious, petrified objects, they must accompany the appropriation we're talking about. The Folies are created; the uses emerge; and then the Folies are appropriated by these new uses. It's all a question of time. Rem Koolhaas' project worked something like that – on paper at least, as we can't know what the result would have been if it had been built.

Rem Koolhaas sees the grid of Folies as out of scale.

The grid of Folies becomes legible as you move about the site: their rhythm is governed by the marking out of boundaries, not by continuity. But then I'm easy to please where La Villette is concerned.

Let's talk about the Grande Halle. What were the basic themes behind the rehabilitation?

First off we had to preserve the identity of the site – the sequential aspect, and the possibility of a global reading of the framework – while creating sub-modules for uses with their own individual constraints. This was a very tricky exercise, given that it was hard to find room for a real architecture between the need for performance-style illusion and the awe-inspiring size of the shelter. The principle we decided on was to first carve out, in the centre of the building, an enormous logistics bay six metres above floor level. This wasn't all that difficult, as the loads involved there tend to push the columns outwards, with each system working as a kind of vault. Then we had to create three thousand square metres of ground-level floor: this explains the lateral studios and balconies, whose arrangement allows for a continuous visual grasp of the building. Inside the studios are the utilities and, beneath some of them, the sanitary facilities.

Last, there was the linearity of the nave and, more particularly, the staging equipment: mobile platforms and travelling cranes mean you can get from one side of the nave to the other and at the same time provide movable staging facilities. All this was necessary to the sound functioning of the building. There were a lot of real technical feats involved, especially the mobile tympanums at each end – they mean the travelling cranes can be moved outside – and the retractable tympanum that

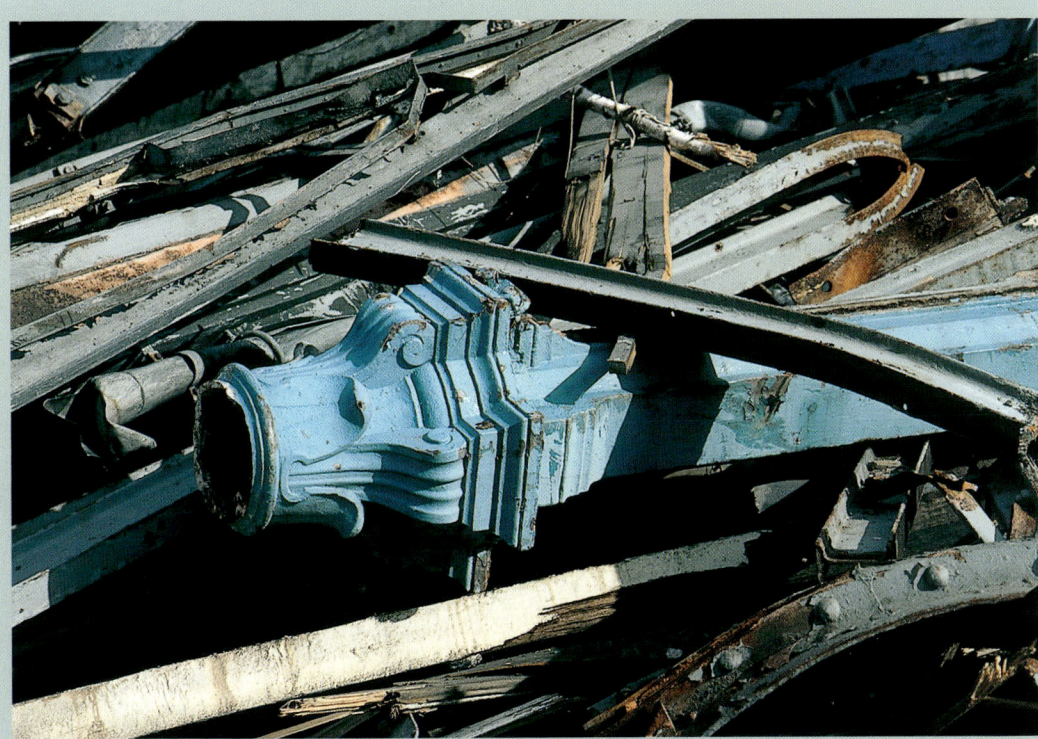

Demolition of the sheep shed, and the swine and calf shed.

INTERVIEW WITH BERNARD REICHEN   225

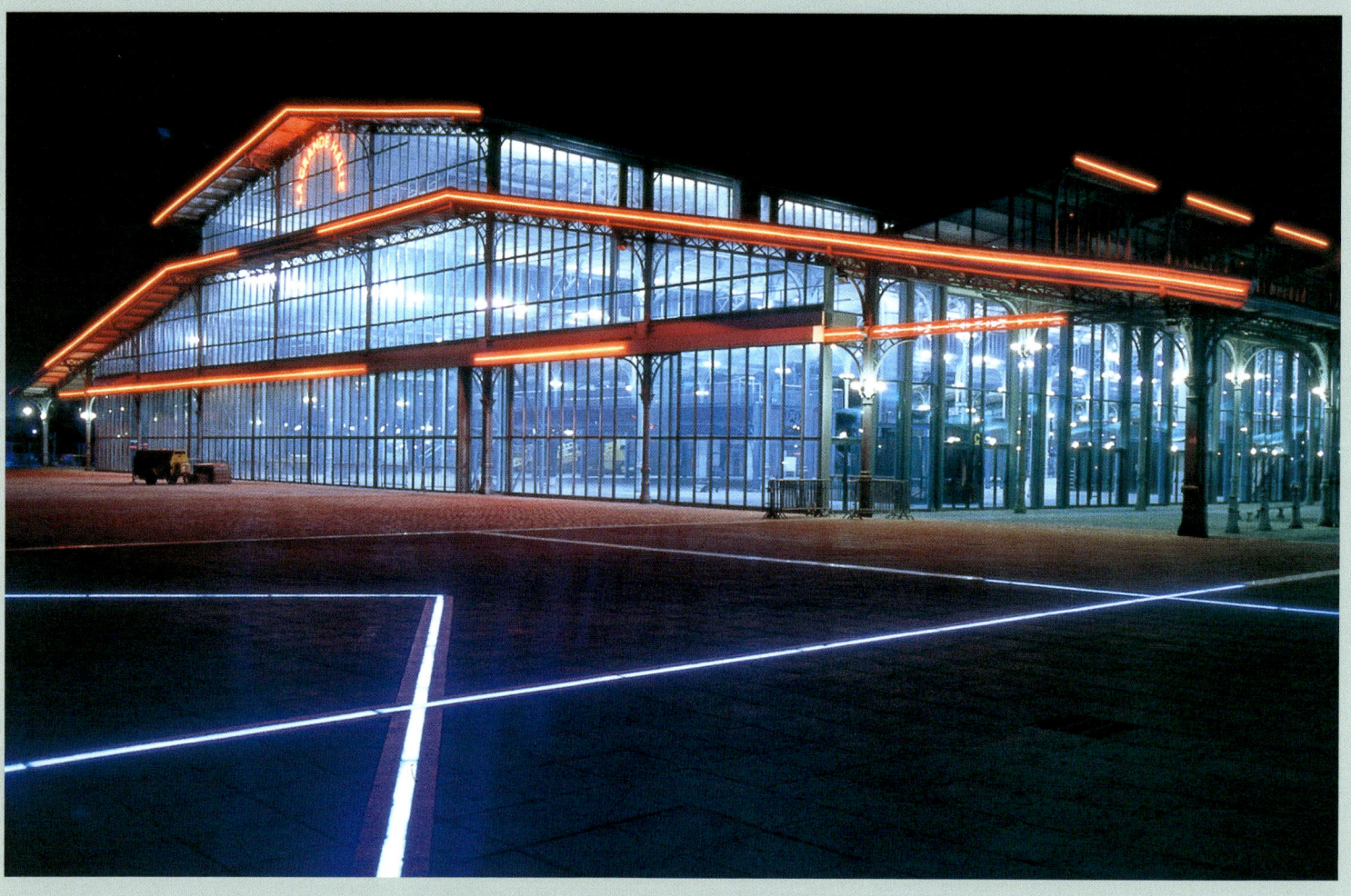

The Grande Halle (architects: B. Reichen and P. Robert). The south façade. Night view from the Pôle Public de Diffusion Musicale et Muséologique (Public Music and Museum Complex).

lets you cut the building in two and create a two thousand seat hall quite separate from the rest of the space. Our contribution was strictly technical – meticulous *and* technical, if you like. We weren't out to make a work of art. If we'd been thinking in terms of an architectural operation, we would certainly have done a lot of damage. So in fact we slipped in between the performance and shelter functions.

What about the façades? Is the use of glass intended to preserve the feeling of transparency that characterised the old cattle shed?

Yes. We wanted to keep the reading of the space that existed before rehabilitation. The long glass façades you mention are "active" façades. Each glass-bearing column is designed like a fishing rod – articulated at the top to ensure that the wind loadings the façade has to cope with are never transmitted to the building. This was a constraint we had to abide by: that the building should not have to bear anything but direct wind. In addition, the size of the façade posts means they can accommodate all air intakes: heating and cooling air arrives via the façade, with a return system in the roof sending the air back down to heat the central part of the building.

Why are the emergency staircases at an angle to the façades?

We wanted to establish a dual perception, a relationship with the building as a shelter and with what I like to call its furnishings: balconies, lifts, emergency exits – everything except the framework, which we refused to touch. The other thing is that the Grande Halle is off-square: it's angled at ninety-three degrees, which is also the case of all the stone buildings in the complex. This gave us something like three metres of skew from one end to the other, which is enormous. In a sense, our job was simply to fit an orthogonal system into a non-orthogonal one. The travelling cranes, for instance, function orthogonally. And then we solved the problems of the points of junction between the two systems by introducing a third kind of system.

Why wasn't the Grande Halle built orthogonally?

At first we thought that Jules de Mérindol had opted for this system as a way of improving the building's wind-bracing. If the cattle shed had been the only example on the site, we could have interpreted the choice in technical terms; but the problem is that the stone pavilions were built the same way. So I don't have an answer to that question.

Was the conversion of the cattle shed absolutely necessary? Looking at the floor area of the old meat market it's fair to wonder whether or not the site wouldn't have been better off without the Grande Halle. And then it's home to just about

The Grande Halle (architects: B. Reichen and P. Robert). The west façade.

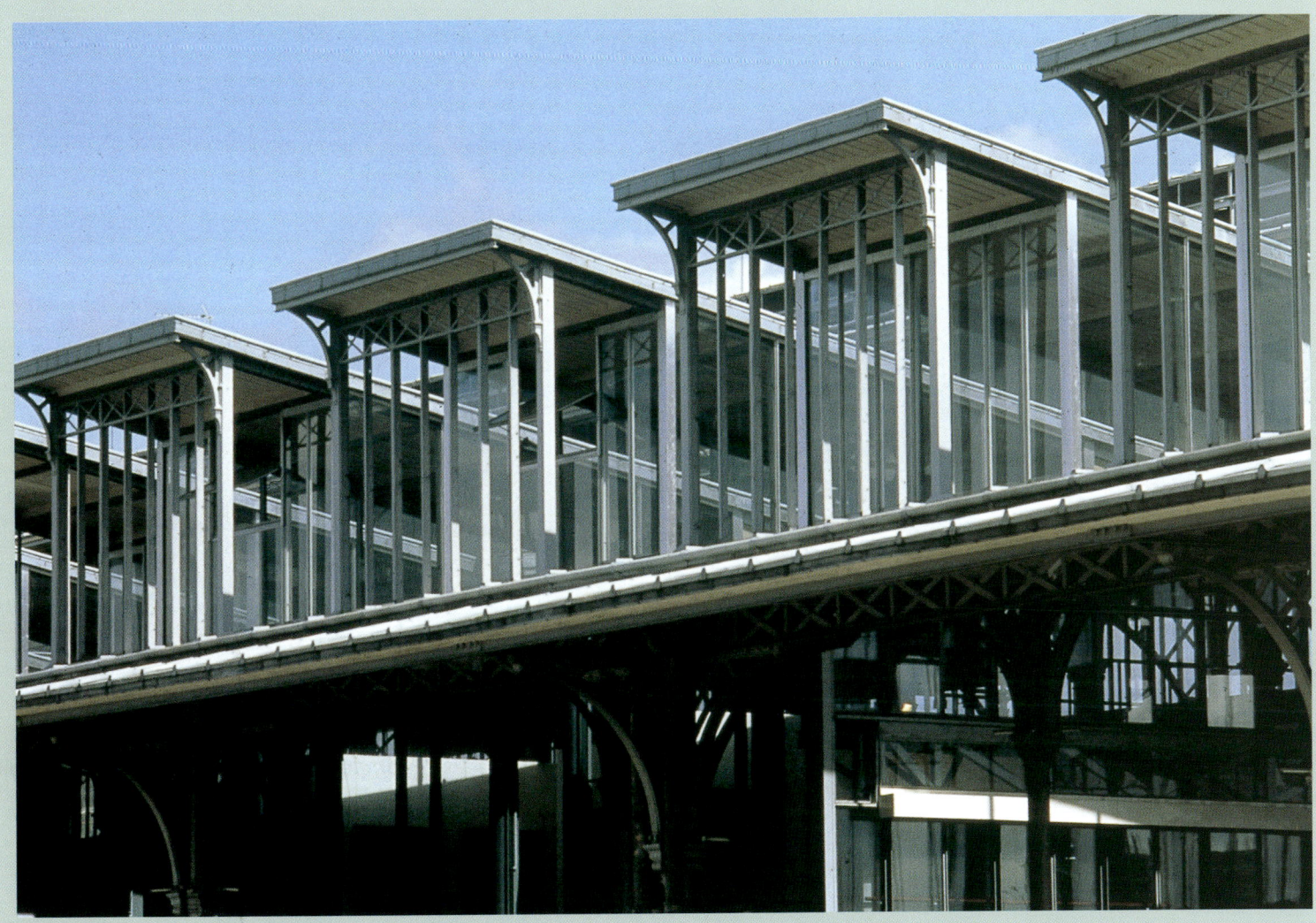

INTERVIEW WITH BERNARD REICHEN

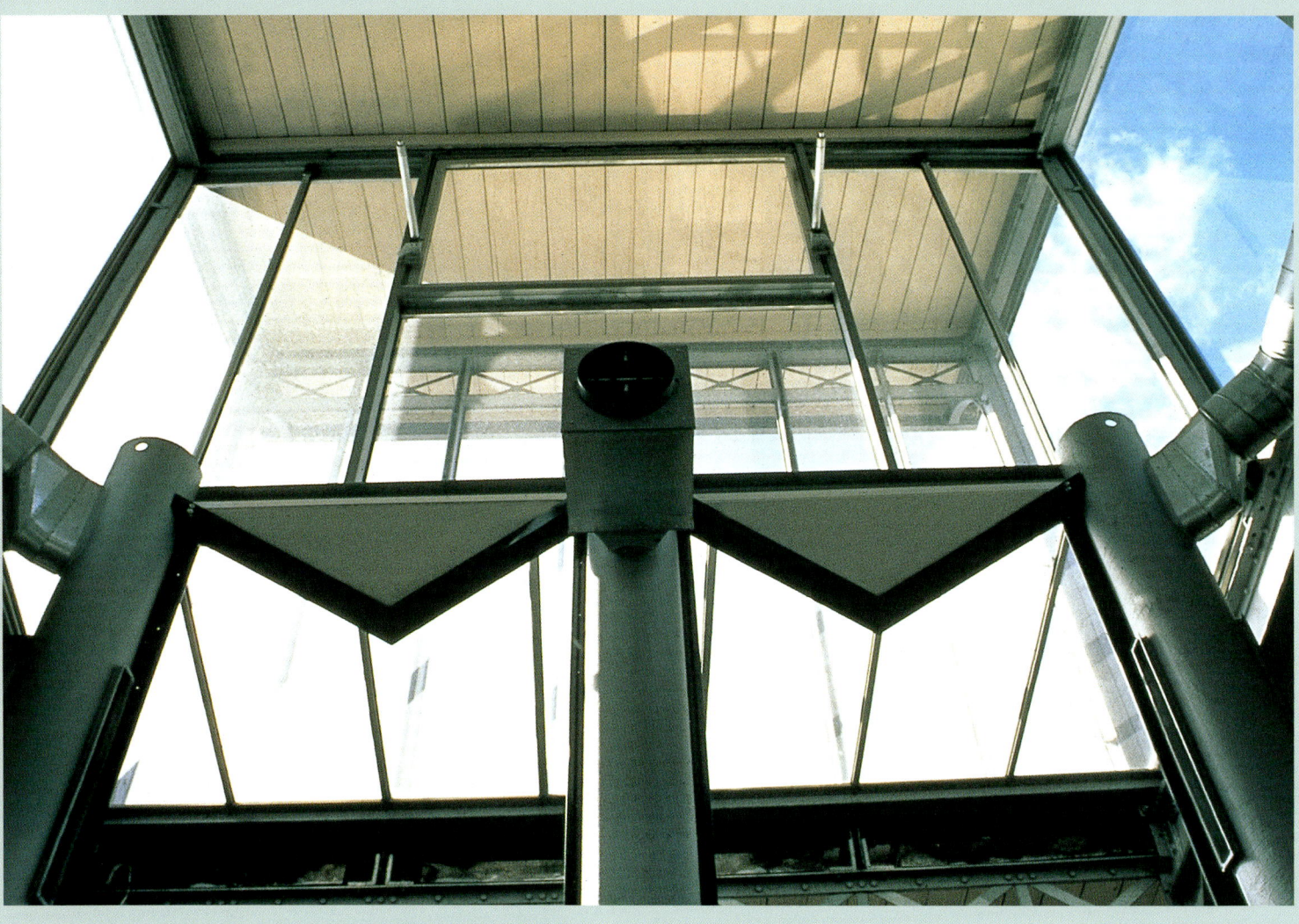

La Grande Halle (architects: B. Reichen and P. Robert). Detail of a façade.

all the site's activities – to the inevitable detriment of the Folies.

Abattoirs have been demolished all over the place, but you don't always end up with La Villette in their place. Sometimes you find yourself stuck with the worst kind of low-grade technology complex. It seems to me that to have a public space of this size – and covered, into the bargain – is a real stroke of luck. And there's no arguing with luck. There's also what I call the right of precedence. The cattle shed determined the original layout of La Villette, so it was important that it should be reincorporated. But there's something else, too: a detailed analysis of the history of the site shows that it was home to two totally different worlds, separated from each other by the Canal de l'Ourcq. To the south were the traders and to the north the butchers: two worlds tied to two quite distinct areas. But while one of these worlds – that of the traders and the cattle shed – never ceased to justify its existence, the other had been directly involved in a national fiasco. When Paul Delouvrier came to La Villette, he had to make people accept the idea that a building like the meat market, a symbol of France's techno-structure, could be rehabilitated in spite of never having been used. So the site was rapidly marked by these two dissimilar worlds: on the one hand the survival of a certain state of mind, with the retention of this enormous, very nineteenth-century metal umbrella, and on the other, the forced-march modernity of the old meat market, now the Cité des Sciences. So I see it as logical that these two enormous buildings, linked by two dissimilar histories, should have been the focus of the same conversion project. Now it seems legitimate to wonder if we could have dismantled the cattle shed and perhaps reassembled it further east, as a way of generating a dynamic out towards the periphery. But in my opinion, if the shed had been pulled down we would never have put it up again. We've become a concrete generation and we've lost the mobility that went with metal. The old world's-fair dynamic involved a system of large-scale events calling for practically unlimited raising and dismantling of this kind of building. That's not so much the case these days.

Interview by Alain Orlandini.

THE ZÉNITH DE PARIS: A VENUE FOR ROCK

The constructional system for the Zénith was conceived so that it would support not only the roofing material but also the technical infrastructure needed for shows (stage lighting, sets, screens) and good internal access for the technicians.

The result was a set of twenty-four poles fifteen metres high, set along the edges of a square with sides of seventy metres. These supported sixty beams, each thirteen and a half metres long and three metres high, which joined to form twenty-five squares. Diagonally across the squares went twenty-five three-dimensional arcs held in place by lacing tubes set at the top of the beams. These are what give the roof its convex form. The great number of double-curved surfaces created by these arcs eliminate any risk of sound concentration. The work began in July 1983 and was completed in January 1984 for a cost of (excluding tax) 28.6 million francs (4.36 million euros). It was financed by the Caisse des Dépôts et Consignations (75%) and by a subsidy from the Ministry of Culture (25%).

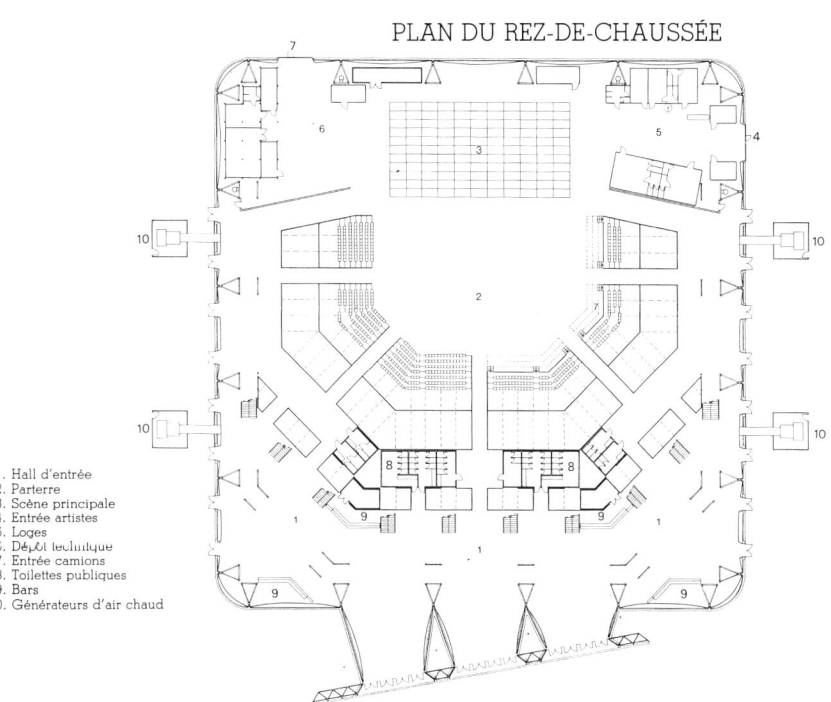

1. Hall d'entrée
2. Parterre
3. Scène principale
4. Entrée artistes
5. Loges
6. Dépôt technique
7. Entrée camions
8. Toilettes publiques
9. Bars
10. Générateurs d'air chaud

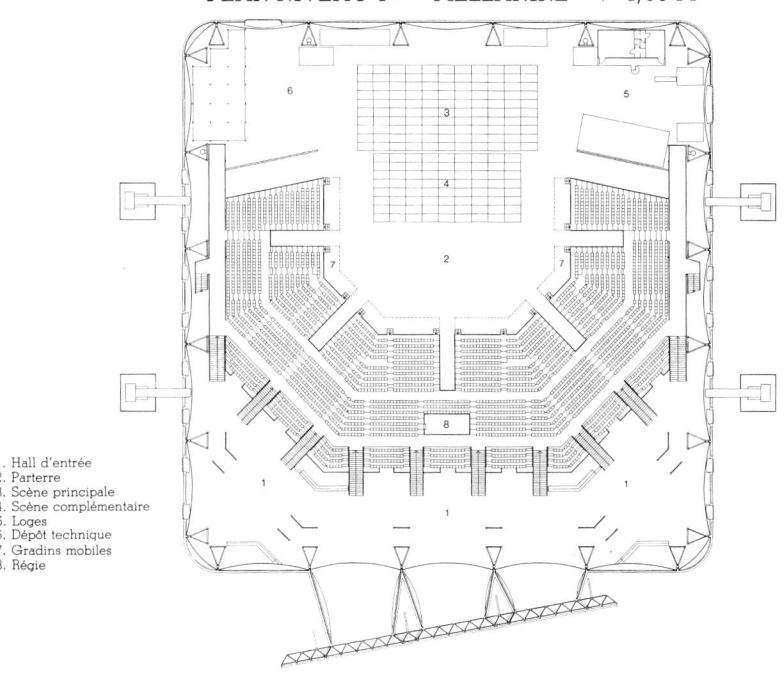

1. Hall d'entrée
2. Parterre
3. Scène principale
4. Scène complémentaire
5. Loges
6. Dépôt technique
7. Gradins mobiles
8. Régie

The Zénith de Paris (architects: P. Chaix and J.-P. Morel). Plans of the ground floor and level one.

PLAN NIVEAU 2ème - MEZZANINE - + 8,00 M

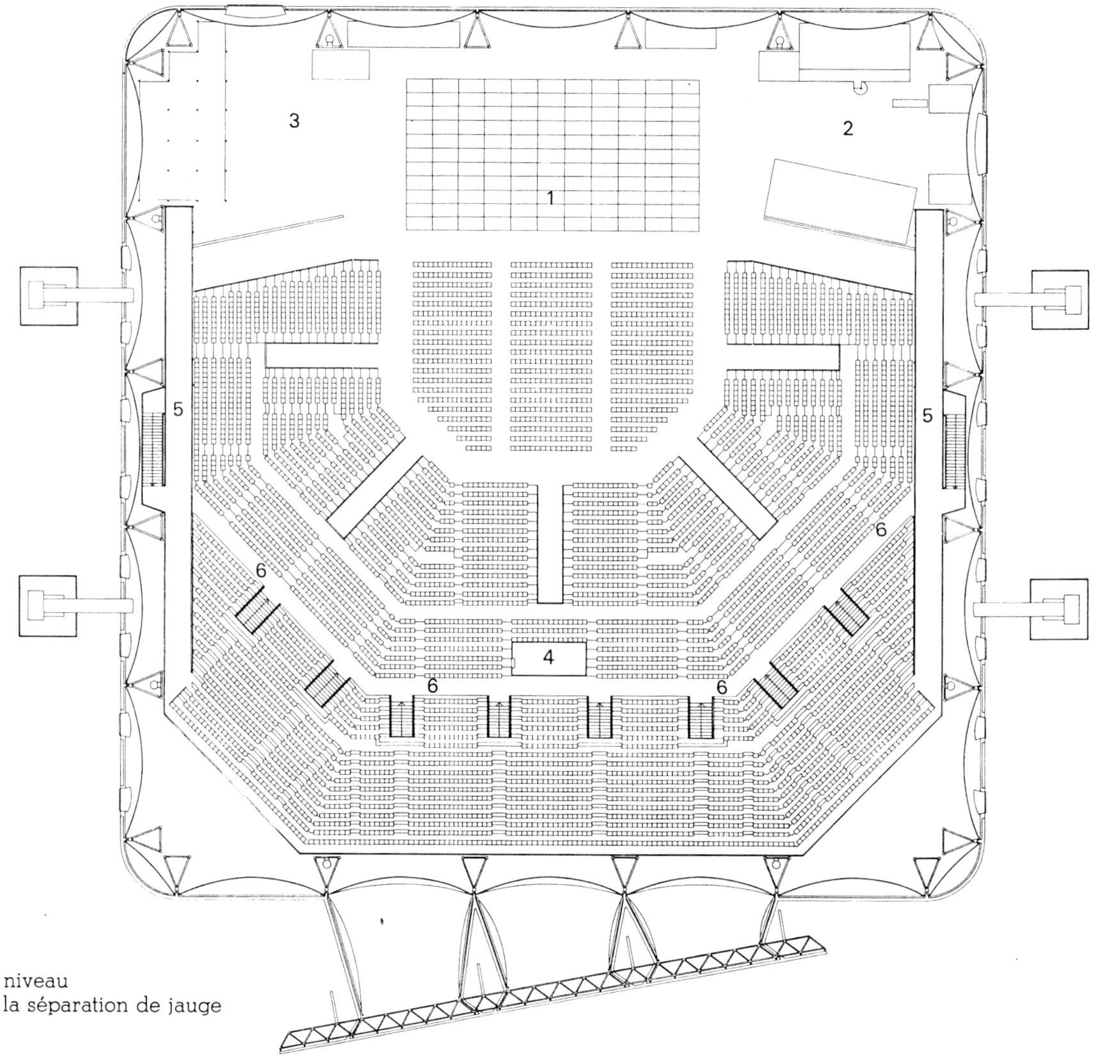

1. Scène principale
2. Loges
3. Zone technique
4. Régie
5. Mezzanine 2ème niveau
6. Emplacement de la séparation de jauge

The Zénith de Paris (architects: P. Chaix and J.-P. Morel).
Above: Plan of level two.
Right: Cross sections.

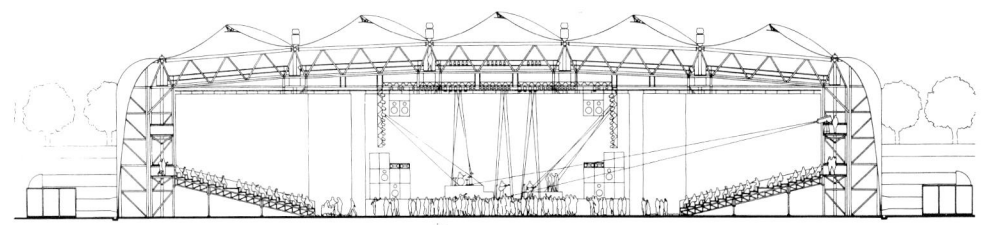

COUPE TRANSVERSALE VERS LA SCENE

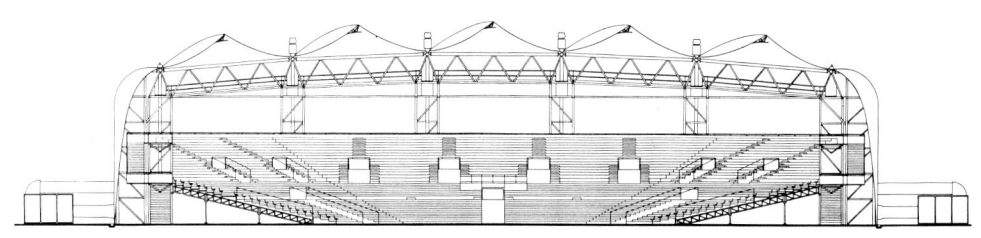

COUPE TRANSVERSALE VERS LE HALL

LA VILLETTE: 1971–1995

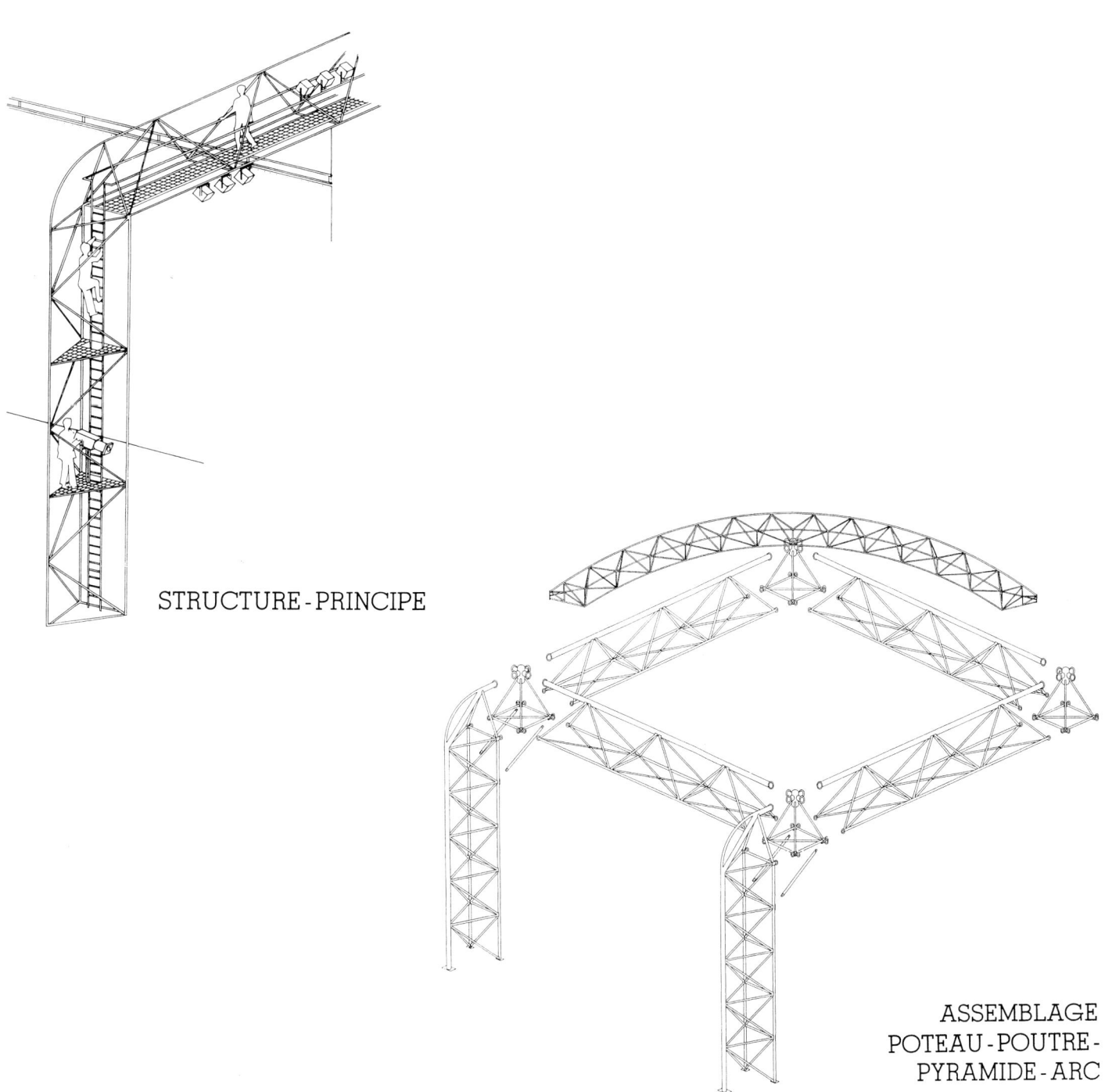

The Zénith de Paris (architects: P. Chaix and J.-P. Morel). Sections and detail drawings.

STRUCTURE - PRINCIPE

ASSEMBLAGE
POTEAU - POUTRE -
PYRAMIDE - ARC

THE ZÉNITH DE PARIS

INTERVIEWS

Daniel Colling

Philippe Chaix

Interview with Daniel Colling

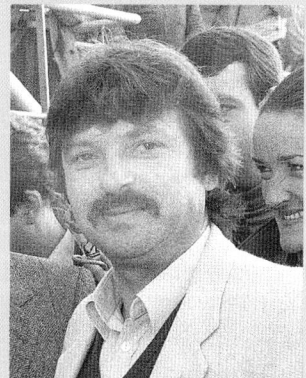

The Zénith de Paris inaugurated by President François Mitterrand. Left to right: Christian Dupavillon, technical adviser to the Ministry of Culture; Jack Lang, minister of Culture; Ségolène Royal, *chargée de mission* to the President's Office; President François Mitterrand; Juliette Gréco, singer; Daniel Colling, *chargé de mission* for the Ministry of Culture; security officer; Jacques Attali, special adviser to the president.

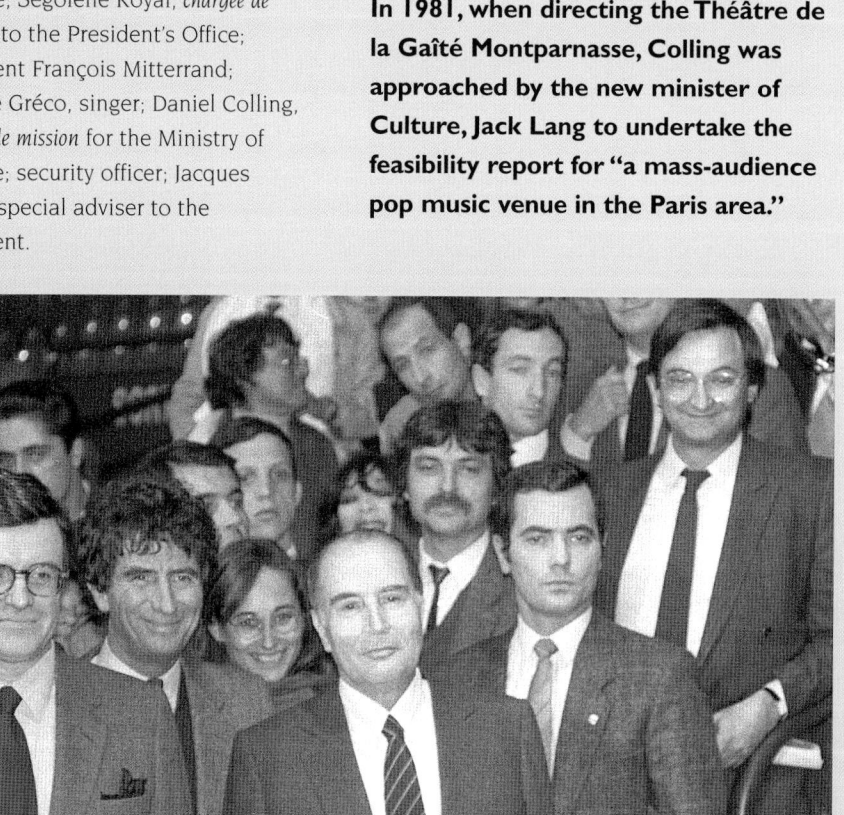

Daniel Colling graduated from the École Nationale Professionnelle in Nancy in 1968. He soon left his native Lorraine, where he had already begun to organise concerts, and "came up" to Paris to co-produce the national tours of the Concerts Mazarine and Alice Productions before setting up his own agency, Écoute S'il Pleut, in 1976. There he promoted the development of a new kind of "song with text." In 1979, he created Speedi, a production company working for, among others, comedian Guy Bedos, and singers Brigitte Fontaine and Jacques Higelin. In 1981, when directing the Théâtre de la Gaîté Montparnasse, Colling was approached by the new minister of Culture, Jack Lang to undertake the feasibility report for "a mass-audience pop music venue in the Paris area."

Three years later, the Paris Zénith was inaugurated with great pomp by President François Mitterrand. The first of many – nine Zéniths have been built around France, and more are on the drawing board – this concert hall with a capacity of six thousand five hundred, welcomes nearly a million spectators every year. It is run by Coker, the company founded by Colling and Daniel Kéravec, in partnership with the SCET and FNAC. Colling himself heads the Zénith development programme. Here this indefatigable and enthusiastic show business professional, founder of the Printemps de Bourges music festival and president of the Centre National de la Chanson, des Variétés et du Jazz (body in charge of programming at the Zénith) looks back on the great adventure of the Zénith.

Could you take me through the origins of the Zénith project?

In September 1981, in my capacity as a music organiser, I was contacted by one of Jack Lang's advisers, Christian Dupavillon. Now, Christian Dupavillon is no ordinary adviser. An architect and writer, he was, if I can put it like this, "responsible" for Jean-Paul Goude's extraordinary parade in 1989. He was also behind that very provocative greeting card showing Victor Hugo clad in leather. Dupavillon had been informed that someone called Colling was championing a certain kind of artistic identity and that, should the ministry decide to talk to the "professionals," he was someone they definitely had to see. In his office, Dupavillon was very direct, "Do you agree with me that the problem for pop music today is the lack of suitable venues?" You should know that before 1981, the Ministry of Culture had never shown any interest in pop and rock music. That, as

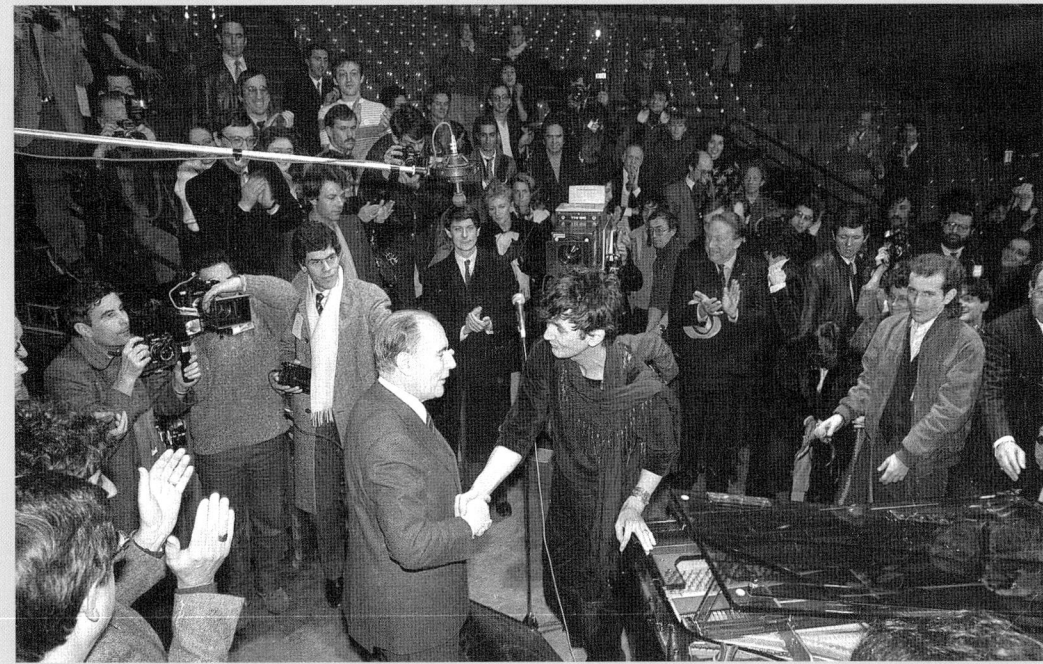

Left: The Zénith de Paris, inaugurated by President François Mitterrand. Here, in conversation with Jacques Higelin (behind, to the right: Charles Trenet).

Below: Johnny Halliday, Jack Lang and Daniel Colling touring the Zénith de Paris during construction.

Jacques Duhamel once put it, was the responsibility of Monsieur Barclay.[1] So, I replied to Christan Dupavillon that the theatre both public and private, had enjoyed special structures for years now. That sports centres had been built for athletes, exhibition centres for exhibitions, and congress centres for congress-goers. But that for pop and rock music, which had become massively popular since the 1970s, there was nothing. We were, I said, forced to "act the migrant cuckoo" in sports and exhibition centres whose acoustics and facilities were often terrible. The minister therefore mandated me to undertake a feasibility study for a high-capacity music venue to be built in or around Paris. At first, my mission was very vague, "A report! A report!" they told me. To do so, I joined up with a friend who specialises in music communication, Daniel Kéravec. We began by making a theoretical study of the market for music in order to determine the capacity of the venue. This general feasibility study led us to the working assumption of about five hundred thousand spectators a year.

Next came the question of the site. We wanted to avoid going outside Paris, except perhaps to La Défense – especially since we realised that Parisians very rarely go out to suburban venues.

So, I started looking for land. I went, among other places, to La Défense – the Grande Arche hadn't been built yet – and at the EPAD they presented me with a list of possible locations. I discovered that there was not much land available. I then thought of locating on the edge of Paris. I went out to the motorway interchange at Bagnolet, which is what was eventually chosen. For us, this enormous "bazaar" designed in the 1950s offered numerous advantages for a large-capacity concert space: a concrete slab of three hectares in the middle of the interchange that could take the auditorium, and covered three levels of parking and the Gallieni Métro station. Bagnolet was very much the fruit of post-war ideas about urban planning. They imagined that motorists coming from the provinces on the future A3 motorway would be prepared to park there and then travel into Paris by Métro. Anyway, because people in high places told me to think in terms of the east-west balance, I thought to myself that Bagnolet could well be the ideal spot. In 1982, the ministry

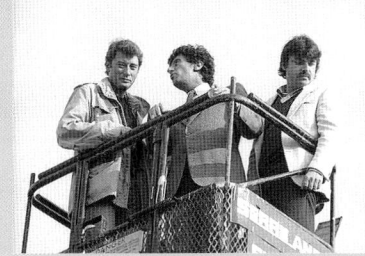

INTERVIEW WITH DANIEL COLLING

organised a limited competition – just ten candidates – for French architects only. Paul Andreu chaired the jury. I was on the technical committee. Claude Vasconi won. In those days there was no talk about the Zénith, only the "Bagnolet rock auditorium." Then François Mitterrand announced the construction officially. The planned capacity was nine thousand. That's what was required for a good match between the capacity and the market. Then Daniel Kéravec and I decided to change directions. The first estimates priced the project at about sixty million euros. A permanent structure with seating for nine thousand over a car park was not easy to build. By way of comparison, Bercy cost one hundred and fifty million euros to build. There was no way that the ministry was going to pay such a sum, so we had to put together a financial package. This involved the Paris town hall (controlled by the right-of-centre RPR), the town of Bagnolet (whose finances were limited), the department (Communist Party) and the regional council (UDF)! In the political climate of the time, there was simply no way you could get all those people to agree, especially about a rock venue. The political upset of 1981 was still fresh in everyone's memory. However, when we were carrying out our report, Daniel Kéravec and I met an architect called Philippe Chaix who designed and built a small cultural centre with nine hundred seats for a town in the provinces. A three-dimensional structure supporting a double canvas, ephemeral and light, certainly, but much more hardwearing than a simple big top, and without a single pole inside it. We asked Philippe Chaix if his structure could be blown up proportionally. His engineers answered in the affirmative. So we went to the ministry with Philippe Chaix to try to persuade them to accept the idea of a preliminary phase because we had lost faith in the idea of building a permanent auditorium at Bagnolet.

Did you expect to build this preliminary project at Bagnolet?

Certainly not! It would have been absurd to do this preliminary project at the site planned for the permanent auditorium. Given that it was a temporary facility, it was easy to fit it into other projects. That's when we were told that La Villette, where Bernard Tschumi had just won the competition to build the park, would be the ideal place. We knew that the construction of La Villette would take place in a time frame of some fifteen years, which turned out to be true. We also knew that its history was in a way linked to that of pop music shows – I am thinking of the Pavillon de Paris, which used to be in the old sheep shed, and Jean Richard's hippodrome. Christian Dupavillon was with us on this, but we had to fight hard to sell the project to Paul Delouvrier, president of the EPPV (public body in charge of the park), and François Barré, director of the Park Mission. But building such a structure was beyond our competence as impresarios. When you are planning to build a concert hall, it's not enough just to question the organisers. You also have to get the views of a developer. So we told Christian Dupavillon that we were grateful to him for thinking of us, but that we wanted him to appoint a project director under whom we could work. Which is how Serge Goldberg was appointed. Serge Goldberg had been in charge of developing the new town of Saint-Quentin-en-Yvelines. He had just been in Africa, where he was mandated to build hospitals. Serge Goldberg was a top-grade civil servant, an alumnus of Polytechnique and the Ponts et Chaussées. Our collaboration was very positive. He particularly appreciated the contents of our feasibility study. The Zénith project was fervently advocated by Christian Dupavillon, Serge Goldberg and myself. François Barré,

Paul Delouvrier and Bernard Tschumi were rather sceptical. Paul Delouvrier kept saying to me, "Why the hell do you keep bugging us with your concert hall?" He was right. "I'm sorry" I told him, "but it's what the minister wants." To which Delouvrier retorted, "And I answer to the president!" Fortunately, we were dealing with intelligent people here. François Barré had a feeling for the thing. We were talking about popular artistic expression. As for Paul Delouvrier, we sold him on the project by saying, "Our auditorium will be built in a year, and last only three years; your project is under construction, and will remain so for many years. You have to find a way of selling its image, and we can make that image positive by bringing in activity." Three years after the Zénith was built, Paul Delouvrier came to see me and said, "You've won, kid. They'll never take down your auditorium." After the construction of the Zénith, Serge Goldberg was made president of the EPPV. He was later mandated to manage the Bibliothèque François-Mitterrand (François Mitterrand Library).

So the Zénith was "sold" to Paul Delouvrier as a temporary project?

Of course! We really had to insist on the fact that the Zénith could be dismantled. Taken down. There was the Bagnolet project, there would be the provisional project at La Villette, merely its prefiguration. But remember: the Eiffel Tower was built with the firm intention of taking it down two years later.

How was the Zénith financed and built?

The operating principle recommended in our report was based on hiring equipment out to producers who would bear the risks of their own shows. Our study demonstrated that the profitability of the Zénith would be such that it would be possible to pay back the loan needed for its construction, priced at the time at under seven and a half million euros. Because it was a state project, we naturally applied to the Caisse des Dépôts et Consignations. Its president, Robert Lion, responded very positively. The Caisse des Dépôts therefore lent the funds needed for the investment, while acting as client through the SCIC, one of its subsidiaries. The outline proposals, full project design, and the tendering happened record fast, between November 1982 and August 1983. The Zénith was built in under four months, between September and December 1983. It was inaugurated by François Mitterrand on 12 January 1984. Three stages were set up for the occasion: one for Charles Trenet, another for Jacques Higelin and a third for Zéro de Conduite (now known as Blankass), a group of kids from Issoudun. But the artist who really inaugurated the Zénith was Renaud, from 15 January to 8 February 1984.

Why did you choose the name Zénith?

When you are choosing a name in this kind of business, it is very important that it shouldn't express the nature of the project too literally, because then it might age prematurely. It absolutely has to be at a tangent. It is the activity that makes the concept powerful. The idea was to evoke an aeroplane, since the Zénith was about live shows. In front of the Zénith there was this famous grain elevator rising up to the sky, a relic from the abattoir days. That made me think of the sky, of aeroplanes, but also of youth, of comics, of emotions and dreams. An aeroplane is something that glides. We suggested "Dakota" to Jack Lang. Dakota is the Indian name of an American state, and it

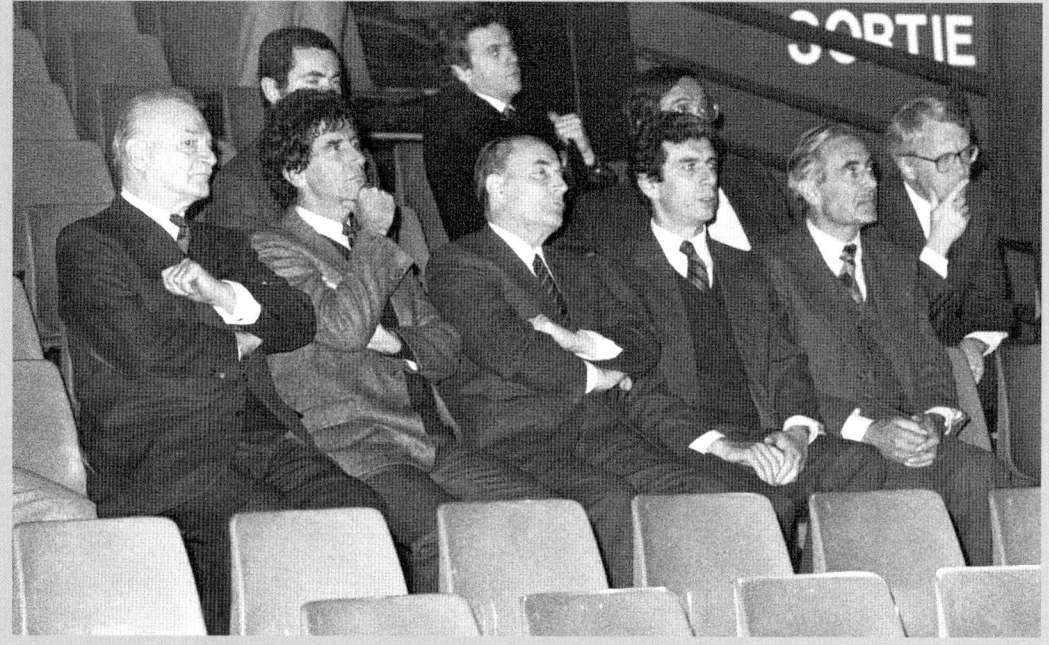

President François Mitterrand inaugurates the Zénith de Paris. Left to right: Paul Delouvrier, chairman of the EPPV; Jack Lang, minister of Culture; President François Mitterrand; Robert Lion, managing director of the Caisse des Dépôts et Consignations; Bertrand Labrusse, chairman and managing director of the SFP; Michel Vauzelle, spokesman for the President's Office.

has a good rhythm to it. It's also the name of the building where John Lennon lived in New York. Jack Lang and Christian Dupavillon weren't very keen. Looking through the Dictionnaire historique des rues de Paris, Christian Dupavillon found out that a zeppelin called the Zénith had taken off from a gas factory located at La Villette in 1875. At Le Bourget there was a general who was willing to give us an old Dakota plane that we wanted to hang from the grain elevator. That's what we ended up doing. That plane, which stayed up there on the grain elevator for six years, is still the logo of the Zénith de Paris today. The name Zénith was registered in autumn 1983 by Coker, the company set up by Daniel Kéravec and myself.

Other halls with the Zénith name have been built since.

The Zénith and Printemps de Bourges brought me close to Jack Lang. I was thus able to suggest to him that it would be useful to repeat the Zénith operation in the provinces, since they too were short of facilities of this kind. He readily agreed.

I persuaded Georges Frèche, mayor of Montpellier, to build a Zénith with the same architectural principles as the one in Paris. The Montpellier Zénith was inaugurated in February 1986. But I told Jack Lang that if we wanted to succeed, it was essential not to impose the "elephant skin," as they called the Zénith in the provinces. They had reservations. People wanted a Zénith too, but a Zénith of their own, not a carbon copy of the Paris one. Local politicians were worried, "But it's canvas," they said. "Kids can cut it up with knives!" And we replied, "What the professionals want is equipment that is up to standard. If Dominique Baudis wants to build his Zénith in red brick,[2] that's his problem. The main thing is that trucks should be able to get to the auditorium, that you can hang up the spotlights. The architectural label doesn't matter." To facilitate the construction of Zéniths around France, Coker agreed to sell the name Zénith to the state for a symbolic franc, but on condition that it should be used in accordance with the specifications appended to the contract of sale. These specifications were drawn up in close collaboration with music professionals.

They now exist in the form of an official document that standardises the "Zénith" concept, in terms of construction and staging and running. If you are a mayor and you want to get a subsidy to build a Zénith, you absolutely have to refer to it. In terms of architecture, it gives no indications concerning the envelope. Only the interior spaces are subject to norms. In terms of running the thing, however, it is clearly stated that the Zénith is to be hired out to producers. We demanded that the management of the Zénith should be handed to professionals who are not allowed to produce. Since 1990, the Ministry of Culture has set up and financed a Zénith programme based on these same specifications. Zéniths have been built in Toulon and Pau (1992), Nancy and Caen (1993), Lille (1995), Orléans (1996), Toulouse (1999), Rouen (2001) and Clermont-Ferrand (2003). Others are being studied, notably for Amiens, Dijon, Limoges, Nantes, Saint-Denis de la Réunion, Saint-Étienne and Strasbourg.

You seem to really enjoy talking about the Zénith.

Yes. In conclusion, I must tell you that the Ministry of Culture's decision to talk to concert organisers and technicians rather than to architects or developers was key to the success of this facility and of the "Zénith" programme. In the name of the entire profession (musicians, producers and technicians), but also in the name of the public, I offer them my thanks.

Interview by Alain Orlandini.

Notes
1. [The founder of Barclay records, Eddie Barclay is France's most famous promoter of pop music.— Trans.]
2. [Dominique Baudis is mayor of Toulouse, a city known for its brick buildings.— Trans.]

Interview with Philippe Chaix

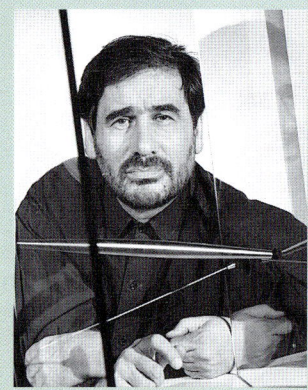

The Zénith de Paris (architects: P. Chaix and J.-P. Morel). The construction site.

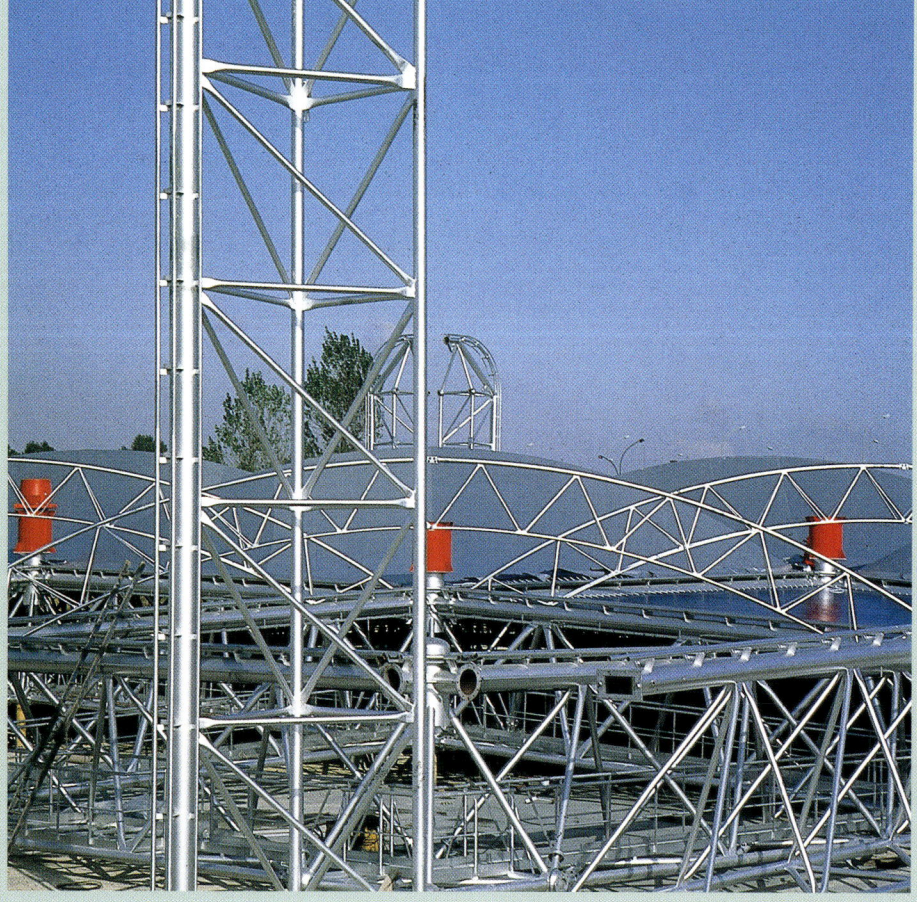

Philippe Chaix and Jean-Paul Morel became associates in 1983, and built the Zénith in 1984. The tremendous success of this six-thousand five hundred seat concert hall at the eastern end of the Parc de la Villette, led to government contracts to build two more venues, in Montpellier and Orléans. The Musée Archéologique in Saint-Romain-en-Gal, and the École Nationale des Ponts et Chaussées and the École Nationale des Sciences Géographiques in Marne-la-Vallée also gave Philippe Chaix and Jean-Paul Morel the chance to continue their pursuit of constructional truth – which is the hallmark of their work. The interview published below gave us an opportunity to go back over the conception of the Zénith, for which Philippe Chaix and Jean-Paul Robert were awarded the Équerre d'Argent in 1984.

On what occasion were you asked to build the Zénith?

At the beginning of the 1980s, the Ministry of Culture wanted to build a big rock venue in Paris. To that end a competition was organised in 1982 and won by Claude Vasconi. The structure was to be built near the motorway interchange at the Porte de Bagnolet. While waiting for it to be built, the ministry wanted to create a temporary venue that would serve to prefigure the future auditorium. It so happened that at the time I had already worked on designing ephemeral spaces in canvas, notably for a small town near Pau. The people from the ministry came to the agency and decided to entrust us with the construction of the Zénith, which absolutely had to be finished in less than a year.

Why did you choose the site of La Villette?

When we decided to locate the Zénith in the park at La Villette, the site of the old abattoir hadn't been developed yet. It was a huge wasteland that could house all kinds of activities. Don't forget that the site of La Villette was often used for rock concerts, and had been for years. The concerts were held in one of the buildings of the livestock market, called the Pavillon de Paris, and in the Jean-Richard circus tent.
To begin with, the Zénith was only temporary. We were only expecting it to be operational

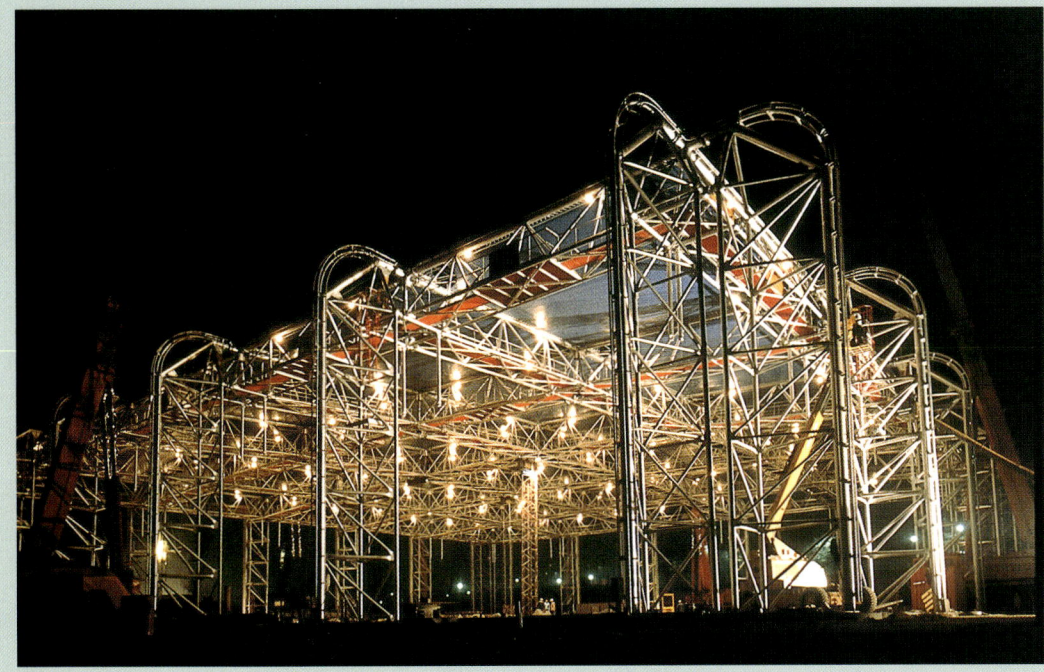

The Zénith de Paris (architects: P. Chaix and J.-P. Morel).
Left: Night view of the construction site.
Below: The roofing canvas.

for two years, after which the venue was supposed to be removed from the site.

When was it decided to keep the Zénith at La Villette for good?

When the Zénith was inaugurated, in January 1984, the Bagnolet project was already virtually written off. Also, the Zénith soon came to be seen as the first of François Mitterrand's *grands projets*. Its success, which was immediate, no doubt explains why they finally decided to keep it at La Villette.

What is the Zénith's constructional system?

Ordinary big tops consist of a structure and the canvas that it supports. So when you organise a concert in one it means that you always have to bring in a second structure that can hold the technical infrastructure. Since we had a paltry budget, we had to come up with something very simple. We therefore thought up a structure that could carry both the technical infrastructure and the canvas. This structure consists of posts and triangular beams that can cover a span of seventy metres.

Does the seating constitute an independent structure?

Yes. The seating stands right on the ground and can be modulated in keeping with the number of spectators.

How did you approach the acoustic problems?

The roofing canvas, which is in polyester fabric coated with PVC, ensures the waterproofing, and on the inner face there is a double acoustic skin comprising sheets of perforated metal and wool.

Interview by Alain Orlandini.

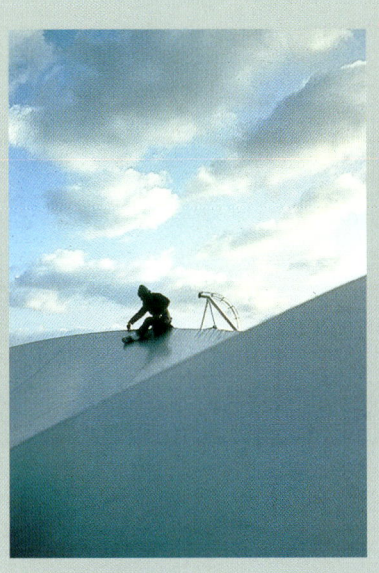

INTERVIEW WITH PHILIPPE CHAIX

THE MAISON DE LA VILLETTE: A PLACE FOR MEMORY

Rehabilitation of the Rotonde des Vétérinaires – the former veterinary checking centre, now renamed the Maison de La Villette – involved two separate operations.

The first had to do with the interior, where the need to maximise usable space led to the removal of all elements not directly related to the load-bearing structure. The outcome is an emptied central area and a technically sophisticated, roof-level substructure providing maximum mobility for exhibition facilities.

The second operation concerned the treatment of the outer shell and enhancement of its contours. The simplicity of the rotunda as volume has been emphasised in a number of ways, including the setting of the windows flush with the façades and the replacement of the old brick roof with an absolutely smooth glass fibre reinforced concrete.

Set on the fringe of the Parc de La Villette, the Maison de La Villette is now home to the history of north-eastern Paris. A history written in blood, but in architecture as well.

The abattoirs.
The Rotonde des Vétérinaires (veterinary checking centre).
Facade, section and plans.

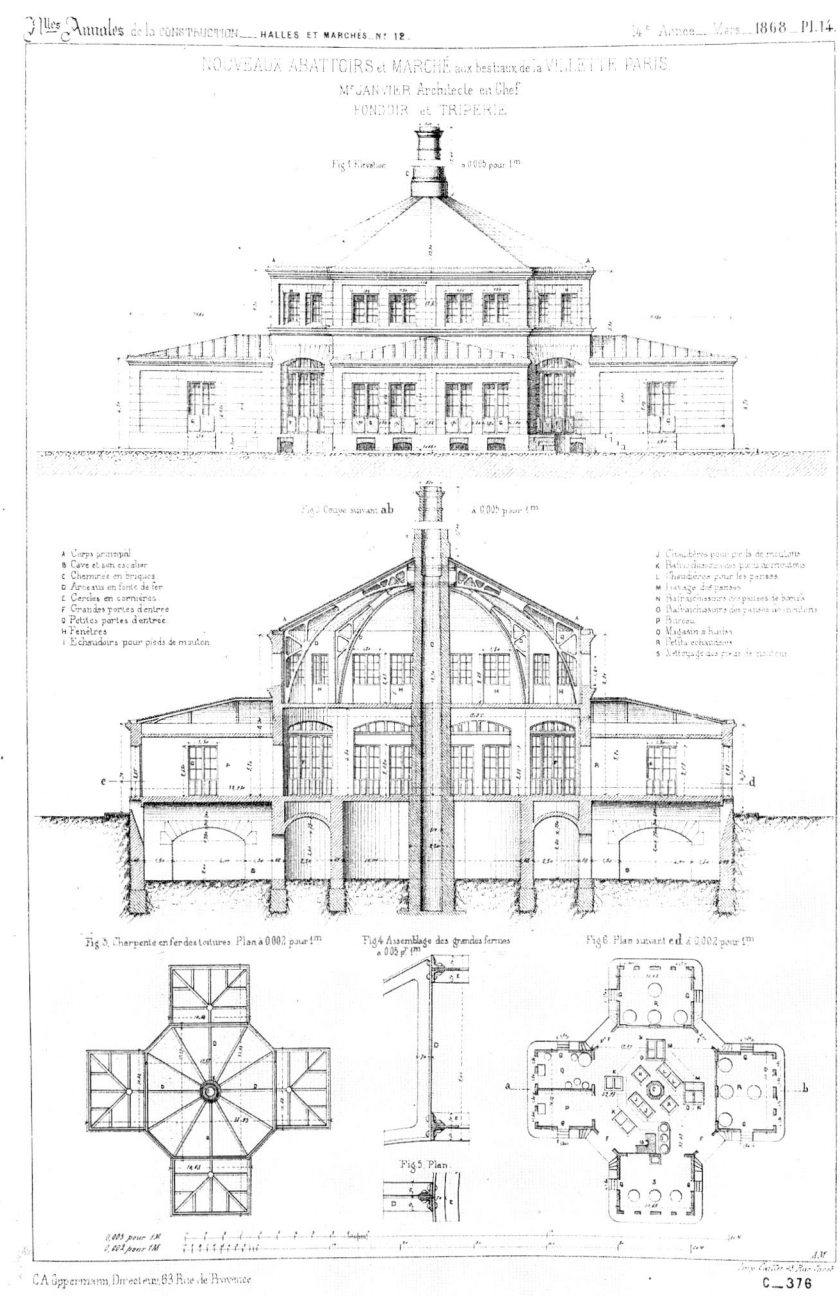

THE MAISON DE LA VILLETTE 245

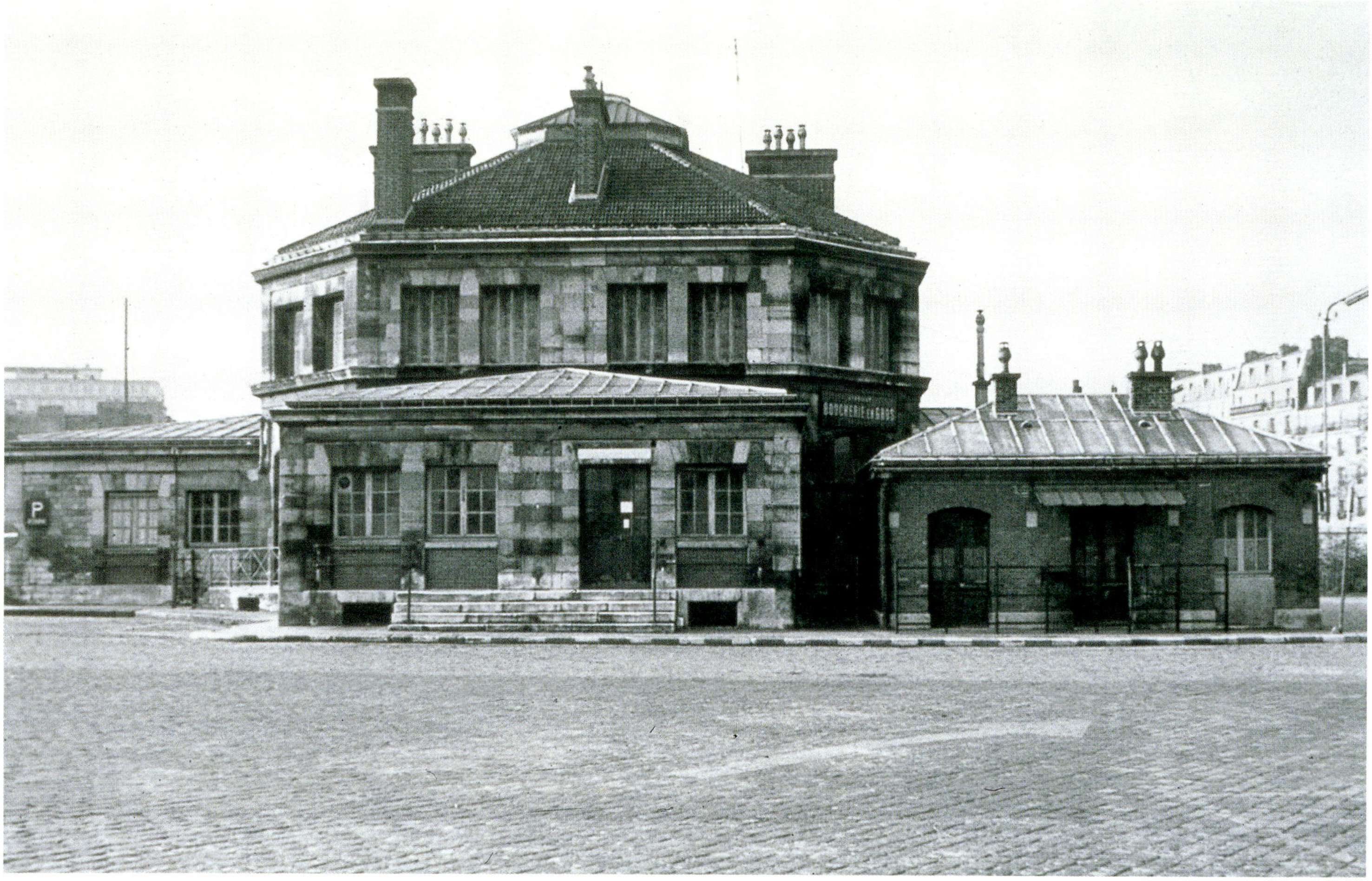

The abattoirs.
Above: The Rotonde des Vétérinaires.
Right: The Maison de La Villette (architects: P. Du Besset, D. Lyon and K. Morita).

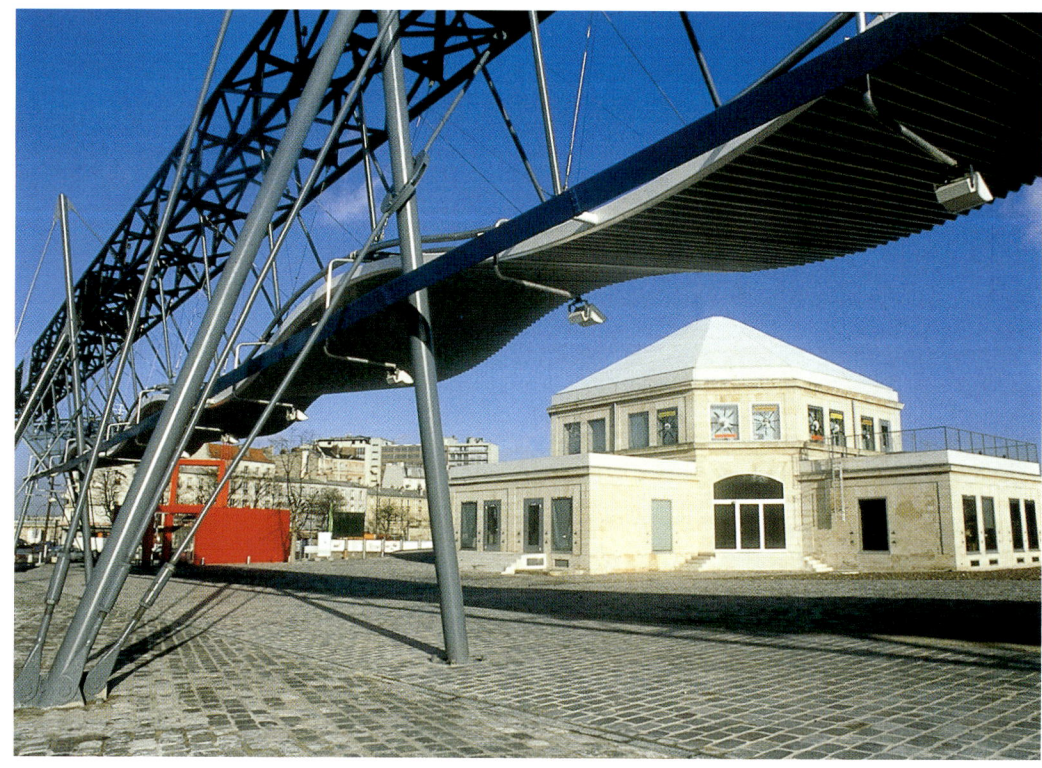

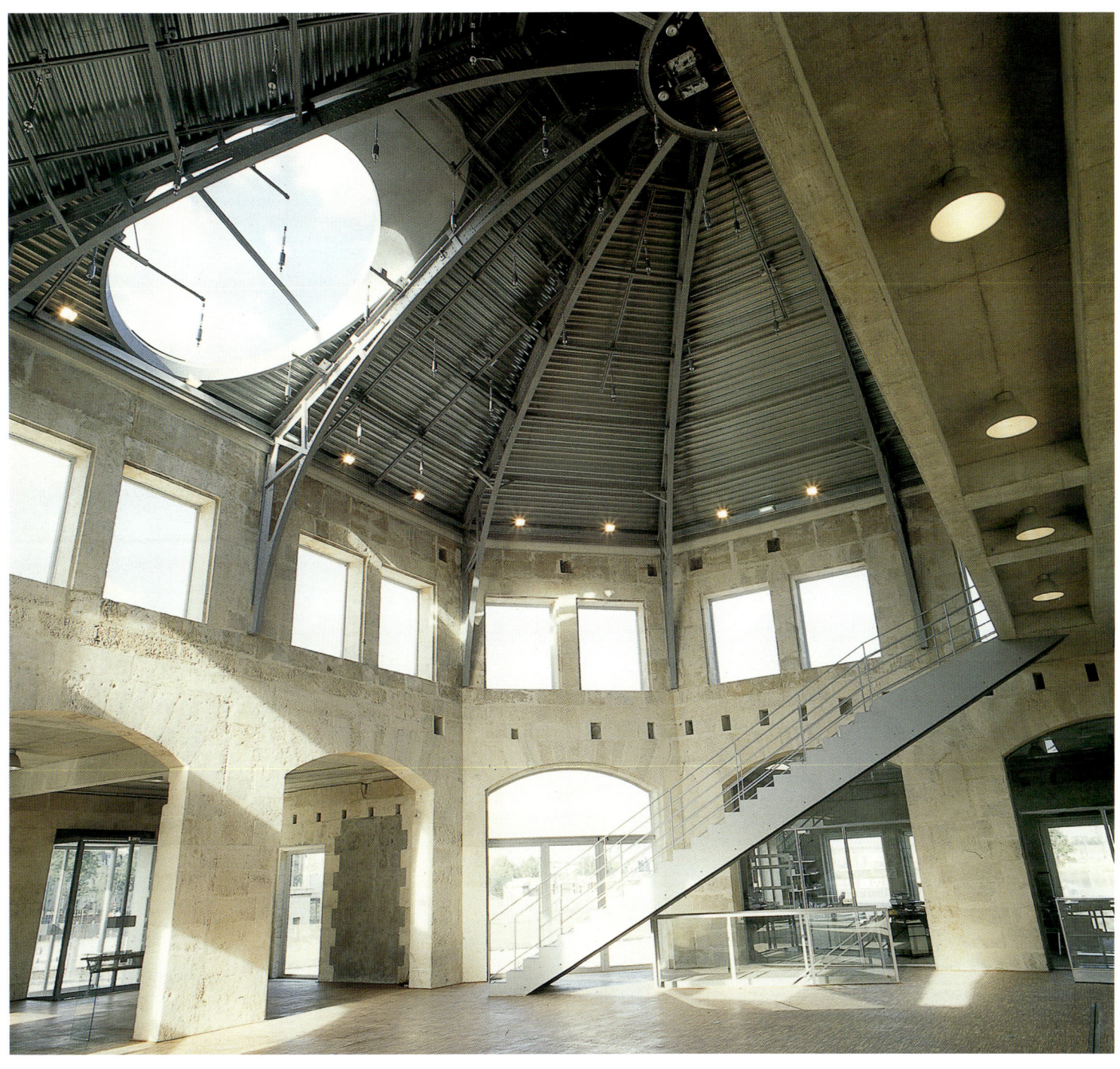

The Maison de La Villette (architects: P. Du Besset, D. Lyon and K. Morita). Interior.

INTERVIEW

Pierre Du Besset

Interview with Pierre Du Besset

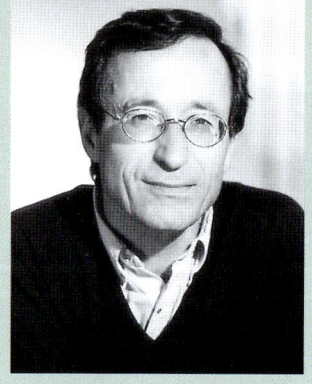

The Maison de La Villette (architects: P. Du Besset, D. Lyon and K. Morita). The metal framework and the large mirror.

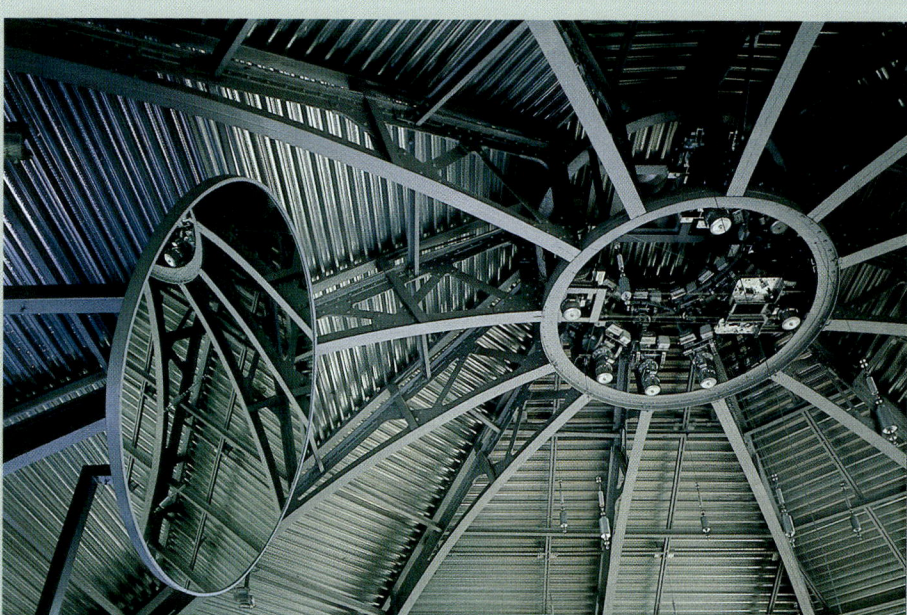

Notable among the buildings of Pierre Du Besset and Dominique Lyon are the headquarters of the Paris daily *Le Monde* and the Médiathèque in Orléans. Dating from 1986–1987 and built in collaboration with the architect Kazutoshi Morita, the Maison de La Villette undertaking involved rehabilitating the Rotonde des Vétérinaires at the former La Villette abattoir. The following interview with Pierre Du Besset provides a general outline of the project.

When were you entrusted with the rehabilitation of the Rotonde des Vétérinaires?

After the competition in 1985. A number of architects were selected by the EPPV, the public body in charge of the park, and finally we were chosen.

What did the brief consist of?

The Rotonde des Vétérinaires was the part of the abattoir complex where the veterinary checks were carried out. The EPPV had the idea of preserving it and turning it into an information collection centre for the history of the Villette site in particular, and north-east Paris in general. So, basically it was seen as an exhibition venue and research centre focusing on the neighbourhood and offering residents as much data as possible on the way things had changed over time.

What about the actual rehabilitation process?

We ripped out the entire interior – partition walls, apartments, intermediate floors and so on – until only the load-bearing structure was left: the walls and the metal frame of the roof. We then introduced a large mezzanine with access via a staircase running at an angle to the central axis. As for the look of the outside of the building, we wanted to stress the idea of a perfectly geometrical object represented by the rotunda. So the new roof is absolutely smooth and the flatness of the outside surfaces is accentuated by windows flush with the façades. A large opening we made in the roof means that a mirror above the lift can reflect the image of the old warehouses along the Canal Saint-Denis, which themselves are part of the neighbourhood's history.

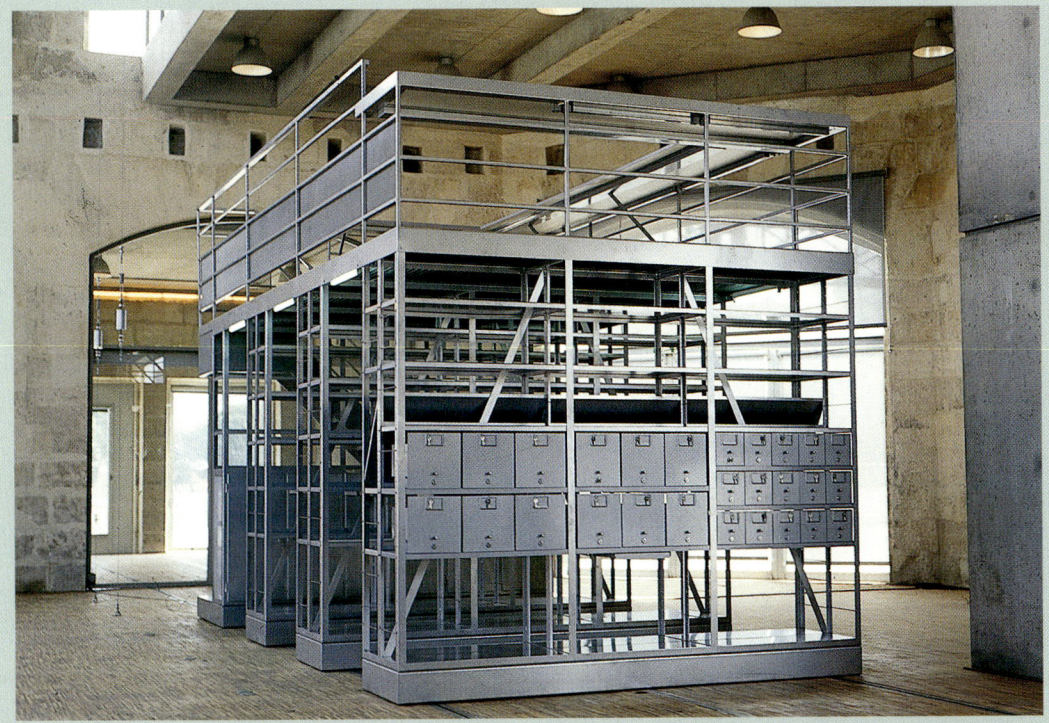

The Maison de La Villette (architects: P. Du Besset, D. Lyon and K. Morita).
Left: The library.
Below: The mezzanine (view from the entrance).

How did you get around the problems relating to the technical substructure?

A system of motors and cables akin to theatre machinery allows for the placing of exhibition panels at any given point on the floor area. It also means an entire exhibition can be lifted out of the way if for some reason the floor area has to be cleared at short notice.

So your contribution was limited to the main structure?

Not at all. We designed the whole technical substructure and the mobile library at the end of the lobby; when necessary the library can be moved back into one of the wings.

Interview by Alain Orlandini.

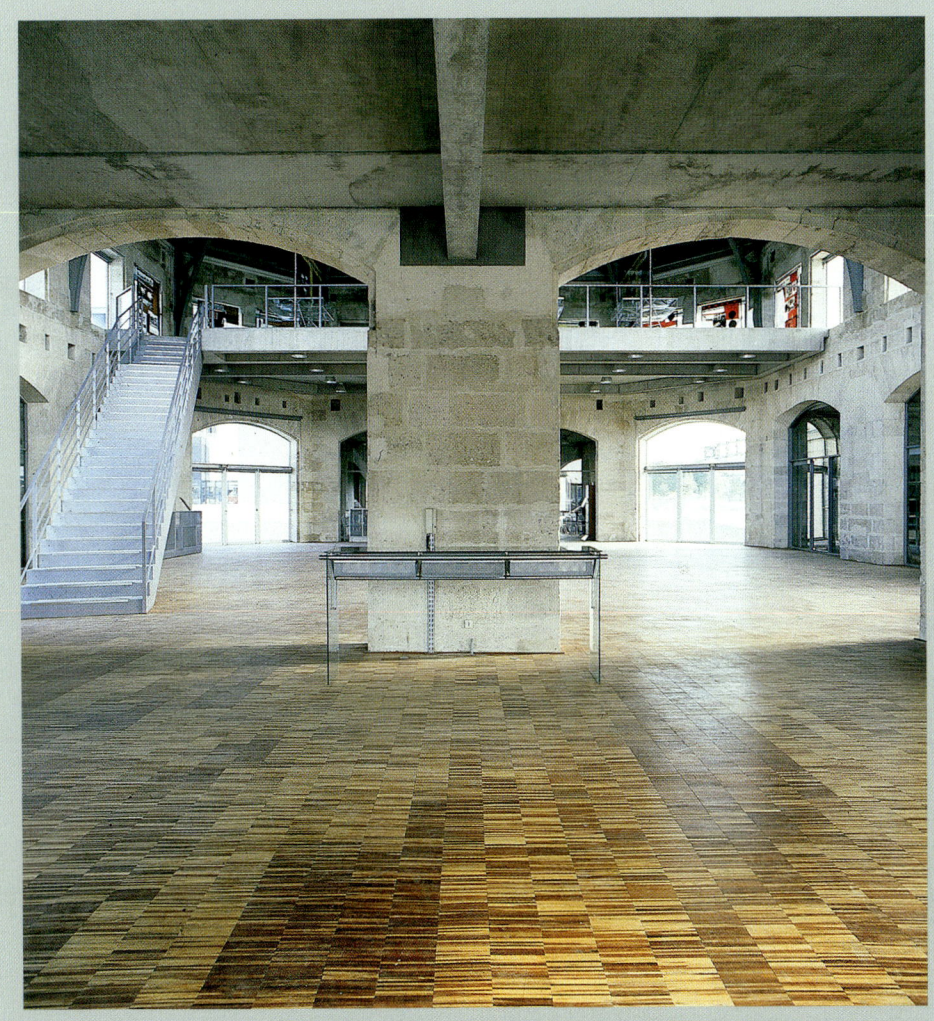

THE CITÉ DE LA MUSIQUE: WHEN ARCHITECTURE MEETS DESIRE

On 19 January 1985, the president of France chose Christian de Portzamparc as architect for the Cité de la Musique. In doing so, he put an end to an epic saga of architecture as a vehicle for utopian programmes the like of which had never been seen before – and for which the site of La Villette had been the principal stage. The Cité des Sciences et de l'Industrie was an enormous neoclassical composition erected to the glory of knowledge whose ever-increasing complexity demanded that it be democratically shared. With its layering of incompatible regulatory systems, the Parc de La Villette itself was a panegyric to fragmentation, a pointer to the new proliferation of ethnicities and cultures and their unpredictable coexistence in a context of endlessly shifting global information. The building of the Cité de la Musique, on the other hand, reflected the French state's urge to call the standard systems of musical training and dissemination into question. At stake in this major project was the fostering of interdisciplinarity via the interlinking of separate fields of activity and the opening up of the classical repertoire to traditional, modern and popular music.

Christian de Portzamparc's architecture fitted perfectly with these lofty purposes. True, the sheer volubility of the man Nietzsche would have put down as a "fanatic of expression" hardly seemed to chime with the temperance usually seen as appropriate to institutional representation; yet the choice of the young architect was not all that surprising in that his sprightly prose seemed to have attained ultimate perfection at La Villette.

Inevitably there were objections: pathological formalism for some and a frivolous digest of an outmoded International Style for others, de Portzamparc's architecture was undeserving of such acclaim. These criticisms, however, were smartly swept aside by the rapturous reception accorded an overt heresy that had wrested free of the straitjacket of a too-dogmatic modernity. True, the École du Ballet de l'Opéra (Paris Opera Ballet School) was already there to accustom the perceptive eye to the undulating Portzamparc line, but the youthful *éclat* of the project laid only the filmiest of veils over what would soon emerge as the essence of its creator's art: vast, enveloping form that keeps the sojourner under a motherly wing as it strives unceasingly towards the sacred.

There was also the staggeringly aristocratic ease with which Christian de Portzamparc reconciled form and function. Whatever may be said of it, his building remains modern in the rationalist sense, each of the spaces within the Cité de la Musique owing its configuration to a rigorous weighing-up of utilitarian and constructional imperatives. Yet for him, form can never be subordinate, can never be mere function. Its place is at the heart of a compromise intended to exalt the essence of the work, with elegance as its medium. Form here is the fruit of a positive intemperance. Savouring the graceful curves of the Cité de la Musique, how can one not think of Nietzsche's artist, immortalising in stone a will to poetry driven by Dionysian rapture? Granted, Portzamparc sometimes runs off track – he is unfailingly effusive and the diversity of the railings in the interior courtyard of the Conservatoire immediately betrays a fondness for embellishment – but his exuberance is never gratuitous. No question, either, of flaunting his unchallengeable gift for the handling of form. Rather he asserts, defiant to the last, a style and a line of thought sometimes capable of perplexing and exasperating his most fervent admirers – even if, *in fine*, they always come round to his way of thinking.

Christian de Portzamparc's architecture commits itself to its setting, tirelessly seeking to mark out a territory, define it, circumscribe it with the presence of stone – stone that sometimes, subtly, yields pride of place to the non-matter of empty space. To an architecture that responds to the advancing abstraction of the contemporary world by making a cardinal value of passionless conceptuality, he prefers the virtues of earthy rootedness and a sound dose of non-transportable art. A mannerist builder out to reclaim a forgotten urbanity, Portzamparc brings to his shaping of city space an urgent quest for light – and shade. Tinged with solemnity, this is an architecture tending to cut free of gravity the better to kiss the heavens; and territoriality is its weapon against the slackening of social bonds.

Crossing the Parc de La Villette is a delightful experience. Once we have passed the approach to the Canal de l'Ourcq and the Grande Halle with its long, glazed façade, we are offered the yawning expanse of Place de la Fontaine-aux-Lions, where empty space and material solidity are adroitly balanced in a dynamically asymmetrical composition. Openness has been the clear choice here: openness towards the east and the too-often ignored outskirts. Then the eye rushes towards the felicitous alliance of volumes at the Pôle Public de Diffusion Musicale et Muséologique (Public Music and Museum Complex): volumes that at first seem so miniaturised you could end up stroking them – but which, after that moment of submission, suddenly assume an awe-inspiring magnitude. Now the tactile and the sensory yield to the silence of the monument, as if the work's materiality had evaporated, making way for the resonance of some higher reality. La Villette is nothing less than the concept of architecture revived.

The Conservatoire National Supérieur de Musique et de Danse

"The plan
is the generator.
Without a plan
there is disorder
and arbitrariness.
The plan contains
the essence
of the sensation."

Le Corbusier

A plan (1)

Perfect fit with an irregularly shaped site, mastery of proportion, harmony of colour: everything combines to make the Conservatoire National Supérieur de Musique et de Danse (National Conservatory of Music and Dance) an impressive success. But the real key to its landmark status on France's architectural scene is the sheer beauty of its plan. For the architecture critic looking to analyse what Blondel termed the "creation of character," in less poetic terms the layout, a pictorial reading is the only natural approach.

First and foremost the plan of the Conservatoire – like all plans – is an abstraction; but an abstraction that seems to have banished graphic austerity in favour of skilled formal interplay. As the painter takes over from the architect, the plan of the Conservatoire emerges as a juxtaposition of four imposing masses matched by a rectangle, a square and a curved surface arranged like the teeth of a comb. The ensemble takes shape around a long, slender space through which there flows, one imagines, the vital current on which the survival of this eminently organic configuration depends.

Beautiful in as much as it is a source of pleasure – pleasure arising from our perception

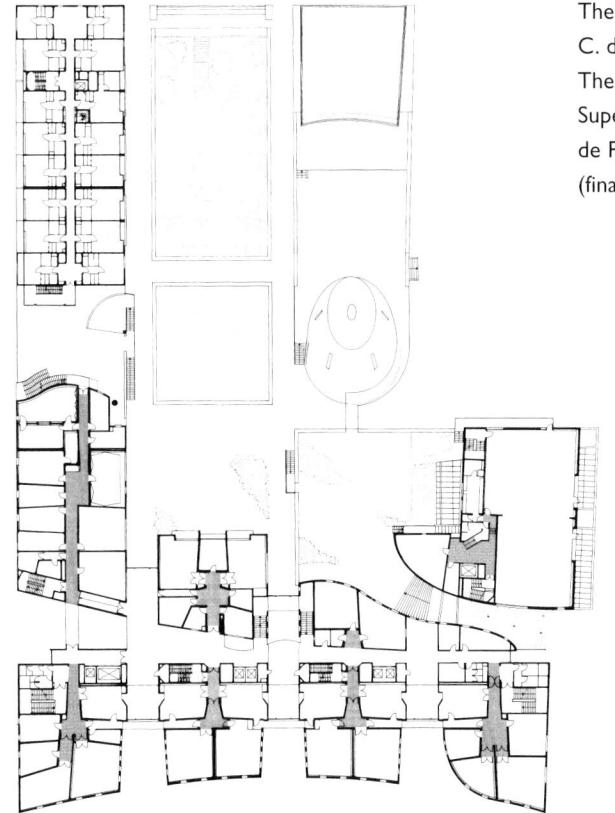

The Cité de la Musique (architect: C. de Portzamparc).
The Conservatoire National Supérieur de Musique et de Danse de Paris (CNSMDP). Floor plan (final project).

The Cité de la Musique (architect: C. de Portzamparc).
The Conservatoire.
Above: Interior passageways.
Below: The main staircase to the upper floors.

of harmoniously organised geometrical forms – the plan of the Conservatoire nonetheless represents a relevant "spatialisation" of functions. Anyone who has familiarised himself with the project will immediately recognise in the plan the indefinable tension that characterises it throughout. Merging to form a homogeneous whole, the different elements seem to exist only via the practical dependency that unites them: the resultant beauty is to be understood as the coexistence of multiple features converging on a specific goal – the creation of a functionally and symbolically liveable space.

Deftly slanted against Avenue Jean-Jaurès so as to let premonitions of the park seep out into the city, the four telluric masses of the Conservatoire's south façade set the architectural scene with absolute assurance. The generous openings between them flood the interior with vivid natural light; in its complex overlapping of volumes the Conservatoire is a lesson in how the need for light can be made to fit with a highly compact plan. Precisely set between the masses of the façade and the volumes opening onto the park runs a frankly axial traffic strip. Broken up by a play of light and shade intensified by a subtle choice of materials – the luminous salvoes pouring in from Avenue Jean-Jaurès are reflected in a floor of polished stone, while the "withdrawal" spaces offer the gentle warmth of wood flooring – the strip sets its varying moods against the discreet compactness of the blocks along the façade. In its allying of the emblematic force of a thoroughfare to a generous conviviality of scale – covering a considerable distance, the spatial distribution it effects echoes the lines of force of the park – this playful strip assumes the role of main artery for the project.

To unify what could easily seem a patchwork of unrelated objects – but ultimately turns out to be the mark of the complex-

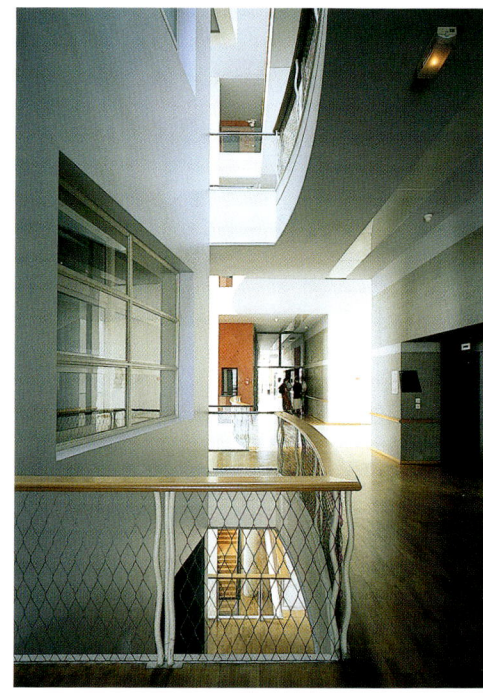

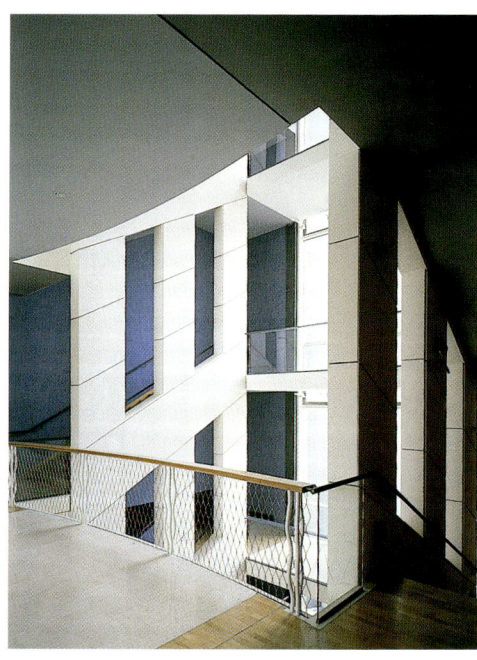

ity proper to all living organisms – there surges upward an immense staircase wedged between the ice-blue cube of the offices and the curving contours of the classroom: a glassed-in breach that is a summons towards a plunging panoramic view of the park. As if free-floating – its pierced structural shells make it look astonishingly light – it imperturbably over-

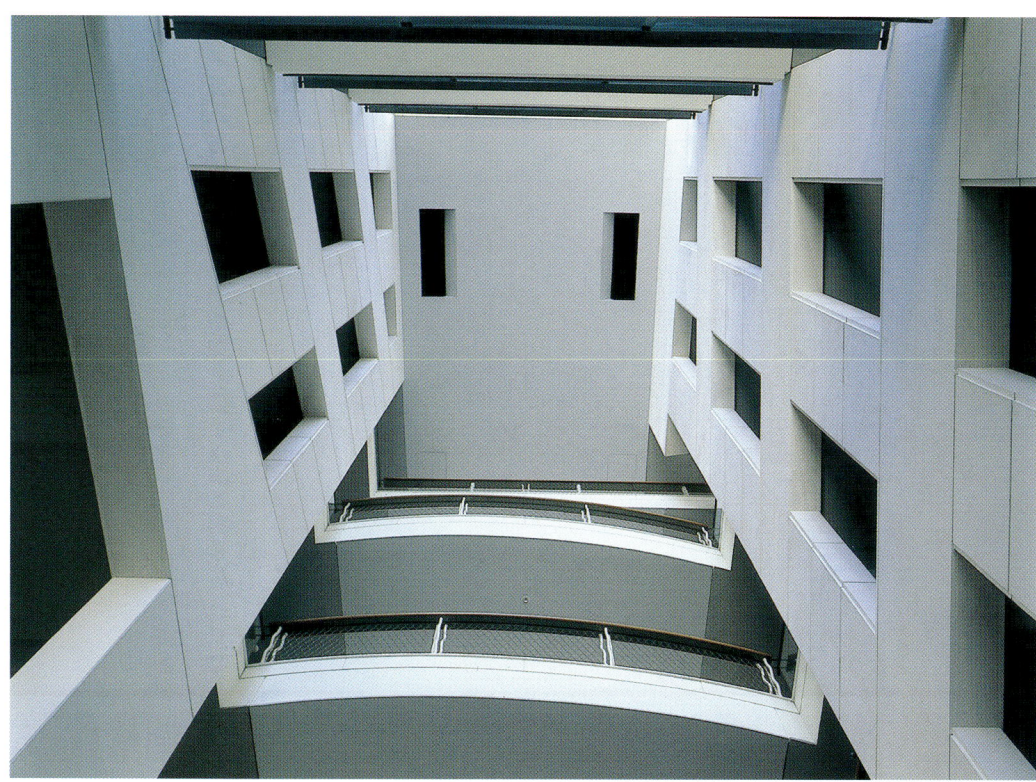

The Cité de la Musique (architect: C. de Portzamparc). The Conservatoire.
Above: The main staircase to the upper floors.
Below left: The entrance hall.
Below right: Passageway leading to the public music rooms (interdisciplinary workshop, organ room and vocal arts room).

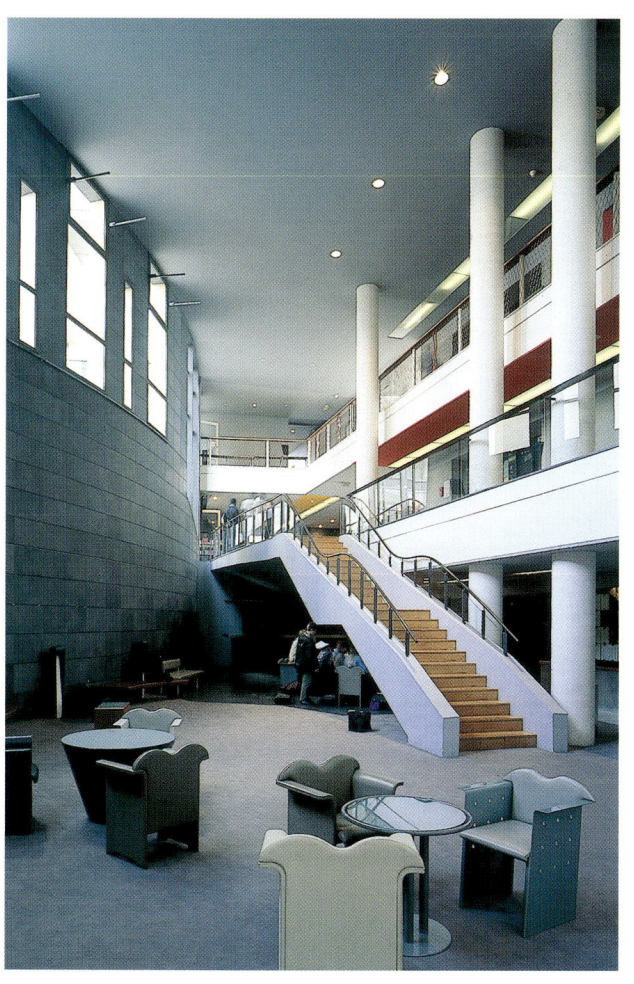
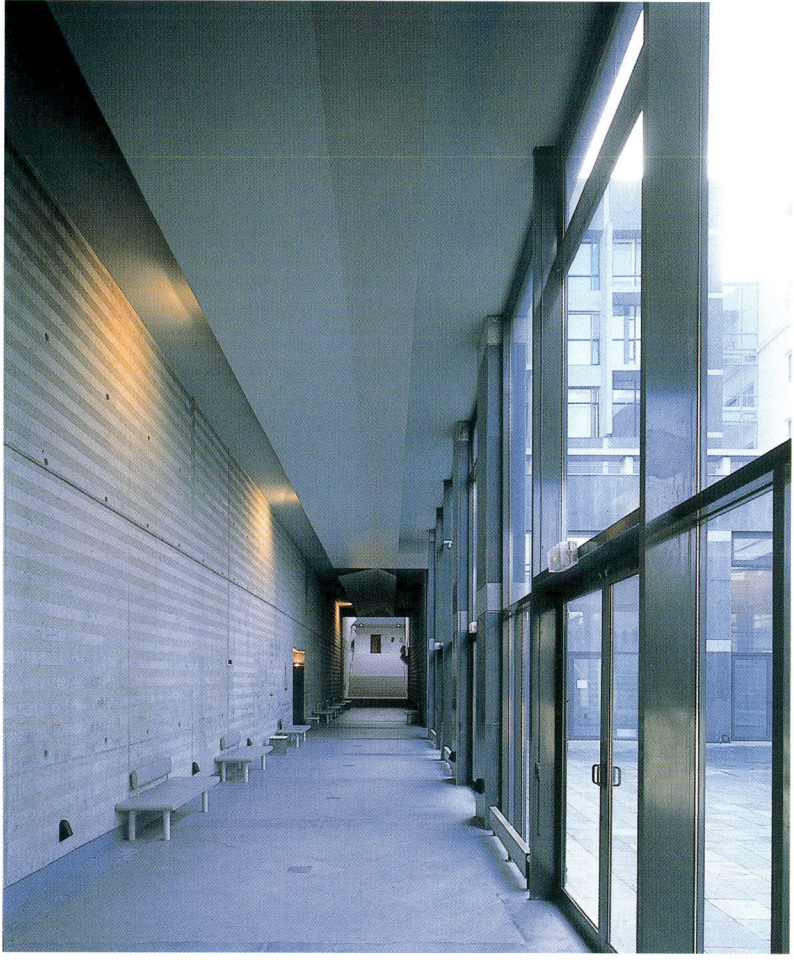

THE CITÉ DE LA MUSIQUE 257

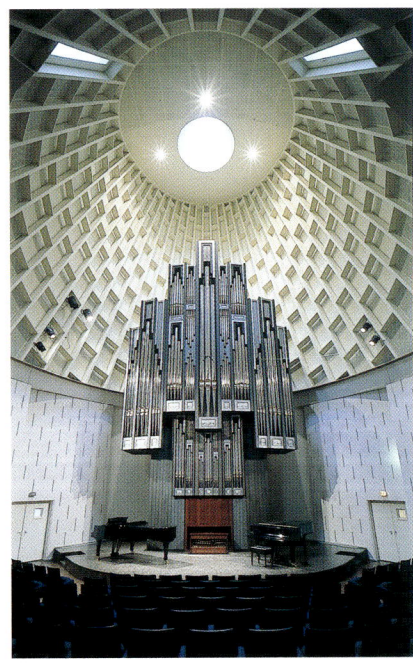

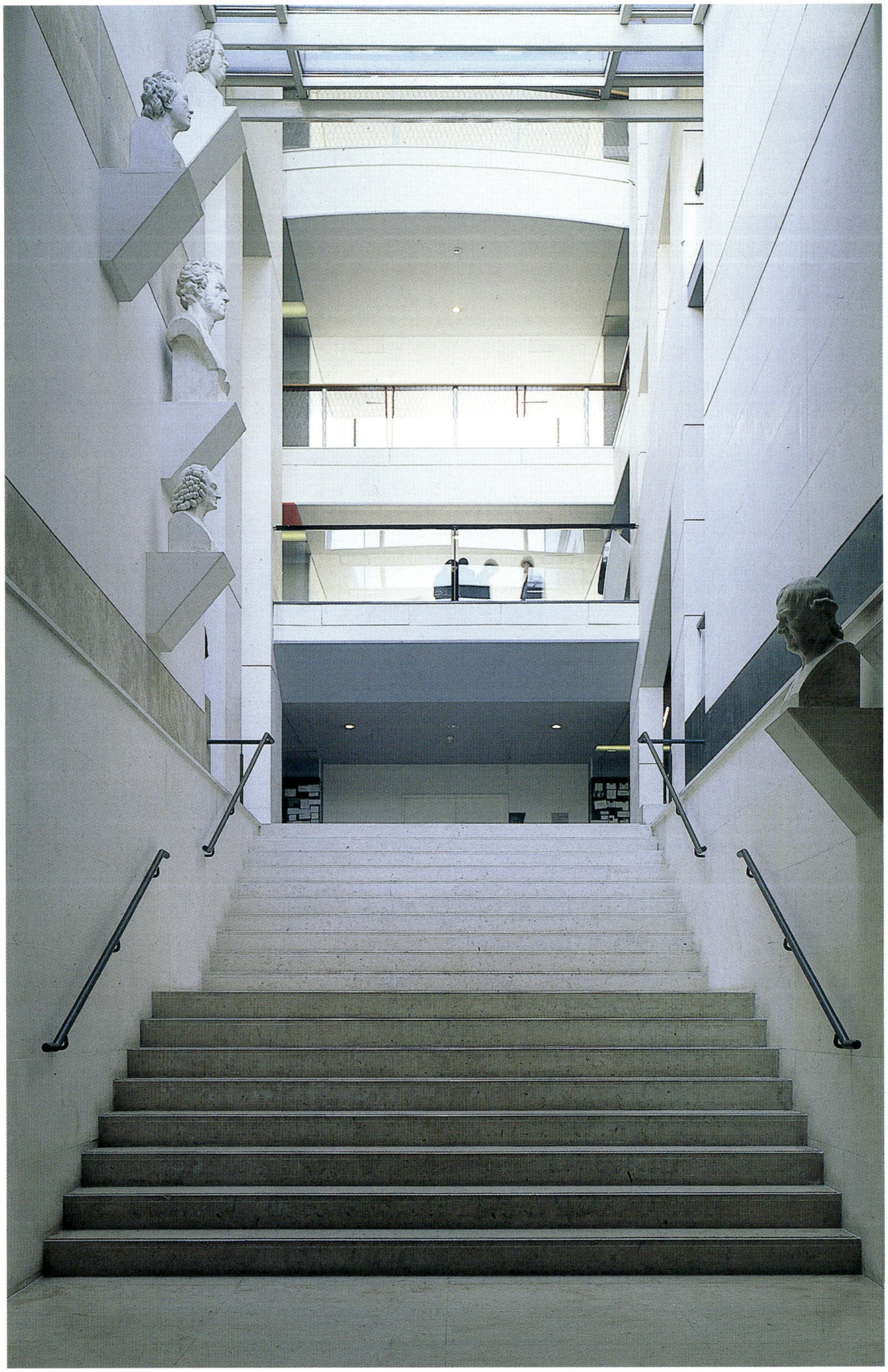

The Cité de la Musique (architect: C. de Portzamparc). The Conservatoire.
Above: The organ room.
Right: The main staircase to the public music rooms.

258 LA VILLETTE: 1971–1995

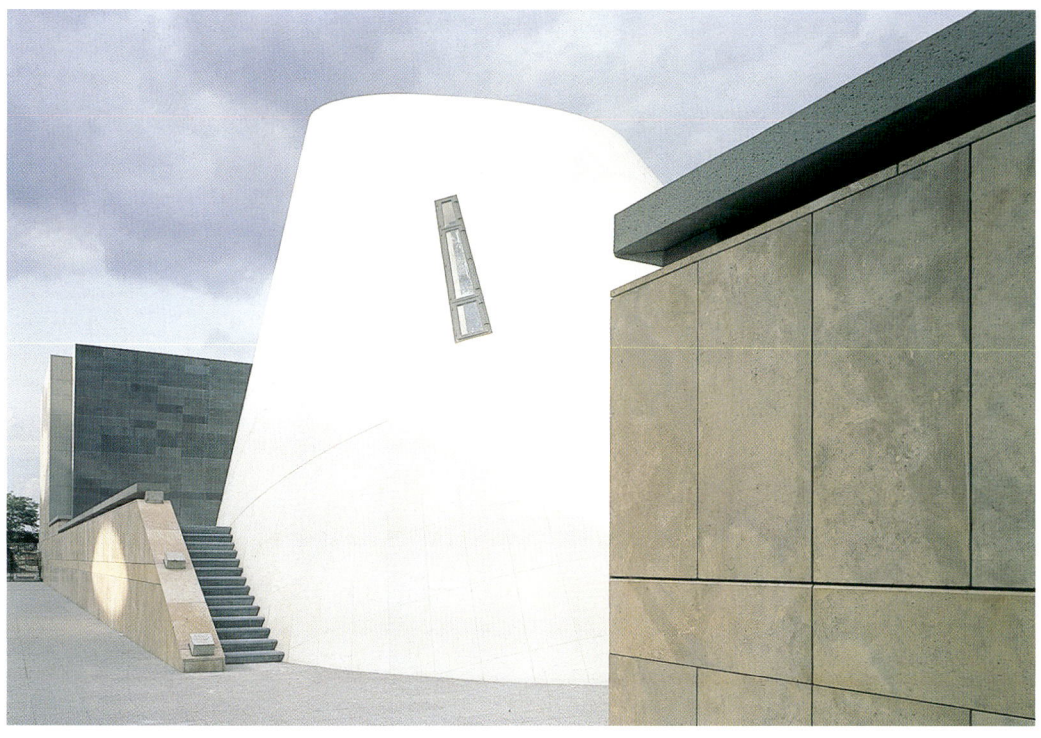

The Cité de la Musique (architect: C. de Portzamparc). The Conservatoire. The interior courtyard.
Above: The roofs of the public music rooms.
Below left: View from the patio.
Below right: The bandstand.

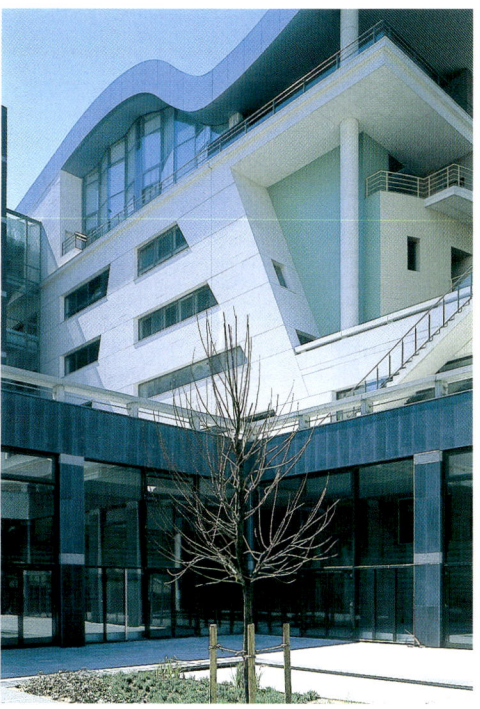

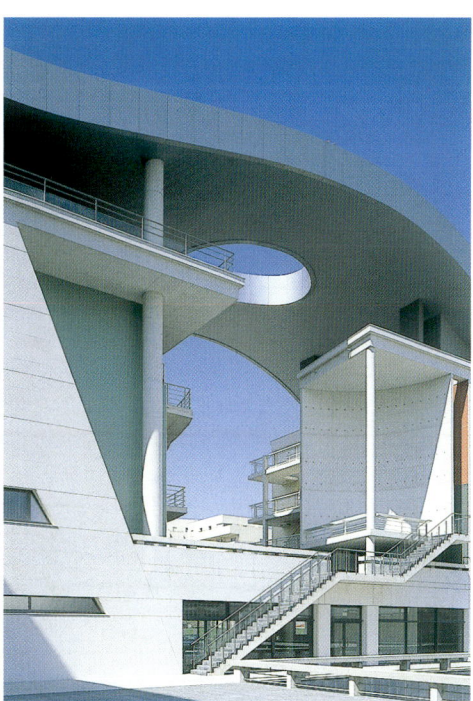

The Cité de la Musique

The Cité de la Musique (architect: C. de Portzamparc). The Conservatoire. A classroom.

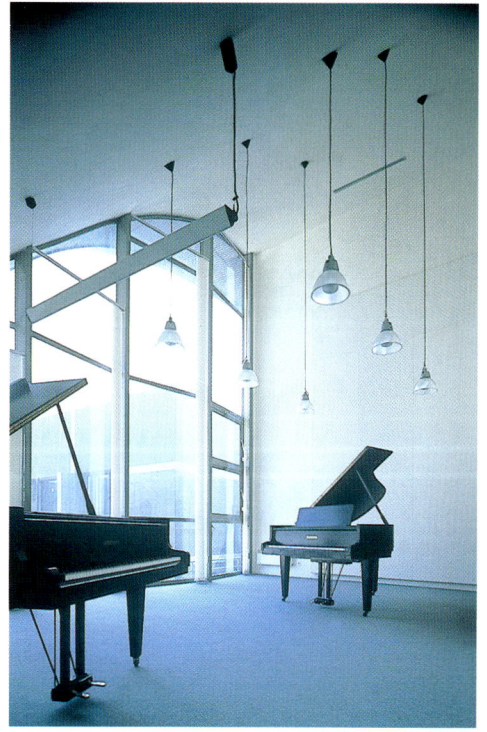

hangs the entry to the public music rooms. To reach the latter, we dive through the softly lit entrance hall and reach a broad interior thoroughfare via a monumental three-flight staircase. Hard up against its right flank, parallel to the Galerie de La Villette walkway – draconian acoustic requirements allowed for no superpositioning – the interdisciplinary workshop, the organ room and the vocal arts room succeed each other, connected to the orchestra stages and percussion rooms by a hypnotic network of passageways. Seven metres below ground level here, but the ensemble floats in the sepulchral dawn of a patio opening onto the gardens of the park. A few more steps to climb and we are in the interior courtyard – this is architecture that calls for muscles and gives staircases back their former nobility. At the undulating summit, a monolith faces the roofs of the public music rooms as they rise out of the depths. Here silence rules supreme.

Both source of pleasure and expression of a "useful" beauty, the Conservatoire plan has successfully led to the hatching-out of an architecture whose form – "signs of character," Blondel would call it – follows from a rigorous spatialisation of its elements.

The Cité de la Musique (architect: C. de Portzamparc).
The Conservatoire. The south façade.

Key architectural moments

The Conservatoire offers itself to anyone willing to walk through it. Here we are at the other extreme from the notion that any building should at first glance yield up its organisation: the design emphasises the *architectural itinerary* and the surprises it can call on us to share. But inside it are spaces – moments? – whose utter poetic power demands that the visitor give in to meditation. These moments are to the project's temporal logic what the static shot is to the language of cinema: a call to suspend the narrative flow, a burst of meaningful intensity that brings the essence of the work vividly to the fore. These are the places – as phenomenological as you can get – I fool myself that I'm analysing here; knowing all the while how dangerous the exercise can be, given that their poetic urgency unfailingly tends to overflow the chronically restrictive framework of critical discourse.

The south façade

The south façade of the Conservatoire is really something. In the Villette context these four substantial volumes, punctuated with loopholes and cut through with a sloping plane whose upper edge slices finely into the heavens, look like an attempt at generating a sense of eternity. Awed by the upward thrust of an image so stunningly poetic, we can only observe respectfully; yet once recovered from the sweet dread induced by what an anonymous critic has termed the "deadly grace" of the composition, we are faced with a curious paradox: the image before our eyes seems to be the very image of the new. The rapidity of its impact, the rumble of its muted violence, and the sheer difficulty of seizing its significance would doubtless have had their effect on perceptual phenomenologist Gaston Bachelard: are not his "image of the first time," "image of the beginnings" and "image sprung from no prior experience" precisely the terms needed to sum up the drama being played out on the fringe of the Parc de La Villette? But will these romantic notions stand up to the analysis of the art historian, bent on laying bare the closeness of the kinship between the south façade of the

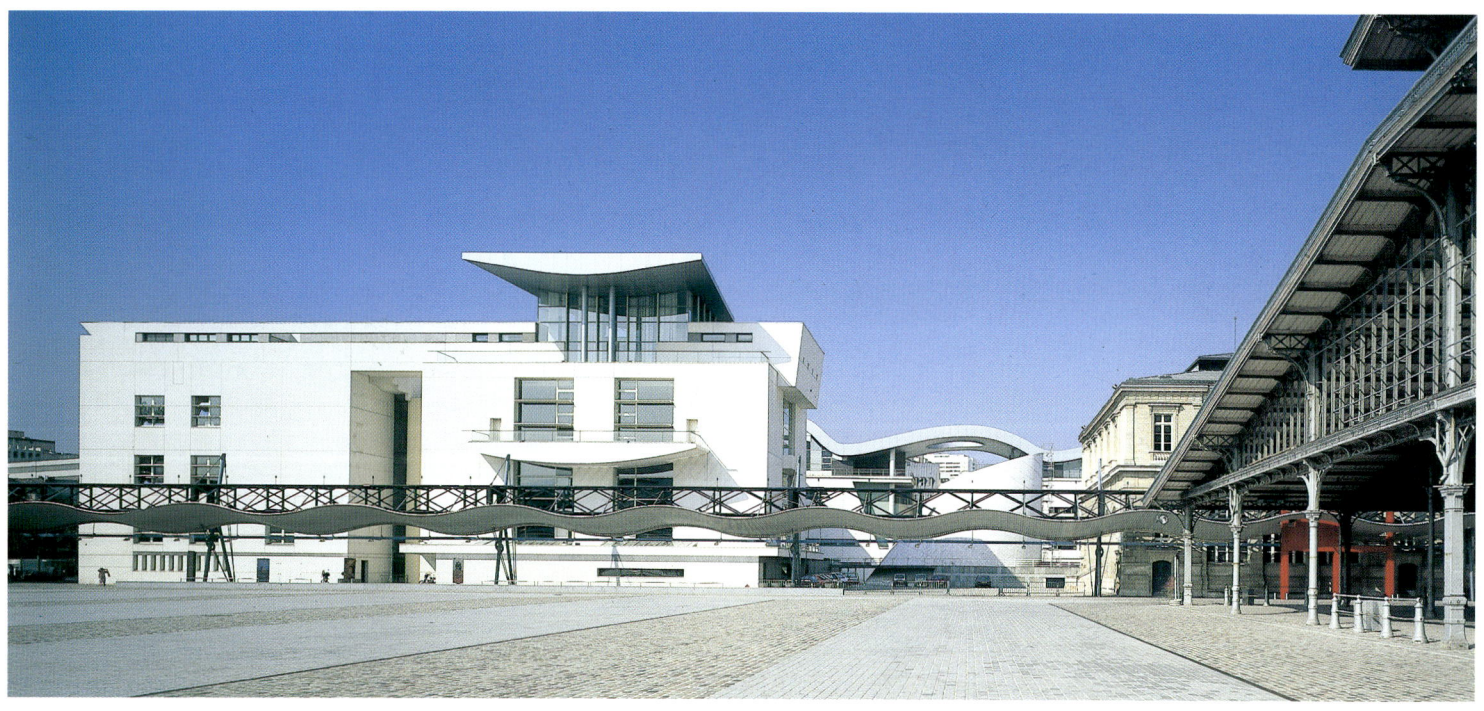

The Cité de la Musique (architect: C. de Portzamparc).
The Conservatoire. The east façade.

Conservatoire and the unforgettable works to be found at Chandigarh, Firminy and Ronchamp? And once we recognise the likelihood that these canonical works have exerted their influence on Christian de Portzamparc, how do we explain our persistent sense of the new and the unique? It is here that Bachelard's theory of poetic images proves crucial.

Those already acquainted with the famous phenomenologist will remember that for him metaphors and poetic images are not at all the same thing. While the former are merely mental constructs and as such only set the soul resonating, the latter have a direct impact: totally acausal in their belonging to an "immemorial" time, they constitute images of the new. Here the quintessence of being is laid bare by the poetic image. As the instantaneous expression of what Bachelard calls the "values of the absolute unconscious" or the "truths of the innermost man," the poetic image breaks free of the control of metaphoric intellectualism to become the pristine mirror of some unfathomable depth.

Once the correlation between poem and building has been recognised – in the final analysis the latter can be considered a succession of spatial *mises-en-scène* linking back to the above-mentioned "values" – we are faced with the following question: in what way does the south façade of the Conservatoire offer us the gift of a poetic image (and by extension, an image of the new)? The reply is self-evident, being the illustration – reduced to its simplest expressive form – of the concept of frontality. For what the south façade offers the eye is nothing less than the resurgence of a shared perceptual reserve: the concept of the plan, taken here as solid matter capable of resisting man's dynamic axis. Laying bare one of the structural elements of our spatial consciousness – the plan as frontier – the south façade has taken on the aspect of what Gaston Bachelard terms a "young language." While "naively conscious," it points the way to an utterly unequivocal meaning; it is this total pared-downness, typical of images born of a moment of abrupt inspiration, that makes it innovative – and in a way indissociable from "trans-subjectivity." Self-evidently right, it generates the communion of souls in a movement of total adhesion to a truth. It is useful at this point to compare it to the Conservatoire's east façade. Shaped as it is by the controlled opposition between horizontals and verticals, the latter is intended as a purely intellectual outcome. The long quest for rightness of proportion has given birth here to beauty shot through with reason. However, its coming having been slowed by the long, winding circuits of thought, it has irretrievably lost all hope of generating an impact on the soul. Petrified by the knowledge it has sprung from, it differs fundamentally from the south façade, which says everything all at once.

Because it has led the unconscious into a "basic experience of life," the south façade can identify with these images that "stand out so clearly from life that life can no longer explain them"[1] and so enter the precious realm of poetic images.

Nonetheless, another thought comes to the observer, who sees the south façade as the underpinning for the emergence of a truth. (It should be noted that the display of the concept involved here already belongs to the register of disclosure.) As the "opening forth" of what the plan truly is – an irreducibly solid frontier element – and a means of enabling it to "achieve its appearance,"[2] the south façade is well and truly the stage for an implementation of the truth, to be taken here as "the hatching-out of being."[3]

In *The Origin of the Work of Art*, Martin Heidegger disconcertingly posits the work as "the opening up of a world," asserting that "The work as work is on its own territory solely within the radius it opens up via its presence."[4] Taken thus, the essence of the work of art lies in its capacity to reveal a reality other than the one usually perceived. Opening a breach in reality, it has something to do with disclosure; but – and this is Heidegger's fundamental point – this disclosure can only take place because it happens on earth, on this "abyssal fundament that underpins everything and on which man lives."[5] Set on a hill as a challenge to the yawning emptiness of the skies, the Greek temple brings forth the earth to us, concealing within itself the possibility of its own upsurging. But this upsurging – Heidegger's third point – goes *ipso facto* with the will of the temple-work to enter "in return" into the mass of the stone and so permeate its immense, mysterious substance. The disclosure, the opening up of a world generated by the Greek temple, thus goes hand in hand with a withdrawal of the temple into the stone, into its most intense sacredness and impenetrability. ("We nonetheless try to penetrate it by breaking up the stone, but its fragments never make any inner quality visible to our gaze: the stone instantly withdraws into its pieces, as mutely weighty and massive as ever.")[6]

The south façade is destined to transmit the trace of this dual movement of upsurge and withdrawal. In its dazzling whiteness and its massiveness we see the breach through which Place de la Fontaine-aux-Lions, the Folie-Accueil (Reception Folly) of the Parc de La Villette and the Haussmannian layout of Avenue Jean-Jaurès approach us. Before our very eyes the south façade creates an entire world; its radius of activity is measurable using the upper ridge of its porch-roof, seemingly intended to call the surrounding space in towards it. As the heart of the whole, the porch-roof reveals itself as the "performer" of the Heideggerian miracle. While clearly meant to unify the four Olympian volumes running along the avenue, and forcefully embodying the frontality concept – a highly utilitarian frontality, as the rooms set back behind it are sheltered from the noise of the street – the porch-roof, like the Greek temple,

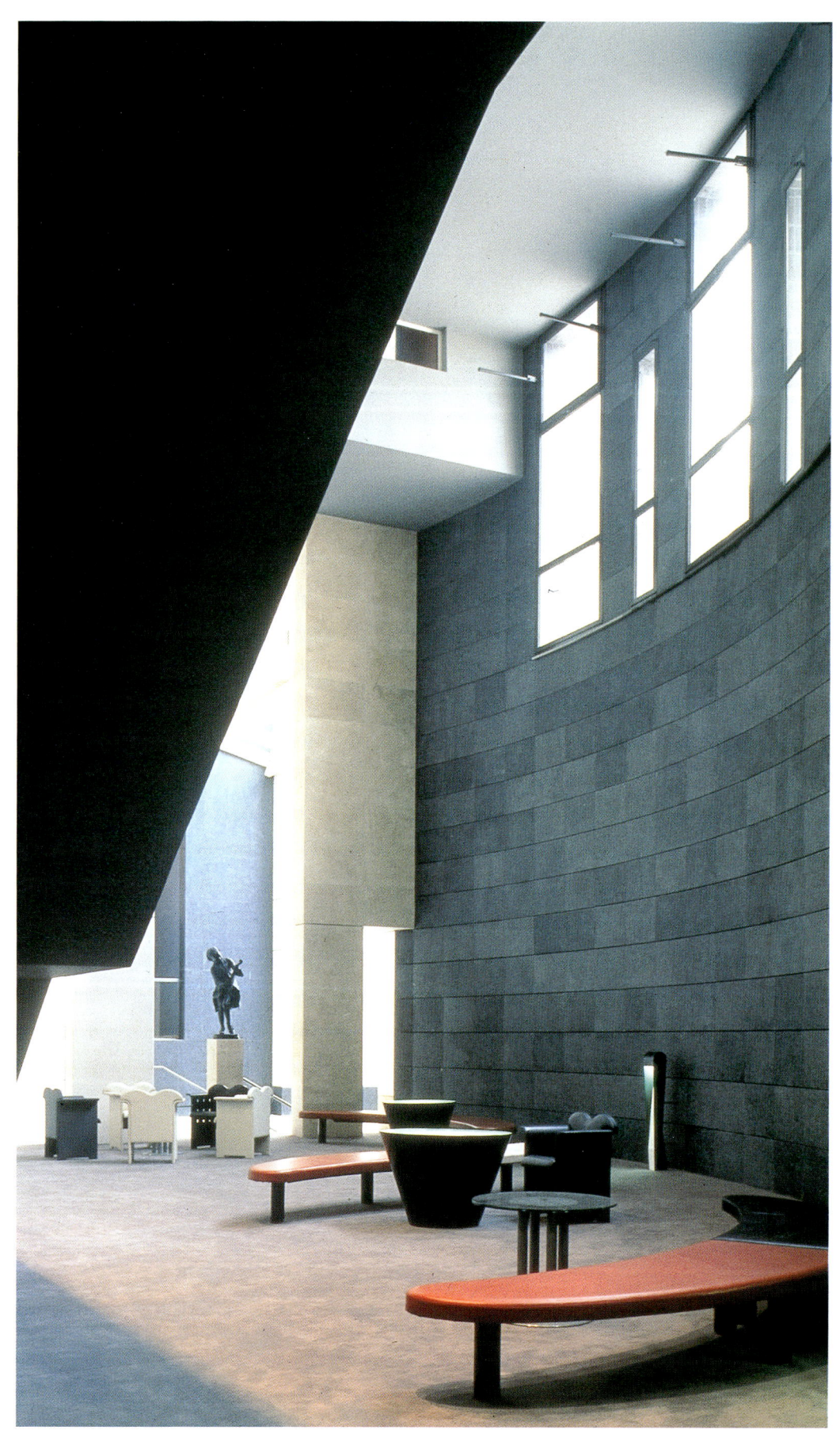

The Cité de la Musique (architect: C. de Portzamparc). The Conservatoire. The entrance hall.

opens up the ground by expanding the foundation of the volumes within which it exists. Here the work of art is the "daughter of the earth,"[7] as is resoundingly demonstrated by the whiteness of the façade's facing material. But the porch-roof wastes no time in extricating itself from its "concretist base"[8] to challenge the infinite space overhanging it: with the entire sky as its terrace, it points up the full measure of the world's ineffable cosmicity. The issue raised, then, is the great original mystery. It goes without saying that this "dynamics of withdrawal" is in no way a negation of the world. At stake, rather, is the opening-up of the world: "This withdrawal of the earth into itself is not at all a uniform, rigid closing-off. On the contrary, it spreads itself in an inexhaustibly simple plenitude of forms and guises."[9]

The Heideggerian temple withdrew into its harsh materiality. The south façade of the Conservatoire opts for a merging with the silently yawning gap of the sky.

The entrance hall

Markedly sunken – some four metres below street level – the Conservatoire entrance hall immediately impinges on our sense of verticality. No sooner have we crossed the little vestibule than the space increases considerably – the entrance hall occupies three levels in their entirety – and the inner part of the building offers itself unstintingly. The hypnotic axiality of the traffic areas is supplanted by the potent attractions of the depths that instead of being relegated to their usual subordinate tasks are here – for once, at least – foregrounded with real enthusiasm. At the same time, we cannot help feeling a childlike curiosity about what makes up the bowels of the building. Yet at the very bottom there awaits no apprehensive *frisson*, but rather the gentleness of daylight filtering in as if by magic among

"The odour of silence is so old."
O.V. de L. Milosz

the columns of a staircase whose straightness is a friendly challenge to the absolute femininity of the area in question. Once recovered from the surprise of seeing the depths of the building take on, like winged heights, a dazzlingly intellectual clarity, we feel the growing conviction that the space enveloping us is shot through with a past, that it resounds with distant echoes from the furthest reaches of memory. As if, through some miraculous capacity for expansion, we were the source of its creation, our bodily envelope having striven to model its contours and ultimately achieved perfect harmony – ideal fusion – between container and content. The time that rolls like thunder here is no longer that of the clockmaker, but an animal time – a time without duration – that sees us totally devoted to the creation of the resting place and merging, almost biologically, with its constituent matter.

Thus at one with the space we find ourselves in, we fill it with our daydreams: by turns a venue for "focused solitude," an enclosure exuding the "primitiveness of the refuge" and a zone of "joyful destitution," it suddenly stands revealed as harbouring pearls of great price: "One only communicates the general bearings of the secret," says Gaston Bachelard, "without ever stating it objectively…One gives the dream-state direction, one does not bring it to completion."[10] Here these words find their perfect illustration as the straight lines and curves marking out the entrance hall rock the visitor nonchalantly between dream and reality: in his imagination, an unbroken section of wall is locked in valiant combat with aggressive heapings of earth, as the levitating overhead walkways call on him to join the ceaseless eddying of the human flow through the building.

The interior courtyard

The Conservatoire has found an image appropriate to its institutional status in the glacial homogeneity of the south façade; but in the interior courtyard, the mind-bending diversity of the programme becomes a pretext for a formal conflagration. A cone with its tip sliced off, a robust rectangle and a cube with one acrobatically incurvated side are distributed like fictional characters across a stage. To the unity achievable with a porch-roof, the interior courtyard prefers the benefits of multiplicity: this is the scene of a meticulous apportionment that stresses the singularity of the volumes while incorporating a spatial concept whose fullness/emptiness dialectic abets their interdependence. Transparency and opacity, matter and antimatter, openness and closedness – these are the pairings around which the interior courtyard is structured.

These are the extremes it must reconcile. This working with contraries first appears in the way the courtyard establishes a linkage with Place de la Fontaine-aux-Lions. Facing the vast esplanade that signals the park beyond, it presents as its sole rampart the roofs of the public music rooms, which have succeeded in extricating themselves from the depths and bursting out into the daylight. Between them the impalpable reality of the void has moved in, and with it an endless chain of sequences. Pared-down solidity and undisguised massiveness, radiant whiteness and muted tints, extravagance and introspection: into this gaping area of contrast comes the Pavillon de la Bourse. Centrally framed by the two roofs and giving substance to the void that separates them, it judiciously reinforces the deliberately porous boundary in the direction of Place de la Fontaine-aux-Lions. Hoodwinking us as to its actual location, and skilfully merging its contours into the breach to form an evanescent barrier, the Pavillon de la Bourse becomes the very emblem of architectural intent: the aim, through the interplay of

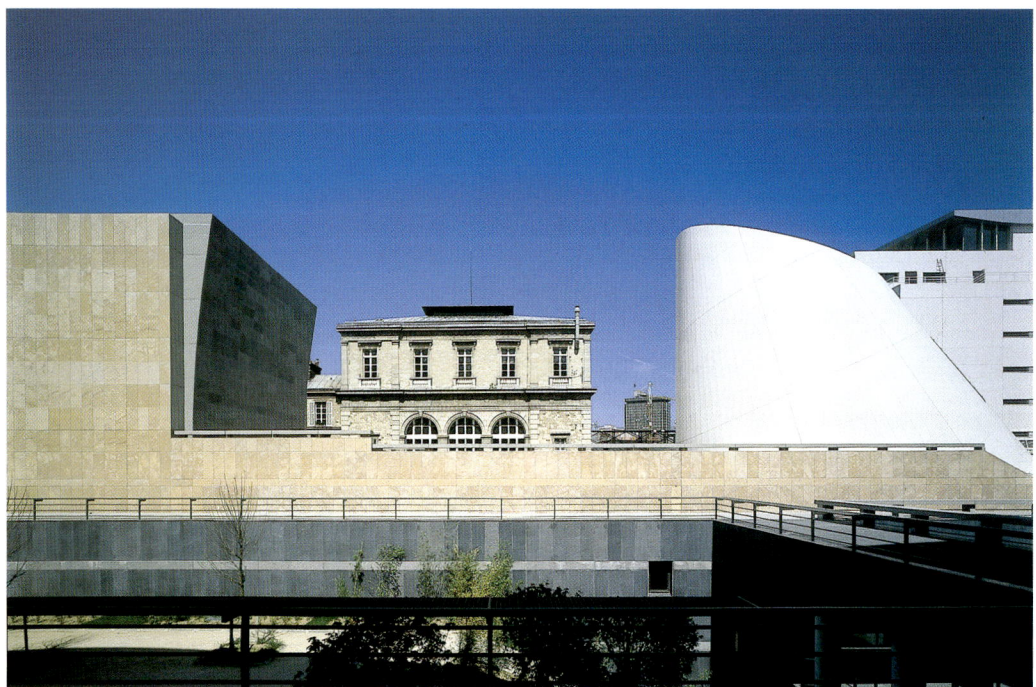

The Cité de la Musique (architect: C. de Portzamparc). The Conservatoire. The interior courtyard. In the background, the Théâtre Présent (formerly the Pavillon de la Bourse).

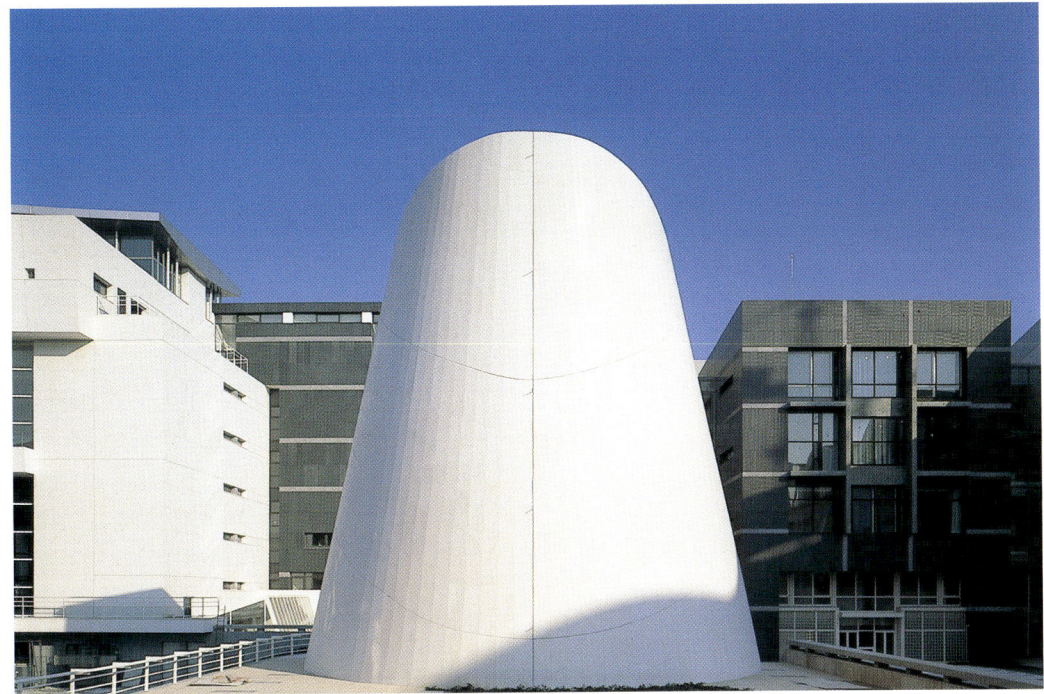

The Cité de la Musique (architect: C. de Portzamparc).
The Conservatoire. The interior courtyard. The roof of the organ room.

fullness and emptiness, is to open out the project eastwards and draw the park, even if only virtually, into the Conservatoire enclosure. (If the Pavillon de la Bourse seems the extension of the park into the Conservatoire, it has the patio as its own extension: its meticulous insertion into the grid of the park intensifies the closeness of the relationship between the Conservatoire and its urban setting.)

The second sequence deserving of comment brings together the roofs of the three public music rooms: the interdisciplinary workshop, the organ room and the vocal arts room. Adroitly graduated from the largest to the smallest, these rooms appropriately remind the casual stroller that the space he is crossing has cosmic roots. Does not their above-ground location imply the existence of elements of the brief hidden in the innermost depths of the project? And in the final analysis, is not the miraculous hatching-out – so scrupulously protected by the opaque façade – the image of an architectonic utopia, of the famous "quest for the precious stone" so dear to Ernst Bloch: a quest that sees man tirelessly delving into the entrails of Mother Earth with the sole objective of discovering the new materials essential to the raising of fresh, inexhaustible forms of architecture? A more theoretical reading of this procession of baroque forms takes us back to the original interpretation made here of the eminently modern concept of "unequivocalness" (or "legibility").

For the moderns, as we know, the façade had to be a faithful expression of plan and section. "The plan," asserted Le Corbusier, "proceeds from inside to outside, and the exterior is the result of an interior."[11] Thus from the outset modernism condemned form as a revisionist blight based on the arbitrary and the sensory. The condemnation was sometimes radical – "The modern man who tattoos himself is a criminal or a degenerate,"[12] declared Adolf Loos in *Ornament and Crime* – and sometimes marked by doubtful compromise: ultimately the façades of Le Corbusier's La Tourette are only a very partial expression of the plan, but the aim was always an objective architecture each of whose elements could justify its existence.

The Cité de la Musique (architect: C. de Portzamparc).
The Conservatoire. The interior courtyard.

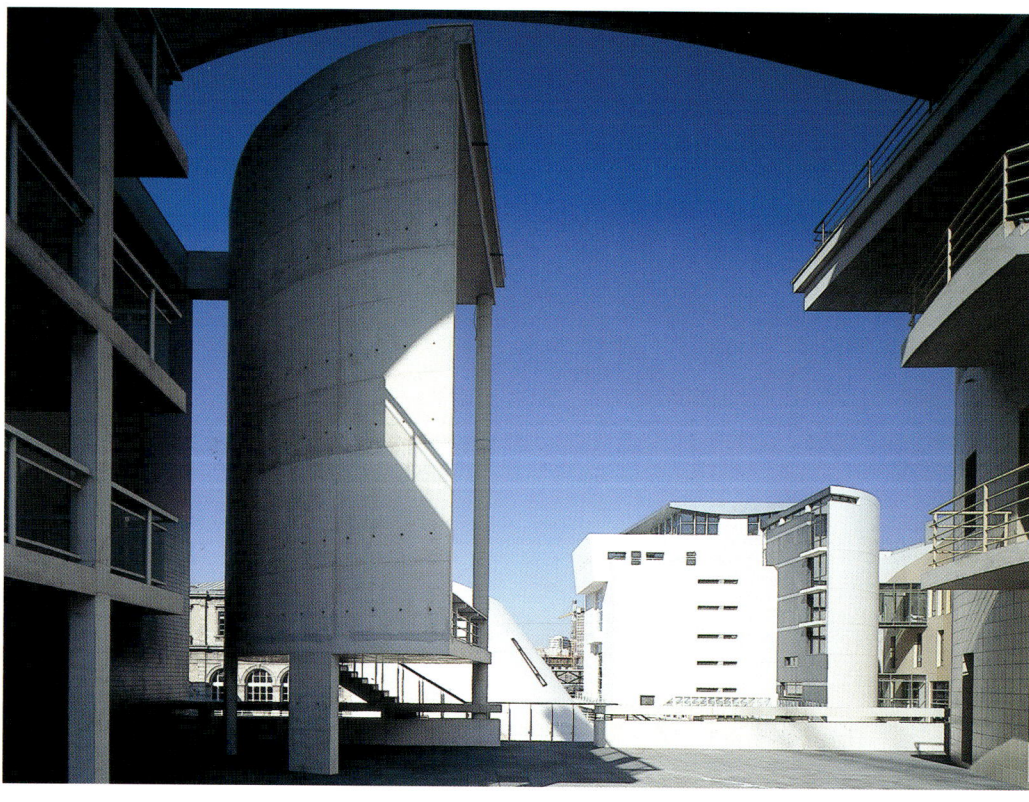

At La Villette this quest for the unequivocal would find highly relevant expression. By making the depths of the plan perceptible at surface level – "at the top" – and making its diversity clear with roofs, each of whose shapes point up an internal component, the courtyard comes out frankly in favour of the modernist discourse: there can be no architecture without "a grasp of the form and construction of all objects according to their strictest elementary logic and their *raison d'être*."[13]

The response to this quest for "transparency" is a luminous illustration of the full/empty duality. Initially trapped between the conical roof of the organ room and the stage of the vocal arts room, the emptiness now completely envelops the three roofs. To the observer wondering whether emptiness or fullness bolsters the border with Place de la Fontaine-aux-Lions, Gaston Bachelard would reply that "nothing is empty" and "the full/empty duality only reflects two geometrical unrealities."[14] Reassured, the observer then turns his gaze to the massive building that closes off the courtyard to the west: as if wounded in the side – its hollowed-out central section seems to gape open – it nonetheless proudly stands guard in a confident face-off with the Aldo Rossi block. For its designer, the issue was to grasp, simultaneously, monumentality and a multifarious programme. The colossal dimensions of the "beast" were met with columns, cornices and staircases designed to relativise its sheer size. The plethoric character of the programme led Christian de Portzamparc to a brilliant resolution of a fundamental question of the architectural creative process, one which at La Villette was formulated as follows: how to achieve a harmonious association of such disparate elements as a media centre, a gymnasium and classrooms? The answer was a vast undulating roof offering a total, instantaneous grasp of the building, with an opening

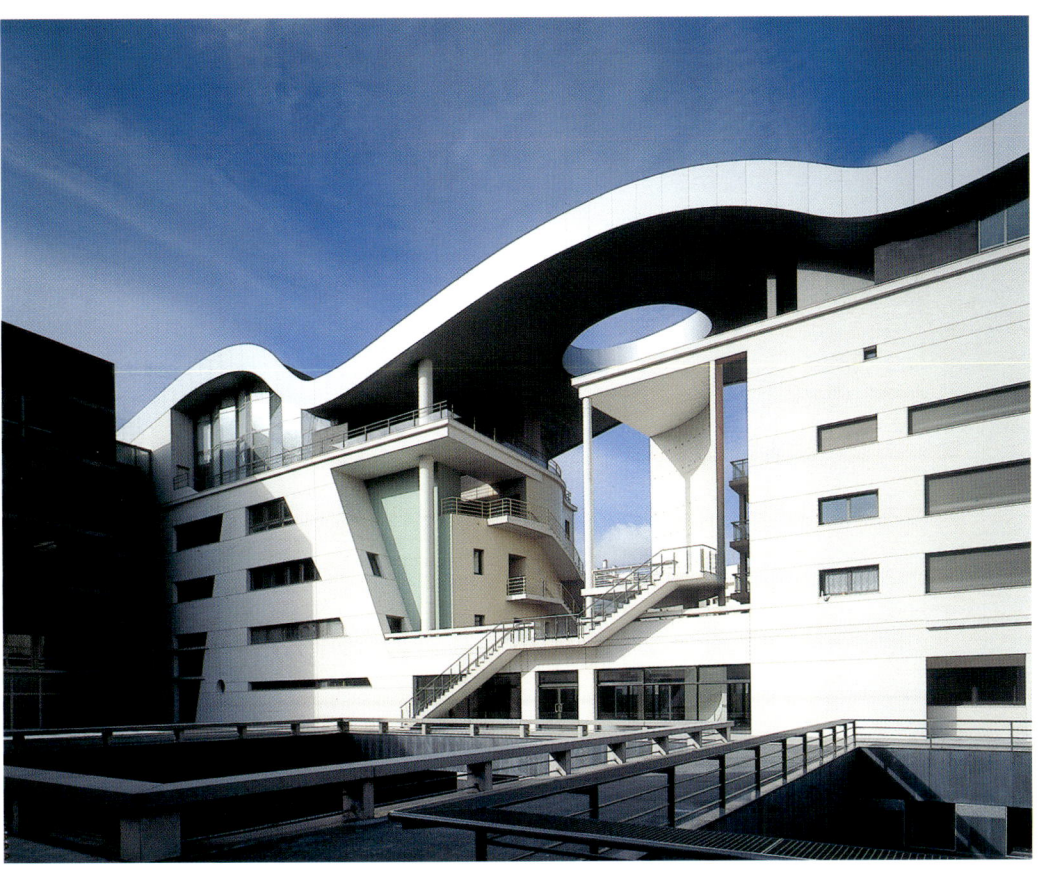

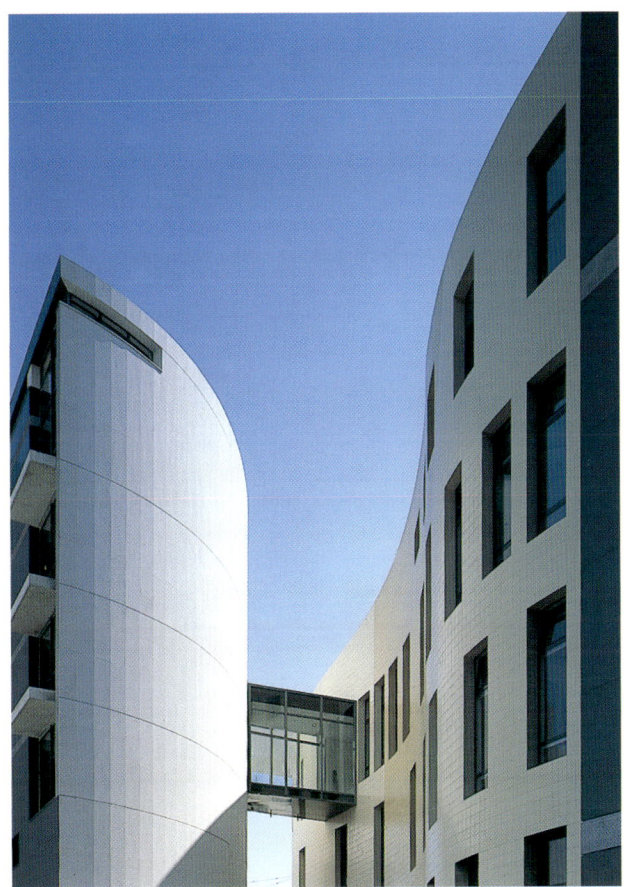

Cité de la Musique (architect: C. de Portzamparc). The Conservatoire. The interior courtyard.

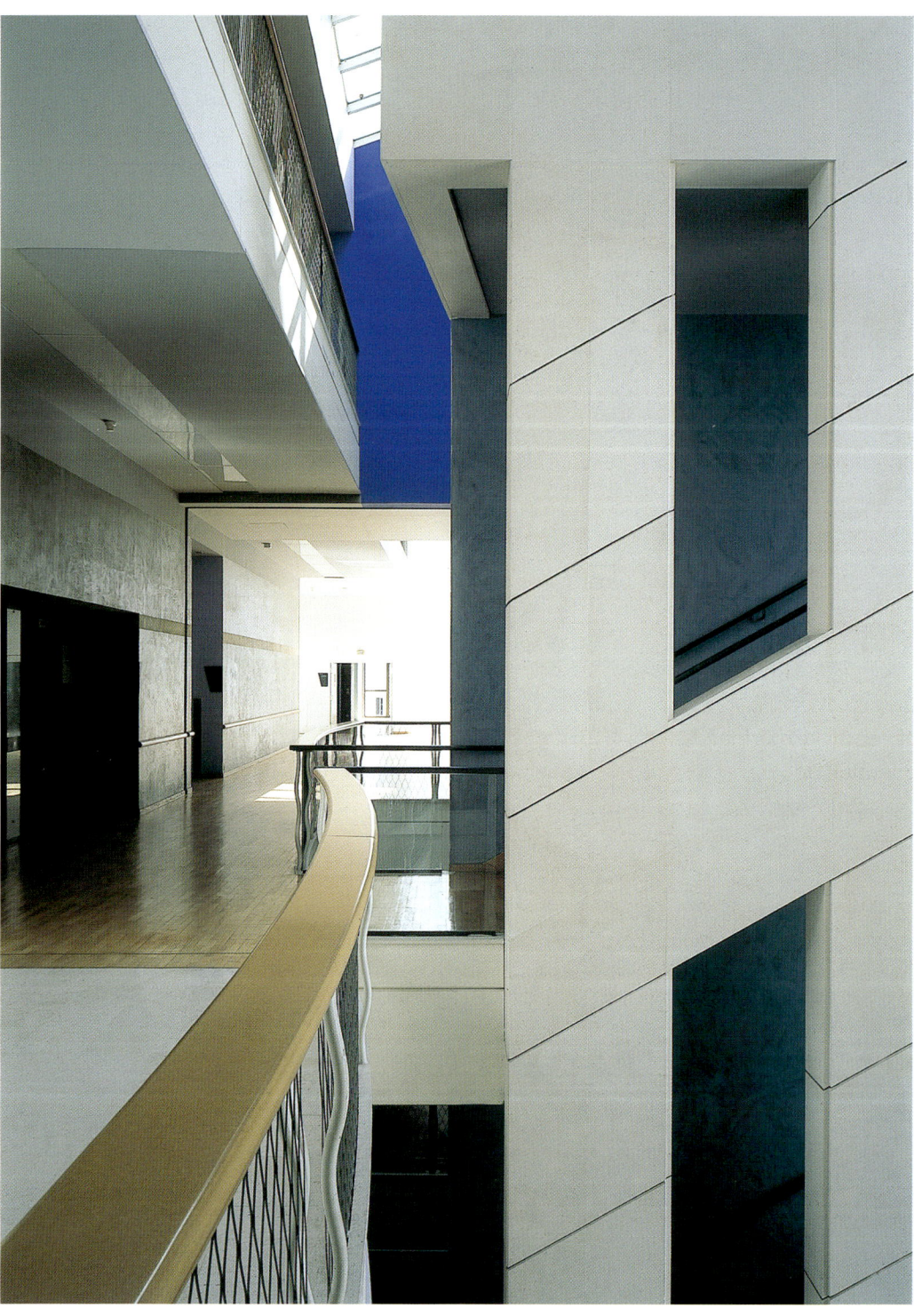

The Cité de la Musique (architect: C. de Portzamparc).
The Conservatoire. The interior passageways.

that splits the latter into two distinct parts, one for the classrooms and media centre, and the other for student accommodation and the gym.

The interior courtyard is the seat of duality. Duality of form, as we have seen, but also of spatial configuration: if the patio is an area for reflection, is not the bandstand a joyous point of focus? And if there is one crucial image, it is that of the troubling contrast between the incitement to movement – symbolised by the undulating crown that shapes the courtyard to the west – and the ancient serenity permeating the roofs of the public music rooms.

Materials

Body, affect, attraction, tropism: Christian de Portzamparc's terminology leaves little room for doubt. Architecture can only exist if it extends a genial welcome to the body, saluting it as the willing victim of an aesthetic vertigo in which sensual euphoria triumphs over the ascesis of critical judgement. In this context, gradual possession of space is like slow immersion in a sensory bath, to be grasped only via a prereflexive synthesis. In this case, the architect who loves to "dramatise spatial impressions" and consequently can identify with phenomenology, will offer the sensualists all the rhetoric of the Cité de la Musique, with its oddly Leibnizian undertones: for any difference between the *"nil est in intellectu quod non antea fuerit in sensu"* so dear to the author of E*thics*, and the "reminiscences of early experiences" mentioned by Christian de Portzamparc, is patently one of form rather than content. Thus an analysis of the Conservatoire entails a

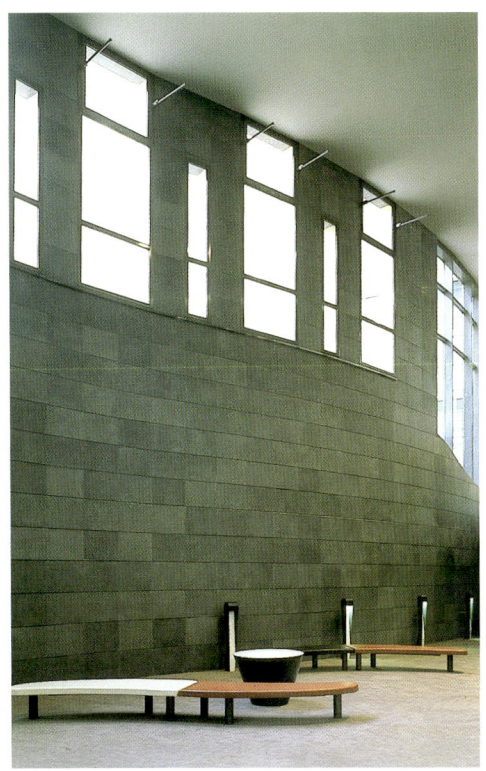

scrupulous inventory of the materials it is composed of, given their role in this quest for a space in which it is the body that "sees."

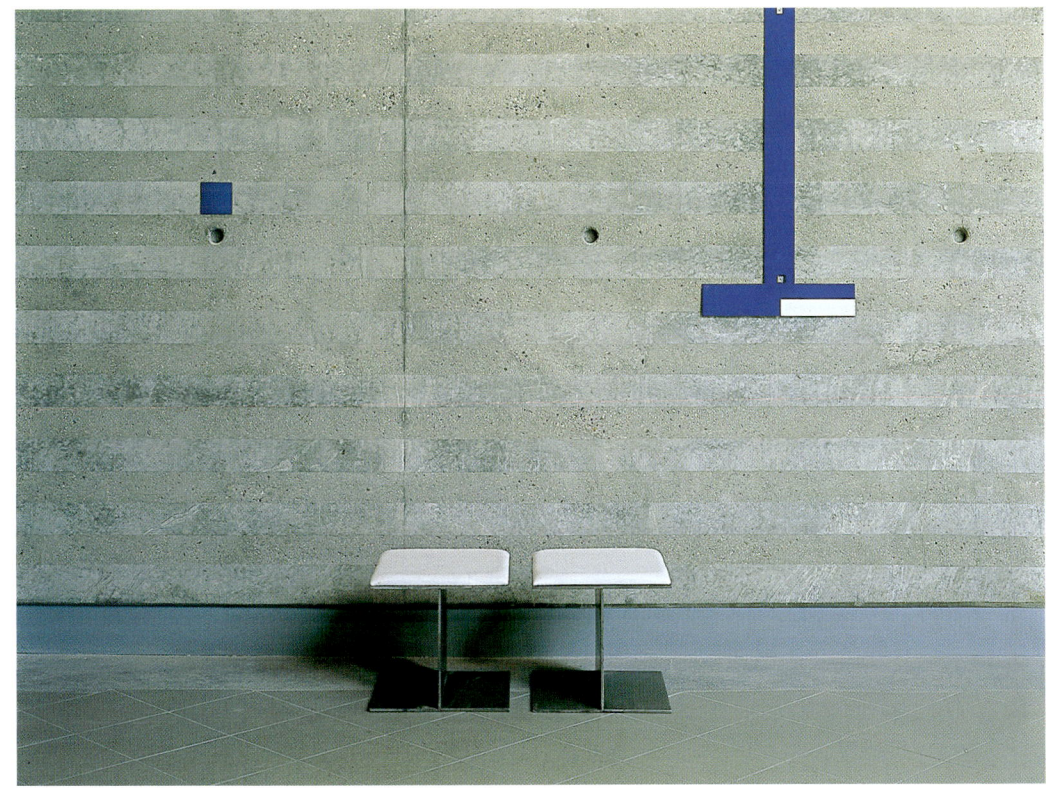

The Cité de la Musique (architect: C. de Portzamparc). The Conservatoire.
Above: The entrance hall.
Left: The entrance way to the public music rooms.

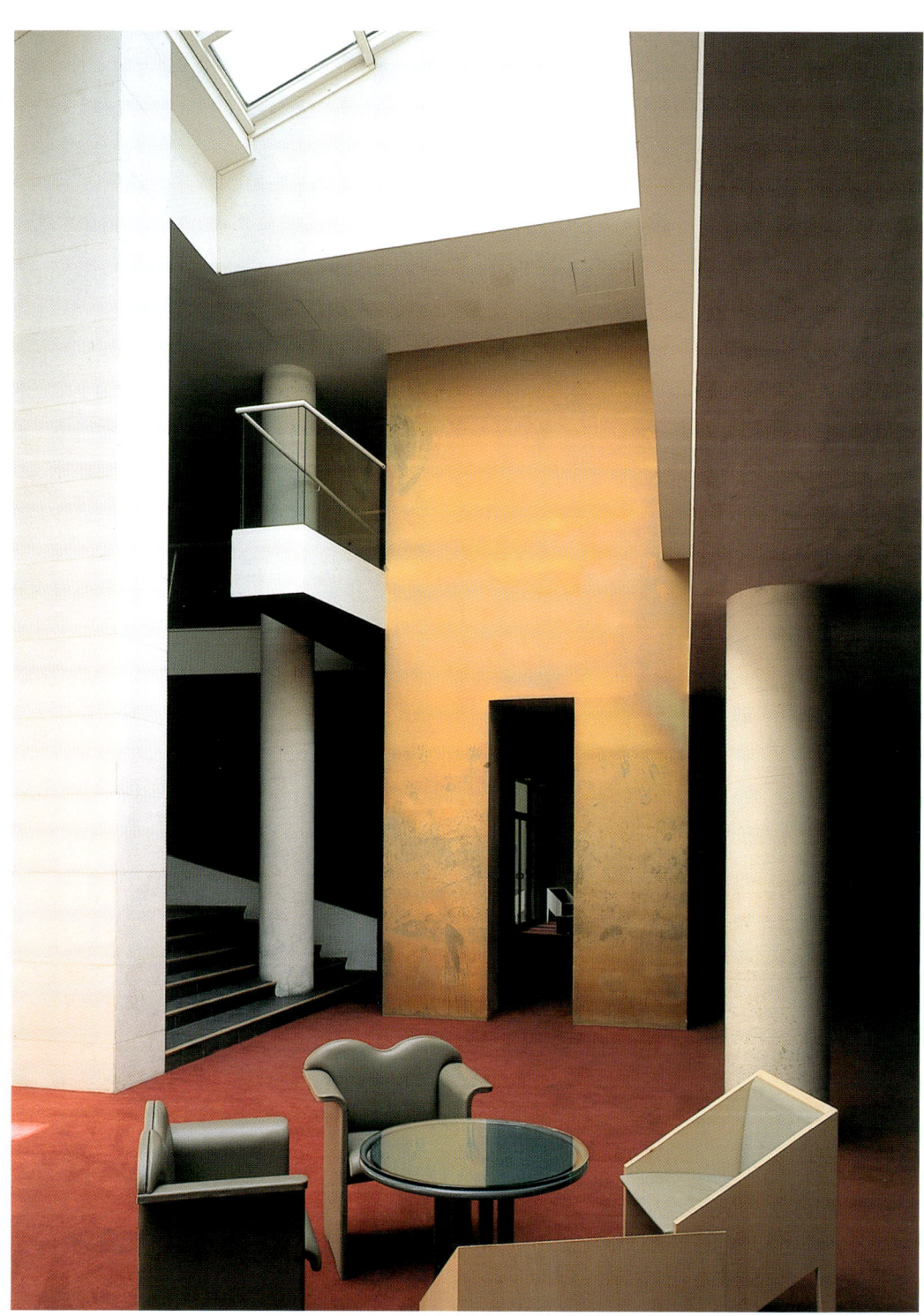

The Cité de la Musique (architect: C. de Portzamparc). The Conservatoire. The entrance way to the public music rooms.

Redoubtably fragmentary, the Conservatoire finds reconciliation in the form of its Spanish Caliza-Capri stone. Under the silent veil of its immaculate whiteness, as if submitting to a supreme, marble authority, the building becomes one and indivisible, utterly achieved. (It should be noted that the all-embracing quietude of this "unifying" material provides a nervous system not only for the Conservatoire, but also for the two sections of the Cité de la Musique, which thus stand revealed as intertwined, intermingled.) However, space within the Conservatoire becomes polymorphous and mutable, structured as it is by a host of enclosed areas the visitor cannot ignore in the course of an architectural itinerary alternating shattering accelerations with cataleptic hiatuses, swollen tempi with deliberate braking. The resultant setting is conducive to the use of a range of materials whose diversity, in return, reinforces the Conservatoire's spatial system. Thus the Belgian Blue limestone from Hainaut, perfectly in tune with the sepulchral entrance hall; thus the green concrete bordering the entrance to the public music rooms, which had to be sandblasted to get rid of irregular traces of shuttering, while the long stripes of the lower-level walls skilfully cancel out the verticals of the formwork in a totally hypnotic space-time continuum; thus the finished concrete used in the breaches on Avenue Jean-Jaurès, whose discreet colouring enhances the sensation of isolation characterising the entrance ways to the individual rehearsal studios.

Yet these heretical materials, in the sense that they maintain a total dissonance with the radiant homogeneity of the façade, sometimes leave room for motifs serving as reminders of the universal whiteness of the Caliza-Capri stone. One thinks here of the white concrete of the patio columns, or the Comblanchien flagstones laid out facing the gaps in the south façade.

An inexhaustible range of materials is on offer, somewhere between Latin fervour and the morose delectation of British dandyism, and rebounding indolently between the expressionless and the incandescent. The concern with detail revealed by this palette is puzzling to say the least, but what does ultimately come through is something of the "organic oneness" so dear to Louis Sullivan: as it was in the Guaranty Building, detail here being the fruit of an "expanded consciousness," the culmination of a "germinal impulse" flowing through the entire structure.

Particularly pleasing are the ochre and blue stucco spattered over the shells of the staircase to the upper levels, and the sea foam-coloured stoneware floor tiles lower down. Both are elements of what could be called an aesthetics of imperfection: the shells of the staircase are smeared with furtive streaks, the mark of some mysterious spatula handed down to posterity, and the stoneware tiling appears to have been cut by a tantalisingly clumsy hand. Then there is the frontal, virtual thrust of the faded Jalsberg stone opposite Place de la Fontaine-aux-Lions and, last but not least, the superb gold glaze, the height of erotic artifice, that embraces one of the columns of the public entrance way to the suave, subdued Eden of the auditoriums. Architecture for the body, then. Or rather *for* the body and *by* the body. But how can the architecture critic settle for an exclusively "plastic" reading of the work, whatever its faithfulness to its subject? After all, almost at once he will have glimpsed, behind the use of the materials, clues to the nature of the methodology. Thus it is that Portzamparc's methodological meticulousness is seen as an indisputable part of an approach seemingly designed to provide an overall view of the project. Like Josef Hoffmann and Joseph Olbrich, both in their time deeply concerned with fullness, Christian de Portzamparc sees archi-

The Cité de la Musique (architect: C. de Portzamparc). The Pôle Public de Diffusion Musicale et Muséologique (Public Music and Museum Complex). The Conque (Conch Shell) and the Rue Musicale (Musical Street).

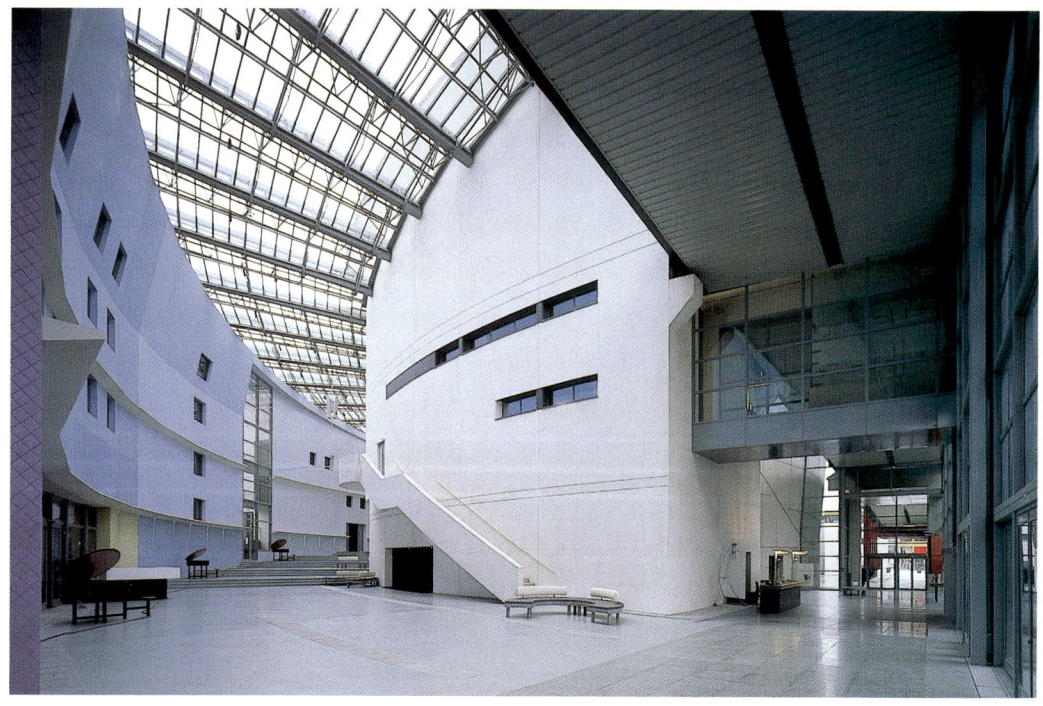

tecture as a global experience in which site, building and furnishings are indistinguishable. Here we could cite the William Morris definition of architecture to which the Secession members so often referred: "Architecture means taking into account the entire physical environment surrounding human life...For architecture is the sum of the modification and variations brought to the earth's surface to meet human needs, with the sole exception of the desert as such."[15]

To see the Conservatoire as a *Gesamtkunstwerk* is to stress the inevitably dramatic aspect of its design; we are reminded of Manfredo Tafuri, who saw in the Darmstadt *Künstlerkolonie* "the sublimated image of a lyrical descent into the fathomless depths of the soul."[16] Architecture, it is now clear, can only emerge out of a sacrificial approach to the creative act, with the price to pay – the solitude of meditative withdrawal – naturally involving its metaphysical dimension.

The Pôle Public de Diffusion Musicale et Muséologique

A plan (2)

In a spirit of Le Corbusier-style good sense, I should like to take another look at the plan and try to perceive the trace of something to do with a conception of architecture – a doctrine. As a necessary prelude, however, I should say that I find the strangely dynamic dimension of the plan troubling and can easily imagine what its preparation must have involved: a pitched battle on a tenacious opponent's home ground, a pitiless struggle to force a semblance of order and regularity on a refractory receptacle. Intractable and perverse, the raw material found itself up against passions which, once set loose, drove into its every nook and cranny as the artist made way for the hardworking craftsman. A mix of modesty and uncertainty, Portzamparc's agenda fed off an endless succession of abortive efforts, momentary victories and shaky compromises which, ultimately and exhaustingly, gave birth to that precious feeling of internal consistency an "accomplished" plan can bring. "Forged by

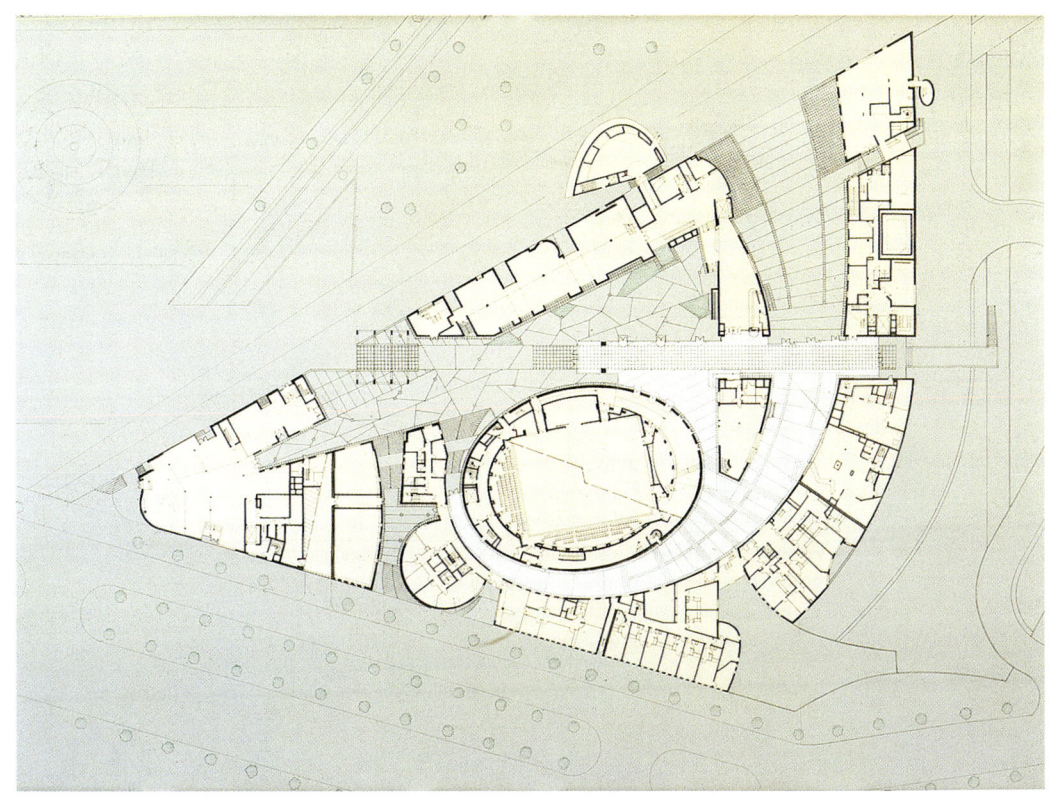

The Cité de la Musique (architect: C. de Portzamparc). The Pôle Public de Diffusion Musicale et Muséologique (Public Music and Museum Complex). The Ground floor plan. Final project.

patience" as the French philosopher Alain put it, yet marked in every respect by the crazed urgency that governed its creation, the plan for the Pôle Public de Diffusion Musicale et Muséologique (Public Music and Museum Complex) became the "battle plan" Le Corbusier was so fond of: "It is a plan of battle. After it comes the battle itself – that's the great moment. The battle takes place between the volumes clashing in space with the morale of the troops, between the cluster of pre-existing ideas and the driving intent."[17] A battle plan, then, a "living," diversity-friendly plan – an ordered diversity, of course – whose component parts, brought together in the resounding collision of their dissimilarity, miraculously find grounds for mutual understanding.

It should not be forgotten that the Conservatoire plan made play with the confrontation of non-matching spaces. But the plan for the Pôle Public, while reapplying the dynamics of antithesis, is nonetheless the product of a fundamentally different programme. The Conservatoire plan drew on abstract painting – on Kandinsky, and more specifically on the motifs of his *Intimate Message* – while that of the Pôle Public looks like the outcome of an empirical process whose formal principle is never provided in advance. "One invents by working," said Alain, the author of *Système des beaux-arts*, adding imperturbably, "from this record of our abiding actions we learn prudence. But through the trustworthy witness that is the least sketch, we also learn confidence."[18]

To the east of Place de la Fontaine-aux-Lions there is no hint of planimetric allegory, the architect having become a modest artist who knows that "the idea comes in the process of doing."[19] Like a violin-maker lovingly working his wood, he has twisted his plan every which way "until, *natura naturans*, it vibrates with a germ of life drawn from its own substance."[20] And could it be that the Conque (Conch), that magisterial spiral street curling around the concert hall, is sister to the giant clam, that denizen of the South Seas whose shell, famed for its curative powers, was used by Chinese mandarins for their bath ritual?

If, to the east the plan is passion – if, to better communicate with the body, it offers itself as the locus of a precipitate formed by an excess of libidinal energy – the task is to tame this evident chaos with a cluster of clearly defined passageways. Like the Conservatoire plan, which arrested its creator's lyrical flight with an internal east-west thoroughfare, the Pôle Public counters the curvilinear dynamics of the Conque with the implacably rectilinear Rue Musicale. The arbitrariness of the curve is confronted with the objectivity of the straight line, the ardour of the *kunstwollen* with the cold abstractness of the concept, the living resources of the organic with the imperturbable silence of the geometrical. The success of the Pôle Public lies in its minutely calculated proportion of what stems from the living – the "moving" – and what is intimately linked to the idea. And when he says that he "plays simultaneously on perception that has no concern with truth, and on knowledge, which craves it,"[21] Portzamparc is simply saying that if it is to work, his architecture must be structured by the two antinomic notions of abstraction and E*infühlung*. On the one hand, the curve brimming with the life of Van de Velde's "force lines" – the famous "presence effect"[22] Portzamparc speaks of – and on the other, the "vitalism" sustained by Riegl's "will to art" and ultimately, naturally producing the "meaning effect"[23] concept so desperately sought by the creator of the Cité de la Musique, and which Kandinsky in his day defined as "transcendental subjectivity."[24]

All this raises a fundamental question: does not this Apollonian/Dionysian duality reflect Christian de Portzamparc's highly ambiguous relationship with a modernity seen as too often doctrinaire? Relevant here is the story of the German architect Mendelsohn returning from Holland, torn between the rationalism of Oud and the Frank Lloyd Wright style of Dudok and declaring that "function without sensibility remains mere construction."[25] Nothing could be more natural here than this reference to Mendelsohn, for in addition to a clear formal similarity – the curves of the Cité de la Musique are the vector for a "life concentrate" oddly reminiscent of the rectangular forms of the Einstein Tower in Potsdam and even of the kinetic hypnotism of the science-fiction architecture sketches once shown at the Cassirer Gallery in Berlin – Mendelsohn's mistrust of modernity is something the Cité's creator seems inclined to share.

Loyalty to modernity, however, comes through in the omnipresence of the architectural itinerary which, without abandoning the curvilinear, firmly establishes the significance of the straight line. The Rue Musicale, as already pointed out, slices through the Pôle Public from east to west. Thus the straight line dominates – and is even the core of – the Cité's typology. Like any follower of Le Corbusier, Portzamparc is aware that "good architecture can be walked through"[26] and one consequence of a structuring process based on dynamic pathways is what Bruno Zevi called the "temporality of space": the work reveals itself over a long period that "dramatises" our perception of it. Le Corbusier was fond of repeating that "Worker housing, detached houses, townhouses, the Palais des Nations, the Centrosoyuz building in Moscow, the World City, the layout of Paris – it all comes down to patterns of movement."[27] While less categorical, Christian de Portzamparc nonetheless sees movement as a core issue.

Although the axis, once it establishes a new relationship with perceptual time, can be seen as expressing a loyalty to modernity, the use of the curve allows its scope to be kept in perspective.

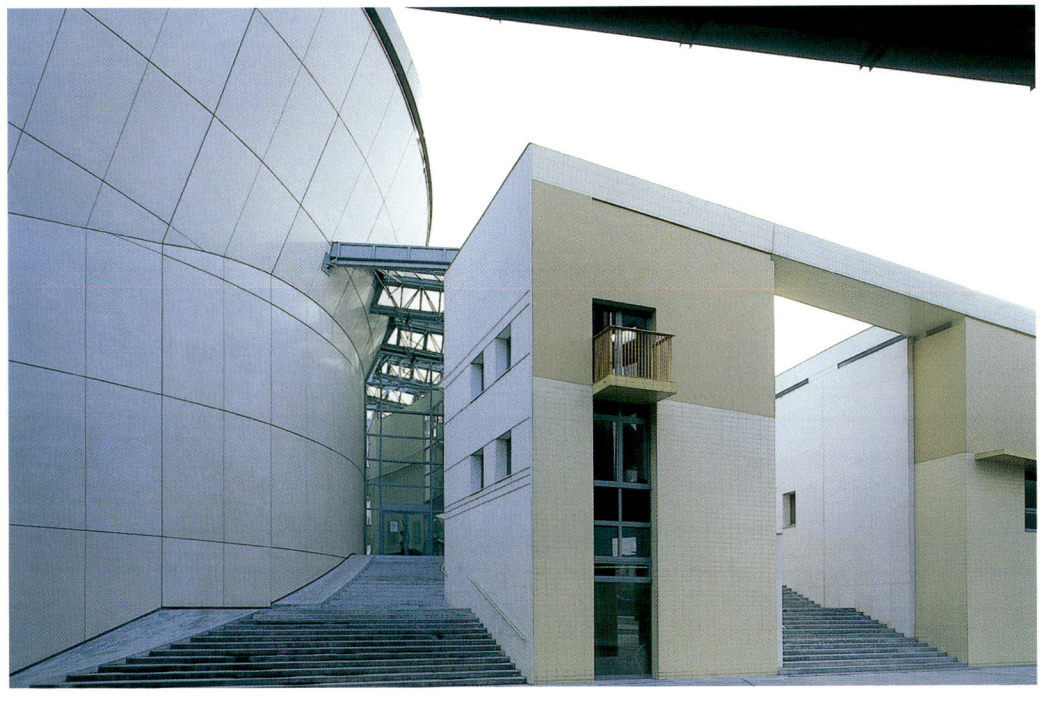

The Cité de la Musique (architect: C. de Portzamparc). The Pôle Public de Diffusion Musicale et Muséologique (Public Music and Museum Complex). One of the entrance ways to the concert hall.

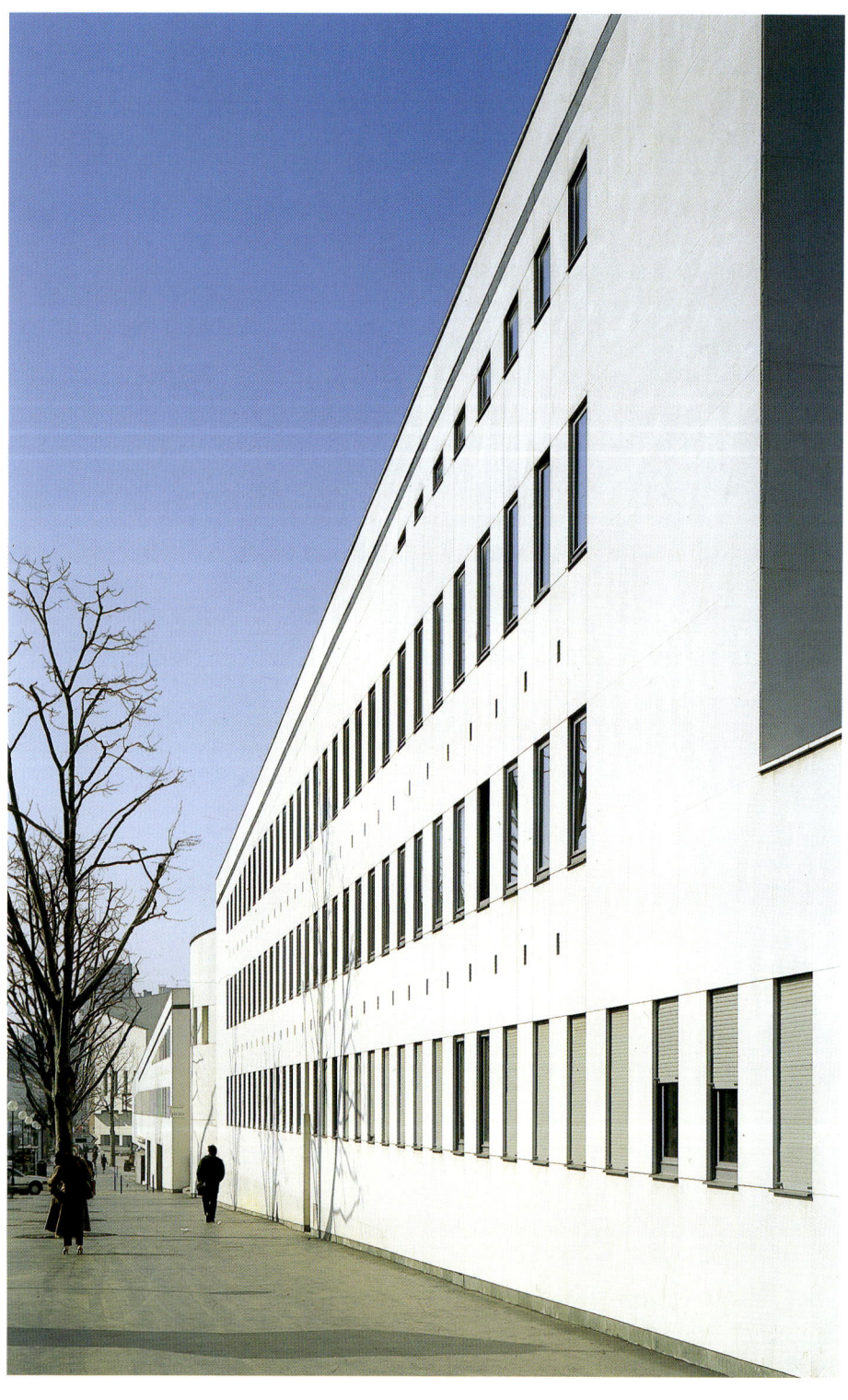

The Cité de la Musique (architect: C. de Portzamparc). The Pôle Public de Diffusion Musicale et Muséologique (Public Music and Museum Complex). The façade on Avenue Jean-Jaurès.

Mendelsohn contradicted Le Corbusier's famous aphorism, "Architecture is controlled by the right angle,"[28] with the smooth curves of his Einstein Tower, exercising a formal freedom not to the taste of practitioners of objective architecture and provoking Mies' stern reminder (made to the future citizens of Palestine) that "a building is made neither of soggy dough nor armour plating, but of skin and bone."[29] It seems unlikely that the joyous shapes of the Cité de la Musique would provoke the same kind of disapproval from today's defenders of an industrial, minimalist approach, but the Cité's undulating lines nonetheless respond to the Folies around the park in the same way as the volumes of Scharoun and Häring – like Mendelsohn, advocates of "organic functionalism" – did to the ascetic creations of the Neue Sachlichkeit architects. Berlin's Siemensstadt district, for example, witnessed pretty much the same fratricidal struggle for architectural leadership as La Villette today: on one side the partisans of what could be called "technological neutrality," and on the other the supporters of something at the very least akin to "redemption through aesthetics."[30] To adopt the curve, take over its life-flow and so become an apostle of Worringer's E*infühlung* – "For us the value of a line or a shape resides in the life value they contain"[31] – became, for Portzamparc, the surest means of escape from the disembodied dryness of dogma. This meant establishing a relationship between architecture and those invited to use it, in which the forces of the mind bow to the immediacy of anti-cognitive perception: a relationship which, because it outlaws any form of intellectualised perception, intensifies the body's receptiveness. In this respect, the dizzy spiral plan of the Pôle Public is reminiscent of the "poetic reaction objects" spoken of by Le Corbusier. Torsion, distortion, retention, outpouring, splitting, liquefaction – everything here springs from an organic dynamic, a "conscious" violence of a distinctly animal cast. Like the shell-roof at Ronchamp, the ear-shaped chapel at La Tourette and the delicately incurvated ventilation outlets at the Marseille Unité d'Habitation, the Pôle

Public plan borrows its shape from the seashell, the butcher's bone and the fossil – all of them forms that have, as it were, captured some ancestral life-thrust. Adopting the curve, then, means seeing what the organic has to offer. But moving into the field of the living means granting a place to emptiness. Here, fullness and emptiness are two interdependent realities, two values arising from the same organic reality. Has not Portzamparc himself defined emptiness as "the other side of fullness?"[32] Let us take this further: if, as the philosopher Alain says, a good musician can be recognised by his "counting of silences,"[33] we can say that the good architect is the one who sets out to establish a relationship of cordial reciprocity between emptiness and fullness. However, the emptiness being sought is not that of the spaces "stripped by speed" that Paul Virilio seems to abhor; nor is it the outcome of a desubstantialisation of the world generated by the proliferation of networks. Because it feeds off gaps, fault lines and breaches, Portzamparc's emptiness is simply a material, or rather a binder – a binder silently and unbudgeably mixed in with fullness.

Here, Christian de Portzamparc is at the opposite pole from Mies. Mies' emptiness is the emptiness of the infinite world. Mies' tireless search for a hypothetical something beyond matter, and his enjoyment in shattering the concreteness of the world, are means of getting closer to the essence of that world – an essence tied to its "aprioristic" character, which the mind quickly buckles down to conquering and dramatising. (In this respect the history of typologies – that unfinished, unfinishable history – is nothing other than the endless inventory of the mind's attempts to appropriate an equally endless space.) Portzamparc's emptiness, by contrast, distances us irrevocably from a lost origin. It summons up a past "outside time" which it would be pointless to try to locate. Mies' emptiness is religious, laying bare an aprioristic world whose existence precedes human action. Portzamparc's emptiness, like a crack in time, is an invitation to "demature" ourselves.

Architecture of the body, architecture of emptiness – all this leads to a further observation: the architecture of the Cité de la Musique is a judicious reminder that it is sometimes a good thing to forget language, that it can be salutary to establish a relationship with reality in which a refusal to formulate is not necessarily a sign of perceptual impoverishment. If the body enjoys primacy in the investigation of reality, we have the chance to reach an original knowledge of the world that language would find very difficult to express. Thus, to acknowledge that "there is a form of thought that does not use language"[34] – to assert, with Bachelard, that "we continuously live solutions to problems for which reflection offers no hope of solution"[35] – means, in Portzamparc's case, declaring oneself a phenomenologist. Any doubt that may have existed in this respect is now dispelled, the creator of the Cité de la Musique having let slip at a recent exhibition that "above and beyond all the explicit justifications for a form, there exists a spatial truth, a specific kind of knowledge, a sanctioning of perception and experience, which are phenomenological."[36] And what lies behind this frantic quest for phenomenological space other than the search for a space of happiness, a space conducive to the "vital outpouring" so dear to Lipps and Worringer? Portzamparc is an epicurean, like the author of *Abstraction and Empathy*, whose celebrated aphorism, "Basically the value of a work of art lies in its ability to make us happy,"[37] could have been written by the architect of the Cité himself.

In conclusion, let us return one last time to the plan of the Pôle Public and check it out for clues to the nature of Portzamparc's relationship not with modern doctrine, but with classicism.

This is clearly a plan intended to keep everyone happy. Within an enormous triangle it has a concert hall, a museum and a music teaching institution rubbing shoulders. As at the Cité Judiciaire in Graz and the Nouvel Équipement Culturel in Rennes, the plan turns out to have a centralising element, in this case the "Trompe" (Hunting Horn): a vast, structuring spiral street winding around the concert hall. But this pursuit of composition leads to a quest for a "grand gesture," a determination to create a celebratory spatial arrangement. It is here that the reference to classicism has its place. The word can mean something other than the "arithmetical tyranny of the Orders" so famously mocked by Zevi long ago. Christian de Portzamparc's riposte to classicism as "synthesis neurosis"[38] is a "funerary monument" classicism. Architecture is unquestionably one of the serious arts, and as such has a duty to make perceptible the sacred dimension of space. Monumentality is doubtless the best way to achieve this. All we have to do here is look at the Pôle Public façade giving onto the park: its sheer size reinforces our solemn reading of the building. But, revealing oneself as a skilled maker of façades, is this not a way of acknowledging oneself as classical (or anti-modern) given that modernity and the inventory principle are known to "exclude the notion of façade"?[39] So, is Portzamparc classical? Unquestionably – but he is anti-classical too, since asymmetry, antiparallelism and dissonance are the very pillars of his architecture.

This love of the "grand gesture" provides, as it did for baroque architects, a guarantee of the merging of building and site. Here architecture and urban planning are the two facets of a single activity: the "urbatecture" spoken of by Zevi. True, the architect has a duty to think out the plan, but he also has a duty to be a *restorator urbis*, an urban planning aesthete skilfully juggling with the various scales of the *Großstadt*. And it is exactly this that the plan of the Pôle Public offers us: something like a Frank Lloyd Wright "open plan," a fleeting mix of Niemeyer's lyrical monumentality, Le Corbusier's Latin-style pathos and Mendelsohn's kinetic fluidity. The outcome is that indefinable something situated at the junction of architecture and town planning.

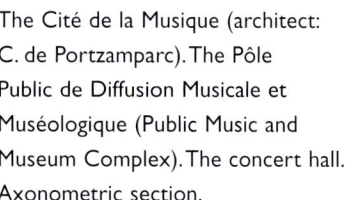

The Cité de la Musique (architect: C. de Portzamparc). The Pôle Public de Diffusion Musicale et Muséologique (Public Music and Museum Complex). The concert hall. Axonometric section.

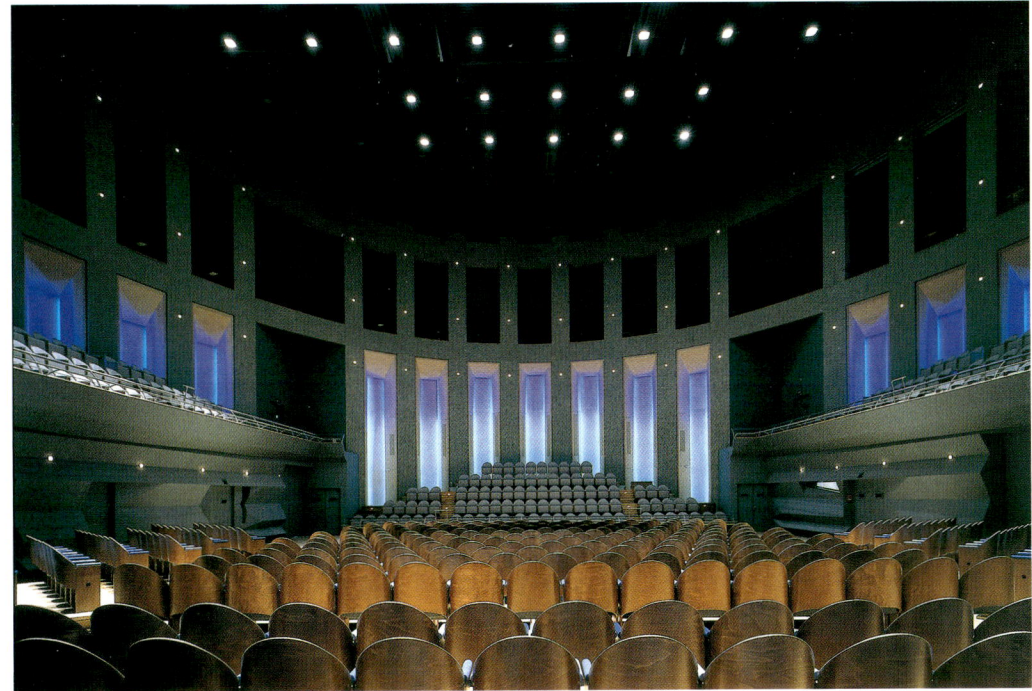

The Cité de la Musique (architect: C. de Portzamparc). The Pôle Public de Diffusion Musicale et Muséologique (Public Music and Museum Complex). The concert hall. Interior view.

The concert hall

With the Musée de l'Instrument (Instrument Museum), the concert hall is one of the major spaces in the Pôle Public; but contrary to the Musée de l'Instrument, whose general outline was established at the sketch phase, its plan evolved appreciably between the first and second rounds of the competition, and then between the second round, and the general and detailed preliminary design phases.

At the close of the first round in April 1984, the plan of the concert hall offered a rectangular shape set in a volume generated by the intersection of an inclined cone and a cylinder, both with circular bases. Six months and a modified brief later, the proposal submitted for the second round revealed a more complex plan based on segments of straight lines and attached to a volume generated by the intersection of an inclined cone and a cylinder, both with elliptical bases.

The general preliminary design phase involved working in conjunction with Pierre Boulez and led to further planimetric modifications. While the shape of the shell remained unchanged, the plan now drew on the overlaying of an ellipse and a large rectangle. The interior volume, expanded at its extremities by the corners of the rectangle breaking out of the ellipse, became larger. On each side of the stalls – where all the necessary configurations are possible – rise four stepped balconies: one of them is motorised and allows for the creation of an orchestra platform that can be set at the same level as the stalls. Above is a gallery-ambulatory set back from the structural points, together with a technical storey suspended from the welded built-up sections of the roof that houses the sound and lighting infrastructure.

For Christian de Portzamparc the choice of an ellipse has to do with its potential, with "the coexistence of a continuous, infinite shell and two immediately identifiable axes which situate us spatially and make possible two totally different kinds of use."[40] Once the ellipse had been settled on, remedies had to be found for the focalisation and whispering gallery phenomena

The Cité de la Musique (architect: C. de Portzamparc). The Pôle Public de Diffusion Musicale et Muséologique (Public Music and Museum Complex). Entrance way to the concert hall.

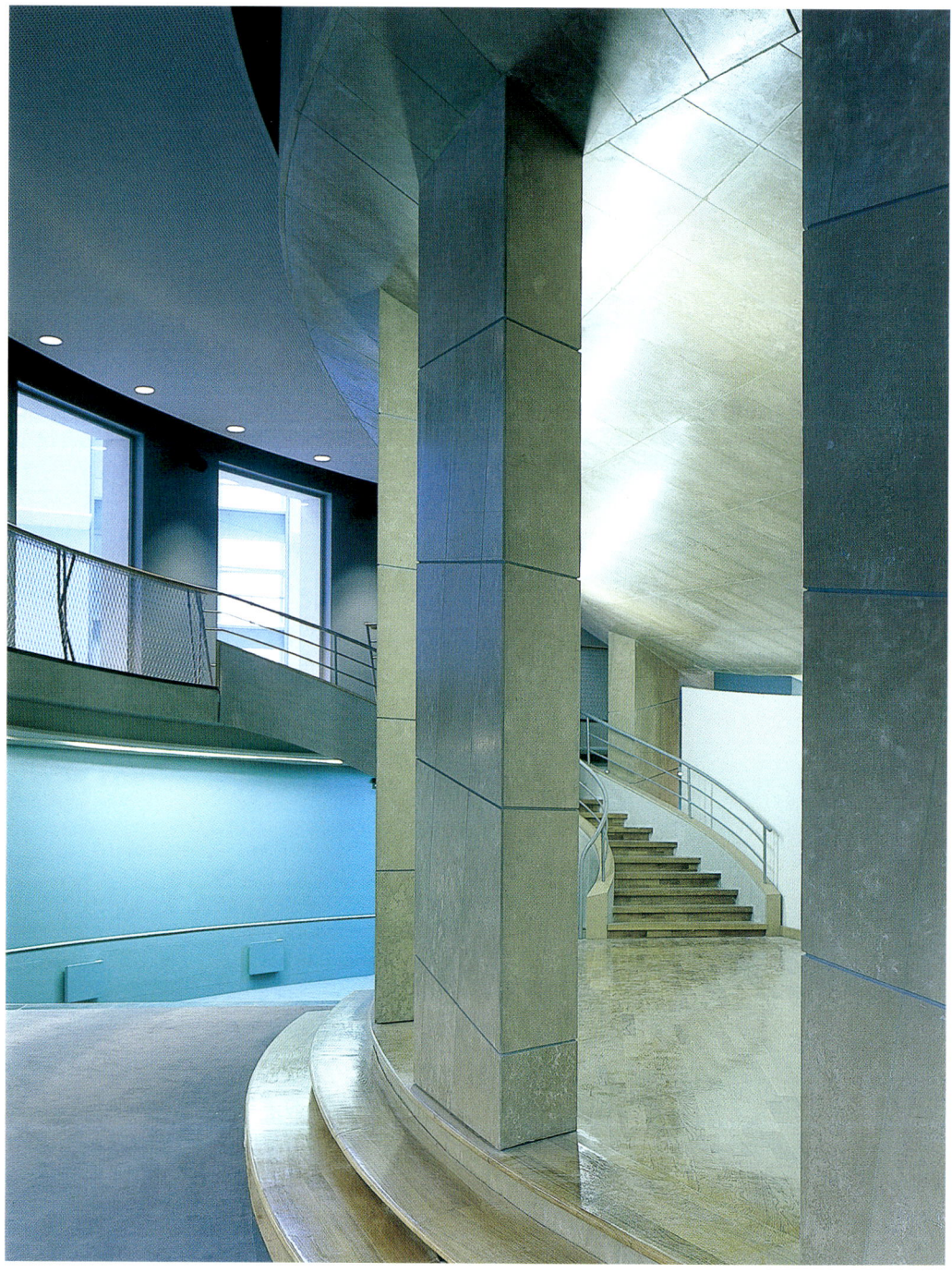

it provoked. With this in mind, the stalls were flanked with open-work partitions, wooden niches were inserted between the load-bearing sections and quadratic residue diffusers were attached to a grid fixed to the ceiling girders.

There then took place an imperceptible shift from elliptical to oval, dictated by the purest building logic. Use of the ellipse, whose radius is continuously variable, would have necessitated making as many moulds as there were concrete tiles in the shell, each of them different from all the others. Since the oval, by contrast, comprises four identical arcs of a circle, grouped two by two, prefabrication was possible.

In addition to acoustics that some find remarkable, the striking thing about the concert hall is its pared-down aesthetic. Two rows of columns set in a ring gravely bear the load allotted to them. A lighting system set in the depths of the niches allows for a spread of light of infinitely varied colours over the surface of the columns. The oblong profile of the roof links back discreetly to the delicately rendered volumes of the Conservatoire. Artifice is limited to the simplest kind, while generating an aura of keen aesthetic precision. In the same way, the technical constraints are skilfully dealt with: the stalls area is a perfect example, allowing an infinite choice of configurations via a compressed air system enabling the lifting of the wooden podiums to which the seats are fixed.

The concert hall is a giant machine that reveals nothing of its inner workings. It is up to musicians, now, to celebrate its beauty and efficiency.

Notes
1. Gaston Bachelard, La Poétique de l'espace (Paris: PUF, 1989), p. 15. (English translation: The Poetics of Space, New York, Beacon Press).
2. Martin Heidegger, L'Origine de l'œuvre d'art (Paris: Gallimard, 1962), p. 36. (English translation: "The Origin of the Work of Art" in Basic Writings, London: Routledge, 1978).
3. Ibid., p. 37.
4. Ibid., p. 43.
5. Jean Lacoste, La Philosophie de l'art (Paris: PUF, 1981), p. 100.
6. Heidegger, op. cit., p. 50.
7. Lacoste, op. cit., p. 100.
8. Heidegger, op. cit., p. 3.
9. Ibid., p. 51.
10. Bachelard, op. cit., p. 31.
11. Le Corbusier, Vers une architecture (Paris: Vincent, Fréal et Cie, 1958), p. 146. (English translation: Towards a New Architecture, Dover, 1986).
12. Adolf Loos, "Ornement et crime" in Ulrich Conrads, Programmes et manifestes de l'architecture du XXe siècle (Paris: Les Éditions de La Villette, 1991), p. 24. (English translation: Ulrich Conrads, Programs and Manifestoes on Twentieth-Century Architecture, MIT Press, 1975).
13. Henry Van de Velde, "À propos de l'art nouveau" in Programmes et manifestes, p. 23.
14. Bachelard, op. cit., note 1, p. 133.
15. Leonardo Benevolo, La Révolution industrielle, vol. I of Histoire de l'architecture moderne (Paris: Dunod, 1978), p. 194.
16. Manfredo Tafuri, Francesco Dal Co, L'Architecture contemporaine (Paris-Milan, Gallimard-Electa, 1991), p. 7. (English translation: Twentieth Century Architecture, Electa, 2004).
17. Le Corbusier, op. cit. note 11, p. 145.
18. Alain, "De l'architecture" in Les Arts et les dieux (Paris: Gallimard – La Pléiade, 1958), p. 292.
19. Lacoste, op. cit., note 5, p. 72.
20. Paul Valéry, Eupalinos ou L'architecte, vol. II of Œuvres (Paris: Gallimard – La Pléiade), p. 105.
21. Christian de Portzamparc, "Questions de forme : entretien avec Richard Scoffier" in Scènes d'atelier (Paris: Centre Georges-Pompidou, 1996).
22. Ibid.
23. Ibid.
24. Wassily Kandinsky, Du spirituel dans l'art… (Paris: Gallimard – Folio Essais, 1989), p. 12. (English translation: Concerning the Spiritual in Art, Dover, 1977).
25. Kenneth Frampton, L'Architecture moderne : une histoire critique (Paris: Ph. Sers, 1985), p. 106. (English translation: Modern Architecture: A Critical History, London, Thames and Hudson, 1985).
26. Jean Jenger, L'Architecture pour émouvoir (Paris: Gallimard–Découvertes, 1993), p. 51.
27. Le Corbusier, Précisions (Paris: Altamira, 1994), p. 128. (English translation: Precisions on the Present State of Architecture and City Planning, MIT Press, 1991).
28. Ibid., p. 151.
29. Ludwig Mies van der Rohe, "Immeubles de bureaux" (1923: Écrits 1, 3) in Fritz Neumeyer, Ludwig Mies van der Rohe : Réflexion sur l'art de bâtir (Paris: Le Moniteur, 1996), p. 242. (English translation: The Artless Word: Mies van der Rohe on the Building Art, MIT Press, 1994).
30. Ibid., p. 77.
31. Wilhem Worringer, Abstraction et Einfühlung (Paris: Klincksieck, 1986), p. 51. (English translation: Abstraction and Intuition, Ivan R. Dee, 1997).
32. Portzamparc, op. cit., note 21.
33. Alain, "De la musique" in op. cit., note 18, p. 292.
34. Portzamparc, op. cit., note 21.
35. Bachelard, op. cit., note 1, p. 11.
36. Portzamparc, op. cit., note 21.f
37. Worringer, op. cit., note 31, p. 50.
38. Bruno Zevi, Le Langage moderne de l'architecture (Paris: Dunod, 1981), p. 26. (English translation: The Modern Language of Architecture, Da Capo Press, 1994).
39. Ibid., p. 7.
40. Christian de Portzamparc, La Cité de la musique (Seyssel: Champ Vallon, 1986), p. 33.

INTERVIEWS

Pierre Boulez

Christian de Portzamparc

Interview with Pierre Boulez

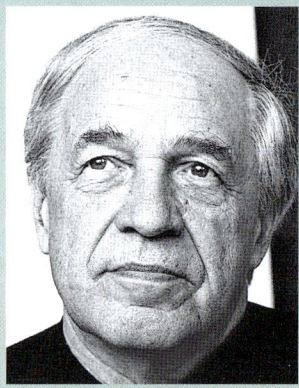

After taking his degree at the Conservatoire National Supérieur de Musique in Paris, where he studied harmony under Olivier Messiaen, Pierre Boulez founded IRCAM (Institute for Research and Coordination in Acoustics and Music) in 1975, and the Ensemble InterContemporain in 1977. He is principal conductor of the BBC Symphony Orchestra. As well, Boulez teaches at the Collège de France. As IRCAM's honorary director, he is a privileged user with the Ensemble InterContemporain, of the Cité de la Musique's concert hall where his works are regularly performed. Here he talks about the design of the hall and the genesis of the Cité de la Musique project.

Could you outline the origins of the Cité de la Musique project for us?

The project goes back to the beginning of the 1980s. At the time we hoped to offer La Villette something resembling the Lincoln Center: a hub for all the main music bodies. Even before François Mitterrand was elected president, we were thinking very seriously about building an opera house, three concert halls – one of them symphonic – and a new building for the Conservatoire. I remember meeting with Jean-Philippe Lecas, then minister of Culture, to try and get across to him that links between the teaching world and professional institutions were urgently needed. So, the first mistake was building the

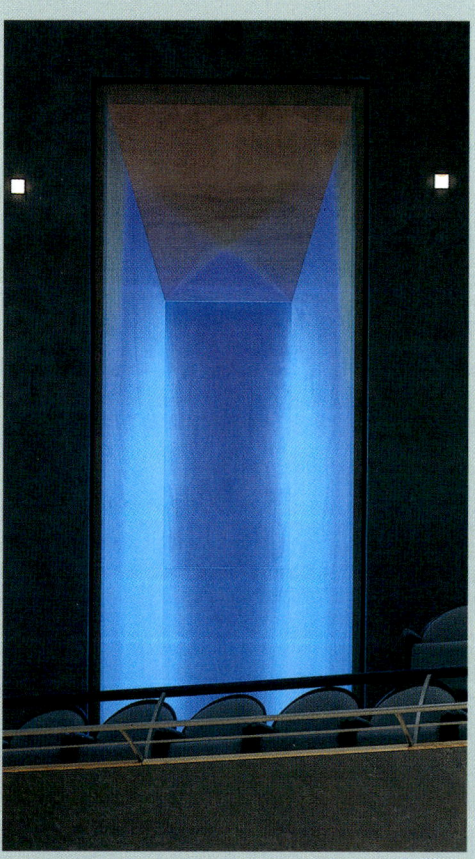
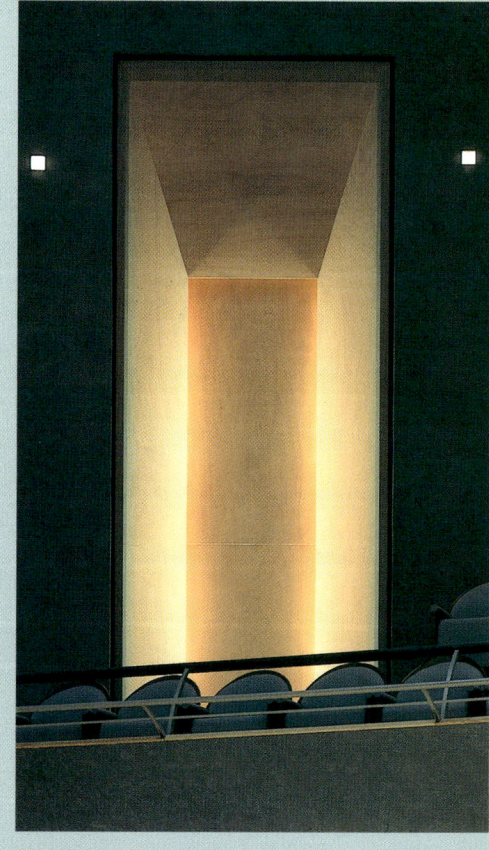

Opera at the Bastille. There were two different and separate competitions, one for the opera and the other for the Cité de la Musique, and this considerably lessened the chances of getting the three halls we had initially planned for. This is how the symphony concert hall came to be dropped, even though it had been included – in a totally utopian way, I should add – in the study for the building of the Cité de la Musique. In fact, with the project for an annex having also been abandoned, all that remains now is the "medium" or "experimental" hall with around one thousand two hundred seats and shared by the Conservatoire and the Ensemble InterContemporain.

So Paris found itself without a symphony concert hall.

In a sense, yes: the Salle Pleyel is no good acoustically and the Châtelet and Champs-Élysées venues are first and foremost theatres.

Should this concert hall still be built now?

Absolutely. Building it would be a godsend architecturally – Christian de Portzamparc's project would at last exist in full – and artistically, because it would make more symphony concerts possible during the season.

Why wasn't the large symphonic hall built instead of the medium-sized one?

Things were done that way at the Opéra-Bastille and we've seen the result: the large hall was built and the small one will assuredly never happen. But let's get back to the genesis of the Cité de la Musique. There

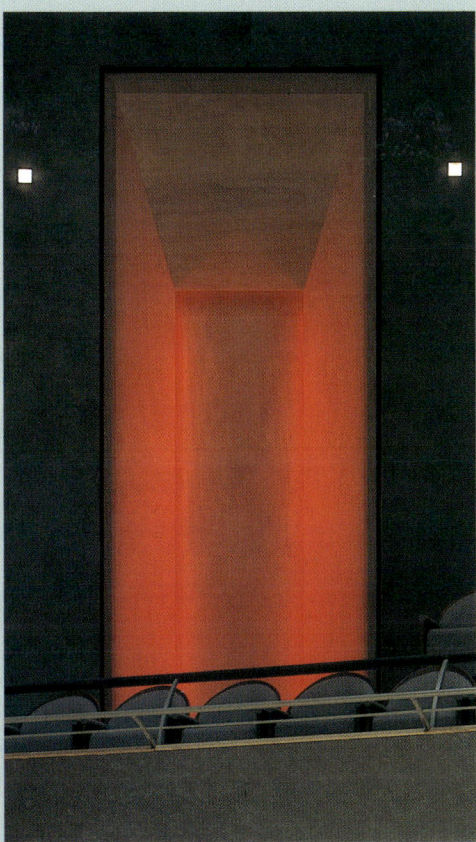 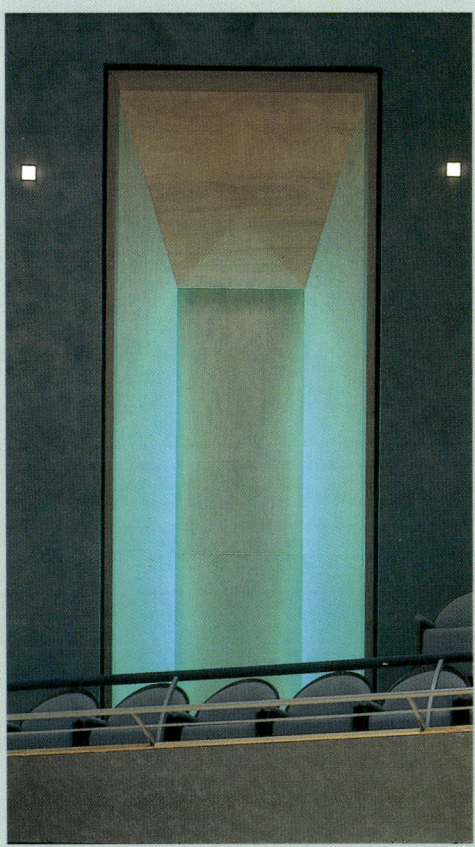

The Cité de la Musique (architect: C. de Portzamparc). The Pôle Public de Diffusion Musicale et Muséologique (Public Music and Museum Complex). The niches in the concert hall.

INTERVIEW WITH PIERRE BOULEZ

came a rapid addition in the form of the museum project – allowing the Conservatoire collection to go on show. So the overall project ultimately came with three sections: the concert hall, the Musée de l'Instrument and the Conservatoire. As far as the concert hall goes, I remember that nobody actually thought about the programming, even though I'd emphasised that it was totally unrealistic to think that the Ensemble InterContemporain and the Conservatoire could handle it on their own. It was at this point that it was decided to appoint a director for the Cité de la Musique and plans were made to organise a musical season including the Conservatoire and the Ensemble.

When big competitions are held, it often happens that major facilities are proposed without any real thought about programming for them. Take the modular hall at the Opéra-Bastille – it's still waiting to be built. When the right-wing won the elections in 1986, the whole thing nearly collapsed. The Chirac government wanted to halt the Cité de la Musique project and transfer part of its programme to the Bastille – an utterly nonsensical idea.

Does the concert hall suit you?

I'm completely satisfied with the concert hall. Acoustic quality is good and the atmosphere inside is warm and friendly. I like it just as much in functional terms because it's mobile – it can be given different configurations and this can be done relatively quickly.

Reading some of the reports from the study period, I noticed that you came out against the concert hall designed by Christian de Portzamparc. What were the reasons for this?

The Technical Committee had asked for my opinion on the concert hall because the Ensemble InterContemporain and I were getting ready to become its principal users. I had reservations about the elliptical shape suggested by Christian de Portzamparc, the ellipse being, in acoustic terms, the most dangerous shape there is. It concentrates sound at its focal points and this makes it a configuration to be avoided when you're thinking in terms of a concert hall.

Once Christian de Portzamparc had been named winner of the competition, how did things work out during the dialogue phase between project management and yourself?

Christian de Portzamparc came to a performance of one of my works, *Répons*. Afterwards we discussed things a lot, mainly mobility problems that I saw as fundamental. I gave him a list of works representative of my generation and asked him to work on suitable architectural configurations. We had to ensure that the changes were not too complex logistically and in this respect the compressed air slide system Portzamparc's agency came up with is just marvellous: I wanted to avoid a system with rails at all costs, because if something jams the whole hall is immobilised until you get the repairs done. We needed a hall where moving things about would be simple. I also insisted that the IRCAM acoustics experts should work closely with Portzamparc. I was very wary of the Comins-bbm consultancy for the simple reason that the director of the Conservatoire was not at all satisfied with the acoustics in his halls.

Do you recall the other projects entered for the competition?

I still remember the Xenakis project, with its odd "potato" shape. As I recollect, his notion of a concert hall didn't seem very strong on function.

What's your happiest memory of this concert hall?

I have a wonderful memory of the day when we performed *Répons* and *Rituel*, which are both works calling for configurations only this hall can provide.

Interview by Alain Orlandini.

Interview with Christian de Portzamparc

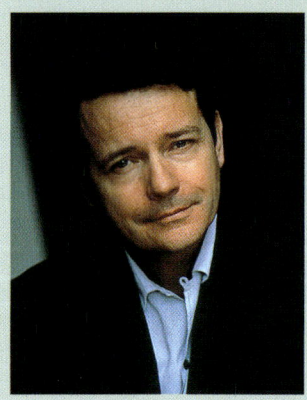

Christian de Portzamparc was born in Casablanca in 1944. He was twenty-seven when his first building – the water tower at Marne-la-Vallée – highlighted the two main strands of his approach: an artistic handling of objects and a personal notion of the relationship between artefact and urban setting. In 1971, he built the Hautes Formes housing estate in the 13th arrondissement in Paris. The 1980s saw him deliver in quick succession three projects in Paris to do with music and dance: the Conservatoire Erik Satie, the École de Danse de l'Opéra and the Conservatoire National Supérieur de Musique et de Danse. Since then he has built a host of projects in France and abroad, and was Pritzker Prize laureate in 1994.

Before we start talking about the Cité de la Musique, what about trying to define the characteristics of your architecture? I'd like to say straight off that one striking feature is the omnipresence of the curve: it seems that for you architecture has to be thought of in dynamic terms. But if we consider the importance movement takes on in dreams – Shelley speaks of dream images as "forces of elevation"; Bachelard stresses the priority of dynamics over form in the dreaming consciousness – we realise the extent to which your work can be perceived as dream-state architecture. It summons us to a linear hypnosis. In the final analysis your architecture is only architecture because it engenders what Bachelard termed "oneiric levitation."

What you've just said is the handsomest compliment my architecture could be paid. I like the way you suggest something that could be related to a kind of relinquishment. Relinquishment is what dreaming is. But that could take us a long way – all the way back to Rimbaud, at least.

I've often wondered why you mention the films of Alain Resnais. Then I realised that his cinema, like your architecture, sets out to invoke the psyche as vector. In Last Year in Marienbad or Hiroshima Mon Amour we find endless travelling shots inviting the viewer to adopt a fluctuating perception of the world. We could say the tracking shot is to Resnais' films what the architectural itinerary is to your work: a means of accessing dreams.

What's interesting is the idea that the body can move. Within an architecture you have to be able to move. That seems to me more important than a shape's dynamic appearance. And anyway, if the body is invited to move, that doesn't necessarily mean that the shapes are dynamic. The shapes of ancient Greece were cubic, but they still contained a call to movement. The Greek city is a succession of assemblages, polarities and attractions that keeps you endlessly moving forward.

As with Alain Resnais, observing your architecture means realising one is

powerless to break down what is perceived into concepts. In the Conservatoire everything seems oddly dilated.

Yes.

But there's a paradox I have to raise here. While your architecture summons movement – and thus dreams – through its recurring recourse to the curve, it is also in search of a point of anchorage. As Hubert Tonka has so nicely put it, your architecture "draws its gravity from its weight of non-transportable art." For example, there's a telluric quality to the south façade of the Conservatoire, with those four imposing masses.

Various perceptual registers exist. There are the weighty and the light, the anchored and the free-floating, the wet and the dry, the vertical and the horizontal. And within each of these interpretative grids you can come up against all sorts of nuances whose possible combinations are infinite. Anchored is classicism, free-floating is modernity. Modernity is less concerned with matter. As far as I'm concerned, though, the two are indissociable. One should be able to make the transition from the prehistoric cave to the aeroplane.

The interior courtyard of the Conservatoire enables this dual perception. On the one hand there are the massive roofs of the public music rooms, and on the other this immense undulating roof heading off towards the park.

Immobility on the one hand, movement on the other.

I've often heard you described as a formalist, doubtless because of the omnipresence of the curve we were talking about just now. What's your reply to this kind of accusation?

Calling an architect a formalist is a clichéd reaction that usually indicates the lack of any theoretical background. Inside every architect there lurks a policeman who comes out into the open as soon as form starts getting used with too much enthusiasm. The formalist is always someone else, someone different from yourself. Accusing someone of formalism can also be a way of saying he's not classical: in this case formalism is identified with the baroque and the weird.
I personally evolved in a highly doctrinaire, anti-formalist milieu. When I came to Candilis I was half-Corbusier, half-Scharoun and ended up interested in ideas that appealed particularly to the rationalists – the grid, for example. Post-war modern architecture was built entirely on a system of moral values: it wanted above all to represent democracy, progress and a new world freed of totalitarianism and everything that went with it. That's why a large part of the modern discourse was doctrinaire and guilt-inducing. And then there was a real problem: the masses needed housing and it was serious business.

You mentioned Scharoun, but it could just as easily have been the Luckhardt brothers or Mendelsohn. I've often compared the undulations of the Cité de la Musique to those of the Potsdam Tower.

That doesn't bother me – the opposite, in fact. But it also needs to be said that if we encouraged students to work with form without any degree of restraint, we'd see projects that would be like enormous, joyous sculptures. I'm always conscious that, as Goethe so aptly put it, architects – unlike theatre designers, whose job it is to enchant us – owe it to themselves to remember the governing principles of their society. In my case, I very quickly adopted the rigorousness of the right angle, and its opposite.

Like Le Corbusier.

Exactly. And it was that complementarity that I found interesting in him.

Adrien Fainsilber has stressed the beautiful paradox of the Le Corbusier approach. He once said to me that "Le Corbusier talks about the poetry of the right angle and ends up building Ronchamp."

True. Let's take the example of the Hautes Formes project. When I work on housing I never try formal stuff. It's more a case of the shapes being induced by the constraints of the site. It's only little by little that I introduce a whole series of elements in which the relation to form is likely to fill out. That's when I decide to allow myself a little leeway regarding the right-angle rule – but without ever forgetting that I must always take into account two basic notions: use and space. Space has to be thought of in terms of interior attributes, and these attributes are going to spill out into the exterior space.

To sum up, I feel we could describe your architecture as elegant. The characteristic of elegance is to highlight a function via a form which, while free, remains faithful to the function it is supposed to contribute to. Seen in this light, being elegant means allowing oneself a few liberties in respect to Sullivan's "form follows function" dogma, but without going formalist.

Absolutely. It must never be forgotten that a space is created first and foremost to be useful. When I say this I always have Joseph Belmont on my back, "What? So you're a functionalist?" To which I reply, "If you like. Except that my notion of function goes far beyond anything the functionalists ever did." Every space has a use, but must be capable of more than that. Capable of becoming festive. All the stuff relating to function is in the brief, and the rest is up to the architect. What the Conservatoire provides in terms of large, fluid traffic areas isn't indicated in the brief. And yet when you see how the students live, you have the feeling that the intense level of interchange there – made possible by a daring interpretation of the brief – has become a specific use and one of the Conservatoire's *raisons d'être*. Interpreting a brief intelligently is a way of being a functionalist, too.

If you stop and think about it, using the term "formalism" betrays a certain lack of culture. To speak of formalism is to forget how important the word "form" is. Where there's perception there's form. Form is what structures our sensory – and thus intellectual – understanding of the world. And this is very important. We're too inclined to feel that understanding is made possible by concepts and language: if this is the case, if interchange is made possible by words whose capacity for communication is rendered unchallengeably superior by the dynamics of abstraction it allows for, we must also learn to perceive the body's relationship with the world and sense the

Page right: The Cité de la Musique (architect: C. de Portzamparc). The Conservatoire. The interior courtyard.

contingent aspect of the "here," "there" and "now." One day in the studio, Josic got annoyed and said to me, "Why are you making an angle like that?" And I replied, "Maybe I can't explain." Today I'd have no trouble in justifying formal choices like that. But we mustn't forget that, formally speaking, the people who preached the dictatorship of the right angle ended up imposing a terribly simplistic world on us.

Repeating our criticisms of some members of the modern movement involves pointing out that several of them sometimes adopted highly formalist approaches. Mies van der Rohe, for instance, is someone who was much concerned with problems of form, even if he claimed otherwise.

Of course. Mies, whom I very much admire, was a great classicist. But whatever happens, the architect – like the musician – can't escape the problem of form.

Don't you see the big problem with architecture as lying in its near-obsession with beauty, when in a sense the craft boils down to pure utility. One has the impression that the architect never settles for the form/function balance that must govern the business of architectural design. One often feels the architect embarrassed by his urge to embellish form. I'm thinking here of a discussion I once had with Jean-Louis Avril, professor of architectural theory at the École d'Architecture de Paris – La Villette, who said, "in architecture the desire for form always wins in the end. But to make beautiful architecture you must always, when preparing a project, postpone as long as possible the

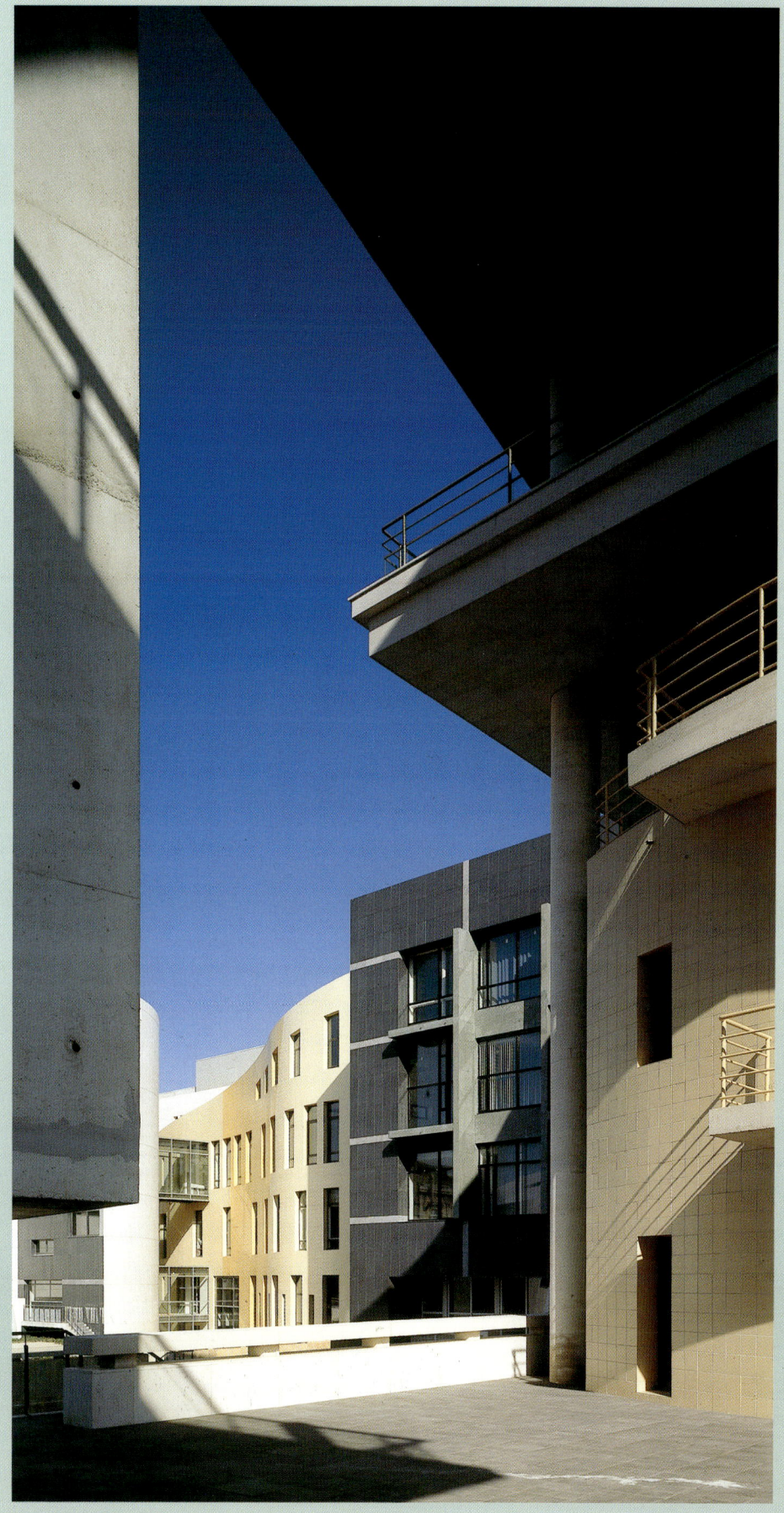

moment of finally having fun." I just loved that. There was something desperate about this way of exorcising the instinct for form that slumbers in every architect.

All of us, at one time or another, have experienced the guilt you're talking about. I understand perfectly what Jean-Louis Avril was trying to say.

His ideas there came from Loos, who said, "Beware of being original, which drawing can make too easy. Often you need to make an enormous effort, when drawing, to chase away all original ideas. But you can overcome the temptation with one simple question: 'How are the people I'm working for going to live in this house or on these premises?'"

Yes.

Let's come back to the notion of the curve. Inherent in the curve is primitive space. And inherent in primitive space is "body space." Your architecture seems to be a quest for a loyalty to the human that our geometry-obsessed civilisation has repudiated: it leads us to understand that the sphere is more tactile than the square, and that the right angle appeared with civilised man.

Architecture is the sign of human presence, and the latter very quickly seeks to rival the natural world. Human beings try to take geometry and use it to make what God could not: the right angle and the flat surface. Geometry is the prose of the modern world. If we synthesised all the drawings made by modern architects, the result would surely be a square. Personally, I like the confrontation between what's flat and what's not, between the regular and the irregular.

Like the south façade of the Conservatoire, which reveals a part-cylinder meeting a sloping plane.

Yes, for example. But sometimes the right angle comes out on top. The Musée Bourdelle is based exclusively on flat surfaces and right angles. I should point out that there are gradations between the straight and the non-straight. A Moebius strip, for example, breaks with angularity, but is less complex than the shape of a cloud.

It's often said that building a tower is every architect's dream, but looking at the forms you create – often curved, as we know – one is inclined to ask if the true architectural space isn't quite simply anthropomorphic. The language you use to describe your spaces has a markedly organic tone: you talk about mountains, hunting horns, canyons and so on.

True, but you have to avoid relationships that are too rigid. Sometimes a snail's shell can be too limiting. That's why I refuse to make this quest for anthropomorphic constancy the only value of my architecture. But what's useful about the phenomenologists, especially Gaston Bachelard, is the way they pinpoint all the things our century was busy unloading: water, earth, fire. Modern man represses them but without being able to forget them completely. I often say there are some things you can't forgo without generating great anxiety. Working as I do on the notion of place is a way of combating a world which, more through lack of culture than for reasons of radicalism, is getting ready to junk a whole set of ideas I see as fundamental. It's because the world is governed by a technico-economic rationale, that the ideas I'm talking about can be disavowed. On the other hand, if I was really convinced that the world was rushing to its destruction, as some say it is, I think that instead of building, I'd write. To build is to give direction, to transform. Ultimately we live with the hope that order will come to the chaos of the world, and that our anguish is due only to the radical change we are experiencing right now.

I would like to talk about the Conservatoire's interior spaces and in particular the entrance hall – which, as we shall see, is also a "body" space. The entrance hall has something of a crypt or a cave about it. You want to nestle into it. It's a place that seems full of history. You mentioned Bachelard just now: I'm convinced that if he visited the Conservatoire he'd find the materialisation of the concepts developed in The Poetics of Space. He'd describe it as a "body-house" or a "belly-house" – unless he opted for terms like "perfect cavity" or "carnal prison" or "mine-sarcophagus."

The first version of the entrance hall had a different layout from the one we ended up with. But it all comes clear once you understand that the idea of an architectural itinerary had to be retained. Doing this meant not having the entry symmetrical in relation to the four blocks set up along Avenue Jean-Jaurès. The symmetrical approach to the point of entry is very deceptive: it leads you to believe, mistakenly, that you'll have a better appreciation of the space. In fact, when your entry is central all mystery evaporates. Once the entry was moved to the east side of the main façade, the plan's balance had to be re-established. This was achieved via the perception of another axis, on each side of which are the patio and the public music rooms, lower down. What it adds up to is a dogleg arrangement. You find this plani-metric figure in certain townhouses in Paris.

Something startling happens when you actually go in to the Conservatoire. You sense intuitively that the entry is off-centre in relation to the façade, but the view of the entrance hall, set lower down, quickly alerts you to an up-down axis that in a way "rebalances" – and thus rationalises – the mental picture one develops of the place. This is a very astute layout.

There's a lot going on seven metres below ground level: the patio, the public music rooms and so on. People had to realise very quickly that they needed to go downstairs. The entrance hall is three metres below ground level and enjoys a privileged position: it can be seen from the ground floor without obstruction from the reception points. The other, very important element here is shade. I wanted the entrance hall to be a kind of haven of shade that would offset the luminous transparency of the floors higher up.

The entrance hall is kind of a hermit's hut. There's something of the primitive shelter about it. "What is a house," asks Bachelard, "if not a sedes – a place to sit down?" The entrance

hall in the Conservatoire is a stopping-place, a little corner of the world just right for a rest – a prenatal rest. Nonetheless, as a space it remains extremely dynamic. The walkways in the upper levels have something very kinetic about them. The entrance hall condenses space, but disperses it as well. Talking about this dual perception you get in the entrance hall, we could quote Bachelard again; in Earth and Reveries of Will *he talks about the cave in terms that fit the Conservatoire entrance hall perfectly: "The cave offers shelter to rest and love, but it is also the cradle of primitive industry. As a rule we find it as the setting for solitary work."*

Yes. But in response to the pertinence of your comments, what I'd like to say is that when you're doing architecture you're thinking with sensations. A lot of philosophers and writers find this very hard to accept – but that's the way it is. And if I want to create this particular place, I don't necessarily have to be able to formulate what you've just said about the entrance hall. When I'm talking to the people I work with, I tell them certain things about materials, and about shade and form, but I would never say all you've just said. During the building process, some people called the entrance hall the chapel. I would never have thought of it that way.

I'd be more inclined to call it a shell. In Victor Hugo's Hunchback of Notre Dame *there's a superb passage describing the near-anthropomorphic relationship between Quasimodo and the cathedral: "One could almost say he had taken on its shape the way the snail takes on the form of its shell. It was his residence, his hole, his envelope. He adhered to it, so to speak, like the tortoise to its shell." Bachelard offers an excellent commentary on these lines, speaking of "this singular, symmetrical, immediate, almost consubstantial coming-together of a man and a building."*

Beautifully put.

In The Bird, *Michelet says: "The real nest-making tool is the bird's body, the breast with which he presses and compresses the materials until he can do as he likes with them, mixing them together and subordinating them to the task in hand." Here we have a fine example of space being created from within.*

I'm fond of quoting Lao-Tse: "The house is not the roofs, not the walls, not the floor, but the emptiness between them, because that's where I live." The important thing is the emptiness. But emptiness isn't vacuity, it's not nothing. Emptiness is the in-between, it's matter without matter.

Emptiness as the "inverse of fullness," to quote one of your favourite expressions.

Right.

Maybe you haven't noticed, but the Conservatoire entrance hall effects an inversion of the cellar-attic bipolarity. Here the brightness of day has abandoned the attic for the depths of the cellar. So down there we've finished with the "suffocation nightmare" or the "nausea of the deep"; instead there's natural, intense light.

Yes.

To sum up, then, the entrance hall is a little house. Bachelard speaks of the house in very poetic terms: "The house of memory, the natal house, is built over the crypt of the house of dreams." This dreamed house could be described as a kind of concentrate of all the houses that occupy the depths of our memory.

The driving force of my work is there. It's made up of all those notions you've homed in on – the irrational, memory, dreams, and so on – which end up being sublimated into aesthetic manifestations. But I have to avoid throwing too much light on that. Otherwise I lose something. Do you know the room Christian Boltanski created in the Conservatoire basement?

No.

Since by law one percent of the budget has to be spent on works of art, I asked Boltanski to do something for the Conservatoire. He works with light a lot, so there was no danger of ending up with something clumsy and cumbersome. But as we strolled through the Conservatoire, he said to me, "This is all too beautiful. I need somewhere dirtier, with shadows." So we went down into the basement, and as we were walking past the enormous concrete footings put in to absorb the vibrations from the Métro, Boltanski suddenly stopped and said, "This is where I want to set up." He moved in next to the enormous stacks of files from the construction site huts that had just been demolished. Then he designed three rooms – an incredible amount of work – dedicated to the Conservatoire dead.

What you're saying backs up our analysis of the entrance hall. The entrance hall is the memory space, calling up a past with no date to it – and to say that, is to acknowledge it as a phenomenological space. So what if we go into this point a little further? Somebody – I don't know who – once described you as "a combination of a sensualist and a phenomenologist"; maybe it was Marc Bédarida, the philosopher, in the book that accompanied the recent exhibition on your work at the Pompidou Centre. When you say that some of your architectural motifs come to you "all of a sudden," "without any prior reflection," I can't help thinking of Bachelard, whom we've already borrowed from extensively and who drew a very clear distinction between the metaphor and the poetic image. For him, a metaphor is the product of a body of knowledge: before it crystallises it makes its way through the long, winding circuits of thought. The poetic image, in contrast, is a kind of sudden inspiration, and owes its trans-subjective import to the fact of being a spark thrown by the soul. It's this instantaneous birth that makes the poetic image archetypal and the sublimation of a shared perceptive capital. I somehow have the impression that you have no trouble accepting that situation specific to the artist, in which he finds himself working with these two quite distinct types of image, the metaphorical and the poetic. The most telling example is that of the Conservatoire's east and south façades. One is the outcome of long, mature reflection – the east; and the other, as you put it, was just born – the south.

Working-out the east façade was heavy going in that the research it entailed required enormous patience. The south façade, on the other hand, came all at once. But to clarify the context I should say that there were prior circumstances behind the speed with which this architectural motif emerged. The fullness/emptiness theme is a part of me: you find it at La Roquette and, to a certain extent, in the Opéra-Bastille project. The large flat section of the Opéra-Bastille façade had been thought of in terms of hollowness. Initially there was a kind of slightly incurved cornice, which I soon found too timid in relation to the size of the façade. I gave a lot of thought to this notion of the slanting plane meeting part of an arched cylinder, but I found my use of it in the Opéra-Bastille competition too formalist.

I see the south façade as the very image of a upsurge, that of the plane concept.

Yes. I think one is constantly confronted with a kind of dual world. There's the attention you give to the inspiration aspect – intuition and chance; and then there's the methodical treatment of such elements as the rationale of the itineraries, the analysis of the specific functions of certain spaces, and other things as well. Obviously there's a coexistence, a linkage between these two worlds.

Nonetheless, Bachelard sees the poetic image as superior to the metaphor. For him "Poetic images stand out from everyday language and thus imply a distinctive meaning. They are not the result of some linguistic outburst or clumsiness. They stem not from the desire to surprise. They bare the mark of a certain primitiveness. They issue forth instantaneously and fully actualised." Further into **The Poetics of Space** *we read: "Poetic images obliterate the world and have no past. They arise out of no earlier experience."*

I agree totally with that point of view.

Bachelard also explains how the encounter with the poetic image represents a kind of founding experience. "The poetic experience," he says, "enables us to dephilosophise ourselves. It allows us to set aside all our cultural influences." He also stresses the fact that philosophy makes us mature too fast, that it "crystallises us in a state of maturity."

Looking at my various buildings, you can very quickly find the reasons behind the ultimate form. But it sometimes happens that I give up trying to explain a form because I'm afraid of losing certain kinds of energy I see as fundamental. Sometimes you find yourself unable to understand everything, and there's nothing wrong with that at all.

Believe it or not, in **The Poetics of Space**, *Bachelard says exactly the same thing: "When you're in the phase of imagining, you don't know how or why you imagine. When you can explain how you imagine, you've stopped imagining." He concludes by saying, "So you have to de-mature yourself."*

Yes. Last year's Pompidou Centre exhibition helped me understand a whole lot of things in this regard. Part of the preparation process involved going back to old sketches that had been in storage, and I could see why, years later, certain arrangements had come back to the surface in my work. Being an architect means having the right kind of sensibility and a stock of intensely lived experiences. A good architect has to start out with a heightened sensitivity to habitat and space – this partially explains why you often find him living in badly organised spaces. Then one day he decides to make use of that sensitivity by turning it into a profession. He's got to be sensitive to places, itineraries and spaces – not just the iconography of the major monuments. This means being able to sense that a given neighbourhood is attractive and another not; that one room has spatial qualities that another lacks. Childhood is full of these spatial experiences and the memory of them ends up functioning as a kind of measuring tool.

I recall something Jean-Paul Sartre wrote – in one of his Situations *volumes, I think – which goes into the question of travel at considerable length. Sartre says that the traveller's relationship with what he perceives, sets knowledge aside in favour of memory – with all the elements of dream and fantasy this implies. In this sense, travelling means dipping into the diversity of forms without there being a relationship that puts the emphasis on reasoning.*

All architects have a passion for cities, and grasp them in different ways. The initial discovery is marvellous because it's exotic. That's the discovery you make in childhood.

A prereflexive discovery, you might say.

Exactly. And the longer the discovery lasts, the more you find yourself in the process of analysing plan structure.

And that's where reasoning takes over.

Yes. Reasoning takes over. But sometimes there are spaces that defeat analysis. I'm thinking of Tokyo, for example. There's something schizophrenic about the relationship one has with that city. Perception often points to spaces you think you know but can't actually situate. When I'm travelling I solve all sorts of problems that crop up at the agency. You could say that travel makes for a good studio.

You often contrast "presence effect" and "meaning effect." On the one hand, there's the idea of the presence of an object with no meaning apart from itself; while on the other hand, there's the idea that this "presence effect" sometimes implies more than the simple here and now presence of the object, and this leads to what you call the "meaning effect." I was rereading The Poetics of Space *recently and came across this: "Language bears within itself the open-closed dialectic. It encloses with meaning, and opens outwards with poetic expression." Is this strange similarity between your ideas and Bachelard's another proof of your fondness for phenomenology?*

This is a core point. There was a time when semiotics was all the rage and people kept saying architecture had to make sense; there was even talk of a semiotic study of the city. My idea was to counter Saussurian linguistics and semiology and Roland Barthes' work on architectural semiotics – which I came across when he was writing *The Pleasure of the Text* – with what I call the presence effect; by which I mean that there are things that ultimately cannot be reduced to language. The entire history of the western world is based on language. One day I met Kevin Lynch at a debate organised by the Institut de l'Environnement and we talked about this idea of a kind of reality that can't be reduced to language. The idea seemed to bother him, as he's used to postulating that the matrix and the model of all meaning are linguistic. Ultimately, it was the incredible brio of Roland Barthes that managed to take us beyond all these linguistic issues. But you have to imagine the ambience of the period, just after May '68, and the kind of doctrinaire tyranny that reigned then: drawing was considered artistic – and thus bourgeois – and had to be got rid of at all costs. Most students handed in theses based solely on texts. I felt it was important for me to emphasise the way of seeing, and of travelling, photographing and drawing. As it happens,

The Cité de la Musique (architect: C. de Portzamparc). The Conservatoire. The entrance way to the public music rooms.

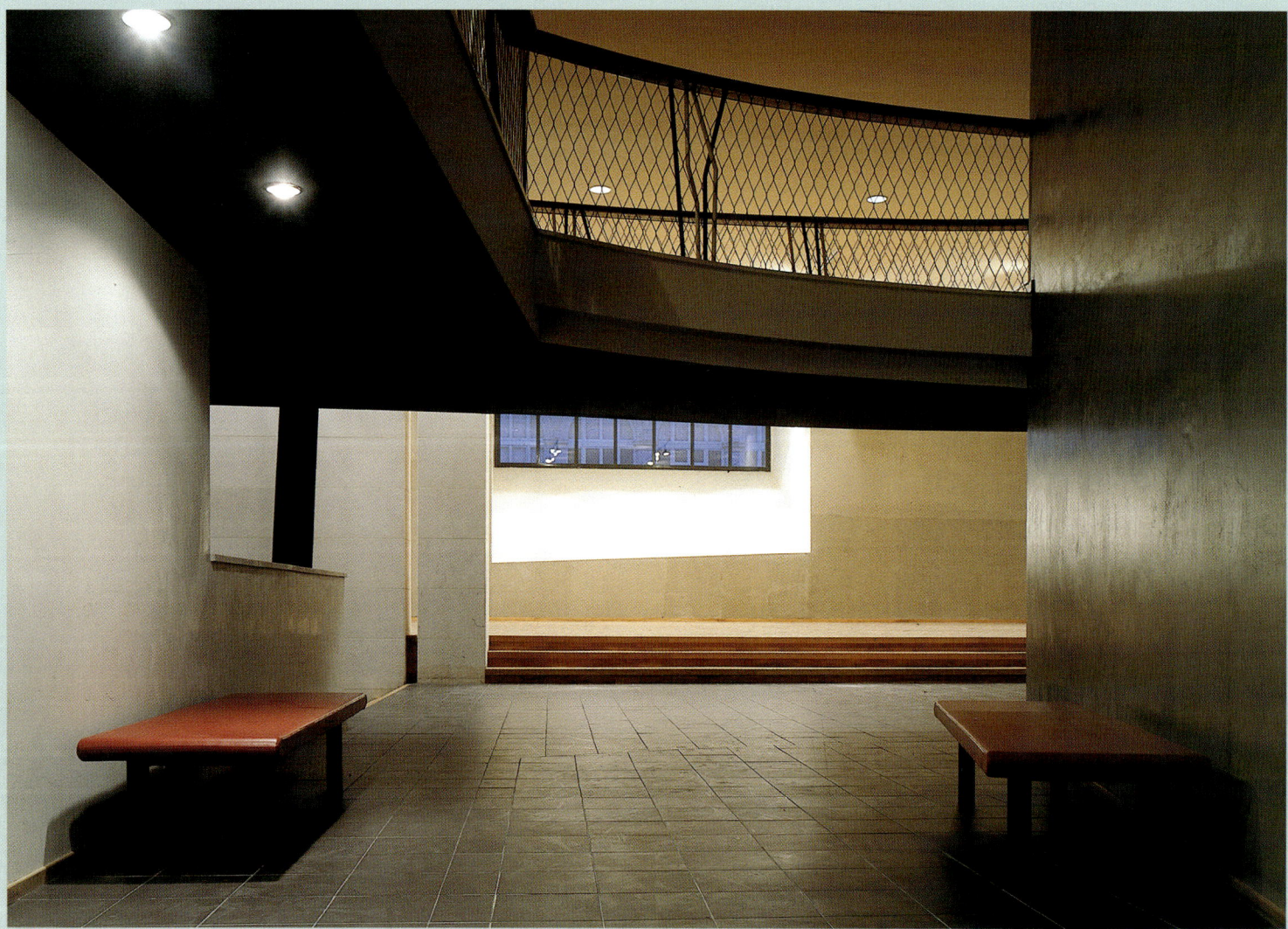

I said to Barthes that I thought it was dangerous that the world of architecture should forget about drawing. He seemed to get my point very quickly. The building of my water tower was in many respects a reflection of these ideas.

Let's talk about your relationship with classicism. As noted earlier, you've been called a formalist, but it's also often said that you're a classicist. I see the situation as more complex than this. It could be said that you're simultaneously Renaissance and baroque. Renaissance because of your stress on perspective, which enables you to focus the observer's eye on one object in isolation and so establish a kind of frozen perceptual time span. But baroque as well, in that you repeatedly use a concept – integration – which, according to Bruno Zevi, is characteristically baroque. The baroque system tries to connect the architectural elements – whether they belong to the plan or the façade – just as the Conservatoire plan seeks to connect its constituent elements by drawing on a series of spatial devices.

Yes. I would have liked to see Le Corbusier's reaction to my work. After all, he was very classical in his own way, too.

Le Corbusier would doubtless have seen you as a passionately rational architect, but one, above all, bent on the emotional charge that every architectural space should also have.

Le Corbusier called this kind of space inexpressible. But to come back to classicism, I'd like to point out that modernism has totally done away with perspective. The modern movement grew out of a series of reactions against everything that might be related to the past. The street, in particular, had to go. The gist of the modernists' message was, "If you don't do this, and if you don't do that, you'll cut free of history and you'll be welcomed into the fold." So they began by outlawing the street, then they outlawed the perspective view in favour of axonometric projection. I included perspective views in my Hautes Formes design, and this made me a classicist in some people's eyes. It's often said that perspective is a ridiculous tool in that it provides only a single point of view; it's often been castigated for its one-eyed – and thus subjective – view of things. I reject this. All you have to do is create four consecutive perspective views. After all, the cinema is just a perspective view in motion. The perspective view is interesting because it includes the observer in the design. The contrary approach had it that axonometric projection replaced monocular perspective with an infinite, more objective view.

It's axonometry that is fictional.

Of course. It's the expression of a perception that doesn't exist. It's also often the cause of enormous errors of judgement. Try an axonometric projection of Hautes Formes: you immediately tell yourself it's unbuildable. It was thanks to perspective that I was able to project myself into the world of exact size, exact height and light. The other modernist taboo was emptiness: the movement didn't like the in-between, spacing, "insideness" and "outsideness." There were people who made fun of Hautes Formes, saying "Christian de Portzamparc thinks emptiness can still be a working concept in modern architecture." For those people, giving shape to spacing meant you belonged to the "old world": to be modern you had to reject this approach out of hand. My reply was the direct opposite: "Emptiness is central to perception. The smallest clearing, the shortest walk in the mountains, is made up of transitions." Candilis and Baudouin taught me how to think about emptiness. Candilis really homed in on the dereliction inherent in modern objects: as he saw it, you had to look for what can link and interweave.

Bernard Tschumi's approach at La Villette appears diametrically opposed to the one you describe. His Folies seem to indicate a search for a purely ad hoc relationship with the earth.

Exactly. But the *plan voisin* did take care to define its boundaries clearly. There was a dialectical kind of relationship between the new infrastructure of the *plan voisin* and the old Paris infrastructure.

Your architecture calls up all the founding elements of classicism: the straight main staircase and the celebratory handling of the façade and layout. Then there's the Conservatoire, with a planimetric configuration resembling that of a Florentine palace. Are these conscious borrowings?

With regard to the staircase, what interests me above all is the dynamism of the subsequent itinerary. The Conservatoire staircase is the *promenade architecturale* so dear to Le Corbusier. And I never draw façades as elevations: I always work them out in three dimensions.

Still, the fanatical care lavished on the Conservatoire's east façade entitles me to see you as a classicist. In his description of the language of modern architecture, Bruno Zevi asserts unequivocally that "the inventory principle excludes the notion of the façade." For the moderns, the façade liberated from axial relationships "ceases to be a closed, autonomous object, an end in itself."

And rightly so. That's what you see when you look at the preliminary sketches for the east façade: more a sculpture in three dimensions than a flat, symmetrical representation. Here the façade becomes an expression of the project as a whole. It emerges once you've defined a specific concept for the project. The "îlot ouvert" (open block) notion I'm currently working on often produces this kind of three-dimensional, dissymmetrical façade. It's true, however, that once the space and the forms are established, there are places that I know are sometimes going to be reworked in search of large-scale pictoriality. I'm tempted to draw a parallel with the human body here: it's symmetrical, but once in motion it stands revealed as a masterpiece of dissymmetry. It's sort of the same with space: it should create an urge for movement, but at the same time you have to be able to get your bearings. A certain kind of stability means movement can be generated, but when there's movement everywhere the richness of mobility is lost.

For Bruno Zevi, asymmetry and anti-parallelism are the two invariants of modern architectural language. They imply "emancipation via dissonance."

Exactly.

There's something very appealing about your remarks on the notion of façade. On the other hand, you seem blatantly out to dramatise it in the classical manner. The layout of the Conservatoire staircase is practically identical to that of the François I staircase in the Château de Blois.

According to Serlio the perfect building is one whose spatial organisation can be grasped at first glance; this means I'm not a classicist, since the Conservatoire only yields itself up via gradual discovery.

As we said earlier, you're more baroque than Renaissance in that you opt more often for the dynamic than the static.

True. But the distinction between the classical and the non-classical is still very tenuous. Does Jean Nouvel's Fondation Cartier make him classical or anti-classical?

Concerning modernity, let's talk a little about Mies van der Rohe. Does it surprise you that I describe your architecture as "anti-Mies"? When we look back to Fritz Neumeyer on the De Stijl approach – knowing the links between Mies van der Rohe and De Stijl – and we read that De Stijl "dissolves the spatial envelope into a complex of independent partitions," we feel that we're at the opposite pole from what you're doing. Mies is looking for "open" spaces, while you prefer to close them.

It needs to be said here that De Stijl and Mies van der Rohe both postdate Frank Lloyd Wright. The publication of the Ernst Wasmuth album influenced a lot of European architects. In answer to your question, though, it doesn't bother me at all to hear my architecture described as "anti-Mies." But I'd like to make it clear that I'm not running an anti-Mies campaign. His contribution is a very enriching one.

You don't think his historical importance has been overestimated?

Of course it has. But his architecture, as I've just said, is very enriching. Fritz Neumeyer's definition of De Stijl is close to the one all the moderns shared at the time: a definition marked by the quest for an isotropic space combining only perpendicular planes. There's no denying that this definition led to works of real quality, but it very quickly became apparent that it was also a modern cliché. When I began my studies, students had to make sure that no two walls ever intersected. One wall arrives, the other one leaves and the outcome is independence for the partitions. As I've already said, this can give rise to buildings of great plastic precision, but it can also become a gimmick, a sort of vacuous chatter. So, is the language defined by De Stijl and Frank Lloyd Wright absent from my architecture? I don't think so. My cultural baggage is hybrid and every heritage inevitably contains contradictions. So we have to avoid pigeonholing my architectural language, which was what Marc Bédarida, Alain Guiheux and Richard Scoffier set out to do, to a certain extent, in their little album marking the Pompidou Centre exhibition. I sensed that they really wanted to lock me into a very specific period – the 1970s – and saw me as a defender of certain values, in particular the return to the urban. This approach put me behind the times. The first article was by

INTERVIEW WITH CHRISTIAN DE PORTZAMPARC

Marc Bédarida and covered the period from the water tower to the late 1970s. It didn't even mention the Cité de la Musique. For him the architecture of Christian de Portzamparc was restricted to La Roquette and Hautes Formes. Anyway, the outcome was that he wrote another article that I find much better.

I can understand someone saying that the Hautes Formes project is historically more important than the Cité de la Musique – which is not to detract in any way from the latter's plastic and urban qualities. Hautes Formes revived a conception of the city that had totally disappeared with the coming of modernity.

I'd like to point out here that I didn't come to a halt in the 1970s. Since then there's been the Cité de la Musique, the "open block" and so on.

What's going to be handed down to posterity, though? The Cité de la Musique or Hautes Formes? The people who organised the Pompidou Centre exhibition must have asked themselves that question – and I'm not at all sure they were wrong in opting for Hautes Formes: in the final analysis the Cité de la Musique is a brilliant restructuring of what had already been said at La Roquette and Hautes Formes.

Schubert was long described as a dwarf walking in Beethoven's shadow – and now he's considered a genius. So there's no once-and-for-all judgement. The Cité de la Musique brief was too atypical to be a vehicle for the universality expressed in Hautes Formes. One day at the studio, a student made an observation I found very relevant: the important thing for him was that I'd been able to come up with the "open block" concept – which he saw as my most enriching contribution, and present in embryonic form in Hautes Formes – after the formalist stage of the Cité de la Musique. He saw the Pompidou exhibition as the closing of the loop – a very intelligent observation.

The important thing is the moment when the new idea breaks through. It doesn't really matter if subsequent ideas take it closer to perfection: the basic thing is planting the seed.

There are artists who restructure idioms not originally of their own making. And yet they do it so well that, historically, they almost come to loom larger than the people they've borrowed from.

So far this interview has foregrounded the elements of contrast between the Conservatoire's east and south façades: one, a sudden inspiration; the other, apparently the outcome of a long, patient process of reflection. Which brings me to another point I see as important: your notion of beauty. Looking at the east façade, one is surprised by its near-mathematical rigour – as if it had been designed by a Grand Prix de Rome winner. This is a façade with something unquestionably classical about it; could the same be said of your notion of beauty?

The Grand Prix de Rome makes me think of a handsome drawing, a "flat" drawing, one unlikely to lend itself to concrete spatial realisation. For me personally, architecture is always a matter of itineraries, volume and perception. More than values of size and relationship, it's the notions of surprise and discovery that move me. Beauty emerges out of unexpected relations and juxtapositions. For my generation, talk of beauty was something of a no-no: the concept of beauty was automatically seen as tied to classicism. Back then we preferred to discuss aesthetic emotion and magnetism. It's true, though, that my projects sometimes provided a chance to get back to considering the importance of dimension and proportion. That way I could combat some of the modern movement's obsessions, one of which was the use of the series to solve the dimension problem.

concepts to bear on architecture can lead to classicism, and vice versa. Sometimes things you haven't composed – the product of something a little mysterious – can look beautiful; and the next day, seen in a different light, they're totally off-putting. You can think about beauty as the classicists did, like aesthetes shut away in their rooms, but observing a neighbourhood or a city inevitably opens you up to other definitions involving chance and conjunction. Doubtless I've often been identified with classicism because my architecture has refinement, but when I need to show photos of the Conservatoire I almost never choose the façade. The façade is a success, but in my opinion it doesn't have the freshness, brilliance and sensuality you can find elsewhere in the building.

When I ask Bernard Tschumi about beauty, he quotes Lautréamont's famous definition: "As beautiful as a chance encounter between an umbrella and a sewing machine on a dissection table." You'll agree with me that this is a far cry from the classical rigour of the east façade of the Conservatoire.

I've often used that quote myself, because sometimes I make this conception of beauty my own. All sorts of movements have borrowed from the Surrealists – Pop Art in particular – but I refuse to offer any definitive assessment of the problem. Architecture is a good school for grasping that there is a whole host of approaches to beauty. Sometimes in the course of a project you find yourself overtaken by concepts that, voluntarily or involuntarily, you would rather have forgotten. As strange as it may seem, for example, bringing phenomenological

When I got my first glimpse of this façade, I thought of the filmmaker Jean-Luc Godard, who once said that "the travelling shot is a moral issue." The same goes for an architectural façade. The east façade was a difficult birth and that's what makes it the success it is. If a project agenda is a relentless battle against chaos – a desperate attempt to impose order on a mass of inputs as inherently contradictory as aesthetic, utilitarian and constructional considerations – it's the architect's business to make this known. The east façade of the Conservatoire carries out this task admirably. There are the two large blocks that seem bent on representing the divergences within the brief, then the long horizontal string course that tries to link them, as if to signal that architecture is also a matter of order and unity.

A number of people, including François Chaslin, have told me they find this façade remarkable. Yet it's the south façade I show in photos.

The south façade is something instantaneous, born of a greater sense of urgency.

Right. At the time of Hautes Formes, I was asserting the interplay of proportion and volume in a near-polemical way – going counter to a period that saw work on the exterior as a matter of pointless frills. This was Josic's opinion, and would doubtless be the opinion of Bernard Tschumi or Frédéric Edelman today.

When Adrien Fainsilber says you're a formalist, what he's really saying is that his conception of beauty differs from yours. He functions more in terms of axes, relationships and sequencing. He's even more classical than you can sometimes be.

Curiously I feel much more in tune with Bernard Tschumi's vision of things than with Adrien Fainsilber's. When Fainsilber calls me a formalist, he's saying he finds me less classical than he is.

Let's continue with the concept of beauty. Your declaration that "space must be thought of in terms of interior quality," and that this quality "must spill over onto the exterior space," is a way of talking about the definition of beauty. What you're formulating is Le Corbusier's beloved concept of the standard. When Le Corbusier brings up the notion of a standard, he insists on the fact that "the envelope is not something preconceived, it is a result." Thus beauty is this something in motion going from the interior to the exterior, like a nucleus of interiority trying to hatch out. Kandinsky puts forward the same idea, but he opts for a different scale. He speaks of the "purely, eternally artistic," by which he means the absolute, eternal – and thus objective – "determination to speak of what is secret via the secret" that characterises art. In encountering the artist's sensibility and that of his time, this determination – Kandinsky calls it "interior necessity" – becomes part of a subjective temporality.

Yes, but the exterior space can in turn be seen as an interior space. When I'm outside, I'm also inside. The modern movement fought against this vision: the modern space was intended to be isotropic.

We also find this thinking about beauty in dynamic terms in Shaftesbury. The famous sentence quoted in all the art history textbooks: "The beautifying, not the beautified, is the really beautiful" is a way of saying that beauty is not to be sought in the thing seen as beautiful, but in the generative process that enabled its disclosure. To define beauty one has to take account of the very act of making, of attaining reality. Shaftesbury's concept of "inward form" suggests Leibniz's monad or the Cambridge School's concept of "plastic power"; but Goethe, whom you often quote, could also be relevant: "For such is the principle of nature: what is valid for

the outside is also valid for the inside." And now, if it's all right with you, let's move from the question of beauty to the buildings at La Villette. What's your verdict on the Parc de La Villette as designed by Bernard Tschumi?

If I'm not mistaken, Tschumi often uses computers in the design process. But what happens is that excessive recourse to computers for visualisation purposes gives the erroneous impression that topological concepts can be modified or expanded at will to fit with various situations. The screen very quickly makes you lose your notion of scale – and the beauty of La Villette site lay in its sheer size. What you look for in a park is vastness and magnitude. It's true that you also want surprises, but generally speaking the main consideration is the idea of having lots of space to let yourself go in. The problem here is that the grid of the Folies really cuts back the opportunities to enjoy all this space. Personally I find that the red of the Folies pulls them towards each other – it's hard to believe there can be a hundred and twenty metres separating one from the other. There's a problem of scale, for sure. So you have to be wary of the image: it can create illusions very quickly indeed. The truth is first and foremost space.

The Conservatoire is a fine example of coexistence between different scales. I'm thinking in particular of the two large interior streets in the lower basement: they furnish a link between the interdisciplinary workshop, the vocal arts room and the organ room; and at the same time re-establish the lines of force of the park – especially the north-south axis of the Galerie de La Villette – within the building itself. You have, so to speak, the impression that the Conservatoire is seeking – successfully – to merge with the site and thus highlight its enormous area. The grid of the Folies, by contrast, looks like the outcome of a purely graphic game, the result being a relationship to the scale of the site that is somehow virtual and fictive. As you say, the rationale here is the computer image.

Bernard Tschumi seems more at ease when he's dealing with more architectural spaces. What I've seen of Le Fresnoy, for example, seems to me a real achievement. But coming back to the way the park is laid out, it needs to be said that its origins lie in a whole series of theoretical explorations dating from the 1960s. The grid is a recurring notion in the history of modern architecture. I'm thinking in particular of Candilis, who liked to get his students thinking about housing typologies involving grid plans that could be reproduced ad infinitum. I find that approach dangerous in that it excluded the dimensional aspect.

You didn't enter the Parc de La Villette competition, but could you give a brief outline of the form your project would have taken if you'd been in the running in 1982? How would you have dealt with the presence of those enormous masses: the Cité des Sciences and the Grande Halle? Would you have put the emphasis on their impressiveness as volumes or, on the contrary, tried to relativise their colossal size via proportionally appropriate spatial configurations?

As I see it, I would have designed the park in such a way as to call attention to the characteristics – in the plural – of the site. I would also have played the diversity card: sheer size here, the axial aspect there. The uncertainty of the maze here, buildings lost amidst vegetation there. Look at the Cité de la Musique: the way it "opens out" towards the periphery lets you see the interplay Adrien Fainsilber has set up between the Cité des Sciences and the Géode. As a result, one of the site's characteristics – its vast size – is readily intelligible. In architecture, you have a whole range of tools that mean you can emphasise or play down the size of a building or a space. But to come back to your question, I think that if I'd been in the competition I wouldn't have felt the need to build more. I certainly would have tried to point up the contrasts, have fun with the ground area. You get the feeling that the layout of the park is the work of an architect who hasn't built very much yet.

When you come down to it, the grid is reassuring.

That's it: reassuring. But it should be said that the competition brief was conducive to this kind of proposal. In the 1982 brief you could spot the weird ideological preconception that a modern park had to be a park without trees – when the cardinal virtue of a park, after all, is to produce vegetation.

That's exactly what I said once to François Barré: that it seemed absurd to have to believe that parks were no longer a space for nature to flourish in.

Right. As a concept, the park is always taken as an alternative to the built – to the city. You could say in this respect that our perception has two major cultural sources: firstly the Franco-Italian, with its emphasis on partial geometrisation of garden spaces, and then the Anglo-Saxon, which puts the accent more on the picturesque. I know that a reasonable approach ought to involve saying that nothing must be reproduced identically – that we must no longer be reliant on the benchmark motifs history has bequeathed us and which nineteenth-century parks were not loath to use in association. But the park should remain a place where the geometrical and the non-geometrical confront each other.

Just like Versailles. On the one hand the buildings and the geometrical park, and on the other, Thetis' grotto.

Exactly. Another thing is that we often forget a point I see as fundamental. If we have an axis and a major motif, that doesn't necessarily mean that's where you have to be. You can be off to one side, or out on the edge.

If Gilles Vexlard heard that, he'd tell you just how close his way of thinking is to yours. He's someone who likes to stress lateralisation and proximity as architectonic components of the act of building, especially in rural architecture. In his recent book, Enseigner la conception architectonic (Teaching Architectural Design) Philippe Boudon seems to share this point of view. He cites Cuisenier, who asserted that "graphic reasoning has taken over from building reasoning" and that "the spaces of

Descartes and Monge helped set the fundamentals of social symbolism on the road to oblivion."

Here I could take the example of the Parc de Saint-Cloud, which has a main thoroughfare and small paths running parallel in the secondary gardens. That's the great thing about this park: the small can live alongside the big. Alain Resnais understood this perfectly when he was shooting *Last Year in Marienbad*: the gardens of the chateau are filmed following lines that are lateral or diagonal, but almost never at right angles. it's interesting to note that sometimes the cinema shows a better grasp of the scope of certain spatial motifs than architects do. When I was given the Pritzker Prize in Columbus, Ohio, I had the opportunity to get to know an absolutely superb park: it's alongside the mayor's house and was designed by an American landscaper called Dan Kyley. The prize was presented to me in the mayor's house – a very Mies-style house, built by Ero Saarinen – and afterwards I went out into the garden, which you could describe as a kind of perfectly contemporary run-through of Le Nôtre's gardens. A very subtle interplay between levels generates a marvellous range of perceptions of scale. There are places where you see the trees as gigantic, when in fact they're relatively small; in the same way the use of foliage sometimes gives the impression that the park is very big – which is not at all the case.

Scale is a core issue. Philippe Boudon has defined the concept of scale as the perceiving subject's "impression of size." As a concept, scale necessarily involves the body as a focus of receptivity.

Right. Ben Kyley's garden is no more than an extremely skilled accumulation of local gardens involving differently scaled readings. It's the opposite of the pastiche of the neoclassical park. In the United States you don't often come across public spaces with this kind of relevance. I'm just back from Washington, where I found that the thoroughfare leading to the Capitol was not always particularly well handled.

We're not sufficiently aware that La Villette is home to architectures whose theoretical bases are totally distinct: an architecture that could be described as phenomenological, which is the one you defend; the simultaneously rationalist and classically-inclined architecture advocated by Adrien Fainsilber; and the Bernard Tschumi one which, like that of Rem Koolhaas, uses the concepts of activity and condensation.

In theoretical terms, Rem Koolhaas' message is extremely rigorous. On the one hand, he states that architecture, because of the excessive complexity of today's cities, can no longer restructure the components of the urban; and that as a result, the architect-designed building now has no choice but to merge into the mesh of the city – this is the Rotterdam Kunsthal. But then he defends the opposite point of view, which is that the building can in a way "swallow" the city by asserting its own monstrous scale and becoming what might be called a mega-architecture – this is Lille–Grand Palais.

The Kunsthal is a very astute piece of building. I particularly like the way all the exhibition rooms are laid out, rolled around an enormous walkway that runs from one end of the building to the other and links the lower, ground-level area – where there's a park – to the upper level, set not far from an expressway.

The spiral itinerary at the Kunsthal is very well handled. Rem Koolhaas has thought out his own personal doctrine and knows how to apply it in each specific instance.

Interview by Alain Orlandini.

Page right: The Cité de la Musique (architect: C. de Portzamparc). The Conservatoire. A classroom.

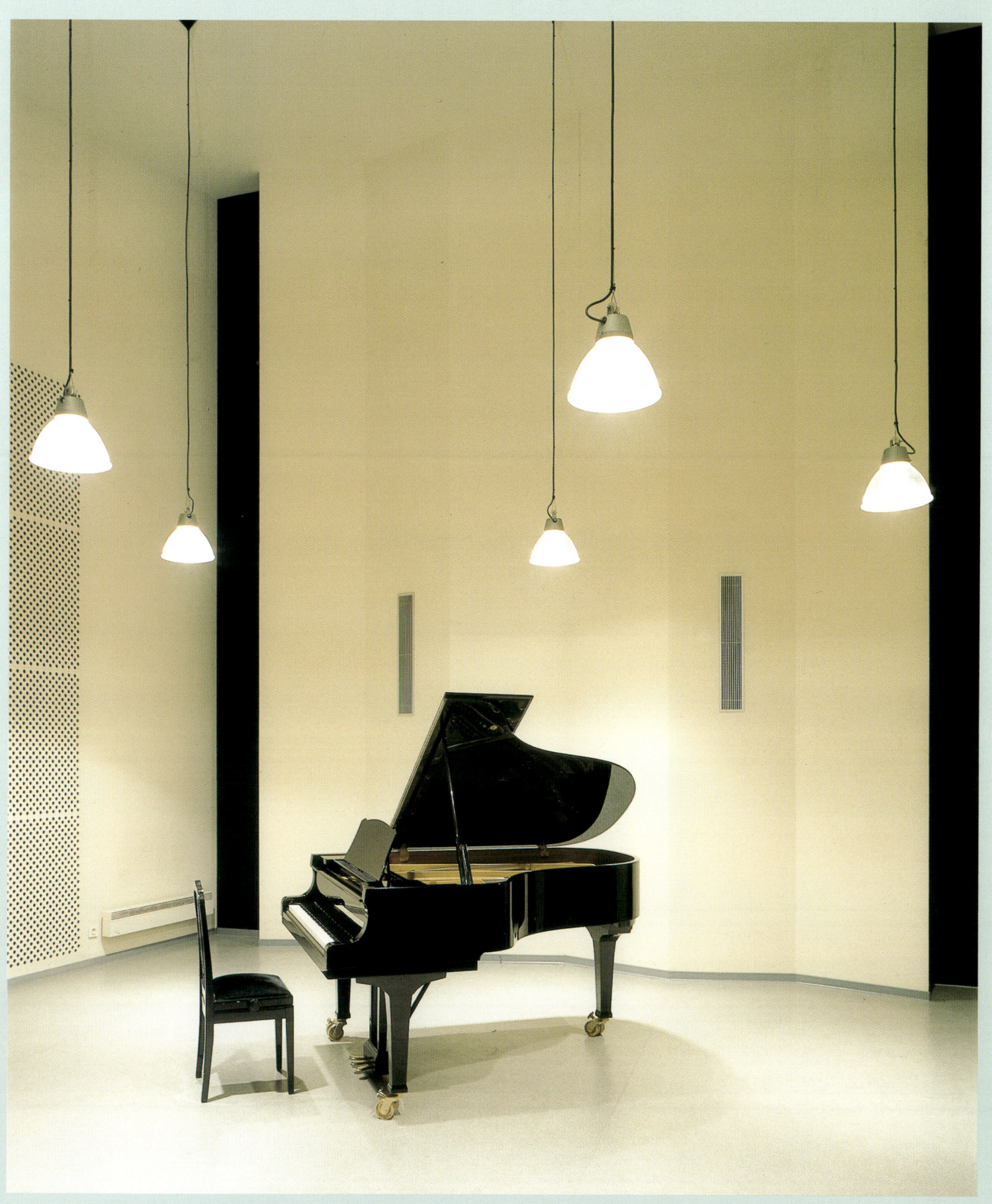

Conclusion

The inevitability of eclecticism

The enduring presence of classical syntax in the work of Adrien Fainsilber; Christian de Portzarmparc's simultaneously expressionistic and phenomenological take on the different concepts bequeathed by modernity; the "programmatic collisions" of Bernard Tschumi: the architecture at La Villette is very much the image of that inevitable eclecticism evoked some time ago now by Leonardo Benevolo. An empirical yet heady collage of distinctive languages, La Villette confirms the irreversible fragmentation of discourses. The dream of a universal metalanguage has faded, but does not this "dis-affiliation" make our architects freer, and therefore more imaginative?

On the usefulness of interviews

Since the stylistic diffuseness in evidence at La Villette dilutes individual practices in a kaleidoscopic plurality of forms and spaces, it seemed appropriate to let the architects themselves do the talking so that their versions of events might yield the information that would explain their approach. We therefore encouraged our architects to express themselves, and sometimes forced them into a spot of self-criticism, but we also remembered to ask "the other people" to talk to us about the architecture. "Other people", meaning those who were not directly involved in the creative process but whose function fully entitled them to formulate a critical judgement. And here I must say that talking to François Barré, Pierre Boulez and Jean Semichon, and getting them to describe, respectively, the Parc de La Villette, the Cité de la Musique and the Cité des Sciences et de l'Industrie, proved just as enriching as the dialogue with Bernard Tschumi, Christian de Portzamparc and Adrien Fainsilber. Here was the best chance to hear what the architects themselves were not always able or willing to say – here, in the course of these engaged, sometimes passionate but always cordial conversations.

For lack of political will/absurd chronology

What with Rem Koolhaas' project being too abstract, and Bernard Lassus' project made illegible by a mediocre rendering, only the teams led by Alexandre Chemetoff and Gilles Vexlard had any real hope of competing with Bernard Tschumi. In the end, the jury voted for

Tschumi. We respect its decision. However, there are two aspects of his project that need to be reconsidered. The first concerns the way the Parc de La Villette relates to the suburbs of Aubervilliers and Pantin. The issue here is the fact that when the competition to build the Parc de La Villette was organised there was no real political determination to get all the players implicated in the rehabilitation of the site pulling together in one common project. The second concerns the links between the park and its extremities. The issue here is the way in which the empiricism of the development process turned out to be a real handicap for all the project leaders in competition at La Villette.

For lack of political will
We know that one of the main requirements put before those competing to build the Parc de La Villette was to create a link between the park and the towns of Aubervilliers and Pantin; that they were asked to show quite clearly how their project would plug into the territories around the periphery. Now, if this link between Paris and its close suburbs was one of the major issues in this competition – and this is a question not for Bernard Tschumi, but for the client organisation and for the presiding authorities – why then were negotiations not started with the municipalities concerned, with a view to allowing the park to extend beyond the Boulevards MacDonald and Serrurier, and over the Périphérique?* And did not the grid-like structure of the project chosen by the jury itself militate in favour of the park overflowing the area originally designated? This makes it hard to blame Tschumi for failing to deal with the linkage of the park and the towns of Aubervilliers and Pantin – even if we are still convinced that more could have been made of the existing roads.

Absurd chronology
The other point that needs to be raised is the way the Parc de La Villette links up with its northern and southern extremities. One could of course point the finger at Bernard Tschumi, holding him responsible for the somewhat tentative way in which his project connects with Porte de La Villette and Porte de Pantin. But that would be to forget that the competition to build the Parc de La Villette preceded the ones for the Cité de la Musique and the development of the north sector of La Villette, and that Tschumi therefore had to deal with an almost insurmountable difficulty: how to find a design that was both flexible and structured. Flexible, so as not to be overly constrictive for the architects awarded responsibility for the coming developments; and structured, so that there would be an overall concept behind the spatial organisation. And so, once again, our question is not so much for Bernard Tschumi as for the client organisation. Why – and this idea is from François Barré – did they not start with the competition to build the Parc de La Villette, and then open the ones to construct the Cité des Sciences, the Cité de la Musique and the Villette-North sector? Some might retort that, if planned in this way, the development of the Villette site would have meant the architect of the park having to grapple with a threefold uncertainty. To them I would reply that, in addition to instituting a "general dynamic of engendering" (these are Barré's words), this way of planning would have had the advantage of putting the architects of the Cité des Sciences, the Cité de la Musique and the Villette-North sector on an equal footing, because they would all have been dealing with the same constraint: the structure of the park. In reality, the rehabilitation of the Villette site first saw Adrien Fainsilber competing to transform

the meat market while sketching out, in the most summary way, projects for a park and music complex – and how could it have been otherwise, since the briefs for these had yet to be finalised? And then Bernard Tschumi competing in complete ignorance of what was going to be built at the northern and southern ends of the site! Perhaps it would have been better to entrust the rehabilitation of La Villette to just one team of architects? Some will argue that such prestigious public commissions are too few and far between to be allotted in so uneven-handed a way. Even so – and I'm sure Adrien Fainsilber won't disagree – such a decision would have led to a more coherent layout on the site than the one we now have.

---

* Likewise, why not get the Paris municipality to agree to the idea of the grid of Folies spreading all the way to Place Stalingrad? I do not think there is much in the argument that the state and city could never have come to an agreement. If, in the 1960s, the latter agreed to sell the fifty-five hectares of La Villette to the state, then why would it refuse to let the Folies in the park come and "nibble" at the banks of its canals? Would that not have provided it with a unique opportunity to see *its* banks at last enjoy the consideration that it had denied them for too long.

Photo credits

t: top; b: below; l: left; r: right; m: middle.

Agence D. Baldani: 33 (3t).

Agence O. Baudry: 59.

Agence P. Chaix et J.-P. Morel: 231, 232, 233.

Agence P. Chaix et J.-P. Morel – E. Valentin: 49t, 242b, 243.

Agence A. Fainsilber: 35, 110, 111, 130, 131.

Agence A. Fainsilber – P. Hurlin: 105.

AFP: 93, 94, 95.

Agence H. Gaudin: 52b.

Agence J. Nouvel: 52t, 52m.

Agence B. Reichen et P. Robert: 216t.

Agence B. Reichen et P. Robert – G.-H. Demol: 222b, 223 to 225.

Agence B. Reichen et P. Robert – T. Williams: 216b.

Agence P. Riboulet: 205 to 207.

Agence R. Taillibert: 27 to 30, 98, 99.

Agence G. Thurnauer: 70tl, 70br.

Agence G. Thurnauer – J. de Gaspary: 71ml.

Agence G. Thurnauer – O. Wogensky: 71mr, 71b.

Agence B. Tschumi: 45tr, 46t, 49b, 138b, 140, 149, 150, 160.

Agence J.-P. Vallier: 48 (4t).

Archipress – J.-L. Boegly: 217b.

Archipress – S. Couturier: 37, 39b.

Archipress – S. Couturier/Atelier de Portzamparc: 68.

Atelier Chr. de Portzamparc: 66t, 275, 280.

Atelier Chr. de Portzamparc – C. Abella: 261.

Atelier Chr. de Portzamparc – N. Borel: 66m, 67, 256 to 258, 259bl, 260, 262, 264, 266, 267, 269b, 270 to 272, 274, 277, 278, 281, 282, 286b, 287, 300, 311.

Atelier Chr. de Portzamparc – J.-M. Monthiers: 268, 269t, 293.

Jean-Luc Bouchart: 237.

Bureau des Paysages: 199.

Gil Cortesi: 236b, 240.

D.R.: 106t, 135b, 154, 182, 190, 198, 208, 217t, 218, 219, 222t, 227, 228, 242t, 250, 259br, 286t, 290.

EPPGHV: 31 to 36, 38b, 39 (3t), 42, 43m, 43b, 44, 45, 46t, 48bl, 48br, 54 to 58, 60 to 65, 66t, 66b, 70 (3 tr), 71t, 97, 102b, 103, 104br, 111, 112, 127, 137, 138t, 139, 177, 183, 184, 187, 191, 192, 209, 255.

EPPGHV – fonds SEMVI: 17, 18 (3t), 19, 40, 77, 81, 122b, 123, 124, 246t.

EPPGHV – J.-L. Berger: 47.

EPPGHV – J.-L. Bohin: 144-145.

EPPGHV – N. Borel: 247, 250b, 251, 259t.

EPPGHV – F.-X. Bouchart: 246b.

EPPGHV – S. Chivet (Agence Vu): 142.

EPPGHV – Dityvon: 146br.

EPPGHV – P. Dolemieux: 51, 146t, 146bl, 151, 203.

EPPGHV – G. Hersant: 143, 148b, 162, 170.

EPPGHV – J.-P. Houdry: 167.

EPPGHV – M. Lamoureux: 50t, 69, 141, 147, 148t, 173, 202.

EPPGHV – J.-M. Monthiers: 46b, 200.

EPPGHV – E. Pinard: 72.

EPPGHV – S. Sautereau: 226.

EPPGHV – J. Vogstschmit: 50b.

EPPGHV – A. Wolf: 195.

OMA – H. Weilemann: 43t, 176, 178, 181.

Les Nouvelles Annales de la construction: 17t, 245.

Photothèque APUR: 20 to 26, 85, 87, 88, 91.

Photothèque CSI: 31b, 32t, 34m, 34b.

Photothèque CSI – G. Basilico: 135t.

Photothèque CSI – P. Carrère: 38t, 38m.

Photothèque CSI – M. Fainsilber: 102t.

Photothèque CSI – A. Goustard: 101.

Photothèque CSI – J.-Y. Grégoire: 104t, 104bl, 113, 115, 118.

Photothèque CSI – P. Hurlin: 106b, 107.

Préfecture de Police: 18b.

Francis Vernet: 236t.

Engraving executed by Labogravure, Bordeaux.
Book printed by RE.BUS srl (Italy) on december 2004.